Gregory J. Watters

Introduction to Peace Studies

Introduction to Peace Studies

David P. Barash

University of Washington

Wadsworth Publishing Company
Belmont, California
A Division of Wadsworth, Inc

Psychology Editor: Ken King
Production Editor: Angela Mann
Designer: Carolyn Deacy
Print Buyer: Barbara Britton
Copy Editor: Tom Briggs
Photo Editor: Bobbie Broyer
Compositor: Thompson Type
Cover: *Tracer* by Robert Rauschenberg (1925–   ).
        Oil and silkscreen on canvas, 84″ × 60″.
        The Nelson-Atkins Museum of Art, Kansas City, Missouri
        (Nelson Gallery Foundation Purchase)
Signing Representative: Karen Buttles

Printed in the United States of America   19

1 2 3 4 5 6 7 8 9 10 — 95 94 93 92 91

Library of Congress Cataloging in Publication Data

Barash, David P.
    Introduction to peace studies / David Barash.
        p.   cm.
    Includes bibliographical references.
    ISBN 0-534-13668-0
    1. Peace.   I. Title.
JX1952.B28   1991
327.1′72 — dc20   90-12237
                                                                    CIP

Brief Contents

Contents

Part I

The Promise of Peace, The Problem of War

Part II

The Causes of War

Part III

Building "Negative Peace"

Part IV

Building "Positive Peace"

Preface

Welcome to Peace Studies. To my knowledge, this book is the first integrated Peace Studies text written by one person in this field, and it is about time. I am also confident that it will not be the last. My hope and expectation is that Peace Studies will soon acquire the academic legitimacy — as well as the enrollments — of such mainstream scholarly enterprises as political science, psychology, and physics. In the meantime, it already has every bit as much intellectual substance, and certainly as much relevance to today's world.

In writing this book, I have been quite aware of the diverse approaches that currently constitute Peace Studies. I have also been aware that Peace Students are, ironically, a fractious lot. Especially because there are no standard introductory textbooks, the field itself has become rather disparate, perhaps even a bit diffuse. In offering the present textbook, I am painfully conscious that it will seem inadequate to some, overinclusive to others, too dry and scholarly to many, too colloquial to the rest. It also reflects my own interests and my own sense of what should constitute an introduction to Peace Studies.

Being aware of the diversity of approaches to Peace Studies, I have sought to err on the side of including somewhat more material and covering somewhat more topics than many instructors might wish to attempt. I hope that you will feel free to pick and choose, treating this volume like a restaurant menu. Personally, I recommend the full-course meal, although others may prefer, for example, to take two from column A, one from column B, and so on. I would be grateful if people using this text would let me know which chapters they have chosen to assign, in what order, and why, as well as offering any suggestions for future revisions. Although this volume is a finished product, I prefer to think of it as a beginning.

Because *Introduction to Peace Studies* is intended for beginning undergraduate students, I have sought to emphasize themes and readability rather than an intensive immersion in the technical literature. Hence, it is not heavily referenced and the "Suggestions for Further Reading" at the end of each chapter direct the interested student toward accessible material rather than "heavy" academic sources. For anyone seriously interested in the subject, this too will come. Sprinkled throughout this book are several brief biographies of people who are especially notable for their contributions to peace, either as scholars or activists (and in most cases as both). I am pleased to tell you that choosing these examples was a difficult task: There are many worthy candidates. I wanted to demonstrate to students that work on behalf of peace is being conducted right now by real people with real faces and real biographies — just like them.

My impression is that most undergraduates interested in Peace Studies tend to be regrettably uninformed about history, often presuming that peace as an issue began with the nuclear freeze movement, or at most the Vietnam War. Hence, I have been relatively generous with historical material, to supplement and, if possible deepen appreciation of current issues such as nuclear weapons, South African apartheid, intervention in Central America, and the greenhouse effect.

In undertaking this project—and revising it for final publication—I have been acutely conscious of the pace of change in the world. The year 1989 in particular was momentous and early 1990 has been no different; I even found myself fantasizing about a loose-leaf notebook, with updates to be mailed out monthly . . . or perhaps daily! As this book is going to the printers, for example, the two Germanies are rushing toward reunification, many years or, for some people, decades earlier than suspected even twelve months ago. Although the precise make-up of the new Germany, and also of Europe, cannot be predicted, several possibilities present themselves: (1) a massive stand-down in the East–West confrontation, at least in Europe, and quite possibly throughout the world; (2) the withdrawal of Soviet troops to within the U.S.S.R.'s borders; (3) the dissolution of the Warsaw Pact and—deprived of a raison d'etre—perhaps NATO as well; (4) the rapid democratization of the Soviet Union and also, not coincidentally, its possible break-up; (5) an increase in ethnic hostilities in Europe and elsewhere; and (6) a transition from military definitions of "national security" to a broader conception of global security that encompasses economic and social issues, with special attention to problems of the world environment, disparities in wealth, and violations of human rights. "Negative peace"—the prevention of war—may well be supplanted by "positive peace" at last. But the world seems likely to continue being convulsed by more than its share of violence and instability as well. Stay tuned.

Finally, let me state that my interest in this project and in Peace Studies goes beyond mere scholarship or pedagogy; that is, I am personally committed to the political and social goals of Peace Studies. As I explain in Chapter 1, the field itself differs from most social science in that it is value-oriented, and unabashedly so. I make no excuses, therefore, for my own bias and orientation, which is frankly antinuclear, antiauthoritarian, antiestablishment, proenvironment, prohuman rights, prosocial justice, pro-peace, and left wing. At the same time, I believe that serious emotional and political efforts are most effective if they build upon serious intellectual effort, including an attempt to understand all sides of complex debates.

Many people have contributed to this book, some knowingly, some not. They include Chadwick Alger, Louis Beres, Kenneth Boulding, Lester Brown, Helen Caldicott, Richard Falk, Roger Fisher, Randall Forsberg, Andre Frank, Jerome Frank, John Kenneth Galbraith, Johan Galtung, Robert Jervis, Michael Klare, Aryeh Neier, Anatol Rapaport, Betty Reardon, Gene Sharp, Ruth Sivard, Richard Smoke, Daniel Thomas, Edward Weisband, Kenneth Waltz, Ralph White, Nigel Young, and my editor at Wadsworth, Ken King. Reviewers Charles Hauss, Colby College; Adrienne Kaufman, The American University, School of International Service; James Keeley, University of Calgary; Robbie Lieberman, University of Missouri; Tom Moody, California State University, San Bernardino; Cheyney Ryan, University of Oregon; and Nigel Young, Colgate University, all provided helpful comments. I especially want to thank my immediate family—Judith, Ilona, and Nellie—for teaching me so much about peace, and suffering so bravely through the wars of completing this manuscript.

Peace to you all,

David P. Barash
Seattle, Washington

Foreword

Peace Research, Peace Studies, and Peace as a Profession:
Three Phases in the Emergence of a New Discipline
by Johan Galtung

You are holding in your hand the first general purpose, single-authored, integrated introductory text to Peace Studies. As research has accumulated this last generation, the field has come of age; it can be taught. This book offers an excellent opportunity to take stock, and, even better, to look ahead. It ranges widely, through time and space, and in understandable language, to educate and to convey what researchers have discovered in the important field of Peace Studies. Rather than repeat what is ably presented here, I will focus on the next step: the emergence of peace as a profession.

My thesis is very simple: *Research and education in Peace Studies have reached the point at which professionalization is now possible and also desirable*. Once research achieves sufficient results, it should be communicated to others, and of course it takes much research to build a body of knowledge sufficiently coherent to be taught. Researchers place lights in the desert; education seeks to use these lights to illuminate dark places. At the same time, education may help us identify the gaps in our knowledge: Students can themselves be experts at looking at things in new ways and their inquisitiveness can open up fresh areas for inquiry.

If researchers are writers who turn into teachers (and thus also into talkers), then professionals are doers. Although to some degree researchers, teachers, professionals, and students all concern themselves with the same basic material, there is a difference in emphasis. With some notable exceptions, we might not expect a peace researcher, for example, to go into the field and really try to build peace, however much he or she may love to write about how to do it. Nor would we expect a professional peace builder to write a first-rate research article or to be an inspiring and well organized teacher. Research, education, and action call for related but different skills. All, however, are important aspects of Peace Studies.

Professionalization is the logical consequence of research with a clear value focus, such as we find in engineering, medicine, or peace research. In the day-to-day workings of research, it is easy to lose sight of the purpose of the whole exercise. And the purpose of peace research is, of course, not only to understand the conditions for peace, but to do something about it. In short, the purpose of both peace research and the peace movement is the same: the abolition of war as a social institution. And beyond this, to contribute to more decency on this small planet.

At this point, we should look at the nature of knowledge in the social sciences. Such knowledge differs significantly from the way we currently conceive knowledge in the natural sciences. Thus, the natural scientist discovers laws and then verifies them; the social scientist chooses laws and then searches for conditions under which they become true. The natural scientist assumes a rigid reality and tests singular hypotheses; the social scientist assumes a more flexible reality and searches for coherence in a web of interrelated propositions, as for instance in the case of a "peace system" or "conflict-solving capacity."

As a result of this unique nature of social reality, the borderline between research, study, and practice becomes less clear than in the natural sciences. There is so much to study, with everything interrelated, that all experiences become relevant. Peace research and peace study therefore often go sideways rather than in depth at a single point. For example, rather than knowing the details of destructive technologies (such as the manufacture of nuclear weapons), the focus is on knowing the conditions that favor research and development of such technologies. Correspondingly, more is gained by knowing the broad circumstances of successful negotiations than by delving in great detail into a single case. The broad wealth of information synthesized in David Barash's *Introduction to Peace Studies* should assist students in grasping this complex interplay, while also providing needed coherence for the field as a whole. It calls for a creative interaction between the researcher's specialized knowledge, the more superficial but broad knowledge acquired by the student, and the professional's holistic knowledge (called "experience") developed in practice.

People in Peace Studies have done enormous amounts of research, which has unleashed creativity and productivity in many people. Clearly, this has been due in part to the international and interdisciplinary character of Peace Studies itself. Few social scientists travel so much and have such large networks abroad. The reason is obvious: We are studying the world system as a whole, which requires extensive travel — both physical and intellectual — across disciplinary borders. The saddest way of doing Peace Studies as an educational practice is making an inventory of the courses given at University X "that have something to do with peace and conflict" and putting them together. However, even this is better than doing nothing; this admirable textbook provides the necessary tool for doing much more.

The time has come to move on, to proceed with vigorous educational efforts, and to start the first training courses for peace professionals. I am not thinking of the baccalaureate level alone, important as it is, or of the Ph.D. level, which remains particularly suited for research, but of the level in between: that of the master's degree, a Master of Peace Studies (M.P.S.). Professionals holding such a degree would have received training in conflict analysis, negotiation, mediation, nonviolence, alternative security, peace economics, peace with the environment, human rights, and so forth.

I would propose one year of training in existing theories with numerous case studies, much like in a business school, and then one year of practice having been exposed to peace professionals as role models, through the UN, other Inter-Governmental Organizations, international peoples' organizations, governmental ministries — particularly foreign affairs, defense, and development assistance — voluntary organizations such as trade unions and religious bodies, municipalities, school districts, media, and so on. There is so much to be done; we could urgently use at least 1,000 such trained peace graduates by the year 2000.

We must undertake this in a spirit of international and interdisciplinary cooperation, based on a global and holistic identification. At the same time, the peace practitioners' dedication must be clear, embodied perhaps in a Hippocratic oath at the end of each M.P.S. program, which will capture the spirit of Gandhi's ethical intuition about the unity of means and ends as well as something equivalent to the medical injunction to "do no harm."

There is much work to do! And with textbooks such as this, Peace Studies has the tools to do it. Let us continue!

Johan Galtung
Professor of Peace Studies
University of Hawaii, Honolulu
Professor of Peace and Cooperative Research
Universitat Witten-Herdecke

Introduction to Peace Studies

Members of UNFICYP (the United Nations Peacekeeping Force in Cyprus) looking out over the countryside. (United Nations)

I

The Promise of Peace
The Problem of War

Human beings are faced with many problems: an increasingly polluted and otherwise threatened planet composed of finite resources whose limits may soon be reached; gross maldistribution of wealth, which prevents the overwhelming majority of human beings from realizing their potential and ensures that vast numbers die prematurely; regrettable patterns of social and political injustice, in which racism, sexism, and other forms of unfairness abound, and in which representative government is relatively rare, and torture and other forms of oppression distressingly common. And this is only a partial list.

Yet, despite all of these difficulties, the remarkable fact is that enormous sums of money and vast reserves of material, time, and energy are expended, not in solving what we might call the "problems of peace," but rather in threatening and actually making war on one another. If it weren't so tragic, the situation would seem so absurd as to be high comedy. Although it seems unlikely that human beings will ever achieve anything approaching heaven on earth, it does seem reasonable to hope — and perhaps even to demand — that we will someday behave far more responsibly and establish a society based on the needs of the entire planet and the beings that inhabit it, a society that is just and sustainable, and not characterized by major outbreaks of self-defeating violence.

In this book, we shall explore some of the needs, prospects, and obstacles involved in achieving such a world. We begin with an examination of war — its causes, prevention, and alternatives. This issue reflects what is perhaps humanity's most serious challenge, because behind the threat of war — especially nuclear war — lies the prospect that human beings may end their civilization, and perhaps their species. This dilemma is also the primary reason for this book, and for the special urgency of establishing an enduring system of peace.

Part I looks specifically at the promise of peace and the problem of war. War and peace are not polar opposites; nonetheless, there is a fundamental tension between them, two differing visions of the way people interact with one another. Part II considers war and its apparent causes, and Part III possible routes toward preventing and abolishing war. Part IV turns to deeper aspects of peace, examining the outlines of our dilemma and considering some solutions, including the creation of positive structures of peace — steps that go beyond the mere prevention of war. Throughout, I hope to challenge you, the reader, both in theory and in the dimensions of your own life.

Chapter 1 begins with an overview of peace as both an ideal and a reality. After grappling with the slippery meaning of "peace," we look at the difficult issue of goals and definitions and ponder another unsettled question: "What is Peace Studies?" Chapter 2 examines the meaning of war, presenting an overview of organized violence through history. Chapter 3 introduces peace movements — their past and current status — including some suggestions as to their future prospects. Peace Studies differs from many other academic disciplines in that its subject is immediately — often painfully — relevant to each of us. Accordingly, Chapters 4 and 5 introduce the reader to some of today's most unpleasant but undeniable realities: what we might call "war movements." Chapter 4 briefly examines so-called conventional trouble spots, and Chapter 5 the problem of nuclear weapons and nuclear war.

1

The Meaning of Peace

Life is a great bundle of little things.
Oliver Wendell Holmes

This text is based on several assumptions: War is humanity's most pressing problem, peace is preferable to war, and moreover, peace can and must include not only the absence of war but also the establishment of positive life-affirming and life-enhancing values and structures. We must also assume, with regret, that there are no simple solutions to the problem of war; most aspects of the war–peace dilemma are complex, interconnected, and often poorly understood. On the other hand, much can be gained by exploring the various dimensions of war and peace, including the prospects of achieving a just, sustainable world—a way of living that will nurture life itself, and of which all citizens can be proud. Throughout, I maintain that there is reason for hope, not simply as an article of faith, but based on the realistic premise that human beings, once they understand the larger situation and recognize their own best interests, can behave rationally, creatively, and with compassion. Positive steps can be taken that will diminish humanity's reliance on organized violence to settle conflicts, and that will begin the construction of a better, more truly peaceful world.

We all think we know what *peace* means. But in fact, different people often have very different understandings of this seemingly simple word. And although most of us agree that some form of peace — whatever it means — is desirable, there are often vigorous disagreements (sometimes violent ones!) over how to obtain it.

HISTORICAL VIEWS OF PEACE

In some cases, the word *peace* has an unpleasant connotation. The Roman poet Tacitus spoke of making a desert and calling it peace, an unwanted situation of sterility and emptiness. Similarly, although nearly everyone desires "peace of mind," the illusory peace that comes from a temporary, drug-based withdrawal from reality, the neutral peacefulness of sleep, or the undesired peace of a coma or even of death may not seem so attractive. To be pacified (from the Latin word for peace, *pax* or *pacis*) often means to be lulled into a false and misleading quietude, and appeasement — buying off a would-be aggressor, thereby achieving a temporary peace by making concessions — has a bad name indeed. By contrast, even the most peace-loving among us recognize the merits of certain war-related attitudes, especially when they refer to something other than direct military engagements: Lyndon Johnson's war on poverty, for example, or the Bush administration's war on drugs, or the medical battle against AIDS.

Eastern Concepts

All this is not simply a matter of playing with words: The truth is that fighting, striving, and engaging in various forms of combat (especially when they are successful) are widely associated with vigor, energy, and other positive virtues. Nonetheless, it is no exaggeration to say that peace is probably the most longed-for and widely desired human condition. The Chinese philosopher Lao Tse (sixth century B.C.), founder of Taoism and author of *Tao De Ching*, emphasized that military force is not the "Tao" or "Way" for human beings to follow. He frequently referred to peaceful images of water or wind — both of them soft and yielding, yet ultimately triumphant over such "hard" substances as

Mohandas K. Gandhi sitting alone. Gandhi became one of the great teachers and practitioners of nonviolence in the twentieth century; he led a very simple personal life and was especially inspired by the Hindu philosophy of "selflessness." (*Gandhi the Man*, by E. Easwaran, courtesy of Nilgiri Press, Petaluma, Ca.)

rock or iron. The teachings of Confucius (approx. 551–479 B.C.) are often thought by Westerners to revolve exclusively around respect for tradition, including elders and one's ancestors. But Confucius did not hold to these ideas because he valued obedience and order as particular virtues in themselves; rather, he maintained that the attainment of peace was the ultimate human goal and that peace came from social harmony and equilibrium. His best-known writings, the *Analects*, also emphasized the doctrine of *jen* (empathy) founded on a kind of hierarchic Golden Rule: Treat your subordinates as you would like to be treated by your superiors.

The writings of another renowned Chinese philosopher and religious leader, Mo-tzu (468–401 B.C.), took a more radical perspective. He argued against offensive war and in favor of all-embracing love as a universal human virtue and the highest earthly goal, yet one that is within the grasp of each of us. "Those who love others will be loved in return. Do good to others and others will do good to you. Hate people and be hated by them. Hurt them and they will hurt you. What is hard about that?"[1]

In what is today India, the Buddhist emperor Aśoka (third century B.C.) is renowned for abandoning his successful military enterprises in mid-career and devoting himself to religious conversion by nonviolent persuasion. The great Hindu epic *Mahabharata* (written around 200 B.C.) contains as perhaps its most important treatise the *Bhagavad-Gita*. This is an account of a great civil war in ancient India, in which one of the principal warriors, Arjuna, is reluctant to fight because many of his friends and relatives are on the opposing side. He is ultimately persuaded to do so by the God Krishna, who convinces Arjuna that he must act, not out of hatred, or hope for personal gain, but out of selfless duty. Although the *Gita* can and has been interpreted as supporting caste loyalty and the obligation to kill when bidden to do so, it also inspired the Indian nonviolent leader Mohandas Gandhi and others as an allegory for the deemphasis of self in the pursuit of higher goals.

Judeo-Christian Concepts

Peace as such is not prominent in the Old Testament. The God of Abraham, Moses, and David is in fact rather bellicose, even bloodthirsty, and the ancient Israelites were successful and merciless warriors. Exceptions exist, however, such as the prophet Isaiah, who praised the reign of peace and described war not as a reward or a route to success, but rather as a punishment to be visited upon those who have failed God. Under the influence of Isaiah and later prophets — and despite the violence of the Maccabees and the Zealots (early terrorist opponents of Roman rule in Palestine), not to mention modern-day Israeli military activities — Jewish tradition has strongly endorsed peacefulness as opposed to the warrior traditions of the Christian and Islamic societies within which most Jews have lived.

Perhaps it is more accurate, however, to say that Jewish, Christian, and Islamic traditions all have bellicose components and periods in their history. A key question, then, for Western thought and faith is whether these warrior activities — often quite persistent and widespread — are part of a pattern of faithfulness to or deviation from their underlying religious traditions.

A deep irony surrounds the concept of peace in all three great Western religious systems. Christianity, for example, gave rise to one of the great warrior traditions of the world, and yet it is unique among world religions in the degree to which it was founded upon a message of peace, love, and nonviolence. "My peace I give unto you," offers Jesus,[2] along with "the peace of God, which passeth all understanding."[3] We shall return to religious as well as ethical conceptions of war and peace in Chapter 19; for now, let us note that most human beings share a positive presumption in favor of peace, although definitions often vary, and hypocrisy is not infrequent.

POSITIVE VERSUS NEGATIVE PEACE

An important distinction must be made between what may be called negative peace and positive peace. *Negative peace* is simply the absence of war. It is a condition in which no active, organized military violence is taking place. The noted French social/political/military thinker Raymond Aron was thinking of negative peace when he defined peace as a condition of "more or less lasting suspension of violent modes of rivalry between political units."[4] His is the most common understanding of "peace" in the context of international politics and issues of "war and peace." It suggests that peace is found whenever war or other direct forms of organized violence are absent. The peace proclamations of Pharaonic Egypt, the *Philanthropa*, were actually statements of a negative peace, expressions of benevolence from a stronger party toward those who were weaker. The *pax* of Roman times really meant no more than an absence of overt violence, typically a condition of nonresistance or acquiescence enforced by legal arrangements and the military might of the Roman legions. The negative peace of the *Pax Romana* was obtained through social repression.

An alternative view, one that has been advanced particularly by Norwegian peace researcher Johan Galtung, emphasizes the importance of *positive peace*. Positive peace is more than merely the absence of war or even the absence of violence. It refers to a condition of society in which exploitation is minimized or eliminated altogether, and in which there is neither overt violence nor the more subtle phenomenon of structural violence.

The Role of Structural Violence

The traditional meaning of violence suggests that it is physical and readily apparent through direct injury or the infliction of pain. But as Galtung notes, it is important to recognize the existence of another form of violence, one that is more indirect and insidious. This *structural violence* is typically built into the very structure of social and cultural institutions. Note that situations of negative peace can be rife with structural violence: both ancient Egypt and imperial Rome practiced slavery, and were in many ways rigid despotisms. There may have been few revolts, and extended periods without wars, but the "peace" that prevailed was a negative peace at best. (In German, the word for cemetery is *Friedhof*, literally "peace yard.")

Structural violence has the effect of denying people important rights such as economic opportunity, social and political equality, a sense of fulfillment and self-worth, and so on. When people starve to death, or even go hungry, a kind of violence is taking place. Similarly, when human beings suffer from diseases that are preventable, when they are denied a decent education, housing, an opportunity to play, to grow, to work, to raise a family, to express themselves freely, to organize peacefully, or to participate in their own governance, a kind of violence is occurring, even if bullets or clubs are not used. Society brings violence upon human rights and dignity when it forcibly stunts the optimum development of each human being, whether because of race, religion, sex, sexual preference, age, or whatever. Structural violence is another

Biography

Johan Galtung

Johan Galtung is one of the great figures in Peace Studies. Born in 1930 in Norway, he holds advanced degrees in both mathematics and sociology. In 1959 he established the first peace research institute, the International Peace Research Institute in Oslo, and served as its director for ten years. He was Professor of Conflict and Peace Research at the University of Oslo from 1969–1977, and founded the *Journal of Peace Research* and the Inter-University Center in Dubrovnik, Yugoslavia. Dr. Galtung has consulted with virtually every United Nations agency and has served as a visiting professor on five continents, including work at Columbia, Duke, and Princeton Universities in the United States, and universities in Japan, China, India, and Malaysia. He is currently Professor of Peace Studies at the University of Hawaii.

Dr. Galtung is fluent in six languages. His prodigious output includes 50 books and more than 1,000 published articles, many of the articles substantial monographs. He has had an immense impact on the discipline of Peace Studies as a thinker, writer, lecturer, consultant, and activist.

way of identifying oppression. And oppression is widespread.

Under systems of structural violence, otherwise "good" people, thinking themselves peace-loving and at peace, may participate in "settings within which individuals may do enormous amounts of harm to other human beings without ever intending to do so, just performing their regular duties as a job defined in the structure."[5] Reviewing the role of normal people, such as Adolf Eichmann, who participated in the Holocaust that murdered six million Jews during World War II, philosopher

Hannah Arendt referred to the "banality of evil" to emphasize the fact that routine, work-a-day behavior by unremarkable people can contribute toward horror.

A shopkeeper in a racially segregated store, for a more pedestrian example, adds directly to the burden of the racially oppressed, even if the segregation is *de facto* — "in fact," because of rigid differences in economic power between the races — rather than *de jure*, specified by laws. Similarly, employees of the Union Carbide pesticide plant at Bhopal, India, did not see themselves as contributing to structural violence, but they did, to the polluted land as well as to a system of economic exploitation, even before the chemical leak that killed thousands in 1984.

Structural violence, including misery, hunger, repression, and alienation, most often works slowly, eroding human values and eventually, human lives. By contrast, direct violence generally works much faster and is more dramatic. In cases of direct violence, even those people not specifically involved in the conflict are inclined to take sides. News coverage is often intense, and because the outcome is often quite real and undeniable — such as dead bodies and property destruction — the viewer is more likely to pay attention and to be concerned. World interest in student-led protests against the Chinese government in 1989, for example, increased dramatically when Chinese troops and tanks opened fire.

Achieving Positive Peace

Despite the prevalence of structural violence, many cultural traditions have identified goals that are closer to positive peace than to its negative cousin. The Greek concept of *irene*, narrowly defined, implies harmony and justice as well as peace.* Similarly, the Arabic *sala'am* and the Hebrew *shalom* embrace not only negative peace but also well-being, wholeness, and harmony within oneself and also among individuals, within a community, and among nations. The Sanskrit word *shanti* refers not only to peace but also to spiritual contentment, an integration of the inward and outward life of human beings, just as the Chinese word *ping* implies harmony or adjustment, the achievement of unity out of diversity (this is comparable to the ancient Chinese concept of integrating seemingly opposed elements, as represented in the classic principles of yin and yang). In Russian, the word *mir* means not only peace but also world, emphasizing the notion that a world at peace would be one that is complete and fundamentally whole.

Attention to negative peace, or the simple absence of war, results in emphasis on peace-*keeping* (the prevention of war) or peace-*restoring* (if war has broken out). By contrast, positive peace focuses on peace-*building*, the establishment of harmonious, nonexploitive social structures, and a determination to work toward that goal even when war is not ongoing or imminent. The former is thus a more conservative goal, as it seeks to keep things the way they are (assuming that war is not actually taking place); the latter is more active and bolder, implying the creation of something that does not currently exist.

Unfortunately, war in the modern world is ongoing in many places and imminent in many others. Moreover, just as there is disagreement among people (most of whom appear to be well intentioned) about how best to avoid war (that is, how to achieve negative peace), there is even more disagreement as to the best route toward positive peace. Positive peace is more difficult to articulate, and perhaps more difficult to achieve, than negative peace. And although there is relatively little debate about the desired end point in the pursuit of negative peace (most people agree that war is a bad thing), when it comes to positive peace, there is substantial disagreement about specific goals and the means of reaching them. Some have argued, for example, that peace should exist only as a negative symbol (the avoidance of war), because once it is defined as a specific ideal system to be achieved, it becomes

---

*Some people have even suggested the term *irenology* for the study of peace. The word has not caught on, however.

Convicts at a Georgia prison farm breaking rocks. A repressive society may be free of overt violence, yet clearly be rife with structural violence and not truly "at peace." (The Bettmann Archive)

something to strive for, even perhaps to the point of going to war in order to achieve it! As one peace researcher remarked:

> Wars have been fought for the sanctity of treaties, for the preservation of law, for the achievement of justice, for the promotion of religion, even to end war and to secure peace. When peace assumes a positive form, therefore, it ceases to be peace. Peace requires that no end should justify violence as a means to its attainment.[6]

Other notable figures, on the other hand, have maintained that a free society may justify — or even require — occasional violence. Thus, Thomas Jefferson wrote in 1787 that "the tree of liberty must be refreshed from time to time with the blood of patriots and tyrants." As we shall see, this tension regarding the acceptability of violence is a recurring theme in the quest for peace.

There are other ways, however, in which peace can assume a positive form, and these are more than mere clichés: cooperation, harmony, justice, and love. Supporters of positive peace uniformly agree that a repressive society, even if it is not at war, can be considered "at peace" only in a very narrow sense. In addition, peace that tolerates outbreaks of violence or that encourages violations of law and order — within political units as well as between them — is acknowledged to be self-contradictory and self-defeating. As we shall see later (Chapter 23), at least one suggestion — nonviolence — holds out the possibility of resolving the tension between means and ends. In other chapters of Part IV, we explore additional aspects of positive peace in detail.

SOCIAL JUSTICE

Having recognized the importance of positive peace, we must now give further attention to it, and to its close kin, social justice. Although everyone agrees that a "just society" is desirable, wide disagreement exists as to what, exactly, such a society would be like. It is useful to identify two fundamental differences in outlook, differences that are largely reflected in the world's two major competing social/economic/political ideologies: capitalism and communism. Capitalism emphasizes opportunity and the doctrine of *earned* benefits. Good work, initiative, independence of mind and spirit, and the rewards of free enterprise are among the bulwarks of capitalist thinking; capitalist societies consider that justice is fundamentally based on individual liberty along with reward for merit. By contrast, communist ideology places great weight on equality. "From each according to his ability; to each according to his need," is considered a guiding maxim of communist society. Whereas capitalism values political freedoms, including the freedom to fail and to be poor, undernourished, unemployed, and so on, communism values economic security — guaranteed jobs, housing, education — but often sacrifices freedom of expression and reward for accomplishment, because the individual takes second place compared to the good of the larger system. Simple as they are, these different

conceptions of social justice permeate many of the East–West conflicts (that is, communist–capitalist conflicts) around the globe.

Social Justice and War

Social injustice, as we shall see, is important not only in its contribution to structural violence but also as a major contributor to war . . . often in unexpected ways. Although the United States of America was originally formed by revolution, it has increasingly emerged as an antirevolutionary force in the world, typically favoring continuation of the status quo. (In a sense, this transition is not really so ironic; the American "revolution" was primarily a struggle for independence and self-government, not a revolution in the system of domestic justice or for a fundamental redistribution of economic, social, or political power.) For most U.S. citizens, as well as conservative Europeans and other privileged people worldwide, their current lifestyles seem fundamentally acceptable. Hence, peace has come to mean the continuation of things as they are, with the additional hope that overt violence will be prevented. For others — perhaps a majority — change of one sort or another is desired. And for a small minority, peace is something to fight for! A Central American peasant was recently quoted in the *New York Times* as saying, "I am for peace, but not peace with hunger."

A long tradition suggests that injustice is a primary cause of war. (We shall examine some of the evidence, and the arguments pro and con, in Chapter 11.) The French philosopher Denis Diderot, for example, was convinced that a world of justice and plenty would mean a world free of tyranny and war. Hence, in his great eighteenth-century treatise, the *Encyclopedia*, Diderot sought to establish peace by disseminating all the world's technical information, from beekeeping to leather tanning and iron forging. And of course, similar efforts continue today, although few advocates of economic and social development claim that the problem of violence can be solved simply by spreading knowledge or even by keeping everyone's belly full.

Problems and Paradoxes

In fact, despite the enormous ills of our planet, there is good reason to believe that our most pressing problem is not hunger, disease, poverty, social inequality, overpopulation, or environmental degradation, but rather the direct violence that human beings commit and threaten to commit against one another. This is especially true with the invention of nuclear weapons. Consider the deep irony of a planet, beset with desperate crises, whose inhabitants nonetheless spend their time and energies fighting with each other, thereby making things even worse. Imagine a small lifeboat, overcrowded, short of food and water, springing leaks, tossed about in stormy seas, and facing a long trip to safe harbor. Imagine further that on this lifeboat there are sufficient resources to patch the leaks, keep everyone nourished, build adequate oars, and makeshift sails so as to complete the voyage safely (and perhaps even enjoyably) . . . but squabbling breaks out among the occupants.* Precious resources get thrown overboard, including the compass, and the boat is in danger of capsizing. Or, try a different image: A space probe headed for Mars has run into serious technical difficulties—the air supply is endangered, the energy source has begun to fail, and the craft has entered an unexpected meteor shower . . . whereupon the astronauts, instead of dealing with their problems, begin a fistfight among themselves!

It is indeed paradoxical that in a time of unique danger and difficulty, the inhabitants of planet Earth waste their time, resources, and energy, as well as their lives, fighting among themselves or preparing to do so. As we shall see, there is nothing new in the human experience about recourse to war. What is new, however, is its profound inappropriateness. With the wolf at the door, we leap to our feet, grab a gun . . . and begin shooting each other.

---

*For an even more disquieting scenario, imagine that resources are *not* sufficient.

THE PEACE–WAR CONTINUUM

"War is not sharply distinguished from peace," wrote Quincy Wright, one of the twentieth century's great students of peace and war, and author of a monumental treatise, *A Study of War.*

> Progress of war and peace between a pair of states may be represented by a curve: the curve descends toward war as tensions, military preparations and limited hostilities culminate in total conflict; and it rises toward peace as tensions relax, arms budgets decline, disputes are settled, trade increases, and cooperative activities develop.[7]

Most people, when pressed, agree that with respect to direct violence, war and peace are two ends of a continuum, with only a vague and uncertain transition between the two. But the fact that two things may lack precise boundaries does not mean that they are indistinguishable. For example, at dawn, night grades almost imperceptibly into day, and vice versa at dusk; yet, when two things are very distinct, we say that they are as different as night and day. The transition from war to peace may be similarly imprecise, but the characteristics of either state are quite dramatic. Consider that U.S. involvement in Vietnam began in the 1950s with economic and military aid to French forces seeking to retain their colonial possessions; it progressed to include the use of small numbers of advisors in the early 1960s, then larger numbers, then direct use of combat troops, massive bombing of the North, and so on. Finally, even though at the height of U.S. involvement more than 500,000 American troops were committed to that struggle, of which about 50,000 died, along with perhaps two million Vietnamese, there was never a formal declaration of war. Yet there was no doubt in anyone's mind that a state of "war" existed.

There is a tendency—especially as happened in the 1980s—for nations to fight wars without formal declarations announcing their beginning or solemn peace treaties signaling their end. The Korean War has never really "ended"; there has simply been a prolonged cease-fire. (That war was never officially declared, either.) Similarly, Israel remains technically at war with most of her Arab neighbors, Egypt excepted. And the most destructive war of recent times, between Iran and Iraq, which produced casualties that may well have numbered in the millions, was never "declared." In fact, most of the world's armed conflicts involve revolutionary and/or counterrevolutionary violence with no declarations of war whatsoever (for example, in El Salvador, Nicaragua, Afghanistan, Angola, Cambodia). This is because in many of these cases, the wars are actually sponsored by major states — often, the superpowers — which prefer to do their fighting by proxy.

The reluctance of governments to declare war, as opposed to their willingness to fight or promote wars, may also be due to the fact that although wars continue to break out, most people are not proud of that fact. And despite the potential for academic arguments over the precise transition points between different stages of armed conflict, most of us undoubtedly know at a gut level what is meant by war. There is also little doubt that given the choice, most of us would prefer peace.

Tennyson expressed an ancient longing:

> Ring out the old, ring in the new.
> Ring out the false, ring in the true. . . .
> Ring out old shapes of foul disease,
> Ring out the narrowing lust of gold;
> Ring out the thousand wars of old,
> Ring in the thousand years of peace.[8]

THE DESIRABILITY OF PEACE VERSUS THE MOTIVATION FOR WAR

Given the positive orientation that most people have toward the word *peace*, it's fair to question why we have never attained it. Perhaps, because we have never known it, we are unsure in our hearts whether it is truly desirable. After all, longing for a "thousand years of peace" is a bit like someone who has never attended a single concert yearning for a paradise in which he or she will spend eternity listening to some heavenly choir! We have not experienced anything approaching a thousand years of peace,

perhaps because in some way we haven't really wanted it. For many centuries, in fact, war has been considered acceptable, even honorable by large numbers of people.

War in U.S. History

Thomas Jefferson once wrote of the United States that "peace is our passion," and its citizens like to think of themselves as peace-loving. But the truth is that even the United States has not been especially peaceful, although like most countries, whenever we employ organized violence, we seek to convince ourselves and others that such actions are merited. Moreover, our society is rife with symbols of war and violence. Guns, for example, have a hallowed place in American folklore: the Kentucky long rifles that opened the frontier, the Winchester repeating rifle that "won the West," and the Colt 45 revolver, the "great equalizer."

"There never was a good war," wrote Benjamin Franklin, "or a bad peace." But Franklin also warned that "even peace can be purchased at too high a price," and indeed U.S. history is often taught as a chronology of major wars, including the War of Independence, the War of 1812, the Mexican–American War, the Civil War, the Spanish–American War, World War I, World War II, the Korean War, and the Vietnam War. How many of us are aware, however, that the United States has also intervened militarily on more than 120 separate occasions, including 18 incursions into China, as well as into Mexico (13), Panama and Nicaragua (9), Honduras (7), Colombia and Turkey (6), Korea, the Dominican Republic, and Japan (5), Argentina, Cuba, Haiti, Hawaii (when it was an independent kingdom), and Samoa (4), Fiji and Uruguay (3), Guatemala, Lebanon, Sumatra, and the U.S.S.R. (2), and once each for the following: Grenada, Puerto Rico, Brazil, Chile, Morocco, Egypt, Formosa, Peru, the Philippines, Cambodia, Laos, Syria, and the Ivory Coast? In most cases, these were relatively minor incursions, intended to protect U.S. economic interests or help maintain compliant governments. But for people caught up in such violence, it was war. And for the current victims, it is war.

Troops of the Fourth U.S. Cavalry Division in Mindanao, the Philippines, in 1906. U.S. troops have often been
engaged in the Philippines, putting down local rebellions aimed at achieving freedom from U.S. rule.
(Thomas Burke Memorial Washington State Museum)

Although the United States cherishes its ideological commitment to peace, and also the separation of military from civilian rule, we have several times chosen our presidents from among our generals: Washington, Jackson, Grant, Eisenhower. Our major leaders have even espoused the desirability of war: Just before the turn of the century, Theodore Roosevelt urged his countrymen not to shrink from acquiring world empire, by war if need be. He wrote that U.S. citizens should value and exercise "the great fighting masterful virtues" and accept imperial responsibilities in Hawaii, Puerto Rico, the Philippines, and Cuba:

> I preach to you, then, my countrymen, that our country calls not for the life of ease but for the life of strenuous endeavor. The twentieth century looms before us big with the fate of many nations. If we stand idly by, if we seek merely swollen, slothful ease and ignoble peace, if we shrink from the hard contests where men must win at hazard of their lives and at the risk of all they hold dear, then the bolder and stronger peoples will pass us by, and will win for themselves the domination of the world.[9]

Biological Justifications for War

Roosevelt speaks for an ancient tradition. War has long been the ultimate arbiter of human disputes, and a way of achieving greatness, both for individuals and whole peoples. Ares, the god of war, was a major Greek deity (Mars was his Roman equivalent); Irene, the goddess of peace, was a minor figure at best. According to Heraclitus, emperor of the

Eastern (Byzantine) Roman Empire during the seventh century A.D., "War is the father of all things." And a potent nineteenth-century viewpoint — no less influential for being fallacious — maintained that war was not only rewarding, virtuous, and manly but also biologically appropriate. This expression of *social Darwinism* attempted to apply the evolutionary concept of natural selection to human political and social activities by providing a biological justification for national conquests, imperialism, military dictatorships, and the subjugation of weaker peoples. After all, went the claim, war and various other human strong-arm tactics were simply the working out of nature's law. But in fact, social Darwinism is not scientifically valid, since natural selection and the process of organic evolution favor living things that are most successful reproductively, not necessarily those that are most aggressive. Moreover, there is no objective basis for assuming that just because something is true in the physical or biological world, it is therefore socially desirable or ethically good. Consider diseases, for example, AIDS or typhoid fever: Both are very "natural" and entirely "organic," and yet most people agree that neither is good.

Social and Political Justifications for War

Some influential thinkers have argued in favor of war, not because it is allegedly natural, but rather, because it is supposed to be beneficial. Thus, Hegel (1770–1831), in *The Philosophy of Right*, suggests:

> War has the higher meaning that through it . . . the ethical health of nations is maintained, since such health does not require the stabilizing of finite arrangements; just as the motion of the winds keeps the sea from the foulness which a constant calm would produce, so war prevents a corruption of nations which a perpetual, let alone an eternal peace would produce.[10]

Although this view is deservedly in disrepute today, the truth is that war has often served to shake things up, producing many changes, not all of them for the worse. Through war, people have "won" their freedom, both by overthrowing despotic governments and by repelling the efforts of others to force them

into subjugation. In some cases, of course, revolutionary wars have resulted in the imposition of new forms of dictatorships — for example, the Cuban Revolution, in which the right-wing dictator Batista was replaced with the left-wing dictator Castro, or the Iranian Revolution, in which the despotic, pro-Western Shah was overthrown, only to be replaced by the despotic Moslem fundamentalist Ayatollah Khomeini. Few people would claim, however, that revolts against oppression should generally be condemned simply because they sometimes go astray.

Consider these facts: In the aftermath of the Cuban Revolution, infant mortality in Cuba has declined to the lowest in Latin America, life expectancy increased from fifty-five years in 1959 to seventy-three years by 1984, per capita food consumption has become the second highest in Latin America, health care is free, literacy exceeds 95 percent (the highest in Latin America), and prostitution, begging, and homelessness — endemic during the Batista years — have been eliminated. This is not to claim that the Cuban Revolution has created an earthly paradise; certain individual rights and liberties are sadly lacking. It simply points out that although opposition governments (such as our own) may criticize Third World revolutions, there is also room to debate whether such efforts necessarily result in worsened conditions, at least for the great majority of the populace.

Especially in societies such as the United States, which tend to support the status quo and to oppose wholesale societal change (whether violent or peaceful), there is a tendency to criticize "failed" revolutions and to point accusingly at the bloodshed that often accompanies revolutionary strife. Writing of the French Revolution, Mark Twain compared "two reigns of terror," the one commonly associated with the revolution, and the other characterizing the regime that was overthrown:

> The one lasted mere months, the other had lasted a thousand years; the one inflicted death upon ten thousand persons, the other upon a hundred million; but our shudders are all for the "horrors" of the minor Terror, the momentary Terror, so to speak. . . . A city cemetery could contain the coffins filled by that brief Terror which we have all been so

diligently taught to shiver at and mourn over; but all France could hardly contain the coffins filled by that older and real Terror — that unspeakably bitter and awful Terror which none of us has been taught to see in its vastness or pity as it deserves.[11]

Although we generally assume that war disrupts society, an alternative view holds that it serves to organize and solidify. Just as social cohesion can be undermined by war, it can also be enhanced by it, as people rally round existing institutions in times of stress, with a sense of closeness that is stimulated by a feeling of shared enemies. Indeed, as we shall see, political elites have sometimes employed the unifying effect of war to distract attention from domestic problems and to prop up or enhance the internal cohesion of their own society.

POLITICAL IDEOLOGIES AND MILITARISM

British military historian Michael Howard has introduced the term *bellicist*, referring to cultures "almost universal in the past, far from extinct in our own day, in which the settling of contentious issues by armed conflict is regarded as natural, inevitable and right."[12] For example, according to Howard, bellicism during World War I "accounts not only for the demonstrations of passionate joy that greeted the outbreak of war but sustained the peoples of Europe uncomplainingly through years of hardship and suffering."[13] On the other hand, many people may be inclined to identify their adversaries as bellicist, while claiming that they, although usually not pacifist, are at least "peace-loving." It is also true that even in modern times there have been ideologies (notably fascism) that have openly glorified war not only as a means but also as a desirable end in itself (more on this in Chapter 9). In fact, the relationship between various political ideologies — conservative, liberal, radical — and war has a long and curious history, as we shall see in the following discussion.

The Conservative Viewpoint

There can be no doubt that in contrast with its more left-wing alternatives, political conservatism has long been more favorable to war. This is especially evident with respect to popular efforts to influence the policy of governments in favor of war avoidance or war termination (see Chapter 3). Nonetheless, even conservative ideologies have espoused a view of peace and war prevention. The conservative tradition traces its conceptual roots to a rather severe, pessimistic view of human nature. At least as far back as the seventeenth century, Thomas Hobbes warned that because of humanity's inherently competitive, sinful nature, primitive life consists of *bellum omnium contra omnes* (war of all against each), which in turn requires the imposition of stringent governmental authority. Socrates, more than two thousand years before, had also argued against democracy, believing that the great majority of people were inherently inclined to misbehavior, which necessitated firm and farsighted leadership from the knowledgeable few, the "philosopher kings." Plato concluded from the Peloponnesian War that states must be tightly organized for survival in a violent, unruly world in which war was an unavoidable fact of life.* As the successor to such Greco-Roman gloominess, the Christian emphasis on original sin provides further conceptual underpinnings for a conservative view of the causes of war, and hence, of the best way to secure peace: through strength and a willingness to use it.

This tradition also suggests that strong moral and governmental controls are necessary if peace is to be secured. For conservatives, war occurs because we are aggressive animals by nature, and because the social order threatens to break or has broken down. Since social groups are seen as basically irrational and unstable, peace can be assured only by appropriate organization and management of power and order. For Hobbes, virtually nothing could justify the overthrow of a monarch, because

---

*Similarly, the Greek philosopher Heraclitus wrote that "all things come into being and pass away through strife." Not all Greek thought was so gloomy and accepting of war, however. Written at about the same time that Plato espoused the inevitability of war, for example, and equally influenced by the Peloponnesian War, Euripides' *The Trojan Women* and Aristophanes' *Lysistrata* reflected an upbeat, distinctly pacifist, and antiwar message.

the "state of nature" is so abominable that anarchy cannot be tolerated. At the same time, ironically, Hobbes recognized that states interact with other states in what is essentially a comparably anarchic situation. "The state of Commonwealths considered in themselves is natural, that is to say, hostile," Hobbes wrote in *The Citizen*. "Neither if they cease from fighting, is it therefore to be called peace; but rather a breathing time."[14]

According to conservative doctrine, if power is properly and securely held, there should be little cause for war, except for occasional brief wars to adjust the world political system — that is, for legitimate "reasons of state" (see Chapter 9). War may be acceptable, even laudable, if it serves to prevent civic breakdown. For example, the Roman historian Livy (59 B.C.–A.D. 17) wrote approvingly in *The Early History of Rome* that the Senate had "ordered an immediate raising of troops and a general mobilization on the largest possible scale" in the hope that the revolutionary proposals that the tribunes were bringing forth might be forgotten in the bustle and excitement of three imminent military campaigns. The Roman general Vegetius is first credited with the phrase *vis paccem, para bellum* (if you want peace, prepare for war), and in more recent times, the doctrines of "balance of power" and "peace through strength" have continued this trend of conservative thought (see Chapter 14).

Probably the most articulate spokesperson for conservative peace strategies was the English orator and statesman Edmund Burke (1729–1797). Burke reflected conservative doctrine in stressing the primacy of community, the importance of preserving the existing institutional order, and skepticism about the perfectability of the human person. At heart, this philosophy has long been motivated by a lack of faith in the potential of the autonomous individual and a deep suspicion of democracy. For conservatives, the traditions of the past must at all costs be respected. Social cohesion is seen to come from reverence and respect for, and deference to, authority (this is why Confucius is also considered to be a conservative social philosopher). Authority and, typically, patriarchy are valued over change, equality, and spontaneity. According to Burke, society is a partnership "not only between those who

are living, but between those who are living, those who are dead, and those who are to be born."[15] In addition, social hierarchies have long been admired by conservative political philosophers, as providing necessary reference points and stability. In more recent times, with the overthrow of hereditary aristocracy, conservatism has shifted from its earlier reverence for the social network and begun advocating rugged individualism, free enterprise, and indeed, individualism over community — in direct opposition to its classical underpinnings. Conservative thought has also become ambivalent toward the state, generally opposing "big government" (except in the realm of military expenditures and in support of large internal police forces, widespread surveillance of dissidents, and so on) and yet also revering patriotism and loyalty to the state.

Not surprisingly, conservatives have long been especially opposed to the threat of disorder coming from abroad. Writing of the traumatic event of his day, the French Revolution, Burke observed: "It is a war between the partisans of the ancient, civil, moral and political order of Europe [the monarchy] against a set of fanatical and ambitious atheists which means to change them all."[16] Burke anticipated the attitude of present-day ideological conservatives when he wrote the following, which could also stand for Ronald Reagan's attitude toward the Sandinistas of Nicaragua:

> I never thought we could make peace with the [French revolutionary] system; because it was not for the sake of an object we pursued in rivalry with each other, but with the system itself that we were at war. As I understood the matter, we were at war, not with its conduct, but with its existence, convinced that its existence and its hostility were the same.[17]

The Liberal Viewpoint

Traditionally, liberals have valued the autonomous individual, free from political, financial, and ecclesiastical authority. Major liberal theorists include John Locke (seventeenth century), Thomas Jefferson (eighteenth century), Jeremy Bentham and John Stuart Mill (nineteenth century), Joseph Schumpeter and John Maynard Keynes (early twentieth century), and John Rawls and Arthur Schlesinger (later twentieth century). According to liberal thought, equality is more desirable than hierarchy. The classical liberalism of the eighteenth century was aligned against monarchism, in favor of egalitarian entrepreneurship and, thus, capitalism; surprisingly to people of the late twentieth century who associate modern conservatism with reverence for "free market" competition and liberalism with belief in the "welfare state," Adam Smith and David Ricardo — economists who are to capitalism what Karl Marx is to communism — were considered among the leading *liberals* of their day. As recently as 1913, liberal theorist Norman Angell claimed that capitalists were necessarily opposed to war: "The capitalist has no country, and he knows . . . that arms and conquests and juggling with frontiers serve no ends of his and may very well defeat them, through the great destruction that such wars will generate."[18]

Another major strand in liberal thought addresses the issue of peace from an economic perspective. In *The Spirit of Laws*, the eighteenth-century political philosopher Montesquieu proposed that international trade and commerce will naturally tend to promote peace: "Two nations which trade with each other become reciprocally dependent; if it is to the advantage of one to buy, it is to the advantage of the other to sell; and all unions are founded on mutual needs."[19] He also argued that trade leads to an improvement in manners and basic civility: "It is almost a general rule that wherever there are tender manners, there is commerce, and wherever there is commerce, there are tender manners."[20] In a similar vein, John Stuart Mill argued that

> It is commerce which is rapidly rendering war obsolete, by strengthening and multiplying the personal interests which act in natural opposition to it. And it may be said without exaggeration that the great extent and rapid increase of international trade, in being the principal guarantee of the peace of the world, is the great permanent security for the uninterrupted progress of the ideas, the institutions, and the character of the human race.[21]

This view soon became a major part of the liberal antiwar credo: By expanding commerce and spreading the political power of capitalism, as well as by working on public opinion, war would be made obsolete. Englishmen Richard Cobden (1804–1865) and John Bright (1811–1889), for example, led the so-called Manchester school, which opposed foreign interventionism and maintained that maximum free trade between people would serve to make war not only unnecessary but also impossible.

In a reversal of roles, however, especially in the United States, twentieth-century liberals have typically placed greater emphasis on social responsibility and community, whereas conservatives have championed individualism and free enterprise . . . except in the area of civil liberties, where liberals champion individual freedom and most conservatives still consider the social unit (that is, the state) to have a higher priority.

With regard to the establishment of peace and the causes of war, liberals have emphasized the excessive power of political states (see Chapter 9), psychological "state of mind" theories as well as the role of misunderstandings (see Chapter 10), and the undue influence of a military/economic/political elite (see Chapter 11). Such concepts may have a good deal of validity, but they have in the past also led to excessive "psychologizing" and a tendency to ignore "wrong-doing," thereby on occasion making war more rather than less likely. For example, noted liberal pacifist Philip Lothian wrote in 1935 that "in some degree the brutality of National Socialists [Nazis] is the reaction to the treatment given to Germany herself since the war," and that "the best way of restoring reasonable rights to the Jews in Germany is not to counter hate with hate, but to undermine the source of the evil aspects of National Socialism by giving Germany her rightful place in Europe."[22] (Nonetheless, it was mainly the conservatives, in Britain and France, who appeased nazism, at least in part because of their greater fear of communism and their hope that Hitler might help destroy European communism in general and the Soviet Union in particular.)

After World War I, the growth of fascism caught liberals, pacifists, and the more radical socialists by surprise, unprepared as they were for its combination of populism, nationalism, and author-

General Francisco Franco salutes passing troops during a victory parade in Madrid, 1939. The fascist forces, opposed by leftists (ranging from liberals to communists) and supported by the right wing (including conservatives and nazis), were ultimately successful in the Spanish civil war. (UPI/Bettmann Newsphotos)

itarianism, its overtly militaristic tendencies and disinterest in world peace. The liberal perspective has had difficulty coming to terms with "bellicist" cultures and ideologies generally; today, conservative critics never tire of accusing liberals of being insufficiently attuned to what conservatives see as the aggressiveness and ambition of world communism. Liberals, in turn, criticize conservatives for taking a narrow, us-versus-them view of foreign events, a view they claim verges on inflammatory war-mongering and often employs a double standard in embracing right-wing — even fascist — regimes so long as they pronounce themselves to be anticommunist. Among most liberals, arms con-

trol — and, more rarely, disarmament — is a prominent goal (see Chapter 15), and much hope tends to be invested in international organizations such as the United Nations (see Chapter 16), as well as international law more generally (see Chapter 17). In addition, in their quest for peace, liberals are more likely than conservatives to consider that governments have a responsibility to achieve such goals as economic well-being, human rights, and ecological harmony (Chapters 20–22). Liberals are also much more inclined than conservatives to be enthusiastic about nonviolence (see Chapter 23).

However, liberalism has also, on occasion, embraced specific wars. The Spanish civil war (1936–1939), for example, was initially seen by the left as an unambiguously just war: A democratic, popularly elected government was under attack by reactionary forces aided by the fascist dictatorships in Italy and Germany. However, the government's unity was quickly compromised by attacks by communists against their rivals on the left, and the loyalist camp was badly split by 1938–1939. This was nothing new: Left-wing political movements have historically succumbed to internal disputes and fratricide (see Chapter 3). By contrast, right-wing movements have traditionally been more united, probably because right-wing ideology, as we have seen, is more likely to respect hierarchy and uniformity. In any event — and ironically for those who associate left-liberalism with opposition to war — the political left sought (although unsuccessfully) to involve Britain, France, and the United States in the Spanish civil war, on the loyalist's side, while the political middle and the conservatives preferred noninvolvement. By the 1980s, those sentiments were reversed: Reagan conservatives were urging greater U.S. involvement in wars in Nicaragua, Afghanistan, Angola, and El Salvador, just as a decade earlier, conservatives had urged vigorous prosecution of the war in Vietnam.

The ultimate factor that decides liberal versus conservative attitudes toward any particular war thus seems to have less to do with general ideological preferences for peace than with the question of who the war would be against: Liberals are likely to condone, even support, wars that oppose right-wing despotisms, whereas conservatives respond similarly to wars against governments of the far left. In short, neither liberals nor conservatives have a monopoly on opposing war and supporting peace.

The Radical Leftist Viewpoint

Political persuasions of the far right—fascism and nazism—did not profess peace as a goal, or even as a virtue. In fact, as previously mentioned, fascist ideology glorified war (see Chapter 11). On the other hand, radical left-wing ideologies have traditionally claimed an association with peace, although often approving of militarism and war under certain conditions. The most extreme and best-known example comes from the Chinese communist revolutionary and political leader Mao Ze-Dong.

> Political power grows out of the barrel of a gun. . . . All things grow out of the barrel of a gun. . . . Some people ridicule us as advocates of the "omnipotence of war." Yes, we are advocates of the omnipotence of revolutionary war; that is good, not bad, it is Marxist. . . . We are advocates of the abolition of war, we do not want war; but war can only be abolished through war, and in order to get rid of the gun it is necessary to take up the gun.[23]

In this view, the end (peace) justifies the means (war). However, it should be noted that such extreme ideologies appear to be increasingly isolated in the world today, and moreover, Maoist actions only rarely matched their rhetoric. Since the death of Mao, the Chinese themselves have largely abandoned such policies.

During the nineteenth century, Europe experienced rapid growth of its military forces, an increase in the number of nation-states, a reduction in the importance of monarchies, and the development of industrial facilities capable of achieving rapid imperialist expansion. Similarly, the United States was undergoing a period of rapid territorial and economic expansion that, by the end of the century, would leave it poised to enter the world scene. In both Europe and the United States, the political left vigorously debated the role of global capitalism: Liberals felt that it promised an interconnected, and thus war-free, world, whereas socialists saw it as immensely dangerous and war-

Mao Ze-Dong, communist leader of China, shortly after the successful revolution of 1949. Mao's rhetoric embraced violence, ostensibly in pursuit of peace. (UPI/Bettmann Newsphotos)

inducing, the engine of a highly militarized and exploitive state system.

In Europe, Karl Marx claimed that capitalism and the ensuing class conflicts had been responsible for war, and that accordingly, a classless, communist society would be warless (see Chapter 11). Note, however, that neither socialism nor communism is necessarily pacifist—both socialist and communist ideologues have often advocated the use of military force in order to gain their ends. There are two diverging traditions in radical left-wing ideology regarding peace: a militarist view associated with Lenin, Mao, and Che Guevara that advocated the use of war—especially revolution— to overcome the evils of capitalism, and an antimilitarist, socialist–pacifist tradition, represented early in the twentieth century by people such as Rosa Luxemburg, Karl Liebknecht, and Dorothy Day, that renounced the use of violence and advocated social change via peaceful evolution, especially through work with labor unions, which—it was hoped — would use massive strikes to oppose war-making by their governments.*

Within the United States, the antimilitarist socialist tradition, under the leadership of men such as Norman Thomas and Eugene V. Debs and women such as Emma Goldman and Rosa Luxemburg, was historically the most pronounced. We should note, too, that much socialist antimilitarism was also anti-Marxist. Religious considerations have also loomed large in many cases, as with the antiwar Catholic activism of Dorothy Day and the Protestantism of A. J. Muste. (Muste is particularly well known for the observations "There is no way to peace; peace is the way" and "Wars will end when men refuse to fight.")

Prior to World War I, in particular, European socialists (who were generally non-Marxist and who favored the nonmilitarist tradition) hoped that "worker solidarity" would prevent the outbreak of war. For example, more than 250,000 people attended an antiwar, socialist rally in Berlin after the first Balkan War in 1912, chanting "War on war, peace for the world." During World War I, the notion of "revolutionary defeatism" briefly took hold as well, based on the hope that armed conflict between capitalist states could be transformed into a liberating, revolutionary conflict between the classes within each state.† On the other hand, even before World War I, many theorists worried that socialist pacifism would be dangerous to the security of the state. For example, in 1914, socialist H. N. Brailsford warned that "the country which had the most socialists would be the first to be devoured and exploited by its neighbors."[24] The outbreak of World War I shortly thereafter was an enormous blow to the forces of pacifist socialism, since the overwhelming majority of socialists, on both sides, elected to support their governments in the war effort, rather than seeking to use the "power of the proletariat" to stifle the war-making efforts of governments and their ruling classes.

In the aftermath of World War I, when socialism could have turned more vigorously antimilitarist, it did not do so; this was at least partly because of a perceived need to defend the first successful socialist revolution — in Russia — from Western hostility and intervention. With the emergence of the U.S.S.R. as a viable political entity, socialist peace movements became increasingly state-oriented themselves. And with the triumph of fascism in the mid-1920s in Italy and the early 1930s in Germany, the socialist "peace tradition" also became increasingly dominated by an often militant antifascism, as it coalesced in opposition to its right-wing opponents. By the same token, socialists have been notoriously self-critical and rocked with fratricidal debate as to the "politically correct" course of action. Thus, for example, a socialist government in France was unable to commit itself to aid the antifascist loyalists during the Spanish civil war, and in modern Spain, a socialist government that initially opposed NATO has become a supporter of that military pact.

In summary, socialists have long advocated opposition to war, although some have felt that the abolition of war was justified by any means, including war itself. For communists, the need for protection of socialism within the Soviet Union also seemed to warrant the use of military force, initially as defense against an overwhelmingly hostile capitalist world. Following World War II, socialists and communists were especially likely to align themselves with anticolonial liberation movements, many of which have been violent. At present, although socialist militarism as such is generally muted, the avowedly antimilitarist tradition within socialism is also relatively weak and uninfluential.

WAR AND PEACE: SOME HOPEFUL HISTORY

Nineteenth-century liberalism viewed war as a regrettable interruption in a progression toward a better, more peaceful world. Even today, liberal

---

*Both Luxemburg and Liebknecht, we should note, were ultimately drawn into an unsuccessful armed rebellion in post–World War I Germany, the so-called Sparticist insurrection (after which both were murdered by the German military).

†To some degree, this is exactly what happened in Russia, where the terrible turmoil of the war contributed greatly to the Bolshevik Revolution.

interpretations of the causes of war (the perspective favored by this author) emphasize the role of misperceptions and errors of one sort or another. War, in this view, is a blunder, the consequence of human fallibility. According to some political scientists, wars occur for the same reasons as automobile accidents. Few people intentionally drive their vehicles into trees or oncoming traffic: More likely, they lose control at crucial times, perhaps because they go too fast, pay insufficient attention, encounter some icy spots, or have a blowout or other malfunction.

By contrast, as we have seen, there is another, sterner perspective, associated with traditionally conservative viewpoints. The emphasis here is on human weakness or sin, the unalterable fact of evil and the need to confront such evil in the interest of morality and human dignity. "The story of the human race," said Winston Churchill, "is war." According to this view, wars do not occur because one side — presumably, the one that is more peace-loving — misunderstands the other, but rather because it understands the other, and the threat it poses, all too well. Wars are thus forced upon human beings by the excesses of those who would do evil; as a result, the righteous must always be alert to defend themselves and others. "The price of liberty," we are told, "is eternal vigilance." According to this view, liberty may also demand a willingness to go to war if need be.

Is War Inevitable?

Regardless of one's thinking about the ultimate causes of war, the belief that war is inevitable carries with it a great danger. Sociologists identify the phenomenon of the "self-fulfilling prophecy," something that is not necessarily true, but that becomes true if believed. For example, if we believe that someone (or some country) is an enemy and we then act on this assumption, our belief may become reality. Similarly, if war is considered inevitable, and societies therefore prepare to fight — for example, by drafting an army, procuring weapons that threaten their neighbors, following a bellicose foreign policy — war may well result. And that fact will

then be cited as proof that the war was inevitable from the start; moreover, it will be used to justify similar behavior in the future. So as we examine the nature of peace and war, and various theories of causation and prevention, bear in mind that these ideas are important. They are literally matters of life and death.

It is also important to remember that social patterns are flexible. Consider that dueling was once a common, and widely accepted, way of settling quarrels: Alexander Hamilton, for example, was killed in a duel. And for thousands of years, it was widely believed that some people — the aristocracy — were of royal blood, and therefore inherently superior to others simply by virtue of their birthright. To cite one more example, cannibalism appears to have been widespread among our human ancestors and in many different societies. It is virtually unknown today.

The most dramatic case of people overcoming a widespread social pattern, however, is that of slavery. Little more than one hundred years ago, slavery was entirely legal in the American South, and also in much of the rest of the "civilized" world. Abolitionists, calling for the immediate end of slavery, were widely considered dreamers, impossible idealists, or dangerous revolutionaries who threatened the very foundations of Western civilization. Slaveowners, on the other hand, argued forcefully that the institution of slavery was necessary for human progress, precisely what some people have claimed for warfare in more recent times. Similarly, slavery was said to be necessary because slaves were so "uncivilized" and "barbarous" that they couldn't be trusted in decent society, just as a nation's enemies today are typically described as so barbarous that they can't be trusted to behave decently toward the rest of the world. Supporters of slavery also claimed that without the economic benefits of slavery (unpaid labor), the agricultural economy of the American South would collapse; again, a similar claim is made today about the economic benefits of military spending, especially in certain regions (the South, the Southwest, the Northwest) that are particularly dependent on it. And finally, it was pointed out that there were "good masters," who treated their slaves

Auction sale for slaves in Charleston, South Carolina (1861 engraving). Scenes such as this were relatively common in the American South. (The Bettmann Archive)

well, just as, ostensibly, there have been certain "good wars." But just as every slave-holder, no matter how "good," was in fact necessarily an enemy of liberty, it can be said that every war, no matter how "good" — and no matter whether it was truly fought for freedom and democracy — serves fundamentally to compromise and sully those principles.

Nonetheless, we must also acknowledge that ending slavery — or dueling or cannibalism or any other once accepted social pattern — may well have been easy compared with the task of ending war, since these earlier changes were feasible without regard to what other people, or other states, were doing. War, however, is in a different category, since a state that renounces war as a means of settling conflicts might find itself vulnerable to others that retain war as an option. In short, an end to war will require more than a modern-day Abraham Lincoln.

An emancipation proclamation to end war could not simply be announced and then unilaterally implemented; it would have to be multilateral and perhaps universal.

Can Nations Change?

There are, however, reasons for optimism. For example, history provides many examples of societies changing dramatically between warlike and peaceful tendencies. During the early Middle Ages, the Swiss were among the world's most bellicose people, fighting successfully against the French in northern Italy, and for their own independence against the Hapsburg ruler of the Holy Roman Empire. Swiss pikemen became the scourge of European battlefields, providing the most effective defense against a charging knight. Although

Switzerland still retains a relatively muscular military force, including mandatory conscription and a comparatively large and well-equipped army, it hasn't participated in an external war since 1515, when it was defeated by the French and adopted a policy of permanent neutrality.

Sweden is another nonbelligerent country that keeps a high military profile, yet has maintained a peaceful neutrality in modern history. In contrast, under King Gustavus Adolphus (1594–1632), Sweden was a militaristic and expansionist state, fighting wars with Denmark, Poland, and Russia. One hundred years later, Sweden fought Russia again, and also became embroiled in the Napoleonic Wars during the early nineteenth century.

Japan has also changed notably. It gave birth to one of the world's great warrior traditions, the code of *bushido* and the highly aggressive *samurai*. Within several decades after European firearms reached Japan via Portuguese traders in 1542, Japanese musketry was the most advanced in the world. But a century later, guns were virtually gone from all of Japan, and when Commodore Matthew Perry "opened" Japan in 1853, Japanese warfare was technologically medieval. The process had been remarkable: The victorious sixteenth-century shogun Tokugawa centralized all firearms manufacture and arranged for all gunpowder weapons gradually to disappear altogether. His decision was not based on a devotion to peace; rather, it reflected the samurais' great distaste for muskets and cannons, which threatened to ruin the cult of the warrior/nobleman. After all, anyone — even a relatively untrained, unskilled commoner — could use a gun to dispatch a great samurai. Although the motives may seem ignoble, the Japanese example is nonetheless inspiring, since it demonstrates that military excess can be curtailed, and whole societies reorganized along more peaceful lines, once the authorities (and in democracies — perhaps — the people) consider such changes to be in their best interest.

It should also be noted that the demilitarization of Japan was itself reversed: During the latter half of the nineteenth century, Japan modernized very rapidly and initiated successful wars against China (1894) and Russia (1904–1905). Japan's aggressive, warlike phase culminated in its defeat during the Second World War in 1945, after which it has kept a relatively small military force while enjoying astounding economic growth. This growth is due at least in part to the small role of military expenditures in the modern Japanese economy, which allows resources to be devoted overwhelmingly to civilian production. (It can be said that the U.S.–Soviet Cold War has had one clear winner: Japan!)

Germany has been similarly variable in its war–peace behavior. About one third of all Germans perished during the devastating Thirty Years' War (1618–1648), many of them innocent civilian victims of that especially brutal conflict. Germany then became the architectural, musical, and philosophical center of continental Europe, although militarism did flourish in Prussia, later the most influential of the German states. Germany itself went through a militaristic phase, beginning around 1860 with the wars of German unification under the direction of Otto von Bismarck, and ending in 1945 with the German defeat in the Second World War. Today, Germany — both the communist East and capitalist West — has large military forces, but neither German state has been expansionist,* at least in part because of political restrictions imposed by the victors in World War II.

Peaceful relationships and traditions can be ruptured by war, just as peaceful societies can become militarized. For example, despite longstanding Jewish advocacy of peace and nonviolence, modern-day Israel expends about 30 percent of its gross national product on its military, and has been involved in four wars (1948, 1956, 1967, and 1974) as well as several invasions of neighboring Lebanon (1978, 1982) during its brief existence.

War can become a national habit, and militarism, a way of life. But so can peace. Traditions of war and conflict can give way to traditions of peaceful alliance: take Great Britain and France, which were bitter opponents for hundreds of years, and

---

*Assuming, that is, that the two Germanies have not already united; even if they have, however, the point is unchanged because if anything German militarism will likely be carefully restrained by the United States and Soviet Union, if not by the Germans themselves.

which have been close allies throughout the twentieth century. As Kenneth Boulding—one of the founders of Peace Studies—has emphasized, a zone of "stable peace" has spread to include western Europe, North America, and Oceania.[25] Within this zone, war is so unlikely as to be essentially inconceivable.

However one judges the preciousness of peace or the legitimacy of war, it should be clear that peace and war are fluctuating conditions, and that neither should be taken for granted. Neither is humanity's "natural state." Our situation—whether to be at peace or at war—is ours to decide. The field of Peace Studies offers help in making this decision.

THE DEBATE OVER PEACE STUDIES

Peace studies is a relatively new discipline. It originated in the aftermath of World War I, a war that shocked Western sensibilities and intellect with its savagery, its cost, and the fact that—even more than most preceding wars—it seemed tragically unnecessary. In the aftermath of the Vietnam War (another conflict that was especially vicious, destructive, and seemingly avoidable) Peace Studies has blossomed as an academic discipline: More than two hundred colleges and universities in the United States currently offer Peace Studies courses or programs. Not surprisingly, however, Peace Studies has also been controversial. We shall therefore examine briefly the two major objections to the subject that have been raised, as well as the responses to those objections. The reader should be warned that (also not surprisingly) this textbook is biased in favor of Peace Studies.

Is Peace Studies Politically and Ideologically Motivated?

Critics argue that the real motivation for Peace Studies is not academic but rather political and ideological. As two conservative scholars put it: "The movement for Peace Studies in schools is part of a trend towards the politicization of education, involving both the lowering of intellectual standards and the assumption of foregone political con-

clusions."[26] Another critic suggests that Peace Studies is

> really designed to do battle with the Strategic Defense Initiative, the MX missile and any other strategic system introduced by the [Reagan] Administration. In the 1920s people who taught such nonsense at least had the courage to define their position as pacifism. Their views didn't masquerade as a new scholarly discipline.

The issue, therefore, is not academics, but advocacy: "These are scholars who intend to win a war for the minds of students."[27] Peace Studies, according to this view, is an effort to indoctrinate students with a particular perspective, one that is left-wing, antimilitary, and anticapitalist. The claim, in short, is that Peace Studies is too politicized and not sufficiently objective. Modern social science is not supposed to advocate particular social goals; rather, social scientists are generally expected to be objective students of social phenomena.

In fact, Peace Studies has a clearly stated value orientation: It is opposed to war and biased toward peace (although not necessarily toward pacifism). As University of Chicago scholar Quincy Wright has put it, there is in modern times

> a more widespread opinion than in any other period of history that war has not functioned well in the 20th Century. Far from being a generally accepted instrument of statesmanship deplored by only a few, war has during the modern period come to be generally recognized as a problem.[28]

Peace Studies is committed to helping solve that problem. "Peace" is thus given a positive value by most students of Peace Studies, while war is given a negative value. Readers will accordingly detect a tone of advocacy in this book, since Peace Studies rather forthrightly proclaims a normative attitude, favoring peace and nonviolence over war and violence.

If such an approach seems unusual for an academic enterprise (even one that is avowedly "relevant" to real-world problems), consider the case of medicine, an applied science committed to addressing the problem of illness. Medical science is objective, in that it seeks to obtain all relevant information, wherever possible minimizing the personal bias of the investigator. When it comes to illness, however, medicine is hardly neutral. Medicine unabashedly seeks to prevent illness or, if prevention fails, to help diminish its ill-effects and, when possible, to provide a cure. Similarly, Peace Studies is an applied science directed toward preventing, diminishing, or curing violence, whether direct or structural. Ultimately, it seeks to establish peace just as medicine seeks to establish health and well-being. Medical researchers and practitioners make no apologies for advocating health; advocates of Peace Studies are similarly committed to the goal of peace and similarly unapologetic.

Although Peace Studies is not neutral, we can still argue that it, like medicine, is objective, taking all relevant factors into account in order to understand the topic as completely as possible. To be neutral is to be lacking in personal preference as to outcome. It is possible, therefore, for Peace Studies to be objective, although it refuses to be neutral. For an example of such nonneutrality, consider this recommendation from one of the leaders of the field, Anatol Rapaport: "A given direction in peace research should be evaluated by the extent to which it contributes to undermining and delegitimizing the global military system."[29]

Regarding the accusation that Peace Studies favors peace over war, then, there is nothing to dispute. It does. A similar argument applies to other disciplines that have recently emerged in the academic world. Environmental Studies, for example, clearly favors an enlightened stewardship of the environment over pollution, despoilation, species extinction, and other forms of ecological abuse, even though the issues addressed in Environmental Studies are often complex, controversial, and intensely political (as with debate over the relative merits of "economic development"). There are similar debates within Peace Studies. For example, just as environmentalists appreciate not only an unpolluted environment but also the jobs provided by an industrial plant, so too, freedom, as well as peace, is recognized as a value. In some cases, as we shall see, freedom — or private possessions, or the right to elect one's government or to celebrate one's ethnic identity — may be judged sufficiently precious to be worth fighting for. In such cases, Peace Stud-

ies has the responsibility to illuminate and clarify the issues.

Specialists and students in a given field may also legitimately advocate their own viewpoint, so long as they are clear and honest in doing so. Scholars always work from a point of view. In psychology, for example, the Freudian is biased (politically biased, one might say) in favor of a particular perspective that emphasizes the role of the unconscious and of early experiences against that of neurobiology or family therapy. Economists tend to see human behavior as motivated primarily by financial considerations; this doctrinal "bias" makes economists less sensitive to the role of genetic factors, historical trends, and so on.

Finally, as for the charge that Peace Studies is too political, it is worth noting that university personnel have, for decades, worked on weapons research (from the atomic bomb to the Strategic Defense Initiative), have designed murderous "pacification" programs during the Vietnam War, and so forth, all projects with direct political significance. It is therefore curious that scholarly activity oriented away from aggression should be criticized as being "too political," simply because it favors peace over war. Most human endeavors, including academic disciplines, are "political." Peace Studies is unusual only in that it admits it.

As we have seen, however, peace is not necessarily part of the left-wing or liberal political agenda, nor is war necessarily more acceptable to those of the right-wing or conservative persuasion. What has been called the "war system" is nonetheless associated with establishment values, if only because war has long been a dominant theme in the behavior of nations. Concern with social justice, human rights, and ecological integrity in general tends to be more evenly distributed across the political/ideological spectrum, but advocates of Peace Studies in particular have been drawn largely from the left-liberal perspective. This is hardly surprising considering that the solutions to these problems generally involve distributing social power more equitably.

The truth is, Peace Studies typically directs students and faculty toward ways of thought that dissent from the mainstream of modern political life, and for that reason the field is perceived (perhaps rightly) as threatening and dangerous to the status quo. In addition, as we have seen, students of Peace Studies generally consider true peace to be more than negative peace, or the simple absence of war. The following passage, from a recent volume concerned with the full scope of peace research, emphasizes the need for Peace Studies to advocate social change:

> As soon as the simple distinction between war and peace is abandoned, thinking about peace necessarily becomes integrated into much broader currents of political thought and practice. Indeed, it hardly seems possible to think seriously about political life in the modern world without some understanding of the way the characteristic forms of contemporary violence challenge so many of our inherited assumptions about what it means to be human, and how we ought to act towards each other. Peace is neither a technical policy problem, nor an easy utopian aspiration. It is a challenge both to prevailing structures of power and to our understanding of what it now means to engage in political life. . . . Not only is it necessary to treat peace as more than just the absence of war, and to refuse to separate peace from injustice, it is also necessary to understand the pursuit of peace as part of a widespread if often inchoate attempt to generate new forms of political practice in the face of fundamental historical change.[30]

Is Peace Studies Redundant?

Critics also argue that Peace Studies is not needed because its material is already covered by existing academic disciplines. Thus, History departments concern themselves with the causes and effects of various wars. Political Science deals with governments and even contains specialized subdisciplines such as international relations, strategic studies, violence, and conflict resolution. Specialists in Psychology investigate individual and group decision making, as well as questions of personal motivation. Programs in Philosophy and in Religion concern themselves with ethics, while Sociology examines social movements including militarism. Economists examine financial and budgetary aspects of war and military spending. International Law is part of the legal curriculum, while concern with the effects of nuclear war has been increasingly reflected in courses within Biology, Environmental Science, Atmospheric Science, and/or Physics. What, then, is left for Peace Studies?

In fact, it is not really important whether Peace Studies is recognized as a new discipline, department, or program. Rather, what matters is that peace (as a necessity and a practical goal) and war, social injustice and ecological destruction (as problems) be established as legitimate areas of concern and inquiry. It is also important that people wishing to direct their studies toward such issues be able to do so within the academic community. Just as with Environmental Studies, Women's Studies, or Black Studies, traditional academic territorial boundaries do not ordinarily permit the interdisciplinary approach that is so desperately needed. Concern about nuclear war, for example, demands attention not just from political science, psychology, economics, history, physics, and so on, but from all of these disciplines. Peace Studies seeks to provide an umbrella under which such attention can be directed. It encourages the systematic integration of disciplines relevant to peace. It also legitimizes the work of scholars who feel that such issues warrant their time and attention, but whose efforts would otherwise be constrained by the traditional limitations of the existing parent disciplines.

No one has a monopoly on wisdom when it comes to the search for peace. However, students of Peace Studies can agree with the maxim of the University for Peace, chartered by the United Nations and located in Costa Rica: "If you desire peace, educate for peace."

THE NATURE AND FUNCTIONS OF CONFLICT

We end this chapter with a brief discussion of various ways of conceptualizing conflict. The word *rivalry*, for example, originated with the Latin *rivus* (river or stream). Rivals were literally "those who use a stream in common." Competitors, by contrast, are those who seek to obtain something that is present in limited supply, such as water, food, mates, or status. But the word *enemy* derives from the Latin *in* (not) plus *amicus* (friendly), and implies a state of active hostility. Rivals necessarily compete, if there is a scarcity of a sought-after resource — this much is unavoidable — but they do not have to be enemies. The word *conflict*, on the other hand, derives from the Latin *confligere*, which means literally "to strike together." It is impossible for two physical objects, such as two billiard balls, to occupy the same space. They conflict, and if either is in motion, their conflict will be resolved by a new position for both of them. Within the human realm, conflict occurs when different social entities are rivals or otherwise in competition. Such conflicts can have many different outcomes: one side changed, one side eliminated, both sides changed, neither side changed, or (rarely) both sides eliminated. Conflicts can be resolved in many ways: by violence, by mutual agreement, by the issues changing over time, and so on.

Conflict, and its more dangerous manifestation, violence, both have a variable, but generally important, place in the history of social thought. In his influential work *The Prince*, the Italian statesman and political philosopher Niccolò Machiavelli (1469–1527) laid out certain basic principles of government. Machiavelli's writing is notable for its unapologetic, even admiring, yet unromanticized advice regarding the uses of conflict, power, and violence. His arguments also serve as a starting point for much of the modern "realist" tradition in political thought (see Chapter 9), and thus as a counterpoint to the central orientation of Peace Studies. Machiavelli's primary assumptions, which give rise to the "Machiavellian" world view, are as follows:

1. *Violence is ever-present and inevitable.* "There is no avoiding war," writes Machiavelli. "It can only be postponed to the advantage of others." In that case, one is justified — indeed, obligated — to employ war and other forms of violence whenever and wherever such application will be most useful.

2. *Violence can be effective, even desirable.* "It is a question of cruelty used well or badly." In addition, military affairs are more important than other political questions: "All armed prophets have conquered, and unarmed proph-

ets have come to grief. . . . The main foundations of every state . . . are good laws and good arms."[31]

3. *The state and its government are the primary actors, and they must be essentially independent of other states, each of which pursue their own vital interests, ultimately using power to determine success or failure.*

It should be pointed out that Machiavelli did not worship violence. However, he emphasized its importance, and had no moral qualms about recommending that it be employed. The perspective of Peace Studies, by contrast, is that violence is not the solution, but rather the problem.

A century after Machiavelli, in 1651, the English philosopher Thomas Hobbes argued that in the absence of an overarching authority, human interactions would degenerate into social unrest and violence; this was his justification for what he called the *Leviathan*, the political state. The ideas of Jean-Jacques Rousseau stand in marked contrast. In his best-known work, *The Social Contract* (1762), Rousseau noted that "man is born free but is everywhere in chains." Rather than championing the state as a means of preventing conflict, Rousseau maintained that conflict is largely a product of civilization, and the state, accordingly, is not so much the solution as a major part of the problem. The eighteenth-century utilitarian philosophers Jeremy Bentham and John Stuart Mill proposed that society should function to minimize conflict by achieving the greatest good for the greatest number of its citizens. Karl Marx developed his theories of history, politics, and economics around the importance of class conflict. Other eighteenth-century theorists, notably the sociologists Georg Simmel and Ludwig Gumplowicz, as well as social Darwinists such as Walter Bagehot and Herbert Spencer, emphasized the positive, creative components of conflict. The pioneering sociologist Max Weber described how conflict serves as an important, although often painful, agent of change. By contrast, twentieth-century American social thinkers such as Talcott Parsons have been especially interested in developing models of social process based on order and consensus, with little attention to conflict as such.

A FINAL NOTE ON THE MEANING OF PEACE

It should be emphasized that the study of peace does not ignore the importance of conflict. Nor does Peace Studies aim to abolish conflict, any more than it expects to eliminate rivalry or competition in a world of finite resources and imperfect human nature. (Analogously, the field of medicine does not seek to eliminate all bacteria or viruses from the world.) Peace Studies does, where possible, seek to develop new avenues for cooperation, as well as an end to *violence*, especially to organized and increasingly destructive violence. It is this violence, by any definition the polar opposite of peace, that has so blemished human history and that — with the advent of nuclear weapons — now threatens the future as well. And it is the horrors of such violence, as well as the elusive, glorious, and perhaps even realistic hope of peace (both negative and positive), that make Peace Studies especially frustrating, fascinating, and essential.

Study Questions

1. Compare conceptions of peace that appear desirable and undesirable.

2. Discuss the relative importance of positive versus negative peace. Which is easier to define? To achieve?

3. There is a striking contrast between the often-expressed longing for peace and the recurring reality of organized violence. Explain, specifically with regard to the United States.

4. What are some presumed benefits of organized violence?

5. How do the fundamental attitudes of conservatism and liberalism toward peace derive from their differing attitudes toward society and the role of the individual?

6. What similarities exist between right-wing and left-wing radicals regarding their commitment toward peace? What differences?

7. What are some practical consequences of the assumption that war is inevitable?

8. Discuss some examples from history that lend credence to the hope that peace is attainable.

9. Assess the validity of some of the primary criticisms of the field of Peace Studies. Can you think of additional criticism beyond those discussed in the text?

10. It is often said that advocates of peace do not necessarily foresee a world without conflict, only one without violence (at least without organized violence). Explain.

Suggestions for Further Reading

Kenneth Boulding. 1978. *Stable Peace.* University of Texas Press: Austin.

Michael Howard. 1978. *War and the Liberal Conscience.* Rutgers University Press: New Brunswick, NJ.

Richard Falk, Samuel S. Kim, and Saul H. Mendlovitz. 1980. *Toward a Just World Order.* Westview Press: Boulder, CO.

Saul H. Mendlovitz and R. B. J. Walker, eds. 1987. *Towards a Just World Peace.* Butterworths: London.

Peter Wallensteen, ed. 1989. *Peace Research: Achievements and Challenges.* Westview Press: Boulder, CO.

Source Notes

1. Mo-tzu. *Mo-tzu, The Writings of Mo-tzu*, XV.

2. John 14: 27.

3. Phil. 4: 7.

4. Raymond Aron. 1966. *Peace and War.* Doubleday: New York.

5. Johan Galtung. 1985. "Twenty-Five Years of Peace Research: Ten Challenges and Responses." *Journal of Peace Research* 22: 414–431.

6. Quincy Wright. 1964. *A Study of War.* University of Chicago Press: Chicago.

7. Quincy Wright. 1968. "War." In D. S. Sills (ed.), *International Encyclopedia of the Social Sciences.* Macmillan: New York.

8. Alfred, Lord Tennyson. 1974. "In Memoriam." In John D. Jump (ed.), *Memoriam, Maude and Other Poems.* Rowman and Littlefield: Totowa, NJ.

9. Theodore Roosevelt. 1910. *The Strenuous Life and Other Essays.* Review of Reviews Company: New York.

10. Georg W. F. Hegel. 1942. *Philosophy of Right.* (T. M. Knox, trans.) Clarendon Press: Oxford, U.K.

11. Mark Twain. 1988. *A Connecticut Yankee in King Arthur's Court.* Morrow: New York.

12. Michael Howard. 1986. *The Causes of Wars.* Harvard University Press: Cambridge, MA.

13. Ibid.

14. Thomas Hobbes. 1949. *The Citizen.* Appleton-Century-Crofts: New York.

15. Edmund Burke. 1961. *Reflections on the Revolution in France.* Doubleday: New York.

16. Ibid.

17. Ibid.

18. Norman Angell. 1913. *The Great Illusion.* Heinemann: London.

19. C. L. Montesquieu. 1977. *The Spirit of Laws.* (David Carrithers, trans.) University of California Press: Berkeley.

20. Ibid.

21. John Stuart Mill. 1958. *Considerations on Representative Government.* The Liberal Arts Press: New York.

22. Quoted in Martin Gilbert. 1964. *Britain and Germany Between the Wars.* Longmans: London.

23. Mao Ze-Dong. 1966. *Basic Tactics.* (Stuart R. Schram, trans.) Praeger: New York.

24. H. N. Brailsford. 1918. *The War of Steel and Gold.* Bell: London.

25. Kenneth Boulding. 1978. *Stable Peace.* University of Texas Press: Austin.

26. Caroline Cox and Roger Scruton. 1985. *Peace Studies: A Critical Survey.* Institute for European Defence and Strategic Studies: London.

27. Herbert London. "Peace Studies—Hardly Academic." From the *New York Times*, quoted in Conrad G. Brunk, "Peace Studies in the University." 1987. *The McGill Journal of Education* 22: 299–306.

28. Wright. *A Study of War.*

29. Anatol Rapaport. 1975. "Approaches to Peace Research." In M. Nettleship, R. Givens, and A. Nettleship (eds.), *War: Its Causes and Correlates.* Mouton: The Hague, Netherlands.

30. R. B. J. Walker and Saul H. Mendlovitz. 1987. "Peace, Politics and Contemporary Social Movements." In S. H. Mendlovitz and R. B. J. Walker (eds.), *Towards a Just Peace.* Butterworths: London.

31. Niccolò Machiavelli. 1977. *The Prince.* Norton: New York.

2

The Meaning of War

Man's body is so small, yet his capacity for suffering is so immense.

Rabindranath Tagore

The great majority of human activities — buying and selling, sowing and reaping, loving, learning, eating, sleeping, worshiping — takes place with a minimum of overt conflict, and certainly without anything even remotely resembling war. Warfare nonetheless has a special importance for human beings, particularly since the invention of nuclear weapons in 1945, which raised the very real possibility that war could extinguish human civilization and, possibly, life on Earth.

Peace researcher Quincy Wright began his classic *A Study of War* by noting that

> To different people war may have very different meanings. To some it is a plague which ought to be eliminated; to some, a mistake which should be avoided; to others, a crime which ought to be punished; to still others, it is an anachronism which no longer serves any purpose. On the other hand, there are some who take a more receptive attitude toward war and regard it as an adventure which may be interesting, an instrument which may be useful, a procedure which may be legitimate and appropriate, or a condition of existence for which one must be prepared.[1]

If war is to be understood, and ultimately overcome, we must first agree as to what it is. In this text, we will consider "hot" wars — that is, overt violent conflict between governments or rival groups hoping to establish governments. In recent times, an official declaration of war has been relatively rare; nonetheless, in many cases, "wars" can still easily be recognized, not only wars between different states but also civil wars and so-called wars of liberation. For the most part, we shall exclude feuds, disputes, or cases of banditry, as well as "trade wars," propaganda wars, or "cold" wars, except insofar as these have a bearing on hot wars.

SOME ISSUES IN DEFINING WARS

Many people have compiled data on war throughout history, both to help pinpoint its characteristics and to test various scientific hypotheses about its causes and/or effects. However, the experts have not always been able to agree on which armed struggles deserve to be included in such a compilation. There is little doubt, for example, that World War I and World War II are major examples, but what about the War of the Bavarian Succession, (1778–1779)? In this "war," fully armed Prussian and Austrian troops marched while drums rolled . . . but not a shot was fired. War was declared, but no one died. By contrast, consider the Korean War, in which more than two million people (military and civilian) were killed: The United States was a major protagonist, and yet war was never declared.* Instead, it was officially known as a United Nations "police action." Or consider the Vietnam War, in which, once again, no official state of "war" was ever acknowledged.

Quincy Wright considered a war to have taken place either when it was formally declared or when a certain number of troops were involved; he suggested 50,000 as a baseline. Lewis Richardson, a Quaker mathematician and another pioneering peace researcher, sought to define wars by the number of deaths incurred.[2] More recently, J. D. Singer and M. Small have focused on a minimum of 1,000

combat-related fatalities.[3] Whatever the technicalities, most people would agree that war can be described in much the same way as the noted jurist's observation about pornography: "I may not be able to define it, but I know it when I see it."

Similarly, there can be debate over exactly when a given war began. The United States entered World War II in December, 1941, after the Japanese attack on Pearl Harbor, just as the Soviet Union had entered the war six months earlier, after being attacked by Germany. Most historians, however, (and virtually all Europeans) consider that World War II began with Hitler's invasion of Poland in 1939, after which France and Britain declared war on Germany. On the other hand, some would argue that World War II began with Italy's invasion of Ethiopia (1935), or even earlier, with Japan's occupation of China (1931). And some experts even maintain that in fact World War II began when World War I ended, with the Treaty of Versailles (1919), which created great resentment among the German people, leading ultimately to a resumption of armed hostilities twenty years later.

Psychologically, the substance of war is found in the intensely hostile attitudes among two or more contending groups. Economically, war involves the emergency diversion of major resources from civilian to military pursuits. Sociologically, it results in a rigid structuring of society, with priority given to military functions. Perhaps the most famous definition of war, however, speaks to its political significance. Karl von Clausewitz (1780–1831), a Prussian army officer best known for the treatise *On War*, defined war as "an act of violence intended to compel our opponents to fulfill our will."[4] He further emphasized that war was "the continuation of politics by other means,"[5] by which he meant war should not simply reflect senseless fury; rather, it should be an orchestrated action, with a particular political goal in mind.

In the last few centuries, several prominent Prussian leaders have advocated the brusque use of force, including war if necessary, to achieve desired ends. Frederick II, also known as Frederick the Great, king of Prussia from 1740 to 1786, wrote that diplomacy without armaments is like music without instruments. In the same vein, Otto von

---

*Neither was peace; that is, the conflict is still officially unresolved, with an ongoing armed truce.

Bismarck, architect of German unification during the nineteenth century, announced to his Parliament: "It is not by speeches and resolutions that the great questions of the time are decided . . . but by iron and blood."

THE FREQUENCY AND INTENSITY OF WAR

By some measures, war has actually been relatively unimportant on the human scene. Based on the number of national states existing since 1815, there have been approximately 16,000 nation-years, and during this time, war has occupied "only" 600 of these nation-years, or somewhat less than 4 percent of the possible total. The twentieth century has been, overall, a very warlike one, and yet modern warfare, even with its enormous capacity for devastation, was directly responsible for fewer than about 2 percent of all human deaths occurring during that time. Note, however, that there have also been many indirect casualties of war, since war and the preparation for war divert resources that might be directed against other causes of death, such as disease and starvation. The particular importance of war derives from its extraordinary violence, its seemingly unnecessary destructiveness, and — in modern times — its potential of wreaking unimaginable havoc.

Scholars estimate that between the years 1500 and 1942 there was an average of nearly one formally declared war per year. This estimate does not include armed revolutions, of which between 1900 and 1965 there were approximately 350, an average of more than 5 per year. According to Lewis Richardson, there were at least 59 million deaths from human violence between 1820 and 1946, of which fewer than 10 million were attributable to individual and small-group violence; the remainder were due to war.[6] Other estimates are comparable.

Indirect Killing

In addition to the direct casualties, war kills indirectly, particularly by disease among armed forces personnel and by starvation as a result of disrupted food production and distribution services. For ex-ample, more than 8 million soldiers and 1 million civilians died during World War I, with approximately 18 million additional deaths resulting from the influenza epidemic of 1918. Historically, in fact, more soldiers have died of diseases and of exposure than from enemy fire: More than eight times as many French soldiers died from cholera during the Crimean War as from battle. Similarly, of Napoleon's forces that invaded Russia in 1812, many more died from the cold and from pneumonia than from Russian military resistance. During the Thirty Years' War, the armies of Gustavus and Wallenstein, facing each other outside Nuremberg in 1632, lost 18,000 men to typhus and scurvy, and separated without a shot having been fired!

In modern times, deaths due to disease have become less prominent during war as a result of improved medical technology. At the same time, however, advances in military technology have made wars themselves more deadly, especially for nearby civilians: Military deaths were roughly the same in World Wars I and II (nearly 17 million), but civilian deaths in World War II (approximately 35 million) were about seven times greater than in World War I. In the past, civilians did sometimes suffer horribly during wars, notably during the Thirty Years' War, when an estimated one third of the German population was killed, and during the sacking of fallen cities, such as Carthage at the end of its long war with Rome. But through most of human history, war casualties have been overwhelmingly concentrated among military forces. With advances in military technology, however, not only have casualties in general increased, but the ratio of civilian to military deaths has risen to unprecedented levels as well. And in the event of nuclear war, in which the casualties could well include essentially all the civilian population on both sides, the numbers would be staggering.

The Waste of War

The sheer wastefulness of war has been appalling, even with non-nuclear weapons. During the Battle of the Somme (1916) in World War I, for example, the British sought to pierce the German lines; they gained a mere 120 square miles, at a cost of 420,000

Front-line trench scene during World War I. During this war, military deaths were exceptionally high, not only from direct combat but also from disease due to relatively primitive medicine as well as unsanitary conditions. (U.S. Signal Corps, U.S. National Archives)

men (3,500 deaths per square mile) while the Germans lost 445,000. At the Battle of Ypres (1917), the British advanced 45 square miles, in the process losing 370,000 men. During World War I alone, Europe lost virtually an entire generation of young men. Here is F. Scott Fitzgerald's description of the Somme battlefield:

> See that little stream—we could walk to it in two minutes. It took the British a month to walk to it— a whole empire walking very slowly, dying in front and pushing forward behind. And another empire walked very slowly backward, a few inches a day, leaving the dead like a million bloody rugs.[7]

Numbers ultimately can be numbing. For example, of the 2,900,000 men who served in the U.S. armed forces in Vietnam (average age 19), 300,000 were wounded and 55,000 were killed. Yet, these figures convey very little of the war's significance or of its horror, both for those who served and for the country at large . . . and especially for the people of Vietnam. They also ignore the war's devastating socioeconomic consequences for Vietnam, as well as for the United States where it prompted an upsurge of inflation as well as profound social effects, including widespread alienation of one generation from the next. There were also political consequences, including a hesitancy to engage U.S. service personnel in subsequent foreign conflicts. In Vietnam itself, the economy was shattered, the natural environment devastated, and several million Vietnamese killed.

Clearly, war has been terribly important to human beings. Like a lurking nightmare, it haunts our consciousness far out of proportion to the numbers of people it has actually destroyed. And regrettably, most of the historical trends in warfare are not reassuring.

HISTORICAL TRENDS IN WAR

The most dramatic changes in warmaking involve technological innovations, which we will examine later in this section. But other long-term changes can also be recognized.

Numerical Trends

The following list of facts and figures should give some idea of how war has evolved over the past five hundred or so years. Consider, for example, these trends:

1. *An increase in the human, environmental, and economic costs of war, and in the number of civilian casualties.*   Three hundred years ago, the Thirty Years' War laid waste to much of what is today Germany; World War II did the same to a large part of Europe, including the western U.S.S.R., as well as Japan and many cities of China. The twentieth century also witnessed the initiation of large-scale destruction of civilian shipping, especially with the use of submarines. Attacks on noncombatants became particularly pronounced with the use of air bombardment — of Ethiopians by Italy prior to World War II; of Spanish Loyalists by German and Italian "volunteers" during the Spanish civil war; of Chinese by Japan; of Poles, Dutch, and English by Germany; of Finns by the U.S.S.R.; and of Japanese and Germans by the United States and Britain during World War II. The ratio of civilian to military casualties at Hamburg, Dresden, Hiroshima, and Nagasaki was on the order of thousands to one.

2. *An increase in the geographical areas involved in the actual battles.*   In ancient times, battles typically took place in or near, and were named for, cities or mountain passes: the Battle of Thermopylae, Waterloo, Gettysburg. By World War I, battles had expanded to encompass entire rivers: the battles of the Marne, the Somme, the Isonzo. During World War II, many of the battles had expanded yet more, to span whole countries or oceans: the Battle of

Britain, the Battle of the Atlantic; on land, the tides of battle swept across the entire continent of Europe. This trend suggests that battles in World War III will almost certainly be global in scope.

3. *An increase in the length of battles, in the number of battles fought per year during the course of a war, and in the number of battles per war.*   The average European war of the sixteenth century comprised fewer than two major battles; the seventeenth century, four; the eighteenth and nineteenth centuries, around twenty; and the twentieth century, more than thirty. Battles once commonly lasted a few hours or an afternoon, and typically did not take place during the winter months or at night; modern battles may last for weeks and occur at any time of day or night and any time of year.

4. *A decrease in the average length of wars and in the ratio of years spent at war to years spent at peace.*   Although the battles are longer, modern wars themselves tend to be briefer but more intense than earlier, more leisurely ones, such as the Hundred Years' War or the Thirty Years' War. During the sixteenth and seventeenth centuries, the major European powers spent about 65 percent of their time in a formal state of war; this percentage has decreased steadily, to 38 percent in the eighteenth century, 28 percent in the nineteenth, and 18 percent in the twentieth. On the other hand, if undeclared "wars" such as colonial expeditions and various armed interventions are taken into account, these figures increase dramatically. The United States, which prides itself (legitimately or not) on its peacefulness, has in fact experienced only twenty years since 1789 when its armed forces were not seeing action somewhere around the globe.

5. *An increase in both the absolute size of armies and in their size relative to the total population increases in peacetime forces-in-being, in the number (both absolute and relative) actually*

*mobilized during war, in the number of combat-
ants engaged in battle, and in the number of
civilians involved in war preparation and conduct.*   European armies during the sixteenth
century were largely made up of mercenaries,
and rarely exceeded 20,000 soldiers. Seventeenth-century armies commonly numbered
around 50,000, which translates into approximately 3 soldiers per thousand population
(about the same proportion as during the Roman Empire). The eighteenth-century armies
of Frederick the Great (Prussia) and Lord
Marlborough (England) approached 100,000
and those of Louis XIV (France) reached
nearly 200,000. During the nineteenth century,
Napoleon fielded as many as 200,000 men *for
a single battle.* And in the world wars of the
twentieth century, armies were measured in the
millions.

6. *A decrease in the casualty rate among combatants — that is, in the proportion of those actually
involved in a battle being injured.*   In the Middle Ages, for example, the defeated side, typically the one that broke and ran, would be cut
down by the victors, often losing as many as 50
percent of its fighting men. By modern standards, however, the actual numbers in question
were small: thousands or, at most, tens of thousands of soldiers involved, as opposed to modern armies numbering in the hundreds of
thousands. Up to the sixteenth century, about
25 percent of combatants died; by the seventeenth century, this proportion was about 20
percent, dwindling to 15 percent in the eighteenth century, 10 percent in the nineteenth,
and 6 percent in the twentieth. This is partly
because with modern technology, a larger proportion of "combatants" are engaged in support and supply rather than actual fighting. In
addition, the proportion of injuries leading to
death has decreased because of better medical
care for the wounded. And disease, once a major scourge during wartime, now causes fewer
fatalities. On the other hand, the proportion of
the civilian population engaged in armed

forces has increased, and since the number and
duration of battles has increased as well, the
percentage of the national population dying in
war has also risen. In France, for example,
approximately 11 out of every 1,000 deaths
during the seventeenth century were due to
military service; in the eighteenth century, this
number had increased to 27; by the nineteenth
century, 30; and in the twentieth, 63.

7. *An increase in the speed at which war spread to
additional belligerents, in the number of belligerents involved in a given war, and in the area
covered.*   During the fifteenth and sixteenth
centuries, each war had, on average, just slightly
more than two participants. By the twentieth
century, the number had jumped to five. As to
geographic area, consider that the Thirty
Years' War took place in central Europe, the
War of the Spanish Succession in Holland, the
Napoleonic wars throughout Europe and parts
of the Near East, and World Wars I and II
throughout the world. (By the same token, the
Seven Years' War has claim to being a world
war, with fighting in Europe, India, and North
America as well as in the Caribbean.)

Considering the increase in world population and in the number of independent political states, no clear-cut evidence exists that war
is increasing, measured either as the number of
wars occurring during a given time period or
as the number of states at war per year. The
frequency of wars has been increasing, but at
about the same pace as the increase in number
of national states. In recent times, there have
actually been somewhat fewer wars than in the
past, with longer periods of peace in between.
On the other hand, when wars have occurred
in modern times, they have been more bloody
overall than in the past, both in the actual number of deaths and in the proportion of the population affected. So, we are having fewer,
shorter wars, but they have become more intense and more lethal.

These generalizations apply only to international wars. Historically, civil wars have

tended to be the most costly of all in terms of lives lost: the War of the Roses (England) during the fifteenth century; the Huguenot wars (France) during the sixteenth century; the Thirty Years' War (Germany) during the seventeenth century; the War Between the States (U.S.) and the Tai'ping Rebellion (China) in the nineteenth century; and the Spanish, Chinese, and Nigerian civil wars of the twentieth century, to name just a few. In such cases, one nation bears the entire cost of war, which tends to produce very high casualties, probably because large numbers of relatively untrained soldiers typically are involved, and because the struggle may occur over wide areas with few prepared defenses.

8. *Since World War II, an increase in the frequency of so-called low-intensity conflicts (LICs) in which the two superpowers especially become indirectly involved in Third World conflicts, revolutions, and counterrevolutions.* Both the United States and the Soviet Union — although the former to a greater degree — have tended to consider that their "national interests" include the outcome of struggles taking place virtually anywhere on the globe. Often, they have interpreted strictly indigenous conflicts, especially those reflecting revolutionary nationalism, as evidence of meddling by the other side, and have regarded the nations involved, therefore, as pawns in the East–West conflict. Moreover, as war has become potentially more destructive and more likely to engulf the superpowers, strategy has focused increasingly on fighting comparatively limited wars — for example, U.S. support for the contras in Nicaragua or the *mujahedeen* in Afghanistan (see Chapter 4) — that are less threatening to the major powers but that nonetheless allow them to carry on their rivalry . . . on someone else's soil. The U.S. experience in the Vietnam War (and quite possibly, the Soviet experience in Afghanistan) also sensitized government leaders to the difficulties of conducting wars that are expensive, in terms of money as well as

lives, and that do not enjoy strong public support. As a result, we can expect increased interest in orchestrating LICs that are comparatively low profile, and hence, less controversial and domestically disruptive.

At the same time, it must be emphasized that the phrase "low-intensity conflict" is very much a euphemism, dangerously misleading with regard to the death and misery it may produce.* Among strategists in the United States, who by the late 1980s seemed especially committed to the concept, an LIC is really a *war*, typically in the Third World, in which the number of U.S. combatants and casualties are kept low; for those directly affected, by contrast, the damage can be staggering. For example, consider the death toll in Nicaragua during the U.S.-sponsored contra war of the 1980s: more than 29,000. To gain a better perspective on this, imagine that Nicaragua's population (3.5 million) was that of the United States (242 million). In that case, a comparable cost to the United States would be more than 2 million lives. Proportionately, the Nicaraguan death toll in this "low-intensity war" exceeded all U.S. losses in all the wars of its history, from the Revolutionary War to Vietnam.

Trends in Style and in Citizen Participation

There have been other trends as well. A major one involves the declining role of personal honor and glory, as well as the end of the so-called code of chivalry. The Battle of Crécy (1346), for example, at which English longbowmen soundly defeated a much larger contingent of heavily armored French knights, is considered one of the major turning points in military history. Following that battle, the victorious Prince of Wales hosted a formal banquet to honor the captured king of France and his son

---

*Similar euphemisms would include the "police actions" in Korea (1950–1953) and Vietnam (1962–1974), "peacekeeping" in the Dominican Republic (1965), and the "rescue operation" in Grenada (1983).

A Nicaraguan family, displaced by the war between the U.S.-backed contra rebels and the Nicaraguan Army, in a temporary shelter. The cost of this war, although relatively low as far as the U.S. economy and population are concerned, has been enormous for the Nicaraguans. (Reuters/Bettmann Newsphotos)

Philip. According to a contemporary historian, the gracious victor offered the following toast:

> In my opinion . . . you have this day acquired such high renown for prowess, that you have surpassed all the best knights on your side. I do not, dear sir, merely speak this way to flatter you, for all those of our side who have seen and observed the actions of each party, have unanimously allowed this to be your due, and decree you the prize and garland for it.[8]

The account continues:

> At the end of this speech there were murmurs of praise heard from every one, and the French said, the prince had spoken nobly and truly, and that he would be one of the most gallant princes in Christendom, if God should grant him life to pursue his career of glory.[9]

Although such delicacy and courtesy still linger on occasion, as with the respectful treatment some-

times accorded captured officers, modern war has become increasingly more brusque and less mannered.

As we shall see in Chapter 7, primitive war among hunter–gatherer bands only rarely involved slaughter, and often resembled disorganized skirmishes. In other cases, it was highly ritualized and organized; nonetheless, the emphasis was typically upon individual accomplishments, especially prestige and revenge. Primitive war had little to do with the acquisition of property or anything resembling modern-day political "power." Among primitive warriors, the idea of conquest was virtually unknown.

Over time, however, as political organization grew more complex and military power brought success — and the absence of such power brought defeat and subjugation — very important changes took place in the relationship of civilians to the military. In the past, entire societies were only rarely organized for war. Raiding parties would be formed on specific occasions, but otherwise, the population was "civilian." It seems likely that, eventually, various forms of local militias were established, to defend grain storehouses, cattle and sheep, and so on. Although the Romans had full-time legionnaires, for centuries, military forces generally were limited by the financial capabilities of the ruler. During the late Middle Ages and early Renaissance, the walled cities of Italy were defended by the *condottierri*, or mercenaries, under contract to the civilian leaders of each city. Eventually, as each city-state found itself increasingly pressured to compete with neighboring military forces, mercenary armies became fixtures. And in the mid-seventeenth century, following the Thirty Years' War in Europe, the modern system of armed nation-states was established.

Following the Italian Wars of the fifteenth century, in which French armies were eventually expelled from the Italian peninsula, the political philosopher Niccolò Machiavelli asserted that citizen-soldiers were preferable to mercenaries. Nonetheless, the major European states generally maintained a distinct class separation between warrior and nonwarrior, with the former coming from the two extremes of society: War*making* became the province of the upper class, which supplied the officers, while actual war-*waging* was done by the lower class, which provided the soldiers. In Prussia, for example, the aristocratic *Junkers* monopolized the upper echelons of warfare, while the lower ranks were filled with conscripts and, occasionally, volunteers.

For centuries, though, the great majority of the human population was relatively uninvolved in wars. During the eighteenth century, for example, war was the sport of kings, who engaged in statesmanship via warfare and the threat of war. Accordingly, many wars were precipitated by disputes over who was to rule after a reigning monarch died, especially if there were no heirs: the War of the Spanish Succession, the War of the Austrian Succession, and so on.

When the monarchical powers of Europe sought to invade France and reestablish the Bourbon monarchy after the French Revolution, the beleaguered French government introduced something new, universal conscription, or the so-called *levée en masse*. The following decree was issued by the Parisian National Convention in 1793:

> From this moment until that in which our enemies shall have been driven from the territory of the Republic, all Frenchmen are permanently requisitioned for service in the armies. The young men shall fight; the married men shall forge weapons and transport supplies; the women will make tents and clothes and serve in hospitals . . . and old men will be brought to the public squares to arouse the courage of the soldiers, while preaching the unity of the Republic and hatred against Kings. . . . The public buildings shall be turned into barracks, the public squares into munition factories. . . . All firearms of suitable caliber shall be turned over to the troops: the interior will be policed with shotguns and cold steel. All saddle horses shall be seized for the cavalry; all draft horses not employed in cultivation shall draw the artillery and supply wagons.[10]

In fact, France did not actually become as thoroughly militarized as this decree suggests. And some forms of conscription had existed before the nineteenth century, although this usually took place on a much smaller scale, such as the so-called press gangs that would descend upon hapless young men and forcibly enlist them in the armed forces. Nonetheless, the *levée en masse* introduced a new twist into modern warmaking: an entire nation in arms. With it, the new French revolutionary government was able to field by far the largest armies ever known, to defeat the invading monarchical powers, and then, under Napoleon, to come close to conquering all of the Western world. It was risky for monarchies at the time to arm their populace, but Napoleon's opponents eventually learned to fight fire with fire, and by the end of the Napoleonic Wars (1815), most major governments had established national armies whose ranks were filled with their own citizens.

An important effect of the *levée en masse* was to devalue the lives of individual troops. "You cannot defeat me," Napoleon once boasted to Austria's famed diplomat, Count Metternich, "I spend 30,000 men a month." In fact, out of a total population of less than 29 million, France lost what was at that time an unparalleled number of soldiers, 1.7 million, during the Revolutionary and Napoleonic Wars. (The trend of increasing militarization has continued among the warlike powers of Europe into modern times; by the end of World War II, for example, two thirds of all German men age 18–45 were in the armed forces.)

The Napoleonic era also initiated another trend with special importance for modern times: the spread of guerrilla warfare. Resistance and terrorist fighters had existed since antiquity; best known, perhaps, were the Zealots, dagger-wielding Jewish opponents of Roman rule in biblical Palestine. But the concept of guerrilla warfare as an organized if rather informal uprising on a national scale originated with the Spanish resistance to Napoleon. In fact, during the five years of French occupation, Spanish guerrillas (aided by English forces in Portugal) accounted for as many casualties as Napoleon suffered in his ill-fated Russian campaign.

Technological Trends

Even if the nearly 5 billion people currently on Earth used only clubs or bows and arrows in organized conflict with one another, war would still be an important and tragic issue in human affairs. What makes war an especially pressing concern, of course, is that people have been extraordinarily inventive in developing fast, efficient, and devastating means of destroying other people (as well as animals, plants, buildings, and land), with ever-increasing ease and at ever-increasing distances. We can identify three major eras of weaponry: (1) the earliest, based primarily on muscle-power, (2) an intermediate era, powered by chemicals, especially gunpowder and the steam and internal combustion engines, and (3) the most recent, featuring nuclear weapons. It is the "advance" from stone axe to hydrogen bomb that gives particular urgency to peace, and that impels us to understand the instruments of war so as to appreciate the need for developing alternative, nonweapon "instruments" of peace.

Muscle-Power Weapons. Primitive people developed stone axes and clubs in the middle Pleistocene (200,000 years ago), and throwing spears and bows and arrows in the upper Pleistocene (about 35,000 years ago). There is no evidence, however, that *weapons* — as opposed to hunting implements — were developed before the Neolithic era, about 13,000 years ago. And for thousands of years, the primary weapons of war — spears, swords, bows and arrows — changed relatively little. Indeed, there is no evidence that the weapons used against other people were any different from those designed for use when hunting animals. But with the accumulation of an agricultural surplus, ancient cities developed where that surplus might be traded for other goods, and these cities in turn became susceptible to attack. Accordingly, by about 5000 B.C., the numerous cities of Mesopotamia (modern-day Iraq) had begun surrounding themselves with complex, walled fortifications. Attackers would besiege a city, often using battering rams or catapults to destroy its walls, or they would simply try to starve it into submission; the defenders would use arrows, boiling water and oil, hot coals, and so on to repel the attackers.

Bronze weapons and armor first appeared in Mesopotamia around 3500 B.C., when the first states were formed. Iron came later, around 1200 B.C. Initially, all fighting was done on foot, but by about 1800 B.C., horses were being employed to draw war chariots carrying at least one driver and one bowman.* Horsemanship improved rapidly, especially among the nomadic steppe dwellers. By around 700 B.C., spurred by the invention of stirrups by Mongol nomads, warriors developed the ability to shoot arrows while moving quickly astride a horse, and to wield sword and lance at high speed. Armored cavalry was introduced around A.D. 100–300, along with the heavy war-horse. The best defense against a cavalry charge was the pikeman, a foot soldier armed with a very long spear, the butt

---

*In the classic Hindu treatise the *Bhagavad-Gita*, the nobleman and warrior Arjuna converses with his driver, who turns out to be the God Krishna.

of which was fixed into the ground with the sharp end pointed at the onrushing horseman. Soldiery consisted largely of archers for long-distance barrages (about two hundred yards), cavalry with lance or swords, footsoldiers wielding swords or clubs, and pikemen. Those who could afford it wore relatively heavy armor.

The Phoenicians and Greeks specialized in the use of ships in war, initially as transport vehicles. Other ships were then designed to ram the transport vessels, thereby disabling them. During the ninth and tenth centuries, the Vikings successfully used ships for surprise raids along the ocean coasts and rivers. Initially, progress in naval design was comparatively slow: The relatively clumsy galleons of the Spanish Armada, for example, would not have been terribly out of place among the warships commanded by Lord Horatio Nelson at Trafalgar 150 years later. However, such ships were ultimately superseded by longer, sleeker, and more heavily armed battleships; these ships dominated until the late nineteenth century when ironclads replaced the older wooden hulls, and steam engines and then diesel power replaced sails.

Firearms and Other Modern Developments.   On land, although the crossbow and longbow increased the range and penetrating power of arrows, the overall conduct of war remained fundamentally unchanged until the fourteenth century, when gunpowder arrived in Europe from China. Swords and bows and arrows were replaced by muskets and bullets, and catapults eventually gave way to cannons. In 1453, for example, the Ottoman Turks successfully captured Constantinople, using cannons to breach that city's great walls. Because such cannons were virtually unmovable, as well as very inefficient, however, they were literally forged on the spot, during the prolonged siege.

Small arms became widely available by the 1550s, thereby gradually offsetting the superiority of nomads (and cavalry in general) on the battlefield. Small arms also eliminated the aristocrat's advantage in war, since a bullet — inexpensive to produce and easy for any trained soldier to fire — could penetrate expensive armor and also stop a

well-trained, carefully bred horse. Early firearms were, however, very inaccurate; in fact, they were generally not fired at a specific target, but rather discharged in the general direction of the enemy. In addition, they were quite difficult to reload: Early musketeers required extensive training in the many movements required to prepare their weapon for refiring. With the invention of the detachable bayonet, pikemen finally became obsolete. And with improvements in hand-held firearms, armor and cavalry also became further outmoded, leading to other changes in the style and substance of warfare. When the flintlock replaced the matchlock, for example, the rate of fire was multiplied threefold. As a result, a larger front could be occupied, resulting in a greater risk of troops being encircled or outflanked. The size of armies therefore increased, from about 70,000 at the beginning of Louis XIV's reign, to more than 200,000 at the end. Simplification of training and standardization of weaponry also made soldiers easier to produce and therefore more expendable.

As firepower has come increasingly to dominate battlefields, military uniforms have become more monotonous and drab, with olive, brown, and gray tones designed to camouflage soldiers replacing the bright capes, sashes, and cockades that were especially characteristic of the cavalry. Even after the military value of cavalry was virtually nullified by the invention of accurate rifles, though, the cavalryman had such a dashing image that many nations continued to maintain cavalry well into the twentieth century.* (The last recorded cavalry charges took place in 1939, when Polish cavalrymen charged — suicidally — against invading German armored divisions.)

King Gustavus Adolphus of Sweden introduced light muskets and small, mobile field artillery

---

*The mounted medieval knight was the predecessor of modern cavalry. The persistence of cavalry long after it was outmoded is testimony to the fundamental conservatism of military planning, as well as the stubborn appeal of a romantic aura combined with a special military role for the aristocracy.

in the early eighteenth century, revolutionizing the European battlefield. Nonetheless, from the mid-seventeenth century until the late eighteenth, war was a highly choreographed encounter, almost like a ritual game. The soldiers were now highly trained professionals, many of whom were considered too valuable to lose in combat. Commanders would maneuver for advantage, and one side or the other would typically then surrender, sometimes with very few shots having been fired.

This rather genteel conception of war was altered not only by the advent of national armies in the late eighteenth and early nineteenth centuries but also by the invention of rifles. Rifling is a process whereby gun barrels are inscribed with a set of spiral grooves that impart a spin to the bullet, which in turn results in greater range and accuracy. Industrial technology also contributed to the changing character of war. For example, by the mid-nineteenth century, breech-loading rifles replaced the older muzzle-loading varieties. This not only allowed quicker reloading because the soldier did not have to ram powder and lead down the muzzle of his gun, but it also enabled each soldier to fire repeatedly while lying on the ground. These new rifles permitted Prussia to defeat a much larger foe, Austria, in the Austro-Prussian War* of 1866 in a period of only six weeks.

Transportation and Communication Advances. The invention of the breech-loading rifle is significant not only in itself, but also in signifying a general and continuing trend: the use of technology to achieve greater range, accuracy, and firepower. Two other technological advantages contributed to that Prussian victory, and also changed the face of modern war: railroads and the telegraph. And in turn, the new-found and crucial reliance upon railroads and telegraphs during the mid to late nineteenth century reflects the importance of technological developments in both transportation and communica-

tion. Railroad transportation enabled very rapid mobilization of troops from reserve status to front-line units. Quick, efficient transportation also permitted each side to concentrate its forces in a small area, thereby achieving the kind of local superiority needed for a breakthrough.

At the same time, the use of communications technology — first telegraph and later radio — permitted single commanders to control vast forces. At one time, commanders had actually engaged in the fighting; Alexander the Great, for example, placed himself at the forefront of his battles, wearing a conspicuous plumed helmet, and Napoleon watched the fighting at Waterloo from astride his horse. In such cases, it was very difficult for a commander to obtain information as to the progress of a battle and thus to plan the disposition of his troops. And it was impossible for him to maintain close and effective control over their behavior. Orders were typically sent by runners, who might be intercepted or disbelieved, and who would often arrive too late to be effective. With the advances in the technology of transportation and communication, on the other hand, commanders could employ much larger armies than ever before: for example, von Moltke, the Prussian commander, directed the entire campaign against Austria without leaving Berlin. Technology, especially railroads, also permitted Prussia to win an even more surprising and decisive victory, this time over France in the Franco-Prussian War. Within two weeks after the declaration of war, in 1870, the Prussians had sent more than a million troops to the front, as compared to the French force of little more than 300,000. Decisive innovations in technology, however, are carefully watched and rapidly emulated. Soon, all European nations had breech-loading rifles, efficient railroad and telegraph systems, etc.

On the other hand, whereas effective technology typically spreads rapidly, it generally takes much longer for these innovations to be incorporated into actual tactics or strategy. Military leaders are commonly accused of being so conservative as to be self-defeating: It is often said, for example, that generals are always ready to refight the last war. For example, many experts anticipated that World

---

*This was the second of Bismarck's three wars of German reunification, the first being the war between Denmark and Prussia, and the last the Franco-Prussian War.

A Polish boy sits atop a heap of ruins near Warsaw in the aftermath of the German blitzkrieg in 1939.
(UPI / Bettmann Newsphotos)

War I would be fought as quickly and decisively as the Franco-Prussian War* had been; instead, the machine gun gave a large advantage to the defense, and the struggle bogged down into interminable trench warfare, with enormous casualties and no quick and decisive victory. The invention of the tank finally hastened the end of that war, by providing a means for penetrating the entrenchments.

Modern Weaponry. It was widely assumed that World War II would largely be a replay of the static trench warfare of World War I; instead, the German army used quick-moving armored forces closely coordinated with air strikes, in a new style of rapidly penetrating attack known as the blitzkrieg, or lightning war, which once again benefited the offense. In contrast with the trench warfare of World War I, there were relatively few casualties in the conquest of Poland, the low countries (Holland and Belgium), and even France. The major loss of life during the Second World War occurred during prolonged fighting on the Eastern front, where the Soviet Union suffered more than 20 million casualties, and Germany sustained nearly 90 percent of its wartime losses.

Toxic gas was used extensively by both sides during World War I. Japan also employed chemical weapons against unprepared Chinese forces during the 1930s; Italy did the same in Ethiopia. Subsequently, advances in chemical and biological warfare (CBW) have raised new fears about the potentially devastating consequences of future wars. Iraqi forces apparently used chemical weapons (mustard

*Interestingly, during the Franco-Prussian War, France had deployed a limited number of primitive machine guns, the "mitrailleuse." Because French authorities misconstrued it as another kind of artillery, however, the mitrailleuse had no real impact at the time.

U.S. Marines test-firing a precision-guided munition, in this case a tube-launched, optically tracked, wire-guided (TOW) antitank missile. Weapons of this sort are relatively inexpensive, yet considered highly effective against large, prized targets. (U.S. Department of Defense)

gases) in their war with Iran during the 1980s, as well as against Kurdish rebels, in both cases violating international law (see Chapter 17).

There have been many innovations in warfighting technology within the last hundred years: breech-loading artillery, landmines, grenades, torpedoes, machine guns, tanks, chemical warfare, powered ships (first steam, later diesel, then nuclear), iron-hulled ships, submarines, and aircraft, including fighters and bombers. Also, advances in rocketry have permitted swift, accurate attacks on distant targets. In general, technological trends have enhanced the capacity to wage war from a distance. The Battle of Leyte Gulf, during World War II, for example, was the greatest naval engagement of all time: In five days, Japan lost four aircraft carriers, three battleships, six heavy cruisers, and eleven destroyers, all by torpedoes launched from submarines or by bombs dropped from airplanes; there were no direct encounters between the surface vessels of the two sides. In the transition to warfare capable of greater destructiveness at greater distance, the role of human courage — once considered foremost among the military virtues — has been almost eliminated.

Other developments in conventional weaponry involve improved armor plating for tanks and ships, as well as highly accurate "precision guided munitions" — relatively inexpensive, highly accurate rocket-propelled devices that can be fired by small groups of soldiers at prized targets such as tanks and aircraft. Analysts believe that in the future even more lethal munitions will be used on an increasingly automated battlefield. These trends have culminated in what is probably the most important technological development in warmaking, the invention of nuclear weapons. Because of the special importance of nuclear weapons and the threat of nuclear war, we shall consider them separately, in Chapter 5.

HAS TECHNOLOGY MADE WAR OBSOLETE?

In the age of nuclear weapons, some people claim that the very destructiveness of these devices has made war obsolete. Actually, this suggestion is neither new nor unique to nuclear weapons: Throughout history, people have claimed that the latest advances in weaponry, by their very deadliness, will somehow prevent war. War has become unthinkable, it has often been said, because of its very destructiveness. And then comes the next war. (This brings to mind Mark Twain's observation: "It is easy to stop smoking; I've done it many times.")

Following the invention of the bayonet, for example, an English editor wrote in 1715 that "Perhaps Heaven hath in Judgment inflicted the Cruelty of this invention on purpose to fright Men into Amity and Peace, and into an Abhorrence of the Tumult and Inhumanity of War."[11] Similarly, Alfred Nobel hoped that his invention, dynamite, would make war impossible. An Englishman, Norman Angell, wrote a bestselling book, *The Great Illusion*, in which he argued that because of the economic interconnectedness of nations, as well as the increased destructiveness of modern military forces, war had finally become impossible.[12] The "great illusion" was that no one could conceive of or wage war in the twentieth century; ironically, World War I began just after Angell's book was published. And in that conflict, the invention of the machine gun led to the deaths of hundreds of thousands, often in just a single battle, such as the Battle of the Somme, or Ypres.

Since the dawn of the nuclear age, observers have once again suggested that since war has become unacceptably destructive — to a would-be aggressor and even to a "victor," if one could be imagined — the likelihood of war has actually decreased.* Although this line of reasoning may be comforting, it is also seriously flawed. Let us grant that nuclear war, because of its potential for mass annihilation, is in a sense its own deterrent. States possessing nuclear weapons (especially the superpowers) may well be very cautious in any conflict with other nuclear weapons states. But at the same time, theories of mutual nuclear deterrence seem to have produced the expectation that because of the seriousness of nuclear war, each side can count on

the other to refrain from anything resembling a nuclear provocation, which in turn makes the world yet more "safe for conventional war." In addition, there is the great danger that in a nuclear confrontation, each side will presume that the other will be deterred by the prospect of annihilation, and therefore, each may expect the other to back down, while remaining determined to stand firm itself. Moreover, as we shall explore further in Chapters 5 and 14, nuclear weapons carry with them an inherent ambiguity: Since the consequences of using them are so extreme, the threat to do so lacks credibility. As a result, although technological "progress" in warmaking has undeniably made war — especially nuclear war — horribly destructive, it remains uncertain whether such developments have actually made war any less likely.

Perhaps most disturbing of all, the fact remains that human beings are influenced by many things beyond a cool, rational calculation of their best interests. As we shall see in Chapter 10, wars have been initiated for many reasons, often involving mistaken judgment, misperception, or faulty information. And when wars take place, the combatants make use of whatever weapons they have. Never in the history of human warfare has an effective weapon been invented and then allowed to rust without at some time being used.

Historically, the impact of "war is obsolete" reasoning has also been ironic: It has not so much discouraged governments from waging war as diminished whatever hesitation scientists, engineers, and industrialists might otherwise have had about lending their talents to the production of ever more destructive weapons. Even the liberal view of the perfectability of human nature (as opposed to the more somber, conservative notion of original sin) helped justify science's contribution to the manufacture of cannons, no less than steam engines or new techniques for producing metal alloys. And during the 1980s, many scientists similarly justified their participation in Star Wars (SDI) research.

Some people even claim that since nuclear weapons states are necessarily advanced technologically, they possess the qualities of judgment that virtually assure that such horrible weapons will never be used. Aside from the hidden racism that

---

*See, for example, John Mueller. 1989. *Retreat from Doomsday*. Basic Books: New York. Mueller argues that war has become unacceptable to modern Western states, and that this process has taken place largely independent of nuclear weapons.

underlies such assertions — the implication that unlike Caucasians, dark-skinned societies lack the intellect or moral rigor to restrain themselves — the fact remains that the only state that has actually used nuclear weapons against other people is the same state whose technological sophistication enabled it to invent nuclear weapons: the United States of America. Even this variant on the theme that "war is obsolete" preceded nuclear weapons. Thus, in the late eighteenth century, the historian Edward Gibbon argued that powerful weapons can only be invented by advanced civilizations, and that such civilizations, because of their advancement, wouldn't allow force to be the arbiter of disputes. Then came the Napoleonic Wars.

TOTAL WAR

One of the most important changes in modern war has been the combination of (1) increased destructiveness of the weapons and (2) decreased selectivity as to their targets. The weapons, in short, have become more deadly, while at the same time, they have been increasingly directed toward civilians. We shall examine the legal implications of this situation in Chapter 17, and the ethical and moral significance in Chapter 19; for now, let us simply note that traditionally, noncombatants have been granted immunity during war . . . in theory, if not always in practice. This was encouraged by the fact that in many cases noncombatants were quite uninvolved in wars that occupied their governments and soldiers. In his book *Sentimental Journey Through France and Italy*, English author Laurence Sterne recounted how, in the eighteenth century, he went to France, entirely forgetting that at the time England and France were fighting the Seven Years' War. There was a time when states would engage in war without the lives of all their citizens being poisoned, corrupted, or otherwise focused by the conflict. In 1808, for example, with the Napoleonic Wars raging, the French Institute conferred its gold medal on Sir Humphry Davy, an Englishman, who blithely crossed the Channel to accept his award, to the enthusiastic cheers of the great scientists of France. However, this separation of civilian and military concerns, of the lives of the people and the behavior of their states, has changed dramatically with the "hardening" of political boundaries as well as the advent of what has come to be called "total war."

The "Home Front"

Although to some extent, military forces have long been financed by taxing the population at large, armies had largely supported themselves once they were in the field, either by foraging, purchasing, or pillaging. With the advent of immense national armies that employed advanced technology and that were unable to provide for themselves, it became necessary for the "home front" to be mobilized to provide the immense amounts of food, clothing, and munitions needed. As entire states were enlisted in the war effort, it became more and more difficult to distinguish between combatants and noncombatants: After all, it was argued, how can the "enemy" be limited to the person who pulls a trigger, ignoring those who build the bombs, guns, ships, and other articles of war? Furthermore, why shouldn't war also be made against those who make the clothing used in military uniforms, or even those who grow the food, without which no military force can be maintained?

During the Russian retreat before Napoleon, partisans destroyed crops and whatever else might have been useful to the invader. And toward the end of the War Between the States, General Sherman led his troops on a destructive rampage through Georgia, punishing the civilians in that part of the Confederacy no less than the rebel military. Total war was therefore not unheard of by the twentieth century; civilians, moreover, have in many cases suffered greatly after their side was militarily defeated, especially if their city was sacked. What was new in total war, however, was the organized use of military force directly and explicitly against an opponent's homeland, in order to win the war.

Total war became institutionalized during World War I, with the first use of the term *home front*, and the direct and deliberate targeting of the people maintaining that "front" — the civilians.

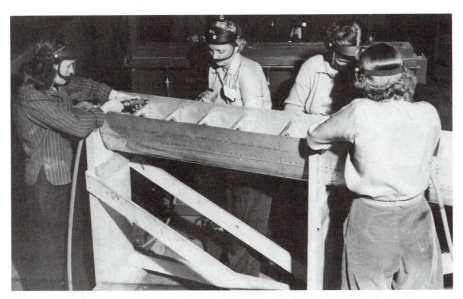

American women manning the "home front" in 1942 while large numbers of men were fighting World War II. "Rosie the riveter" became a symbol of womens' contribution to the war effort; transitions of this sort also made strategic bombing of enemy civilians (by both sides) more acceptable. (UPI/Bettmann Newsphotos)

Italy had actually initiated military bombing during its 1911 campaign in Libya, but Germany's use of zeppelins to bomb London was the first major attack on a home front. In order to appreciate some of the ambivalence this tactic raised, consider the following letter from Captain Peter Strasser, chief of Germany's naval airship division, to his mother:

> We who strike the enemy where his heart beats have been slandered as "baby-killers": and "murderers of women." . . . What we do is repugnant to us too, but necessary. Very necessary. Nowadays there is no such animal as a non-combatant; modern warfare is total warfare. A soldier cannot function at the front without the factory worker, the farmer and all the other providers behind him. You and I, mother, have discussed this subject, and I know you understand what I say. My men are brave and honorable. Their cause is holy, so how can they sin while doing their duty? If what we do is frightful, then may frightfulness be Germany's salvation.[13]

Loosening of Restraints

The tendency toward total war at this time was widespread, and certainly not limited to Germany. For example, the British naval blockade of Ger-

many during World War I caused great suffering and widespread malnutrition, leading to an estimated 800,000 civilian deaths above the normal mortality figures. As one critic puts it:

> One consequence [of industrialization] was to loosen the restraints upon war. With the growing material power to make war, what was needed was more politeness, more art, more wit in the conduct of international relations. What came was more grossness.[14]

What also came, as a result of national commitment to total war, was an inability on the part of the belligerents to call a halt to the carnage. Thus, for example, the disputes leading up to World War I were in their own way no more serious than those of the eighteenth century, which were resolved with much less bloodshed. What happened, in part was that

> the techniques of war had completely overpowered the ability of governments to limit their commitment to it. The axiom that force can only be overcome by greater force drove them to make war total, and the scale of the sacrifices they then had to demand of their citizens required that the purposes of

the war must also be great. When sixty million men have been ordered into uniform and sent off to risk their lives; when in France, for example, one in three of the male population (including infants and old men) has been killed or wounded in a period of four years; when the people's willingness to go on making sacrifices has been sustained in every country by hate propaganda that depicts the war as a moral crusade against fathomless evil — then governments cannot just stop the fighting, sort out the petty and obscure Balkan quarrel that triggered it, swap around a few colonies and trade routes, and thank the surviving soldiers and send them home. Total war requires the goal of total victory, and so the propaganda has become the truth: the future of the nation (or at least the survival of the regime) really does depend on victory, no matter what the war's origins were.[15]

Strategic Bombing

The invention of airplanes, and with it the possibility of long-range, strategic bombing, opened up yet another phase in the march of total war. Following the horrors of trench warfare in World War I, theorists initially welcomed the possibility of attacking an enemy's homeland as a means of guaranteeing that future wars would be short and, on balance, less destructive than in the recent past. Foremost among these theorists was the Italian air force general Giulo Douhet (1869–1930), who emphasized that air power, applied directly to an enemy's industry and to the workforce that sustained its war effort, would destroy that side's "will to resist" and break its morale, resulting in a relatively quick and painless victory:

> A complete breakdown of the social structure cannot but take place in a country being subjected to . . . merciless pounding from the air. The time would soon come when, to put an end to horror and suffering, the people themselves, driven by the instinct of self-preservation, would rise up and demand an end to the war.[16]

In pursuit of total war, during the 1930s and continuing through World War II, numerous civilian targets were attacked. German bombers targeted Rotterdam (Holland) as well as Coventry and London (Britain), while British and American strategic bombers eventually retaliated and then exceeded the initial German bombings, conducting large-scale raids against many German urban areas, including the dreadful fire-bombings of Hamburg and Dresden. In the Far East, U.S. bombers attacked Japanese civilian targets, culminating in the use of atomic bombs against the cities of Hiroshima and Nagasaki.

With the exception of these latter two cases, no evidence suggests that the national will to resist was ever seriously shaken by total war; on the contrary, national will was typically hardened by such attacks, even as the death toll shot up. It is estimated, for example, that German bombs killed 60,000 British civilians during World War II, and that Allied bombs killed more than 300,000 Germans and 500,000 Japanese. Perhaps most troubling of all is that, today, we take civilian casualties for granted, although perhaps we have not yet reached the sorry state Shakespeare predicted for us in *Julius Caesar* 3.2:

> Blood and destruction shall be so in use,
> And dreadful objects so familiar,
> That mothers shall but smile when they behold
> Their infants quartered with the hands of war.

WAR AND EMPIRES

It is beyond the scope of this book to review the entire history of war and its relationship to the rise and fall of empires. To some extent, the history of war *is* the history of civilization . . . or more accurately, a history of failures in our struggles to be civilized. The rise and fall of empires and states has been marked — if not specifically caused — by a pattern of military successes followed eventually by defeats. The relative peace that followed the establishment of a military empire has always been temporary (decades or, at most, hundreds of years): Empires that rose by the sword generally died by the sword. By contrast, empires that were founded on fundamentally peaceful tenets, like the Chinese, have tended to be long-lived (thousands of years).

Some Ancient Empires

In the Near East, for example, the Sumerian empire was established around 2500 B.C., and replaced by that of Sargon of Akkad, which in turn eroded around 2000 B.C. Hammurabi then forged a Babylonian empire that lasted about two hundred years, until it was conquered in turn by the Mitanni and the Assyrians around 1400 B.C. Egypt began uniting in approximately 3000 B.C., whereupon it spread via conquest and contacted the Mitanni, signing a nonaggression pact with them and with the Hittites around 1400 B.C. But the Assyrians eventually conquered Egypt as they did the Babylonians. In turn, the Assyrian capital of Nineveh was destroyed by the revivified Egyptians and Medes in 612 B.C.

Next to rise to prominence were the Persians, who conquered Babylon in 538 B.C. The Persian Empire under Darius I in the fifth century B.C. extended from what is now southern Russia to southern Egypt, and from the Danube to the Indus rivers. But the Greeks held off the Persians, and following their rather unexpected victory, Greece entered into its golden age, 500–400 B.C. However, this period of prosperity and influence was shattered by the devastating Peloponnesian War between Sparta and Athens, and the Greeks never regained their civic and military glory.

Ultimately, the Greeks were defeated by the Macedonians under Philip. Philip's son, Alexander (the "Great"), enabled the Greeks to conquer Egypt and virtually everything previously held by the Persians. Meanwhile, Rome developed as a major force, conquering Macedonia and Greece, and defeating its rival Carthage in the Punic Wars by the third century B.C. The ensuing *pax Romana* lasted about five hundred years, but the western Roman Empire ceased to exist after A.D. 476, because of successful attacks by such "barbarians" as the Huns, Visigoths, and Vandals. The eastern (Byzantine) part of the Roman Empire came under attack by Moslem Saracens, and ultimately fell to the Turks in 1453. Before this, Islamic forces had conquered Egypt, North Africa, Palestine, and Spain, and were engaged in periodic wars with the Christian Crusaders.

Medieval to Modern

Moslem armies, however, were stopped in their advance into Europe at Tours, in modern-day France, by forces under the leadership of Charles Martel. Charlemagne, Martel's grandson, was subsequently crowned Holy Roman Emperor by the pope, in forlorn hope of rekindling the power of ancient Rome. Several centuries later, in the twelfth century, Genghis Khan, leader of nomadic Mongol herdsmen from Asia, established the largest land empire ever known, and although he was never conclusively defeated, the Mongol empire eventually gave way as well, largely because the various subjugated peoples retained their cultural identity even as they assimilated various Mongol traditions as well.

As the Mongol empire receded, other empires gained prominence, each relying heavily on military power, and each relatively short-lived. Thus, the Italian city-states as well as Spain, Portugal, and Holland have all had their periods as major world powers, especially through their trading activities, secured by naval power. England and France (modern successors, in part, of the Holy Roman Empire) contested for centuries, essentially to a draw. Napoleon and, in more recent times, Hitler have attempted to conquer large parts of the known world, and although they succeeded briefly (at least in continental Europe), their ambitions were defeated by military force. From the eighteenth to the early twentieth century, Britain was the supreme world power, but the British empire has also declined, in large measure hastened by the bloodletting and economic costs of World Wars I and II. Neither the "thousand year Reich" (Hitler's grand design) nor the "greater east-Asia coprosperity sphere" (Japan's) succeeded for more than a few years.

War and Change

Wars have also marked many of the major transitions in modern society. The Thirty Years' War was the last of the great wars of religion; the Treaty of Westphalia, which concluded it, marked the beginning of the modern system of political states. The Seven Years' War reflected European competition for overseas colonies, and the Napoleonic and

U.S. (left) and Soviet troops (right) shaking hands at the Elbe River, in April, 1945. This historic meeting (and historic photo) marked the end of World War II in Europe; it also indicates the kind of global cooperation that will be needed if peace is to be deep and lasting. (The Bettmann Archive)

French Revolutionary Wars signaled the initiation of European democracy. Bismarck's three wars for the unification of Germany during the later part of the nineteenth century spurred the rise of nationalism, while World War I brought about the end of monarchism. World War II left the United States and the Soviet Union as the two preeminent powers, thereby initiating the Cold War between them. The end of colonialism in the mid to late twentieth century has been hastened by numerous wars of national liberation.

The military systems of Europe may well have contributed to the rapid growth of European power:

> A well-drilled army, responding to a clear chain of command that reached down to every corporal and squad from a monarch claiming to rule by divine right, constituted a more obedient and efficient instrument of policy than had ever been seen on earth before. Such armies could and did establish a superior level of public peace within all the principal European states. This allowed agriculture, commerce, and industry to flourish, and, in turn, enhanced the taxable wealth that kept the armed forces in being. A self-sustaining feedback loop thus arose that raised Europe's power and wealth above levels other civilizations had attained. Relatively easy expansion at the expense of less well organized and disciplined armed establishments became assured, with the result that Europe's world-girdling imperial career extended rapidly to new areas of the globe.[17]

Although war has been crucial to many of the major political changes on the world scene, it has also, paradoxically, served to prevent change. In that sense, the threat of war has helped maintain the status quo. The *pax Romana*, during the period of Roman hegemony, was due largely to the ability of Rome to act essentially as (Western) world policeman. The same was true, but to a lesser extent, during the so-called *pax Britannica*, from the late eighteenth to the early twentieth century. Following World War II, the United States attempted — with even less success — to initiate a kind of *pax Americana*. It may well be that the only kind of peace likely to be truly lasting will have to be something as yet unknown, a *pax mundi* — that is, a global peace associated not with individual nations, but with the world.

WAR AND COLONIALISM

Owing largely to their advantage in technology, the major European powers — and to a lesser extent, the United States — were able to conquer large areas of the globe. First Spain and Portugal, then Holland, France, and England succeeded in establishing vast overseas empires. In some cases, competition among would-be colonial powers resulted in military confrontations, such as the Seven Years' War between England and France (known as the French and Indian War in America). Mostly, however, the colonial powers exercised their military domination over colonial peoples, such as the British in India and east Africa, the French in western Africa and southeast Asia, the Dutch in Indonesia, the Spanish in much of the New World, and the colonists in America.

In the early stages of colonial expansion, native peoples such as the American Indians, Africans, and Chinese had numerical superiority, but they lacked modern firearms and the necessary social and political organization to resist effectively. Cortez, for example, conquered 8 million Aztecs with four hundred men with muskets, sixteen horses, and three cannons. Pizarro was similarly successful in Peru, and Clive in India. Commodore Perry "opened" Japan with a handful of naval vessels. An Englishman, Hillaire Belloc, offered this sardonic commentary on the crucial role of technology in nineteenth-century British imperial conquest:

> Whatever happens we have got
> The Maxim gun, and they have not.[18]

But just as American Indians eventually obtained rifles during the nineteenth century, rebels in El Salvador during the 1980s have captured large amounts of military hardware, provided initially by the United States to the repressive, neocolonial Salvadoran government. Indeed, virtually everyone in the world now has access to modern technology. Shoulder-held Stinger missiles, for example, supplied by the United States to Afghan rebels (the so-called *mujahedeen*) in the late 1980s, have stymied modern Soviet helicopter gunships. Revolutionary nationalism, especially in the form of guerrilla warfare, has been very successful, particularly since World War II, in evicting the weakened European powers from such regions as East Africa, Algeria, Vietnam, and Indonesia. By contrast, revolutionary forces have only rarely succeeded against locally based, nationalist governments, except where those governments were corrupt and generally out of touch with their citizenry, as happened with Russia in 1917, China in 1949, Cuba in 1959, and Nicaragua and Iran in 1979.

A FINAL NOTE ON WAR

Only rarely do today's armed conflicts involve a formal declaration of war, probably because in general, diplomatic formalities are less prominent and, more than ever before, war is widely considered an illegitimate way to settle grievances. However, just as a cesspool by any other name still would stink, wars — call them what you will — are still taking place, causing immense destruction and misery. Moreover, the threat of war remains very great, with its likely consequences more severe than ever (see Chapters 4 and 5).

Even "small" conventional wars can be devastating: For example, the Six Days' War between Israel and its Arab opponents in 1967 resulted in 21,000 battle-related deaths, which is far greater than the rate of killing per day that occurred during the Korean War. And between 1980 and 1988, the war between Iran and Iraq, generally considered a minor conflagration on the world scene, appears to have claimed more than a million lives. (This war has been atypical, incidentally, in involving relatively few civilian casualties.) In absolute terms, worldwide military expenditures are now higher than ever before, exacting an enormous toll on civilian economies, although relative to such measures as gross national product, military expenditures are relatively stable since national economies have also been growing.

Although life may not have become cheap, the experience of war and of military planning shows that it certainly is *not* considered to be priceless. It also shows that some lives are valued more than others.* Moreover, a great danger lurks in a very special kind of calamity — nuclear war — that could be catastrophic not only for humans but also, perhaps, for the global ecosystem.

Study Questions

1. War is difficult to define. Is this an important problem? Why or why not?

2. Considering the various historical trends in war, what — if anything — does this portend for the future?

3. What have been some of the primary effects of the nation-state system upon warmaking?

4. Compare and contrast the personal and social significance of the following technological innovations in warfare: cavalry, rifles, aircraft, nuclear weapons.

5. Trace the importance of nonlethal technology in war (notably, advances in communication and transportation).

6. Do you feel that technology has made war obsolete? Defend your point of view.

7. What is meant by "total war"? What is its relevance to the study of peace? Compare total war with the *levée en masse*.

8. If, as Heraclitus said, "War is the father of all things," what specifically are some of its offspring, aside from death and destruction?

9. What evidence, if any, is there that war is limited in its ability to achieve political ends? What evidence, if any, is there that war is effective in this regard?

10. Some scholars would not have included this chapter in a Peace Studies text, reserving such material for courses on war, instead. Do you feel it is important or relevant to Peace Studies? Why or why not?

Suggestions for Further Reading

William McNeill. 1982. *The Pursuit of Power*. University of Chicago Press: Chicago.

Gwynne Dyer. 1985. *War*. Crown: New York.

Robert L. O'Connell. 1989. *Of Arms and Men: A History of War, Weapons and Aggression*. Oxford University Press: New York.

Paul Seabury and Angelo Codevilla. 1989. *War: Ends and Means*. Basic Books: New York.

Martin van Creveld. 1989. *Technology and War: From 2000 B.C. to the Present*. Macmillan/Free Press: New York.

Source Notes

1. Quincy Wright. 1964. *A Study of War*. University of Chicago Press: Chicago.

2. Lewis Richardson. 1960. *Statistics of Deadly Quarrels*. Boxwood Press: Pittsburg.

3. J. D. Singer and M. Small. 1972. *The Wages of War, 1816–1965*. John Wiley: New York.

---

*This was dramatically demonstrated, for example, during the rebel offensive in El Salvador in late 1989. When rebels occupied poor residential neighborhoods, government military forces responded with aerial bombing, which resulted in heavy civilian casualties; by contrast, when the rebels occupied wealthy neighborhoods, no such bombing took place.

4. Karl von Clausewitz. 1984. *On War*. (Michael Howard and Peter Paret, trans.) Princeton University Press: Princeton, NJ.

5. Ibid.

6. Richardson, *Statistics*.

7. F. Scott Fitzgerald. 1934. *Tender Is the Night*. C. Scribner's Sons: New York.

8. John Froissart. 1336; 1901. *Chronicles of England, France, Spain and the Adjoining Countries from the Latter Part of the Reign of Edward II to the Coronation of Henry IV*. The Colonial Press: New York.

9. Ibid.

10. J. F. C. Fuller. 1961. *The Conduct of War, 1789–1939*. Eyre and Spottiswode: London.

11. Quoted in Gwynne Dyer. 1985. *War*. Crown: New York.

12. Norman Angell. 1914. *The Great Illusion*. Heinemann: London.

13. From A. Norman. 1968. *The Great Air War*. Macmillan: New York.

14. John C. Nef. 1950. *War and Human Progress*. Harvard University Press: Cambridge, MA.

15. Gwynne Dyer. 1985. *War*. Crown: New York.

16. Giulo Douhet. 1942. *The Command of the Air*. Coward-McCann: New York.

17. W. McNeill. 1982. *The Pursuit of Power*. University of Chicago Press: Chicago.

18. Hilaire Belloc. 1940. *Cautionary Verses*. Duckworth: London.

3

Peace Movements

It is only through a conscious choice and through a deliberate policy that humanity can survive.
   Pope John Paul II

Famed historian Will Durant was once asked by a television interviewer if he could summarize the history of the world in about five minutes. Responding that he could do so in even less time, he then said:

> History books describe the history of the world as a river red with blood. Running fast, it is filled with the men and events that cause bloodshed: kings and princes, diplomats and politicians. They cause revolutions and wars, violations of territory and rights. But the real history of the world takes place on the riverbanks where ordinary people dwell. They are loving one another, bearing children, and providing homes, all the while trying to remain untouched by the swiftly flowing river.[1]

Perhaps this is a bit romantic; after all, people don't always love one another, and sometimes — as we shall see — they have jumped rather enthusiastically into the river of war. But by and large, even when preparing for war or actually engaging in it, human beings have yearned for peace. They have even expended substantial effort seeking to achieve it. In this chapter, we briefly consider some efforts to build dikes — or at least, place sandbags — to channel the warlike river and keep it far from people's homes. Even, perhaps, to dry it up altogether. (Later, in Parts III and IV, we examine specific proposals and their prospects.)

Just as there have been wars and changes in warmaking throughout history, there has also been peace and efforts toward peacemaking. If we judge by the number of years spent at war versus those at peace, or even by the number of wartime deaths versus peacetime deaths, we would have to conclude that the peacemakers are far ahead. And yet, if we consider that any war is an unacceptable blemish on the human record, we must agree that the work of peacemaking is not only unfinished, but woefully unsatisfactory. As we have seen, by many measures wars have become more serious, making the work of the peacemaker all the more urgent. There have, however, been numerous efforts at peace, raising many possibilities and opportunities, some long-standing and others quite recent; there have also been hints of success. In fact, whereas the toll of war can be tallied, it is impossible to assess how many wars, or how much destruction during wars, have been prevented by the efforts of various peace movements.

POPULAR ATTITUDES TOWARD PEACE

One difficulty faced by the would-be peacemaker is that although most people claim to be in favor of peace, the great majority seem to be far more interested in war. Many people find peace boring, and war exciting. We can readily identify a war novel, a war movie, a war song, a war painting, or a war toy; by contrast, how many of us can identify clearly a *peace* novel, movie, song, painting, or toy? When war is mentioned on the daily newscasts, people prick up their ears; when peace is mentioned, people are more likely to yawn.

On the other hand, there has been *antiwar* poetry (notably the works of Wilfred Owen and Siegfried Sassoon after World War I), novels (such as *All Quiet on the Western Front, Catch-22*), songs such as "Where Have All the Flowers Gone?", and films (including *Platoon* and *The War Game*).

Opposition to war, interestingly, seems easier to express than commitment to peace. Thus, not surprisingly, most "peace" movements, as we shall see, have been fundamentally antiwar movements.

The Semantics of Peace and Peace Movements

Human beings tend to use a variety of different terms to identify things in which they are particularly interested. The Eskimos, for example, have eleven different words for what in English is known simply as "snow," and the Bedouins have over a hundred distinct words for "camel," depending on an animal's age, sex, health, temperament, and so on. Similarly, we assign titles to all our different wars: the Punic Wars, the War of the Roses, the Seven Years' War, the Balkan Wars, and so on. By contrast, the word *peace* is a generic term, used only in the singular, even though the "peace" that obtained, say, in Europe between World Wars I and II must have differed markedly from that of the 1950s or the period immediately after the defeat of Napoleon. Perhaps when our interest in peace equals our interest in war, we shall begin to identify not only "wars" but also "peaces," as something more substantial than simply the intervals between wars.

Once again, let us reemphasize that peace entails more than the absence of war. However, there seems little doubt that historically—and even at present—the defining characteristic of "peace movements" has been their antiwar stance. Efforts to achieve ecological balance, economic fairness, and human rights are important, and they certainly fall within the purview of Peace Studies, but they are not what is generally meant by a peace movement.

At the present stage of human development (technological no less than moral), even advocates of so-called realism are increasingly recognizing that war is not a viable instrument of national policy. Accordingly, there are virtually no "war movements"—at least, none that would identify themselves as such! Instead, a wide variety of doctrines and organizations espouse various (often contradictory) ways of achieving peace: Advocates of "peace through strength," for example, claim that states

Antinuclear rally — the largest in United States history — in New York City, in June, 1982. (United Nations/Paulo Fridman)

must maintain large military forces, along with a willingness to employ them if necessary (see Chapter 14). For the present, however, we shall consider "peace movements" as they are more traditionally identified — that is, as sources of popular opposition to war and to militarism. As such, they can be seen as representing one aspect of the more practical and results-oriented side of the academic discipline known as Peace Studies.

Most students of peace and war agree that in the twentieth century, war has reached its nadir: It has become less useful and less desirable than ever before. Modern wars have been unacceptably wasteful, destructive, and cruel. Moreover, in many cases, the state initiating a given war has not achieved its aims. In the twentieth century most aggressors have been either defeated or stymied in their goals: the Central Powers in World War I, the Axis in World War II, North Korea in the Korean War, Pakistan in the India–Pakistan Wars, Iraq in its war with Iran. The most recent trend, however,

is to diffuse "blame," with relatively few clear-cut aggressors or innocent victims; moreover, these wars have ended, most commonly, in stalemate. But there have also been some successful wars, notably wars of national liberation, such as those for independence in Indonesia, Algeria, and Kenya. The Vietnam War can also be seen as a successful war of unification, with distinctly anticolonial overtones as well.

Historical Versus Current Perceptions of War

Although modern readers may be surprised to learn this, the truth is that, until recently, war has not generally been recognized as a serious human problem; nor has it been widely or deeply deplored. Indeed, war has not even been considered particularly unseemly. Rather, it has been accepted as an instrument of statesmanship, to be utilized under appropriate circumstances. Several factors seem to be involved in the new public perception that war is a problem and that peace is not only a desirable goal but one that is — or must be — attainable:

1. *The potential for global destruction.* The development of increasingly destructive weapons, including various forms of conventional explosives, chemical and biological substances, and most especially nuclear weapons, has given all people a stake in the permanent abandonment of armed hostilities. Peace has come to be increasingly important; some might say, essential.

2. *The social and economic toll.* The enormous economic and social costs of war and war preparations have given people a direct interest in reducing the role of the military in daily life, even in the absence of the actual threat of war. Peace has become domestically desirable.

3. *The evolution of Earth into a "global village."* The increased speed of communications and transportation has enhanced the interconnections among human beings, economically, socially, and emotionally. More than ever before, people are directly affected by the experiences of others. Peace on the planet Earth has become indivisible: There is no peace so long as war is raging anywhere.

4. *The increase in political involvement.* With the growth in literacy and the spread of more democratic forms of government, people are more likely than ever before to accept personal responsibility for the actions of their country. To an extent not seen in the past, war is no longer considered a visitation of some god, or an acceptable consequence of a monarch's whim. Likewise, peace is increasingly seen as everyone's business, something that is attainable, if enough people want it and are willing to work for it.

Before 1914, states were relatively unashamed to acknowledge their own offensive goals in starting a war. But since 1945 in particular, such brazen aggression has become more and more rare. States now feel obligated to proclaim their *defensive* motivations, and even if their *behavior* is not dramatically different, this difference in emphasis may well be meaningful. Prior to 1947, for example, the United States had a War Department; its name was subsequently changed to the Defense Department. Indeed, the military branch of government of virtually every state in the world employs the word *defense* rather than war. Perhaps the switch is merely cosmetic. But even so, it reflects a significant change of attitude: Defense is acceptable, offensive war is not.

The Malleability of Public Opinion

On the other hand, people commonly espouse peace in times of peace, then switch to war as soon as it breaks out. The propaganda apparatus of the state has long been very effective in changing people's views of allies and enemies. The famed essayist and commentator Edmund Wilson deplored

> how a divided and arguing public opinion may be converted overnight into a national near-unanimity, an obedient flood of energy which will carry the young to destruction and overpower any effort to stem it. The unanimity of men at war is like that of a school of fish, which will serve, simultaneously and apparently without leadership, when the shadow of an enemy appears, or like a sky-darkening flight of grasshoppers, which, also compelled by one impulse, will descend to consume the crops.[2]

This sort of flexible militancy has been essential to the conduct of wars, since states have few if any "natural" enemies, but rather shifting alignments that are influenced by economic, political, or other factors, some of which are likely to undergo rapid and sometimes dramatic fluctuations.

Of course, just as enemies can be created almost at will, so can friends and allies. The United States had long considered itself a friend of China, until the communist revolution of 1949, when "Red" China suddenly became a serious enemy. But when President Nixon acted to normalize relations, Red China became good old China once again, and public opinion toward the Chinese changed dramatically. George Orwell's portrayal, in *1984*, of a fictional situation involving three superstates —

Oceania, Eurasia, and Eastasia — is a powerful indictment of the malleability of public opinion. As Orwell's account begins, Oceania is at war with Eurasia:

> On the sixth day of Hate Week, after the processions, the speeches, the shouting, the singing, the banners, the posters, the films, the waxworks, the rolling of drums and squalling of trumpets, the tramp of marching feet, the grinding of the caterpillars of tanks, the roar of massed planes, the booming of guns — after six days of this, when the great orgasm was quivering to its climax and the general hatred of Eurasia had boiled up into such delirium that if the crowd could have got their hands on the two thousand Eurasian war criminals who were to be publicly hanged on the last day of the proceedings, they would unquestionably have torn them to pieces — just at this moment it had been announced that Oceania was not after all at war with Eurasia. Oceania was at war with Eastasia. Eurasia was an ally.[3]

Peace activists are often frustrated at the ease with which public animosity can be evoked and manipulated. But there is a hopeful message to be found here as well, since the levers of public opinion can, at least in theory, also be worked to the advantage of peace and the delegitimization of war.

SOME CONCEPTUALIZATIONS OF PEACE

Not surprisingly with something as irrational, destructive, and hateful as war, many people through history have opposed it. Because certain individuals are so strongly associated with particular strategies of peace, we will consider them in the context of their specific proposals: Gandhi and nonviolence (Chapter 23), Dag Hammarskjöld and the United Nations (Chapter 16). Here, we briefly consider some efforts to conceptualize peace, in hope of conveying not only information about but also the flavor of the endeavor. One of the problems with peace plans generally is that, almost invariably, they are far less specific and detailed — and typically, less workable as well — than a military staff's plans for war.

For centuries, leaders and citizens alike have spoken out strongly against war. Whereas many have urged a "war against war," or a "national campaign to make war obsolete," the truth is that such campaigns have only rarely gone beyond the level of well-meaning exhortation. And peace campaigns, even the best organized and most generously funded, have never come close to rivaling the organization and funding behind even the smallest, most run-of-the-mill wars.

Religious and Renaissance Traditions

The Dutch theologian Erasmus, writing early in the fifteenth century, was one of the most prominent Renaissance Christian scholars to condemn the institution of war. He recoiled at the "mad uproar, the furious shock of battle, and the wholesale butchery, the cruel face of the killers and the killed, the slaughtered lying in heaps, the fields running with gore, the rivers dyed with human blood."[4] It should be emphasized that his views went counter to the prevailing climate of opinion, which tolerated and frequently even reveled in warfare as good and noble, so long as it met the necessary requirements of a "just war" (see Chapter 19). Erasmus even went so far as to heap scorn on military leaders as "military idiots, thick-headed lords . . . not even human except in appearance."[5] Although a religious thinker, Erasmus embodied perhaps the first substantial humanistic efforts in the West to question the divine right of kings to engage in war. "Among the soldiers," he pointed out, "the one who has conducted himself with the most savagery is the one who is thought worthy to be captain in the next war."[6]

Thomas More, by contrast, concluded that the inhabitants of his Utopia would engage in defensive war, albeit in a manner to minimize general suffering and only when necessary. His futuristic vision of the Utopians was not entirely pacifist, however, and it foreshadowed imperialism: "They account it a very just cause of war if a people possess land that they leave idle and uncultivated and refuse the use and occupancy of it to others who according to the law of nature ought to be supported from it."[7]

Many religious traditions have had a clear conception of peace, although relatively few have specifically elevated peace to a central position in their dogma or practice. A notable exception, within Christianity, is the Society of Friends (also known as the Quakers), established by George Fox in the mid-seventeenth century. Quakers have maintained a tradition of peacemaking and, notably, opposition to military conscription and resistance to taxes for military purposes that continues to this day. (We shall examine religious and ethical attitudes toward war and peace in Chapter 19.) Numerous attempts have also been made to design systems of world government, in the hopes of making war less likely (see Chapter 18).

Democratic Theory

Many thinkers have sought to combine political theory with opposition to war, arguing that democracy would be inherently less war-prone than other forms of government. In *The Rights of Man*, Thomas Paine pointed out that

> government on the old system is an assumption of power, for the aggrandisement of itself; on the new, a delegation of power for the common benefit of society. The former supports itself by keeping up a system of war; the latter promotes a system of peace, as the true means of enriching a nation.[8]

Paine went on to argue that "man is not the enemy of man, but through the medium of a false system of government." Monarchies were "false," but democracies, he felt, were "true."

In 1849, noted British statesman Richard Cobden carried on the tradition of associating democracy with peace and despotism with war. In a famous speech, he asked:

> Where do we look for the black gathering cloud of war? Where do we see it rising? Why, from the despotism of the north, where one man wields the destinies of 40,000,000 of serfs. If we want to know where is the second danger of war and disturbance, it is in that province of Russia — that miserable and degraded country, Austria — next in the stage of despotism and barbarism, and there you see again

the greatest danger of war; but in proportion as you find the population governing themselves — as in England, France, or in America — there you will find that war is not the disposition of the people, and that if Government desire it, the people would put a check upon it.[9]

Significantly, just a few years later, England was locked in the Crimean War against Russia (although Russia had not attacked England, and sought to avoid the conflict). Moreover, Cobden lost his seat in Parliament for opposing this war which — at least in its initial stages — was very popular with the English public.

Political leaders, especially in democratic societies, have persistently maintained that democracy is inherently favorable to peace. In 1951, U.S. Senator Robert Taft wrote: "History shows that when the people have the opportunity to speak they as a rule decide for peace if possible. It shows that arbitrary rulers are more inclined to favor war than are the people at any time."[10] In fact, political rhetoric notwithstanding, the evidence is overwhelming that democracies are no more peaceful than other forms of government. Over the past two hundred years, they have been every bit as likely as dictatorships to find themselves at war. What is striking, however, is that democracies have never gone to war against other democracies, a potentially important finding that we shall explore further in Chapter 9.

As we discussed previously, a complex relationship seems to exist between social/political ideologies and the perceived desirability and feasibility of peace. Probably most individuals have opposed war, but this opposition has been largely personal, sometimes religious, and often rather narrowly focused. Peace movements, by contrast, have been organized opposition movements, derived overwhelmingly from the political left. On occasion, however, (notably, in recent times, with the opposition to the Vietnam War and to nuclear weapons) they have enjoyed substantial support from the political middle and those lacking a clear ideological affiliation.

With this very brief historical and ideological overview, we turn now to peace movements themselves, activist efforts that have sprung from a variety of ideological roots and that have a diversity of agendas, but that share a common opposition to war and other forms of violent conflict.

A BRIEF HISTORY OF PEACE MOVEMENTS

An important distinction must be made between the peace proposals of specific individuals and the history of peace movements in general. Although peace movements, as we understand them today, are relatively recent developments (since the early nineteenth century), they have traditionally drawn on a vast reservoir of popular discontent with war, and have been nourished, in large part, by a belief in "universalism," a cosmopolitan ethic that sees shared humanity and a common interest in peace underlying and uniting political and ethnic distinctions among people.

Perhaps the first organization specifically devoted to achieving lasting peace was the Amphictyonic League, organized among a number of city-states in ancient Greece; the members agreed not to attack one another or to cut off one another's water supply. The Olympic Games also served a peacemaking function in ancient Greece. Every four years, any ongoing hostilities were halted by a one-month truce, during which Greeks were prohibited from bearing arms or making war.

Religious Peace Movements

The early Christian church clearly was strongly pacifist. During the first few centuries A.D., Christians were persecuted by the Roman Empire for refusing to serve in the Roman legions. Renunciation of arms was inspired by the teachings of Jesus, notably as presented in the Sermon on the Mount. In addition, early Christian writing specifically rejected service in the Roman legions as "idolatry." Pacifism also seemed especially appropriate to many early Christians because it involved renunciation of the secular world, in anticipation of the Second Coming. Subsequently, with the conversion of the emperor Constantine, mainstream Christianity also experienced a dramatic conversion toward a state-supportive view of the legitimacy of war and of military service (see Chapter 19). Earlier pacifist views came to be considered heresy by the so-called Christian realists, who believed that the Second Coming was not imminent, and that therefore, one must come to terms with the world of power and politics — that is, the world of "Caesar," as in the biblical injunction to "render unto Caesar that which is Caesar's." In short, Christian realists granted a certain legitimacy to the secular world of military force.

During the Middle Ages, the Roman Catholic church made some efforts to limit war, at least among Christians: The "Truce of God" forbade warfare on Sundays and certain other holidays (the word *holiday* originally referred to "holy day"), and the "Peace of God" forbade fighting in certain holy places, while also granting immunity to specific persons, such as priests and nuns. (However, the church also promoted the Crusades, and supported the prosecution of so-called just wars, even among Christians; see Chapter 19.) Traditions of absolute pacifism nonetheless reemerged during the Middle Ages, most of which carried a strong antistate flavor as well: The Waldensians of the twelfth century and the Anabaptists of the sixteenth were notable in this regard, and were aggressively persecuted by both church and state. In spite of such persecution, vigorous, if small-scale sects such as the Quakers, Mennonites, and the Brethren, sometimes known as the "prophetic minorities," maintained religiously oriented peace traditions. Much of their activity was centered around individual statements of religious and ethical conscience, an individual refusal to participate in war often referred to as "personal witness."

Secular Peace Movements

By contrast, secular peace movements, as we know them today, are less than two centuries old. Numerous organizations sprang up during the nineteenth century. The New York and Massachusetts Peace Societies, for example, were both founded in 1815, and the following year, "The Society for the Promotion of a Permanent and Universal Peace" was established by the Quakers. Soon, other organizations were founded, on both sides of the Atlantic, including the American Peace Society and the Universal Peace Union in 1866. Many international peace conferences were held toward the mid-nineteenth century, including gatherings in London (1843), Brussels (1848), Paris (1849), and Frankfurt (1850).

These efforts received some attention from governments, but were largely fringe events. Other than legitimizing the concept of peace, and spreading hope among those attending, they had virtually no concrete accomplishments. Later, the Hague Peace Conferences (circa 1890–1909) had more influence with government leaders, generating widespread expectations among many citizens as well. (Subsequent meetings, notably those that focused more specifically on arms limitation, will be considered in Chapter 15.) Although measurable successes have been rare, it can be argued that by placing the concept of international peacemaking on the world agenda and keeping it there, international peace meetings helped set the stage for such achievements as the eventual establishment of the League of Nations after World War I and the United Nations after World War II (see Chapter 16). They also helped generate a growing international mood in which war was seen as uncouth, and recourse to war became increasingly unpopular.

Probably the first organized efforts by any peace group to *prevent* a war took place in the United States, prior to the Mexican–American War (1845). Although the effort failed, peace groups did succeed in getting the two parties to negotiate their differences, and a propeace viewpoint was forcefully expressed. And during that war, Henry David Thoreau was jailed for refusing to pay a poll tax, which, in his judgment, indirectly supported that conflict. His essay "Civil Disobedience" has been enormously influential ever since. In it, Thoreau argued that citizens of a democracy have a higher obligation than to the policies of their government. He maintained that the conscientious citizen is obliged to do what is right, and to refuse personal participation in wrong-doing — even if the wrong-doing is sanctioned by the legal authority of govern-

ment, and even if defiance leads to government retribution. The idea of civil disobedience has been greatly enlarged on by modern practitioners of nonviolence (see Chapter 23).

Within the past one hundred years, the dominant periods of peace movement activism within the United States, and the primary themes of each, can be identified as follows:

1890–1914: alarm about modern armaments such as breech-loading artillery, machine guns, and heavily armed naval vessels

1916–1921: opposition to World War I and Western interventionism in the Soviet civil war

1920s: a variety of movements based on revulsion to World War I

1930–1939: concern about a second world war and anxiety about the risks of aerial bombardment

1957–1963: opposition to nuclear weapons, notably atmospheric nuclear testing with its resulting fallout

1965–1972: opposition to the Vietnam War

1980–1985: opposition to nuclear weapons, military bellicosity, and a perceived growing danger of nuclear war; support for a nuclear freeze

Early 1980s to present: opposition to military involvement in Central America; since 1988, continued (but reduced) concern about nuclear weapons, notably underground testing and the deployment of new "generation" weapons, and about the militarization of space.

The worldwide antiwar movement probably reached its peak after World War I. This was because, despite the mutual distrust and the long history of military and economic competitiveness that preceded that war, the fact remains that before World War I actually began, the two sides had no grudges or antagonisms that in any way justified the immense slaughter that ensued. Neither side was obviously aligned on the side of "good" or "evil,"

Marchers demonstrating in support of a nuclear freeze in 1982. Antinuclear activism reached an all-time high around that time, fueled largely by a militarized cold war climate, massive increases in military spending, and heightened public concern about nuclear war. (The Nuclear War Graphics Project)

and indeed, that war itself appears to have been largely a consequence of blunders, on both sides. Hence, World War I has widely been labeled "the war nobody wanted." The public understanding of "pacifism" derives largely from opposition to World War I, and the widespread movement against conscription that it stimulated. People who considered themselves peace-loving, but who supported President Wilson's "war to end wars," began calling themselves internationalists; they placed their long-term hopes on international agreements between states. By contrast, pacifists were (and still are) associated with a firm personal refusal to fight in any war, a stance that typically is based on personal religious or moral convictions.

In the United States, the antiwar movement of 1917 was eventually destroyed by wholesale arrests, brutal police raids (most notorious among these were the Palmer Raids in 1919, named for the Attorney General at the time), and vigilante mobs. The leaders were given long prison terms or expelled from the country.

Peace Movements in Historical Context

Historically, periods of war have tended to be followed by periods in which peace is espoused with particular vigor. This is apparently due in part to simple physical, economic, and social exhaustion, as well as the literal inability of devastated societies to mobilize the resources—both emotional and material—necessary to prosecute a lengthy war. The Greek historian Herodotus, called the "father of history" for his masterful treatment of the Greco–Persian Wars (500–479 B.C.), pointed out that "in peace, children bury their parents; war violates the order of nature and causes parents to bury their children."[11] Insofar as such experiences are what psychologists describe as "aversive stimuli" (events, such as corporal punishment, that are supposed to have the effect of reducing one's inclination to repeat the immediately preceding behavior), people are especially likely to favor peace after they have buried their children — that is, in the immediate aftermath of war.

For example, after the Peloponnesian War, Greece experienced an upwelling of pacifist sentiment. Again, following the chaotic civil and imperial wars toward the end of the Roman Republic, a widespread yearning for peace contributed to the consolidation of the relatively peaceful Roman Empire. The Truce of God and Peace of God, orchestrated by the Catholic church in the early Middle Ages, were stimulated in large part by the loss of life following coastal raids by Vikings, bloody squabbles among feudal lords, and inland assaults from steppe-dwelling nomads. Later in the Middle Ages, the costly Crusades and the various wars among dynastic rivals, including the murderous Hundred Years' War between England and France, led to the pacifism of humanists such as Erasmus, as well as numerous suggestions for doctrines of international law (see Chapter 17).

The Thirty Years' War ended in 1648 with the establishment of the modern state system; statesmen were motivated in part by the recognition of how devastating the most recent war had been. But of course, the new system of states did not prevent war, at least not for long. One hundred fifty years later, the ruinous Napoleonic Wars led not only to the so-called Holy Alliance and the balance of power "peace" of mid-nineteenth century Europe but also to an increased interest in international prohibitions on war and in the various and scattered peace conferences of that century. The wars of nationalism, especially the Franco–Prussian War (1871), led to renewed concern with the structure of international law (see Chapter 8). And of course, the horrors of World War I were directly responsible for creation of the League of Nations and various disarmament efforts during the 1920s and 1930s (see Chapter 15), just as World War II led to the establishment of the United Nations (see Chapter 16) as well as renewed interest in world government (Chapter 18). The threat of nuclear war, which developed during the U.S.–Soviet Cold War, has been responsible for unprecedented concern about limiting and, if possible, abolishing a whole class of weapons.

Unlike the experience of World War I, support for World War II was much more widespread. To some extent, in fact, World War II legitimized war in the minds of many, and led to a lull in peace movement activity. In part, the Second World War was widely viewed as having occurred because the Western democracies had been unwilling to confront Germany and Japan strongly enough and early enough (the so-called "lessons of Munich"). In addition, because the aggressive militarism of Germany and Japan had represented an obvious threat, pacifism became widely discredited as a way of coping with international evil. Moreover, during the decades following World War II, anticolonial liberation movements gave further credence to the legitimacy of organized violence, so long as it was for a good cause.

The resurgence of peace movement concerns during the 1950s and 1960s was due largely to growing anxiety about nuclear weapons, as well as opposition to specific wars, such as in Korea and, to a much greater extent, Vietnam. The peace movement also was influenced by activity in the Third World, notably the nonviolence of Gandhi and the antinuclear awareness promoted by the *hibakusha*, Japanese survivors of Hiroshima and Nagasaki.

A TYPOLOGY OF PEACE MOVEMENTS

Peace movements may be concerned with opposition to a specific war (the Vietnam War, intervention in El Salvador or Nicaragua), to a particular weapon or weapons system (cruise missiles, neutron bombs, the MX missile, chemical weapons), to an aspect of the war system (conscription, war taxes), to the prevailing socioeconomic system (capitalism), or simply to the institution of war itself (pacifism). One useful classification of peace movements divides them into three categories:

1. Movements to eliminate war in general

2. Movements to stop particular aspects of war

3. Movements to stop particular wars[12]

It is easier to stop specific wars than to stop war in general; not surprisingly, efforts to banish war altogether are also most likely to be associated with efforts to reshape public opinion, and to establish firm structures of positive peace as well. Such efforts are also more likely to be persistent, as opposed to opposition to particular wars or to specific means of waging war, which typically end along with the war in question or with the banning (or deployment) of the contested weapons.

Movements to eliminate war altogether have spawned secular groups such as the Peace Pledge Union in England and the Women's International League for Peace and Freedom (WILPF), as well as various religious organizations and traditions such as the Fellowship of Reconciliation (FOR), Pax Christi, the Quakers, and numerous advocates of nonviolence. Movements to stop particular aspects of war have included, in the past, opposition to poison gas, to specific weapons delivery systems such as the MX missile and the B-1 bomber, to nuclear weapons themselves (SANE, the freeze campaign, CND, and END), to conscription (the War Resisters' League), as well as campaigns in support of converting military industries to civilian production. Movements to stop particular wars included widespread mobilization to oppose the Vietnam War, notably in the United States (often known at that time as the "Mobilization," or the "Mobe"), and, more recently, to U.S. intervention in Central America, especially Nicaragua and El Salvador.

The following list suggests a different typology, identifying some of the major traditions, and an example of each:[13]

Tradition	Example
1. religious pacifism	conscientious objection: Society of Friends (Quakers), Pax Christi (Catholic), Fellowship of Reconciliation
2. liberal internationalism	United Nations associations, National Peace Councils, world disarmament campaigns
3. anticonscription	War Resisters' League, Amnesty International
4. socialist internationalism	no modern equivalents, but very active until World War I, including the International Workers of the World (the "Wobblies")
5. feminist antimilitarism	Women for Peace, Women's International League for Peace and Freedom
6. radical ecological pacifism	The Green Party (especially in West Germany)
7. communist internationalism	World Peace Council
8. nuclear pacifism	Europe: CND (Campaign for Nuclear Disarmament), END (European Nuclear Disarmament) U.S.: SANE/Freeze, Physicians for Social Responsibility, and many others

Note that liberal internationalism has sometimes been called "pacificism," as distinct from "pacifism"; although the former seeks to prevent war, it does not entirely renounce it as an instrument of policy in extreme circumstances. Note, too, that this is necessarily a very incomplete list. It does not, for example, include groups opposed to specific weapons, of which there have been many (Campaign Against Euromissiles, Live Without Trident, Coalition Against the MX, and so on). Numerous other organizations could also be identified within any one of these traditions; moreover, the traditions often overlap, both conceptually and in terms of membership.

The Communist Role

The Soviet Union has occasionally attempted to influence peace movement directions, largely through its World Peace Council and various other peace councils, located in other countries. And it has, on occasion, had some minor impact. Certain international petitions, such as the Stockholm Peace Appeal of 1950—which accumulated millions of signatures in support of the abolition of nuclear weapons as well as universal disarmament—received major sponsorship from the U.S.S.R. The Soviet Union was also favorably disposed toward the antimissile demonstrations in Europe during the early 1980s. However, of the millions of people who opposed these missiles, and nuclear weapons in general, communists composed a very small fraction. Within the United States, the influence of the Communist party within labor unions, as well as in civil rights and peace movement activities, is negligible. Nonetheless, government leaders in the West have often sought to portray peace movements in particular as communist dominated or, at minimum, communist influenced. Such accusations greatly exaggerate the strength of the Communist party, immensely understate the depth of grass roots, nonideological antiwar sentiment, and also reveal the desperation of Western governments to destroy the credibility of indigenous movements critical of their own policies.

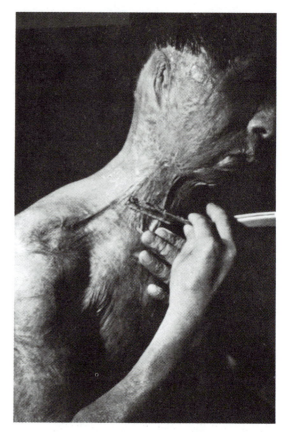

A severely scarred burn victim from Nagasaki, twenty-five years after the bombing. The *hibakusha*—survivors of the atomic bombing of Hiroshima or Nagasaki—have done much to increase antinuclear awareness around the world. (United Nations)

Interconnections

It should also be emphasized that although peace activists have tended to align themselves with specific organizations, there are numerous and important interconnections between them and between certain peace traditions and other popular social movements. For example, feminist antimilitarism, which emerged in the early years of the twentieth century, was strongly infused with energy and leadership from the women's suffrage movement. Opposition to nuclear power—in the late 1960s and throughout much of the 1970s—contributed to broader antinuclear sentiment in the 1980s. Many people active in feminism, socialism, gay and lesbian rights, religious nonviolence, and so on participate in peace movement activities as well. Environmental organizations such as Greenpeace and Friends of the Earth have found themselves increasingly involved in antinuclear protests; such groups express their antiwar, and particularly antinuclear, concerns because of the threat of environmental destruction they perceive as arising from nuclear war and also from ongoing radioactive contamination emanating from nuclear weapons facilities, even while "nuclear peace" prevails.

Other groups that focus primarily on economic justice have found themselves increasingly drawn to the peace movement agenda through recognition of the economic cost of military expenditures. While military spending does create jobs, people are coming to recognize that comparable spending in the civilian economy would generate even more jobs, and also address critical social needs. The era of avowedly conservative federal government policies, ushered in with the election of Ronald Reagan, has resulted in massive federal budget deficits, a hesitancy to raise taxes, and belt-tightening with respect to social expenditures. As a consequence, activist groups have become increasingly aware of the "opportunity costs" of military spending — that is, the degree to which military expenditures diminish a country's opportunity to invest money in other, socially more productive ways. Insofar as the Cold War appears to be winding down during the 1990s, if not ending altogether, we can expect that antiwar pressure — or at least opposition to military spending — will if anything increase. On the other hand, one consequence of the West "winning" the Cold War may be that peace movement forces will become relatively quiescent, at least in the short term. Ironically, this could diminish the pay-off of "victory," if military forces and expenditures are therefore permitted to remain high.

CURRENT PEACE MOVEMENTS

As we have seen, modern peace movements — both in the United States and worldwide — tend to be pluralistic; that is, they are influenced by a variety of traditions, motivated by a range of concerns, and guided by diverse strategies. Some peace movement activities are closely associated with feminists, as indicated by the Greenham Common's women's camps, formed in Britain to protest deployment of U.S. ground-launched cruise missiles; others are allied with environmentalists, as the antinuclear work of Greenpeace and Friends of the Earth demonstrates. In addition, occasional coalitions are formed between peace movement activists, gay rights activists, and opponents of nuclear power. In the mid-1960s, against the advice of some of his associates, who feared diluting the domestic focus of his work and also alienating some supporters, the

Reverend Martin Luther King Jr. came out forcefully in opposition to the war in Vietnam, arguing that the struggle for civil rights was inextricably linked to a halt in unjust and destructive warfare.

The United States

Despite these interconnections, however, the modern peace movement in the United States has often been accused of being excessively a concern of middle-class white people. The antinuclear movement begun in the 1980s has made efforts to reach out to other groups, to broaden its appeal and deepen its commitment. Nevertheless, antinuclear protesters — the freeze campaign, supporters of a comprehensive test ban, opponents of Star Wars — as well as feminists and environmental activists, remain largely drawn from the relatively well educated and well-to-do. By contrast, opposition to U.S. intervention in Central America and to apartheid in South Africa, and support for civil and gay rights, is more likely to derive from a wider socioeconomic cross section. Organizations such as CISPES (Committee in Solidarity with the People of El Salvador), and others seeking more peace-affirming policies toward Nicaragua, have regularly undergone FBI scrutiny and harassment; despite this, they have persevered and grown.

Peace movements (and left-wing movements within the United States in general) have tended to focus largely on one issue at a time, as earlier concerns are abandoned and the latest issue — cynics would say, the most recent fad — attracts most of the energy and outrage. Thus, in the late 1950s, it was opposition to McCarthyism; in the early 1960s, atmospheric testing, fallout shelters, and arms control; in the mid-1960s, civil rights; in the late 1960s, the Vietnam War; in the early 1970s, the environment; in the late 1970s, feminism and human rights; in the early to mid-1980s, nuclear weapons; and in the late 1980s and early 1990s, South African apartheid and interventionism in Central America. To some extent, it can be argued that these shifting priorities were appropriate, reflecting shifting threats: It should come as no surprise that the Reagan administration, for example, with its verbal

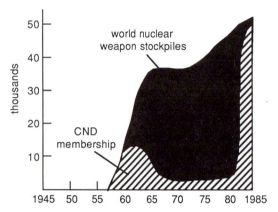

Changes in membership of CND, a British antinuclear organization, compared with growth of world nuclear weapon stockpiles.
Antinuclear membership increased rapidly along with increases
in nuclear arsenals in the late 1950s, and again in the early
1980s, but declined dramatically in the mid-1960s following the
Partial Test Ban Treaty and throughout the 1970s, even though
world nuclear weapons remained high and even increased during
that time. (Modified from SIPRI, 1985.)

bellicosity and cavalier attitude toward nuclear war,
generated the most vigorous antinuclear peace
movement in U.S. history.

Often, however, peace movements have been
motivated by a surge of popular anxiety that
quickly subsides, even though the underlying problem remains as serious as ever; for example, the
antinuclear movement of 1958–1963 diminished
rapidly after the Partial Test Ban Treaty was
signed, although nuclear testing and the nuclear
arms race simply went underground, intensifying
rather than diminishing. In other cases, peace
movements that were narrowly focused around opposition to something specific tended to disband —
perhaps appropriately — when "their issue" was resolved. A good example is the resistance to the war
in Vietnam, which ended when U.S. ground forces
eventually withdrew. European opposition to the
deployment of nuclear missiles by NATO sparked
a virtual firestorm of antinuclear protest during the
early 1980s. With the signing of the INF Treaty of
1988 banning such missiles on both sides, the European antinuclear movement has been much more
quiet.

However, several notable peace movement traditions have emerged from the 1980s, all of them
emphasizing grass-roots efforts and organization.
Within the United States, the nuclear freeze movement was remarkably widespread, all the more so
because it was virtually devoid of national leadership and also subjected to wholly unfounded red-
baiting from the Reagan administration. On one
level, this peace movement — which advocated a bilateral, verifiable U.S.–Soviet freeze on the testing,
production, and deployment of nuclear weapons
and their delivery systems — was a failure, in that its
program did not become national policy, and the
meetings, protests, and political clout of its heyday
seem but a memory just a decade or so later. However, the freeze campaign still exists, and has
merged with the older, more centrally organized
Committee for a SANE Nuclear Policy, forming
SANE/Freeze.

In addition to its structural institutionalization,
freeze supporters can point to the fact that many
freeze goals have also been institutionalized in a
less concrete, but more important manner: into
mainstream political thought. (In this way, the path
of the U.S. antinuclear movement has been similar
to that of the environmental movement of the early
1970s, many of whose goals and ways of thinking
have progressed from "radical" to "mainstream.")
During the presidential election of 1984, for example, the Democratic party adopted a nuclear freeze
as part of its national platform; at the freeze movement's inception in 1979, few would have dared
dream of such an outcome.

Europe

Several important peace movement traditions have
also developed in Europe. One is the Green Party
(*Die Grünen*), which originated in West Germany,
where it remains most influential. The Green movement has also given rise to other Green parties
throughout Europe, and has begun spreading to
the United States as well. The Green movement's
underlying philosophy represents a synthesis of
ecology, feminism, political decentralization, community and workplace democracy, antiauthoritar-
ianism, and a determined antimilitarism; the

movement is based on grass-roots coalitions of local groups, most of which remain largely autonomous. Counterculture politics are strongly established in the Federal Republic of Germany (West Germany), perhaps in part as a reaction to the role of Germany in World War II, and also in part because the divided nature of Germany serves as a constant reminder of the Cold War, as well as of Germany's position as the likely battlefield and initial victim of any "theater" nuclear war on the European continent.

Peace movements in Europe have long been dominated by direct opposition to war, and this trend continued throughout the 1980s. Anticonscription advocates, for example, known as the Ploughshares Movement and the Berlin Appeal, became especially popular in both Germanies. Nearly 20 percent of those eligible for military service applied for conscientious objector status in West Germany, while the evangelical Lutheran churches of the German Democratic Republic (East Germany) had growing influence in this regard. These church groups were also particularly influential in organizing opposition to the hard-line East German Communist government, resulting in the dramatic events of late 1989, when it (and other East European Communist governments) was toppled, and the hated Berlin Wall was essentially dismantled.

Also in Europe, the English-based Campaign for Nuclear Disarmament (CND) was founded in 1958, stimulated initially by opposition to nuclear testing. During the 1980s, largely in response to the intensification of the Cold War during the early Thatcher and Reagan years, the CND experienced dramatic expansion as a broad-based, populist movement. CND membership was about 3,000 in 1979; by 1984, it exceeded 100,000. In 1981, massive street demonstrations involving tens of thousands — sometimes hundreds of thousands — of people convulsed the cities of Bonn, Brussels, Athens, London, Rome, Madrid, and Amsterdam, largely in opposition to NATO's nuclear weapons policies. These demonstrations were part of a peace movement revitalization that united antinuclear protesters with antinuclear power activists, the women's and ecological movements, gay and lesbian rights supporters, socialists, and internationalists of a variety of orientations, ranging from supporters of the United Nations, to a sprinkling of pro-Kremlin peace fronts, to advocates of world government.

In addition, a new organization originated in the early 1980s — European Nuclear Disarmament (END) — that seeks a nuclear-free Europe (from "Poland to Portugal," or alternatively, from "the Atlantic to the Urals") and an end to the post–World War II division of Europe into western and eastern blocs. Unlike antinuclear movements in the United States, European antinuclear peace movements tend to advocate unilateralism — that is, ending the arms race and other vestiges of the Cold War regardless of how the other side responds. "Unilateralists," they say, "are multilateralists who mean it."

Another peace movement goal, the establishment of nuclear-free zones, has long had substantial support, in the form of a Nordic nuclear-free zone (the Scandinavian countries), a Balkans nuclear-free zone (Greece, Bulgaria, Romania), and so on. In the 1980s, this geographic approach spread to other regions, including Africa, the Middle East, and notably, the South Pacific, where continued French nuclear testing and U.S. insistence on nuclear weapons bases has combined to generate an increasingly unified antinuclear stance among indigenous Polynesian peoples.

Certain issues remain unresolved, however, and troublesome: the lack of a nonaligned peace movement in France, the "top-down" nature of the peace movement in the Soviet Union (where a group known as the Committee for the Establishment of Trust has been suppressed), the repression of anything approaching truly independent peace movement efforts in Turkey, the apparent lack of such movements in China or India, and so forth. But against this, the rapid democratization of Eastern Europe has not only revealed the extraordinary brittleness of governments based on military repression, it has also opened up the prospect of ending the NATO–Warsaw Pact confrontation, while releasing political space for a genuine citizen-based pursuit of peace.

SOME INTERNAL DEBATES WITHIN PEACE MOVEMENTS

Peace movements, as we have seen, are not homogeneous. They have fluctuated substantially over time, in numbers of members and groups as well as in goals. They have periodically been galvanized by opposition to especially atrocious wars (Vietnam) or weapons (poison gas, nuclear), only to recede somewhat when the war is terminated (Vietnam) or certain major provocations have been removed (above-ground nuclear testing, Euromissiles). One observer of the European peace movement during the 1980s suggests that peace movements are like whales, which periodically break the surface then disappear under the waves. "When the whale disappears in a dive, those on the right believe the movement no longer exists. Supporters of the movement, on the other hand, see the leaping whale and claim it can fly."[14] The truth is somewhere in between.

In addition to their fickleness, peace movements are notorious for their ideological heterogeneity: The truth is that peace activists fight a lot, at least with each other. (Not actual violence, mind you, but often with substantial verbal and conceptual aggressiveness.) Aside from the distinct orientations of different groups and the diverse personal agendas of the individuals who constitute these groups, certain sources of debate and tension have persisted within "the movement" (which — it should be apparent by now — is actually much more plural than singular). In part, this may be due to the fact that such movements, themselves generally advocating social change, tend to attract adherents who are antiestablishment, strong-willed, and inclined to rebel against authority. In any event, here are some of the major controversies that have caused substantial splintering within peace movements, but that have also contributed to the vibrancy that comes from vigorous internal debate.

State-Centeredness

Supporters claim that since states are the primary actors in the international war–peace arena, it is essential to reform the way states behave toward one another — for example, by encouraging trade, democracy, disarmament conferences and agreements on the rules of war, the abolition of certain weapons, and the establishment of international agencies such as the League of Nations and the United Nations. Critics object that focusing on the behavior of states merely perpetuates such behavior by exacerbating rather than alleviating nationalist biases. They feel that states are the problem, and that solutions must necessarily be less "state-centered."

This argument leads us into an important debate regarding the merits of nonalignment: Especially in Europe, public opinion tends to favor the peace movement perspective overwhelmingly with regard to nuclear weapons, yet also to identify strongly with the NATO alliance. Accordingly, some European peace activists argue that an anti-nuclear, anti-NATO stance might alienate public opinion that would otherwise support major initiatives in denuclearization. Others maintain that by adhering to the Western alliance, peace groups buttress the Cold War and undermine their own prospects for ultimate success. With the virtual breakup of the Warsaw Pact as the 1990s begin, it seems likely that pressures will mount for a parallel dismantling of NATO, or at least a diminution in its military role.

The Use of Military Force

Opponents of any use of military force (absolute pacifists) disagree with those we might call "relative pacifists," or "pacificists," who believe that a "good" or permissible war (such as the Spanish civil war or World War II) may still be possible, but who often oppose specific wars, such as in Vietnam or Central America. Even with so-called good wars, the question must be posed: Is the evil to be overcome (slavery in the Civil War, nazism in World War II) greater than the evil of the war that had to be waged to overcome the evil? A similar debate attends the use of smaller military forces: Was the "liberation" of Grenada worth the loss of life that resulted from the 1983 invasion of that island by the United States? And did the removal of Panama's Noriega warrant another invasion in 1989? Some self-styled "realists" argue that under certain conditions, the use of force is appropriate; others —

Biography

William Sloane Coffin

William Sloane Coffin has a distinguished history of antiwar activism and involvement in religion, government, and the academic world. After musical studies with Nadia Boulanger in Paris, he served as a U.S. Army liaison officer to the French and Russian armies and worked for the CIA from 1950 to 1953. He then attended divinity school and was chaplain of Yale University from 1957 until 1975. During that time, he advised the Peace Corps, cofounded Clergy and Laity Concerned for Vietnam, and became prominent as an opponent of the Vietnam War, especially through his efforts on behalf of draft resistance and conscientious objectors.

Rev. Coffin has continued to be very active in both the civil rights and antiwar movements. He has written numerous books (including *The Courage to Love* and *Speaking the Truth in a World of Illusion*) and has spoken to hundreds — if not thousands — of audiences around the world. He became senior minister of Riverside Church, New York, in 1977, and founded its highly regarded Disarmament Program. The program's goals include ending intervention, reversing the arms race, and redressing the international North-South economic imbalance. In 1988, shortly after SANE and the Nuclear Freeze Campaign merged to form SANE/Freeze, Rev. Coffin became president of that organization. He argues that "disarmament, ecology, and economic justice are inextricably linked; and only by serving the first can sufficient funds be freed to serve the other two."

---

equally "realistic" — maintain that violence is ultimately self-defeating. Absolute pacifists also typically object to the idea of ever institutionalizing a worldwide military force, even one designed for peacekeeping (see Chapter 16). Others worry about the potential for despotism (see Chapter 18). And still others regret the absence of such an international force.

Centralization Versus Grass-Roots Organization

One antiwar tradition favors the development of strong leadership and central authority; the other prefers local, grass-roots organizing. Within today's antinuclear movement, the former would include such organizations as SANE, the Union of Concerned Scientists, and the Council for a Livable World; grass-roots activities, by contrast, have characterized the nuclear freeze movement and the Mobilization for Survival. The merger of SANE and the nuclear freeze movement in 1987 might presage an integration of these tactics along with a new organizational philosophy.

In a related vein, it is unclear whether peace movements have historically had greater success when they were composed primarily of large numbers of people, mobilized as "objects," or relatively fewer, but more strongly motivated individuals, who see themselves as "subjects" of their own intense actions and protests. Thus, the peace movement mobilization of a million people in New York City in June 1982 had an undeniable impact on the world and national psyche, but so did the handful of Buddhist monks who, a decade or so earlier, immolated themselves to protest the Vietnam War.

Single Issue Versus Broader Social Agenda

Many groups have opposed specific aspects of war — weapons (the MX missile, Trident submarines, neutron bombs, "refuse cruise" in Europe), conscription, war taxes — or specific wars (Vietnam, U.S. involvement in El Salvador or Nicaragua), whereas other groups have emphasized the importance of broadening their agenda to embrace economic aspects of social justice (e.g., employment

Buddhist monk immolating himself in downtown Saigon to protest religious oppression as well as the conduct of the Vietnamese War. Acts of this sort attract attention not only because they are violent in themselves but also because of the deep personal commitment that they reflect. (UPI/Bettmann Newsphotos)

at decent wages, medical care, affordable housing and child-care), environmental concerns (wildlife conservation, clean air and water, preservation of open space, renewable energy sources, protection of tropical forests, mitigation of the greenhouse effect), support for gay rights, opposition to racism and sexism in the United States and to apartheid in South Africa, and so on.

In some cases, peace movements have become closely associated with a single political party, such as Labour in Britain or the Communist party in Italy. Supporters of the single-issue approach emphasize that by concentrating on a small number of manageable concerns, they are more likely to have a demonstrable effect, which will also provide them with successes upon which to build; supporters of a broader agenda counter with the argument that specific issues come and go and that the peace

movement can actually be weakened whenever a single issue is resolved, whether won or lost. In addition, peace advocates are increasingly aware of the importance of pointing out the linkages between various "single-issue" considerations. For example, the nuclear freeze campaign during the 1980s received relatively little support from the black community, at least in part because the U.S. underclass was more concerned with immediate issues of economic and social justice. On the other hand, more success has been achieved by combining calls for jobs with antiwar programs — there is a natural linkage here, since a military economy actually creates fewer jobs than would similar expenditures in the domestic sector (see Chapter 11).

Single-issue politics offer the advantage of bringing sharp, substantial pressure to bear on a narrow point, thereby perhaps penetrating deeply. However, such thrusts are also susceptible to being turned aside. Broad, programmatic, consensus-building blueprints for social change, by contrast, bring pressure across a much wider societal front, but with less visible impact in any one area.

Practicality Versus Idealism

How far should peace movements aim? Is there danger that by setting their sights too high, they will make "the best an enemy of the good?" On the other hand, don't peace movements have an obligation to be something above normal politics, which bills itself as the "art of the possible"? In this time of unique danger and opportunity, perhaps peace movements must, as some peace advocates put it, "be realistic — demand the impossible." Realism on the part of the U.S. nuclear freeze campaign, for example, appears like a step backward to much of the European peace movement, which has long demanded substantial *unilateral reductions* in nuclear weapons.

Here is another dilemma of practicality versus idealism: As the Green party in West Germany has enjoyed modest electoral success (up to about 10 percent of the popular vote), it has had to confront the political process as members of the German government, that is, as insiders rather than as

English police arresting antinuclear protestors who were blockading the Greenham Common Airbase. NATO insistence on deploying cruise missiles here evoked an extensive program of nonviolent civil disobedience, notably on the part of a courageous and dedicated group of English women. (UPI/Bettmann Newsphotos)

protesters from the outside. This has generated two factions within the Green movement: the "fundis" (or "fundamentalists"), who hold out for idealized goals such as the total abolition of nuclear weapons and a refusal to form coalitions with more conservative parties, and the "realos" (or "realists"), who are willing to make certain practical concessions in the interest of immediate, although incomplete, successes. There can be substantial tension here between "doing what can be done and attempting to do what needs to be done."[15]

In one view, effectiveness per se is not the relevant criterion by which peace movements should be judged. Rather, peace movements have a special role, as keepers of society's collective conscience. Peace movements should therefore hold to exemplary values and goals, thereby providing a counterweight to the supposedly practical politics of repression and violence that have caused the world

so much misery. In one extension of this argument, perhaps peace movements should fashion themselves after Sisyphus, the character from Greek mythology who was condemned to spend eternity rolling a heavy rock up a steep hill, only to have it roll back down again every time. Advocates of this approach do not applaud the rock's downhill roll, but neither do they get discouraged by it; their efforts are not attenuated by the mere fact that the rock is heavy, or the hill steep. Moreover, according to the existential philosopher Albert Camus, Sisyphus was happy, because in the course of his impossible labors, he at least defined himself as a human being by his opposition to a malign and uncaring universe.

On the other hand, as noble as it might be to say no, and to struggle valiantly but hopelessly, the stark importance of the need for peace makes an impressive case for getting something done, even if it is less than one might hope. It also helps to say yes on occasion — that is, to maintain a vision of positive peace that goes beyond mere opposition to war. Thus, an important criticism of peace movements is that

> they are reactive, that is they are despairing responses to the fact that our social and political systems are controlled by people who are incapable of giving us peace — and so occasionally we erupt in protest against the latest illustration of this sad truth, but never do we manage to get to the roots of the problem and succeed in constructing a social and political system which will give us peace.[16]

A useful — although negative — view of peace movements is that they serve as grit in the cogwheels of the world's war machines, preventing them from running smoothly, and perhaps eventually causing them to break down altogether. Another analogy — and a more positive one — compares peace movements to bread yeast, helping dough to rise. In any case, peace movement activists remain divided as to whether they ought to compromise their principles in the interests of real but ambiguous "progress," such as support for conventional "modernization" of military forces, especially in Europe, in return for denuclearization.

Civil Disobedience

Supporters of civil disobedience maintain that when the government is engaging in morally unacceptable behavior — often counter to the tenets of international law — it is acceptable and even essential to oppose these practices, even if opposition of this sort involves breaking domestic law. Opponents of civil disobedience worry about the morality of law-breaking, and also about the possibility that such acts may alienate the majority of the citizenry and ultimately prove counterproductive. This is actually part of a broader debate about tactics, especially between those who advocate grass-roots activism, "in the streets," by as many people as possible, versus a top-down approach that focuses on working within the political system to influence decision-makers. In turn, the debate about tactics is part of an even larger issue: whether to *oppose* war by the electoral process, writing, speaking, orga-

nizing and attending meetings, passing resolutions, and so on, or actively to *resist* it, by strikes, nonviolent (or violent) civil disobedience, tax resistance, and so on.

AN ASSESSMENT OF PEACE MOVEMENTS

Although this book clearly supports peace movements, we must also acknowledge that peace movements have not always contributed positively toward peace. In some cases, public opinion has been mobilized by peace movement efforts, but it has also been alienated; in some cases, wars have been made more unpopular, but in other cases they have also actually been prolonged. Peace movement efforts nearly always have unseen, latent consequences as well as visible, immediate ones. This makes it difficult to pronounce a specific peace "campaign" — or the movement as a whole — a "success" or "failure."

Some Criticisms

In the famous Oxford Peace Union Pledge during the 1930s, many students in England declared that they would not "fight for king and country," which in turn appears to have emboldened Hitler by suggesting that his aggressive designs might not be resisted. Similarly, it can be argued that the other vigorous European peace movements of the 1930s not only made nazi and fascist aggression more likely, but also diminished the degree of Allied preparedness when war finally did come.

More generally, peace movements, by excessive wishful thinking, may sometimes blind their fellow citizens to the provocative and dangerous behavior of others. "Nothing is more promotive of war," writes peace researcher Quincy Wright, "than diversion of the attention of the prospective victims from the aggressor's preparations."[17] As we shall see, however, there are many contributing causes to war; of these, the occasional counterproductive effects of peace movements are quite insignificant. Nothing is more disruptive of peace, we might conclude, than blaming well-intentioned peace movements for the war-prone behavior of states and their leadership.

Mothers and children from Khabarovsk, U.S.S.R., protesting against nuclear weapons. Antiwar demonstrations in the Soviet Union have traditionally been limited to those the government approves; they have, however, been enthusiastic and well-attended. (United Nations)

Nonetheless, peace movements often have a difficult time. During war, they are typically denounced and often banned or even attacked as unpatriotic, cowardly, or traitorous for giving "aid and comfort to the enemy." And during times of peace, they often are hard-pressed to make a dent in public complacency. A sociopsychological view of peace movement activism puts special emphasis on the personal needs presumably being met by such activity: acting out youthful rebellion, opposing authority as a predictable "age-appropriate" stage in personal development, exercising the opportunity of behaving outrageously while remaining relatively free of social or family responsibilities. This line of argument can readily be overused, especially by right-wing critics eager to discredit peace movement activism. But it would also be a mistake to ignore the diverse personal motivations of peace movement activists. In addition, current peace movement activists in fact represent a rather wide cross section of ages; many are peace movement veterans, some of whom may have "dropped out" for a while to develop careers or start families, only

to return when the issues appear especially acute, or when their conscience forces them to.

In recent years, the antinuclear and antiinterventionism peace movements have been called naive, actively subversive, or unwitting dupes of international communism. Critics often suggest, for example, that peace movements, by exerting pressure on the U.S. government, weaken the position of the United States vis-à-vis the U.S.S.R., because the U.S.S.R. does not permit a comparable indigenous peace movement to exercise similar pressure from within its own society. Peace movements, it is said, should therefore keep quiet.

This is a curious argument, and one that warrants a rebuttal. Essentially, the claim is that since the Soviet Union is not a full-fledged democracy, the United States must stifle its own democratic tradition. Moreover, it assumes that if peace movement goals are achieved (modulating or ending the arms race, restraining intervention in Central America or the Middle East), the Soviets will gain a unilateral advantage at the expense of the United States. Most devotees of Peace Studies would reject these propositions, pointing out that world peace, demilitarization, and an end to violence are not "zero sum games," in which one side must lose if the other wins. Rather, both sides stand to come out ahead if a peace agenda is actually realized.

Moreover, peace movement goals definitely include modifying the behavior of the Soviet Union (no less than the Republic of South Africa and a variety of other states). It is a simple and practical fact of life, however, that citizens are most able to influence the polities of which they are members: for U.S. citizens, this is the government of the United States, just as for Russians it is the Soviet Union, or for Filipinos the Philippines. In most cases, governments are all too happy to have their citizens — whether members of a peace movement or not — criticize and demonstrate against rival foreign governments. But in doing so, they are unlikely to have much impact.

To some degree, peace movement activists accept the proposition that human beings all share important common bonds, and are therefore mutually responsible for whatever happens on their shared planet. But they also operate on the reasonable assumption that people — especially those fortunate enough to be living in a democracy — have a special responsibility to evaluate critically and, if necessary, to seek to reform the behavior of their own government. In this respect, citizens of the United States have much to do.

Some critics also point to what they see as a conflict between peace movement policies and support for human rights, especially within Soviet-bloc countries. Thus, certain Soviet emigrés, such as Alexander Solzhenitsyn, have joined right-wing politicians and commentators in urging a hard-line U.S. stance vis-à-vis the Soviet Union, such that any "concessions" regarding peace are linked to Soviet "concessions" regarding human rights, including economic decentralization, increased political freedom, and the right to emigrate. Others view the issue differently, emphasizing that internal Soviet reforms — as well as political liberalization within the Soviet client states of Eastern Europe — are much more feasible in an atmosphere of diminished Cold War tensions than when the U.S.S.R. is made to feel pressured and threatened.

Maintaining the Momentum

It is all too easy for peace activists to fall victim to personal fatigue, despair, and cynicism. But in fact, peace movement activists worldwide have already accomplished a great deal. In the twentieth century, for example, conscientious objection has become widely recognized as a basic human right, although the exercising of that right is sometimes perilous.* The Vietnam War was terminated in large part because of U.S. discontent with the war fueled by immense pressure from the domestic peace movement. Similarly, as of 1990, nuclear weapons appear to be undergoing a process of delegitimization, much to the dismay of militarists and cold warriors. The political and economic barriers between Eastern and Western Europe are rapidly coming down, and accordingly, cold war fear and hostility are evaporating. War itself may be the next to go, along with systems of interpersonal and structural violence in society more generally.

Peace movements have typically grown when the threat to peace was great, and/or when the memory of recent carnage was particularly acute and painful. Ironically, they have done best — in terms of enthusiasm, membership, and financial contributions — when the situation has seemed darkest, as during the early years of the Reagan administration when anticommunist rhetoric was particularly inflammatory and the domestic military build-up (both conventional and nuclear) reached record levels. As we have seen, peace movement activism has largely been reactive, swelling in response to crises, then readily being co-opted by partial successes (the Partial Test Ban Treaty of 1963, the INF Treaty of 1988). It remains to be seen whether the modern peace movement can sustain its momentum when immediate, readily perceived

---

*It is interesting to note that within peace movements themselves, even anticonscription was not universally accepted as an appropriate goal: A segment of socialist antiwar activists actually applauded conscription, hoping it would create a "people's army," whereas others feared that it would simply contribute to an "army against the people."

threats do not exist and when governments modulate their rhetoric but not their policies, or co-opt the peace movement agenda by showy, but relatively trivial concessions to peace.

More specifically, it remains to be seen whether antiwar sentiment in the United States will outlast specific crises in Central America and elsewhere, and whether the antinuclear movement will continue to be prominent when and if national policies become less controversial, or if such policies lead to significant reductions in strategic nuclear forces. An important historical reason for the decline in peace movements has been their tendency to focus on too narrow an issue. Thus, the signing of the Atmospheric Test Ban Treaty (1963) virtually demolished an antinuclear movement that had focused largely on the dangers of radioactive fallout. Similarly, when NATO partially deployed its Euromissiles, the European peace movement was first defeated, then left bereft of an issue when the INF Treaty — eliminating these missiles on both sides — was negotiated. On the other hand, we should note that the European peace movement contributed mightily to the elimination of these missiles; the point here is that when a movement focuses narrowly on a specific weapon, it can readily be co-opted or left feeling empty-handed and uninspired, even when it has been successful.

Accordingly, contemporary peace movements need to develop alternative foreign policy concepts, alternative defense strategies, a positive view of social goals, broader motivations beyond single-issue rallying points, a workable model of a disarmed (or at least, substantially demilitarized) economy, and staying power. In addition, successful peace movements will have to achieve realism in confronting the power of the state, while also, when possible, breaking out of a strictly state-centered model of politics.

The overriding goal of many peace movement activists is not so much the elimination of states as their transformation. Specifically, demilitarization could serve not only as a goal but also as a method. And demilitarization, as such, is independent of specific weapons or specific "hot spots" around the world. The peace movement of the 1980s called for the denuclearization of military policy as well as the demilitarization of defense policy. It called into question the fundamental rationality of "national security" based on military means alone. In addition, it called not only for widespread participation but also for empowerment on the part of ordinary citizens. The peace movement of the 1990s would appear to have a full agenda.

Peace movements are sometimes seen as quixotic, hopeless quests, peopled by refugees from the 1960s, a view held especially by many in the conservative, self-satisfied "me generation" of the late 1980s. Yet evidence abounds that such movements, especially in recent times, have influenced national policy: Both supporters and opponents of the war in Vietnam, for example, agree that the United States terminated its involvement in that sorry conflict because of an ebbing of political will to continue prosecuting the war. In addition, there seems little doubt that the Reagan administration, during its latter years, grew increasingly antinuclear under movement pressure that was widespread, vocal, and highly visible. To cite another example, national policy in New Zealand was strongly influenced by peace movement sentiment in that country. The result was a ban on all nuclear facilities, including visits by nuclear-armed or nuclear-powered naval vessels, much to the consternation of the United States.

Moreover, history offers many examples of successful movements that initially appeared to be facing impossible odds: support for women's suffrage, opposition to monarchy, to dueling as a means of settling personal disputes, or to the institution of slavery, which was an ancient and firmly rooted practice, at one time virtually worldwide and considered by many to be an immutable and irrevocable part of human society. More recently, few people would have imagined that India would win its independence from Britain through a campaign of militant but nonviolent protest, that decades-old fascist dictatorships in Spain and Portugal would give way to modern parliamentary democracies, that bloody tyrannies in the Philippines and Haiti could have been overthrown peacefully, that the Soviet Union would renounce its Stalinist heritage and institute massive democratic restructuring (*perestroika*) and political/ideological openness (*glasnost*), that South Korea, Argentina, and Brazil would become democratic republics, that the "captive nations" of Eastern Europe would throw off their shackles and emerge as fledgling democracies eager to embrace free-market economic reforms. Maybe sometime in the future, people will look back wonderingly at the latter part of the twentieth century, noting with amazement that such a war-prone world, aided by persistent, widespread peace movements, could mount so successful a campaign against war itself.

"If we examine successful social movements that transformed unfavorable power balances," writes one important peace movement theorist,

> we find they possessed certain common features: a vision of a promised land; a leadership dedicated unto death; a set of tactics that produced illuminating encounters with the established order and resulted in some kind of blood sacrifice; a widely endorsed moral passion; and developments that weakened the old order in decisive respects and made its maintenance appear impractical or illegitimate to an expanding constituency of its former upholders.[18]

A FINAL NOTE ON PEACE MOVEMENTS

In recent times successful peace movements have led to such tangible events as independence for India, the civil rights movement in the United States, an end to above-ground nuclear testing, and the democratization of Eastern Europe, among others. It remains to be seen whether a successful movement for peace—both negative and positive—will be similarly constituted, or similarly rewarded. The alternative is to continue "business as usual" in a world of war, injustice, and deprivation. Many people have long recognized that this old way is unacceptable, a perception that has become even more widespread with the advent of weapons of mass destruction. Yet, progress toward a different and more peaceful world has been painfully slow, if indeed there has been any such progress at all. Not surprisingly, therefore, it often seems that we have been, as Matthew Arnold put it,

> Wandering between two worlds, one dead,
> The other powerless to be born.[19]

The special hope of peace movements is that they might serve as midwives for that newer world, providing it with the impetus and power to be born at last. Just as birth may be difficult, often painful, even dangerous, we have seen that the course of peace movements has not run altogether smoothly, nor have peace movements been unidirectional or universally welcomed. But just as birth is natural and necessary if life is to continue, it seems equally certain that peace is necessary (whether or not it is natural), and that peace movements may contribute mightily toward success. If so, there may be real hope that humanity, through conscious choice and deliberate policy—as Pope John Paul II put it—might yet survive and even flourish.

Study Questions

1. Do you believe that there has been a change in public attitudes toward war? Why or why not?

2. Discuss examples of substantial changes in public attitudes, and show how such changes may be relevant to the actions of peace movements.

3. What relationships have been claimed between democracy and war?

4. Compare pacifism with "pacificism."

5. What relationships appear to exist between peace movements and the conduct of actual wars?

6. Suggest at least one classification of peace movements other than that proposed in this text.

7. Sketch the complex and often ambivalent attitude of socialist movements toward war.

8. What considerations other than opposition to war have been merging with modern peace movements?

9. What are some notable differences between modern European-based peace movements and those in the United States? Some similarities?

10. Describe your personal position regarding the various controversies within modern peace movements. Support your position with examples, either from history or the current world situation.

Suggestions for Further Reading

Peter Brock. 1970. *Twentieth Century Pacifism*. Van Nostrand Reinhold: New York.

Geoffrey Nuttall. 1971. *Christian Pacifism in History*. Seabury Press: New York.

Richard Taylor and Colin Pritchard. 1981. *The Protest-Makers*. Pergamon Press: Oxford, U.K.

Robert Cooney and Helen Michalowski. 1987. *The Power of the People*. New Society Publishers: Philadelphia.

Pam Solo. 1988. *From Protest to Policy*. Ballinger: Hagerstown, MD.

Source Notes

1. Quoted in Kermit Johnson. 1988. *Realism and Hope in a Nuclear Age*. John Knox Press: Atlanta.

2. Edmund Wilson. 1962. *Patriotic Gore: Studies in the Literature of the American Civil War*. A. Deutsch: London.

3. George Orwell. 1949. *1984*. Harcourt, Brace, Jovanovich: New York.

4. Desiderius Erasmus. 1967. "*Dulce Bellum Inexpertis*." In M. M. Phillips (ed.), *Erasmus and His Times*. Cambridge University Press: Cambridge.

5. Ibid.

6. Ibid.

7. Thomas More. 1965. *Complete Works*. Edward Suntz and J. H. Hexter (eds.). Yale University Press: New Haven, CT.

8. Thomas Paine. 1984. *The Rights of Man*. Penguin: New York.

9. Quoted in Kenneth Waltz. 1959. *Man, the State, and War*. Columbia University Press: New York.

10. Ibid.

11. Herodotus. 1910. *History*. (George Rawlinson, trans.) E. P. Dutton: New York.

12. Bob Overy. 1982. *How Effective Are Peace Movements?* Housmans: London.

13. Based on Nigel Young. 1984. "Why Peace Movements Fail." *Social Alternatives* 4: 9–16.

14. Philip P. Everts. 1989. "Where the Peace Movement Goes When It Disappears." *Bulletin of the Atomic Scientists* 45: 26–30.

15. Overy. *How Effective?*

16. Overy. *How Effective?*

17. Quincy Wright. 1964. *A Study of War*. University of Chicago Press: Chicago.

18. Richard Falk. 1987. "The State System and Contemporary Social Movements." In S. H. Mendlovitz and R. B. J. Walker (eds.), *Towards a Just World Peace*. Butterworths: London.

19. Matthew Arnold. 1934. "Stanzas from the Grande Chartreuse." *Essays and Poems of Matthew Arnold*. Harcourt Brace Jovanovich: New York.

4

War Movements: Conventional Trouble Spots

Wars begin when you will, but they do not end when you please.
  Niccolò Machiavelli

In the first three chapters of this book, we examined some general principles of peace and war, including a description of the problems involved in avoiding war and attaining peace, as well as some likely causes and potential solutions. It can be argued, however, that just as the nature of peace — and the pursuit of peace — differs from one occasion to another, there is no such thing as *war*, but rather specific *wars*, each distinct and with its own unique precipitating causes, circumstances, personality, and history. Moreover, the reader's attention in the coming years is likely to be drawn to one or several areas of conflict, not only to test the validity of these generalizations about peace and war, but also because these are real-life places where actual people will be living, struggling, and dying. And yet students, even college students, tend to be woefully uninformed about the basic dynamics, historical background, and geographical setting of the various violent conflicts around the world. Hence, there is a need for a primer, a kind of guidebook to areas of war and violent conflict. Even though much of this material will be overtaken by events, it should nonetheless provide a kind of grounding, to help understand the tumultuous world of the 1990s.

In this chapter, we shall therefore take a brief tour through some major trouble spots, places where conventional war has recently taken place, is now going on, and/or seems likely to occur in the future. Our tour will be necessarily brief, selective, and undetailed: The goal is to help underline the reality of war as a pressing and immediate human problem, as real as tomorrow's headlines, thereby emphasizing the importance of Peace Studies in a war-prone world. This chapter also should give the reader a sense of the diversity of armed conflict and war-related tensions present in today's world. Finally, it should provide a smattering of basic information simply to help make the reader a better-informed citizen.

Even though new sources of armed strife will doubtless arise, we can have a certain grim confidence that certain areas probably will remain more troubled than others. Thus, while it is unlikely that Bolivia and Thailand, for example, will find themselves at war in the foreseeable future,* we can also anticipate that certain trouble spots — Central America, the Middle East, India and Pakistan, South Africa — will remain troubled for some time to come. (Because of the special importance of nuclear war, especially between the two superpowers, we shall consider that issue separately, in Chapter 5.)

A CLASSIFICATION OF MODERN WARS

Wars occur for many different reasons, and are of many different types. Although the following list represents a rather crude classification of wars as either interstate, interventionist, civil, or "warlike," it seems more meaningful to categorize wars according to these broad types than to list contemporary wars alphabetically or by geographic region. It should also help place into context the confusing,

kaleidoscopic array of organized, armed violence in the world.

1. *Interstate wars.* These involve wars in the classic sense, between two or more recognized political entities that both enjoy the same degree of political sovereignty. In the past, such wars were formally declared at their outset, and were terminated with official peace treaties. As we have seen, however, wars are rarely "declared" these days; nonetheless, in most cases, we can still recognize the classic interstate nature of such conflicts. They often involve efforts by one state to gain territory at the expense of the other, although other factors may also be involved, such as punishment for past wrongs or various economic or political motivations. Well-known examples include the Napoleonic Wars, as well as World Wars I and II.

2. *Interventionist wars.* In certain cases, such as the Soviet invasion of Afghanistan and the Vietnam War (which many consider to have been a U.S. invasion of Vietnam), an outside state becomes actively involved in support of one faction in a civil war. When the extent of the outside involvement becomes such that it overshadows the original local warring factions, we can distinguish these wars from either interstate or civil wars, although of course the distinction is somewhat arbitrary. Another form of interventionist war should also be identified, the relatively brief injection of military forces (typically from a much stronger state) into another state. Such interventions typically occur to prevent governments from changing, or to induce a change. Examples include the Soviet interventions in Hungary (1956) and Czechoslovakia (1968), and U.S. interventions in the Dominican Republic (1965), Grenada (1983), and Panama (1989).

3. *Civil wars.* In these wars, organized fighting occurs between two segments within the same state. Civil wars are by far the most common wars now taking place, and it seems likely that

---

*Such assurance may be misleading, however; prior to 1982, not many people would have anticipated a war between Argentina and Great Britain.

this will continue to be the case. They can usefully be subdivided by the goals of the civil war, whether (1) revolutionary, that is, attempting to overthrow an existing government, or (2) secessionist, in which a group — typically occupying a distinct region — seeks to secede from an existing government. Historical examples of revolutionary civil wars include the Spanish civil war of 1936–1939 (in which the fascist Francisco Franco gained power), the Chinese Revolution (culminating in 1949 with the establishment of communism in China), the Cuban Revolution which brought Fidel Castro to power, and the Nicaraguan Revolution, through which the Sandinistas took control of that country in 1979.* Secessionist civil wars would include the American War of Independence (which was successful) and the American Civil War (which was not). Most secessionist civil wars have been unsuccessful.

It is tempting to recognize another category of war, the anticolonial war, in which people seek independence from a remote occupying power. In the late twentieth century, most anticolonial wars have already been successfully fought. Not uncommonly, they have given rise to interventionist or civil wars, which often continue to have a strong anticolonial flavor.

4. *Warlike situations.*   If the previous categories are subjective, this one is even more so. It involves situations in which organized, armed violence simmers or appears imminent, even if it is not presently occurring on a large scale.

As we shall see, this extremely simple classification ignores much of the complexity of contemporary wars. For example, in virtually all cases of civil wars, the forces in conflict receive support from other states. Sometimes, this outside support is so significant as to constitute virtually the primary reason for the war; in such cases, outside powers are using local actors as pawns for their own designs. In many situations, racial and ethnic antagonisms, and/or religious and ideological differences add fuel to the fire.

INTERSTATE WARS

Libya and Chad

Background.   Libya, a former Italian colony in north Africa, is small in population, wealthy in oil revenues, relatively undeveloped economically, Arab-speaking, and Islamic. King Idris was overthrown in a military coup in 1969, whereupon Colonel Muammar Qaddafi emerged as political leader. He is widely considered to be a sponsor of international terrorism, directed against Israel as well as many of Libya's neighbors, upon whom Qaddafi has had territorial designs. Libya has sponsored rebels in each of the states bordering it: Egypt, Sudan, Chad, Niger, Algeria, and Tunisia. Libya also had a short border war with Egypt in 1978 and another battle with the Tanzanian army in Uganda in 1979; in both cases, the Libyans were soundly defeated.

Chad, like Libya, occupies a relatively large area and has a small population (about 5 million). It is part of the former French Equatorial Africa, and retains close economic and cultural ties with France. Following a military coup in 1975, the Chaddian government experienced considerable instability, mediated on occasion by Nigeria. France has also maintained strong military ties with Chad, as with many other former French colonies in central and west Africa, including Gabon, the Congo, and Cameroon. Northern Chaddians are primarily Arabic-speaking Moslems, while the southerners — where the seat of the government is located and most political and economic power lies — are French-speaking, and largely animist and Christian. Chad is very poor and arid.

---

*Many famous revolutions — such as the French (1789) and Russian (1918) — were actually closer to *coups d'état* than to revolutionary wars. It may be significant, however, that both led to extensive fighting within a few years between the revolutionaries and supporters of the old regime.

The Conflict.   Libya has a territorial dispute with Chad that dates back several hundred years, to when the Ottoman Turks controlled the Libyan desert. The disputed area lies along northern Chad, a possibly mineral-rich region known as the Anzou Strip. Libyan troops were operating in the northern half of Chad sporadically during the 1970s, and with increasing frequency and in greater numbers during the 1980s, supporting a Moslem insurgency there. France responded with military supplies as well as a limited number of paratroopers to support the central Chaddian government.

In addition to its territorial demands, Libya claims to be providing fraternal support to the rebel Islamic forces in northern Chad. The result has been continuing desert warfare, largely between Chaddian forces backed by France and Libyan forces supplied by the Soviet Union. Libya suffered a major military defeat in the Anzou Strip during 1987, but the "war" goes on. It is also noteworthy that the Sudan, Chad's neighbor to the east, is divided along similar geographic/ethnic lines: Christian and animist in the south, Islamic in the north. But in this case, political power rests in the north. Accordingly, the Sudan has also experienced a history of secessionist warfare, with the Libyans alternately shipping arms to Islamic extremists in the north, and then Christian/animists in the south, seeking to destabilize the pro-Western Sudanese government.

Ethiopia and Somalia

Background.   Ethiopia was one of Africa's oldest independent kingdoms, ruled for many decades by the pro-Western emperor Haile Selassie. He was overthrown in 1974 in a military coup led by left-leaning officers, after which Ethiopia became a Marxist state. The Somali republic, on the other hand, was formed only recently, in 1960, from a union of British Somaliland in the north and Italian Somaliland in the south. The government of Somalia, like that of Ethiopia, is Marxist, and has been since a military coup in 1969. Many Somali-speaking people live in Ethiopia and, to a lesser extent, northern Kenya; the Somali government has

long sought to unite all ethnic Somalis within the same country. Border fighting broke out several times between Kenya and Somalia during the 1960s.

The Conflict.   The most serious conflict has centered on an arid region in eastern Ethiopia known as the Ogaden, which is inhabited largely by Somali-speaking herders and desert nomads. Ethiopia and Somalia went to war over the region in 1977. Somali forces, backed by the Soviet Union, invaded the Ogaden and achieved early success. However, in 1978, Ethiopia, supported by Cuban troops and with the assistance of the Soviet Union (which had switched sides after the United States refused to come to the aid of Marxist Ethiopia), repulsed the Somalis. Somalia accordingly tilted toward the United States. Somali rebels within the Ogaden continued to fight, and to receive assistance from the government of Somalia. By 1988, Ethiopia and Somalia reached a tentative peace settlement, at least partly because Ethiopia was also simultaneously fighting secessionist civil wars in its northern provinces of Tigre and Eritrea. Shortly thereafter, however, serious fighting broke out between the Somali dictatorship (now U.S.-leaning) and rebels in the very arid northern part of that country.

This struggle was especially notable because it greatly exacerbated a widespread famine in the region, which itself was due to a prolonged drought. However, in the absence of war, relief agencies would have been able to provide substantial assistance; as it happened, both the rebels and government forces used food as a weapon, cutting off supplies to civilians in regions thought to be sympathetic to the other side. The result is that hundreds of thousands died of starvation and malnutrition, despite the mobilization of worldwide assistance efforts, including such U.S.-backed fund-raising efforts as "USA for Africa."

Iran and Iraq

Background.   For more than two thousand years, Arabs and Persians (Iranians) have contested control of the Shatt-al-Arab, the combined mouths of

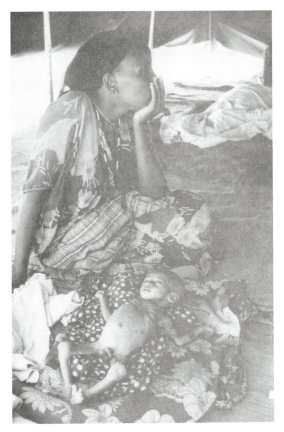

An Ethiopian woman and her severely undernourished child at an emergency refugee camp. Natural drought was directly responsible for widespread famine in Ethiopia; warfare has interrupted delivery of vitally needed food supplies. (United Nations/ O. Monsen)

the Tigris and Euphrates rivers. Iraqis are ethnically Arabs, and Arabic-speaking; Iranians are ethnic Persians, and Farsi-speaking. Although both countries are overwhelmingly Moslem, different sects predominate in the two: Iraq's political leadership is predominantly Sunni, while somewhat more than 50 percent of its population is Shiite. By contrast, Iran is primarily Shiite. About 90 percent of the world's Moslems are Sunni; Shiites constitute an underclass in most Moslem countries except for Iran. The antagonism between Sunni and Shiite branches of Islam dates from a seventh-century dispute over the rightful successors of the prophet Mo-

hammed. The followers of Mohammed's son-in-law were known as the "shia," and they have long cultivated an underdog emphasis on suffering and martyrdom. By contrast, Sunni Moslems are somewhat more secular and establishment-oriented. Each considers the other to be heretical.

The Conflict. During the 1970s, Iran (and the United States) supported Kurdish tribes seeking to secede from Iraq and form an independent Kurdistan. At the same time, Iraq demanded control over Arab-populated areas of Iran, known as Kuzistan. This dispute was ostensibly settled in 1975 by a mutual noninterference agreement between Iran and Iraq (although this did nothing to address the Kurds' demands). At the time, Iraq harbored an Iranian revolutionary and religious leader, the Ayatollah Ruholla Khomeini. Iraq agreed to deport Khomeini to France, in return for which the Shah of Iran would close the Iranian border to Kurdish rebels. With the fall of the (U.S.-backed) Shah in 1979, and the ensuing chaos in Iran following the return of Khomeini, the Iraqi leader, Saddam Hussein, felt that he had an opportunity to win victory in his long-standing border dispute with Iran. Iraq invaded Iran in 1980, and was initially successful. Eventually, however, the Iranians counterattacked, using human wave tactics that produced enormous casualties but that also reestablished the borders in their prewar positions, with some slight gains for the Iranians. A long and painful war of attrition resulted.*

Iran has the larger population and greater resources, as well as continuing revolutionary and religious fervor. Many thousands of teenage boys, for example, martyred themselves willingly, clearing minefields for following troops. Iraq relied instead

---

*In such a war, each side seeks to wear the other down by applying continuous pressure; in many such cases, the goal is not so much to win the war outright on the battlefield, but to undermine popular support for the conflict within the opponent's homeland through accumulated economic pressure as well as the mounting number of casualties.

on superior firepower and technology, as well as the use of chemical weapons such as mustard gas. Iraq received the support of most Arab states (except, notably, Syria, which has long been an Iraqi rival). Nonetheless, the long-term prospects were widely thought to favor Iran. In 1983, Iraq therefore began the "tanker war," attacking Iranian oil shipping in the Persian Gulf, in an effort to damage Iran's economy and possibly involve the superpowers in a negotiated settlement. In response to Iranian retaliation, especially against Kuwait (a pro-Western Iraqi ally), the United States began escorting selected oil tankers in the Persian Gulf. In 1987, Iran and Iraq also began the "war of the cities," firing relatively inaccurate missiles at Bagdad and Teheran; these have had no military significance but have produced civilian casualties. This bloody and destructive war has claimed upwards of one million lives.

Efforts by the United States to arrange for a UN-sponsored arms embargo of both sides were largely unsuccessful. Earlier, the Reagan administration was greatly embarrassed by the revelation that it had secretly shipped arms to Iran, in the hope of gaining release of American hostages held by pro-Iranian groups in Lebanon. (Some of the profits had also been used to support — illegally — the contra rebels in Nicaragua.) Both the Soviet Union and the United States tried to play both sides of this war, since both superpowers have retained an interest in keeping either side from becoming dominant in the region. In 1988, the United Nations Secretary General, Javier Perez de Cuellar, succeeded in persuading the governments of Iran and Iraq to agree to a cease-fire, with a United Nations observer force designated to oversee the armistice. Final resolution will require, among other things, agreement as to which state controls the disputed Shatt-al-Arab waterway, which, in the past, has constituted part of the Iran/Iraq border.

Israel and the Arab States

Background.   Zionism is a political movement dedicated to the establishment of a Jewish homeland in a region long claimed by Jews and occupied and ruled by just about everyone else. However, there are also several million Palestinians (Arabs living in the region historically known as Palestine — essentially the land between the Jordan River and the Mediterranean Sea) who also claim the same area as their home. This rivalry dates back, in a sense, to the conflict between Jew and Moslem over the legacy of their reputed common father, Abraham.*

Historically, the Romans were followed by the Turks as rulers of the region, with an intervening period of rule by Christian Crusaders. Jews began immigrating in large numbers during the late nineteenth century, fleeing especially from persecution by the Russian czars. However, Arabs at that time constituted more than 90 percent of the population. Then, with the defeat of the Turkish Ottoman Empire in World War I, Britain was granted a mandate to control the region. The British "Balfour Declaration" of 1917 promised a homeland for the Jews; but previously, Britain's Henry McMahon, high commissioner to Egypt, had promised British support for Arab independence in the region, in return for Arab assistance in the war against Turkey (which had been allied with Germany and Austria-Hungary during World War I). Zionists purchased land in British-administered Palestine, and many additional settlers immigrated, leading to clashes with the resident Arab population. Following the Holocaust during World War II, additional Jewish refugees arrived, swelling the Jewish population to about 40 percent of Palestine. Worldwide Zionism, political agitation, sympathy for Jewish suffering under Hitler, and pro-Zionist terrorism within Palestine (which Jews considered their biblical "promised land") eventually persuaded Britain to partition Palestine into Jewish and Arab sectors in 1948.

The Conflict.   Partitioning led to open warfare between the newly declared state of Israel and its neighbors: Egypt, Lebanon, Syria, and Jordan. Israeli gains in that first Palestine war of 1948 led to

---

*Abraham is said to have had a son, Isaac, who became the ancestor of the Jewish people, and another, Ishmael, an outcast, who was the ancestor of the Arabs.

A Palestinian family standing near the remains of their West Bank house, which was bulldozed by Israeli armed forces. The homes of persons suspected of participating in the intifada have been summarily destroyed. (Curt Borgwardt)

the displacement of hundreds of thousands of Arabs, who became homeless, embittered refugees. In addition, their humiliation, anger, and insistence upon having their own Palestinian state (whether within the current borders of Israel or in some other area, such as the West Bank or Gaza Strip) has contributed to much of the hostility and unrest in the Middle East today.

A second Arab-Israeli war was fought in 1956, when, in response to growing threats from Egypt's nationalist leader, Gamal Abdel Nasser, Israel invaded the Sinai and occupied the Gaza Strip while France and Britain invaded the Suez region. Opposition from the United States, however, led to Western and Israeli withdrawal. Then, in 1967, Egypt's president Nasser sent forces into the Sinai and closed the Strait of Tiran to Israeli shipping. Israel responded with an "anticipatory counteroffensive" against Egypt, Syria, and Jordan — the Six Day War that gave Israel control of the Sinai, the Golan Heights (previously part of Syria), and the West Bank, including the old city of Jerusalem (previously part of Jordan). This war was ended by United Nations Security Council Resolution 242, which called for eventual Israeli withdrawal from the occupied Arab lands in return for peace and the recognition of Israel's right to exist. The exact amount of territory to be returned was not specified, however; similarly unresolved was the question of whether or not there was to be an Arab Palestinian state.

In 1973, during the Jewish holiday of Yom Kippur, Egypt and Syria surprised Israel with a sudden attack across the Suez Canal and along the Golan Heights. Eventually, the Arab armies were repulsed, but not before inflicting heavy casualties on Israel, thereby restoring Arab pride and tarnishing the image of Israeli military invincibility. Egyptian president Sadat subsequently visited Jerusalem in 1977; this event, plus the Camp David accords of 1979, orchestrated by President Carter, led to Israeli withdrawal from the Sinai in return for an Israeli-Egyptian peace treaty and normal diplomatic relations (see Chapter 13). However, Israel has remained to this day in a formal state of war with many other Arab states.

Throughout this time, displaced Palestinians conducted commando and terrorist operations against Israel, while Israel refused to negotiate with the major Palestinian political unit, the Palestine Liberation Organization (PLO), claiming that it was a terrorist organization dedicated to Israel's destruction. In 1982, Israel invaded southern Lebanon, from which PLO guerrillas and terrorists had been harassing northern Israel. This precipitated an air war with Syria, which Israel won handily, but it enmeshed Israel in a difficult situation from which it has been unable to extricate itself. In the process, the Lebanese state has been effectively dismantled, with Israel establishing a so-called security zone in the south, Syria controlling much of the east, and the rest of the country divided among various armed militias, leaving the nominal Lebanese government with little real authority.

Various Arab states remain committed, at least rhetorically, to the destruction of Israel. And Israel has annexed the Golan Heights and has been introducing Jewish settlers into the West Bank, which some Israelis claim as their own, the biblical Judea and Samaria. At the same time, more than one million Arabs live in the West Bank, chafing under Israeli rule. Their determination to end twenty years of occupation led in December 1987 to escalating protests and riots on the part of young Palestinians — the so-called *intifada* or "uprising." It has led to rough — some say, brutal — repression by the Israelis, and appears to make the Israeli occupation increasingly untenable. In 1988, King Hussein of Jordan renounced all Jordanian claims to the West Bank. The PLO, which Israel does not formally recognize, thereupon declared the existence of a free and independent Palestinian state in this area. Although the overwhelming majority of countries do not acknowledge the existence of such a Palestinian state at this time, most agree that, eventually, such a state will have to be established; Israel, however, resists world pressure in this regard.

Israel continues to be the dominant military power in the Middle East, and has received substantial military, economic, and political support from the United States (which also provides aid to Egypt and to the conservative Arab states of Saudi Arabia and Jordan, as well as the "oil ministates" of Bahrain, Qatar, Kuwait, and the United Arab Emirates). The U.S.S.R. is allied with the Arab world, especially in providing weapons and diplomatic support; in the Middle East, however, with its long and tangled history of plots, counterplots, and betrayals, nearly everyone is suspicious of everyone else. Furthermore, it is widely acknowledged that Israel possesses nuclear weapons. In 1981, Israel bombed and destroyed an Iraqi nuclear facility that the Israelis claimed was intended to produce nuclear weapons. The economic and social cost of an ongoing state of war has also been enormous, and yet, the issues are so deep-rooted and seemingly intractable that further hostilities seem likely.* Given the high emotional involvement of the superpowers (especially the United States) in the region, any serious local clashes probably will involve them as well.

Vietnam and Cambodia

Background. During the 1950s and 1960s, Cambodian leader Prince Norodom Sihanouk maintained a neutral posture and kept Cambodia out of the war in Vietnam. However, during the Nixon administration, the United States and South Vietnam charged that Vietnamese communists had established bases and supply routes in eastern Cambodia, along the South Vietnamese border. The United States began bombing these regions in 1969. The following year, Prince Sihanouk was overthrown by the pro-Western general Lon Nol, and U.S. and South Vietnamese troops entered Cambodia to clear out North Vietnamese and Viet Cong (insurgent South Vietnamese) base camps. The communist forces retreated deeper into Cambodia, and by the end of 1970, the entire country was at war. By 1975, after the United States had withdrawn from Vietnam, the most extreme and violent faction of the Cambodian Communist party, the Khmer Rouge, led by Pol Pot, had won control.

---

*The following story comes to mind: A scorpion, who wanted to cross the Jordan River, asked a frog to carry him on his back. The frog refused, claiming that the scorpion would sting him. The scorpion explained that of course he wouldn't do so, since this would mean the scorpion's death as well. The frog, seeing the logic in this, agreed, but half-way across the river, the scorpion could restrain himself no longer and stung the frog. With his dying breath, as both he and the scorpion began to slip under the waves, the frog croaked out, "Why?" and the scorpion explained, "Because this is the Middle East."

An estimated one million Cambodians subsequently died of starvation, disease, and outright murder during the forced relocation and brutal collectivization that occurred during the next five years. The movie *The Killing Fields* depicts some of the horror of those times. By 1979, the Khmer Rouge were driven from power by their former allies, the communist Vietnamese.

The Conflict. It is not clear why Cambodian forces initiated a hopeless conflict with Vietnam in the late 1970s. In any event, Vietnam responded by invading Cambodia in 1979 and tossing out the Khmer Rouge. Throughout the 1980s, Vietnam maintained more than 200,000 troops in Cambodia, seeking to keep their puppet regime in power. It has been opposed by a mutually distrustful coalition of Cambodians, including the Khmer Rouge (still led by the murderous Pol Pot), as well as royalists supporting ousted prince Sihanouk and rightists (who had previously deposed Sihanouk) receiving aid from the United States. China has supported the Khmer Rouge, largely, it seems, out of antagonism to the Vietnamese and their ally, the Soviet Union. The United States, similarly, has refused to support the Cambodian government installed by Vietnam, largely, it seems, out of antagonism to the Vietnamese. In the meantime, more than 250,000 Cambodian refugees live in squalor in neighboring Thailand. Thailand, for its part, has winked at the presence and brutal recruiting tactics of anti-Vietnamese rebels, in part because it hoped to establish a buffer between itself and Vietnam. It should also be noted that in 1979, China attacked Vietnam to "punish" it for its occupation of Cambodia; this brief but violent war resulted in perhaps 8,000–10,000 Vietnamese casualties and upwards of 35,000 Chinese casualties.

The Vietnamese economy was faltering badly during the 1980s, during which time the maintenance of Vietnamese troops in Cambodia became a painful financial and social burden. Vietnam consequently began withdrawing its forces, completing the process by late 1989. As a result, many persons are fearful that the Khmer Rouge, as the most powerful opposition group, will regain control. The possibility also exists that given the bickering, distrust, and widespread distaste among the feuding anti-Vietnamese factions, the Cambodian government initially installed by Vietnam will ultimately consolidate power in that long-suffering country.

Britain and Argentina (The Falklands/Malvinas War)

Background. The Falkland Islands, small, remote, and windswept, about the area of Connecticut and with a population of less than 2,000, are among the few vestiges of British colonial power still remaining. The government of Argentina, however, has long claimed these islands, calling them the Malvinas. The inhabitants consider themselves British subjects, although geography clearly favors Argentine control. The Argentine government, a military dictatorship led by General Galtieri, was under pressure from the following sources: an inflation rate exceeding 100 percent, an ongoing dispute with Chile over the Beagle Channel and Tierra del Fuego, and a declining sense of legitimacy within the country at large, owing in part to the tortures, murders, and other acts of repression directed at political dissidents. The British government of Margaret Thatcher, meanwhile, was facing an election that it was expected to lose.

The Conflict. In 1982, with negotiations over the eventual return of the islands to Argentina dragging on, Argentine forces landed and declared ownership. The British people were outraged, and a naval task force was dispatched. The United States sought, unsuccessfully, to mediate between the two sides, both of which are U.S. allies. Within a few months, the Falklands had been retaken by the British, at a cost of 1,100 lives and about £4 billion, as well as several major ships and a number of aircraft. Prime Minister Thatcher was overwhelmingly re-elected to her second term in Britain; the "Falklands factor" — British pride in their recapture of the islands — was considered to have played a major role. The Argentine military, further discredited by the war, was replaced by a democratic government, but one that still places a high priority on regaining the "Malvinas."

It is interesting to note that unlike most recent wars, this one involved virtually no civilian casualties, since it was fought at sea and on essentially unoccupied land; also, Britain refrained from attacking the Argentine mainland. This brief war revealed the political uses of modern war, as well as demonstrating the effectiveness of precision-guided conventional munitions (so-called smart rockets). It also demonstrates that the possession of nuclear weapons does not necessarily make a country immune to military challenge from a nonnuclear state: Britain possesses nuclear weapons, whereas Argentina does not . . . yet.

India and Pakistan

Background. The entire Indian subcontinent had been under British imperial rule since the eighteenth century. However, the antagonism that existed between Hindus and Moslems was such that when the region achieved independence in 1947, two separate states were created, at the insistence of the Moslem minority: India, the largest and most populous, primarily Hindu, was distinguished from Moslem Pakistan, which was in turn divided into western and eastern halves. Millions of Hindus and Moslems, fearful of persecution, fled to their respective states, and bloody rioting ensued.

In addition to their religious and cultural differences, Indians and Pakistanis both claimed sovereignty over Kashmir, a mountainous region adjacent to both West Pakistan and India; the ruler was Hindu, but the majority of the population was Moslem. In 1947, Pakistani invaders were repulsed by Indian troops, and Kashmir became a bitterly contested part of India. In its search for allies against its larger and more populous neighbor, Pakistan became increasingly associated with the United States, and to some extent China. (China, in turn, has had an ongoing border dispute with India, which led to a brief Sino-Indian war in 1962, in which the Indians were decisively defeated.) India became a leader of the nonaligned nations, although edging in some ways toward closer cooperation with the Soviet Union.

The Conflict. In 1965, another India–Pakistani war erupted, over yet another disputed territory, the Rann of Kutch, an uninhabited delta region that is virtual desert in the dry season and flooded marsh during the monsoon season. Pakistani forces defeated India's, whereupon Pakistan's leader, Ayub Khan, sent Pakistani-trained guerrillas into Kashmir on sabotage missions. India responded by occupying Pakistani supply routes into Kashmir, which Pakistan then invaded. The two armies fought to a virtual standstill, after which a ceasefire was negotiated by Soviet premier Kosygin.

Meanwhile, Pakistan was a single nation in name only. Not only were East and West Pakistan separated by 1,000 miles, they were culturally different as well: in West Pakistan, tall, light-skinned Punjabis, who honoured warriors; in densely populated East Pakistan, short, dark-skinned Bengalis, who respected intellectuals and traders. The two people shared a belief in Islam, but little else; they did not even speak the same language. Western Punjabis dominated the Pakistani union and the eastern Bengalis felt exploited. Most government and army posts, for example, were occupied by West Pakistanis and the federal government seemed indifferent to a devastating cyclone that struck East Pakistan in 1970. Also in 1970, a political party that supported greater autonomy for East Pakistan — the Awami League led by Sheikh Mujibur Rahman — was overwhelmingly elected, whereupon it was banned by the Pakistani federal government. The Awami League then declared East Pakistan to be an independent state, known as Bangladesh ("Bengal nation").

The Pakistani army responded by arresting Bengali leaders, massacring hundreds of thousands of people, and causing millions of refugees (most of them Hindu) to flee into neighboring India. The Indian government, which had long favored the partition of her old enemy, was further inflamed by the plight of the Bengalis, who were ethnically allied to India; furthermore, caring for the refugees had overtaxed the Indian economy. In late 1971, India entered Bangladesh in support of the Bengalis and decisively defeated the Pakistanis, who were outnumbered and also surrounded by a hostile population. Bangladesh became a sovereign, independent state, and the fearful antagonism between India and Pakistan (formerly West Pakistan) was if anything enhanced.

The 1971 India–Pakistan war could certainly be considered an interstate interventionist war, since India was intervening in a Pakistani civil war; however, it seems more accurately viewed as only one stage in an ongoing interstate conflict. India detonated a nuclear explosion in 1974, whereupon Pakistan has been eagerly seeking to develop its own nuclear weapons. By the late 1980s, this quest has apparently been fulfilled.

In the following cases, interstate wars have recently occurred, are continuing at a low level, and/or generate a degree of ongoing tension:

Guatemala/Belize.   Guatemala claims the tiny Central American state of Belize (formerly British Honduras). As a result of Guatemalan threats, Britain several times has reinforced its supporting garrison in Belize.

El Salvador/Honduras.   In 1969, El Salvador and Honduras fought the so-called Soccer War, a five-day conflict sparked by rivalry over a series of soccer matches. The underlying issue, however, concerned alleged Honduran mistreatment of Salvadoran migrants.

Greece/Turkey/Cyprus.   The island of Cyprus lies close to Turkey, with a population consisting of a Greek majority (Greek Orthodox Christians) and a Turkish minority (Moslem). The Turks especially have felt oppressed. Greece and Turkey have long been at odds over other issues, including navigation and oil exploration rights among certain islands in the Aegean, as well as a bitter history dating from when Greece was part of the Ottoman Empire. Cyprus became independent from Britain in 1960, and Greece and Turkey nearly went to war in 1964 and then again in 1967, both times with the "home" countries seeking to defend the rights of their Cypriot compatriots. In 1974, the Cypriot leader Archbishop Makarios was overthrown by a coup led by militant Greek army officers, after which Turkey, fearing for the Turkish minority, invaded Cyprus; this resulted in a *de facto* partition of Cyprus into a Turkish-held northern section and a Greek-held southern section. Animosity between Turkey and Greece continues to this day, stimulating military preparations on both sides, and periodically erupting into crises, despite the fact that both countries, as members of NATO, are ostensibly allies.

Yemen/South Yemen/Oman/Saudi Arabia. A communist regime in South Yemen, which receives Soviet support, is considered a mild threat to its conservative northern neighbor, Saudi Arabia; several pitched battles were fought during the 1970s. South Yemen also supported the so-called Dhofar rebels in Oman, who were eventually defeated with the assistance of Iranian forces sent by the Shah. Meanwhile, the South Yemenis have also fought with Yemen (a conservative, Moslem state sometimes known as North Yemen), which has in turn received aid from Saudi Arabia as well as the United States.

Western Sahara.   In 1976, Spain relinquished control of its colonial possession Spanish Sahara (now Western Sahara) to Morocco and Mauritania, both of which claimed the area. In addition, insurgents known as the Polisario, supported by a third adjacent country, Algeria, have engaged in guerrilla warfare with Morocco in particular over control of Western Sahara.

Sino-Russian Conflict.   Clearly, there would be nothing minor about war between these two giants were it ever to break out. Even without war, each country's anxiety about the other influences a wide range of events. China and the U.S.S.R. have a common border of 4,500 miles, and tensions have flared into actual combat more than a dozen times, most seriously in

1969 along the Amur River on the northwestern Sino-Soviet border. China maintains about one million troops and militia along this border, facing a force of nearly 500,000 Soviets. Both sides also possess nuclear weapons aimed at the other. Recently, Sino-Soviet tensions appear to be defusing, and both sides have announced plans to reduce military forces along their border.

REVOLUTIONARY CIVIL WARS

Angola

Angola had been an African colonial possession of Portugal since the seventeenth century. Bloody guerrilla warfare erupted in the 1960s. In 1974, the long-standing right-wing Portuguese dictatorship of Antonio Salazar was overthrown in Lisbon; a year later, Angola was granted independence. Two major rebel groups fought for control in Angola: the Marxist MPLA (Popular Movement for the Liberation of Angola), which received Soviet military supplies along with Cuban troops, and UNITA (National Union for the Total Independence of Angola), a group of pro-Western rebels from the southern provinces. The MPLA defeated UNITA in 1976 and established a socialist government, but UNITA continued a guerrilla war seeking to overthrow the Angolan regime. The Cuban troops remained to help support the Marxist Angolan government (where, ironically, they protect American-owned, Gulf Oil facilities from destruction by U.S.-sponsored insurgents). In addition to substantial backing from the United States, UNITA receives direct logistical and combat support from the Republic of South Africa, which has made periodic aerial and land incursions into southern Angola, hoping to destabilize the Angolan government. The situation in Angola is closely entwined with that of Namibia, which we examine next.

Namibia

South Africa fought on the side of the democracies during World War I. As a reward, it was given a League of Nations mandate over the former Ger-

A Kenyan military policeman arriving at Windhoek as part of the United Nations Transition Assistance Group, which helped supervise free elections in Namibia during 1989. (United Nations/ M. Grant)

man colony of South-West Africa, today known as Namibia. Following World War II, the United Nations embraced a policy of eventual independence for all former colonial territories. When it became apparent that South Africa was reneging on this commitment, the UN terminated South Africa's mandate over Namibia in 1966, and several years later, recognized a leftist independence movement, SWAPO (South-West Africa People's Organization), as the legitimate representative of Namibia. Although Namibia remained under South African control, SWAPO cooperates with the embattled Angolan government. Its war for Namibian independence from South African occupation cost upwards of 10,000 lives. South Africa used the presence of approximately 45,000 Cuban troops in Angola as a pretext for not granting independence to Namibia, with the Cubans and Angolans claiming that the former were invited in response to the

South African threat. In late 1988, with the Soviet Union, the government of the Congo, and the United States serving as mediators, an agreement was finally reached that called for the following: South African withdrawal from southern Angola and Namibia, independence for Namibia, and the departure of the Cuban troops from Angola, with a phased withdrawal of all parties in accord with a UN resolution drafted ten years earlier. The United Nations has supervised free and independent elections and has monitored compliance with the accord. However, it remains to be seen whether this agreement can be implemented; in addition, U.S. support for the UNITA insurgency within Angola was not affected by this pact, and so civil war in Angola may very well continue, with the ongoing possibility of further South African and Cuban intervention.

Mozambique

After nearly one hundred years as a Portuguese territory, Mozambique (like Angola) finally won its independence in 1975, following ten years of revolutionary guerrilla warfare. The socialist Mozambican government opposed the white minority government of Rhodesia during the late 1970s, and fighting occurred between Mozambican and Rhodesian troops. Mozambique was used as a base for black rebel attacks against white Rhodesia. The government of Mozambique has been engaged in an increasingly devastating civil war of its own, battling rebels originally sponsored by the minority white government of Rhodesia's Ian Smith. When that government became the black majority state of Zimbabwe, South Africa adopted the insurgents, known as "Renamo,"* to harry the Mozambican state. Renamo has been responsible for widespread atrocities, including the murder of more than 100,000 Mozambicans, nearly all of them civilians. Even the Reagan administration, which eagerly embraced nearly any anticommunist organization, found Renamo distasteful.

---

*For "Mozambique National Resistance" in Portuguese.

Nicaragua

The United States has a long history of dominating the politics of Central America, via heavy-handed economic influence including the support of a small but very influential number of upper-class landowners, often backed by direct military intervention. In Nicaragua, the United States placed the increasingly corrupt and brutal Somoza family in political control. (Of Somoza, President Franklin Roosevelt once said, "He may be an SOB, but he's our SOB.") This family dynasty was finally overthrown in 1979 by a group known as Sandinistas, named after a legendary Nicaraguan anticolonial leader of the 1920s, who fought against one of many interventionary forces of U.S. marines. Since their revolution, the Sandinista government has become increasingly Marxist, receiving aid from the Soviet bloc and Cuba, and enlarging its armed forces. Much of this — supporters of the Sandinistas say all of it — was due to the opposition of the United States, which organized and equipped counterrevolutionaries, widely known as "contras." The contras consisted of landowners, mercenaries, disaffected peasants, and other rightists who opposed Sandinista land reforms, and included some participants in the 1979 Sandinista revolution.

The contras were originally established in part through the efforts of Argentina's right-wing military dictatorship, with the approval and assistance of the United States. They waged a terror campaign and guerrilla war against the Managua government through most of the 1980s, with the financial and logistical support of the United States. Although the Reagan administration strongly supported the contras, calling them "freedom fighters" and the "moral equivalent of our founding fathers," much domestic opinion within the United States considered them U.S.-created terrorists and thugs who were unable to achieve any substantial backing among their own people. A group of Latin American states, including Venezuela, Colombia, and Mexico, known as the Contadora group, sought for years to defuse the conflict and achieve both U.S. disengagement and improved human rights within Nicaragua; the Reagan administration, while paying lip service to the goals of the Contadora group, continued to undermine peace efforts while pressing for a military solution that was never achieved.

In 1987, Costa Rican president Oscar Arias proposed a general Central American peace plan, which was agreed to by Honduras, Guatemala, El Salvador, Nicaragua, and Costa Rica. In 1988, contra and government leaders reached a tentative cease-fire plan, calling for domestic reforms on the part of the government, release of prisoners, and eventual incorporation of the contras as opposition forces into a peaceful, democratic process. Whether such an accommodation will be lasting remains uncertain; unlike all other insurrections that have ultimately been successful, the contras enjoy very little domestic support within Nicaragua. The contras have instead been entirely dependent on outside (U.S.) assistance, having received virtually no support within their own country. The right-wing argued that the Sandinistas sought only to tighten their authoritarian regime and extend Marxism to the rest of Central America; the left-wing countered that the contras were unwilling to abide by the popular will of Nicaraguans, seeking instead to overthrow the Sandinistas by force. By 1990, the Bush administration signalled that it was prepared to terminate U.S. support for the contras, switching instead to economic and political pressures against the Nicaraguan government. This strategy appeared successful when the Sandinistas were defeated in an election in 1990 by a coalition led by Violetta Chamorro and strongly supported by the United States. It indicates what might eventually become known as the "Nicaragua syndrome," whereby attempts by Third World countries to break away from U.S. domination are met by severe military and economic pressure, after which the population — exhausted by the prolonged sacrifice — chooses a path of greater accommodation.

El Salvador

El Salvador, like all the countries in Central America except for Costa Rica, has a long history of right-wing military suppression (abetted by the United States) as well as frequent coups and revolutions. The major guerrilla group, the leftist FMLN, has been fighting to overthrow a right-wing government supported by the United States. In addition to the overt guerrilla war, a vicious terrorist war has been waged, in which far-right "death squads" in particular have summarily murdered their moderate and left-wing civilian opponents. Under pressure from the United States, however, death squad activities diminished somewhat during the late 1980s. An ultra-right-wing group in El Salvador known as the Arena Party, closely associated with the economic oligarchy that controls the Salvadoran economy, favors more vigorous prosecution of the war against the rebels, whereas a center-right coalition has made some efforts to achieve a negotiated peace. In 1989, an Arena government was elected in El Salvador, after the rebels urged their supporters to boycott the election. The United States continues to send hundreds of millions of dollars in aid, much of it military, in support of the Salvadoran government, which appears unable to control extremist violent elements within its own military forces.

The Catholic Church in El Salvador has been increasingly sympathetic to the poor and dispossessed; that is, to the political left. The far right has responded with violence, notably the assassination of priests, nuns, various church workers, and even the Archbishop of San Salvador, Oscar Romero.

The Philippines

The Philippine islands became a Spanish colony in the sixteenth century when they were claimed by the explorer Magellan. The United States gained control over the Philippines as part of the spoils of the Spanish-American War (1898). Filipino military units had fought alongside the United States against Spain, thinking they would be granted independence after that war. However, they rebelled upon learning that the United States intended to administer the Philippines as a U.S. colonial possession; U.S. marines were sent in, and the rebellion was put down, with much bloodshed. The United States intervened militarily on several other occasions to suppress various insurgencies, but after the Japanese occupation of World War II, the Philippines were finally granted independence. The Filipino government, closely allied with the United States, defeated the communist-influenced Huk rebellion during the period 1945–1953. Ferdinand Marcos, after first being elected democratically, ruled as a dictator for more than twenty years until he was overthrown in a peaceful, popular uprising in 1986, with political leadership passing to Corazon Aquino.

The Philippines face two major insurgency campaigns. One rebellion comprises a Moslem uprising in the south, especially on Mindanao, where Moro tribesmen (the MNLF, or Moro National Liberation Front) seek secession from the rest of the Philippines, which is overwhelmingly Catholic. The second rebellion, which aims at overthrowing the central government, is being fought by the New People's Army (the NPA), the military arm of the outlawed Philippine communist party. Shortly after taking office, Corazon Aquino's government entered into negotiations with the NPA; these talks broke down, however, and the government in Manila — under substantial pressure from right-wing elements within the army — reverted to armed counterinsurgency warfare.

The United States has substantial interests in the Philippines, including financial investments, a history of alliance, and political involvement throughout the twentieth century, as well as two major military bases, Clark Air Base and Subic Bay Naval Station.

The following countries are not experiencing full-fledged civil war, but rather, small-scale revolutionary insurgencies, most of them on the level of organized resistance (according to supporters) or terrorism (according to opponents):

Guatemala.   Officially a democracy, but with strong military influence and substantial, brutal repression of opposition political groups; insurrection is most strongly developed among Indians who have been pushed into the mountains and who have been subjected to what amounts to government-sponsored genocide.

Honduras.   The basic revolutionary call here, as in Guatemala, is for economic justice; public sentiment has been further inflamed by the rather supine attitude of the Honduran government toward United States policies, especially support for U.S.-backed contras in Nicaragua.

Peru.   A romantic and very violent Maoist insurgency, once again emphasizing economic justice and restructuring of the local economy, with support among middle-class intellectuals, is known as the *Sendero Luminoso*, or Shining Path; this organization of several thousand has especially sought to capitalize on unrest among Peru's mountain-dwelling Indians.

Colombia.   Leftist rebels known as M-19, motivated in large part by the very unequal distribution of Colombian wealth, have employed terror and kidnapping; they are also accused by the government of indulging heavily in cocaine trafficking, while the rebels, in turn, accuse the government of doing so.

Burma.   More than a dozen different ideologically and ethnically oriented rebel groups oppose the socialist government; many of them (including, it appears, the government itself) are also involved with the lucrative opium trade.

Thailand and Malaysia.   Both these countries are facing persistent low-level communist insurgencies, which have stimulated them to cooperate across their common border.

Laos.   As in Cambodia but on a smaller scale, royalist and rightist forces oppose a communist regime imposed by the Vietnamese.

Sudan.   The Islamic government, in power in the north, fundamentalist by inclination and generally supported by the United States, has been fighting an on-again, off-again civil war since 1983 with the leftist, Christian/animist Sudanese People's Liberation Army, which has received aid from Soviet-backed Ethiopia; both sides have used food as a weapon in this struggle, denying emergency relief to civilians suspected of sympathizing with the other. It is estimated that in 1988 alone, 260,000 Sudanese died of hunger; most or all of these deaths could have been prevented if the civil war was not taking place.

INTERVENTIONIST WARS

The United States in Vietnam

Background.   Prior to Japanese occupation during World War II, France had been the dominant colonial power in Indochina since the 1870s. Ho Chi Minh, who had led the Vietnamese resistance against the Japanese, turned to the Western democracies, expecting them to honor the long-standing demands for Vietnamese independence. However, when France refused to grant independence to its Indochina possessions, the Vietnamese, led by Ho Chi Minh, fought a revolutionary war that finally succeeded in 1954. During that period, the insurgent Vietnamese, known as the Vietminh, received assistance from the Soviet Union and China, and were increasingly perceived by the West as agents of international communism. The insurgency appeared to be ended when the French were defeated at Dienbienphu; by that time, the United States was providing substantial aid to France.

The Geneva Conference in 1954 arranged for the establishment of three states in what had been French Indochina: Laos, Cambodia, and Vietnam. It was further agreed that a "provisional military demarcation line" would separate Vietminh forces in the north from French-supported forces in the south, with political unification to be achieved by a general election within two years. The United States never signed the Geneva Accords, however, and began to treat South Vietnam as an independent, anticommunist state. At the time, it was widely acknowledged that in any free election, the Vietnamese would overwhelmingly have chosen unification under Ho Chi Minh's leadership. The United States proceeded to back Ngo Dinh Diem, a Roman Catholic from a Mandarin family, who proclaimed an independent Republic of Vietnam in the south.

The Conflict.   The Vietminh perceived that the Americans had basically replaced the French as colonial occupiers of (south) Vietnam, seeking to deny them politically what they had won on the battlefield. The United States, in turn, gripped by the Cold War mentality, saw the likely "loss" of Vietnam as part of a worldwide communist conspiracy, orchestrated by Moscow and Peking. Diem refused to permit unified elections, claiming that Ho Chi Minh would not permit a free campaign. The Vietminh in the north, backed by aid from China and the U.S.S.R., began sending insurgent forces into the south; the United States responded by providing growing numbers of military advisers to the increasingly unpopular Diem. At the time of President Kennedy's assassination in 1963, 17,000 Americans were serving in Vietnam.

Antigovernment guerrillas in the south (known as the Vietcong) made continual gains, as did the Vietnamese National Liberation Front, formed in 1960. Diem was subsequently overthrown, mainly by a Buddhist-led and largely nonviolent movement, and then assassinated — an act that was probably inspired by the United States — and ultimately replaced by leaders in whom the United States had greater confidence. The United States hoped that the post-Diem leadership would be more popular with the Vietnamese people, but this did not prove to be the case. U.S. military involvement increased, both in number of troops and in military assistance to the increasingly hard-pressed South Vietnamese military. The United States became further committed to direct participation in the fighting in Vietnam during the Johnson administration (1963–1968), leading to massive bombing of North Vietnam and the introduction of more than 500,000 American troops.

Claims were regularly made that the war was about to be won, that there was "light at the end of the tunnel," if only more military muscle were to be brought into play. But the North Vietnamese kept infiltrating forces into South Vietnam, where the government and the American military failed to win "the hearts and minds of the people." The war became increasingly controversial within the United States as well. Supporters of the war in Vietnam saw the issue as one of stopping communist expansionism and also saving face — that is, maintaining U.S. credibility as an ally. Opponents of the war objected to the brutal and inhumane way it was being fought, especially the widespread use of napalm, and the establishment of "free-fire zones," within which all inhabitants, most of them civilians, were considered "legitimate targets." They also argued that the United States had no business

U.S. Marines fighting to retake part of the city of Hue during the Tet offensive of 1968. (UPI / Nik Wherler)

interfering in Vietnam in the first place, since the conflict was essentially a local, nationalist, and anticolonial dispute, not part of the U.S.-Soviet international tug-of-war. The Vietnam War became the longest and most divisive war in U.S. history, and ultimately, the first one in which the United States was to be defeated. A massive North Vietnamese and Vietcong offensive during the Buddhist Tet holiday in 1968 ended most illusions about the United States' ability — even with advanced technology and massive military force — to impose a military solution on a determined, indigenous people. Although the United States had the wherewithal to stay in Vietnam indefinitely (as Britain stays in Northern Ireland, for example, or the Soviets in the Baltic and Caucasian republics), U.S. public opinion increasingly demanded a termination to this unpopular and unsuccessful war.

But the bombing and killing continued for many years, including mining of the North Vietnamese harbors of Hanoi and Haiphong, which introduced the possibility of conflict with Soviet forces. Finally, a peace agreement, calling for U.S.

withdrawal, was reached in Paris in 1973. Prior to that, President Nixon, who had won election in 1968 with the promise of a "secret plan to end the war," revealed that his plan was "Vietnamization": turning the conduct of the war over to the South Vietnamese, but with large amounts of U.S. aid. By 1975, after U.S. troops had departed, the South Vietnamese government fell to a combination of the northern armies and the Vietcong, and a united communist Vietnam was established. The United States had lost 55,000 men, and had dropped more than 7 million tons of bombs on Indochina, eighty times the amount that had been dropped on Britain during World War II. Vietnamese casualties are difficult to assess, but may have reached 2 million. Vietnam continues to be economically and ecologically devastated as well.

The Soviet Union in Afghanistan

Background.   Afghanistan has long been plagued by wars, invasions, and blood feuds. It has never had a strong central governmental authority, but rather a loose confederation of fiercely independent tribal warlords, traders, and nomads, occupying separate regions of a very arid, mountainous land. Many outside powers have attempted at one time or another to control the country and the independent Moslem Afghans, but none have succeeded for long. The British in particular fought in several Afghan wars during the nineteenth century, achieving no lasting success and suffering some embarrassing defeats. Throughout much of the twentieth century, Afghanistan was a monarchy and was also essentially "Finlandized" (that is, like the Scandinavian country of Finland, it kept mainly to itself and avoided antagonizing its large neighbor, the Soviet Union).

Then, in 1973, the Afghan king was ousted in a military coup. After a series of intrigues and countercoups, a militant communist government eventually took power in 1978, and sought to implement a number of Marxist social and economic reforms: redistribution of land, institution of a secular society, voting and economic rights for women. The conservative, Islamic fundamentalist tribesmen revolted against such radicalism, and began receiving covert assistance from China, Pakistan, Saudi Arabia, and the United States. As the situation became increasingly unstable, the Soviet Union invaded Afghanistan (ostensibly at the request of the Afghan government) in December 1979.

The Conflict.   At the height of Soviet intervention, more than 125,000 troops were committed to Afghanistan, opposed by a wide array of anticommunist resistance fighters known as the *mujahedeen*. The Soviets employed air and armored power, and were able to control most of the cities; the *mujahedeen* controlled much of the countryside through effective guerrilla fighting. Afghan society was seriously disrupted, with more than 2 million refugees fleeing to Iran and 3 million to Pakistan. The United States became the major supporter of the Afghan resistance, providing more than $650 million in covert military aid during 1987 alone.

The American experience in Vietnam and the Soviet experience in Afghanistan differ in significant ways: Unlike the United States, the U.S.S.R. never had to cope with a vigorous antiwar movement, and unlike the case of Vietnam, Afghanistan

shares a thousand-mile border with the Soviet Union. However, the Soviet intervention in the Afghan civil war and the earlier U.S. intervention in Vietnam share striking similarities as well. For instance, in both cases, a superpower — after initially intervening in a civil war — found itself increasingly committed to fighting with a smaller, weaker nation, which could easily be outgunned but could not be defeated. In both cases, the superpower seriously underestimated the courage and tenacity of Third World nationalists, and sought unsuccessfully to acquire local supporters for an unpopular puppet government.* And in both cases, the superpower, as it became more and more frustrated by the guerrilla tactics of the local population, grew more brutal in its conduct.

The Soviet invasion of Afghanistan was widely portrayed in the West (especially in the United States) as indicating Soviet aggressive designs for world conquest; more likely, however (as in the case of the United States in Vietnam), it was a consequence of weakness, fear, and miscalculation rather than aggressiveness and strength. The U.S.S.R. evidently feared the prospect of "losing" Afghanistan to anti-Soviet, rightist forces, just as the United States had feared "losing" Vietnam. And in both cases, the superpower withdrew after being successful on the battlefield, but unsuccessful in achieving its goals, which in the Soviet case was the stabilization of a communist — or at least, not virulently anti-Soviet — regime in Afghanistan. In the process, several hundred thousand Afghans were killed, and over a million injured, along with perhaps 20,000 Soviet dead.

In a treaty signed in Geneva, the U.S.S.R. agreed to withdraw its forces from Afghanistan, and to turn the fighting over to the Afghan army ("Afghanization," we might call it). All Soviet ground forces left Afghanistan in early 1989. Pakistan and Afghanistan also agreed to refrain from

---

*As with Diem in Vietnam, the U.S.S.R. also toppled a particularly unpopular Afghan leader, Babrak Karmal, and replaced him with another, hoping to establish leadership more acceptable to the local people.

interfering in each other's internal affairs, and to facilitate the return of Afghan refugees. The Soviets, however, reserved the right to continue sending military supplies to the communist regime in Kabul, while the United States, in turn, announced that it would provide comparable aid to the *mujahedeen*, largely through Pakistan. As of this writing, most experts anticipate that the communist Afghan government will not survive long without its Soviet protectors. On the other hand, the Afghan resistance is so bitterly divided that fighting among the major groups likely will continue for some time, even if and when the Soviet-backed Kabul government is toppled. Also, the government that eventually emerges in a noncommunist Afghanistan quite possibly will be a fundamentalist Islamic theocracy, not unlike that of Ayatollah Khomeini in Iran, and hence, one that is not particularly appealing to the United States.

SECESSIONIST CIVIL WARS

Secessionist struggles are relatively common forms of civil war that, in many cases, involve long-standing racial and ethnic animosities and — perhaps for this reason — tend to be particularly brutal. In 1967, for example, the Ibo people of Nigeria sought to secede and establish their own state of Biafra. The resulting war between the Ibos and the Hausas of Nigeria lasted for three years, and produced about one million combat-related deaths, as well as severe malnutrition for approximately 500,000 children. Frequently, an outside state will encourage the secessionists, especially if the two groups share some ethnic affinity, and hold out the prospect that the seceding region will eventually become part of the other state. (Somali assistance to anti-Ethiopian rebels in the Ogaden, discussed previously, would be an example.)

Tamils Versus Sri Lanka

The majority of the population of Sri Lanka (formerly Ceylon) are Sinhalese; their religion, Buddhist. Among the minority Tamils (who are Hindu), a group of separatists known as the Tamil Tigers have conducted guerrilla and terrorist warfare in support of their demand for an independent Tamil state. Nearby India, which dwarfs Sri Lanka in population as well as military and economic power, has long been sympathetic to the Tamils, not only because of religious affinity, but also because about 50 million Tamils also live in southern India. In 1987, the Sri Lankan government reached an accord with the Tamil separatists providing for limited autonomy for Tamil regions; Indian armed forces were invited into the country to supervise the agreement and the disarming of Tamil rebels. However, serious fighting broke out between diehard Tamils, who opposed the agreement, and their erstwhile supporters, the Indians.

Sikhs Versus India

India is made up of literally hundreds of ethnic groups, often speaking their own language and practicing different religions. The most disaffected are probably the 15 million Sikhs living mainly in the Punjab, India's most prosperous province. (Sikhism is a monotheistic offshoot of Hinduism.) Sikhs generally are disproportionately represented in Indian agriculture, trade, academia, and the military; Sikh zealots have long sought to secede from India to establish their own state of Khalistan, between India and Pakistan. In 1984, militant Sikh extremists seized the Golden Temple in Amritsar. This building, the most holy place in Sikhdom, was subsequently stormed by the Indian Army, resulting in the deaths of about one thousand people, and outraging many Sikhs throughout India. Subsequently, Indian prime minister Indira Gandhi was murdered by her own Sikh bodyguard, which touched off waves of anti-Sikh rioting in which thousands were killed. Militant Sikhs have responded with terrorist tactics such as bombing airplanes and killing bus passengers, as well as armed clashes with Indian forces.

Eritreans Versus Ethiopia

In northern Ethiopia, the province of Eritrea is largely Moslem, a former Italian colony annexed by Ethiopia in the early 1960s. Forces representing the Eritrean People's Liberation Front, believed to be receiving assistance from some Arab states, seek to secede from the central government. Out of an Eritrean population of approximately one million, about 30,000 are rebels; both the rebels and the central government are Marxists. Severe drought and famine have struck Ethiopia during this rebellion, and both sides have used food as a weapon in their struggle.

Kurdistan

Ethnic Kurds — largely nomads and pastoralists — living primarily in eastern Iraq, western Iran, and eastern Turkey have long sought to secede and establish their own state of Kurdistan. Iran has assisted Kurdish rebels against Iraq, as part of the Iran-Iraq War, while for a time, Turkey had an unusual arrangement permitting its troops to operate in northern Iraq. With the cessation of the Iran-Iraq War, both governments have been able to devote more attention to their Kurdish rebellions; the Iraqis have even resorted to poison gas, killing thousands of civilians in rebel-controlled areas.

Tibet Versus China

Tibet was annexed by Chinese forces in 1952. Although Tibet continued to enjoy some internal autonomy, China took charge of all external affairs. After a Tibetan uprising in 1959, the Dalai Lama, spiritual leader of Tibet's Buddhists, fled to India, and China stepped up its occupation. Many monasteries and other components of indigenous Tibetan culture were destroyed during the excesses of the Chinese Cultural Revolution (1966–1976), although Chinese authorities made some efforts at rebuilding the Tibetan infrastructure beginning in 1979. Violent pro-independence riots occurred in 1987, and then again in 1989; discontent seems likely to continue, although most observers give the Tibetans, who are poor even by Chinese standards, little chance of ever seceding from the Chinese empire.

Some other, occasionally violent secessionist efforts include the following:

Ethnic republics versus the Soviet Union. The Soviet Union is the last of the great empires, having forcibly incorporated various ethnically distinct regions as republics within the Union of Soviet Socialist Republics. Most of these republics retained their ethnic identity, including language and customs, and many desire independence. The Baltic republics (Lithuania, Latvia, and Estonia) have been especially active in seeking secession by peaceful, political means and secessionist sentiment is also high in the Ukraine, Moldavia, and parts of Kazakistan and Uzbekistan. Violence erupted when Soviet authorities used brutal force to suppress pro-independence demonstrators in the republic of Georgia. Most dramatic, however, has been the situation in the trans-Caucasus republics, Armenia and Azerbaijan. Christian Armenians and Moslem Azerbaijanis have feuded for centuries; in early 1990, a virtual civil war began and Soviet armed forces entered the region to quell the fighting. The Azerbaijanis in particular responded with intensified nationalist demands for secession, seeking either to establish an independent state or to merge with neighboring Iran. It is quite possible that the 1990s will see substantial secessionist activity within the Soviet Union; it is less certain whether such activity will be peaceful, and whether the Kremlin leadership will show restraint.

Basques versus Spain. The Basque inhabitants of northern Spain (and to a lesser extent, southern France) along the Pyrenees Mountains speak a distinct language and are ethnically unrelated to the Spanish majority. An ongoing terrorist* campaign, along with a nonterrorist separatist movement, seeks to establish an autonomous Basque state.

---

*It should be noted that this word is used — and often overused — to describe almost any violent activity that is not authorized by a nation-state's government. By contrast, terrorism when conducted by governmental authorities is more likely to be called repression, counterinsurgency, nuclear diplomacy, or even business as usual.

Ethnic Albanians versus Yugoslavia. Yugoslavia is a composite state, established after World War I and made up of many different nationalities, the major ones being Serbs and Croats. Among the minorities, 1.2 million inhabitants of Kosovo Province are ethnically Albanian, and seek, occasionally violently, to secede from Yugoslavia, and perhaps eventually to join with the existing state of Albania. Yugoslavian authorities have, in turn, responded violently against Kosovo. Yugoslavia is a nonaligned communist state that is also experiencing additional ethnic unrest among its constituent republics, notably an upsurge of Serbian nationalism. Albania is a peculiarly isolated, formerly Maoist state. Although both governments are communist, neither is part of the Warsaw Pact.

Moluccans versus Indonesia. Inhabitants of the Molucca islands in Indonesia believe they were promised independence when Holland withdrew from what had been the Dutch East Indies. They now fight an on-again, off-again guerrilla war, which sometimes includes attention-getting destructive acts against Dutch facilities in Europe.

East Timorese versus Indonesia. The western half of the island of Timor has been part of Indonesia since that country achieved independence in 1949; the eastern half, however, had been a Portuguese colony since the sixteenth century. Following Portuguese withdrawal, East Timor has been under military occupation by Indonesia since 1975. It is estimated that more than 200,000 rebellious East Timorese have been massacred by the occupying forces.

WARLIKE SITUATIONS

Northern Ireland

Great Britain is comprised of Scotland, Wales, England, and Northern Ireland. The English and the Irish have been fighting for centuries, essentially since the Norman conquest in 1066. The conflict between English occupiers and the indigenous Irish intensified after Henry VIII sought to impose Protestantism on an overwhelmingly Catholic population. Northern Ireland is about two-thirds Protestant, consisting for the most part of descendants of English and Scottish settlers, who maintain a strong identity as British subjects. By contrast, the Republic of Ireland (or Eire), to the south, is a separate, independent nation-state composed almost entirely of Catholics who harbor resentful memories of English oppression and appropriation of Irish land, especially as part of (largely successful) efforts to populate Northern Ireland with English and Scottish Protestants.

In 1920, after years of rebellion on the part of the Irish and brutal repression on the part of English authorities, the English government established Ireland and Northern Ireland as separate entities within Great Britain. After the Republic of Ireland became totally independent, in 1949, the conflict continued over Northern Ireland. The Catholic minority claims that it is economically, socially, and politically discriminated against by the Protestant majority; many Catholics accordingly seek a union of Northern Ireland with the south. The Protestant majority, not surprisingly, opposes this and wishes to remain part of Britain, or to be independent. Guerrilla fighters, associated with the revolutionary Irish Republican Army — a successor to the group that had been active in battling the English before the time of Irish independence — continues to launch terrorist attacks against English armed forces and Protestant civilians in Northern Ireland, which in turn leads to counterterrorism directed at Catholics.

South Africa

The predominant white group in the Republic of South Africa is the Boers, descendants of Dutch immigrants, some of whom arrived in South Africa during the seventeenth century. The late eighteenth century saw the arrival of British settlers and military forces, and during the nineteenth century, the British fought numerous Zulu wars, after which they turned their attention to the Boers. During the Boer War (1899–1902), a British army of 290,000 eventually defeated a guerrilla force of 35,000 Boers, in the process causing the deaths of more than 26,000 Boer women and children who had been herded into history's first organized concentration camps.

The Republic of South Africa, now independent of Britain, consists of more than 3 million Boers, more commonly known as Afrikaaners (who speak primarily a Dutch dialect known as Afrikaans), about 2.5 million people of British descent, 1 million Indians and Asians, and perhaps 20 million black Africans, most of them Bantu-speaking, with Zulus and Xhosas the major groups. The government practices a particularly repressive form of segregation known as *apartheid* that denies the black majority political representation and economic and social rights. The avowedly racist South African government is increasingly isolated in world affairs, and opposed by nearly all of black Africa, especially the so-called frontline states that directly border that country: Mozambique, Zimbabwe, Zambia, Botswana, Lesotho, and Swaziland. However, although the Republic of South Africa is widely detested and greatly outnumbered, it remains the major economic and military power in the region.

The main opposition group, the African National Congress, has been banned,* but continues antiapartheid activities, both violent and nonviolent, operating within South Africa and nearby. The South African government has traditionally shown little interest in political compromise; most often, it responds with domestic repression and occasional military forays into the adjoining frontline states. The government has also carried out forced resettlement efforts directed toward the black majority, seeking to relocate much of the population into so-called homelands of little economic value. It is also widely believed that South Africa has developed a small arsenal of nuclear weapons, probably in collaboration with Israel.

Lebanon

Despite an enormously diverse populace squeezed into a very small country, as well as a proximity to areas of geopolitical tumult, Lebanon was remarkably peaceful through the first half of the twentieth century. It was something of a Middle Eastern Switzerland,† populated by Maronite Christians (Roman Catholics), Greek Orthodox Christians, Sunni Moslems, and Shiites, along with a sizable population of Armenians and other groups including the Druze (an offshoot of Islam). There are also Syrians, Kurds, and other minorities. Historically, French and Syrian influence has been strong. U.S. marines entered the country in 1957, in response to threats from Syria and Egypt, but generally, Lebanon was tolerant and wealthy, a major banking center.

In the early 1970s, fighters and refugees from the PLO entered Lebanon, after having been defeated by the Bedouin forces of Jordan's king Hussein during the so-called Black September War. Essentially, chaos has reigned ever since, as various factions have fought among themselves, maintaining private armies in the nature of medieval warlords. The federal government has very little power and authority, especially after an Israeli invasion in 1982, which had an effect similar to the U.S. invasion of Cambodia during the Vietnam War: The country was destabilized and fractionated. Shiite Moslems are the largest single group, and are influenced to varying degrees by Iran. Since the late 1970s, Syria has stationed about 30,000 troops in the Bekaa Valley in east-central Lebanon, at least partly to keep the peace among feuding factions. By the late 1980s, Israel still had not entirely withdrawn; it continues to maintain a buffer zone in

---

*This ban was lifted in 1990 and the most prominent ANC leader — Nelson Mandela — was released after twenty-seven years in jail. Accordingly, hopes have arisen for an easing of apartheid, although there is doubt whether the greatly outnumbered South African whites will ever permit a true democracy based on "one man, one vote."

---

†That is, a prosperous multi-ethnic state that was an island of tranquility amid violently contending neighbors.

southern Lebanon. Christian Lebanese and Syrian-backed Islamic units have also engaged in highly destructive fighting and artillery bombardments within Beirut itself, and among themselves.

A FINAL NOTE ON CONVENTIONAL TROUBLE SPOTS

Few useful broad conclusions can be derived from such a heterogeneous mass of unrest and bloodshed. Indeed, our goal in this chapter has been to examine and describe the trees rather than to generalize about the forest. Two points stand out, however. First, the world has more than its share of man-made — and to a much lesser extent, woman-made — misery. And second, even without considering the immense problem of nuclear weapons, Peace Studies has its work cut out just in confronting war, let alone tackling the additional task of building peace. Nonetheless, it is also worth emphasizing that along with all the anger, violence, and misery in the world, an undercurrent of hope exists: Some people have been able to achieve independence and a degree of freedom; warring factions have shown themselves capable of reconciling their differences. Just as long-standing historical antagonisms such as those between Britain and France or Japan and Korea have been largely resolved, the possibility exists that most — and someday, perhaps, all — of the tensions around the world will be defused, so that this chapter can be read as history rather than as current events.

Study Questions

1. What are some general differences between interstate and civil wars?

2. Describe the current status of some of the major recent interventionist wars.

3. The Soviet Union has historically allied itself with various "wars of national liberation." More recently, the United States has also begun actively supporting insurgent movements, notably counterrevolutionary ones. Discuss the current status of this shift of roles.

4. To what extent are secessionist wars independent of the East–West conflict?

5. Are there any common characteristics shared by those conventional trouble spots that have recently been settled? By those that have not?

6. To what extent is racial/cultural intolerance involved in contemporary wars and warlike situations?

7. To what extent is your appreciation of the subtleties involved in the following conflicts enhanced by considering their history: Israel and her Arab neighbors, Vietnam and the United States, India and Pakistan?

8. Describe at least one important conventional trouble spot not considered in this chapter.

9. Select one of these trouble spots, and make a cogent argument as though you were a spokesperson for one of the contending sides. Now do the same for the other side. Can you also propose an equitable settlement, likely to be acceptable to both?

10. Describe how at least one trouble spot described in this chapter is now essentially quiet, and suggest whether or not a comparable settlement appears to be feasible for at least one that is currently unsettled.

Suggestions for Further Reading

Richard Alan White. 1984. *The Morass: United States' Intervention in Central America.* Harper & Row: New York.

Dilip Hiro. 1985. *Iran Under the Ayatollahs.* Routledge & Kegan Paul: London.

James F. Dunnigan. 1985. *A Quick and Dirty Guide to War.* William Morrow: New York.

Amin Hewedy. 1989. *Militarization and Security in the Middle East.* St. Martin's Press: New York.

John D. Brewer (ed.). 1989. *Can South Africa Survive?* St. Martin's Press: New York.

5

War Movements: Nuclear Weapons

Grown-ups can't be trusted with guns and bombs.
Cynthia G. (age 8)

Albert Einstein once noted that as a child, he had been taught that modern times began with the fall of the Roman Empire. But everything changed with the atomic bombing of Hiroshima and Nagasaki: Now, Einstein observed, we would have to say that modern times began in 1945, a watershed in human history. There is indeed something unique about nuclear weapons. They represent a dramatic discontinuity in human history, and they offer the possibility of an even more dramatic break: a canceling of the past, an end to the present, and a negating of the future. As destructive as conventional warfare has been — and continues to be — it pales next to the sheer terror and horrific consequences of nuclear war. In this chapter, we conclude our survey of the basic dimensions of war and peace by reviewing some issues that are unique to the phenomenon of nuclear war.

At least four factors must be understood if one is to grasp the nature of nuclear war and the urgency as well as the prospects of preventing it: (1) the weapons (bombs and warheads) themselves and their effects, (2) the so-called delivery systems (the means by which nuclear weapons are to be fired at their targets), (3) so-called strategic doctrine, which is concerned with the plans and strategies for the use of nuclear weapons, and (4) the problem of nuclear proliferation. Our goal in this chapter is to consider these four factors; in subsequent chapters, we shall seek to integrate some remaining nuclear issues into our consideration of peace–war questions more generally.

THE NATURE OF NUCLEAR WEAPONS

Nuclear weapons derive their explosive power from the conversion of matter into energy. This takes place according to the well-known equation $E = mc^2$, in which E = the amount of energy released, m = the mass to be converted into energy, and c = the speed of light. Since the speed of light is itself a very large number, and is squared in the equation, the resulting energy release is truly enormous. Nuclear energy drives the sun and the stars; prior to 1945, however, its explosive power had never before been brought to Earth. Hence, it is something entirely new to the human experience.

The power of nuclear weapons exceeds that of conventional explosives by approximately a factor of one million. Consider, for a moment, the result of multiplying anything by a million: If you have a few dollars in your pocket, and increase that tenfold, or even a hundredfold, the difference may be appreciated, but it is unlikely to be long-lasting. Multiply by a million, on the other hand, and your life will probably be changed forever. Similarly, you may normally walk at about two miles per hour; multiply by ten or a hundred, and you are at automobile or even airplane speed. But multiply by a million, and you are heading for outer space. Herein rests the underlying significance of nuclear weapons and nuclear war: something radically new and unfathomably destructive, something qualitatively different from previous human experience.

Atomic bombs result from nuclear fission, the splitting of large, unstable atoms, most commonly uranium-235 (a radioactive isotope of the element uranium) or plutonium-239 (another radioactive element, one that is essentially man-made). When enough fissionable material is gathered together in one place, and exposed to a barrage of neutrons, some of the unstable nuclei are split, releasing en-

ergy as well as additional neutrons. These neutrons, in turn, split the nuclei of other atoms, releasing yet more energy and yet more neutrons, which continue to split additional nuclei in a chain reaction that accelerates geometrically, and thus at extraordinary speed. We say that the material has reached "critical mass" when each nucleus, after being split (or "fissioned"), releases enough neutrons to split approximately two nearby nuclei. From one fissioned nucleus, we get 2, then 4, then 8, 16, 32, 64, and so on, with the number doubling with every "generation" of nuclei that split. As a result, an immense amount of energy can be released in a very short time: In 0.00000058 seconds, 2^{57} nuclei (approximately 2 followed by 24 zeros) will have been split, releasing the energy equivalent to 100,000 tons of TNT.

Atomic, or fission, explosions are typically measured in kilotons—that is, the equivalent energy that would be released by the detonation of thousands of tons of TNT. Thus, a 12-kiloton atomic explosion—the size that destroyed the Japanese city of Hiroshima—releases the same amount of energy as the detonation of 12,000 tons of TNT.

The first nuclear weapons were based on fission. Most nuclear weapons today, however, are fusion, or thermonuclear, devices. They derive much of their energy from the squeezing together of very small atoms, notably deuterium and tritium, two isotopes of hydrogen. In the process, the element helium is produced, and once again, through the conversion of mass into energy, vast amounts of energy are released. When plutonium, for example, is split, the total mass of the medium-sized fission products that are formed—such as iron, cobalt, and manganese—is slightly less than that of the parent nucleus with which we started. Similarly, the total mass of the helium nuclei produced by fusion is slightly less than the mass of the hydrogen isotopes with which a fusion reaction begins. This mass has not really been "lost." Rather, it has been converted into energy.

Fusion is more efficient than fission in that more energy per starting mass is released. But fusion is also more difficult to initiate than fission, since great heat and pressure are required literally to squeeze the hydrogen nuclei together. Therefore, fusion explosions — or "hydrogen bombs," as they are often called — start with a relatively small "atomic" explosion, which serves as a trigger to initiate the much more powerful fusion reaction. This requirement of great heat and pressure is why fusion reactions are also known as *thermo*nuclear explosions. Fusion explosions also are typically boosted with an additional fission component, as the energy released by the fusion is captured by a lower-grade form of uranium, usually U-238, which is induced to split as well. So, the typical thermonuclear (H-bomb or hydrogen bomb) explosion is fission–fusion–fission, all occurring in a minuscule fraction of a second. The energy released in such detonations can often extend into the range of megatons, equivalent to millions of tons of TNT.

Although nuclear explosives are often referred to as "bombs," they are in fact more likely to be carried by a missile, in which case they are known as "warheads." In addition, nuclear weapons are often designated as either "tactical" or "strategic." The former refers to weapons intended for use on a battlefield, the latter for use against an adversary's homeland. In some cases, however, these distinctions are not so clear-cut. For example, NATO's intermediate-range nuclear missiles were considered tactical by the United States, since they were intended for use in the European "theater," whereas the Soviet Union considered them to be strategic, since they could reach the U.S.S.R.

THE EFFECTS OF NUCLEAR EXPLOSIONS

Immediate Consequences

Given that nuclear weapons have been exploded only twice in wartime (at Hiroshima and Nagasaki), it may seem strange that they should command so much attention. The reason is simple, and related entirely to their effects: Nuclear explosions are extraordinarily powerful and devastating. Nothing even remotely like them has ever been experienced on this planet. Consider this account of the first atomic bomb test, at Alamogordo, New Mexico, in July 1945:

> No man-made phenomenon of such tremendous power had ever occurred before. The lighting ef-

fects beggared description. The whole country was lighted by a searing light with the intensity many times that of the midday sun. It was golden, purple, violet, gray and blue. It lighted every peak, crevasse and mountain range with a clarity and beauty that cannot be described but must be seen to be imagined. It was the beauty the great poets dream about but describe most poorly and inadequately. Thirty seconds after the explosion came, first the air blast pressing hard and against people and things, to be followed almost immediately by the strong, sustained, awesome roar which warned of doomsday and made us feel that we puny things were blasphemous to dare tamper with the forces heretofore reserved to the Almighty. Words are inadequate tools for the job of acquainting those not present with the physical, mental and psychological effects. It had to be witnessed to be realized.[1]

For insight into the effects of a nuclear explosion on the world as we live in it, however, we must consider eyewitness accounts of the actual use of atomic weapons, such as this one describing the impact on Nagasaki:

> For some 1,000 yards, or three-fifths of a mile, in all directions from the epicenter . . . it was as if a malevolent god had suddenly focused a gigantic blowtorch on a small section of our planet. Within that perimeter, nearly all unprotected living organisms — birds, insects, horses, cats, chickens — perished instantly. Flowers, trees, grass, plants, all shriveled and died. Wood burst into flames. Metal beams and galvanized iron roofs began to bubble, and the soft gooey masses twisted into grotesque shapes. Stones were pulverized, and for a second every last bit of air was burned away. The people exposed within that doomed section neither knew nor felt anything, and their blackened, unrecognizable forms dropped silently where they stood.[2]

As Soviet premier Nikita Krushchev once said, following a nuclear war, the survivors would envy the dead.

Nagasaki and Hiroshima were both hit with atomic bombs, carrying the explosive power of about 20 and 12 kilotons, respectively. It must be emphasized that these are very small compared to the bombs and warheads now available: Hydrogen bombs have been produced in the multimegaton range. Since one megaton is equivalent in energy to

Remains of the city of Hiroshima, two days after the atomic bombing of that city. (United Nations)

one million tons of TNT, it follows that a 9-megaton bomb (the largest currently stockpiled in the U.S. arsenal) is slightly less than one thousand times more powerful than the one that destroyed Hiroshima. Most bombs and warheads in the strategic arsenal of the United States and the U.S.S.R. are about 100 to 500 kilotons, or approximately eight to forty times more powerful than the Hiroshima bomb. The total U.S. strategic arsenal is about 3,200 megatons; by comparison, the entire explosive force detonated by both sides during World War II was approximately 3 megatons.

Let us now proceed with a (mercifully) brief discussion of the immediate effects of nuclear explosions. At the instant of detonation, approximately 35 percent of the energy released in a typical thermonuclear detonation is emitted as heat, 50 percent as blast, and 15 percent as radiation.

Heat.   Unlike a conventional explosion, the heat from a nuclear explosion lasts for a relatively long time. An explosion of one megaton, for example, will have released only about 60 percent of its heat after a duration of three seconds. Hence, it gives rise to a persistent blast of heat that continues for a remarkably long time—up to ten seconds for a

multimegaton explosion. Some of the most nightmarish injuries suffered by the residents of Hiroshima and Nagasaki were severe burns. People close to the epicenter were literally vaporized; those at a greater distance were charred; those further yet were often seriously burned, especially if they were out in the open.

In addition to injuries resulting from direct exposure to heat rays, a large proportion of the burns at Hiroshima and Nagasaki resulted from the combustion effects of the explosions; that is, they derived secondarily from the radiant heat released by the explosion, as a result of the immense fires ignited by that heat. At Hiroshima, a firestorm was created; this occurs when the strong updrafts of a large, intense blaze cause air to rush in horizontally, causing it to roar like a blast furnace and reach great temperatures. (Firestorms were also created by the conventional incendiary bombings of Dresden, Hamburg, and Tokyo.)

Severe burns are among the most painful injuries that people can sustain; moreover, the care and treatment of such injuries requires enormous investment in money, technology, and highly trained personnel . . . precisely what will *not* be available in the aftermath of even a very "small" nuclear war. There are only about one thousand highly specialized "burn beds" in the United States, all of them located at major metropolitan hospitals, and therefore likely to be obliterated by a nuclear war.

Blast.   The energy released as blast occurs in two forms. Dynamic overpressure is felt as strong winds, of greater than hurricane force. More remarkable, however, and unique to nuclear explosions, is static overpressure, which results from the rapidly expanding fireball and the compression it produces. Static overpressure is a force that presses on all surrounding structures like a great hand, maintaining its pressure for several seconds. As with radiation and heat, the exact effects depend on the size of the explosion as well as the distance from the epicenter. Static overpressure is measured in pounds per square inch (psi). Two psi will cause severe damage to most houses; 5 psi will collapse all but concrete, steel-reinforced, and some brick structures. An area subjected to 5 psi or greater is generally viewed as the lethal area of a nuclear explosion, the area within which everyone can be assumed to be killed. Thus, for a one-megaton airburst, the 5-psi radius would extend about five miles from the epicenter, covering an area of approximately eighty square miles. (Actually, some people within the 5-psi region would probably survive, at least initially, but some people outside that region would die, with the two being roughly equal.) Most deaths due to blast would result not so much from the blast itself as from the collapsing buildings and flying chunks of wood, glass, concrete, and metal, all traveling at lethal speeds. The blast effects of a single large thermonuclear bomb, for example, detonated over any major city would be sufficient to collapse virtually all of the buildings within a radius of several miles. It would be, in a sense, as though hundreds of thousands of people experienced a gigantic head-on automobile accident, at upwards of 60 mph, simultaneously . . . only much worse.

Radiation.   Of the energy released as radiation from a nuclear explosion, about two-thirds (10 percent of the total) appears as radioactive fallout (to be discussed in the section on medium-range effects), with the rest emitted instantaneously, at the speed of light. The major forms of this "prompt" radiation are X-rays, gamma rays, and neutrons. Radiation is measured in many ways; the most useful for our purposes is the rem, a measure of the amount of biological damage caused. Most Americans generally receive about .13 rem per year as a result of background radiation plus medical exposures (a chest X-ray contributes about .05 rem). In large quantities prompt radiation can be fatal: It is generally estimated that exposure to 450 rem will kill approximately one half of all healthy adults.

Intense radiation exposure (5,000–10,000 rem) results in death in a matter of minutes as a result of the swelling of the brain and central nervous system. Doses of 1,000 to 5,000 rem are also invariably fatal, usually because of the destruction of the cells lining the digestive system, although death may take several days. In the 200 to 1,000

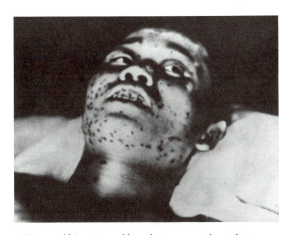

A 21-year-old Japanese soldier who was exposed to radiation approximately 3,000 feet from the Hiroshima explosion. He initially appeared uninjured; the subcutaneous hemorrhaging developed more than three weeks later. The young man died two hours after this photo was taken, on September 3, 1945. (United Nations)

rem range, death occurs from the so-called hematopoietic syndrome, which causes the destruction of the bone marrow. Victims die of a condition not unlike AIDS, since their immune system is destroyed or severely compromised, and they typically succumb to various diseases, especially pneumonia. Treatment not only entails bone marrow transplants but also requires a carefully controlled, germ-free environment. Even then, it may be impossible to determine whether a victim has received a small dose (and is therefore likely to recover) or a lethal dose, for which no treatment will be effective. In the aftermath of nuclear war, this inability to discriminate between those who can and who cannot be saved may prove important, since it will be very difficult to practice "triage," in which victims are divided into three groups: those who will recover regardless of treatment, those who will die regardless of treatment, and those who might profit from treatment.

Prompt radiation is a significant factor in cases of nuclear reactor accidents (such as the 1986 disaster at the Soviet nuclear power plant at Chernobyl) or "small" nuclear explosions, such as occurred at Hiroshima and Nagasaki. In dealing with larger detonations, however, prompt radiation is less important than heat or blast, since the lethal radius for the former is less than for the latter. In other words, with explosions larger than about 20 kilotons, people who would otherwise die from the initial radiation will be killed first by the heat and/or blast effects. And even in a nuclear war, people can only die once.

Combined Immediate Effects.   Most estimates of nuclear war fatalities are lower than they should be, because the relevant effects are generally considered separately. In reality, all would occur simultaneously. People would be trapped in collapsing buildings (blast), which would probably then burn (heat), while the survivors would also have to contend with radiation. Infections are a serious complication of burns, and radiation reduces the body's ability to ward off infection. Not only would many victims be burned and irradiated, but they would also suffer from crushing and/or piercing injuries. In addition, most hospitals and most medical personnel are located in major cities, which would almost certainly be targeted and destroyed, and pharmaceuticals would be almost entirely unavailable. Finally, firefighting would be virtually impossible, because streets would be blocked with the debris of collapsed buildings, water pressure would be nonexistent because of the rupture of pipes, and potential firefighters would likely be dead or contending with their own personal tragedies.

Of the approximately 200,000 fatalities resulting from the bombing of Hiroshima, about 50 percent were due to burns, while about 30 percent were due to lethal doses of radiation. Another 75,000 people perished in Nagasaki. Although technical knowledge of this sort is important, such sanitized data are grossly inadequate for conveying the full horror of nuclear war — even the very small nuclear war that took place in August 1945. Another kind of knowledge, more personal and visceral, is probably more meaningful.

There are harrowing accounts of people with empty eyesockets whose eyeballs were literally melted, infants attempting to nurse at the corpses of dead mothers, burn victims with their skin hanging in loose strips, family members trying to rescue relatives who had been trapped under collapsed and burning buildings. One survivor gives this testimony:

> The sight of the soldiers was more dreadful than the dead people floating down the river. I came upon I don't know how many, burned from the hips up; and where the skin had peeled, their flesh was wet and mushy. . . . And they had no faces! Their eyes, noses, and mouths had been burned away, and it looked like their ears had melted off. It was hard to tell front from back.[3]

Even for those not physically injured, the psychological effects of such an immense and sudden disaster were overwhelming. A Hiroshima physician describes some survivors leaving the city:

> Those who were able walked silently toward the suburbs in the distant hills, their spirits broken, their initiative gone. . . . They were so broken and confused that they moved and behaved like automatons . . . a people who walked in the realm of dreams. . . . A spiritless people had forsaken a destroyed city.[4]

To this we can only reiterate that the Hiroshima and Nagasaki bombs were very small by today's standards; moreover, there was an "outside," from which aid eventually reached the miserable survivors. In the event of a full-fledged nuclear war today, the experience would be many times worse, with no outside and virtually no prospects of recovery.

Midrange Consequences

Fallout.   The best-known midrange effect of nuclear war would be fallout. We mentioned that of the 15 percent of a nuclear explosion's energy that is released in the form of radiation, one third — or 5 percent of the total release — appears as immediate radiation. The remaining 10 percent occurs as radioactive fallout.

Fallout looks like a fine grayish dust. It is made up of pulverized dirt and other materials, which are rendered radioactive by the nuclear explosion, sucked up into the mushroom cloud, and deposited at various distances from the epicenter. The intensity of fallout depends on many factors, among

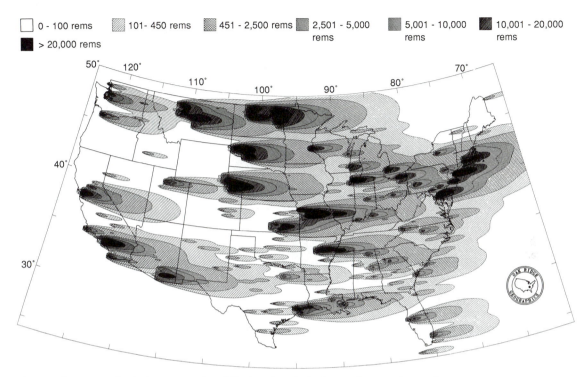

| | 0 - 100 rems | | 101- 450 rems | | 451 - 2,500 rems | | 2,501 - 5,000 rems | | 5,001 - 10,000 rems | | 10,001 - 20,000 rems |
| | > 20,000 rems |

Fourteen-day integrated radiation exposure doses following a hypothesized counterforce attack, assuming a west wind at 20 mph. (Oak Ridge National Laboratory)

them whether the explosion is an air-burst or a ground-burst — that is, whether it detonates over a target (perhaps as high as several thousand feet) or directly on the target at ground level. Air-bursts are preferred for destroying relatively large, unprotected targets such as entire cities, because the blast and heat effects would be more widely distributed instead of being absorbed by the mass of the target itself. On the other hand, strategic planners look to ground-bursts for destroying heavily armoured or reinforced structures, such as underground missile silos or command and control bunkers. Ground-bursts produce significantly more fallout than do air-bursts.

The actual distribution of fallout is determined not only by the kind of explosion but also by wind patterns. Fallout tends to be deposited in a cigar-shaped plume extending downwind from the epicenter; the stronger the winds, the longer and thinner the fallout pattern. And the closer to the

epicenter, the higher the radiation level. Fallout would make itself felt perhaps within hours of a detonation, certainly within days. Since most land-based missile sites within the United States are located near agricultural land, crop-growing regions would likely be severely affected. Fallout would produce substantial increases in cancer rates (especially leukemias) and in the proportion of birth defects and induced abortions. If long-running nuclear reactors were vaporized in a nuclear attack, additional vast amounts of long-lived radioactivity would be released; for example, one year after the event, a destroyed one-gigawatt nuclear reactor would have released about one hundred times more radioactivity than a one-megaton bomb.

Social, Economic, and Political Organization.   In addition to the fallout, a major midrange effect of nuclear war would be its impact on social, economic, and political organization. Food storage regions would likely be destroyed or rendered inaccessible; cities would be devastated, with rescue, fire-fighting, and medical services largely unavailable; transportation might well cease altogether. Electricity-generating plants would almost certainly be destroyed, along with oil refineries. Most sources of power—for communication, transportation, manufacturing, agriculture—would be eliminated, perhaps permanently. A simple barter system would probably replace traditional money-based economies. As economist John Kenneth Galbraith has emphasized, communism and capitalism might well be indistinguishable in the ashes. Diseases such as cholera would spread rapidly, with sanitation and public hygiene virtually eliminated, and billions of insects and trillions of bacteria would multiply in the rotting, unburied corpses.

Shortly before he was assassinated in 1979, Lord Mountbatten gave a speech in which he asked:

> And when it is all over, what will the world be like? Our fine great buildings, our homes will exist no more. The thousands of years it took to develop our civilization will have been in vain. Our works of art will be lost. Radio, television, newspapers will disappear. There will be no means of transport. There will be no hospitals. No help can be expected for the few mutilated survivors in any town to be sent from a neighboring town—there will be no neighboring towns left, no neighbors, there will be no help, there will be no hope.[5]

By contrast, there have always been those who calculate that nuclear war might be survivable, at least for some people and with appropriate precautions, such as (in the early 1960s) blast and/or fallout shelters and (in the 1980s) crisis relocation plans, which were intended to organize the evacuation of the citizenry from high-risk areas to other regions, thought to be untargeted. Such thinking is especially prominent among some nuclear strategists who fret that "excessive" concern for the effects of nuclear war might erode U.S. willingness to stand up to the Soviet Union. They worry also about the possibility that antinuclear anxiety will diminish the credibility of the stated U.S. intention to resort to nuclear weapons under certain circumstances, such as an invasion of western Europe. In addition, right-wing politicians have worried that

nuclear fears—especially of the sort that motivate people in Peace Studies, and that, in turn, are promoted by their work—will undermine a national commitment to evermore weaponry, as well as undercutting a "better dead than red" mentality.

By the late 1980s, however, such thinking had become increasingly difficult to defend, largely as a result of the widespread publicity concerning the horrific prompt and intermediate effects of nuclear war, as well as revelations concerning long-term effects. The peace movement, both in the United States and worldwide, can take substantial credit for awakening government leaders to the unacceptable consequences of nuclear war, as epitomized in the belated observation by President Reagan that a "nuclear war can never be won and must never be fought."

Long-Term Consequences

Ozone Depletion. Ozone is a chemical form of oxygen (O_3) that exists in the upper atmosphere. It absorbs much of the sun's ultraviolet light, which would otherwise strike the Earth and cause great damage to biological systems. Nuclear explosions produce large amounts of nitrogen oxides, which would react chemically with the ozone, depleting it by perhaps 50 percent within about six months. (Again, the exact amount would depend on the size and number of detonations, whether they were air- or ground-bursts, and so on.) Substantial ozone depletion would lead to a significant increase in skin cancer and blindness, the latter being especially severe among animals, who could not readily be persuaded to wear sunglasses. Pollinating insects, such as bees, which use vision to locate flowers, might well be unable to function; the result would be severe and widespread ecological disruption, and possible collapse. In addition, photosynthesizing plants could be severely affected, notably the oceanic phytoplankton that are responsible for the bulk of the planet's oxygen production. Ozone levels would rebuild naturally, but only after an interval of several years.

Nuclear Winter. Undoubtedly, the most serious long-term consequence of nuclear war is the phenomenon of nuclear winter. This refers to the cooling and darkening of the planetary environment that many experts believe will result from a widespread nuclear war. The basic concept of nuclear winter is as follows: A nuclear war would produce not only immense amounts of dust but — far more important — enormous fires, which in turn would generate huge quantities of smoke and soot. Rising into the upper atmosphere, this material would absorb incoming heat and light from the sun, thereby making the Earth cold and dark.

Some estimates show that nuclear winter could be triggered by the detonation of as "little" as 100 megatons, a tiny fraction of the world's arsenals. The effects would be worldwide and catastrophic: Temperatures could plummet as much as 50 degrees F, which would result in extreme freezing over widespread areas and total disruption of agriculture and natural ecosystems, as well as perhaps making fresh water unavailable for people, plants, and/or animals for prolonged periods of time. Certainly, such an event would greatly complicate the problems of survival in what is sometimes, in a sanitized way, referred to as the "postattack environment."

Another striking finding of the nuclear winter researchers is that there appears to be a threshold phenomenon. Thus, although the amount of cooling and darkening likely to result from nuclear war will almost certainly increase as the megatonnage increases, the detonation of as little as 100 megatons would precipitate nuclear winter.

The nuclear winter scenario has generated some controversy, as specialists have questioned some of its assumptions, such as how much smoke would actually be produced, how it would be distributed globally, and how intense and how persistent the climatic darkening and freezing would therefore be. There is also debate over the possible modulating effect of the oceans and the effect of increased cloud cover, as well as questions as to what proportion of the targeted cities would actually burn. Thus far, however, most of the assumptions of nuclear winter scientists have proven to be quite robust, although we must concede that the prospect of nuclear winter is still theoretical. We probably will never know if it is entirely valid . . . until it is too late.

ANXIETY AND NUCLEAR POLICY

Numerous studies have been conducted on the likely effects of nuclear war. The findings vary, depending on the assumptions made. However, even a small-scale nuclear war undeniably would be a human and environmental catastrophe unknown in human history, and a full-scale nuclear war between the superpowers would dwarf anything that has occurred on Earth in many millions of years. Tens of millions of people would die immediately, perhaps more than a hundred million on each side. The worldwide effects, even making minimal assumptions regarding nuclear winter, would also be catastrophic. Calculations show that the disruption of agricultural, trade, medical, and hygienic facilities would result in the deaths of hundreds of millions more, and in the debilitation of most of the remaining survivors. Most specialists agree, however, that the species *Homo sapiens* probably would persevere, especially in parts of the Southern Hemisphere, and perhaps in small, desperate bands in isolated areas elsewhere.

For many of us, such assurances give scant comfort. The grotesque and utterly unacceptable consequences of nuclear war are a major motivating force for people concerned with the maintenance of peace and the prevention of war, especially nuclear war. Nuclear hawks accuse peace movement adherents of exaggerating the likely horrors of nuclear war in order to increase popular revulsion against these weapons and to make governments especially cautious about ever employing them. Peace movement activists reply that if so, this tendency to dramatize has been a justifiable response to the dangerously cavalier attitude of government officials — especially during the Reagan administration — toward the prospect of nuclear war.

It might be useful to contrast the likely results of being wrong, in either direction. Thus, what if the effects of nuclear war have been overestimated? In this case, the United States might find itself unduly wary of asserting military power — with the possible consequences of "losing" some geopolitical confrontations. In the words of Richard Perle, an influential hawk and assistant secretary of defense in the Reagan administration, "I've always

Biography

Helen M. Caldicott

Helen M. Caldicott is an Australian-born physician who has been one of the world's most effective antinuclear activists. She credits Nevil Shute's novel *On the Beach* with awakening her to the dangers of nuclear war. In 1971, she led a one-woman campaign to halt French nuclear testing in the Pacific Ocean. She also labored to educate Australian uranium miners about the medical and military dangers of their work. She moved to the United States in 1977 and wrote *Nuclear Madness: What You Can Do!*, which was published only a few weeks before the near meltdown at the Three Mile Island nuclear power plant. A year later, she began to revitalize Physicians for Social Responsibility (PSR), an organization that was previously instrumental in campaigning against above-ground nuclear testing and that grew rapidly in membership and impact.

Under Dr. Caldicott's leadership, PSR became one of the leading antinuclear organizations in the United States; during the 1980s it was especially successful in raising consciousness about the medical consequences of nuclear war. Dr. Caldicott is a passionate and inspiring speaker, whose primary message is that the world is in peril and that each of us must take personal responsibility for ending the nuclear menace. She has been nominated for a Nobel Peace Prize, and starred in the Academy Award winning documentary "If You Love This Planet." Helen Caldicott founded Women's Action for Nuclear Disarmament (WAND) in 1980 and wrote the influential book *Missile Envy* in 1984. Helen Caldicott moved back to Australia in 1986 but plans to spend extensive time in the United States, continuing her efforts on behalf of nuclear disarmament and environmental preservation.

---

worried less about what would happen in an actual nuclear exchange than about the effect that the nuclear balance has on our willingness to take risks in local situations."[6] Alternatively, what if those who minimize the effects of nuclear war are wrong? Virtually everyone pays lip service to the fact that nuclear war would be terrible. The fact remains, however, that the intensity with which people will seek to avoid nuclear war, and hence, the willingness of policymakers to forgo possible short-term gains in order to prevent a potential nuclear holocaust, will vary with their judgment of just how terrible nuclear war would be. Those who consider that it would be an overwhelming and utterly unacceptable disaster are less likely to persevere in policies or confrontations that might conceivably result in such a disaster. Those who, by contrast, take a more sanguine and perhaps minimizing attitude will be more liable to practice "brinksmanship." If the nuclear hawks are wrong, then the consequence of being too willing to risk nuclear war might be catastrophic for the nation, and for the planet as well.

At present, and despite a growing consensus that nuclear war is an unacceptable option, some aspects of nuclear strategy depend on the willingness of governments to employ nuclear weapons, or at least, on the belief by an adversary that such willingness exists. Hence, we encounter such statements as the observation by Henry Kissinger that nuclear diplomacy "requires strong nerves," and that accordingly, the United States should "leave no doubt about our readiness and our ability to face a final showdown."[7]

During the early years of the Reagan administration in particular, official pronouncements appeared to minimize the likely consequences of nuclear war. For example, in 1982, Deputy Undersecretary of Defense T. K. Jones claimed that "Everybody's going to make it if there are enough shovels to go around. . . . Dig a hole, cover it with a couple of doors and then throw three feet of dirt on top. It's the dirt that does it."[8] Other pronouncements of this sort, combined with a massive and unprecedented military build-up of both conventional and nuclear weapons, stimulated renewed interest in — and anxiety about — the effects of nuclear war.

By the late 1980s, antinuclear peace movement activities apparently had succeeded at least in making it unacceptable for politicians and strategic planners to speak lightly of precipitating a nuclear holocaust. Toward the latter years of the Reagan administration, official pronouncements on this topic became much more circumspect, which is testimony to the impact of a populace and a peace movement that had become increasingly antinuclear, largely because of that administration's own policies. Nonetheless, whether there have actually been any changes in U.S. nuclear procurement policies, or in the actual operational plans for using nuclear weapons, is debatable.

NUCLEAR DELIVERY SYSTEMS

The technology — and the peace–war implications — of delivering nuclear weapons to their targets is almost as important as that of the weapons themselves. The strategic nuclear forces of both the United States and the Soviet Union are based on a triad of three distinct components: long-range bombers, land-based intercontinental missiles, and missile-carrying submarines, as well as a more recent fourth component, cruise missiles.

Bombers

Bombers were originally intended to attack targets by dropping gravity bombs. That role has to some extent been superceded by the use of bombers as "launch platforms" for a variety of air-to-land missiles. More recently, however, interest has been revived in using bombers as "penetrating aircraft," having them fly very low, thereby ducking under radar detection.

Compared to the other legs of the triad, bombers are quite slow: It would take six hours or so for these aircraft, flying over the North Pole, to traverse the distance between the United States and the Soviet Union. However, they have a pronounced advantage in that, because they are manned, they can be recalled. This is not true of either land-based or submarine-launched missiles.

The Soviet Union does not have a tradition of using strategic bombers; unlike Britain and the United States, for example, during World War II the U.S.S.R. did not engage in massive bombing raids against Germany. The Soviet Union currently maintains a relatively small fleet of about 150 strategic bombers. These aircraft are widely acknowledged to be far inferior to their American counterparts, which, despite frequent complaints as to their age, are without question the world's premier strategic bombing fleet. The backbone of the U.S. bomber force continues to be approximately 260 B-52s, which have been updated in various ways including new engines and sophisticated electronics warfare capabilities, plus 100 of the new B-1 penetrating bombers. Another model, the so-called Stealth or B-2 bomber (designed to be almost invisible to hostile radar) should enter service some time in the 1990s.

Land-Based Missiles

Ballistic missiles are rockets. They travel very rapidly, reaching speeds of greater than 10,000 mph, and during intercontinental flight they actually leave the Earth's atmosphere and then reenter to strike their targets. Intercontinental ballistic missiles, or ICBMs, are located underground, in steel and concrete-reinforced silos. The United States maintains about 1,000 ICBMs (as with all such weapons for all countries, the exact numbers keep changing, when older models are phased out and new ones brought into service). The U.S.S.R. has invested especially heavily in ICBMs, and currently has about 1,600.

Most ICBMs are MIRVed, which means they are equipped with *m*ultiple, *i*ndependently targeted *r*eentry *v*ehicles. A single MIRVed missile can be equipped with ten or more warheads, each of which can be aimed at a different target. The fifty MX missiles in the active U.S. arsenal, for example,

The B-1 bomber, designed to penetrate Soviet airspace and deliver nuclear weapons. (U.S. Department of Defense)

each carrying about ten warheads of 350 kilotons (nearly thirty times the power of the Hiroshima bomb), can destroy 500 distinct targets. Soviet missiles tend to be larger than their U.S. counterparts, a fact that has caused great consternation to some in the United States, and that has buttressed claims that the United States is "behind" in ICBMs, thereby helping to generate support for additional missile programs. In fact, the smaller size of U.S. ICBMs is an indication of the *superiority*, not inferiority, of U.S. missile technology. According to the physics of nuclear explosions, the accuracy of a warhead is far more important than its explosive size: A small increase in accuracy is equivalent — in the probability of destroying a given "hardened" target* — to a very large increase in total explosive

force. The U.S. arsenal has achieved very high degrees of accuracy; as a result, it has been possible to decrease the megatonnage, and also to employ ICBMs that are somewhat smaller than the first, relatively primitive missiles.

Missile accuracy is measured by circular error probable (CEP), which is taken to be a distance, with the target at the center, such that one half of all warheads will fall within a circle produced by this radius. Thus, a large CEP indicates inaccuracy, and vice versa. Soviet ICBMs tend to have larger CEPs than their U.S. equivalents; hence, the U.S.S.R. has sought to compensate for this deficiency by building larger rockets, capable of lifting larger warheads. In recent years, both superpowers have achieved great increases in the accuracy with which ballistic missile warheads can be directed; as we shall see in the section on strategic doctrine, this is a very troubling development.

It would take approximately thirty minutes for ICBMs fired by one superpower to devastate the

---

*One that has been reinforced with steel and concrete so as to withstand several thousand psi.

other. The Soviets have begun deploying mobile ICBMs,* while the United States is seriously considering doing the same.

Strategic Submarines

Nuclear submarines can be nuclear in two senses: They are typically propelled by nuclear power plants, and they also carry nuclear missiles, known as SLBMs, for *submarine-launched ballistic missiles*. These missiles are designed to be fired while the submarine remains submerged. The particular advantage of strategic submarines is that, unlike bombers or ICBMs, they cannot be targeted by an adversary once they are on deep-ocean patrol. In terms of strategic doctrine, they have therefore long been considered an ideal deterrent weapon, in that they offer the prospect of a secure retaliatory force. (Curiously, the relative inaccuracy of their missiles has also been an advantage, since they could only be used to retaliate against cities, and not to initiate a disarming first strike.) However, SLBMs have certain disadvantages, notably the fact that communication with deeply submerged submarines is quite difficult. And the present generation of SLBMs — notably the U.S. Trident or D-5 missile — is expected to be as accurate as the most accurate ICBMs.

Strategic submarines carry many SLBMs; the U.S. Trident submarine, for example, carries twenty-four missiles. Like ICBMs, SLBMs tend to be MIRVed, although the United States has progressed further than the Soviet Union in this regard. In addition, whereas the Soviet Union has a larger number of strategic submarines than does the United States (roughly sixty to forty), and more SLBMs as well, the United States has more submarine-based warheads (about six thousand to three thousand). And at any given time, the United States maintains nearly ten times more warheads on deep-ocean patrol than does the U.S.S.R. The United States also enjoys an immense geographic advantage over the U.S.S.R., because of its extensive, ice-free ocean coastlines. U.S. strategic submarines are far quieter than their Soviet counterparts, and the United States is also acknowledged to have a substantial lead in antisubmarine warfare.

Cruise Missiles

Cruise missiles have become increasingly prominent in recent years, and have become in a sense the fourth leg of each superpower's "triad." Cruise missiles are pilotless, jet aircraft that travel comparatively slowly (about the speed of sound), but stick close to the ground and are therefore difficult for radar to detect. They are also relatively inexpensive to produce. Equipped with modern navigational and homing devices, they are also becoming extremely accurate. In addition, note that cruise missiles are quite small, perhaps twenty feet long. Thus, once they are deployed in large numbers, verification of their elimination at any time in the future, even if countries possessing them muster the political will to do so, becomes difficult if not impossible. Cruise missiles can be armed with conventional or nuclear warheads, and at present there is no way to distinguish the two kinds.

Cruise missiles come in three different modes: air-launched cruise missiles (ALCMs, pronounced "alk'ems"), which are carried by bombers; ground-launched cruise missiles (GLCMs, or "glick'ems"); and sea-launched cruise missiles (SLCMs, or "slick'ems"). The INF Treaty removed ground-launched cruise missiles that NATO had stationed in Europe (see Chapter 15); air- and sea-launched cruise missiles, however, are being deployed in dizzying numbers, by both superpowers. As is so often the case in the nuclear arms race, the United States appears to have a substantial lead over the Soviet Union in the technology of cruise missiles, although the Soviets may well have produced more of them.

---

*ICBMs that travel around the countryside (usually on trains) are therefore more difficult for an opponent to target.

Comparing the Superpower Arsenals

Each superpower maintains about 25,000 bombs and warheads, of which about 11,000 are designated for strategic use. The American triad is better balanced, that is, less vulnerable to preemptive attack, than that of the U.S.S.R. The United States has about 50 percent of its strategic warheads on submarines, 25 percent on bombers, and 25 percent on ICBMs. By contrast, the Soviets have perhaps 70 percent of their strategic warheads on ICBMs, 25 percent on submarines, and 5 percent on bombers. The United States has generally led in the nuclear arms race, maintaining a five- to ten-year lead in most technological innovations. Typically, however, the Soviet Union has caught up, in many cases ultimately compensating for its qualitative inferiority by deploying its version in larger numbers.

U.S. ballistic missiles (submarine- and land-based) are all solid-fueled, relatively reliable, and highly accurate; the Soviets, by contrast, still use large numbers of less reliable, cumbersome, liquid-fueled missiles, and their accuracy is not as great. We have already considered the important and often misleading issues of U.S.-Soviet accuracy, megatonnage, throw weight, and missile size. In other important measures — readiness and reliability — the United States is also widely acknowledged to hold a substantial lead.*

---

*It is interesting to note that some conservative analysts, confronted with the fact that Soviet missiles are maintained at a lower state of readiness than their U.S. counterparts, respond that this fact — which would seem to suggest a relatively low level of hostile intent — actually shows just the opposite: The Soviets don't need a high level of readiness, they argue, because they know that the United States would never initiate an attack against them. When the Soviets choose to attack the United States, it is claimed, they will simply increase their readiness as needed. If Soviet readiness, on the other hand, had turned out to be greater than that of the United States, it is virtually certain that this fact would also have been used as evidence of Soviet aggressiveness. When one's mind is already made up, any data serve to confirm the preconception.

STRATEGIC DOCTRINE: DETERRENCE

Strategic doctrine refers to the plans that underlie the accumulation of nuclear weapons, the justifications for their existence, and the expectations as to their use. The major component of U.S. strategic doctrine is said to be deterrence, the idea that nuclear war will be prevented by the threat that any attacker would suffer unacceptable retaliation. Realizing this, the would-be attacker would therefore be deterred. Deterrence as such is not unique to nuclear weapons (we shall examine the concept of "peace through strength," including more detail on nuclear deterrence, in Chapter 14). What is unique to nuclear deterrence, however, is the consequence of failure, and the fact that heretofore, military forces that ostensibly provided deterrence also did double duty in providing defense, should deterrence fail. For centuries, for example, the Roman legions kept the peace by deterring would-be attackers, but when attacks nonetheless occurred, the legions were also available to defend Rome. In the nuclear age, despite efforts at achieving strategic defense (see Chapter 14), the fact remains that the offense is all-powerful; if nuclear deterrence should fail, there would be no defense. Shortly after World War II, American strategic analyst Bernard Brodie recognized the qualitative change in deterrence ushered in by nuclear weapons:

> The first and most vital step in any American security program for the age of atomic bombs is to take measures to guarantee to ourselves in case of attack the possibility of retaliation in kind. The writer in making this statement is not for the moment concerned about who will *win* the next war in which atomic bombs have been used. Thus far the chief purpose of our military establishment has been to win wars. From now on its chief purpose must be to avert them. It can have almost no other useful purpose.[9]

Deterrence theory has been modified and adjusted many times in accordance with the state of U.S.-Soviet weaponry. (Variations in U.S.-Soviet relations, interestingly, have had very little effect on nuclear doctrine; it will be worth noting whether the Gorbachev-era thaw in U.S.-Soviet relations ultimately produces changes in nuclear weapons policy.) The basic premise of deterrence has remained that neither side will use nuclear weapons against the other so long as the victim retains the ability to cause unacceptable damage to the attacker. In such thinking, the initial attack is referred to as a first strike, and a first-strike capability is generally taken to mean the ability to conduct a first strike that will render the victim unable to retaliate. Neither the United States nor the U.S.S.R. currently has an effective first-strike capability, although some people worry that this may change in the near future as both sides deploy weapons of increasing accuracy.

According to deterrence theory, therefore, it behooves each country to maintain a second-strike capability, the capacity to absorb a first strike and still retaliate. If one side has a second-strike capability, then the other, by definition, lacks a first-strike capability. The result is considered to be strategic stability,* a situation in which neither side can profit by striking first; thus, war should not occur.

SKELETONS IN THE CLOSET OF DETERRENCE

Unfortunately, deterrence theory is not as cut-and-dried, or even, perhaps, as reliable, as its enthusiasts might wish. Several factors — or "skeletons in the closet" of deterrence — have consistently undermined the presumed goal of strategic nuclear stability based on mutual deterrence.

Skeleton 1: How Much Is Enough?

No simple rule of thumb or straightforward quantitative measure can assure national leaders that they have accumulated enough retaliatory force to deter an adversary. Indeed, if one side is willing to be annihilated in a counterattack, then it cannot be deterred. And if one side is convinced of the other's implacable hostility, then no amount of weaponry

can ever be "enough." So long as money can be made from building weapons, so long as prestige and careers are served by designing, producing, and deploying new "generations" of nuclear forces, there will be continuing insistence on yet more weapons. Furthermore, insofar as nuclear weapons serve symbolic, psychological needs, such as conveying legitimacy to otherwise insecure leaders and countries, demonstrating the scientific and technological accomplishments of a nation, or simply "flexing one's muscles," then once again, there is no rational way to put a cap on the optimum size of one's arsenal.

Nonetheless, in the early 1960s, Defense Secretary McNamara attempted to establish a reasonable criterion that would enable the United States to make some assessment of its deterrent needs, thereby — it was hoped — avoiding a never-ending accumulation of nuclear arms. It was estimated that approximately 400 megatons would destroy roughly one quarter of the Soviet population and two-thirds of its industry. Beyond that amount, a process of diminishing returns sets in, such that (as Winston Churchill commented with regard to strategic bombing in World War II), additional explosions simply "made the rubble bounce." Strategic planners further judged that to be prudent, each leg of the strategic triad should be able to deliver 400 megatons. However, because of the many factors that drive the nuclear arms race — and to some extent, arms races in general (see Chapters 9, 12, and 14) — the arsenals of both sides have expanded to many times this amount.

Skeleton 2: Credibility

A second major difficulty of deterrence theory is the problem inherent in basing security on the threat to do something that is grossly self-destructive, and therefore lacking in credibility. Thus, granted that one side would be irrational to attack a nuclear-armed opponent that had a second-strike capability, the victim would be equally irrational to reply with nuclear weapons. Not only would retaliation be useless, but it might also be counterproductive, adding to worldwide destruction (through

---

*It is worth noting that in the arcane and bloodless language of strategic discourse, there is no such word as *peace*. The closest approximation is "strategic stability," which is not peace at all, but rather a kind of suspended animation in which overt warfare is merely postponed.

Defense Secretary Robert McNamara (left) conferring with General Maxwell Taylor and President John F. Kennedy. Under McNamara's leadership, the United States formalized its doctrine of nuclear deterrence and sought to determine how large a nuclear arsenal was needed. (John F Kennedy Library)

fallout, ozone depletion, nuclear winter, and so on) while also bringing the possibility of yet another attack from the aggressor's remaining nuclear forces. In addition, given the moral issues raised by a willingness to commit mass murder on the largest scale in all human history (Chapter 19), there might be additional reason to doubt either side's willingness to do so.

This problem caused by the inherent incredibility of nuclear deterrence is magnified yet more when deterrence is extended to cover not only nuclear attacks against the United States, but also at-

tacks against our NATO allies in Europe, oil supplies in the Persian Gulf (the so-called Carter Doctrine), the state of Israel, and so on. "Extended deterrence" implies that the United States will respond, with nuclear weapons if necessary, to situations in which vital U.S. interests are engaged, but that fall short of actual attacks against U.S. territory. In order to enhance the credibility of this doctrine, the United States has also developed theories and weaponry for the fighting of so-called limited nuclear wars, under the assumption that if the threat of World War III is not believable, the threat to initiate limited use of nuclear weapons might suffice.

"One cannot fashion a credible deterrent out of an incredible action," wrote former Defense Secretary Robert McNamara. "Thus, security for the United States and its allies can only arise from the possession of a range of graduated deterrents, each of them fully credible in its own context."[10] Such thinking has led, in turn, to the notion of "flexible response," according to which NATO should possess a range of military options, including a diversity of nuclear responses short of all-out nuclear war.

There are, however, some serious problems with doctrines of limited war-fighting. First, in order to be credible, such doctrines must be based on weapons and tactics that are in fact usable — generally missiles, bombs, and warheads that are smaller and more accurate and that produce relatively less "collateral damage" (the killing of innocent civilians and their property). So in order to be effective, which in the case of nuclear weapons means in order *not to be used*, these weapons must be made *more usable*. But this poses a major paradox, and one that may someday be catastrophic: the more usable, hence credible, they are, the more likely they are actually to be used. And numerous studies have suggested that in the event of nuclear war, no matter how small and controlled the opening shots, the confrontation probably will escalate into an all-out strategic exchange, with catastrophic consequences for all involved. Moreover, even without such escalation, a "limited" nuclear war, in Europe for example, would appear quite unlimited to the Europeans, for whose benefit the war was ostensibly being fought. As a result of all this, even "limited nuclear war"—hence, nuclear deterrence—may be seen as lacking in credibility after all.*

Skeleton 3: Vulnerability

As we have seen, deterrence entails the possession of a second-strike capability. And this, in turn, requires that the nuclear weapons of each side remain invulnerable to attack, or at least, that the probability of their being destroyed in a first strike be very low. Over time, however, as nuclear missiles have become increasingly accurate, concerns have been raised about the growing vulnerability of these weapons. Such vulnerability has been enhanced by the development of so-called counterforce doctrines, policies that favor the targeting of an adversary's weapons rather than population centers. Although counterforce appears to be more ethical than its alternative, countervalue targeting (see Chapter 19), it carries with it the threat that the other side may be planning a first strike.

Great accuracy is not a prerequisite for deterrence: A thermonuclear bomb could destroy Leningrad or Chicago whether or not it lands within 100 meters of its target. Such accuracy is important, however, if the goal is to destroy ("take out") ICBMs and command centers within their reinforced steel and concrete silos, since these can only be destroyed by a virtual direct hit. The problem is that there is no logical reason to attack these structures in retaliation, after their missiles have been

fired; hence, as each side threatens the weapons of the other, the increasingly vulnerable "superpower" worries that its opponent—rather than planning to retaliate if need be—is instead planning to strike first, thereby initiating a potentially deadly spiral of paranoia leading ultimately to an attempt at a preemptive strike by one side or the other. In fact, other justifications exist for counterforce targeting, including the following:

1. The supposed greater morality of aiming at weapons rather than people.

2. A desire to limit the opponent's ability to cause further damage, by destroying weapons that could theoretically be used in a second wave of attacks.

3. The presumption by some hawkish strategists that the Soviets value their weapons more than their population; hence, that they would be more deterred by threats to the former than to the latter.

4. The persistence of a rather deadly but well-established military tradition of "target practice," wherein accuracy has always been stressed as a virtue.

5. The fact that deterrence by threatening the destruction of the opponent's cities requires much fewer nuclear weapons, and less technology than is needed to threaten the opponent's military assets. The latter are more difficult to hit and are much more abundant than cities or industrial centers; thus, a counterforce strategy helps justify an expanded role for both the military and the nuclear weapons industry. Whereas there are only about a hundred Soviet cities with a population over 100,000, U.S. strategic analysts have been able to identify many thousands of Soviet missile silos, military depots, and other potential counterforce targets.

Whatever its origin, the result of counterforce is the perception of vulnerability, which in turn leads to strategic instability. On the one hand, the side possessing a first-strike capability may be tempted to make such an attack, especially under

---

*Against all this, some analysts—such as McGeorge Bundy, who served as national security advisor to Presidents Kennedy and Johnson—have emphasized what has been called "existential deterrence." The idea is very simple: Whatever the elaborate technical and theoretical arguments over strategic nuclear theory, the mere existence of these terribly destructive weapons, combined with deep uncertainty over the consequences of their use and the likelihood of catastrophic escalation, must result in extreme caution and a high degree of deterrence.

Coordinated multiple launch of Minuteman III ICBMs from Vandenburg Air Force Base, California. A first strike, by either side, would require a precisely coordinated launch of thousands of missiles. (U.S. Department of Defense)

at least two warheads to have any confidence of destroying an opposing missile, because of possible malfunctions.) But if each missile is armed with, say, ten warheads, then an attacker could destroy — in theory — ten of the other side's missiles (and 100 warheads) while only expending one of its own. To "cover" each victim missile with two warheads would still require only two attacking missiles; in return, there would be a relatively high probability of destroying ten of the opponent's missiles. The result is very dangerous in that it threatens to undermine deterrence yet further. It should be emphasized that deterrence rests on creating a situation in which neither side would be tempted to shoot first; MIRVing, combined with accuracy, leads to crisis instability, in which, during conditions of crisis — when each side fears that the other may gain an advantage by making a preemptive attack — either side may be tempted to strike first.

Although both the United States and the Soviet Union adhere to various degrees of counterforce strategies, the fact remains that neither side is currently capable of conducting a disarming first strike against the other. There are simply too many imponderables for any sane leader to anticipate complete success in anything so complicated and incalculably risky as a first strike; moreover, the ocean-going SLBMs of each country are effectively invulnerable. Nonetheless, the *perception* of vulnerability could be destabilizing, and both countries seem determined to deploy new missiles that are ever more accurate, while resisting restrictions on MIRVing.

Skeleton 4: Human Psychology

Deterrence theory assumes rationality. It also assumes that leaders will always retain control over their nuclear forces, and over their emotions as well, making decisions based solely on a cool calculation of the costs and benefits associated with each course of action. Deterrence theory assumes that each side will scare the other with the prospect of the most hideous, unimaginable consequences, and that the persons thus terrified will then behave with

conditions of crisis when war seems likely and perhaps inevitable. On the other hand, the vulnerable side might well calculate that since the opponent has the ability to strike a devastating first blow, it should preempt such an attack by striking first. This is also more likely during an international crisis. (There is no limit to this chain of reasoning: Side A, fearing that side B is about to preempt in this way, may be tempted to pre-preempt . . . leading side B, which anticipates such a pre-preemption, to consider pre-pre-preempting, and so forth. The result of all this is a high level of *in*stability, precisely opposite the goal of deterrence.)

The phenomenon of MIRVing has further added to concerns about vulnerability to a first strike, for the following reason: With all missiles armed with only a single warhead, it would take a missile to destroy a missile. (Actually, it would take more than one, since the attacker would have to use the utmost in cool, precise rationality. Ironically, everything we know about human psychology suggests precisely the opposite outcome: Intense fear is incompatible with careful cognition (see Chapter 10 for a discussion of war-related errors, both emotional and cognitive, on the part of national leaders).

Deterrence theory also ignores the fact that even without intense fear, people often behave in ways that are irrational, even spiteful (that is, hurtful to themselves as well as others). Moreover, they may be the victims of insufficient or faulty information, or various other perceptual distortions that cause them to make incorrect judgments as to the intentions of others, the probabilities of various alternative courses of action, and so on. It requires no arcane strategic wisdom to know that people often act out of anger, despair, insanity, stubbornness, or fixed religious conviction. And finally, in certain situations — such as when either side is convinced that war is inevitable, or when the pressures to avoid losing face are especially intense — an irrational act, even a lethal one, may appear quite rational, or otherwise appropriate . . . even unavoidable.

HOW A NUCLEAR WAR COULD START

There are many possible scenarios (imagined sequences of interactions) in which nuclear war could occur. Here are some examples.

Bolt Out of the Blue

Although most laypeople imagine a surprise, middle-of-the-night attack, most experts agree that a so-called bolt out of the blue, or BOOB, attack is the least likely scenario of all. Neither side would come out ahead, and unless other factors are operating, deterrence should prevent any such calculated madness. On the other hand, strategic analysts worry constantly that one side may be tempted to attack preemptively (to jump through any open "windows of vulnerability") if it becomes convinced that the opponent's weapons could be destroyed in a surprise first strike. Realistic scenarios

for BOOB attacks generally depend upon some combination of the various other scenarios discussed below.

A "Game" of Chicken

A teenage "game," captured memorably in the 1950s James Dean movie *Rebel Without a Cause*, was to play "chicken" in automobiles. Two drivers would drive toward each other at high speed, straddling the white line. The one who swerved lost; the one who persevered in racing straight ahead was the winner. In a game of chicken, therefore, the goal is to induce the opponent to swerve, and not to do so oneself.

The most dramatic example of nuclear chicken occurred during the Cuban Missile Crisis in 1962, when the Soviet Union attempted to install medium-range nuclear missiles in Cuba. The United States demanded that the missiles be withdrawn; the Soviets refused. After considering and rejecting various options — including a conventional attack on the missile sites, an invasion of Cuba, and a preemptive nuclear strike against the Soviet Union — President John Kennedy decided on a naval blockade (designated at the time as a "quarantine"). The situation was exceedingly tense, and President Kennedy subsequently stated that he thought the chances of nuclear war had been between one in two and one in three. Premier Khrushchev eventually ordered Soviet naval vessels to turn back, and an accommodation was reached, in which the offending missile site was dismantled and the United States promised not to invade Cuba.

As then Secretary of State Dean Rusk put it, "We were eyeball to eyeball, and the other guy blinked." In other words, the Soviets turned aside in that game of nuclear chicken. They may have been induced to do so, at least in part, by the fact that the U.S.S.R. was militarily inferior to the United States, both in conventional forces in the Caribbean and in nuclear arms. (One way to win a game of chicken is to drive a Mack truck while your opponent is driving a Honda Civic.) However, the United States and the U.S.S.R. are now roughly equal militarily, and neither side is likely to accept the ignominy of being the one to swerve. In contests of nuclear chicken, when each side insists that the other one turn aside, the result is likely to be fried chicken.

Escalated Conventional War

Military forces of the United States and the U.S.S.R. have not fought each other since the United States — along with the other Western powers — tried unsuccessfully to undo the Bolshevik Revolution (1918–1920). It is quite possible (some would say, likely) that such restraint has been due to the shared possession of nuclear weapons. Nonetheless, each side has been engaged in conventional fighting — the Soviets, for example, in Hungary (1956), Czechoslovakia (1968), and Afghanistan (1979–1988) and the United States in Korea (1950–1953), Vietnam (1962–1974), Beirut (1982), Grenada (1983), the Persian Gulf (1987–1988), and Panama (1989) to mention just a few.

The United States apparently has seriously considered the use of nuclear weapons in many cases, from 1946, when President Truman insisted that Stalin withdraw his forces from Iran (which he did), to 1968, when military leaders sought ways to help lift the siege of Khe Sanh in Vietnam. Thus far, such threats and confrontations have been resolved short of nuclear war, but there is no assurance that this will continue indefinitely.

There is also an ongoing threat that during conventional warfare, nuclear weapons will be used in a last-ditch effort to win the war, or simply to prevent their being overrun. Nearly twenty years after leaving the Defense Department, Robert McNamara warned that

> we face a future in which for decades we must contemplate continuing confrontation between East and West. Any one of these confrontations can escalate, through miscalculation, into military conflict. And that conflict will be between blocs that possess fifty thousand nuclear warheads — warheads that are deployed on the battlefields and integrated into the war plans. . . . In the tense atmosphere of a crisis, each side will feel pressure to

delegate authority to fire nuclear war weapons to battlefield commanders. As the likelihood of attack increases, these commanders will face a desperate dilemma: use them or lose them.[11]

Catalytic and Proxy Wars

Both the United States and the U.S.S.R. have supported other nations that have in some ways functioned as proxies for the two superpowers. When one superpower or the other offers security guarantees to an embattled third party, the possibility exists that nuclear weapons might be employed if the ally is losing. Or at least, the "protector" feels the need to threaten such use, which could elicit a comparable threat from the other superpower, leading once again to nuclear chicken. Early in the 1973 October War between Israel and the Arab states, for example, Israeli forces were doing poorly, and Israel may well have been on the verge of employing its own nuclear arsenal. The U.S.S.R. began military preparations — suggesting the possible use of nuclear weapons — as a guarantee to the Arabs, which in turn led the United States to order a worldwide nuclear alert. The October War was eventually concluded by the successful Israeli use of conventional weapons (assisted by massive U.S. military aid, especially tank ammunition), but not until both superpowers again came close to being drawn into the fray. When the Israelis had eventually turned the tide and threatened to overrun Cairo, the Soviets mobilized forces in support of Egypt, whereupon the United States again instituted a nuclear alert. The crisis was eventually defused by the United Nations.

Nuclear Accidents

An accidental nuclear detonation has never taken place, although both sides may have come close. In several cases, the conventional explosive that is part of a nuclear weapon has detonated, scattering large amounts of radioactive material. Furthermore, nuclear-armed bombers and submarines have crashed, exploded, and/or sunk. Given the chaos that would doubtless follow an accidental nuclear explosion, it is always possible that such an event would lead to "retaliation." A full-fledged nuclear detonation would dwarf such episodes as occurred at the Three Mile Island (U.S.) or Chernobyl (U.S.S.R.) nuclear power plants. Moreover, if a nuclear explosion occurred during a time of high international tension, the consequences may well be more serious yet.

Unauthorized Use

Both the United States and the U.S.S.R. keep relatively tight, centralized control over their nuclear weapons, in an effort to make certain that they will only be employed if appropriate orders are given by the highest level of political leadership. Numerous fail-safe devices are incorporated into U.S. weapons design, and we assume that comparable controls exist on the Soviet side as well. However, there is no guarantee that something could not go wrong, and as a result, someone relatively low in military/political rank could wind up starting a nuclear war.* Drug abuse is reported to be high among the personnel of strategic submarines, for example, and because communications with submerged submarines is so restricted, crews do in fact have both the authority and the capability to initiate use of nuclear weapons without necessarily having received orders to do so from higher in the chain of command.

Irrational Use

It can readily be argued that *any* use of nuclear weapons constitutes irrational use. Beyond this, however, the possibility also exists that those persons exercising the highest political authority may themselves go insane or behave irrationally. Many famous leaders throughout history were psychotic or experienced psychotic episodes: Caligula, Nero, Ludwig of Bavaria, and probably Adolf Hitler and Joseph Stalin as well. Woodrow Wilson and Dwight Eisenhower suffered serious strokes while in office,

which compromised their ability to perform their duties and to think clearly. During his final days before resigning the presidency in 1974, Richard Nixon is said to have acted irrationally under the stress of the Watergate investigations. No precedent, and no set of guidelines, currently exists for countermanding the orders of a sitting president, no matter how dangerous or unwise such orders might be . . . and the use of nuclear weapons could legally be ordered without a formal declaration of war by Congress, and even without any prior consultation.

False Alarms

Perhaps the most chilling—because the most likely—scenario for nuclear war involves failure in the C³I (command, control, communications, and intelligence) systems of either side. Before the nuclear age, countries worried about being the victims of a surprise attack, as happened to the United States at Pearl Harbor and to the Soviets when Germany suddenly invaded in June 1941. In the era of nuclear weapons, a danger even greater than surprise attack, paradoxically, is that one side—thinking it is under attack—may "retaliate" when in fact it had not actually been attacked at all.

Because the extreme destructive power of nuclear weapons is combined with exceedingly high speed and short warning times—literally, a matter of minutes—there is great pressure to know quickly whether such an attack is under way, and if so, to respond immediately. In addition, as nuclear delivery systems become increasingly accurate, counterforce weapons have made it more and more feasible (at least in theory) for the attacking side to demolish the victim's nuclear forces. And as that feasibility increases, reports of such an attack become more believable. The result is great pressure on the victim to respond decisively to any reported attack.

At present, U.S. policy calls for the use of strategic nuclear weapons only after the country has undeniably been struck by an opponent's nuclear weapons. As we have seen, nuclear deterrence depends, essentially, on the other side believing that, if attacked, the victim will retaliate in kind. But as

---

*It is an interesting question, on the other hand, whether someone high in a nation's hierarchy is any more entitled! (See Chapter 19.)

Combat operations center at NORAD, deep under Cheyenne Mountain in Colorado. Reported attacks against the United States would be analyzed here. (U.S. Department of Defense)

we have also seen, nuclear deterrence must deal with a major problem: credibility. Having suffered immense destruction in an initial attack, literally nothing can be gained by retaliating, and moreover, a great deal can be lost, if the attacker responds to the victim's retaliation by firing yet more missiles. In addition, the great speed and increasing accuracy of strategic missiles have led some analysts to conclude that, at least in theory, an opponent could target a large proportion of the victim's land-based missiles. So, it has been argued that in order to shore up the credibility of nuclear deterrence, it will be necessary to employ a system known as "launch on warning," in which the decision to launch is made upon warning of an attack, rather than waiting until the attacker's warheads have literally begun exploding on U.S. soil. Moreover, in order to bolster the credibility that the victim will actually make such a retaliation, launch on warning is also often taken to mean that the "decision" to launch will be removed from human beings, and placed in the hands of computers, preprogrammed to launch when warned of an impending attack.

Launch on warning, the supremely logical consequence of nuclear deterrence theory itself, carries immense dangers, however. First, it drastically reduces the time span in which a decision must be made . . . perhaps the most fateful decision in the history of the world. Second, it places our fates in the hands of potentially fallible sensor and warning systems. And third, it makes us all dependent on the correct functioning of our computers (as well as Soviet computer systems, which are widely acknowledged to be less efficient than our own). Indeed, the world's future will be seriously in jeopardy if launch on warning ever becomes a reality, and yet, high-ranking analysts from both superpowers have indicated that trends in nuclear weapons technology and doctrine are pushing strongly in this direction.

Even without launch on warning, the leadership of both superpowers is essentially hostage to the correct functioning of their warning systems. And during times of international stress or crisis, this connection may be especially perilous. Thus, there have been many false alarms: According to the Senate Armed Services Committee, there were 151 "serious" nuclear false alarms and 3,703 lesser alerts during a (presumably representative) period between January 1979 and July 1980. In the past, radar signals bouncing off the newly risen moon have been taken for enemy missiles, migrating geese have been similarly misinterpreted, and a fire in a Siberian natural gas pipeline set off a satellite sensor, which identified it as the exhausts of a Soviet missile launch. In 1980, a practice war-games tape was erroneously read by military computers as an actual attack, and faulty microchips have several times generated unnecessary alerts.

The Hotline — installed after the Cuban missile crisis — and the recently instituted Crisis Control Centers are supposed to reduce the danger that similar false alarms, in the future, will lead to war by miscalculation. But it remains unclear what sort of communication would reassure a side that believes it is being attacked and feels that it must respond immediately.

NUCLEAR PROLIFERATION

We have focused on the two superpowers because between them the United States and the Soviet Union account for about 98 percent of the world's nuclear weapons. In addition, the United States and the U.S.S.R. are primarily responsible for the qualitative as well as the quantitative dimensions of the nuclear arms race. U.S. citizens also have a much greater opportunity to influence the behavior of their own country than those of any other country. Moreover, because of the reciprocating effects of the nuclear arms race, U.S. policy is also likely to influence the Soviet Union as well. We have accordingly focused on what has been called vertical proliferation, the accumulation of weapons and delivery systems by the superpowers. However, there is substantial reason to be concerned about horizontal proliferation, the acquisition of nuclear weapons by other, nonnuclear countries, as well.

But there is also another view: Since nuclear weapons, in the hands of the superpowers, have ostensibly helped "keep the peace," then these same weapons, widely proliferated, might actually be a stabilizing influence on world affairs. (After all, if the U.S. and Soviet public is supposed to accept that nuclear weapons are good for them, then why wouldn't nuclear weapons be equally good for, say, Pakistan, or Argentina?) This is the so-called porcupine theory, that a world composed of many nuclear-armed states would be a safe one, because each state would carefully avoid antagonizing its neighbors, just as porcupines walk in relative safety through the forest. It should be emphasized that this is distinctly a minority position.

In addition to the United States and the Soviet Union, acknowledged nuclear weapons states are Britain, France, and China. India conducted a successful nuclear test in 1974, but claims that it has not accumulated a nuclear arsenal. Israel has not admitted possessing nuclear weapons, but it is known to have a nuclear arsenal of perhaps 200 warheads. It consistently claims that it "will not be the first to introduce nuclear weapons into the Mideast." South Africa and Pakistan are on the brink of nuclear capability (many people believe that both states, like Israel, have crossed that brink but maintain a polite fiction that they have not).

In this very brief section, we shall first consider the technological means of horizontal proliferation,

and then examine the political motivations for developing, and refraining from developing, nuclear weapons.

Technological Means

Fissionable materials could be stolen, and then fabricated into nuclear weapons. It is widely acknowledged, for example, that Israel commandeered a shipload of enriched uranium in the late 1960s. Also, governments or terrorist groups conceivably could steal ready-made bombs or warheads while they are in transit or in storage depots. Or, governments could purchase ready-made nuclear weapons; Libya, for example, attempted unsuccessfully to buy nuclear bombs from China.

Fissionable materials can be obtained from the so-called front end of the nuclear cycle; this is how the acknowledged nuclear powers have obtained theirs. Natural uranium ore consists of only 0.7 percent U-235, whereas for use in nuclear explosives, the U-235 concentration must be about 90 percent. (Nuclear power plants, by contrast, require about 3 to 10 percent U-235.) The process of "enriching" uranium ore to bomb-grade involves a difficult and costly technology in which the unwanted U-238 is winnowed out, most commonly using a gas diffusion process. Enormous amounts of electricity are required, and the gas diffusion plants of nuclear weapons states are immense installations. Other, cheaper techniques — "poor man's" enrichment processes — have been described, and may be operating in South Africa.

The "rear end" of the nuclear cycle is an easier route for obtaining fissionable materials. All nuclear reactors, whether ostensibly designed for research purposes or as power plants, produce plutonium as an unavoidable consequence of their operation. Although the plutonium present in spent reactor fuel is too diluted to be used directly in explosives, this plutonium can be extracted and concentrated via various reprocessing technologies; plutonium reprocessing is much cheaper and easier than is uranium enrichment. India obtained a nuclear capability by reprocessing spent fuel from a Canadian research reactor, using materials originally supplied by the United States. The relationship between nuclear reactors and nuclear weapons was made dramatically clear when Israeli jets in 1980 destroyed a French-built Iraqi research reactor that the Israelis claimed was intended for producing plutonium for use in nuclear explosives.

Political Motivations

Perhaps even more significant than *how* to "go nuclear" is the question of *whether* to do so. Numerous countries that could readily go nuclear have not done so — Sweden, Canada, Germany, Japan, Australia, Holland, Switzerland — while others, with a much less developed economy and technological base — Pakistan, South Korea, Taiwan, Iraq — are on the verge of joining the nuclear club. Of the first group — states that have the ready capacity to obtain their own nuclear weapons, but do not appear likely to do so — there are four main categories:

1. States that are closely associated, politically and militarily, with the United States and are thus under the American "nuclear umbrella": Canada, Holland, Belgium, Italy, and the other nonnuclear NATO states.

2. States that are aligned with the Soviet Union, which does not permit them to develop an independent nuclear capability: the Warsaw Pact countries.

3. Neutral states, or those that do not see themselves as significantly threatened or that calculate that their security would be *decreased* by possessing nuclear weapons: Sweden, Switzerland, Australia.

4. Germany and Japan, states that by virtue of previous painful experience with nuclear weapons, sensitivity about their own past, and post–World War II legal and constitutional restraints, seem unlikely to develop nuclear weapons, and whose nuclearization would not be tolerated by others.

This group may be useful in illuminating factors that may help thwart nuclear proliferation. The second group — nonnuclear states on the verge of going nuclear — shows the other side of the coin. They also fall into several categories:

1. Lonely and "outlaw" states that find themselves relatively friendless and seriously outnumbered by their opponents: Israel, South Africa, Taiwan.

2. States with long-standing competitive and sometimes hostile relationships with a close neighbor: Brazil and Argentina, Pakistan and India, North and South Korea.

3. States with highly ambitious leaders: Libya, Iraq.

Among the existing nuclear powers, the proliferation path has been very much like a chain of dominos: The United States initiated a nuclear weapons program out of a fear of being "beaten to the punch" by Germany during World War II; the Soviet Union followed suit, in response to the U.S. nuclear monopoly; China went nuclear largely because of the U.S.S.R.; India developed nuclear weapons primarily because of China; and Pakistan is currently developing a nuclear arsenal, because of India. (The United States, in turn, has been unwilling to cut off aid to Pakistan, as required by U.S. law when evidence of attempted proliferation is overwhelming, because of Pakistan's value to the United States in helping to channel aid to the Afghan *mujahedeen* rebels.)

In some of these cases, states "went nuclear" after they discovered that the superpowers could not be counted on to provide a "nuclear guarantee" — that is, to risk nuclear war on their behalf. For example, during a tense confrontation between China and the United States over the islands of Quemoy and Matsu (small islands off the coast of China and fortified by Taiwan) during the 1950s, the U.S.S.R. failed to back China after the United States issued a nuclear threat. In addition, the Soviets reneged on an earlier pledge to share nuclear weapons technology with Mao's government. China then proceeded on a crash program to develop its own nuclear capability. When India was badly defeated by China in its brief war over Ladakh in 1962, the Soviet Union did not issue any nuclear ultimatums in support of India, even though by this time, the U.S.S.R. was increasingly friendly to the Indian government. Similarly, the Pakistanis felt badly let down by the United States during the India–Pakistani war over Bangladesh, after which they seem to have accelerated their own efforts toward nuclear independence. The superpowers cannot, however, really be blamed for hesitating to run such a grave risk as nuclear war, even on behalf of an ally. The problem — a nearly intractable one — is closely intertwined with that of state sovereignty: States insist on their absolute sovereignty and freedom of action in a world that is increasingly interdependent. (Chapter 9 discusses the problem, and Chapters 15–18 present possible solutions.)

Former Pakistani Prime Minister Ali Bhutto also pointed to a kind of religious domino effect in explaining the urge of certain nonnuclear states to cross the nuclear threshold. He noted that there was already a Christian bomb, a Marxist bomb, a Jewish bomb, and a Hindu bomb. Why, then, he asked, shouldn't there also be a Moslem bomb? (And for that matter, we might continue, why not separate Sunni and Shiite bombs, a Shinto bomb, a Buddhist bomb, a Catholic bomb, a Lutheran bomb, a Methodist bomb, a Zoroastrian bomb, an agnostic bomb, a neo-American Church bomb . . . ?)

There is also another, more general motivation behind would-be proliferators: pride. Britain and France, for example, had little strategic motivation for developing their own nuclear arsenals, but both countries in the 1950s and 1960s were contending with the dismantling of their overseas empires, and with the psychological stress of having to forgo their previous position as "great powers."* If it pos-

sesses nuclear weapons, a state is guaranteed a place in world councils, and, not surprisingly, many Third World leaders feel that their country, their people, and their culture deserve the same recognition, and are capable of the same responsibilities, that certain Caucasian powers have arrogated to themselves. In this respect, those who oppose nuclear proliferation ought to ask themselves whether there is any unacknowledged racism in the assumption that nuclear weapons are acceptable in the hands of white-skinned people of European descent, but intolerable if possessed by those whose skins are dark or whose religion or ideology is foreign to their own.

Nonetheless, many legitimate reasons for opposing nuclear proliferation exist, including the following:

1. As more people and organizations have their "finger on the button," the probability increases that someone, somewhere, will for some reason press it.

2. In many Third World countries, political power is held by military dictators who are not accountable to their citizenry, who have obtained power without democratic scrutiny, and who may be psychologically unstable.

3. Countries with a limited technological base may hesitate to invest heavily in various "failsafe" protective devices, thereby increasing the danger of accidental detonations, unauthorized use, and/or war by false alarm.

4. According to standard deterrence theory, states with a very small nuclear arsenal may actually be more at risk of preemptive attack than those having an ability to absorb such an attack and then retaliate.

5. Many would-be proliferators are currently engaged in active or smoldering hostilities directly on their borders; unlike the United States and the U.S.S.R., which in fact are not currently fighting directly over anything. Extremist elements or terrorist groups might well make use of nuclear weapons if they obtained them.

---

*In the case of France in particular, the problem of nuclear "credibility," discussed earlier, was also involved: President DeGaulle emphasized that France — and by extension, other countries of Europe — could not count on the American "nuclear umbrella," in that a U.S. president would be unlikely to risk the nuclear destruction of New York, for example, to save Paris. His answer was for France to develop its own independent deterrent, the "force de frappe."

The superpowers have a shared interest in restricting nuclear proliferation, and have established an international framework toward that end, the Nonproliferation Treaty (see Chapter 15). However, today's nuclear powers are ill-situated to criticize other countries for seeking to obtain nuclear weapons so long as they continue to accumulate their own vast arsenals. "Do as I say," they appear to be pronouncing, "not as I do."

OTHER PROLIFERATION PROBLEMS

In addition to the problem of proliferation in the narrow sense, attention has begun to focus on other, related issues, notably the growth of ballistic missile technology and of chemical weapons. When China detonated its first nuclear explosion, in 1964, U.S. officials sought to reassure its citizens that the Chinese were far behind in modern delivery vehicles—that is, ballistic missiles. Since that time, China has developed several generations of its own ballistic missiles, and numerous other states, nuclear as well as nonnuclear, have followed suit. Both Brazil and Argentina have active ballistic missile research programs (Argentina's Condor II missile, for example, is nearing completion). India has launched its own space satellites, and has also developed a ballistic missile, the Agni, with a range of up to 1,500 miles and a payload of one ton. The most serious and dangerous region for ballistic missile proliferation, however, is the Middle East. An Iraqi missile, the Al Abbas, can reach Jerusalem or Cairo; the Saudis have obtained Chinese East Wind missiles, capable of reaching anywhere in the Middle East, as well as southern Europe. And Israel's Jericho II missile, with a 900-mile range, can threaten even the Soviet Union. Since 1987, the United States and six of its allies have been party to the so-called Missile Technology Control Regime. Restrictions are lax and difficult to enforce, however, and—as with the nuclear nonproliferation regime—many important states are not members.

Chemical weapons have been called the "poor man's atomic bomb," and in fact, the manufacture of highly toxic chemical munitions is relatively easy and inexpensive. Iraq used such weapons against Iran, and also against its own Kurdish rebels; Libya—assisted by a German chemical firm—has been accused by the United States of constructing a chemical warfare facility. France, the Soviet Union, and the United States maintain large chemical weapons stockpiles. Of these, the U.S. arsenal is probably the most sophisticated, consisting of "binary" chemicals, two subcomponents that are not lethal in themselves, but that become highly toxic when combined immediately prior to use. The U.S.S.R. has indicated its intention of destroying its chemical arsenal, and both the United States and U.S.S.R. appear to be moving in this direction.

A FINAL NOTE ON NUCLEAR WEAPONS

There is an ancient Chinese proverb: Unless we change direction, we shall end up where we are headed. The proliferation of nuclear weapons—both vertical and horizontal—poses the most serious imaginable threat to human beings and to the planet. As we have emphasized, a world that is truly at peace must be more than one that is not actively at war. It is our planet, and our lives, and we have the right, even the duty, to aim high. And yet, when it comes to nuclear weapons, the narrow goal of simply preventing war is so essential that it seems satisfactory as an end in itself. Given the extraordinary dangers of nuclear war, however, mere prevention—from day to day, year to year—is not sufficient; most people in Peace Studies believe that we must aim for a higher degree of confidence. Undoubtedly, any satisfactory solution to the nuclear dilemma must be political, and not just technological. But at the same time, peace in the nuclear age demands the elimination of the nuclear threat itself. In the long run, nothing less will do.

Study Questions

1. Present an argument that, as Einstein suggested, the invention of nuclear weapons has changed the nature of the modern world. Present an argument that, to the contrary, things are still fundamentally the same.

2. Compare nuclear fission with nuclear fusion, in terms of physics, effect, and strategic consequences.

3. In what respects are the effects of nuclear weapons unique, and in what respect do they represent continuation of effects already found with conventional weapons?

4. It is often said that Mutually Assured Destruction is not so much policy as a statement of reality. Explain.

5. Present an argument in support of nuclear deterrence, and one in opposition to it.

6. Compare the U.S. and Soviet nuclear arsenals with respect to delivery systems.

7. What is meant by "limited nuclear war"? Why is the concept so cherished by nuclear hawks and opposed by nuclear doves?

8. Explain the relationship between missile accuracy and counterforce. How is this distinction important with regard to first- and second-strike capability?

9. Nuclear proliferation has actually proceeded somewhat more slowly than many authorities predicted in the 1960s. Why?

10. Define each of the following terms: catalytic war, proxy war, countervalue, horizontal proliferation, vertical proliferation, the IAEA, launch on warning, the rear end of the nuclear fuel cycle, MIRVing.

Suggestions for Further Reading

Lawrence Freedman. 1983. *The Evolution of Nuclear Strategy*. St. Martin's Press: New York.

Jack Dennis (ed.). 1984. *The Nuclear Almanac*. Addison-Wesley: Reading, MA.

Herbert M. Levine and David Carlton (eds.). 1986. *The Nuclear Arms Race Debated*. McGraw-Hill: New York.

Dan Kurzman. 1986. *The Day of the Bomb*. McGraw-Hill: New York.

David P. Barash. 1987. *The Arms Race and Nuclear War*. Wadsworth: Belmont, CA.

Source Notes

1. Quoted in L. Groves. 1962. *Now It Can Be Told*. Harper & Row: New York.

2. Frank Chinnock. 1969. *Nagasaki: The Forgotten Bomb*. World: New York.

3. From John Hersey. 1946. *Hiroshima*. The Modern Library: New York.

4. From M. Hachiya. 1955. *Hiroshima Diary*. University of North Carolina Press: Chapel Hill.

5. From a speech delivered by Lord Mountbatten in Strasbourg, France, 1979.

6. Quoted in Robert Scheer. 1982. *With Enough Shovels*. Random House: New York.

7. Henry Kissinger. 1957. *Nuclear Weapons and Foreign Policy*. Norton: New York.

8. Quoted in Robert Scheer. 1982. *With Enough Shovels*. Random House: New York.

9. Bernard Brodie. 1946. *The Absolute Weapon*. Harcourt Brace Jovanovich: New York.

10. Robert McNamara. 1968. *The Essence of Security*. Harper & Row: New York.

11. Robert McNamara. 1986. *Blundering into Disaster: Surviving the First Century of the Nuclear Age*. Pantheon: New York.

Italian dictator Benito Mussolini addressing an adoring crowd. (UPI/Bettmann)

II

The Causes of War

In Part I, we took an overview of peace and war. As the logicians might put it, the absence of war is a necessary but not sufficient condition for the realization of peace. It is insufficient because a life without war can nonetheless also be lacking in peace. But at the same time, the prevention of war is absolutely necessary if any meaningful peace is ever to be achieved. And so, our hopes for peace, and our work toward it, must take account of war; in particular, we must examine the causes of war, if our ultimate search is to be based on reality, and if our suggestions, means, and goals are to enjoy any realistic prospect of success.

For too long, in my own view, students of peace — in their legitimate eagerness to embrace a new and more peaceful world — have abandoned the understanding of war to their "hard-headed, realistic" colleagues in the more traditional academic disciplines of political science and international relations. Perhaps I am too hard on my friends, but I fear that as a result of this division of responsibility, while Centers for Strategic Studies and the like engage in the planning and legitimation of war and other acts of government-inspired violence, many devotees of peace have spent altogether too much time striving to understand peace, while avoiding the very real problem of war. In doing so, they have kept themselves unsullied, but have run the risk of becoming increasingly marginalized, not only in academic circles, but also with respect to their potential influence in the real world.* This is not to propose that Peace Students should become servants of the academic war establishment, whether cold or hot; rather, they should get to know their enemy. And that enemy, more than anything else, is war.

As we have discussed, "war" does not exist, but rather, individual wars, just as the species *Homo sapiens* does not, in a sense, exist; rather, there are individual people. In addition, it is far easier to understand individual people than to encompass the complexity and diversity of the 5 billion souls that constitute the human species. Just as we can make useful generalizations about the human species, however, we can do the same about the "species" of violent human conflict known as war.

In doing so, it is helpful to distinguish between the *causes* of war — or of a particular war — and the ostensible *reasons* for such wars. The former refers to the underlying factors that actually give rise to the war, the latter to the propagandistic excuses frequently enunciated by governments to justify their actions. We shall be primarily concerned in Part II with the causes of war, insofar as they can be identified. Then, in Part III, we shall be in a position to assess the practicality of the various suggestions for preventing war. Nonetheless, the task is daunting. Indeed, trying to specify the causes of war generally, or even just the causes of any one war, is

a bit like the famous story of the blind men and the elephant, as told by nineteenth-century American poet John Saxe,

> It was six men from Industan, to learning much inclined,
> who went to see the elephant (though all of them were blind),
> that each by observation might satisfy his mind . . .[1]

Not surprisingly, each one felt a different part of the elephant, so that the one touching the legs thought they were tree trunks, the one touching the tail thought it was a snake, and so on. And so, at the end, they

> disputed loud and long, each in his opinion stiff and strong,
> though each was partly in the right, and all of them were wrong.[2]

In reviewing the various proposed causes of war, we shall proceed from the most reductionistic interpretations to the most inclusive. Thus, we shall begin with an examination of war causation at the personal level (Chapter 6), move through a consideration of war among small groups of nontechnological people (Chapter 7), to the functioning of large, advanced units (that is, nationalism) and political states (Chapters 8 and 9, respectively), an examination of decision making by leaders (Chapter 10), the role of social and economic factors (Chapter 11), and finally, the special case of U.S.-Soviet relations (Chapter 12). Although we shall necessarily consider these explanations one at a time, let us try to avoid the blind men's blunder, by recognizing at the outset that war is a complex and integrated phenomenon that, to be understood, must be studied in its entirety, and with a hefty dose of humility.

Consider, for example, that someone has just died. We might ask, "Why did this happen? What was the cause of death?" And perhaps we are told, "He died of disease."

---

*In all fairness, this criticism applies more to students and others who support the ideal of peace than to the hard-working and, typically, equally hard-headed scholars who have long been toiling to create Peace Studies as a viable discipline.

"What kind of disease?" "Heart disease." "What was the nature of the heart disease?" "Hardening of the arteries leading to a massive stroke — that is, a coronary thrombosis." And if we then inquire, "What was the cause of that?" we will get any number of "answers": He had poor dietary habits, he had a genetic predisposition to high cholesterol levels, he didn't get regular medical care, he was under a great deal of stress, he smoked too much, he didn't get enough exercise, and so forth. One of these might be the major cause, but chances are, several of them, taken in combination, were ultimately responsible. The causes of war can be at least as complex as the causes of death.

We should also keep in mind the logician's distinction between "necessary" and "sufficient" conditions. Thus, for war to occur, it may be necessary for human beings to exist in societies, but it certainly is not sufficient — some human societies apparently have never known war. Similarly, it may be necessary for individuals to be motivated so as to participate in the preparations and conduct of war, but once again, this is not sufficient — people often get angry, but this does not necessarily mean that their country goes to war as a result. Moreover, wars often occur without very much personal anger being involved.

Every scholar of peace and war, it appears, has a different framework for understanding the causes of organized human violence. Peace researcher Quincy Wright, for example, identified four major factors: idealistic, psychological, political, and legalistic, arguing that

individuals and masses have been moved to war 1. because of enthusiasm for ideals expressed in the impersonal symbols of a religion, a nation, an empire, a civilization, or humanity, the blessings of which it is thought may be secured or spread by coercion of the recalcitrant [idealistic]; or 2. because of the hope to escape from conditions which they find unsatisfactory, inconvenient, perplexing, unprofitable, intolerable, dangerous, or merely boring [psychological]. Conditions of this kind have produced unrest and have facilitated the acceptance of ideals and violent methods for achieving them. Governments and organized factions have initiated war 3. because in a particular situation war appeared to them a necessary or convenient means to carry out a foreign policy, to establish, maintain, or expand the power of a government, party, or class within the state; to maintain or expand the power of the state in relation to other states; or to reorganize the community of nations [political]; or 4. because incidents have occurred or circumstances have arisen which they thought violated law and impaired rights and for which war was the normal or expected remedy according to the jural standards of the time [legalistic].[3]

Although there is mild disagreement as to the most useful way to categorize the causes of war, there is consensus that every war — just like every human being — must have progenitors. Efforts at identifying war-mongering culprits, as individuals rather than impersonal forces, have been especially frequent in the aftermath of every major war. One scholar described the chronology of such culprit-hunting as follows:

In the eighteenth century many philosophers thought that the ambitions of absolute monarchs were the main cause of war: pull down the mighty, and wars would become rare. Another theory contended that many wars came from the Anglo-French rivalry for colonies and commerce: restrain that quest, and peace would be more easily preserved. The wars following the French Revolution fostered an idea that popular revolutions were becoming the main cause of international war. In the nineteenth century, monarchs who sought to unite their troubled country by a glorious foreign war were widely seen as culprits. At the end of that century the capitalists' chase for markets or investment outlets became a popular villain. The First World War convinced many writers that armaments races and arms salesmen had become the villains, and both world wars fostered the idea that militarist regimes were the main disturbers of the peace.[4]

Similarly, the Vietnam War — to take just one example — was said to have been caused by the desire of United States' capitalists for markets and investment outlets, by the pressures for markets and investment outlets, by the pressures of American military suppliers, by the American hostility to communism, by the crusading ambitions of Moscow and Peking, the aggressive nationalism or communism of Hanoi, the corruption or aggression of Saigon, or the headlong clash of other aims.[5]

Clearly, for the Vietnam War — or for just about any other war — a host of different causes can be identified, many of which might be operating simultaneously, some of which may involve individuals, and others more frustrating and faceless considerations. In our yearning for Truth — which most people would like to be simple and unadorned — we tend to be dissatisfied with complex, multifactorial explanations. For example, it is tempting to say that the country initiating a war is the one that "started" it, and therefore, the one that "caused" it — that is, the culprit. But the real world is only rarely this simple. For example, England declared war on Napoleon's France in 1803, but this was at least in part because France had invaded Switzerland, to which England felt committed. When the United States "started" the War of 1812 with Britain, it was at least partly in response to the impressment of American sailors by British naval forces. (It was also in part because of U.S. imperialistic designs on British Canada.) And although nearly everyone agrees that Nazi Germany initiated World War II, the fact remains that Britain and France first declared war on Germany, not the other way around . . . but only after Germany invaded Poland in 1939.

Wars, in short, often result from preexisting provocations, so that the underlying causes of a war may lie fur-

ther back. And of course, those provocations are themselves the result of yet earlier causes; the German invasion of Poland was itself "caused" in part by Britain and France's earlier appeasement of Hitler, which convinced the German leader that aggression against Poland would go unpunished. Meanwhile, Hitler's aggressive and expansionist policies were also "caused," at least in part, not only by his own personal makeup but by German anger over the terms of the Treaty of Versailles, which ended World War I. And so it goes. The Western conception of causality requires that for every effect (including war), there must be a preexisting cause. It also suggests that this cause should be clear-cut, direct, and linear. Even if we grant the legitimacy of cause and effect,* however, there is no reason why "causes" — especially causes of something so complicated as war — should not be diffuse, indirect, curvilinear, and multifaceted. In short, war is at least as complex and potentially confusing as an elephant, with many dimensions and components.

But this is not to claim that a search for the cause (or causes) of war is a waste of time, even though the results can sometimes be misleading. Out of that search can come a deeper appreciation of the dilemma that is war. Moreover, our judgment as to the causes of war will have great influence on our preferred methods for preventing specific wars, and our hopes for eliminating war altogether.

---

*Something that can, in fact, be disputed, especially when it comes to complex social phenomena.

6

The Personal Level

Everything that is alive forms an atmosphere around itself.
  Wolfgang von Goethe

Wars require the organized activity of large numbers of people. But even the facts of complex organization and massive numbers do not eliminate the personal involvement and responsibility of individuals. To some degree, individual people acquiesce to war, prepare for it, and often participate in it, either passively (by permitting it to occur) or actively (by providing material assistance or actually doing the fighting). If people didn't allow, encourage, or engage in them, wars wouldn't happen. Hence, without denying the importance of other levels of causation — which we shall explore in subsequent chapters — our search for the causes of war might reasonably begin by looking to the inclinations and behavior of individual people. The preamble to the constitution of UNESCO states that "wars begin in the minds of men" (and, we must add, women as well, although to a lesser extent). It takes no great stretch of imagination to charge the human psyche with prime responsibility for the initiation of war. Former Senator J. William Fulbright emphasized the personal dimension of warmaking (and thus, war-preventing) when he wrote:

> The first, indispensable step toward the realization of a new concept of community in the world is the

acquisition of a new dimension of self-understanding. We have got to understand, as we have never understood before, why it is, psychologically and biologically, that men and nations fight; why it is, regardless of time or place or circumstance, that they always find *something* to fight about.[1]

When we concern ourselves with peace and war, we talk about the actions of large social units, often entire countries. But at least in part, when we say that a social unit "acts" in a particular way, what we really mean is that the people within those units act in such a manner. As one scholar has put it, we say that the state acts, often meaning that the people within it — more importantly, within the government — act, just as we say that a teapot boils when we really mean that the water in it boils.[2] It is the behavior of the water molecules that determines the "behavior" of the larger vessel; a similarly "molecular" approach looks for the causes of war at the personal level.

First, we shall examine four major perspectives on the causation of war at the personal level — instinct, sociobiology, Freudian psychiatry, and innate human depravity — that share an emphasis on the role of inborn, biological factors. Then, after considering some criticisms of these "human nature" approaches, we shall consider a variety of other factors operating at the personal level, all of which involve greater attention to the role of learning and other social experiences. In succeeding chapters, we take up the question of causation at increasingly broader levels.

INSTINCT

Many thinkers have assumed that human beings are instinctively aggressive. A particularly influential version of instinctivist theory has developed around presumed biological traits of the human species. Thus, one of the most influential U.S. textbooks on international relations begins as follows: "The drives to live, to propagate, and to dominate are common to all men."[3] According to such notions, human warfare can be traced to our evolutionary heritage, attributable directly to genetic mechanisms, including tendencies to form dominance

hierarchies, to defend territories, and to behave aggressively toward others. Much emphasis is placed on the existence of comparable behavior patterns among certain animals, and the presumption that the behavior of animals reflects underlying principles that hold for the human species as well.

The Lorenzian Approach

Perhaps the most influential exponent of this perspective was the Nobel Prize–winning Austrian ethologist (student of the biology of animal behavior) Konrad Z. Lorenz. Lorenz helped conceptualize a view of instinctive behavior according to which animals are endowed with certain behaviors, called "fixed action patterns," whose actual physical performance is genetically fixed and unvarying from one individual to another. Over time, a kind of behavioral energy accumulates, which is discharged when an appropriate stimulus is presented. Or alternatively, it may "overflow" even without any environmental cues being present, simply because the accumulation of unspent energy creates a need to perform the behavior in question. In his book *On Aggression*, Lorenz argued that certain species-preserving aspects of aggression applied to human beings as well; they include the following:

1. Providing an opportunity for competition within a species, after which the most fit will emerge to produce the next generation.

2. Achieving spacing and population control, to minimize the disadvantages of overpopulation.

3. Establishing a means whereby the pair bond can be strengthened, as by shared aggression of a mated pair against competitors.

It should be emphasized that Lorenz was not concerned with extolling human aggression, but with understanding it. He noted that in moderate amounts, aggression may well be functional and healthy, but at the same time, he deplored its occurrence in excess, especially when combined with what he called "militant enthusiasm," the tendency of people to lose their normal inhibitions against violence when united with others similarly motivated. Lorenz also pointed out that animals such as

Konrad Z. Lorenz, founder of the modern science of ethology and a major proponent of the view that human aggressive behavior is largely instinctive. (*The Bettmann Archive*)

wolves or hawks — which have lethal natural weapons — also tend to possess innate inhibitions against employing these weapons against members of the same species. By contrast, animals such as rabbits, doves, or human beings — not naturally equipped with lethal weapons — lack such inhibitions. According to this line of thought, the human situation is especially perilous because, while we have developed the ability, by technological means, to kill our fellow human, quickly, easily, and in great numbers, our biological evolution remains far behind, so we continue to lack genetically based mechanisms to keep our new-found lethality in check.

The Lorenzian approach, seeking to "extrapolate war from human instinct," is in some ways a caricature of biological (ethological) views. According to what we might call the "classical ethological" approach, aggression is genetically controlled behavior, such that the actual behavior patterns are rigidly stereotyped, invariant, and independent of learning. Aggression can also emerge spontaneously; that is, individuals have a *need* to discharge this instinct by behaving aggressively.

Lorenz suggests that one way to deal with our instinctive penchant for uninhibited aggression and militant enthusiasm is by rechanneling this biological energy into socially useful (or at least nondestructive) forms of competition, such as athletics, the space race, or medical research. Nonetheless, Lorenz is pessimistic in assessing the human future:

> An unprejudiced observer from another planet, looking down on man as he is today, in his hand the atom bomb, the product of his intelligence, in his heart the aggressive drive inherited from his anthropoid ancestors, which this same intelligence cannot control, would not prophesy long life for the species.[4]

Other members of the "war in our genes" school have also contributed to the instinctivist approach. "Was my response to Pearl Harbor innate or conditioned?" asked the writer Robert Ardrey.

> Was it something I had been born with or something I had been taught? Was it truly a command of genetic origin, an inheritance from the experience and natural selection of thousands of generations of my human and hominid ancestors?[5]

In this book and in his earlier *African Genesis*, Ardrey clearly associates himself with the Lorenzian view, arguing that since human beings evolved from anthropoid apes that hunted at least occasionally, and were probably at least somewhat carnivorous, then we must be genetically aggressive as well.

Is War in Our Genes?

Although biology may well carry valuable insights for the current human condition, such simplistic extrapolations from animal to human can also be dangerously misleading. For example, it is no more valid to argue that human beings are "naturally" murderous because baboons sometimes kill other baboons, than it is to conclude that human beings

Relaxed social scene among chimpanzees at the Gombe Stream Reserve in Tanzania. Although chimps — and other nonhuman primates such as baboons — sometimes engage in aggressive behavior, they also spend much of their time in highly affiliative, prosocial interactions. (Hank Klein)

are naturally vegetarians because gorillas exclusively eat plants, or that humans can fly because birds have wings.

There is also a danger that by accepting war as part of "human nature," we justify war itself, in part by diminishing our own human responsibility to behave more peacefully. If war is "in our genes," then presumably, we cannot act otherwise, so we should not be blamed for what we do; maybe, in fact, we shouldn't even bother trying to do anything about it. At minimum — and perhaps, at its most pernicious — such biological fatalism supports a pessimistic perspective on the human condition, one that provides an excuse for the maintenance of large military forces and leads to profound distrust of others. There is, indeed, evidence that people who are generally right-wing and promilitary tend disproportionately to be believers in the doctrine that war is somehow etched in our genes.

Accordingly, in 1986, a group of prominent behavioral scientists from twelve nations met in Seville, Spain, and agreed on the "Seville Statement," which has since been endorsed by the American Psychological Association and the American An-

thropological Association, among others. Some excerpts from this statement are as follows:

- It is scientifically incorrect to say that we have inherited a tendency to make war from our animal ancestors. Warfare is a peculiarly human phenomenon and does not occur in other animals. War is biologically possible, but it is not inevitable, as evidenced by its variation in occurrence and nature over time and space.

- It is scientifically incorrect to say that war or any other violent behavior is genetically programmed into our human nature. Except for rare pathologies the genes do not produce individuals necessarily predisposed to violence. Neither do they determine the opposite.

- It is scientifically incorrect to say that in the course of human evolution there has been a selection for aggressive behavior more than for other kinds of behavior. In all well-studied species, status within the group is achieved by the ability to cooperate and to fulfill social functions relevant to the structure of that group.

- It is scientifically incorrect to say that humans have a "violent brain." While we do have a neural apparatus to act violently, there is nothing in our neurophysiology that compels us to.

- It is scientifically incorrect to say that war is caused by "instinct" or any single motivation. The technology of modern war has exaggerated traits associated with violence both in the training of actual combatants and in the preparation of support for war in the general population.

- We conclude that biology does not condemn humanity to war, and that humanity can be freed from the bondage of biological pessimism. Violence is neither in our evolutionary legacy nor in our genes. The same species . . . [that] invented war is capable of inventing peace.

SOCIOBIOLOGY

A more sophisticated version of instinctivism is associated with the new scientific discipline of sociobiology, whose best-known practitioner has been the zoologist Edward O. Wilson. The sociobiological approach differs from instinctivism in that it places new emphasis on evolution as a process rather than a historical event. That is, sociobiologists are particularly concerned with the *adaptive significance* of behavior, the way in which particular behavior patterns are maintained and promoted in a population because they contribute to the reproductive success of individuals (not species) that possess these traits.

A sociobiological view of human war examines such phenomena as ecological competition (for food, nesting sites, and so on), male–male competition, and the role of kinship patterns in directing aggressive behavior in particular ways. Among many species, for example, males tend to be larger, showier, and more aggressive than females. In addition, biological differences between males and females mean, among other things, that one male can successfully fertilize many females. Sexual differences of this sort, in turn, convey a reproductive

pay-off (enhanced evolutionary fitness) to individuals — especially males — who succeed in defeating their rivals, whether in symbolic displays or outright combat. Consistent with this theory, men are significantly more aggressive than women, and much more likely to be involved in violence of all sorts, including war.

Another important tenet of sociobiological theory is the role of genetic relatedness: Individuals who share genes probably will behave benevolently (altruistically) toward one another, because such behavior tends to contribute to the success of genes predisposing toward such behavior; conversely, a low probability of genetic relatedness will be associated with aggressiveness. Consistent with this theory, appeals to patriotism often involve what anthropologists term "fictive kinship," calling upon citizens to stand up for "motherland," "fatherland," "Uncle Sam," "brothers and sisters," and so forth.

As for competition, it can be defined as "the active demand by two or more individuals . . . for a common resource or requirement that is actually or potentially limiting."[6] Many studies have pointed to the role of primitive war in gaining access to mates, animal protein, and social prestige, such that warfare among nontechnological peoples, which in the past appeared to be irrational and nonadaptive, is now increasingly seen to possess an internal logic of its own . . . although, to be sure, not necessarily a logic that is consciously appreciated by the participants.

Sociobiologists tend to back away from the simplistic "either/or" dichotomy of instinctivism. It is misleading to ask, as Robert Ardrey did in the selection quoted earlier, whether a given behavior is instinctive or learned, since all behavior is considered to result from the interaction of genetic potential and experience, or nature and nurture. "In order to be adaptive," writes E. O. Wilson,

> it is enough that aggressive patterns be evoked only under certain conditions of stress such as those that might arise during food shortages and periodic high population densities. It also does not matter whether the aggression is wholly innate or is acquired part or wholly by learning. We are now sophisticated enough to know that the capacity to

learn certain behaviors is itself a genetically controlled and therefore evolved trait.[7]

Finally, another important evolutionary perspective, represented notably by anthropologist
Robert Bigelow, considers war to have had a prominent role in the early evolution of the human species. Human brain size, for example, has more than
tripled in one million years of evolution. Conceivably, proto-human warrior bands were a major selective force in our own early evolution, with
successful bands killing off those that were less successful. Large brains could well have contributed to
success in lethal intergroup conflicts — that is,
primitive war — by promoting relatively sophisticated communication, formation of social alliances,
and effective use of weapons. Those enjoying such
success would presumably have left more descendants, who in turn would be likely to possess these
favored traits and capacities. If so, then the early
stages of war itself, over evolutionary time, would
have contributed to our large brains, and thus to
the fundamental nature of *Homo sapiens*.

FREUDIAN PSYCHIATRY

Sigmund Freud was in many ways the founder of
modern psychiatry, and is particularly noteworthy
for his emphasis on the role of the unconscious in
human behavior. Freud himself was a pacifist, and
he especially deplored what he saw as a vicious,
lethal streak among human beings. Freud interpreted much of humanity's more "inhumane" behavior to the operation of "Thanatos," or the death
instinct, which, in his view, was opposed to "Eros,"
the life instinct. In a famous letter to Albert Einstein, he noted, "We are led to conclude that this
[death] instinct functions in every living being,
striving to work its ruin and to reduce life to its
primal state of inert matter."[8] Freud maintained that
both Eros and Thanatos are manifestations of the
"pleasure principle," a more fundamental drive that
inclines people to minimize pain, whether through
death (Thanatos) or the intensification of life and
love (Eros). When Thanatos is thwarted by Eros,
its energy is displaced outward onto subjects other

Sigmund Freud, the father of psychoanalysis and one of the
premier students of the human subconscious. (National Library of
Medicine)

than oneself, resulting in aggression between individuals or among groups.

Although Freud subsequently revised his conception of the death instinct, it remains associated
with his thought. But Freud also argued that, regardless of whether Thanatos exists within the human psyche or whether we are simply aggressive by
nature, civilization demands that people repress
their primitive tendencies toward destructive and
aggressive behavior if they are to live together
peacefully. Parents must provide discipline for their
children, society must restrict its citizens, and ultimately, some form of supranational authority will be
necessary to enforce a system of world government
over individual states that would otherwise function anarchically. Hence, civilization demands
repression, which in turn necessarily produces discontent (and neurosis) among its populace.

Another important Freudian concept especially relevant to war is that of "narcissistic injury";

narcissism involves infatuation with oneself and, in moderation, is considered a normal stage in personality development.* When the individual associates him- or herself with a larger group (see Chapters 7 and 8), including the nation-state, slights or injuries to the group are easily interpreted as injuries to oneself. The resulting "narcissistic rage" involves an unrelenting compulsion to undo the hurt; in the pursuit of this vengeful "justice," great violence may be self-righteously employed. Some of the most destructive wars have been perpetrated by people seeking to reconnect territory that has been separated (for example, the French yearning to recapture the provinces of Alsace and Lorraine, captured by Germany in the Franco-Prussian War, or the Vietcong and North Vietnamese, who sought in the Vietnam War to reunite their country), or to achieve such separation, when governments have forced an unnatural connection (as in various wars of secession, such as in Nigeria or Ethiopia). In addition, insults to the flag or other aspects of national pride can evoke violent responses, because of the narcissistic injury they inflict.

Like the Lorenzian and (to a lesser extent) the sociobiological approaches, the Freudian perspective is pessimistic. Thus, Freud maintained that we really shouldn't be so disillusioned about atrocities during wartime, because the notion that humankind was fundamentally civilized is itself illusory: "In reality our fellow citizens have not sunk so low as we have feared because they have never risen so high as we have believed."

INNATE DEPRAVITY, NASTINESS, AND EVIL

Some thoughtful people have long maintained that human beings are innately depraved, nasty, and evil, basing this claim on a loosely connected blend of biology and moral outrage. Looking over the

bloodletting of the English civil war (1642–1649), Thomas Hobbes concluded that there was "a general inclination of all mankind, a perpetual and restless desire for power after power that ceaseth only in death."[9] To some extent, Hobbes's pessimism can be traced to a biblical — especially Christian — tradition which teaches that human nature is inherently flawed. Suffused with original sin, we are inherently incapable of becoming good until we are eventually reunited with God in heaven. Consider these sentiments from the sixteenth-century theologian John Calvin, perhaps the most influential advocate of this perspective:

> Even infants themselves, as they bring their condemnation into the world with them, are rendered subject to punishment of their own sinfulness. . . . For though they have not yet produced the fruits of their iniquity, yet they have had the seed of it in them. Their whole nature is, as it were, a seed of sin and therefore cannot but be odious and abominable to God.[10]

Because of our innate human sinfulness, we were cast out of the Garden of Eden, doomed to death. We deserve — indeed, we are required — to be treated sternly and punished vigorously. Some students of human behavior have concluded that much human misery, including even the penchant for war itself, derives in part from the consequences of being mistreated as children.[11] It is further argued that many acts of violence toward children — whether overt, such as beatings or sexual abuse, or more subtle, such as criticism and belittling — have in turn been buttressed by this view that human beings are inherently sinful. In any event, according to the pessimistic Christian perspective, a true state of personal peace can only be achieved by grace, just as a state of political peace requires the Second Coming of Christ. Until then, war is inevitable. As we have seen, Machiavelli had based his political philosophy on a similar assumption, although without the theological underpinnings.

This attitude is not limited to fundamentalist Christians, however. Another approach, rarely articulated but widely held, views human beings as having not only a capacity for violence, but also a

---

*According to Greek mythology, Narcissus was a youth who fell in love with his own image, and was eventually transformed into the flower that bears his name, condemned to look eternally at his own reflection in a pond.

deep-seated love of bloodletting and carnage. In his letter to Albert Einstein, Sigmund Freud observed that "man has within him a lust for hatred and destruction. . . . It is a comparatively easy task to call this into play and raise it to the level of a collective psychosis."[12] And in the seventeenth century, John Milton wrote that, even if our species were rendered somehow impervious to injury from all outside forces,

> yet the perverseness of our folly is so bent, that we should never cease hammering out of our own hearts, as it were out of a flint, the seeds and sparkles of new misery to ourselves, till all were in a blaze again.[13]

War is an evil unique to humanity because human beings are considered to be uniquely the root of all evil, especially by philosophically inclined theologians such as Luther, Saint Augustine, John Calvin, and Reinhold Niebuhr, as well as religiously motivated political leaders such as Oliver Cromwell or satirists such as Jonathan Swift. In "A Tale of a Tub," Swift wrote that "the very same principle that influences a bully to break the windows of a whore who has jilted him, naturally stirs up a great prince to raise mighty armies, and dream of nothing but sieges, battles and victories."[14] And nearly three hundred years later, Reinhold Niebuhr argued that it was the "sinful character of man" that necessitated "the balancing of power with power."[15] Others, notably the philosopher Spinoza, locate the evils of human violence in the fact that our rational faculties are regularly overwhelmed by our irrational and untamed emotions.

This is only a very limited sampling of a widespread notion. Although it is difficult (perhaps impossible) to prove, the idea of innate human weakness and depravity remains very popular, especially among the lay public, as well as among those who are sympathetic to military force, often including war itself. Thus, if human nature is inherently nasty and bloodthirsty, then we can never have any confidence in morality, or law, or anything else to deliver us from war, since these are only rather frail, artificial institutions constructed by

fundamentally flawed human beings. Because human nature presumably cannot be changed, the only recourse — albeit a regrettable one — is to arms.

CRITICISMS OF "HUMAN NATURE" THEORIES

The various "human nature" theories on the causes of war all contain flaws. For example, human beings undoubtedly have the biological capacity to kill one another . . . given that they have often done so. The danger is that such a broad generalization may be useless when analyzing the past or predicting the future. Other, more specific flaws in these theories exist as well. For example, consider the following:

1. Although war is a widespread human trait, it is not a universal one; certain cultures, such as the Tasaday of the Philippine Islands, the South African bushmen (or San), and the Eskimo, apparently never engaged in war. Explanations based on human nature should apply to them no less than to others. Although some societies are clearly more war-prone than others, no evidence whatsoever indicates that such warlike tendencies reflect inherent differences in human nature.

2. Even among war-prone cultures, there have been many years of peace; if human nature caused World War II or the Vietnam War, then what about the peace that preceded and followed these wars? If human nature causes war, then it must also cause peace; consider the neutrality of Sweden, the demilitarized U.S.-Canadian border, Gandhi's nonviolence. Any explanation that is so broad becomes useless; to paraphrase a military metaphor of Carl von Clausewitz, he who seeks to explain everything, explains nothing.*

3. Even within war-prone cultures, there have been war-resisters, peace advocates, and the

---

*Clausewitz used the word *defend* instead of *explain*.

Eskimo children in Nome, Alaska. Although Eskimos sometimes are individually violent, war as a social institution is unknown to them. (Thomas Burke Memorial Washington State Museum)

maintenance of long-time nonviolent traditions by groups such as the Mennonites and the Quakers; are they less human, or less natural, than their more violent fellow citizens?

4. The fact that animals behave in certain ways does not necessarily mean that human beings do so; we are unique in possessing language as well as the capacity for complex, abstract, and symbolic thought, which gives us the opportunity to reason, to analyze, and to rise above our unpleasant or dangerous inclinations. (Of course, the fact that we have the ability to do something does not in itself guarantee that we do so.)

5. If war is a result of human nature, then it is predestined and unavoidable, since we cannot — by definition — behave counter to our own nature. The belief that war is inevitable is particularly dangerous because it is likely to discourage people from seeking to end war and to promote peace. Moreover, it can serve to *justify* war by making it appear somehow "good," because it is natural.

The above criticisms are all valid to a degree, especially when applied to naive or crude instinctivism. But they also oversimplify the more sophisticated "human nature" arguments. Thus, most biologically inclined theorists recognize that genetic factors do not irrevocably commit a person, or a society, to a given course of action. Rather, they create predispositions for behaving aggressively or violently when circumstances are appropriate; similarly, nothing in biological thought suggests that such predispositions could not be overridden by religious beliefs, historical circumstances, and so on. There is nothing inconsistent about suggesting that human beings can say "No" to their genes.

Analogy and Homology

With regard to the relevance of animal studies, a distinction should be made between *analogy* and *homology*. Analogy refers to a superficial similarity. For example, the wings of a bird and the wings of a butterfly are analogous, but not homologous: They derive from entirely different structures in terms of their evolutionary history, embryological development, and anatomy. By contrast, the wings of a bird and the wings of a bat are homologous, because they derive from a similar evolutionary past and even involve modification of the same muscles and bones.* For our purposes, the point is that animal studies — interesting though they may be — do not

---

*They are analogous as well, since bat and bird wings both assist in flying. It is also possible for characteristics to be homologous but not analogous, as, for example, the wings of a bird and the forelegs of a horse.

necessarily offer any meaningful insight into the human condition if the behaviors in question are merely analogous. The fact that ants make "war" may tell us virtually nothing about war among *Homo sapiens*. On the other hand, if such underlying principles as ecological and sexual competition or the genetics of altruism are homologous, then animal studies could point out useful principles that might be operating among human beings as well. Here, one compromise appears worthwhile: to rule out the two extremes. Thus, we can reject the following arguments: (1) "People are just like other animals; if animal *x* does something, human beings must therefore do the same"; and (2) "People are entirely different from animals. What we know about the latter cannot tell us anything at all about the former."

Human Nature and Genetic Determinism

There is also a great difference between a possible genetic *influence* and a doctrine of genetic *determinism*. The former implies the existence of tendencies, likely to be subtle and capable of being overridden, whereas the latter implies rigid, iron-clad automatic responses. There may well be genetic influences that human beings, if they are to be peaceful, must overcome; this is not to say that our genes predetermine our behavior, condemning us to violence. As to morality, advocates—and critics—of biologically based arguments should be wary of what the philosopher David Hume called the "naturalistic fallacy," the mistaken belief that "*is* implies *ought*." In other words, whatever insights biological sciences might provide into the workings of the natural world, these are distinct from ethical guidelines as to what is good. Typhoid is natural; this does not mean that it is good. War may or may not be natural; whether it is good is an entirely different question. In any event, if typhoid, or war, is to be cured or prevented, we must understand its causation, whether or not we are pleased by what we find.

There can, nonetheless, be real dangers in adhering too strongly to an instinctivist model of human warfare, especially if it counsels that we must await substantial changes in human nature. The problem is that human nature changes only as a result of the evolutionary process, which is necessarily very slow. Accordingly, whether or not instinctivism yields insight into the human condition, we must look toward other, more active interventions if we are to effect any meaningful changes.

FRUSTRATION

Among explanations for war that do not depend upon explicit assumptions about human nature, one of the most influential has been the frustration–aggression hypothesis, which seeks to explain individual aggressiveness as well. According to this theory, first proposed by the psychiatrist John Dollard and his colleagues, aggressiveness is produced by frustration, which in turn is defined as "an interference with the occurrence of an instigated goal-response at its proper time in the behavior sequence."[16] Thus, if a hungry rat is presented with food, after which a glass wall is interposed between the animal and its desire, the rat is likely to become aggressive. A similar phenomenon occurs with frustrated human beings, people who have been unsuccessfully seeking something—food, political freedoms, access to a disputed territory, union with others who practice the same customs—or who have obtained partial success only to be prevented from achieving their ultimate goals.

In its early statement, frustration theory was presented rather dogmatically (if not aggressively): "The occurrence of aggressive behavior always presupposes the existence of frustration, and contrariwise, the existence of frustration always leads to some form of aggression."[17] This rigidity of thought led to problems comparable to those encountered with certain human nature theories: The argument can become circular if all cases of aggression are defined as requiring preexisting frustration, and vice versa if any behavior that follows frustration is defined to be aggression.

Frustration theory has subsequently been modified to recognize that frustration creates a predisposition or readiness for aggression, by producing an intervening emotional state: anger. In addition, environmental stimuli—targets and/or cues—are necessary for aggression to be produced. And finally, an individual's learning experiences and society's expectations are recognized to exert a powerful influence on the connection between frustration and aggression. Of course, other responses to frustration are also possible, namely, submission, resignation, alienation, withdrawal, avoidance, or even acceptance, but this does not in itself argue against the potency of the frustration–aggression link.

Frustration can also result in resentment, which (like the above responses) may or may not subsequently produce aggressive behavior. Frustration may be especially high when a discrepancy exists between expectations and realities; bad conditions, such as poverty or political repression, are made even worse by high expectations that conflict with unpleasant realities. Accordingly, the "revolution of rising expectations," particularly in the Third World, has been associated with frustration and violence.[18] Authorities often respond with increased repression, but the forceful repression of strongly felt needs (such as the yearning of Palestinians for self-determination, and before that, of Zionists for a Jewish state) can in itself be highly frustrating, and thereby ultimately increase hostility and aggression. In some cases, frustration finds its outlet in aggressive behavior against others who are not actually the frustrating agent. For example, the frequency of lynchings and tribal violence by blacks against other blacks in the Republic of South Africa have increased dramatically in recent years, at least partly in response to frustration with the white minority government, which remained racist, repressive, and recalcitrant, while also being militarily and economically powerful enough (at least thus far) to frustrate black ambitions for self-determination.

There is another possible twist to the connection between frustration and war, namely, boredom. It has been suggested that war is especially appealing to those whose lives are lacking in excitement and interest. "The absence of delight in daily living," writes one notable authority, "has helped to leave many lives empty and sterile and so, fair game

for any excitement, including the most terrific of worldly excitements, that of war."[19] Furthermore, once a society has elevated military values, trained men and boys (rarely women and girls) to be warriors, and institutionalized and mythologized the war experience, people may be especially prone to being frustrated and bored with peace. Of course, warfare itself actually involves prolonged periods of boredom and monotony: The endless repetition, drill, and "hurry up and wait" that characterize military routine are hardly antidotes for civilian ennui. Military boredom may lead, however, to frustration, which in turn leads to greater willingness to go to war, if only to "see action" and thereby finally break the monotony.

SOCIAL LEARNING

Clearly, human beings are very strongly influenced by their experiences—those that occur early in development and those that characterize later socialization—as well as society's norms and expectations. Most psychologists and sociologists maintain that human violence arises in response to experiences, rather than bubbling up out of our genetic constitution. "The important fact," writes psychologist John Paul Scott, "is that the chain of causation in every case eventually traces back to the outside. There is no physiological evidence of any spontaneous stimulation for fighting arising within the body."[20] Scott has emphasized that individuals are particularly likely to fight if they have fought successfully in the past, and that aggression often results from a breakdown in social structures. (It is also noteworthy, on the other hand, that some of the most aggressive societies have been highly structured: Nazi Germany, Fascist Italy, Napoleonic France.)

Conditioning

One of the most important developments in twentieth-century psychology revolves around the learning phenomenon known as "conditioning," associated especially with the work of B. F. Skinner. The basic idea is that behavior will be influenced by its consequences for the individual. Thus, certain behaviors tend to be "reinforcing"; that is, they make it more likely that the individual will repeat the previous behavior.* Some authorities employ the phrase "instrumental aggression" to refer to aggressive behavior that is oriented primarily toward attaining some goal, such as winning a war or recovering territory, rather than causing injury as such.

In any event, conditioning theory applied to human aggressiveness suggests that people will behave aggressively when such behavior leads to reinforcing (that is, positive) results, and that, conversely, the likelihood of aggression will be reduced if it leads to negative results. By extrapolation, members of whole societies presumably can be influenced similarly, making war more probable if their previous behavior has been positively reinforced (rewarded) and less probable if it has been negatively reinforced (punished). For example, the international aggressiveness of Nazi Germany was positively reinforced during most of the 1930s by the appeasement policies of the West; by contrast, it can be argued that a taste for international adventuring on the part of the United States was negatively reinforced by its divisive and ultimately unsuccessful experience in Southeast Asia (the so-called Vietnam syndrome). Generally, such actions affect different groups of society in different ways; in the case of the Vietnam syndrome, however, negative reinforcement seems to have been about equally shared by the American people and by many (perhaps most) government leaders. Insofar as this argument is valid, however, it might suggest concern about the most recent trend of U.S. armed incursions: in Libya, Grenada, and Panama.

---

*In layperson's language, we say that the behavior is somehow "rewarding," since it provides something that the individual appears to find gratifying, such as food, rest, or sex. However, most psychologists shy away from such language, emphasizing the more objective effects on behavior rather than subjective experiences.

Socialization to Aggressiveness

Some societies actively encourage aggressiveness from early childhood. For example, consider the Fulani people of northern Nigeria, among whom males seek to embody the ideals of "aggressive dominance." As young boys, they are taught to beat their cattle to prevent them from wandering off, and to fight back unhesitatingly whenever they have been attacked. If they refrain from retaliating, they are mocked as cowards. They show virtually no emotion when struck with sticks during increasingly serious fights, and by the time they are young men, they are proud of their battle scars. Not surprisingly, they are also prone to personal fighting as well as warfare.[21]

An influential American social psychologist summed up the dominant view more than a generation ago when he wrote that "Men [and, we must add, women] not only learn when it is best to fight or not to fight, whom to fight and whom to appease, how to fight and how not to; but they also learn whom, when and how to hate."[22] He went on to discuss the phenomenon of social learning for group aggressiveness:

> Learning to fight and to hate involves much more than learning to box, to duel, or to participate in other forms of group violence. Systematic education for aggressive warfare in ancient Sparta or in modern Germany [note: this was written in 1943] includes, besides physical education in games and contests, universal compulsory military training; the inculcation of certain attitudes, prejudices, beliefs; and devotion to leaders and ideals. The whole purpose and direction of such education is toward group aggression.[23]

Similar processes of socialization can also produce a group characterized by peace rather than aggression. In such a group,

> there is the minimum amount of physical violence among the members. Antagonism, hostilities, and conflicts are held in check by customs, laws and rules which are enforced in part by duly constituted authorities and in part by inner compulsions of loyalties and the sense of social responsibility. Peace

between groups as well as within a group is maintained by the joint action of external authority and social attitudes of tolerance and good will.[24]

Also important in this context is the phenomenon of "imitative learning," whereby individuals are especially prone to do something if they witness others doing the same thing. Thus, aggressiveness and hostility — or alternatively, an inclination to settle disputes peacefully — can become part of the ethos of a society.

Self-Fulfilling Behaviors

An important sociological concept is the "self-fulfilling prophecy," according to which a belief becomes true if people believe that it is true. In the realm of aggressive behavior, hostility begets hostility on the part of others, which in turn not only reinforces the initial hostility but also intensifies it. People create their own interpersonal environments simply by behaving with a certain expectation: If someone is suspicious, secretive, and blameful, he or she is likely to elicit comparable behavior. This pattern has the makings of a "paranoid cycle," in which hostility becomes self-reinforcing. A similar pattern might apply to international relations as well. For example, if country A, convinced of the hostility of country B, increases its armaments, then country B may well respond in kind. This, in turn, reinforces the "enemy image" already present, leading to yet further militarily oriented actions, each of which may truly be intended to be "defensive," but which, taken as a whole, diminish the security of all participants. As we shall see, such a process characterizes much of the history of arms races.

Redirected Aggression

Other patterns in behavioral development also take place, often without the explicit intent of producing aggressiveness. In James Joyce's short story "Counterparts" we meet a man who is browbeaten by his boss, and who then stops at a pub after work and is defeated at arm-wrestling, after which he finally

goes home . . . and beats up his young son. This phenomenon is known as "displaced" or "redirected" aggression, wherein anger — often generated by other sources — is displaced or redirected to different targets. Biblical tradition describes how the ancient Israelites would designate one animal as a "scapegoat," which would be abused and driven from the herd, taking with it the sins (and angers) of those who remained behind, uninjured.* Frequently, the victims of redirected aggression are smaller or weaker, or already the objects of social abuse: a religious or racial minority, advocates of unpopular political doctrines, and so on. Blacks, communists in the United States, Arab immigrants in France, Christian Evangelicals in the Soviet Union, all have borne the brunt of redirected aggression by people who have themselves been deprived or disadvantaged. Although local minorities provide convenient "targets of opportunity," foreign nations especially lend themselves as objects of redirected group anger, predisposing toward war.

The "Authoritarian Personality"

Following World War II, and the Holocaust in which 6 million of Europe's Jews were murdered, a group of researchers sought to identify those personal traits and experiences that predispose people toward anti-Semitism. Their work resulted in the so-called F-scale (for fascist), which gave a crude measure of tendency toward authoritarianism. The "authoritarian personality" was found to be correlated with a view of the family in rigidly hierarchical terms: the husband dominant over the wife, and parents demanding unquestioned obedience and respect from their children and partaking of moralistic and disciplinarian styles of child rearing. This was combined with a strongly nationalistic

---

*Ironically, Jews — perhaps more than any other people — have in historical times served as scapegoats for other cultures.

outlook, ready submission to powerful external authority, and fear of weakness and of moral contamination. The resulting "autocratic personality structure" often engenders an autocratic, xenophobic, and militaristic approach to both social problems and foreign relations.[25] Such people often have a relatively poor self-image, which makes them especially prone to following orders blindly, even if these orders involve inflicting injury on oneself or others, and even if the behaviors involved go counter to fundamental precepts of morality that (in a nonmilitary context) are also part of a traditional upbringing.

Closely connected is the psychiatric concept of "identification with the aggressor," in which the victim tends to adopt the attributes of a powerful punishing agent (parent, government) in order to alleviate anxiety; in the process, the victim is transformed into an aggressor, either directly or indirectly by supporting aggression on the part of others. Perhaps significantly, permissive societies seem to be less warlike than those that have high levels of physical punishment of children and of sexual repression.

Alienation and Totalism

Psychoanalysts Erich Fromm and Erik Erikson have focused on the role of painful experience operating through nonrational psychic processes. Fromm distinguishes between "defensive aggression" and "malignant aggression," with the latter involving a passionate drive to hurt others (sadism) or oneself (masochism).[26] But unlike the "human nature" theorists, he attributes malignant aggression to social conditions rather than to innate human traits. In particular, Fromm blames "alienation," a terrible loneliness and sense of disconnectedness from others. Alienated people and alienated groups are inclined to avenge their pain by acts of godlike destruction; they are also ripe candidates for inclusion in violent organizations where they can lose themselves in a group united by hatred of others. This might include the Ku Klux Klan and other neo-nazis in the United States and "skinheads" in Great Britain, as well as other terrorist and hate

groups worldwide. Such factors could also influence the behavior of mainstream political groups and their leadership, although with less intensity and a better-hidden, more subtle pathology.

In a similar vein, Erik Erikson has pointed out that, especially when it is changing rapidly, society generates ambiguities and unresolved stresses that combine with the individual's developmental problems to produce "totalism," or a susceptibility to all-or-nothing simplifications: us versus them, good versus evil, God versus the devil.[27] Given the sacrifices that war demands—not only economic and political but also personal, as in the willingness to sacrifice one's life and to go against the standard societal prohibition against taking another's life—it is not surprising that totalistic thinking and war should go hand in hand.

THE ATTRACTION OF WAR

In his novel *Notes from Underground*, Dostoyevsky wrote that "In former days we saw justice in bloodshed and with our conscience at peace exterminated those we thought proper to kill. Now we do think bloodshed abominable and yet we engage in this abomination, and with more energy than ever."[28] This energy derives at least in part from the fact that some people find war a positive experience. Many have extolled the sheer intensity of confronting the basic phenomena of life and death, and in the process, exploring the boundaries of one's capacities. There is something exhilarating about meeting death face to face, perhaps even heroically and for a noble cause, rather than being overtaken alone in the night. Teilhard de Chardin (who served in World War I), wrote:

> The front cannot but attract us, because it is, in one way, the extreme boundary between what you are already aware of, and what is still in the process of formation. Not only do you see there things that you experience nowhere else, but you also see emerge from within yourself an underlying stream of clarity, energy, and freedom that is to be found hardly anywhere else in ordinary life. . . . This exaltation is accompanied by a certain pain. Nonetheless it is indeed an exaltation. And that is why one likes the front in spite of everything, and misses it.[29]

For others, there is a compelling sexual component, as revealed in this passage from Norman Mailer:

> All the deep, dark urges of man, the sacrifices on the hilltops, the churning lusts of night and sleep, weren't all of them contained in the shattering, screaming burst of a shell? The phallus-like shell that rides through a shining vagina of steel. The curve of sexual excitement and discharge, which is, after all, the physical core of life.[30]

And most significant of all, perhaps, is the satisfaction of "belonging" and the companionship, particularly a kind of male bonding that most men do not experience during civilian life. Shakespeare's Henry V rhapsodizes about the pleasure the forthcoming battle holds for

> We few, we happy few, we band of brothers;
> For he to-day that sheds his blood with me
> shall be my brother.

Or consider this commentary, from a combat veteran of World War II:

> We are liberated from our individual impotence and are drunk with the power that union with our fellows brings. In moments like these many have a vague awareness of how isolated and separate their lives have hitherto been. . . . With the boundaries of the self expanded, they sense a kinship never known before. Their "I" passes insensibly into a "we." . . . At its height, this sense of comradeship is an ecstasy.[31]

The American philosopher William James (1842–1910) believed that the raw emotional appeal of war constituted one of the greatest difficulties in overcoming it. In his renowned essay "The Moral Equivalent of War," James argued the case for war's attractiveness:

> The war against war is going to be no holiday excursion or camping party. The military feelings are too deeply grounded to abdicate their place among our ideals until better substitutes are offered that the glory and shame that come to nations as well as to individuals from the ups and downs of politics and the vicissitudes of trade. . . . Modern war is so expensive that we felt trade to be a better avenue to plunder, but modern man inherits all the innate

A wounded rifleman being helped to an aid station by one of his buddies during the Korean War. For all its horror, war fosters a companionship that many men find deeply rewarding. (United Nations / Army photo)

> pugnacity and all the love of glory of his ancestors. Showing war's irrationality and horror is of no effect upon him. The horrors make the fascination. War is the *strong* life; it is life *in extremis*. . . . Inordinate ambitions are the soul of every patriotism, and the possibility of violent death the soul of all romance. . . . If war had ever stopped, we should have to reinvent it, on this view, to redeem life from flat degeneration. . . . Its "horrors" are a cheap price to pay for rescue from the only alternative supposed, of a world of clerks and teachers, of . . . consumer's leagues and associated charities, of industrialism unlimited, and feminism unabashed. No scorn, no hardness, no valor any more! Fie on such a cattle-yard of a planet. . . . Militarism is the great preserver of our ideals of hardihood, and human life with no use for hardihood would be contemptible. Without risks or prizes for the darer, history would be insipid indeed.[32]

He then suggested that these attractions could only be overcome by substituting another crusade:

> a conscription of the whole youthful population to form for a certain number of years a part of the army enlisted against Nature . . . would preserve in the midst of a pacific civilization the manly virtues which the military party is so afraid of seeing disappear in peace. We should get toughness without callousness, authority with as little criminal cruelty as possible. . . . So far, war has been the only force that can discipline a whole community, and until an equivalent discipline is organized, I believe that war must have its way.[33]

None of these selections should be seen as reflecting enthusiasm for war, but rather, a grudging recognition that war has not only its horrors but also its attractions. A famous *bushido* text from ancient Japan advises that "When all things in life are false, there is only one thing true, death."[34] The most war-prone ideologies generally claim that their long-term goal, however, is to eliminate war. But there is a notable modern exception: fascism. Fascism has unblinkingly glorified war, and (judging by its success in the twentieth century) has struck a favorable chord in many people. "War alone," wrote Italian dictator Benito Mussolini,

> brings up to their highest tension all human energies and puts a stamp of nobility upon the people who have the courage to meet it. All other trials are substitutes, which never really put a man in front of himself in the alternative of life and death. A doctrine, therefore, which begins with a prejudice in favor of peace is foreign to Fascism.[35]

Of course, the fact that someone may be a fascist does not in itself constitute a satisfactory explanation for his or her inclinations toward war. Rather, one must also consider those factors that presumably have made him or her embrace such a warprone ideology: frustration, authoritarian personality structure, social learning, biological influences, and so on.

A final contributing cause of war, working at the personal level, may well be a kind of sanitized romanticizing of battle, found in many children's cartoons and toys, as well as in movies, music, art,

Sergeant H. A. Marshall, a sniper with the Calgary Highlanders of the Canadian Army, in Belgium, 1944. The image of the dashing military hero — whether knight in shining armor, cavalry officer, Green Beret, "top gun" fighter pilot, and so on — has a powerful hold on the human imagination. (National Archives of Canada)

and literature. For example, consider the following, by English poet A. E. Housman:

> I did not lose my heart in summer's eve,
> When roses to the moonrise burst apart:
> When plumes were under heel and lead was flying,
> In blood and smoke and flame I lost my heart.
>
> I lost it to a soldier and a foeman,
> A chap that did not kill me, but he tried;
> That took the sabre straight and took it striking
> And laughed and kissed his hand to me and died.[36]

To be sure, there also exists a rich catalog of antiwar songs, stories, movies, and poems, ranging from the delicate and plaintive (as in the song "Where Have All the Flowers Gone?") to the unrelentingly realistic and grotesque (as in *All Quiet on the Western Front* or *Catch-22*). Opponents of war, however, are obliged to recognize those aspects of war, currently out of vogue, that have long exercised positive appeal for the human psyche.

INHIBITIONS AGAINST WAR

The history of warfare shows that people are capable of the most heinous acts of brutality. From American history alone, consider the nineteenth-century massacre of Sioux Indians at Wounded Knee in South Dakota, or the twentieth-century massacre at My Lai in Vietnam: In each case, hundreds of men, women, and children were slaughtered wantonly. Indeed, the preceding sections may leave the impression that war exerts a virtually irresistible attraction to human beings at the personal level, whether through our innate characteristics, our experiences, or via the lure of excitement, camaraderie, and ideology. But in fact, even beyond ethical and religious strictures (see Chapter 19), many inhibitions serve to check the personal propensity for war and to moderate individual conduct in war.

One of these is fear for one's own life. In Euripides' *The Supplicants*, the Theban Herald points out that "if death had been before their own eyes when they were giving their votes, Hellas [Greece] would never have rushed to her doom in mad desire for battle."[37] There are, in fact, very few heroes during a war; most soldiers seek to do the minimum necessary to save themselves and their close colleagues; their own behavior is often ignoble.[38]

And as to blood-lust and war fever, consider this: During World War II, rarely did more than 25 percent of American soldiers fire their guns in battle; more often, even during intense firefights, only around 15 percent did so. And this applied to intensely trained combat infantrymen. A study sponsored by the U.S. Army concluded that "It is therefore reasonable to believe that the average and healthy individual—the man who can endure the mental and physical stresses of combat—still has such an inner and usually unrealized resistance towards killing a fellow man that he will not of his own volition take life if it is possible to turn away

This Confederate soldier—Private Edwin Francis Jennison of the Second Louisiana Cavalry—was barely a teenager when photographed on July 1, 1862. The youth and inexperience of soldiers makes them no match for powerful, well-organized military systems. (Library of Congress)

from that responsibility."[39] It can even be argued that fear of killing, rather than fear of being killed, is the largest cause of battle failure.

By the Korean and Vietnam Wars, however, the percentages of soldiers willing to fire their weapons had gone up significantly, largely because of improved training and greater emphasis on establishing within-group solidarity among individual combat units. Army discipline has long been recognized as crucial, largely because the side that broke and ran historically has been the one that was butchered. A major part of military training, of course, seeks to countermand the basic moral teaching (not limited, incidentally, to Western tradition): "Thou Shalt Not Kill." The goal of basic training, in the armed forces of all countries, has been not so much the teaching of new techniques and skills as the inculcation of new attitudes: unquestioning obedience and a willingness to kill. Despite some resistance, most people can in fact learn

Major-General R. F. L. Keller exhorting personnel of the Third Canadian Infantry Division during the invasion of Normandy in June of 1944. Officers typically carry at most a pistol that is very rarely used; enlisted men are expected to do the actual killing. (National Archives of Canada)

these things, usually in just a few weeks. This should not be surprising, since a profound asymmetry of power exists between the recruit and the armed forces: "Recruits usually have no more than twenty years' experience of the world, most of it as children, while the armies have had all of history to practise and perfect their techniques."[40]

It is also interesting to note that actual killing during combat is widely considered the role of enlisted men or, at most, junior officers; by 1914, for example, lieutenants and captains in the British army led men into battle carrying only a swagger-stick or, at most, a pistol. Officers, it was understood, do not kill; there is reason to believe that if they had had the choice, most enlisted men would not have done so either.

George Orwell, who fought as an antifascist volunteer on the Loyalist side during the Spanish civil war, recounted that he was unable to shoot an enemy soldier whom he observed "half-dressed and . . . holding up his trousers with both hands. . . . I did not shoot partly because of that detail about his trousers. . . . A man who is holding up his trousers isn't a 'Fascist,' he is visibly a fellow-creature, similar to yourself, and you don't feel like shooting him."[41]

ISSUES IN NUCLEAR PSYCHOLOGY

Because of the special features of nuclear war, it also merits special consideration at the level of individual psychology. Many of the most cogent issues in nuclear psychology operate at the level of decision makers (see Chapter 10). Other aspects, however, affect the psychological functioning of all citizens.

When it comes to nuclear war, both attraction and revulsion are at their most intense. Some people, as we shall see, evince a strange love for weapons of such all-encompassing power (hence, the title of the famous satirical movie *Dr. Strangelove, or How I Learned to Stop Worrying and Love the Bomb*). Others, by contrast, are especially repelled by the grisly prospect of ending life on so massive a scale. And yet, because a full-fledged nuclear war has never occurred, and because, in addition, the effects of nuclear explosions are so powerful as literally to defy human imagination, most people have difficulty focusing their minds and energies on such a topic, which is at once horrifying and yet strangely unreal.

When confronted with deeply unpleasant information, for example, people often respond with denial, a refusal to confront such reality. This process is particularly well known with respect to personal death: Virtually everyone recognizes that, eventually, he or she will die. However, most of us go about our lives as though our own death holds little reality. When confronted with the facts, we concur; otherwise, we practice denial. Something similar can be identified with respect to the nuclear danger: Most of us go about our daily lives as though the prospect of instantaneous nuclear holocaust does not hang over us, simply because such an overwhelming threat is too painful and emotionally disruptive to admit into our moment-to-moment consciousness.

This behavior, although presumably adaptive for the individual, also has unintended and potentially dangerous consequences. By refusing to confront unhappy truths, people who might otherwise become mobilized in opposition to nuclear weapons generally direct their attention and energy elsewhere. Moreover, they abandon the field to those who have insulated themselves from the negative consequences of nuclear activities, and who, by virtue of career advancement and/or ideology, have committed themselves to a more pronuclear, and possibly prowar, orientation.

Denial is encouraged by the fact that nuclear weapons tend to lack psychological reality: They are kept in secret or restricted installations, and in the United States, the Department of Defense refuses, as a matter of policy, to "confirm or deny" their presence.* Hence, for most people, nuclear

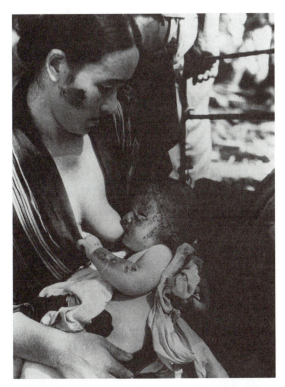

Mother and child shortly after the bombing of Hiroshima. The stunned look on the woman's face is suggestive of "psychic numbing." (United Nations)

weapons cannot be seen, touched, smelled, or heard, and so it requires a conscious effort to consider that they exist at all.

Closely related to denial is another personal psychological phenomenon of the nuclear age, often referred to as psychic numbing. This phrase, originally applied to the *hibakusha*, the victims of the atomic bombing of Hiroshima and Nagasaki,[42] refers to a loss of emotional sensitivity and awareness that appeared to result from the immersion in death that characterized those events. It can be argued that to some extent, we are all victims of Hiroshima and Nagasaki, in that all of us suffer from some degree of psychic numbing, as the nuclear menace pervades our unconscious.

Another important psychological mechanism of the nuclear age has been called the "more is better syndrome."[43] In some ways, it appears to be

---

*This policy has ostensibly been adopted so as to keep information from would-be nuclear terrorists; regardless, one important effect of official secrecy clearly is to keep the American public uninformed and, to some extent, to facilitate denial.

a vestige of prenuclear times, when security was obtained (at least in some cases) by accumulating more weapons than one's opponent. In a world bristling with nuclear overkill, it seems unlikely that "more" is even meaningful, let alone better, and yet the tendency persists to think in this way.

A FINAL NOTE ON "PERSONAL LEVEL" EXPLANATIONS

Approximately 1 to 2 percent of human deaths during the past century have been inflicted by other human beings. In other words, 98 to 99 percent of human deaths are not caused directly by violence operating at the personal level. Moreover, of those deaths that are caused by other people, the greatest majority are due to collective violence rather than individual aggression.

Many social scientists — notably, Margaret Mead — have insisted that war is a human invention, not a biological necessity. They cite the high level of social organization and structuring involved in any military enterprise, and the fact that different societies make war, if they do so at all, in very different ways, depending on their social structures and technological devices. Different societies also make war for different reasons, including pride, prestige, revenge, and resources (see Chapter 7).

It can also be argued that decisions regarding war, especially in large, modern societies, are not made at the personal level, or at least not at the level of the average citizen. Certainly, they do not involve the simple summation of the individual inclinations within a population; rather, war is decided by political (and often military, economic, and intellectual) elites, after which the populace generally goes along, sometimes eagerly, but sometimes only after considerable manipulation or even outright coercion. In other cases, as we shall see, war isn't really "decided" at all; it just seems to happen, often by mistake or misjudgment (Chapter 10).

In addition, although war typically *arouses* great passions, war is not always the *result* of such passions. In some cases at least, wars appear to have been chosen by highly intelligent, rational individuals, after carefully calculating the costs and benefits of alternative courses of action. According to military historian Michael Howard:

> In general, men have fought during the past two hundred years neither because they are aggressive nor because they are acquisitive animals, but because they are reasoning ones: because they discern, or believe they can discern, dangers before they become immediate, the possibility of threats before they are made.[44]

Men also fight when they perceive — whether accurately or not — that they will gain substantially by doing so.

One view, then, is that, rather than being a result of wild, instinctive human drives, war can be the consequence of our coolest, most cerebral calculations. Individuals may fight with passion when placed in warring situations, but in fact, throughout history, authorities have often had to manipulate or otherwise coerce their supposedly vicious, hot-headed, war-loving citizens to fight in the first place. Traditionally, many soldiers have been forced into battle with guns at their backs, hating and fearing their officers and military discipline more than the "enemy." There have been many more draft-dodgers and deserters than people rioting because they have not been provided with sufficient opportunity to go to war.

In any event, any serious effort to prevent war — and even more, to establish peace — clearly must take account the inclinations and behavior of individual people, especially people with power. However, it should not limit itself to this level, since, as we shall see, the "behavior" of socially organized groups differs substantially from that predicted by personal psychology or biology.

Study Questions

1. What are some reasons for thinking that the individual level is crucial to an understanding of the causes of war? What are some reasons for thinking that this level may be misleading?

2. Compare the Lorenzian ethological model of human aggressiveness with the sociobiological one. What are potential disadvantages of either biological approach? Advantages?

3. What is the potential relationship between war and each of the following: narcissistic rage, Thanatos, frustration, denial?

4. Present the case that war is a result of innate human depravity. Make an alternative case that it results precisely from the actions of our higher mental functions.

5. If war results in part from patterns of social learning, what would this suggest about how to engineer a war-free world?

6. Explain the relevance to personal motivations toward aggressiveness of the following: conditioning, self-fulfilling prophecies, socialization patterns, redirected behavior, alienation.

7. How are fascism and romanticism occasionally allied in their attitudes toward war?

8. Is there any evidence for human *dis*inclination toward killing and war?

9. To what extent are the psychological processes associated with nuclear war different from those associated with conventional war? To what extent are they similar?

10. What parallels, if any, appear to exist between interpersonal violence and war? What differences?

Suggestions for Further Reading

Eric Fromm. 1973. *The Anatomy of Human Destructiveness*. Holt, Rinehart & Winston: New York.

Jerome D. Frank. 1982. *Sanity and Survival in the Nuclear Age*. Random House: New York.

Ralph K. White. 1984. *Fearful Warriors*. Free Press: New York.

David P. Barash and Judith Eve Lipton. 1985. *The Caveman and the Bomb*. McGraw-Hill: New York.

Andrew B. Schmookler. 1989. *Out of Weakness*. Bantam: New York.

Source Notes for Part II

1. John Saxe. 1892. "The Blind Men and the Elephant." *The Poetical Works of John Godfrey Saxe*. Houghton: Boston.

2. Ibid.

3. Quincy Wright. 1966. "Analysis of the Causes of War." In R. Falk and S. Mendlovitz (eds.), *Toward a Theory of War Prevention*. World Law Fund: New York.

4. Geoffrey Blainey. 1973. *The Causes of War*. Free Press: New York.

5. Ibid.

Source Notes for Chapter 6

1. J. William Fulbright. Preface to Jerome D. Frank. 1967. *Sanity and Survival*. Random House: New York.

2. Kenneth Waltz. 1959. *Man, the State and War*. Columbia University Press: New York.

3. Hans Morgenthau. 1967. *Politics Among Nations*. Knopf: New York.

4. Konrad Lorenz. 1966. *On Aggression*. Harcourt, Brace & World: New York.

5. Robert Ardrey. 1966. *The Territorial Imperative*. Atheneum: New York.

6. Edward O. Wilson. 1971. In J. Eisenberg and W. Dillon (eds.), *Man and Beast: Comparative Social Behavior*. Smithsonian Institution Press: Washington, DC.

7. Edward O. Wilson. 1975. *Sociobiology: The New Synthesis*. Harvard University Press: Cambridge, MA.

8. Reprinted in James Strachey (ed.). 1964. *The Standard Edition of the Complete Psychological Works of Sigmund Freud*. Hogarth: London.

9. Thomas Hobbes. 1930. *Selections*. F. J. E. Woodbridge (ed.). Scribner: New York.

10. John Calvin. 1956. *On God and Man*. F. W. Strothmann (ed.). Frederick Ungar: New York.

11. See, for example: Andrew Bard Schmookler. 1988. *Out of Weakness*. Bantam: New York. Alice Miller. 1984. *For Your Own Good*. Farrar, Straus & Giroux: New York.

12. Strachey. *The Standard Edition*.

13. John Milton. 1953–1982. "The Doctrine and Discipline of Divorce." In *Complete Prose Works*. Yale University Press: New Haven, CT.

14. Jonathan Swift. 1930. *A Tale of a Tub*. Columbia University Press: New York.

15. Reinhold Niebuhr. 1940. *Christianity and Power Politics*. C. Scribner's Sons: New York.

16. John Dollard et al. 1939. *Frustration and Aggression*. Yale University Press: New Haven, CT.

17. Ibid.

18. See T. R. Gurr. 1970. *Why Men Rebel*. Princeton University Press: Princeton, NJ.

19. John Nef. 1950. *War and Human Progress*. Harvard University Press: Cambridge, MA.

20. John Paul Scott. 1975. *Aggression*. University of Chicago Press: Chicago.

21. Dale Lott and B. Hart. 1977. "Aggressive Domination of Cattle by Fulani Herdsmen and Its Relation to Aggression in Fulani Culture and Personality." *Ethos* 5: 174–186.

22. Mark May. 1943. *A Social Psychology of War and Peace*. Yale University Press: New Haven, CT.

23. Ibid.

24. Ibid.

25. T. W. Adorno et al. 1950. *The Authoritarian Personality*. Harper & Row: New York.

26. Erich Fromm. 1973. *The Anatomy of Human Destructiveness*. Holt, Rinehart & Winston: New York.

27. Erik Erikson. 1964. *Childhood and Society*. Norton: New York.

28. Fyodor Dostoyevsky. 1960. *Notes from Underground*. E. P. Dutton: New York.

29. Pierre Teilhard de Chardin. 1965. *The Making of a Mind: Letters from a Soldier-Priest, 1914–1919*. Harper & Row: New York.

30. Norman Mailer. 1968. *The Armies of the Night*. New American Library: New York.

31. J. Glen Gray. 1967. *The Warriors: Reflections on Men in Battle*. Harper & Row: New York.

32. William James. 1911. "The Moral Equivalent of War." In *Memories and Studies*. Longman, Green: New York.

33. Ibid.

34. Z. Tomatsu Iwado. (trans. and ed.). 1937. *Cultural Nippon*. Nipon Cultural Federation: Tokyo.

35. Benito Mussolini. Quoted in Seyom Brown. 1987. *The Causes and Prevention of War*. St. Martin's Press: New York.

36. From A. E. Housman. 1936. *More Poems*. A Knopf: New York.

37. Euripides. 1955. *Euripides*. University of Chicago Press: Chicago, IL.

38. See, for example, Paul Fussell. 1989. *Wartime*. Oxford University Press: New York.

39. S. L. A. Marshall. 1947. *Men Against Fire*. Morrow: New York.

40. Gwynne Dyer. 1987. *War*. Crown: New York.

41. George Orwell. 1968. *Homage to Catalonia*. Harcourt Brace Jovanovich: New York.

42. R. J. Lifton. 1964. *Death in Life*. Random House: New York.

43. D. P. Barash and J. E. Lipton. 1985. *The Caveman and the Bomb*. McGraw-Hill: New York.

44. Michael Howard. 1984. *The Causes of War*. Harvard University Press: Cambridge, MA.

7

The Group Level: "Primitive" Wars

Man is a social animal who dislikes his fellow men.
 Delacroix

Regardless of precisely how important individual factors may be, war remains fundamentally a group activity. A single person may be able to cause a war (as, in a sense, the assassin who killed Archduke Ferdinand "caused" World War I, or Adolf Hitler "caused" World War II by his personal ruthlessness and aggressiveness), just as individuals can go "to" war, by enlisting or being conscripted. But an individual, by him- or herself, cannot "make" war. War is a group endeavor. As such, it has changed dramatically in the details of its conduct, though less so in the motivations for it and the functions it serves.

Let us therefore take a closer look at the early history of war, and then briefly review its occurrence among nontechnological peoples, not necessarily because war was responsible for shaping our innermost selves, but rather because it has characterized much of human endeavor for many thousands of years.

THE EARLY HISTORY OF WAR

War and Human Evolution

Very little is known about the earliest human warfare. It seems likely, however, that social grouping among primitive human beings was highly adaptive — that is, it probably contributed to their cultural and biological success. By associating with other individuals, our ancestors were able to share information and resources, to gain assistance in caring for their young, and to defend themselves against predators. Presumably, social grouping also enabled primitive human beings to bring down larger prey than would have been possible for a solitary individual. Some anthropologists have suggested that the early stages of human social evolution were promoted by selection for effective hunting, which favored the ability to use and fashion tools, to walk upright (thereby freeing the hands), and to communicate effectively with one's fellow hunters. This "hunting hypothesis" has been disputed, however, by others who emphasize the importance of gathering and digging roots. Interestingly, the hunting hypothesis focuses on the dominant role of men, whereas the "foraging" hypothesis places more importance on the role of women.

The role of war in early human evolution has also been disputed. One extreme view holds that war — even "primitive" war — is a very recent development, and one that exerted essentially no influence on the human species. The other view, and one that may be equally extreme, claims that warfare was an essential component of human evolution, perhaps the major selective force operating in our early history.[1] According to this proposal, groups that were more successful in hostilities with other groups were more likely to leave offspring who themselves possessed traits contributing to such success.*

---

*Note that this view is still compatible with the perspective that war — or violence generally — occurs in part when social problems arise that cannot be resolved through human intelligence. Ironically, then, war (which requires intelligence and may even have helped create human intelligence) also represents a failure of intellect.

The dispersion of early human groups may have made contact — and thus, hostility — rare. Nonetheless, significant interactions probably still took place at regions of common interest: waterholes, areas of local food abundance, and so on. We may never know whether early war was important in shaping human evolution; even if it was, however, it seems unlikely that this would somehow doom the human species to unending war in the future. After all, war entails such positive elements as communication, coordination, self-restraint, and self-sacrifice. A winning group would presumably be one that cooperated well. Making airborne missiles, for example, whether spears or ICBMs, is not a frenzied act of passion but rather a labor of considered intelligence. (Launching them, on the other hand, may involve mental processes that are much more primitive.)

No clear evidence of organized warfare — as opposed to fighting and skirmishing between mobile bands — can be found during the Paleolithic (early Stone Age) or even Mesolithic times, from 10,000 to 8,000 B.C. At this point, hunting and gathering societies were replaced by economies based on the domestication of plants and animals. War is first discernible during the early Neolithic, which began around 8,000 B.C. The remains of the ancient city of Jericho (dating from 7,500 B.C.) show clear signs of fortified towers and walls, suggesting military defenses, no doubt necessitated by the accumulation of wealth via trade, which in turn created targets for aggressive raiding or war.

Why Study Primitive War?

Anthropologists studying modern-day people have, however, found examples of primitive war that may in some ways reflect traditions that predate the maintenance of fixed and fortified cities for the defending of accumulated wealth. It must be borne in mind that the actions of certain twentieth-century nontechnological people, even if primitive by Western standards, are not really the same as those that occurred in earlier stages of human history. Nonetheless, by examining primitive "war" among contemporary human beings, we may learn something about our ancestors' behavior in

Members of the nomadic Warramunga tribe of Central Australia. These people are typical hunters and gatherers. (Thomas Burke Memorial Washington State Museum)

pre-Neolithic days, thereby gaining some insight into underlying tendencies among *Homo sapiens* more generally, including all of us, today. The goal of this chapter is historical as well as analogic: to present a brief overview of war among nontechnological people so as to learn something about our own roots, and also to see other forms of war in microcosm, so as to learn something about our own current behavior. In addition, we shall try to extract some insights into the relationship of group association to military enthusiasm, because, after all, war is distinguished from assault or homicide by the fact that it is not done single-handedly. (In Chapter 10, we will consider the special case of small-group decision making on the part of leaders.)

It may be hoped that a study of the diversity of human warmaking would lead to some useful generalizations beyond the following, most clearly articulated by the historian Arnold Toynbee: Extremes of climate (both very hot and very cold) are less conducive to the development of large-scale warmaking than are temperate climates; prairie and seacoast dwellers tend to be more war-prone than

mountain or forest inhabitants;* pastoralists (nomads) are more war-prone than are settled agriculturalists. We can also go beyond the simplistic (and misleading) generalizations that human beings have always fought wars, or that they have hardly ever fought wars, or that they always fight wars for practical reasons, or that they never do so.

FUNCTIONS OF PRIMITIVE WAR

Virtually all observers of war, whether technological or nontechnological war, agree that it is in most cases ethically a "bad thing." But there is legitimate disagreement, among sociologists studying Western war and among anthropologists studying its nontechnological counterpart, about whether war

---

*Such generalizations are always risky; for example, the following people are all mountain-dwelling, and traditionally militaristic: the Swiss, Scots, Gurkhas, Sikhs, and Dani.

is adaptive or maladaptive. (A phenomenon is considered adaptive or functional if it contributes positively to the success of the individual, or society, that manifests it.) Thus, advocates of the latter, "dysfunctional" perspective emphasize the disruptive and retrogressive aspects of war: how it retards growth, development, and material and social progress, as well as the obviously negative effects of increased suffering and death. Proponents of the former viewpoint claim that primitive war can be "eufunctional" — that is, it can serve a positive role in providing social solidarity within each competing unit.*

Economist Walter Bagehot expressed the eufunctional perspective when he wrote that "Civilization begins because the beginning of civilization is a military advantage."[2] Herbert Spencer also emphasized the prosocial aspects of war: "From the very beginning, the conquest of one people over another has been, in the main, the conquest of the social man over the antisocial man."[3] This is an interesting argument to consider, especially for those of us who think of war as the extreme in antisocial behavior.

William McDougall, an influential American psychologist of the early twentieth century, expressed a view that long prevailed among social scientists, and still has many adherents today:

> When in any region social organization had progressed so far that the mortal combat of individuals was replaced by the mortal combat of tribes, villages or groups of any kind, success in combat and survival and propagation must have been favored by, and have depended upon, not only the vigor and ferocity of individual fighters, but also, to an even greater degree, the capacity of individuals for united action, good comradeship, personal trustworthiness, and the capacity of individuals to subordinate their impulsive tendencies and egoistic promptings to the ends of the group and to the commands of an

accepted leader. Hence, wherever such mortal conflict of groups prevailed for many generations, it must have developed in the surviving groups just those social and moral qualities of individuals which are the essential conditions of all effective cooperation and of the higher forms of social organizations. For success in war implies definite organization, the recognition of a leader, and faithful observance of his commands, and the obedience given to the war chief implies a far higher level of morality than is implied by the mere observance of the primal law. . . . Such conflict of groups could not fail to operate effectively in developing the moral nature of man; those communities in which this higher morality was developed would triumph over and exterminate those which had not attained it in equal degree. And the more the pugnacious instinct impelled primitive societies to warfare, the more rapidly and effectively must the fundamental social attributes of men have been developed in the societies which survived the ordeal.[4]

This passage has been reproduced at length not because it is necessarily correct (such matters are largely speculative, although it is useful to understand the arguments), but rather because it reflects an important bias among many students of peace and war, namely, that war contributes to humanity's "higher morality."

War is not a simple or unitary phenomenon among modern nation-states; neither is it readily explained among nontechnological peoples. The following functions of primitive war have been suggested:

1. Provide outlets for the aggressiveness of young men, and in the process, reduce within-society tensions

2. Provide opportunities for social advancement via enhancement of prestige

3. Gain access to food resources, notably animal protein

4. Obtain women from neighboring groups

5. Obtain land from neighboring groups

6. Correct an imbalance in the sex ratio — among certain societies, female infanticide creates

---

*Note: This advocacy should be distinguished from advocating war itself; it is one thing to claim that war has some positive virtues, quite another to *recommend* it on balance.

Maori ceremonial war dance. (Thomas Burke Memorial Washington State Museum)

an excess of males, which can be corrected by a war

7. Achieve revenge, which often carries both symbolic and social payoffs

8. Provide the opportunity for enlargement of the tribal domain and (rarely) for certain individuals to establish large kingdoms or empires

At its simplest level, primitive war appears to be largely concerned with interpersonal competition and struggles to obtain individual prestige, rather than with large-scale conflicts between social groups or even the accumulation of land, women, or other resources. Thus, in primitive war, the involvement and motivation tends to be at the personal level, as compared with modern warfare, which is directed toward conquest or the advancement of state interests. In the modern, technological case, personal involvement and motivation tend to be relatively less intense, because the benefits to be derived are more diffuse, and often ideological rather than practical and immediate.

To take one example, an authority on primitive war suggested that before contact with Caucasians, warfare among the indigenous Maori tribes of New Zealand was adaptive in that it served to distribute population, thereby preventing local overexploitation of natural resources, while also opening up new land for occupation. European settlers brought muskets, however, which increased the costs of warfare to the point where they exceeded the benefits.[5] It should be noted, however, that anthropologists are divided over the degree to which ecological forces are responsible for human war, and if so, which forces might be predominant.

One group of explanations for primitive war emphasizes material objects of competition (animal protein, women, land), access to which "ensures the well-being of the living."[6] By contrast, another viewpoint focuses primarily on cultural factors, with special attention to the role of ideologies and symbolic structures in giving social meaning and value to acts of organized violence.[7] Still another theory seeks to integrate these hypotheses into an explanation for the evolution of the state (see Chapter 9). This influential theory is based on the assumption that increasing populations exert ever-increasing pressure on resources, which may create conditions favorable for people to organize into ever-larger competitive units.[8] Despite their frequent disagreements, however, most anthropologists are united in rejecting the idea that primitive war is a genetically driven need:

> The possibility of armed conflict has been embedded in the social and cultural experience of humankind at least since the palaeolithic era, when the spear and spear-thrower were developed, presumably for the purposes of hunting game. What does this mean for the future? It certainly does not mean that human societies are in some sense "programmed" for war, nor does it mean that the history of human progress tells Hobbes' grim story after all. We do know that war is an aspect of many cultural ideologies, but we also know that ideologies — that is, people's statements about their beliefs — are flexible idioms that express selectively the cultural propositions that are capable of life in human minds. This is cause for hope, since cultural analysis suggests that the causes of war lie not in the land, nor in some implacable demand for blood or honour, nor in human genes, but in imaginations that tolerate both the image and the reality of wholesale violence, at least for the moment.[9]

CHARACTERISTICS OF PRIMITIVE WAR

The renowned anthropologist Bronislaw Malinowski identified six categories of armed aggressive behavior among nontechnological peoples:

1. "fighting, private and angry," which serves as the prototype of criminal behavior

2. "fighting, collective and organized," among groups within the same cultural unit

3. "armed raids, as a type of man-hunting sport, for purposes of head-hunting, cannibalism, human sacrifices, and the collection of other trophies"

4. "warfare as the political expression of early nationalism, that is, the tendency to make the tribe-nation and tribe-state coincide"

5. "military expeditions of organized pillage, slave-raiding and collective robbery"

6. "wars between two culturally differentiated groups as an instrument of national policy"[10]

Primitive war can be understood not only by examining the kinds of activities involved, as in Malinowski's list, but also by considering its functions. "Among almost all American Indians," suggested one authority, "war existed to bring glory to the individual, and since war was relatively safe, everyone was happy even though few tactical, strategic and economic advantages for a whole people were obtained."[11] Even the causing of death or injury was not always a goal, and in fact, mortality appears generally to have been low; indeed, primitive "wars" often end after a single death or even a serious injury. The Dani people of New Guinea traditionally do not use feathers on their war arrows, thereby reducing accuracy and keeping casualties down. And the Ibo of Nigeria used to count up their dead after a war, after which the side losing fewer warriors compensated the "losers" with money, to avoid any grudges.

Among the rather warlike American Plains Indians, the social group was represented by a peace chief; the war chief, by contrast, served only during an actual campaign. And even then, among many of the Plains tribes, a much more glorious deed than killing one's enemies was to "count coup," or touch an opponent with either one's hand or a special, ritual stick, thereby humiliating the opponent and bringing great credit to the successful warrior. Self-renown, rather than death to one's enemies, was widely considered the highest goal. (Modern people generally persist in valuing the "war-hero." The difference is that personal aggrandizement — either wealth or glory — is not supposed to be the reason for engaging in modern warfare; rather, the individual warrior is ostensibly an altruist or public protector.)

Trophy-taking was, and still is, widespread in primitive war: heads among the New Guinea highlanders and the Jivaro of South America, scalps in the Plains Indian conflicts (especially with white invaders), foreskins among the ancient Israelites. Vestiges of this custom can be seen in modern times, in notches on guns in the Wild West or "kills" painted on his plane's fuselage by a fighter pilot. However, the indiscriminate killing of old people,

Gathering of war chiefs of the South Dakota Sioux. (Thomas Burke Memorial Washington State Museum)

women, and children is rare, even in the most heated of wars; the Mongols in the Middle Ages and the ancient Israelites were exceptions. Even the notoriously fierce Yanomamo of the Amazon and Dani of the New Guinea highlands usually exempt women and children, as well as anyone who has a personal relationship with a would-be attacker. (This has made it advantageous to spread marriages among many different groups; as we shall see, the establishment of such protective networks of relationships is a frequent pattern.)

Primitive war typically is governed by numerous rules, which are specific to different tribes. For example, the Nuer of Sudan are forbidden to use spears against anyone living within a given proximity; beyond that distance, such lethal weapons are allowed. Among the Dani, truces automatically occur at nightfall, although the battle is considered unfinished until at least one person is killed on either side (and ambushes occasionally occur at night as well).

Among the most widespread customs associated with primitive warfare are those involving the extensive use of ritual to signal the initiation of warfare and the change of one's status, from "civilian" to warrior. Magic amulets are common, as are special ways of shaving and adorning the body, typically with paints and/or feathers. Such techniques ostensibly help ward off evil and bad luck, but their more practical function appears to be the promotion of group solidarity. This includes modern-day uniforms and "totemic" symbols such as insignias, regimental banners, and national flags. Ritual abstinence, notably from food or sex, apparently helps relieve the guilt of killing, while also signifying that one is "pure" and different, and thus permitted to act in ways that in a context of peace would be forbidden. Repetitive dancing and singing, often accompanied by the use of drugs, was characteristic of warfare preparation among people in Asia, Africa, Polynesia, and certain American Indians; this apparently reduced fear and helped cement commitment among members of a war party, while also providing a buttress against panic. And ritual rehearsals of battle served to diminish anxiety, and also to provide practice.

Typically, elaborate rituals are also performed after a battle, especially if the warrior has actually killed somebody. The great majority of societies consider that anyone who kills — even in war — has thereby become "unclean," and must be ritually purified before being readmitted into civilian life.

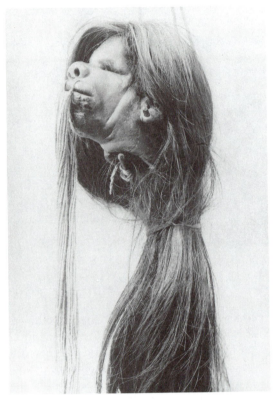

Trophy head taken by the Jivaro people of the Upper Amazon.
(Thomas Burke Memorial Washington State Museum)

Again, fasting or abstinence are most common, often with varying periods of isolation from the home group. In modern societies, returning soldiers are often accorded medals, parades, or membership in special veteran's organizations.

EXAMPLES OF PRIMITIVE WARS

As an example of "war" among nontechnological, stateless societies, consider this case study occurring among the Arunta, a group of hunters and gatherers living in the desert of central Australia.[12] A band of Arunta had suffered several inexplicable deaths. The old men leading the band decided, by mystical means, that these deaths were caused by malevolent magic being perpetrated by a neighboring band of Arunta. So, they organized an *atinga*, or revenge group, the members of which—after

undergoing various purification rituals—painted their bodies and set out after the neighboring band, carrying their spears and fighting boomerangs. The other band discovered the approaching *atinga*, and recognizing that they were outnumbered, sent out a delegation of young women as a token of peace. This peace offering was rejected, however. (Had the attackers copulated with the delegation, this would have meant that they accepted the offer, in lieu of bloodshed.) Next, the threatened group sent two men to negotiate with the attackers; these discussions took two entire days, during which an agreement was eventually reached allowing a battle to take place. Part of this agreement, however, was a secret understanding as to who would be killed by the attackers: three young men in the offending group, and no one else. These three had been making trouble for their elders by taking inappropriate sexual liberties, violating rules for the sharing of food, and otherwise being disobedient. The following day at dawn, according to the agreement, a fire was lit by the elders of the group under attack; the attackers advanced quickly, speared two of the prearranged targets (the third had sensed danger and escaped during the night), and took their wives as booty. Elders of the group under attack put up a show of resistance, but the attackers quickly retreated, with the two marked men being the only casualties.

Although every episode of war—just like every human society—is to some extent unique, the Arunta example reflects widespread patterns of warfare in nontechnological peoples, including the following:

1. *Social control.* In systems where formal machinery for resolving conflict is absent or weak, and no legal means exist for enforcing conformity, war serves as a method of social control. Thus, social unity within each band was enhanced, as was the influence and position of the elderly leaders in each case.

2. *Limited destruction.* Resorting to stylized symbols and agreements served to limit the destructiveness of the conflict, maintaining a rough balance between the adversaries, who

Ceremonial dance by members of the Arunta tribe of central Australia. (Thomas Burke Memorial Washington State Museum)

will, after all, continue to be neighbors. There is no direct parallel to the "total wars" of modern Western society.

3. *Internal logic.* Although the justification for the attack may seem irrational to the modern Westerner, it is consistent within a certain kind of cause-and-effect reference system, and is not necessarily any less rational than wars fought to determine the dynastic succession of an obscure line of royalty or trading rights that will only influence a tiny minority of the population on either side.

4. *Bargaining.* The process of bargaining is readily understandable cross-culturally, as is the sly way the elders of the attacked tribe turned a potential disaster to their own benefit.

5. *Limited goals.* The above "war" was fought for limited goals, and in a very limited way. Warfare among nontechnological peoples is typically of this sort — over revenge, women, animal protein, prestige, or, occasionally, ac-

cess to physical space for hunting, farming, or living. Only very rarely does lethal group conflict erupt over conflicting ideologies. In fact, neighboring groups, which are overwhelmingly the opponents in primitive war, typically share the same culture, language, and world view.

For another example of primitive war, consider the Yanomamo of the Brazilian and Venezuelan Amazon basin.[13] They call themselves the "fierce people," and members of a given village (perhaps 50–250 people) spend considerable time and energy making war on their neighbors. Most wars apparently take place over women, although Yanomamo men are highly pugnacious within their own villages as well; social interactions involve a large amount of bluff and bluster, and disputes (which break out frequently) are often settled by chest-pounding duels or club fights in which the contestants take turns smashing each other over the head. Men strut about, throwing tantrums and seeking to establish a reputation as a warrior with courage and a "short fuse." They even spend hours memorizing defiant death speeches to be uttered if mortally wounded. The ultimate test of pugnacity, however, occurs during surprise raids on neighboring villages.

In the case of the Yanomamo, although casualties generally are not high during any one engagement, the long-term effect may be significant; one village studied by the anthropologist Napoleon Chagnon, for example, was raided twenty-five times during a fifteen-month period, during which a total of ten people, or 5 percent of the village population, were killed. If a village's size is so depleted that it can no longer defend itself, its remaining members may be forced to join a larger village for protection. This is not considered a desirable option, however, because the host village is likely to demand substantial payment — notably, women — in return for such assistance.

Blood revenge appears to be an important cause of war among the Yanomamo. Thus, of all males twenty-five years of age or older, 44 percent have participated in the killing of someone, and 30 percent of all adult male deaths are due to such violence. In the aftermath of a killing, the victimized group — and especially the relatives of the victim — feel obligated to retaliate against the killers, or at least against the village or relatives of the killers. This, in turn, promotes a never-ending cycle of retribution; nearly 70 percent of all adults over forty years of age have lost a close genetic relative due to violence, and they generally feel obliged to retaliate in kind. Once caught in a cycle of quid pro quo of this sort, it is difficult to become extricated. Failure to respond, for example, invites additional attacks because the group is then seen as weak and vulnerable to further aggression. Moreover, participating in the system of blood feuds may provide reproductive benefits: At least among the Yanomamo, men who have killed have more wives and more offspring than do men who have not.[14]

ALTERNATIVES TO PRIMITIVE WAR

There are a variety of seemingly peaceful societies, defined variously as (1) not experiencing wars fought on their soil, (2) not fighting wars with other groups, or (3) not experiencing any civil wars or internal collective violence. (Interestingly, the frequency of external war has very little correlation with that of internal war.) Some examples of the most peaceable societies include the Semai of Malaysia, the Siriono of Bolivia, the Mbuti pygmies of central Africa, the !Kung bushmen of the African Kalahari Desert, and the Copper Eskimos of northern Canada.

It is increasingly recognized that certain nontechnological people are notable not so much for their lack of aggression as for their effective and nonviolent way of coping with it. For example, the Eskimos of central Greenland slap each other's faces; in western and eastern Greenland, they engage in prolonged singing duels, with individuals competing to be more imaginative, and to engage their audience more effectively. Many inhabitants of Alaska, Siberia, and Baffin Island have traditionally settled their disputes by wrestling. The Kwakiutl Indians of the northwest coast of America competed by holding potlatch feasts, in which chiefs sought to outdo each other by demonstrating how much wealth they could sacrifice. And the African bushmen (the !Kung) and pygmies use laughter and ridicule, only rarely resorting to outright physical violence.

In many other stateless human societies, war is either absent or quite rare. Among those factors that help prevent the outbreak of organized violence, the following appear to be especially important in preventing civil warfare (although not all are present at the same time): (1) socialization toward the peaceful settling of conflicts and disapproval of the use of violence or force; (2) the presence of a decision-making system for the group or tribe that is capable of applying effective sanctions against violent transgressors; (3) the opportunity for dissidents to emigrate to other groups; and (4) the existence of economic interdependence within the group.

As to the maintenance of peace between groups, several factors can be identified, although the enormous diversity of human cultures makes any generalizations hazardous. The perception of shared ancestry among different groups tends to inhibit violence between these groups, just as an

Early stage of potlatch ceremony among the Kwakiutl people of Alert Bay, British Columbia, in 1918. The bowls contain coins and the sticks correspond to blankets being offered for destruction. (Thomas Burke Memorial Washington State Museum)

emphasis on relatedness within a group (motherland, fatherland, "brothers and sisters," and so on) tends to produce greater internal solidarity combined with an increased willingness to close ranks against other groups perceived as unrelated, foreign, and thus, enemies. Similarly, peaceful relations among groups are often enhanced by establishing kinship ties through marriage. For example, among the Mundurucu of Brazil, men reckon their kinship through the male descent line ("patrilineal"), but after marriage, husbands live in their wives' home community ("matrilocal"); as a result, attacks upon different villages might require that men take up arms against their relatives.*

According to a school of thought led by the anthropologist Claude Levi-Strauss, a primary reason for the incest taboo is that, by marrying outside

the family, people establish cooperative relationships with other groups, thereby minimizing the likelihood of destructive warfare between these groups. The phenomenon of establishing politically useful alliances via marriages has a long history in Western affairs as well, at least at the level of ruling houses among the European monarchies.

PRIMORDIAL GROUP PROCESSES

The Psychology of Groups

Human beings are highly social creatures. One of the most powerful human tendencies is to aggregate into groups, and somehow to distinguish the members of each group from members of other, comparable groups, using language, customs, patterns of adornment, shared mythologies, and so forth. Other groups who speak different languages (or even the same language, but with a different accent), who worship different gods, or who follow a different political or economic system are readily identified as dissimilar, and often threatening as

---

*It is worth noting that the great Indian epic, *The Bhagavad-Gita*, revolves around the internal conflict of a warrior, Arjuna, forced to make war upon his relatives.

well. Sigmund Freud wrote of the "narcissism of minor differences," whereby people tend to focus upon, and exaggerate, cultural traits that distinguish themselves from their neighbors.

Clearly, group life entails important and empowering aspects: the ability to share effort, to pool resources, to cooperate, to achieve division of labor, to learn and to teach, and simply to receive stimulation from the presence of one's fellows. As William James once wrote, "All the qualities of a man acquire dignity when he knows that the service of the collectivity that owns him need them. If proud of the collectivity, his own pride rises in proportion."[15] There is a powerful allure in being needed and appreciated, and a strong tendency to associate oneself with a larger whole, thereby enhancing one's sense of worth and importance.

But there are also disadvantages. Of these, one of the most significant is the loss of inhibitions that can result from immersion in a crowd, as a result of which a "mob psychology" can take over, through which individuals engage in acts that would be virtually inconceivable if they were acting alone. It can be debated whether warmaking groups literally produce a new kind of entity, a social one having its own tendencies and characteristics, or whether groups simply give social sanction to preexisting individual tendencies, notably aggressiveness, intolerance, and the like. Freud once commented that he could shame a single German stormtrooper, sent to search his apartment in Vienna, but when two were sent together, they became "good Nazis."

This process of "deindividuating" seems to involve three major components:

1. *The effect of validation by one's peers.* Members of homogeneous groups are more likely to respond to conflicted situations with hostility than are groups whose membership is more heterogeneous.* Individual aggressiveness, when validated by the expressed aggres-

siveness of others, is more likely to be released. One of the most important innovators in military science was the Dutchman Maurice of Naussau, prince of Orange (1567–1625), who was the originator of the close-order drill. According to a renowned historian, this innovation not only permitted closely coordinated maneuvers by large numbers of people, it also introduced an important psychological and sociological dimension, which largely explains why modern armed forces still use these techniques in basic training, some four hundred years after Maurice introduced them:

> When a group of men move their arm and leg muscles in unison for prolonged periods of time, a primitive and very powerful social bond wells up among them. This probably results from the fact that movement of the big muscles in unison rouses echoes of the most primitive level of sociality known to humankind. . . . Military drill, as developed by Maurice of Naussau and thousands of European drillmasters after him, tapped this primitive reservoir of sociality directly. Drill, dull and repetitive though it may seem, readily welded a miscellaneous collection of men, recruited often from the dregs of civil society, into a coherent community, obedient to orders even in extreme situations when life and limb were in obvious and immediate jeopardy.[16]

2. *Diminished individual profile.* Biologists have identified something known as the "selfish herd" phenomenon, whereby animals as diverse as fish or starlings appear to flock together because, by doing so, each individual increases the chances that its neighbor — rather than itself — will fall victim to an approaching predator. Animals in groups are also able to accomplish things, such as killing a prey animal or driving off a would-be predator, that could not be achieved by a solitary individual. Similarly, a human crowd seems to provide not only a feeling (as well as the reality) of strength in numbers, but also a shield of protective anonymity. In addition, groups are usually associated with highly visible and persuasive leaders, who may provide the impetus for group hostility by actively fomenting as well as directing violence that might not otherwise occur if

---

*The most strike-prone industries, for example, are those whose workers are isolated from the rest of the community and are drawn from ethnically similar backgrounds.

Зря стараешься, акула!
Просчитаешься, акула,
Подплывая к берегам.
Хоть под самым носом Куба,
А тебе не по зубам!

FIGURE 7.1   Dehumanization: The United States (as a shark) threatening Cuba in a Soviet poster of the early 1980s.

individuals were left to their personal inclinations. And finally, the simple presence of leaders also tends to suggest to the group members that the leaders, rather than the followers, are likely to be at risk for retaliation, which in turn diminishes reluctance of the followers to participate.

3. *Contagious or imitative behavior.* A frustrated or angry person is much more likely to behave aggressively if he or she experiences others who are doing so. This may involve not only "getting the idea" of violence, but also gaining a kind of social "permission" to behave in this way. Thus, it is well known that violence (or, to put a more favorable cast upon it, resistance to oppression) tends to spread when oth-

ers witness or hear about the events: the French Revolution of 1789, the Luddite uprising in early nineteenth-century Britain, the U.S. ghetto riots of the late 1960s, the Polish "Solidarity" strikes, and the Palestinian uprisings of the 1980s.

Dehumanization

Another prominent and troublesome characteristic of group functioning is the ready tendency to "dehumanize" members of other groups, that is, to give the impression — to colleagues, and at least on a subconscious level, to oneself — that the others are not really human at all. Such dehumanization is especially easy to apply to those who are recognizably different because of language, appearance, cultural practices, and so on. Among various non-technological peoples, even the word *human* is the same as the name for the tribe; members of different tribes are thus denied their humanity, as a result of which they can be killed with little or no remorse. Among modern technological peoples, language patterns during times of hostility reflect this tendency, especially with the use of animal terms to describe an opponent: vermin, insects, rats, pigs, dogs, and so forth. Even nonanimal slang terms have a similar effect: wogs, slants, kikes, niggers, krauts, honkies, and so on.

The following news item appeared in the *San Francisco Bulletin* during the 1860s. It is a telling example of dehumanization in action:

> Some citizens of this city, while hunting in Marin County yesterday, came upon a large group of miserable Digger Indians. They managed to dispatch 30 of the creatures before the others ran away.[17]

This encounter—which apparently was a frightful massacre—is reported matter-of-factly, even proudly. Note that the perpetrators were "citizens," not even duly constituted military authorities, and that no questions were raised about the propriety of their acts. Furthermore, the language employed— "miserable" (implying lowly, not unhappy), "dispatch," and "creatures"—suggests that in killing them, the San Francisco citizens had performed a civic duty; certainly, they had not really slaughtered thirty innocent and defenseless human beings!

Group associations may also contribute to war by engaging people in a tragic process by which the hostility of a few serves essentially to contaminate most, if not all, others. One writer poses the question as follows: "Imagine a group of tribes living within reach of one another. If all choose the way of peace, then all may live in peace. But what if all but one choose peace?"[18] The problem could be that, like the proverbial rotten apple, a single highly aggressive tribe would either dominate its less aggressive neighbors or catalyze a conversion to aggressiveness by any of the others. Such a transition could also occur, of course, as a result of a single aggressive individual, and indeed, perhaps

that is part of the reason for aggressiveness on the part of social groups. It remains to be seen, however, whether the means of control would also be comparable.

A FINAL NOTE ON PRIMITIVE WARFARE

We may never fully know the earliest history of human warfare, nor do we know whether "primitive" war among today's nontechnological, stateless societies casts much light upon the evolution of human warfare more generally. In addition to its intrinsic interest, however, "primitive" war undoubtedly illuminates at least some facets of modern, technological war that might otherwise be obscured by the complexity of modern war and by our own subjective involvement in current affairs. Moreover, certain fundamental underlying principles of personal motivation, group association, and intergroup hostility appear to be prefigured in an examination of nontechnological war. Perhaps we can derive insights that apply both to modern war and to peace.

Study Questions

1. Discuss the implications—if any—of the theory that human warfare was responsible for the evolution of the human brain.

2. What are some arguments for and against extrapolating from present-day "primitive" people to the origins of human war?

3. Distinguish between the concepts that war is adaptive and that war is good.

4. To what extent can you distinguish between the functions of war among nontechnological peoples and the functions of war among advanced societies?

5. Compare the nature of individual motivation for war among nontechnological people and in the modern nation-state.

6. What are some implications to be derived from the existence of human societies in which war has apparently been unknown?

7. How is the phenomenon of "deindividuating" encouraged in military training? Is it limited to such situations?

8. Define dehumanization and give recent examples.

9. What are some apparently primitive group processes that can reasonably be extrapolated to modern technological warfare?

10. Make an argument that students of Peace Studies should understand the anthropology of war. Make the alternative case, that it is not terribly relevant.

Suggestions for Further Reading

M. Fried, M. Harris, and R. Murphy (eds.). 1967. *War: The Anthropology of Armed Conflict and Aggression.* Natural History Press: New York.

Robert Bigelow. 1969. *The Dawn Warriors.* Atlantic/Little, Brown: Boston.

Jerome D. Frank. 1982. *Sanity and Survival in the Nuclear Age.* Random House: New York.

Andrew B. Schmookler. 1984. *The Parable of the Tribes.* University of California Press: Berkeley.

Source Notes

1. Robert Bigelow. 1969. *The Dawn Warriors.* Atlantic/Little, Brown: Boston.

2. Walter Bagehot. 1953. *Economic Studies.* Stanford University Press: Stanford, CA.

3. Herbert Spencer. 1967. *The Evolution of Society.* University of Chicago Press: Chicago, IL.

4. William McDougall. 1915. *An Introduction to Social Psychology.* Methuen: London.

5. A. P. Vayda. 1968. "Hypotheses About Functions of War." In Fried, Harris, and Murphy (eds.), *War: The Anthropology of Armed Conflict and Aggression.* Natural History Press: Garden City, NY.

6. R. Brian Ferguson (ed.). 1984. *Warfare, Culture and Environment.* Academic Press: Orlando, FL.

7. See, for example, Andrew Strathern. 1984. *A Line of Power.* Tavistock: London.

8. Robert Carneiro. 1970. "A Theory of the Origin of the State." *Science* 169: 733–738.

9. Carol J. Greenhouse. 1987. "Cultural perspectives on war." In R. Vayrynen (ed.), *The Quest For Peace.* Sage: Beverly Hills, CA.

10. Bronislaw Malinowski. 1941. "An Anthropological Analysis of War." *American Journal of Sociology* XLVI: 521–550.

11. H. H. Turner-High. 1949. *Primitive War.* University of South Carolina Press: Columbia.

12. B. Spencer, F. J. Gillen. 1927. *The Arunta* (2 vols.) Macmillan: London.

13. Napoleon Chagnon. 1967. "Yanomamo Social Organization and Warfare." In M. Fried, M. Harris, and R. Murphey (eds.), *War: The Anthropology of Armed Conflict and Aggression.* Natural History Press: New York.

14. Napoleon Chagnon. 1988. "Life Histories, Blood Revenge, and Warfare in a Tribal Population." *Science* 239: 985–992.

15. William James. 1911. "The Moral Equivalent of War." In *Memories and Studies.* Longman, Green: New York.

16. William H. McNeill. 1982. *The Pursuit of Power.* University of Chicago Press: Chicago.

17. Quoted in R. Heizer and A. Almquist. 1970. *The Other Californians.* University of California Press: Berkeley.

18. Andrew B. Schmookler. 1984. *The Parable of the Tribes.* University of California Press: Berkeley.

8

The Group Level: Nationalism

Whatever you may be sure of, be sure of this: that you are dreadfully like other people.
James Russell Lowell

Primitive, nontechnological war warrants our attention, both for its own sake and for what light it may shed on wider (and possibly deeper) human patterns. The fact remains, nonetheless, that the fundamental issues of peace and war in the modern world are played out in a different arena, that of larger groups, often functioning at the level of nations.

NATIONS, STATES, AND NATIONALISM

In a sense, nations are primitive groups writ large. Just as tribal groups are composed of individuals sharing a strong sense of personal and social identity, nations are similarly united, only the populations are much larger and, typically, more complex internally. The term *nation* derives from the Latin *natio*, referring to birth (as in prenatal or native). Although the word *nation* is often used loosely to indicate a state — that is, a political and geographic entity — in fact the term refers more precisely to a large group of people, ideally united by a common language, origin, history, and culture. No formal process exists for identifying nations; rather, a nation exists when a group considers itself to be a nation.

A *state*, by contrast, is a political unit, an area of land whose people are governed independent of other, comparable states. A nation-state exists if a nation and a state have the same geographic boundaries. (In this book, we shall use the term *international* in its most common, although technically incorrect, usage: referring to exchanges or interactions across the boundaries of different states. The term *interstate*, however, would actually be preferable.) For example, for a brief period after World War I, Lithuanians, Latvians, and Estonians each constituted separate nation-states, the Baltic states of Lithuania, Latvia, and Estonia. Then, they were forcibly incorporated into a larger state, the U.S.S.R. By and large, these Baltic peoples still consider themselves nations unto themselves, but they are not states. The Soviet Union, on the other hand, is a large state, but not a single nation; rather, it is composed of many nationalities, including not only ethnic Russians but also Armenians, Azherbaijanis, Georgians, Ukrainians, Tatars, Turkmen, and so on.

The phenomenon of *nationalism* is one of the most powerful forces of modern times. It refers to the yearnings of people to constitute themselves as part of a nation, typically to form a nation-state, and often to adjust geographic boundaries so as to increase the size of their domain, to incorporate others who share the same sense of national identity, and frequently to establish their nation as significant, if not preeminent. According to one definition, nationalism comprises "a people's sense of collective destiny through a common past and the vision of a common future."[1] This hints at an important component of nationalism, one that transcends such comparatively academic concepts as an analysis of language, history, or shared cultural traditions; namely, the emotional appeal of belonging, of shared deeds, and of extending the boundaries of oneself to comprise a larger and seemingly more glorious whole. In the words of nineteenth-century French philosopher and historian J. Ernest Renan, "What constitutes a nation is not speaking the same tongue or belonging to the same ethnic group, but having accomplished great things in common in the

past and the wish to accomplish them in the future."[2] In perhaps the most famous definition, Renan also suggested that nationalism is

> a grand solidarity constituted by the sentiment of sacrifices which one has made and those that time is disposed to make again. It supposes a past, it renews itself especially in the present by a tangible deed: the approval, the desire, clearly expressed to continue the communal life. The existence of a nation is an everyday plebiscite.[3]

Increasingly, however, the sense of national identity has moved beyond the textbook definition, which emphasizes cultural unity. To a great extent, large nation-states are not so much natural social constructs as arbitrary groupings of people, cobbled together for political and economic purposes. The result has been a strong tendency to establish national symbols that can be shared by many persons regardless of their ethnic identity, thereby conferring unity. National flags, national heroes, national myths, national anthems — all have a remarkable hold over most people, and all nations seek to inculcate recognition of and respect for such symbols, typically requiring oaths, pledges, or other specific acts of allegiance. In some cases, nationalists have successfully appropriated other, preexisting symbols and traditions: Consider German nationalism and the Nordic race; Irish nationalism and Catholicism; American nationalism and democracy, liberty, and free enterprise; Russian nationalism and communism; Japanese nationalism and Shintoism; Israeli nationalism and Judaism and the Old Testament; Iranian nationalism and Shiite Islam.

During times of stress — especially if the stress comes from an external threat — nationalist sentiments are likely to become particularly intense. Often, the threat serves to inflame pronational emotions that may previously have been dimming. The German invasion of the U.S.S.R., for example, enabled Stalin to build upon a "war nationalism" that overcame much disaffection with his purges and heavy-handed dictatorship. (At the same time, some nationalists — notably in the Baltic states and the Ukraine—attempted in the early stages of World War II to ally themselves with Nazi Germany, hoping thereby to fulfill their own nationalist aspirations of separating from the Soviet Union.) The Japanese attack on China similarly evoked a kind of solidarity born of war nationalism, causing the government of Chiang Kai-shek and the revolutionary forces of Mao Ze-dong to make common cause, in the interest of Chinese national survival, against the invader. Even long after national struggles have ceased, the existence of martyrs and of regular days for remembrance also serves to whip up nationalist sentiment and keep it fresh. There is not a single nation-state that does not designate at least one day for the celebration and reaffirmation of its nationhood: July 4 in the United States, July 14 (Bastille Day) in France, October 1 in China, and so on.

Nationalism can, in theory, be limited to love for one's nation; in practice, however, it is often combined with antagonism toward other nations. "By nationalism," wrote George Orwell,

> I mean first of all the habit of assuming that human beings can be classified like insects and that whole blocks of millions or tens of millions of people can be confidently labelled "good" or "bad." But secondly—and this is much more important—I mean the habit of identifying oneself with a single nation or other unit, placing it beyond good or evil and recognizing no other duty than that of advancing its own interests.[4]

This occurs, in part, because the nation provides a way of submerging the comparatively small, vulnerable self into a much larger, more powerful, and ennobling other. As theologian H. Richard Niebuhr describes the ardent nationalist,

> The national life is for him the reality whence his own life derives its worth. He relies on the nation as a source of his own value. He trusts it; first, perhaps, in the sense of looking constantly to it as the enduring reality out of which he has issued, into whose ongoing cultural life his own actions and being will merge. His life has meaning because it is part of that context, like a word in a sentence. It has value because it fits into a valuable whole.[5]

Unfortunately, as we saw when considering the dynamics of small groups (see Chapter 7), the tendency to identify one's group as a "valuable whole" carries along with it another tendency—nearly as strong—to devalue other, similar groups, or worse yet, to see them as threatening to oneself, one's group, and thus, one's fundamental values. Therefore, the Others become suitable targets for competition, conflict, and often violence.

THE HISTORY OF NATIONALIST WARS

The sense of nationhood, as opposed to tribal affiliation, is relatively recent. During the Middle Ages, for example, individuals typically felt that they belonged to a city, or to a local reigning monarch. The loyalty of someone whom we now identify as "French" might have included affiliation with family and village and personal fealty to the duke of Lyons, the king of France, the Holy Roman Emperor, and the pope, but not to "France" as such.

Nation-states began to develop during the late Middle Ages. After the Treaty of Westphalia (1648), which ended the Thirty Years' War, and with increased travel and communication, people became more aware of the existence of others who were similar to themselves, as well as yet others, generally farther away, who were quite different. Moreover, centralized authorities—abetted by gunpowder—were able to demolish the castles of local rulers and enforce a broader allegiance: to kings, whose domains also expanded to include greater numbers of similar people. At the same time, loyalty to local rulers and religious leaders tended to diminish. Spain, Portugal, France, and England were nation-states by the sixteenth century; later, the phenomenon of nationalism received an enormous boost from revolutionary and Napoleonic France.

In the course of its revolution in the late eighteenth century, France developed the first truly national anthem, the stirring "La Marseillaise," and substituted adherence to the nation for fealty to a monarch. In addition, Napoleonic conquests of other nations helped generate strong counterfeelings of national pride on the part of those who had been invaded. Nationalistic emotions were wide-spread by the early nineteenth century, largely co-alescing around the doctrine of national self-determination, the belief that each national group had the right to form its own state. Under this im-petus, Greece won its independence from Turkey in 1829, and Belgium was declared independent from The Netherlands in 1830. (The Dutch repub-lic, in turn, had achieved its own national self-determination several centuries earlier, breaking away from the Spanish empire after a protracted and bloody conflict; this republican revolt was the first modern successful war of national liberation.)

Within the United States, the Revolutionary War was largely a war of independence rather than of nationalism. Nonetheless, nationalism ultimately expressed itself through the doctrine of "manifest destiny," which claimed that it was manifestly the destiny of the American people to expand across all of North America. Moreover, dreams of a major worldwide role for the United States led to other adventures, including, for example, the War of 1812. Senator Henry Clay of Kentucky, leader of an ultranationalist group known as the "Warhawks," expressed both local pride and nationalist fervor when he proclaimed:

> It is said that no object is attainable by war with Great Britain. . . . I say that the conquest of Canada is in your power. I trust that I shall not be deemed presumptuous when I state that I verily believe that the militia of Kentucky are alone competent to place Montreal and all of Upper Canada at your feet.[6]

The resulting war was one of the smallest in U.S. history — 1,877 Americans killed, 9,700 taken pris-oner, and a cost of $200 million, including the burn-ing of Washington, D.C., by the British. And no territory was gained. Nonetheless, U.S. nationalist sentiment contributed to such expansionist adven-tures as the Mexican-American War and the Span-ish-American War, as well as a growing series of armed interventions, notably in Latin America and the Far East.

By the late nineteenth century, nationalism in western Europe had become pronounced in Ger-many and Italy, each of which was divided into

Otto von Bismarck, architect of German unification during the nineteenth century. (The Bettmann Archive)

numerous states. Italian unification was eventually achieved in 1870, after a militant struggle primarily against the Austrian empire (which continued to be a state comprised of many nations). Meanwhile, bu-reaucratic unification of such German "ministates" as Saxony, Hanover, and Silesia was completed in 1871, with Prussia the undisputed leader of the new German nation-state. This unification was achieved by the Prussian leader Otto von Bismarck, who successfully engineered a series of wars, first against Denmark, then Austria, and culminating in the Franco-Prussian War.

Whereas western European nationalism pri-marily involved the amalgamation of previously dis-united regions and states, nationalism in eastern Europe took a somewhat different form, seeking to carve nation-states out of the large, heterogeneous Ottoman (Turkish), Austro-Hungarian, and Rus-sian empires. These demands, especially on the part of the newly created Balkan states — and the tensions they provoked, especially within the Austro-Hungarian empire — played a major role in initiating World War I. The Austrian leadership, for example, was desperately worried that it would not be able to hold together its rickety, heterogeneous assemblage of restive nations, consisting of Hungarians, Serbs, Croats, Montenegrins, Slovenes, and so on. Following the assassination of Archduke Franz Ferdinand of Austria by a Serbian extremist in 1914, the Austrians particularly feared that the demand for Serbian nationalism ultimately would result in the disintegration of the Austrian empire. And so, it was decided to "punish" the Serbs. Russian stood by tiny Serbia, in a show of national solidarity (Serbs, like Russians, are ethnically Slavic). Germany, in turn, stood by its ally, Austria. France was already allied to Russia, and was independently hungering to regain the provinces of Alsace and Lorraine, lost to Germany forty years before, in the Franco-Prussian War of German reunification. Furthermore, as we shall see in Chapter 10, the rigid war plans of Germany demanded an invasion of neutral Belgium, which in turn brought Great Britain into the war. As novelist Kurt Vonnegut might have written, "and so it goes." Or rather, so it went, with national passions, fears, demands, and misunderstandings resulting in the first great modern war.

But even following World War I (or as it was called at the time, the Great War), numerous nations were not granted self-determination. The state of Yugoslavia, for example, is a patchwork quilt of seven "national republics," Serbs, Croats, Bosnians, Macedonians, Slovenians, Montenegrins, and Albanians, each of which consider themselves nations. (These factions were held together at least in part by a powerful leader, Josip Broz Tito, a renowned anti-Nazi partisan during World War II. National unrest in the years following Tito's death in 1980 have led some observers to question whether Yugoslavia will be able to cohere as a state.)

Czechoslovakia, also created after World War I, consists of Bohemia, Moravia, Ruthenia, and Slovakia, which in turn consist mainly of Czechs, Slovaks, and so-called Sudeten Germans. (This latter group was to constitute Hitler's excuse for annexing Czechoslovakia in 1938, under the guise of providing for their welfare and furthering a greater German nationalism.) In addition, whereas Polish and Baltic nationalism were honored at the end of World War I, national sentiments were (as they often are) subordinated to Great Power politicking and map-drawing according to the spoils of war rather than the desires of the people involved: Germans were annexed to Poland, Austrians to Italy, Serbs and Hungarians to Romania, Bulgars and Albanians to Serbia (now Yugoslavia), and so on. As a general principle, the national aspirations of defeated peoples are often trampled upon.

Nonetheless, nationalist sentiment can be extraordinarily resilient. For example, Poles retained their national identity for decades when "Poland" didn't exist on the map (it was gobbled up in the late eighteenth century by Germany, Russia, and Austria). Citizens of Venice considered themselves Italians even while part of Austria; French-speaking residents of Quebec have effectively resisted "Anglicization" of their culture by the rest of English-speaking Canada; Basques consider themselves Basques rather than Spaniards; and so forth. To be sure, there have been some instances of "assimilation," in which isolated national groups lose their identity in favor of a larger group in which they are embedded; native American Indians, for example, despite awareness of their non-U.S. national heritage, typically think of themselves as Americans. But in most cases, intrastate nationalism has resisted the efforts — even the violent efforts — of state governments to deprive them of their identity.

By the nineteenth century, the colonizing activities of the European powers had created a situation in which large segments of the globe were under military domination by people who had little similarity to, or cultural affinity for, the much larger number of "natives" being subjugated. Wars of national liberation were notably successful in Latin America during the 1800s as the Spanish empire crumbled in the south and the brief French ascendancy in Mexico was also ended. Revolutionary nationalism during the nineteenth century was less successful, however, in Africa and Asia: The Zulus were eventually crushed by the British in southern Africa, for example, and despite bloody uprisings (of which the so-called Sepoy Mutiny is best known), Britain maintained control over India as well as Egypt and, indeed, a large proportion of the inhabited planet. Although China was not directly occupied by imperialist powers, the weak and decentralized Chinese government was regularly humiliated and forced to submit to economic ravishment, including the forced "opening" of the country to opium trading; the resulting Opium Wars caused yet more resentment, if anything adding to the growing demand for Chinese nationalism, as did the Boxer Rebellion and the ill-fated Tai-ping Rebellion. (It has been estimated that this latter struggle, little known in the West, resulted in some 20 million fatalities.)

In the aftermath of the two world wars of the twentieth century, revolutionary nationalism has essentially triumphed throughout the world, in some cases through protracted conventional war, in others by guerrilla operations, and in yet others by peaceful transitions, whereby the occupying colonial power granted independence, albeit grudgingly. In most cases, colonial holdings were not bounded in ways that were naturally (that is, nationally) meaningful. As a result, many of the newly independent former colonies, especially those established since the end of World War II, have had to cope with substantial national divisions of their own, many of which have led to war.

TYPES OF NATIONALIST WARS

National Independence

National independence need not always be preceded by war. India, Pakistan, Burma, and Malaya achieved statehood and self-determination with relatively little bloodshed. On the other hand, warfare is a frequent prelude to national independence, as witnessed by the birth of the United States. Indonesia fought for four years to gain independence from Holland, and Algeria became separate from France only after eight years of fighting that cost 250,000 Algerian and French lives.

National Prestige

Many of the classic interstate wars of modern history have been stimulated by issues of national prestige. Enthusiasm within the United States for the Spanish-American War was generated by American desire to enter the arena of worldwide colonial acquisitions. The government of Spain, for its part, appears to have fought back largely because it would have been embarrassing to give up without doing so! Similarly, the aggressive appetite of both Germany and Japan in the twentieth century was whetted by a pervasive sense that these great nations had not achieved world status commensurate with their economic or technological accomplishments, or their self-proclaimed racial superiority.

During the lengthy Anglo-German naval arms race that preceded World War I, to take another example, the German chancellor, Bethmann-Hollweg, said that Germany needed a navy not only to protect her seacoasts and commerce, but for the "general purposes of her greatness." India has long taken the lead in condemning worldwide militarism in general, and the nuclear arms race in particular. But when Prime Minister Rajiv Gandhi announced in February 1988 that his country had successfully developed and tested a surface-to-surface liquid-fueled missile — entirely with Indian technology — he received a standing ovation in the Indian Parliament.

Pride and prestige, sometimes on a personal level as well, became a major factor in the U.S. decision to prosecute the Vietnam War. President Johnson persevered in that war in large part because of his private determination not to be "the first U.S. president to lose a war," and for President Nixon, the worst outcome for the United States in that conflict was "humiliation." "If, when the chips are down," he announced,

> the world's most powerful nation, the United States of America, acts like a pitiful, helpless giant, the forces of totalitarianism and anarchy will threaten free nations and free institutions throughout the world. It is not our power but our will and character that is being tested.[7]

American frustration was acute during the period from late 1979 to early 1981, when revolutionary

Iranians held the staff of the U.S. embassy captive. The resulting sense of national humiliation contributed greatly to the election of Ronald Reagan, and to the military buildup and increasing bellicosity that followed: the U.S. invasion of Grenada (which served partly to assuage the emotional pain of a devastating car-bomb attack on the temporary U.S. Marine barracks in Beirut, Lebanon, just a few days before), U.S. bombing attacks on Tripoli in retaliation for Libyan sponsorship of terrorism, and the sinking of Iranian naval vessels in the Persian Gulf. All these provided an outlet for frustration and an opportunity to redeem a sense of diminished national pride.*

The United States is not necessarily any more vulnerable than other countries to stains upon its national honor, nor is it unusually likely to respond violently to affronts. On the other hand, being a superpower means that the United States possesses great military strength (notably, nuclear weapons) that it is generally unable to use; and yet, the presumed deterrent benefits of possessing these weapons depends entirely upon the perception that, if need be, they might be used. Hence, a superpower attaches great importance to issues of national "credibility," and sees large consequences in what might otherwise be considered minor tests of will. (This issue will be discussed further in Chapter 14.)

The maintenance of national prestige and the avoidance of humiliation looms large in the calculation of every state. For example, Arab pride had been sorely wounded by Israel's string of military victories; the October War of 1973, although technically yet another Arab defeat, came close enough to victory to demolish the myth of Israeli invincibility. It so restored Egyptian self-respect and prestige that President Anwar Sadat felt empowered to make his stunning trip to Jerusalem in 1977, to conclude the Camp David accords in 1978, and actually to sign an Egyptian-Israeli peace treaty (the first and only one between Israel and an Arab state) in 1979.

Secessionism

Sentiments of national unity are often associated with yearnings of a group of people to secede from a larger collectivity of which they do not feel a part. In 1967, for example, about 50,000 Ibos, who had migrated to northern Nigeria, were slaughtered by the more numerous Hausas, who resented Ibo economic success. Another one million Ibos were driven out of the north, after which the Ibo "nation" sought to secede and form their own nation-state of Biafra. The result was a civil war in which many hundreds of thousands died and many more suffered from severe malnutrition and starvation. The war ended, unsuccessfully for the would-be secessionists, in 1970. As we have already noted, secessionism remains a major contributor to armed violence today (see Chapter 4).

Reintegrationism

In this case, people in a region seek to become associated with a "homeland" in which their nationality is represented. The Greco-Turkish hostilities over Cyprus were sparked by Greek Cypriot efforts to reintegrate their population into the Greek nation. Similar sentiments are shared by Catholics of Northern Ireland, who would like their country to rejoin Eire (the Republic of Ireland) to the south.

Irredentism

After the political unification of Italy in the nineteenth century, the new government claimed that there remained other areas containing ethnic Italians that were "not yet redeemed" (*irredenta*), and that should eventually be incorporated within the Italian state. These regions were within the boundaries of other states, who, not surprisingly, were less than enthusiastic about acceding to the Italian demands. Irredentist claims have often led to war: historically, as when French armies in the fifteenth century, led by Joan of Arc, sought to unite the French "nation," or when the Spanish regions of

---

*At the same time, it must be noted that what redeems the pride of one nation typically diminishes that of another, leading in turn to a felt need for revenge, which creates yet more need to assuage the reinjured pride, and so on.

Castile and Aragon fought the occupying Moors, also in the fifteenth century; or more recently, when Hitler claimed Czechoslovakia and Poland in part because they contained German-speaking minorities. Irridentism continues in the modern world. Thus, at present, Japan claims the Kurile Islands, seized by the Soviet Union at the end of World War II, Ghana claims all of Togo, and Morocco claims Mauritania.

International or Transnational Solidarity

The sense of "nationhood" often extends across political boundaries, resulting in strong feelings of empathy and connectedness with fellow nationals living in another state. When these people are considered to be abused, war can be evoked by a felt need to extend protection to fellow nationals living elsewhere. Thus, India felt especially justified entering the 1971 Pakistani civil war because India's Bengali population found it intolerable to stand idly by during Pakistan's slaughter of its own Bengalis. The various Arab states send money and fighters in support of Palestinian nationalism, thereby expressing solidarity with fellow Arabs. The states of black Africa are especially opposed to South African apartheid because of the oppression of its black population. Turkey has come to the aid of the Turkish population on Cyprus, just as Greece has been seen as the protector of the Greek population there.

Of course, this is not the whole story, and the extending of international solidarity can also be a pretext for aggression; for a clear example, take Hitler's annexation of Czechoslovakia and his invasion of Poland, using the alleged mistreatment of Czech and Polish "Germans" as an excuse. The U.S. invasion of Grenada in 1983 was officially excused at the time by the claim that American medical students on that island were in danger of being taken hostage, just as the U.S. invasion of Panama in 1989 was ostensibly undertaken, in part, to protect American lives in that country. In short, national solidarity has often been used to provide legal and political justifications that rationalize a conflict or intervention whose roots may well lie elsewhere, as with Hitler's ambitions for territorial expansion, the U.S. need to "stand tall" in 1983

after the car-bomb attack on U.S. marines in Beirut, or U.S. frustration with the drug-dealing of Panama's General Noriega.

In many cases, states stop short of war, but nonetheless provide "fraternal" aid to ethnic groups in other states. This is often done largely to promote their own interests, which may be limited to satisfying restive, kindred national elements within their own borders. India, for example, with its large Bengali population, could not stand idly by while West Pakistanis were slaughtering the Bengalis of East Pakistan. India was similarly drawn into the fighting in Sri Lanka (formerly Ceylon) because both India and Sri Lanka had a large Sinhalese population. The Soviet Union, like India an amalgamation of many national identities, has been especially sensitive to events in Iran and Afghanistan because these states, adjacent to the U.S.S.R.'s own borders, contain national groups that are also represented within the U.S.S.R. The Soviet leadership is legitimately concerned, for example, that rampant Islamic fundamentalism might well spread to the U.S.S.R.'s large Islamic population. In some cases, a chain of "solidarity" can be forged, which more resembles a game of dominoes; for example, the following pattern emerged in northern and eastern Africa during the 1970s:

> Libya supported Muslim Arab rebels against a Christian and animist Negro regime in Chad. The Chad government supported animist Negro rebels against the Muslim Arab regime in Sudan. The Sudanese regime supported Muslim rebels against the Christian regime in Ethiopia. And Ethiopia supported, along with Chad, the rebels in the Sudan.[8]

In Chapter 4, we considered several examples of ongoing wars that could be cited as primarily nationalist in character: irredentist disputes between Ethiopia and Somalia over the Ogaden, and between Morocco and Algeria over West Sahara; secessionist warfare by Kurdish inhabitants of Iran, Iraq, and Turkey, and by Bengalis against Pakistan; or wars of national prestige and ideology such as the Vietnam War. Although other factors—from the personal to the socioeconomic—are relevant as well, any consideration of the causes of war clearly must give special attention to the powerful and varied impulses of nationalism.

Nationalist Threats to States

One might ask why governments so strenuously resist the various secessionist, irredentist, and reintegrationist national movements. Aren't the (West) Pakistanis better off not being artificially united to 100 million resentful Bengalis? What would be the harm to Spaniards if the troublesome Basques seceded and formed their own tiny nation-state? Part of the answer may itself reflect a kind of national pride, the hope for a larger and therefore greater state. In addition, the resisting people are typically those who profit economically and socially from the presence of the would-be seceders. British support for national self-determination in Kuwait (threatened by Iraq shortly after its independence) and Brunei (eyed hungrily by Indonesia) derives in part from their oil resources; Belgium's enthusiasm for attempts by residents of Katanga to secede from the Congo (now Zaire) was keyed to the copper wealth of that province; had Biafra been carved out of Nigeria, much of that state's industrial capacity and natural resources would have gone, along with the Ibo people; when Hitler seized the Sudetenland, he not only "liberated" three million Sudeten Germans, but also about three-quarters of Czechoslovakia's industrial capacity.

When states are heterogeneous (composed of many nations), leaders also worry that successful demands for national self-determination will lead to additional demands and ultimately to the breakup of the home country. Such fears drove the Austrian government at the onset of World War I and Soviet officials are deeply worried about a similar "domino effect" in the early 1990s. Furthermore, it is not clear that further "Balkanization" — of Africa, India, or anywhere else — will necessarily further the cause of peace. Certainly, the Balkan peninsula, known as the "tinderbox of Europe," has not been a good advertisement for the peaceful benefits of nationalist sentiment.

RACIAL AND CULTURAL INTOLERANCE

Whenever individuals associate with one another, and especially if they do so on the basis of shared characteristics that exclude others and distinguish between "Us" and "Them," there is the danger of racism and other forms of intolerance, which can themselves contribute to war. Many of the world's hostilities involve different nationalities in conflict. Of course, the mere fact of ethnic difference is not a sufficient cause for war; after all, many pluralistic societies live peacefully, both intranationally — the multiethnic population of Hawaii, for example, or multilingual Switzerland — and internationally. In addition, distinct racial or cultural differences are not necessarily a precondition for war, either: Paraguay and her racially and culturally similar neighbors fought some extraordinarily bloody wars in the nineteenth century, as did Austrians and Prussians, North and South Koreans, and North and South Vietnamese, not to mention the long and tragic history of civil wars within ethnically homogeneous nations such as Spain or China.

A very high proportion of armed conflicts, however, do involve members of different ethnic/religious/cultural/linguistic groups, such as Iraq (Arab) versus Iran (Persian), Jew and Arab in the Middle East, Irish Catholic versus Protestant in Northern Ireland, Tamil versus Sinhalese in Sri Lanka, and so on. In the tiny, land-locked African state of Burundi, for example, the government is largely controlled by the Tutsis, a tribal and racial group that tends to be relatively tall and slender, and who comprise only about 15 percent of that country's population of about 5 million. By contrast, the Hutus, shorter and stockier, and of Bantu derivation, comprise the remaining 85 percent. In 1982, frustrated and vengeful Hutus murdered approximately 2,000 Tutsis, in many cases by amputating their legs (thereby making them "shorter"). In retaliation, about 150,000 Hutus were slaughtered.

In a sense, there is nothing new about this. Hatreds based on ethnic and religious differences were at the root of many wars throughout history, including notably the Crusades of the Middle Ages (European Christian versus Arab Moslem) and the Thirty Years' War (largely Catholic versus Protestant), which devastated Europe in the seventeenth century. To a degree, no clear distinction can be made between national antagonisms based on religion and those based on differing race and ethnicity. Many of the recent African wars (Ibo-Hausa,

Hutu-Tutsi) have been more ethnic than religious; the India-Pakistan wars, on the other hand, have been primarily religious, although the differences between Hindu and Moslem are so fundamental to Indian and Pakistani society that they merge into ethnic distinctions as well. The Iran-Iraq and Arab-Israeli conflicts involve both religious and ethnic differences, although the former is more ethnic, and the latter more religious.

Clearly, many other factors have been operating in each of these conflicts: border disputes, a history of antagonism based at least partly on generations of real or perceived oppression, economic rivalries, and the like. And typically, these various "causes" provide the immediate stimulus for each outbreak of violence. At the same time, national and often racial sentiment commonly linger in the background as a crucial underlying "cause," and also as an explanation for the persistence and intensity of many conflicts. In addition, once war erupts — even if for other immediate reasons — the belligerents quickly seize on any discernible differences between themselves and their opponents, typically magnifying these differences, elevating their own traits, and devaluing those of the other side. Often, it is sufficient just to point to the opponents as different — that is, as Hondurans rather than Salvadorans, or Koreans rather than Japanese — to evoke potent antagonisms. As we have seen, dehumanizing language is often introduced at this point as well.

A year after the beginning of World War I, Einstein lamented humanity's insistence on primitive hatred and its use of nationalism as the vehicle for that hatred:

> When posterity recounts the achievements of Europe, shall we let men say that three centuries of painstaking cultural effort carried us no further than from the fanaticism of religion to the insanity of nationalism? It would seem that men always seek some idiotic fiction in the name of which they can hate one another. Once it was religion; now it is the state [for "state," read "nationalism"].[9]

It is worth emphasizing that "state worship" and nationalism, of the sort that Einstein so decried, come together especially in fascism and other ultranationalist ideologies of statism.

NATIONALISM AND THE PUBLIC MOOD

Opinions count, especially when it comes to issues of peace or war, and this is even more true in a democracy. "Opinion," wrote Alexander Hamilton, "whether well or ill founded is the governing principle of human affairs." And Abraham Lincoln noted that "he who molds public sentiment goes deeper than he who enacts statutes or pronounces decisions."

Inflaming Public Sentiment

Wars can be provoked for many reasons, including so-called reasons of state (see Chapter 9), which, at the outset, evoke very little nationalist passion on the part of the participants; rather, they proceed in large part from the machinations of leadership (see Chapter 10). In order to prosecute wars, however, especially in the modern era, it has proven necessary to inflame the public, after which states have often found that it is easier to start a war than to stop, or even control, it.

In 1853, for example, Britain and France entered a war between Russia and the Ottoman empire, on the side of the Turks. They took this step after Russia had annexed the principalities of Wallachia and Moldavia (now divided between Romania and the U.S.S.R.) from the Ottoman empire and then resoundingly defeated the Turks in a famous naval battle at Sinope. After this Crimean War began, Austrian diplomacy successfully maneuvered the Russian troops out of the two contested principalities, thereby removing the main political basis for the war. But its emotional basis remained unresolved: In the war fever occasioned by outrage over the "massacre at Sinope,"* as well as the excitement over launching an expeditionary force to punish the evil czar, the British and French governments soon found that they had a tiger by the tail. The Western allies therefore decided to attack the Russian city of Sebastopol, on the Crimean

---

*A major reason for British outrage over the Russians' naval success was that it raised fear that British mastery of the oceans might eventually be contested.

Peninsula, a seemingly vulnerable region that would provide the dramatic victory needed to satisfy the aroused British and French publics. Instead of the anticipated quick and easy victory, however, they lost 500 (out of 700) British cavalrymen in the heroic but incalculably stupid Charge of the Light Brigade (which subsequently was immortalized in Tennyson's poem), as well as tens of thousands of additional lives, mostly from disease. Without the pressure of nationalist sentiment, there probably wouldn't have been any Crimean War at all, or, at worst, a brief and inconsequential war.

Manipulating Public Opinion

In modern times, most governments recognize that war requires the mobilization of national sentiments, and so, if real affronts to national dignity, honor, or well-being are not available, pretexts are typically arranged. Even Hitler, who clearly hankered to invade Poland in 1939, found it necessary to stage a phony "incident" to justify his actions and help arouse German national indignation: He staged an attack, allegedly by Polish forces (but actually by Germans wearing Polish uniforms), against a German radio station. The so-called Gulf of Tonkin incident, in which U.S. destroyers were supposed to have been attacked by North Korea, is now acknowledged to have been exaggerated and manipulated by the U.S. government, so as to induce congressional authorization and public support for the direct involvement of U.S. combat units in Vietnam.

Effective orators and publicists have long been able to sway public mood, often generating enthusiasm for war. The ancient Greek historian Thucydides recounts that the Athenian general Alcibiades stirred up irresistible public demands for glory, booty, and adventure. "With this enthusiasm of the majority," notes Thucydides, "the few that liked it not feared to appear unpatriotic by holding up their hands against it, and so they kept quiet."[10] The result was an expedition against Syracuse (in modern-day Sicily) that ultimately proved disastrous.

In the second century B.C., when Carthage had long ceased to be a threat to Rome, the elderly and eloquent Cato would repeat, after every one of his speeches, *Carthago delenda est* ("Carthage must be destroyed"). And in the ensuing Punic War, it was. The U.S. entry into the Spanish-American War was promoted by lurid and often exaggerated accounts of Spanish atrocities in Cuba: the so-called yellow journalism of the Hearst newspaper chain, which favored war. The U.S. battleship *Maine* was blown up while in Havana harbor, allegedly by Spanish agents; this inflamed American passions, and "Remember the Maine" became a slogan of that war, just as "Remember the Alamo" had served in the Mexican-American War. Some historians now maintain that the *Maine* was actually sunk by a prowar group, to provide a pretext for the hostilities that followed.

One of the most famous cases of the manipulation of public mood was the handiwork of Otto von Bismarck, prime minister of Prussia and later the first chancellor of a unified German nation-state. His machinations are worth examining. Eager for a war with France as a means of uniting the German "nation," Bismarck wanted France to appear the aggressor so as to ensure the enthusiastic cooperation of the various German ministates. He managed to goad the French into declaring war, as follows: Prince Leopold, a member of the Prussian Hohenzollern royal family, had fortuitously been offered the vacant throne of Spain. The French government objected, not wanting to be surrounded by two powerful states that were so closely allied; Leopold relented and refused the crown, whereupon France insisted on a guarantee that no Hohenzollern would ever rule Spain. This demand was presented to the Prussian king, Wilhelm I, at the city of Ems. Wilhelm agreed in principle, but responded politely that the rigid French demand could not be accepted as written, since this would appear to be an abject capitulation. Wilhelm sent a telegram to Bismarck, informing him of these events, whereupon Bismarck edited this "Ems dispatch" so that it appeared to be an insulting response to the French demand. The Ems dispatch aroused enormous fury in France when it was published, and with all the passion of aroused national indignation, France promptly declared war . . . which was precisely what Bismarck wanted. Listen to this account of how Paris responded to the outbreak of the Franco-Prussian war:

> I saw people running along the Rue Vivienne; I promptly ran after them. The steps of the Stock Exchange, from top to bottom, were a sea of bare heads, with hats flung into the air and every voice raised in a tremendous Marseillaise, the roar of which drowned the buzz of noise from the stockbrokers' enclosure inside the building. I have never seen such an outburst of enthusiasm. One kept running into men pale with emotion, children hopping around in excitement and women making drunken gestures. Capoul was singing the Marseillaise from the top of an omnibus in the Place de la Bourse; on the Boulevard, Marie Sasse was singing it standing in her carriage, practically carried along by the delirium of the mob.[11]

In the resulting war, Bismarck's forces achieved decisive victories, and the loose German confederation became solidified as greater Germany. The French province of Alsace, as well as part of Lorraine, was ceded to Germany, and France was also forced to pay substantial financial reparations. France subsequently seethed with national resentment toward Germany, which contributed ultimately to World War I . . . which contributed to World War II . . . which contributed to the fracturing of Europe into Eastern and Western "blocs" that continued for another forty-five years.

Quenching Public Passions

There was one period in European history — the eighteenth century — when wars, although frequent, were notably restrained. "The fundamental reason why war was less atrocious in the eighteenth century, than either before or since," writes historian Arnold Toynbee,

> was that it had ceased to be a weapon of religious fanaticism and had not yet become an instrument of nationalist fanaticism. During this interval it was merely a "sport of kings." Morally, the use of war for this more frivolous purpose may be all the more shocking, but the effect in mitigating the material horrors of war is undeniable. The royal players knew

quite well the degree of licence that their subjects would allow them, and they kept their activities well within these bounds. Their armies were not recruited by conscription;* they did not live off the country they occupied like the armies of the Wars of Religion, nor did they wipe the works of peace out of existence like the armies of the twentieth century. They observed the rules of their military game, set themselves moderate objectives and did not impose crushing terms on their defeated opponents.[12]

With the onset of nationalist passions, however, the comparative delicacy of eighteenth-century warfare became history.

As we have seen, there is a tradition of hoping and expecting that public opinion — acting through democratic government — will serve as a check on war. Once public opinion is mobilized in support of a war, however, a rational conclusion to that war apparently becomes virtually impossible; even reasoned debate about ending the conflict becomes difficult, since in the nationalist passion it arouses, those who urge a more conciliatory course are often branded as unpatriotic or downright treasonous. In addition, although a kind of exhaustion often sets in during a war, in most cases there is also an enhanced sense of determination as well as a malicious feedback loop whereby sacrifice demands yet more sacrifice. During the Vietnam War, for example, advocates argued that the fighting should be continued, and in fact, intensified, to assure an outcome favorable to the United States, which would in turn justify the loss of so many lives and the expenditure of so much revenue.

When wars were fought out of allegiance to the person of the local lord, king, emperor, pope, shogun, or maharaja, it was relatively easy to call a halt to the proceedings once the leaders in question decided to do so. But when wars are fought out of allegiance to national imagery, prestige, or ideology, against a rival seen to embody a detested alternative

---

*We should note here that whereas universal conscription did not exist in the eighteenth century, conscription and impressment, on a smaller scale, were common, as were militias and feudal levies before them.

"Do You Want This?" German World War I poster intended to evoke fear, hatred, and a desire to defend German womankind against the Allied enemy, pictured here as brutish and (of course) non-Aryan. (Department of Rare Books and Special Collections, McGill University Library)

image—and when the efforts and emotions of an entire citizenry have been aroused—it becomes much more difficult to quench the flames. Never has a nation's leadership, after declaring war, subsequently announced that it had changed its mind!

We criticize giving "aid and comfort to the enemy," and we have many terms, such as *treason, traitor, betrayal,* to describe the act of undermining one's country by collaborating with an opponent, especially during war. By contrast, we are conspicuously silent about those who, by their actions, create enemies, and we have no terms to describe those who err on the other side: who undermine their country by being excessively eager to fight or unwilling to seek an equitable peace. During World War I, for example, the government of Britain resolutely refused even to consider examining on what terms—short of unconditional surrender—peace with the Central Powers might be negotiated, not even breaching the possibility that such peace might have been achieved by German agreement

to withdraw from France and Belgium, as well as return Alsace/Lorraine.*

A further consequence of evoking public passions is that many present-day nationalist wars remain unresolved, partly because relatively few recent wars have been successful in ending the underlying conflict that generated the war itself: Korea remains divided and heavily armed; India and Pakistan are still hostile and suspicious (although Bangladesh is independent); the Middle East remains a tinderbox; even the Falklands/Malvinas still lingers as an unresolved dispute between Britain and Argentina, despite Britain's decisive military victory. Nationalist passions keep long-kept rivalries simmering, interfering with the prospects of reconciling old disputes or healing old injuries. Moreover, modern nation-states have many more

---

*Ostensibly, this was one of the main reasons why Britain and France were fighting.

resources available than they had in the past. Finally, superpower allies of the contestants, reluctant to permit their clients to suffer an unconditional defeat, often prolong hostilities: The U.S.S.R. keeps resupplying the Arab states, the United States and China keep Pakistan armed against India, and so on. In some cases, however, closure on a nationalist war has been achieved, generally when the most intensely pronationalist side won: This happened in Vietnam, as in most anticolonial wars of national liberation. In other cases, a decisive move by an inspired national leader — as with Sadat's overtures to Israel — can overcome the prowar drift of nationalist passion.*

NATIONALISM VERSUS POLITICAL IDEOLOGY

Even so potent a force as political ideology (see Chapter 9) can appear pallid compared to the energies of nationalism, which is in a sense a primitive and widespread ideology of its own. The Russians and the Chinese are both Marxist, but they are Russians and Chinese first, as witnessed by their armed border clashes and persistent antagonism in recent decades.† Similarly, the Vietnamese and the Khmer Rouge of Cambodia have been bitter enemies, despite their shared communist ideology, as have been the Vietnamese and the Chinese, who fought a short but vicious war in 1979.

Perhaps the most dramatic case, however, of the triumph of nationalism over political ideology occurred in the early days of World War I. (More accurately, nationalist and imperialist ideology clashed with internationalist and socialist ideology . . . and the former won.) In the years prior to World War I, the European Socialist parties were

powerful, seemingly united, and for the most part committed to opposing the institution of war, which was viewed as part of capitalist exploitation of the proletariat. Through various international resolutions as well as others within each major European country, the large Socialist parties (most influentially, those of Germany and France) asserted that if war ever appeared imminent, their memberships would smother it by general strikes and, if necessary, insurrections. Solidarity among the working class would make war impossible: "They" might declare a war, but no one would come.

Before war was in fact declared, however, French socialists worried that German socialists would be unable to restrain German militarism, which would leave France fettered while Germany triumphed; German socialists, in turn, feared that success on their part would leave Germany at the mercy of regressive Russia. In the end, an overwhelming majority within the Socialist parties of each nation announced support for the war, because for *their* country, such a war would be defensive. The following declaration, by the Social Democratic Party of Germany in 1914, shows the tenor of thinking at the time:

> We are menaced by the terror of foreign invasion. The problem before us now is not the relative advisability of war or peace, but a consideration of just what steps must be taken for the protection of our country. . . . As far as concerns our people and its independence, much, if not everything, would be endangered by a triumph of Russian despotism, already weltering in the blood of her own noblest sons. It devolves upon us, therefore, to avert this danger, to shelter the civilization and independence of our native land. Therefore, we must to-day justify what we have always said. In its hour of danger Germany may ever rely upon us. We take our stand upon the doctrine basic to the international labor movement, which at all times has recognized the right of every people to national independence and national defense, and at the same time we condemn all war for conquest.[13]

On the other hand, sometimes ideology and nationalism go hand in hand, producing a combination that is especially potent. The war-prone imperialism of France during the eighteenth and nineteenth centuries, for example, was enhanced

---

*It must also be noted that several years after his courageous initiative, Sadat was assassinated by outraged Arab/Islamic nationalists.

†Of course, there are also examples that go the other way, such as the conflict between North and South Koreans, North and South Vietnamese, Nicaraguan Sandinistas and contras, and East and West Germans. In all these cases, however, ideological differences are fanned by the competition between the United States and the U.S.S.R.

by the French commitment to their *mission civilisatrice*, the notion that France had a special mission to civilize the non-French world. Similarly, German national militarism in the twentieth century was buttressed by Nazi yearnings for a "thousand year Reich" peopled by a triumphant "Aryan race." Part of the Soviet Union's enthusiasm for expansionism, as well as support for Third World national revolutions, has come from devotion to Marxist ideology, just as the American ideology of democratic capitalism and the vision of the United States as the "new Jerusalem," a shining "city on the hill" uniquely pleasing to God and man, undergirded U.S. territorial expansionism during the nineteenth century, and overcame a penchant for isolationism in the first half of the twentieth century.

In most cases, peace movements fare poorly during wartime, overwhelmed by militant national enthusiasm. There are exceptions, however: Notably, a kind of "war weariness" can set in, especially when the war itself is controversial and/or appears to be stalemated. The Vietnam War was such an example, controversial from the start and terminated in large part because the enthusiasm of the American citizenry was insufficient, and turned increasingly to public outrage. World War I turned out to be much bloodier than expected, and after several years, seemed nowhere near resolution. Although citizen support remained generally high (except in Russia), mutinies became frequent: Fifty-four divisions (about one half the total) of the French army mutinied in April 1917; 25,000 men were eventually court-martialed. Such behavior proved contagious: One month later, in May 1917, 400,000 Italian troops deserted the field at Caporetto, and around the same time, German and Russian troops were fraternizing openly.

THE TENSION BETWEEN PEACE AND FREEDOM

Some of humanity's most stirring visions and most memorable sacrifices have been made on behalf of freedom, typically efforts of national groups to achieve self-determination. Consider, for example, the blood-tingling sentiments of these lines from Robert Burns's poem (later put to music) "Scots Wha Hae," originally written in support of renewed Scottish national independence (Scotland was once an independent state, before being incorporated into Great Britain):

> By oppression's woes and pain! By your sons in servile chains!
> We will drain our dearest veins. But they shall be free!
>
> Lay the proud usurpers low! Tyrants fall in every foe!
> Liberty's in every blow! Let us do or die.*[14]

Historical Background

Many people today think of nationalism as a cause of war (and as we have seen, they are at least partly correct). Certainly, nationalist sentiments such as those expressed by Burns—whether laudable or not—are not likely to lead to the peaceful resolution of disputes. It may therefore be surprising to learn that through much of the nineteenth and early twentieth centuries, nationalism was widely viewed as a potentially strong contributor to *peace*. After all, intense and homogeneous nationhood should guarantee unity within a state, and diminish the likelihood of civil war.

Moreover, by producing a cross-cutting loyalty—one that transcends connections of economic class, local leadership, even religion—feelings of national identity apparently have sometimes contributed to peace and stability. Nationalism has helped end many instances of endemic subnational conflict. Following the establishment of nation-states in western Europe, for example, the low-level feuding and banditry, as well as the religious and class violence, that had long characterized that region was virtually terminated. The same can be said for much of prenational India, China, and Japan. Perhaps, if feelings of national identity were stronger, the destructive violence of the Spanish, Chinese, or Nigerian civil wars would not have occurred. The War Between the States, the bloodiest war in U.S. history, took place because feelings of regional identity (especially in the South) were

---

*Pronounced in Scottish to rhyme with "free."

Three Confederate soldiers during the United States Civil War. For these men, and much of the American South, regional identity was stronger than national identity. (Library of Congress)

stronger than those of national identity. The idea of nationalism as a route to peace is nonetheless ironic in that the first nation-state to achieve what is generally regarded as the modern level of national self-consciousness — Napoleonic France — embarked almost immediately on the most expansionist domestically fueled wars that Europe had experienced up to that time.

Nationalist leaders, like the apostle of Italian unification Giuseppi Mazzini (1805–1872), continued to maintain that peace would ensue when every nationality constituted its own state. However, not surprisingly, advocates of national self-determination typically considered that peace itself was subordinate to freedom as an immediate goal. Mazzini himself, perhaps the most literate and charismatic of the many young evangelists of nationalism in Europe during the nineteenth century, maintained that education and insurrection would liberate Italy:

> Education must ever be directed to teach by example, word and pen the necessity of insurrection. . . . Insurrection — by means of guerilla bands — is the true method of warfare for all nations desirous of emancipating themselves from a foreign yoke. . . . It

forms the military education of the people and consecrates every foot of the native soil by memory of some warlike deed.[15]

Twenty years later, he was still calling for "War, in the noble intention of restoring Truth and Justice, and of arresting Tyranny in her inhuman career, of rendering the Nations free and happy and causing God to smile upon them benignly."[16]

Nationalist wars did in fact follow Mazzini's call. In 1859, France defeated Austria and helped liberate Italy. Prussia and Austria "freed" Schleswig and Holstein from Denmark; then Prussia defeated Austria to help unite the German states, and followed this up by "liberating" Alsace and Lorraine from France to form Germany in 1871. Throughout the nineteenth century, the various "captive nations" of Europe made numerous appeals to European conscience; Montenegro, Romania, Serbia, Bulgaria, and Greece succeeded in gaining their independence from Turkey, although the Poles (under Russia) and Hungarians (under Austria) failed.

Much of European liberal thought of the nineteenth century reflected an important question that continues to be debated by students of peace even now: What is the right course when two cherished goals — freedom and peace — conflict? Thus, more than a century ago, there was widespread sympathy (and not just among ardent nationalists) for the struggles of Eastern Christians against Turkey, Poles against Russia, the Irish against England, Italians against Austria, and before that, much of Europe against Napoleon. At the same time, it was recognized that the fight for freedom may require breaches of the peace. There was real tension, therefore, in reconciling a cherishing of peace with a commitment to freedom. This conflict caused substantial difficulty, for example, for the British Peace Society, whose leader complained at one point that "this idea of nationality is a poor, low, selfish, unchristian idea, at variance with the very principles of advanced civilization."[17]

The International League for Peace and Freedom was established in Paris in 1867. The guest of honor at its first meeting, the Italian patriot Garibaldi, called for replacing monarchy with democracy, separating church and state, and establishing, ultimately, a United States of Europe, if need be by war. There were also disillusionments. Widespread enthusiasm for the Balkan League (Greece, Bulgaria, and Montenegro*) in their 1912 struggle with Turkey was dampened when the victorious states refused to cooperate and began fighting among themselves, in part over conflicting claims to the newly established state of Albania. This in turn precipitated the Second Balkan War of 1913. It doesn't take a genius to recognize that more states means more boundaries, and hence more opportunities for antagonisms to proliferate. By the turn of the century, therefore, the attitude toward nationalism had become ambivalent: support for oppressed minorities — captive nations within oppressive empires — tempered by anxiety about a world divided into numerous feisty, competing, and independent units. The derogatory term often applied is "Balkanization"; indeed, the Balkans were long known as the "tinderbox of Europe."

The Post–World War II Scene

In the sense of avoiding major armed conflict, Europe has been largely "peaceful" since World War II, perhaps partly because of the existence of nuclear weapons. But Europe has also achieved a fair degree of national self-determination: just about all French live in France, virtually all Germans in one Germany or the other (or in Austria), nearly all Poles in Poland, and so forth. There are, however, Austrians in northern Italy (the Tyrol), Hungarians in Romania, and Albanians in Yugoslavia; in each case, the presence of the minority group has led to substantial unease and occasional violence today. In addition, there are simmering separatist movements among the Spanish Basques and Catalans, the Catholics in Northern Ireland, and occasionally, the Swiss in the Jura region, as well as tension between Flemings, who speak a Dutch/German dialect, and French-speaking Walloons in Belgium. With the weakening of centralized communist controls following the democratic "revolutions" of 1989, there is some risk that long-suppressed nationalist antagonisms, such as between the Bulgars and ethnic Turks in Bulgaria, will emerge violently. But by and large, European states have become nation-states, and they may be more peaceful (internally, at least) as a result.†

Other regions are less fortunate. Palestinians currently strive — violently and nonviolently — for national self-determination that has been denied them. India is a patchwork of dozens, perhaps hundreds, of potential nations speaking more than a thousand languages. China contains more than 50 million non-Chinese, of which the Tibetans are notably oppressed and resentful. The U.S.S.R. is a vast heterogeneous assemblage, increasingly restive as

---

†Yugoslavia is a notable exception, because it was cobbled together after World War I, consisting of many nations united primarily by a fear of Germany. Resentments among the Yugoslav nationalities are nearly as strong as the pressures making for a unified state; conflicts between Serbs and ethnic Albanians have been violent, and prosperous Slovenia threatens to secede altogether.

---

*Today part of Yugoslavia.

the Kremlin seeks to permit greater political freedom and openness while still maintaining the Soviet Union as a single state. The boundaries of the postcolonial African states are nothing less than a disaster, since they were drawn (by Europeans) with virtually no regard to the nationality of their people.

The Effects of Political Ideology

Finally, there is the prickly question of fundamental values: Peace, admittedly, is immensely important, but is it infinitely valuable? Is peace so worthy an end that it should be maintained at all costs? And what of the connection between peace and freedom, or justice? What if justice — including national self-determination — cannot be obtained without war? In the latter part of the twentieth century, many Western advocates of peace tend to view nationalism as an evil if it is practiced by the Western powers, not only because it has in the past led to imperialism, but also because it may contribute to a growing danger of nuclear war. At the same time, there is a tendency to look favorably on wars of national liberation, if directed by the oppressed against their oppressors: the Algerian struggles against France during the 1950s and 1960s, the Mau-Mau movement for independence of Kenya from Britain during that same time, and even the Vietnamese conflict with the United States. Currently, many people, while considering themselves supporters of peace, are reluctant to condemn revolutionary wars directed against rightist regimes, as in El Salvador, or against remnants of colonial oppression, as in Namibia.

At the same time, right-wing anticommunists, while deploring revolutionary nationalist violence (which they typically see as communist-inspired and therefore especially illegitimate), applaud various equally violent counterrevolutionary wars, such as that of the contras in Nicaragua, UNITA in Angola, or the *mujahedeen* in Afghanistan. Seemingly, both right- and left-wing ideologies are willing to value freedom over peace, so long as "freedom" is defined as either (in the first case) freedom from Marxist governments or (in the second) freedom from colonial or right-wing military dictators.

Within the United States, partisans of the political right (that is, conservatives) tend to see antiestablishment revolutionary movements as necessarily aligned with "worldwide communism." By contrast, centrists and leftists are more likely to emphasize the nationalist, rather than the ideological, underpinnings of such activities. They point out, for example, that Josip Tito, anti-Nazi partisan leader and later president of Yugoslavia, was a nationalist first and a communist second (he withdrew Yugoslavia from the Warsaw Pact, for instance); similarly, Ho Chi Minh was more committed to Vietnamese nationalism than to communism of either the Chinese or Soviet variety.*

There can be no doubt that the effort to achieve freedom via national struggle has produced many wars (of liberation and, more recently, of counter-liberation). Moreover, enthusiastic adherence to the goals of the nation-state has also generated additional wars (of conquest), while setting the stage for a possible showdown between nuclear-armed nation-states.

THE QUESTION OF "NATIONAL CHARACTER"

No evidence whatsoever points to any genetically influenced behavioral differences among people of differing nationality. Nonetheless, the belief persists that a nation, like an individual, can in some cases be characterized by certain summed personality traits. In fact, numerous errors of political judgment have resulted from a misreading of the "national character" of a prospective opponent. Hitler, for example, and Napoleon before him, felt that the English were "soft," a "nation of shopkeepers," and

---

*Nationalists are not necessarily benign, however, even though they may be less threatening to the United States; Romanian dictator Nicolai Ceausescu, for example, was a nationalist first and a communist second, but nonetheless very much a despot.

Adolf Hitler being hailed by the German people. Hitler evoked powerful positive emotions among his followers. (Brown Brothers)

therefore neither willing to resist aggression nor capable of doing so. During the eighteenth century, Germans were widely considered to be either philosophical metaphysicians or incurable romantics, not cut out for heavy industry or any other practical undertakings; the Italians, by contrast, were seen as highly rational and scientifically inclined. Today, these stereotypes have reversed.

Often, such perceptions are self- (or rather, nation-) serving, as well as incorrect. During World War II, for example, part of the Allied justification for bombing German cities was that, unlike the British moral fiber, which was by definition indomitable, the German will to persevere would crumble under bombardment, leading perhaps to revolt and thereby shortening the war. Official government documents claim that

the evidence at our disposal goes to show that the morale of the average German civilian will weaken quicker than that of a population such as our own as a consequence of direct attack. The Germans have been undernourished and subjected to a permanent strain equivalent to that of war conditions during almost the whole period of Hitler's regime, and for this reason also will be liable to crack before a nation of greater stamina.[18]

There is debate about whether strategic bombing actually shortened World War II by creating shortages of critical materials, notably ball bearings and petroleum, in the final months; however, it is widely acknowledged that, if anything, bombing increased the German will to resist. Certainly, the German national character did not "crack." Twenty-five years later, the United States similarly underestimated the ability and willingness of the North Vietnamese to absorb punishing bomb attacks, and yet persevere in a war to which they, as a nation, were committed.

The persistence of the idea of "national character" is probably due to the fact that, while it is incorrect biologically, it has a certain short-term psychological and sociological reality. Thus, a "national style," in speech, clothing, even responses to stress or to potential enemies, can be exhibited. These styles can and do change over time, but they nonetheless have some limited consistency. For example, Mediterranean people (Italians, Greeks) tend to be relatively more voluble and excitable than people of more northern climes (Scandinavians, Germans, British). Latin Americans and Arabs tend to maintain less interpersonal distance than do Americans or Europeans, which sometimes leads to misunderstandings at international gatherings. By American standards, Japanese are unusually concerned with politeness and social formality, and Russians annoyingly secretive and mistrustful, while by Russian standards, Americans are insufferably brash and outspoken. When Premier Khrushchev arrived in the United States for a summit conference with President Eisenhower, he unwittingly antagonized many Americans by clasping both hands above his head, in a gesture used to signal "victory" by U.S. prizefighters; in the U.S.S.R., the same action is used to communicate friendship and solidarity.

Patterns of family life and personal development can also influence behavior patterns characteristic of the nation as a whole. According to the psychoanalyst Erik Erikson, the political appeal of nazism to Germans in the 1930s was based at least partly on the authoritarian style of the typical German family, in which the father was both tyrannical and remote:

> When the father comes home from work, even the walls seem to pull themselves together. The children hold their breath, for the father does not approve of "nonsense" — that is, neither of the mother's feminine moods nor of the children's playfulness. . . . Later, when the boy comes to observe the father in company, when he notices his father's submission to superiors, and when he observes his excessive

sentimentality when he drinks and sings with his equals, the boy acquires . . . a deep doubt of the dignity of man — or at any rate, of the "old man."[19]

Such confusion makes social maturation difficult. Erikson opines that if the "Fuhrer" had sought to appear as a straightforward father figure, he would have evoked ambivalence from the German citizenry. Instead, Hitler appealed to the German "national character" as a glorified, indomitable older brother.

Take another example: Europeans developed one of the world's most bloodthirsty warrior traditions. They also traditionally raised large numbers of cattle and pigs, but because of a shortage of fodder during the long, cold winters, for centuries European pastoralists — especially those in the northern regions — had to slaughter all but a few of their animals every fall. According to one renowned historian, "This may have had a good deal to do with their remarkable readiness to shed human blood and think nothing of it."[20]

Whatever the role of "national character," and of shared national experience in molding such traits, the role of national self-image is undeniable. Nations invariably see themselves as well meaning and motivated only by the purest of goals; their opponents, on the other hand, typically see them in a rather different light (see Chapter 10). For example, Americans generally viewed their efforts on behalf of postwar reconstruction (the Truman Doctrine and the Marshall Plan), which included assistance to defeated Germany and Japan, as generous and laudable. To the Soviets, it was entirely self-serving: a form of economic imperialism, a device to relieve American postwar overproduction, as well as a political weapon directed against their country and their nation.

A FINAL NOTE ON NATIONALISM

Undeniably, nationalism can be beautiful, especially when it evokes compassion and love and serves as a positive force for human cooperation and even ecological awareness. Love of the land, the people, the culture, the ecosystem can contribute toward dignity, caring, altruism, and some of the finer emotions of which human beings are capable. At the same time, however, nationalism can become malevolent when it fosters intolerant chauvinism, when it creates violent divisions between people, when it threatens to destroy the values it supposedly venerates. Nationalism pumps people up, generating conditions that often bring them down as well. In his essay "Christianity and Patriotism," Leo Tolstoy pitied "the good-natured foolish people, who, showing their healthy white teeth as they smile, gape like children, naively delighted at the dressed-up admirals and presidents, at the flags waving above them, and at the fireworks, and the playing bands."[21] Tolstoy warned that this euphoria is typically short-lived, since the flags and cheerful bands are quickly replaced by "only the desolate wet plain, cold, hunger, misery — in front of them the slaughterous enemy, behind them the relentless government, blood, wounds, agonies, rotting corpses and a senseless, useless death."[22] One of the great challenges to students of peace thus is to channel the benevolent aspects of nationalism, while guarding against its horrors.

Study Questions

1. Distinguish between a nation and a state; give examples, including states that aren't nations and nations that aren't states.

2. Describe some advantages and disadvantages of nationalist sentiment.

3. Trace, briefly, the role of nationalism in causing World War I.

4. Is there any indication that nationalism is a less powerful — and potentially disruptive — force today?

5. Give modern-day examples of secessionism, reintegrationism, and irredentism other than those described in this text.

6. Discuss similarities and differences between nationalist, racial, and cultural intolerance and the tribal warfare described in the previous chapter.

7. It is sometimes said that war is not really a result of anger and aggressiveness, but rather the consequence of a great deal of serious rational thought; even if this is true, especially of leadership decision making, discuss the use of nationalist sentiment, through history, to appeal to apparently primitive human emotions.

8. In this chapter, you read that "Even so potent a force as political ideology . . . can appear pallid compared to the energies of nationalism." Give some current examples that both support and contradict this proposition.

9. During the nineteenth century, many people felt that nationalism could be a potent force for peace. Explain. Could it be, today?

10. Give arguments for and against the concept of "national character."

Suggestions for Further Reading

Hans Kohn. 1946. *Prophets and Peoples: Studies in Nineteenth Century Nationalism*. Macmillan: New York.

Louis L. Snyder. 1976. *Varieties of Nationalism*. Holt, Rinehart & Winston: New York.

Karl W. Deutsch. 1979. *Tides Among Nations*. Free Press: New York.

Benedict Anderson. 1983. *Imagined Communities*. Verso: London.

Colin H. Williams and Eleonore Kofman. 1989. *Community Conflict, Partition and Nationalism*. Routledge: New York.

Source Notes

1. John Stoessinger. 1962. *The Might of Nations*. Random House: New York.

2. J. Ernest Renan. 1882. *Qu'est-ce qu'une nation?* Calmann-Levy: Paris.

3. Ibid.

4. George Orwell. 1953. *Such, Such Were the Joys*. Harcourt, Brace: New York.

5. H. Richard Niebuhr. 1970. *Radical Monotheism and Western Culture*. Harper & Row: New York.

6. Quoted in G. G. Van Deusen. 1937. *The Life of Henry Clay*. Little, Brown: Boston, MA.

7. Radio and TV address to the nation, April 30, 1970.

8. David W. Ziegler. 1977. *War, Peace, and International Politics*. Little, Brown: Boston.

9. Albert Einstein. 1979. *Einstein: A Centenary Volume*. Harvard University Press: Cambridge, MA.

10. Thucydides. 1919. *History of the Peloponnesian War*. Cambridge University Press: London.

11. Quoted in John Keegan and J. Darracott. 1981. *The Nature of War*. Holt, Rinehart & Winston: New York.

12. Arnold Toynbee. 1935. *A Study of History*. Oxford University Press: London.

13. Quoted in Kenneth N. Waltz. 1959. *Man, the State and War*. Columbia University Press: New York.

14. Robert Burns. 1927. *The Complete Writings of Robert Burns*. Houghton Mifflin: Boston.

15. Giuseppe Mazzini. 1891. *Life and Writings of Joseph Mazzini*. Smith, Elder & Co.: London.

16. Ibid.

17. Michael Howard. 1978. *War and the Liberal Conscience*. Rutgers University Press: New Brunswick, NJ.

18. Quoted in C. Webster and N. Frankland. 1961. *The Strategic Air Offensive Against Germany*. HMSO: London.

19. Erik Erikson. 1950. *Childhood and Society*. Norton: New York.

20. William McNeill. 1982. *The Pursuit of Power*. University of Chicago Press: Chicago.

21. Leo Tolstoy. 1987. *Writings on Civil Disobedience and Nonviolence*. New Society Publishers: Philadelphia, PA.

22. Ibid.

9

The State Level

Nothing appears more surprising to those who consider human affairs with a philosophical eye, than the easiness with which the many are governed by the few.
  David Hume

As we explore the various levels at which wars originate, we come now to the question of states. As we have seen, popular usage often makes no distinction between the terms *nation* and *state*, although the former correctly refers to a collection of people (see Chapter 8), and the latter to an entity that functions in the world political arena. Inhabitants of the United States are especially likely to be careless in this usage, since, unlike other states, which typically refer to their subdivisions as provinces, regions, republics, and the like, we use the word *state* to mean the level of political division ranking just below the U.S. federal government (for example, New York, Texas, or California).

DEFINING THE STATE

More generally, however, a state can be defined as a sovereign political unit that may include many different communities and that operates via a centralized government, which has the authority and power to decree and enforce laws, collect taxes, and act as the legally recognized representative of its citizens in exchanges with other states, including the waging of war.

The relationship between nations and states is complex. Although, as we have seen, there have long been efforts to make national and state borders coincide (creating nation-states), states also tend to suppress national movements within their borders: It has been estimated that there are 200 states containing more than 800 nationalist movements (more than 7,000 if ethnic identity alone is taken as the criterion for nationalism). At the same time, states promote their own, dominant nationalism. When nations are not organizing themselves into states, states seek to create nations by trying to unify the diverse peoples living within their borders.

The concept of statehood has often been imbued with an idealistic and almost metaphysical significance (so, for that matter, has the concept of nationhood). "What is the State essentially?" asked one scholar.

> The more closely we examine it, the more mystical and personal it becomes. On the Nation we can put our hand as a definite social group, with attitudes and qualities exact enough to mean something. On the Government we can put our hand as a certain organization of ruling functions, the machinery of law-making and law-enforcing. The Administration is a recognizable group of political functionaries, temporarily in charge of the government. But the State stands as an idea behind them all, eternal, sanctified, and from it Government and Administration conceive themselves to have the breath of life.[1]

This rather ethereal description notwithstanding, the modern state performs numerous specific functions and has immense power, in particular the power of war. When discussion of the state is not enveloped in emotional rhetoric ("wrapping one's self in the flag"), states justify their existence by appeals to rationality, and principles of efficiency and regularity. And yet, scholars increasingly recognize that perhaps the most crucial characteristic of the state is its monopoly on the use of legitimate physical violence within a specific physical territory. That is, states reserve unto themselves the privilege of taking human life, without being answerable to any higher secular authority:

> The state claims the privilege of killing people for such crimes as treason, sedition, and murder and in

such activities as wars, reprisals, and pacifications. The state also tries to prevent any other person or organization from killing within its jurisdiction by enforcing municipal laws against homicides, insurrections, and invasions and from killing its nationals abroad by diplomatic protection and intervention. Since this monopoly in killing is conceived as a characteristic of the state in the abstract, the recognition by each state of other states implies recognition of the equal right of every state to exercise the monopoly within its jurisdiction. This jurisdiction, however, is not easy to define because of the migratory character of nationals and armies and the frequent instruction of armies to kill foreigners abroad and to protect nationals abroad from being killed.[2]

Interestingly, the two political ideologies that particularly value the state, elevating it above the individual, are of the far left and the far right. Thus, in the communist world, individuals are held to be less important than the collectivity, typically represented by the state. Although Marxist theory calls for the eventual "withering away of the state," in practice, the governments of Marxist states are notably intrusive and generally intolerant of alternative forms of government. On the far right, Benito Mussolini wrote:

> The fascist conception of life stresses the importance of the State and accepts the individual only in so far as his interests coincide with those of the State. . . . The fascist conception of the State is all-embracing; outside of it no human or spiritual values can exist, much less have value.[3]

Mainstream liberals and conservatives seem also to be placing greater emphasis on the state, with liberals looking toward the promise of a benevolent "welfare state," and conservatives lauding the role of patriotism and the "national security state."* Peace activists, however, frequently criticize what they see as excessive emphasis on states; they argue that an inordinately state-centered view of world politics makes the continuation of states a foregone conclusion, thereby shutting out the prospects for other kinds of political "space," such as

---

*Sometimes derided as the "warfare state."

citizens' groups, bioregionalism, religious, ecological, or feminist alliances, and so on. But however the state is imagined, whether we like it or not, and whatever may be our goals for states in general and our own state in particular, states undeniably are the primary actors on the world stage today, and so we had better understand what they are about.

STATE SOVEREIGNTY

A very important concept related to theories about and practices of states is sovereignty, defined by French political economist Jean Bodin (in 1576) as "the state's supreme authority over citizens and subjects."[4] In other words, under the doctrine of sovereignty, states are the final arbiters of earthly disputes and issues. There is no higher recourse. This is supposed to be true during peacetime, but it is, if anything, exaggerated during war. Writing during the time of reigning monarchs, Bodin conceived of sovereignty especially in the sense of one's "sovereign lord," emphasizing the relationship of a subject to his or her ruler.

The Dutch jurist Hugo Grotius, writing a century later, made major contributions to the development of international law by considering the relationship of sovereign rulers to other such rulers; he contended that given the concept of state sovereignty, no ruler could be subject to legal control by another state. This principle, which still applies today, means that in theory the United States is legally on a par with, for example, Malta, an island state in the Mediterranean Sea one tenth the size of Rhode Island and containing about one third as many people.

The Price of State Sovereignty

A crucial consequence of state sovereignty is international anarchy. In a world composed of separate states, each of which is sovereign and, thus, legally equal, there cannot be — by definition — any recourse to higher authority in the solving of disputes. Conflicting claims among cities can be adjudicated by the government of a province, or whatever we call the next higher administrative unit. Conflicts among provinces can be adjudicated by the federal government that in some sense sits "above" these provinces. If different federal governments are truly sovereign unto themselves, however, there is no guarantee of orderly process — never mind harmony — when these entities quarrel. They may agree to submit their disputes to arbitration, mediation, or other forms of negotiation, or seek to employ diplomacy (see Chapter 13). But such efforts depend entirely on the voluntary goodwill of the states involved; that is, they involve temporary, and readily revoked, surrender of sovereignty. The Charter of the United Nations, for example, clearly states that it does not seek to restrict the sovereignty of the states making up this international organization (see Chapter 16).

When states disagree seriously, given that they are legally coequals, they are in theory "free" to engage in a violent test of strength, that is, war. (Or, looking at it differently, one might say that sovereign states engage in war when in fact they agree that war is the best way to resolve the issue between them.) In short, the doctrine of state sovereignty results in international — really, interstate — anarchy. Note that this does not necessarily imply disorder; in fact, much of the diplomatic exchange between states is highly structured. Rather, anarchy results from the absence of any overarching authority superior to that of states themselves. Bodin as well as Hobbes recognized that interstate violence, or war, is the price we pay for the system of state sovereignty, which, they claimed, maintains a degree of peace within states.

Others have placed much of the blame for war at the doorstep of the state system, although this has not necessarily led to rejection (even in theory) of the system of nation-states. More often, the mood is one of resignation:

> With many sovereign states, with no system of law enforceable among them, with each state judging its grievances and ambitions according to the dictates of its own reason or desire — conflict, sometimes leading to war, is bound to occur.[5]

It is sometimes claimed that the blood of martyrs has been the seed of the Christian church; in any event, the blood of soldiers has long been the seed of the state.

Violations of State Sovereignty

The doctrine of state sovereignty is very powerful, and all states claim to support it (although, in fact, efforts at spying and subversion represent frequent and sometimes continual violations of that doctrine). Thus, when Marshall J. Pilsudski, Polish nationalist and dictator, advised the French government in 1933 to overthrow the German government while Hitler was still weak, it was judged that under the doctrine of state sovereignty, Germany had the "right" to choose its own government.

This "right" has only been selectively respected, however. In 1979, for example, when the government of Tanzania, with the aid of Ugandan exiles, invaded Uganda and ousted the Ugandan despot Idi Amin, other governments generally applauded or remained silent. In 1956, the U.S.S.R. trampled on Hungarian sovereignty, putting down efforts at liberalization; Czechoslovakia suffered the same fate in 1968, and Poland was threatened with it in 1981. The U.S.S.R. may also be said to l.ave violated the sovereignty of Afghanistan following the 1979 invasion; supporters, however, can claim that the Soviets were merely responding to requests for assistance by the legitimate, Soviet-backed Afghan government. The U.S. government sought to arrange for the assassination of Cuba's Fidel Castro early in the 1960s, and attempted to kill Libya's Moammar Qaddafi by bombing his residence in 1986. The CIA engineered the forcible overthrow of democratically elected governments in Guatemala and Iran in the 1950s, and Chile in 1973 . . . and these are only some of the more widely acknowledged examples whereby state sovereignty has been violated.

When Britain, France, and Israel invaded Egypt in 1956, capturing the Suez Canal, international outrage (especially from the United States) forced them to withdraw and to respect Egyptian sovereignty. In 1984, the United States secretly and illegally planted mines in certain Nicaraguan harbors, despite the fact that Nicaraguan sovereignty is no less "real" — at least in theory — than Egyptian

sovereignty. In 1988, the U.S. government arranged for the extradition of an accused drug smuggler from Honduras, in clear violation of the Honduran Constitution and Honduran sovereignty. Outraged Hondurans rioted in response. In 1989, when the United States invaded Panama in clear violation of Panamanian sovereignty, worldwide condemnation was widespread but ineffectual. In short, while all state governments pay lip service to it, the doctrine of sovereignty is not consistently observed in practice.

Limitations of State Sovereignty

States have traditionally been very hesitant to allow the armed forces of another state to be stationed within their territory, or even to pass through. During World War II, for example, Spain's fascist government under Francisco Franco, although sympathetic to Nazi Germany, would not permit German troops to cross its territory. However, sovereignty can be surprisingly flexible. The government of South Korea hosts tens of thousands of U.S. troops and several hundred U.S. nuclear weapons; South Korean military forces are essentially under U.S. command, largely as a consequence of the Korean War. The United States, along with Britain and France, still maintains large military forces in West Germany, as does the U.S.S.R. in East Germany, consequences of the German defeat in World War II, which has limited the sovereignty of the two Germanies. (A strong desire to reestablish such sovereignty seems likely to lead to both Soviet and Western troop reductions, especially now that communism has been discredited in East Germany.) In a remarkable, if limited, surrender of sovereignty, the government of Sri Lanka invited Indian troops to enter that country, so as to police an attempted truce with Tamil separatists; this led to Indian troops becoming engaged in hostilities with Sri Lankans on Sri Lankan soil.

Since the late 1940s, the Soviet bloc countries of Eastern Europe experienced a limited kind of sovereignty: Their governments were administered entirely by their own nationals (Bulgaria by Bulgarians,

U.S. and South Korean soldier direct a Korean civilian during the annual U.S.-Korean joint military maneuvers in that country. The sovereignty of South Korea has, in a sense, been abridged by the stationing of U.S. troops on Korean soil. (U.S. Army)

Poland by Poles, and so on) but with the ever-present shadow of Soviet military might in the background. Even then, Romania had carved out an increasingly independent foreign policy for itself, while retaining a hard-line, Stalinist domestic stance. Hungary reversed the pattern, being quite loyal to the U.S.S.R.'s goals in external affairs, while liberalizing its internal economy considerably. (Some observers have suggested that a parallel situation applied to many NATO states, especially in Greece and Italy, just after the Second World War, when U.S. military and economic force was used to crush labor and antifascist resistance groups and install pro-Western, procapitalist governments.) In any event, the democratization of Eastern Europe appears to carry with it an enhancement of state sovereignty, as the U.S.S.R. announced its "Sinatra Doctrine": encouraging its former satellites to do things "their own way."

Finland offers an interesting case of compromised sovereignty, although less severe than had prevailed in the states of Eastern Europe. Finland is officially neutral, but its geographic proximity to the Soviet Union has led to the phenomenon of "Finlandization," whereby that state studiously refrains from antagonizing the U.S.S.R., especially in its foreign affairs.

The states of Western Europe are experiencing a kind of reduction in sovereignty, although this appears to be entirely voluntary. The European Parliament sets some economic and legal policy, in a sense over the heads of its constituent states; and the same can be said for the Western European economic union, the Common Market. For example, by eliminating tariffs between, and setting rules for the conduct of trade among, their member states, the rules of the Common Market circumscribe the economic sovereignty of each participant, ultimately for the good of all. In 1992, all trade barriers among the Common Market countries are scheduled to be lifted. Some suggest that this may be a preliminary to the eventual establishment of a "United States of Europe" (see Chapter 16).

Other economic unions — such as OPEC, the Organization of Petroleum Exporting Countries — have been less successful in getting their member states to subordinate their desires to those of the group as a whole. When Saudi Arabia, for example, refuses to restrict its crude oil production, thereby foiling OPEC efforts to drive oil prices up, it assigns primacy to the principle of state sovereignty.

As to the basis for sovereignty, it is to some extent enshrined in international law, since part of international law relies on the notion that a procedure, if customary, has legal validity (see Chapter 17). Historically, states have consistently supported the concept of sovereignty, even if not its practice in all cases. But underlying the legalities, the fundamental legitimacy of sovereignty appears to rest on force: Just as states have a monopoly on sanctioned violence within their borders, there do not now exist any suprastate structures capable of overriding a state's claim of sovereignty. In *The City of God*, Augustine tells the story of a pirate who had been captured by Alexander the Great. Alexander asked him what was his justification for "infesting" the sea.

And the pirate answered, with uninhibited insolence, "The same as yours, in infesting the earth! But because I do it with a tiny craft, I'm called a pirate. Because you have a mighty navy, you're called an emperor."[6]

THE STATE SYSTEM

The Origins of States and the State System

Many theories have been proposed to explain the origin of the state. Aristotle maintained that it was "natural," and therefore needed no explanation. Rousseau viewed it as a historical curiosity. Some anthropologists have suggested a relationship between the early production of agricultural surpluses (made possible by division of labor) and the presence of centralized organization to store, ship, and protect that surplus.[7] Others have emphasized the early association of primitive civilization with arid environments (as in Babylonia and Egypt) and the possible advantage of economies of scale* in providing for irrigation canals,[8] although, as has been pointed out, in some cases (China, Mexico) states developed before irrigation. Marxists maintain that states originated to police the dominance of one class over another. Most social scientists and historians, however, ascribe special importance to interactions among states, leaning toward what may be called the "conquest" theory to explain the origins of the state: Larger, well-integrated sociopolitical groupings succeeded in conquering smaller, less-integrated competitors, leading to the modern state system.

As noted in the previous chapter, the modern state system is generally thought to have originated with the Peace of Westphalia (1648), which ended the Thirty Years' War in central Europe. This was the last of the major European wars of religion, as various principalities of northern Europe defied the Holy Roman Emperor (Catholic and centered in Vienna) by becoming Protestant. At the Peace of Westphalia, the following formula (negotiated a century earlier) was reaffirmed: *cuius regio euius religio* ("whose the region, his the religion"). In

other words, the religion of the ruler would determine the faith to be sanctioned within each region. The effect of this arrangement was to elevate political states above the Holy Roman Emperor, even above the Roman Catholic church, and to establish the presumption that individuals owe personal loyalty to something relatively new, namely the state as embodied by the local ruler.

But even before this, states constituted a powerful force over their subjects. In Sweden, during the Thirty Years' War, for example, five-sevenths of the taxes raised were appropriated for the war effort. The state began rationing food to the civilian population, as well as establishing armaments monopolies, appropriating private lands, and selling war bonds. In the pursuit of armed might, the state began to penetrate nearly every aspect of civilian life. Several centuries earlier, distinctions had been blurred between the sacred and the secular, between religion and society; similarly, in the conduct of modern war, boundaries were erased between state and society. Just as the medieval knight was intimately connected with the Catholic church, the seventeenth-century armies (especially the Protestant forces) made virtually everyone into a functionary of the state.

War and the State System

Whatever its origins, the organization of people into states represents a major fact of life today, and the "state system" is crucial to the issues of peace and war. Even though people are organized in other ways — racially, vocationally, religiously, and so on — the state system has achieved a virtual monopoly not only on power (executions, wars), but also on political discourse and even our ability to imagine solutions to the problem of war. To a large extent, proposed courses of action within most peace movement traditions are "state-centered," and within traditional governmental circles policy options are focused entirely on the behavior of states.

Increasingly, as states came to be accepted without question as sovereign over the individuals within their boundaries, they were left free to interact with other states so as to maintain and enhance

---

*Economies of scale refer to the greater efficiency that is often achieved by doing things in a larger volume; for example, installing a new sewer line is cheaper, per household, if each family connects to the same system rather than installing its own.

their position. According to military historian Michael Howard, as often as not states fight "not over any specific issue such as might otherwise have been resolved by peaceful means, but in order to acquire, to enhance, or to preserve their capacity to function as independent actors in the international system at all."[9] And French philosopher Raymond Aron argued that "The stakes of war are the existence, the creation or the elimination of states."[10] In short, the wars between states, which characterize so much of the state system, are typically about states and the state system itself. On the other hand, since the end of World War II, the number of states in the world has tripled, largely because of decolonization, and yet the frequency of wars (as opposed to their intensity) has not increased comparably.

Certain states have been disproportionately involved in wars. These tend overwhelmingly to be the "Great Powers," especially those of Europe. According to Quincy Wright, of the 2,600 most important battles involving European states between 1480 and 1940, France participated in 47 percent, Austria-Hungary in 34 percent, Great Britain and Russia in 22 percent, Turkey in 15 percent, and Spain in 12 percent. Of 25 interstate wars since 1914, the Great Powers were involved in 19. Today, the United States and the U.S.S.R. together spend about two-thirds of all military budgets expended worldwide, and the Great Powers (the United States, the U.S.S.R., Great Britain, France, Germany, Italy, China, and Japan) nearly 90 percent. Several centuries ago, Spain, Turkey, Holland, and Sweden were involved in a high proportion of wars; with their decline as world powers, they have become substantially more peaceable as well.

These observations suggest that perhaps the problem of war is not so much a function of the system of states, but rather of certain states, and particularly, of the relative importance of these states. Furthermore, it can be argued that there is not, in fact, a "system" of states, but rather simply a number of separate entities, each pursuing its own interest (*realpolitik*). And yet, states apparently often act not only to preserve themselves but also to maintain the predominant international fabric of which they are part. A seeming counterexample

was the third and final partition of Poland (in 1793); in this case, a state was dismembered through the actions of other states. However, the parties to the partition — Prussia, Austria, and Russia — were all absolute monarchies, and Poland's system of elected rather than dynastic rulers was a particular challenge to the monarchical system. This was especially true since the just-completed French Revolution had called the legitimacy of hereditary monarchs into question.

Similarly, the French monarchy was enthusiastically reestablished by the Congress of Vienna — composed of the victorious, monarchical states of Europe — following Napoleon's defeat. The "Holy Alliance" at that time was dedicated to suppressing democratic stirrings, which threatened to disrupt the current "community of states." Thus, Austria and Russia cooperated to put down a Hungarian revolution in 1849. And following the Bolshevik Revolution, the Western allies sent an expeditionary force (1918–1920), which attempted to undo the fledgling Soviet Union's foray into communism and away from the prevailing system of capitalist states. Troops from Germany — just previously a sworn enemy — were also used to help put down democratic revolutionary forces in Finland and the Baltic states. And following World War II, the United States and its allies essentially set up the governments of Japan and especially West Germany as members of the anti-Soviet state system.

This leads us to identify two rather different ways of thinking about the causes of wars: (1) a kind of *system analysis*, in which the most significant factor is considered to be the preexisting organization — of states, of ideologies, or of individual or group inclinations — all of which inquire into the deep causes of war, versus (2) a *situation analysis*, which considers that each crisis is attributable largely to the situation presented by the crisis itself, a function of specific events and actors and unique situations. For example, we can view the Eritrean-Ethiopian secessionist war as a consequence of the state system, which created an artificial entity known as Ethiopia, and which also contains states (such as Somalia as well as the United States, Cuba, and the U.S.S.R.) that eagerly meddle in the affairs

Leaders of the four Western "Great Powers," meeting at the Versailles Conference at the end of World War I. Pictured here are, from the left, Orlando of Italy, Lloyd George of Great Britain, Clemenceau of France, and Wilson of the United States. (U.S. Signal Corps, The National Archives)

of others. Or, we can examine more closely the gripes of the Eritreans, as well as the counterarguments of the Ethiopian government, taking the conflict as bounded by its own particularities.

Finally, it should be emphasized that the system of states is not irretrievably wedded to war. After all, there have been numerous peaceful boundaries between states, such as the United States and Canada since 1812 and the United States and Mexico since 1846, and Norway and Sweden since their peaceful separation in 1905. In addition, war between France and Germany, or Britain and France, is almost inconceivable today, although the animosity between these states goes back literally hundreds of years.

ALLIANCES BETWEEN STATES

States form alliances. They do so to increase their security, assuming that in unity there is strength. Surprisingly, perhaps, large states (such as the United States, the U.S.S.R., Britain, and France) are

if anything more likely to enter into alliances than are small ones. Apparently, large states consider themselves to have large responsibilities and commitments, with their obligations often exceeding their resources; hence, they seek to ally with others. Alliances are also often formed among states that share common cultural or ideological features, and typically involve mutual pledges of assistance, often including the willingness to go to war in support of another alliance member.

Alliances as a Cause of War

It has been claimed that alliances can help deter war by presenting a would-be aggressor with stronger opposition (see Chapter 14). It has also been claimed, however, that overall, alliances have served more as a cause of war. Even the signing of an alliance can be a serious provocation, leading to efforts to test, undermine, or break rival alliances. The evidence is equivocal, although certainly, alliances have a very strong influence on who goes to war and on which side, when and if war breaks out.

The events leading up to World War I provide the most dramatic example of alliances among states contributing to war. We shall now recount some of these events, so as to emphasize how alliances among states can be double-edged swords: bringing about or preventing wars, increasing or reducing tensions, tying states together in ways that may not be anticipated by the leaders and can only with difficulty be understood, later, by historians.

As the nineteenth century drew to a close, France and Germany had been engaged in an arms race over the size of their armies, and Britain had been in naval arms races independently with both Germany and France. Britain and France were the major colonial powers in Africa, and Germany had been largely excluded from colonial acquisitions. Following a tense confrontation between British and French forces at Fashoda in modern-day Sudan, along the upper reaches of the Nile, the two states only narrowly averted war. They agreed to divide their spheres of influence in Africa, with Britain gaining uncontested control of east Africa and Egypt, and France occupying northwest Africa, including Algeria and Morocco.

This emerging *entente cordiale* was seen by Germany as a threat, although it was not in fact intended as such. The German kaiser, hoping to drive a wedge between Britain and France, then precipitated a crisis in 1905 when he sailed into the port of Agadir and gave an inflammatory speech, demanding independence for Morocco. Kaiser Wilhelm's plan backfired, however, as the other Western powers closed ranks against Germany. France gained a firmer hold on Morocco, and moreover, Britain and France, perceiving German antagonism, transformed their fledgling alliance into a military pact against Germany. Meanwhile, Russia and Britain had long been rivals for the disintegrating Ottoman empire in the Balkans and Near East; France helped these two states to overcome their antagonism, so that the three joined to form the Triple Entente.

Germany, not surprisingly, felt surrounded and more threatened than ever. It negotiated a competing pact — the so-called Triple Alliance — with Austria-Hungary and, ostensibly, Italy (although in fact, Italy ultimately wound up fighting against Austria). Austria-Hungary was at this time a patchwork empire, a state comprised of fourteen or fifteen different nations, nervous about the various nationalist movements then spreading through eastern Europe. Hoping to shore up its prestige, Austria in 1908 annexed the Serbian provinces of Bosnia and Herzegovina, ignoring the strong protests of Russia, which felt a sense of Slavic national protectiveness for the region. Russia, however, had recently suffered a humiliating defeat at the hands of Japan in the Russo-Japanese War (1905), and was in no position to start another.

Austria-Hungary, however, continued to worry about its future as a state, and Germany continued to feel surrounded by hostile neighbors. The Triple Alliance's successful power play in Bosnia/Herzegovina also led to a hardening of will among the Entente. (Typically, a success by one alliance leads to a compensatory stiffening by the other.) So, when the Archduke Ferdinand of Austria was murdered by a Serbian nationalist at Sarajevo (now part of Yugoslavia), Austria felt a need to reassert its power as an effective and united state, while Russia in particular felt compelled to back up tiny Serbia. The German kaiser promised full support to Austria, Russia promised support to Serbia, and France (because of its alliance commitment as well as a long-held grudge over Alsace and Lorraine) pledged to fight along with Russia. Shortly afterward, when Germany followed its long-prepared war plan and invaded neutral Belgium to attack France, Britain felt compelled to enter the war as well.

Many other factors were involved in precipitating World War I, which deserves to be known as the War Nobody Wanted (see Chapter 10). There can be little doubt, however, that the web of opposed alliances was crucial in dragging most of the states of Europe into war.

The Absence of Alliances as a Cause of War

Ironically, just as World War I was caused in part by the state system of alliances, World War II was caused by the absence of such alliances. Through much of the 1930s, Stalin sought to involve the Western democracies in an alliance against Nazi Germany, but Britain and France, apparently

Participants at the now-infamous Munich Conference in 1938. Pictured here, from the left, are Chamberlain of Great Britain, Daladier of France, Hitler of Germany, and Mussolini and Ciano of Italy. (The Bettmann Archive)

disliking Stalin's Soviet Union even more than Hitler's Germany, resisted. Then, in 1938, French premier Edouard Daladier and British prime minister Neville Chamberlain agreed in Munich to allow Hitler to occupy the Sudetenland of Czechoslovakia. When Hitler also annexed Bohemia and Slovakia in the spring of 1939, Britain and France were finally ready to reinstitute the World War I Triple Entente against Germany. By this time, however, Stalin had given up on the West and had engineered his own pact with Hitler, calling for Germany and the U.S.S.R. to carve up Poland between them. When Germany invaded Poland in September 1939, France and Britain — having warned Hitler that they could not stand idly by — finally declared war on Germany. However, the ultimately successful alliance of Britain, France, the Soviet Union, and the United States did not come about until 1941, after Germany attacked its purported ally, the U.S.S.R. and Japan — allied to Germany — attacked the United States, after which Germany declared

war on the United States as well. Just as the rigidities of the pre-1914 alliances in Europe helped precipitate World War I, the failure of the anti-Nazi states to organize a united opposition seems to have encouraged German expansionism.

In more recent times, supporters claim that NATO (and presumably the Warsaw Pact as well) has kept the East-West peace; an alternative view is that these alliances have heightened tensions that might otherwise have subsided. In any event, it is noteworthy that the ebbing of the Cold War has led to anxiety among NATO officials that their alliance has become increasingly outdated.

Alliances and the State System

Winston Churchill, for all his opposition to Hitler, detested Stalin and the Soviet Union at least as much — until Hitler's attack on the U.S.S.R. provided the opportunity for Britain to ally with the Soviets against Nazi Germany. In short, alliances have been based primarily on matters of state convenience and power (see the next section on *realpolitik*). Hence, they have shifted readily, depending on current perceptions of mutual advantage. As Great Britain's Lord Palmerston put it, "Great states have no permanent friends, only permanent interests." Thus, during the First Balkan War of 1912, Bulgaria, Greece, and Serbia were allied against Turkey. Less than three months later, Serbia, Greece, and Turkey then fought Bulgaria in the Second Balkan War. And less than two years after that, World War I (which began as the "Third Balkan War") featured Bulgaria and Turkey fighting together as allies of Germany and Austria-Hungary, while Serbia fought on the other side. And in the wake of growing threats from Germany in the early twentieth century, as we have seen, Franco-British animosity quickly turned to alliance. Similarly, the thaw in Sino-American relations was initiated by President Nixon as a way of strengthening the U.S. hand vis-à-vis the U.S.S.R. (and presumably, sought by Mao for the same reason).

Orthodox political scientists have attempted to characterize the state system — both past and present — in terms of the shifting pattern of major state actors and their alliances. Two primary dimensions are generally considered: polarity and connectedness. Thus, a bipolar system consists of primarily two states (such as the United States and the U.S.S.R.) with their associated allies as minor accompaniments. By contrast, a multipolar system might consist of many states (such as the United States, the U.S.S.R., Japan, China, and the "super-state" of Europe). The dimension of connectedness refers to the closeness with which the various states are linked, and the probability that a perturbation in one will cause some change in another. If this probability is high, the states are said to be "tightly" connected; if low, they are "loosely" connected. Thus, the state system at any given time could conceivably be "tight and bipolar," "tight and multipolar," "loose and bipolar," or "loose and multipolar."

Much effort has been expended trying not only to assess the nature of the world state system, but also to predict its future. Theories also abound as to which patterns are most war-prone and which are most peace-stable. For example, perhaps bipolar systems are more stable because each side can attend more accurately to the behavior of the other; or perhaps multipolar systems are more stable for the same reason that biologically diverse ecosystems are more stable than monocultures — there are more different players available to take up the slack and to prevent catastrophic breakdown. Many other interpretations are possible; the jury is still out on the war–peace significance of differing patterns of interstate alliances and connections.

In any event, such issues are particularly the concern of political scientists or specialists in international relations, fields that are closely supportive of, and often apologists for, the state system. The field of peace studies, by contrast, tends to distance itself from analyses of this sort, considering instead that the state system is part of the problem, and thus unlikely to be part of the solution.

REALPOLITIK AND RAISON D'ÉTAT

States, as we have seen, are major actors on the world stage. When a state behaves in a particular way, acting supposedly for its own good, the French say that it is demonstrating "raison d'état," the state's own reason for its actions. The term actually has a double meaning, implying not only the rational justification for acting in a particular way, but also the "right of a state" to act in its own best interests. Insofar as states are totally sovereign, raison d'état is sufficient justification unto itself, legally if not morally.

Closely related to raison d'état is the concept of "realpolitik," derived from the German, and referring to the conduct of international affairs under the assumption that a state's policy should be oriented toward and based upon considerations of power rather than ideals. Realpolitik is not necessarily any more "real" than other styles of international politics, but it fancies itself to be so.

In the late Middle Ages, Niccolò Machiavelli was a major proponent of realpolitik; during the eighteenth century, Prussia's Frederick the Great, and in the nineteenth century, Austria's Metternich, Britain's Palmerston, and especially Germany's Bismarck practiced the tradition with particular success; in the twentieth century, Henry Kissinger (a student of Metternich) has been a well-known practitioner. These leaders, and many others, have taken the position that realpolitik requires governments to base policy decisions on issues of power and state self-interest; in other words, raison d'état.

Realpolitik and Power

The political philosopher Hans Morgenthau was especially concerned with outlining the realpolitik bases for state conduct in world affairs. He maintained that the primary national interest was the quest for national security, and that this was to be achieved fundamentally through state power. The goal of international politics, in Morgenthau's very influential view, was therefore the maximization of state power. According to Morgenthau, "universal moral principles cannot be applied to the actions of states in their abstract, universal formulation, but they must be filtered through the concrete circumstances of time and place."[11] Politics is reducible to one of three basic goals: "to keep power, to increase power, or to demonstrate power."[12] Power is to the national leader what wealth is to the economist, or morality to the ethicist. And states are assumed to be concerned — almost exclusively — with enhancing their power, and not hesitant about going to war to achieve that end.

Note, however, that power is not strictly limited to military power. In 1941, the United States was far more powerful than Japan realized, not because of its military but because of its population, industrial potential, and determination not to be defeated. Japan, similarly, is very powerful today, despite a relatively modest military force, because of its immense economic strength, its social cohesion, and its ability to compete in international markets. (This, in turn, may be due partly to the fact that Japan has invested in domestic productivity rather than weaponry.) Certain neutral states also wield moral power, such as Sweden and, to some extent, India because of its history of Gandhian nonviolence. The power of a state can be defined as the ability of that state to influence the behavior of other states. As such, power can derive from unity, ideology, effective leadership, geographic position, and health and educational level of its citizens, as well as from access to resources, no less than from raw military force and the willingness to use it.

Realpolitik and War

In the rough and tumble world of realpolitik, however, military power — however achieved, and whether direct or implied — is the "name of the game." Carl von Clausewitz, spokesperson for the military aspects of realpolitik, made the renowned observation that war is "the continuation of politics by other means."[13] He emphasized the subordination of military to political goals, and wrote that although war is often brutal, it should not be senseless, but rather "an act of violence to compel the enemy to fulfill our will."[14] According to Clausewitz, "Violence is therefore the means; imposing our will on the enemy, the end."[15]

Part of the realpolitik tradition in statecraft, accordingly, is the view that war is, ideally, not a consequence of error or irrational factors, but rather a result of the cool-headed decision that more can be gained by going to war than by remaining at peace. By extension, wars also begin when two parties disagree as to their relative strength, and end when they are in agreement, that is, when the victor is revealed to be stronger than the vanquished. (Of course, given that most wars have a loser, it can be argued that 50 percent of the time, states are wrong, or their decision processes less than ideal.)

It would be simplistic, however, to assume that practitioners of realpolitik are necessarily warmongers. Rather, they advocate a constant and (as they see it) hard-headed sense of the ways of international power, limiting war only to those cases in which it will contribute to the "national interest"; Morgenthau, for example, strongly opposed the Vietnam War, but only because it was hurtful to the United States, not because it was wrong. "The concept of the national interest," wrote Morgenthau, presupposes neither a naturally harmonious, peaceful world nor the inevitability of war as a consequence of the pursuit by all nations of their national interests. Quite to the contrary, it assumes continuous conflict and threat of war to be minimized through the continuous adjustment of conflicting interest by diplomatic action.[16]

As we have seen, when the realpolitik of interstate behavior comes into conflict with general moral principles, the latter almost always takes a back seat. Bismarck set about intentionally to forge a German nation-state (the Second Reich) in the crucible of war. He had no doubt that the formation of a powerful, unified Germany was worth the suffering and death that would unavoidably accompany a few wars. Following the assassination of the Austrian archduke Franz Ferdinand in 1914, Conrad von Hotsendorf, Austrian chief of staff, argued for war with Serbia, not because it was somehow right, but because it was necessary, in order to maintain the power of the state of Austria:

> It was not a question of a knightly duel . . . nor of punishment for the assassination. It was much more the highly practical importance of the prestige of a Great Power . . . which, by its continual yielding and patience . . . had given an impression of impotence and made its internal and external enemies continually more aggressive.[17]

Sometimes, a sense of moral obligation may tend to push a state toward war, with realpolitik acting as a brake. Thus, it was probably in Britain's moral interest to come to the assistance of Finland when it was attacked by the Soviet Union in 1939; the British national interest, however, was to refrain, because aiding the embattled Finns might have fatally weakened Britain vis-à-vis Germany, while also embroiling Britain in a devastating war with the U.S.S.R. So, in this case, realpolitik probably helped prevent war.*

---

*It is uncertain whether this was to the disadvantage of the Finns as well, since there would doubtless have been much more suffering had their "winter war" with the U.S.S.R. been prolonged.

On the other hand, realpolitik considerations have long been used to justify war, although often using terms of morality or idealism. Consider the following argument from nineteenth-century liberal British prime minister William Gladstone: "However deplorable wars may be, they are among the necessities of our condition; and there are times when justice, when faith, when the failure of mankind, require a man not to shrink from the responsibility of undertaking them."[18] Gladstone argued with special passion that Britain had a moral obligation to aid the Bulgarians, at the time oppressed by the Turks, whose rule, according to Gladstone, involved "the basest and blackest outrage upon record within the present century, if not within the memory of man."[19] Yet, it should be noted, just twenty years earlier, Britain had gone to war in support of that same Ottoman empire, against Russia (the Crimean War). The issue at the time, far from the abuses and outrages of Turkish policy, was in fact the realpolitik competition between Britain and Russia for influence in the Black Sea region. (It should be pointed out, however, that Gladstone's attitude represented something of an ethical advance over previous principles of realpolitik in that he emphasized the relationship of war to the common interests of humankind, rather than simple considerations of state power.)

Realpolitik and Morality

Realpolitik transcends ideology. Thus, British liberal statesman James Bright resigned from the cabinet in 1882, in protest of Britain's bombardment of Alexandria and occupation of Egypt: "Be the Government Liberal or Tory much the same thing happens: war, with all its horrors and miseries and crimes and cost."[20] Moral and ethical considerations loom large in today's world as well (see Chapter 19), and yet, when they conflict with realpolitik, the latter has generally triumphed. Immediately after World War II, for example, U.S. government officials harbored certain former Nazi war criminals — especially those who had expertise as rocket scientists or knowledge about left-wing resistance movements in Europe — because it was felt that they could help the United States compete against the Soviet Union. The United States has refrained from criticizing the oppressive tactics of China in forcing its rule upon captive Tibet, and in brutally suppressing the prodemocracy movement in the late spring of 1989, because alliance with China has been useful to the United States in its larger struggle against the U.S.S.R. Similarly, the United States has been willing to wink at Pakistan's violation of nuclear nonproliferation obligations because of Pakistan's value as a conduit for aid to the anti-Soviet *mujahedeen* guerrillas in Afghanistan.

On a wide scale, the United States has collaborated with right-wing dictators and despots, essentially ignoring their often abominable human rights record, because their anticommunist stance has been judged useful in confrontation with the Soviet bloc (see Chapter 20). There is growing evidence that U.S. policy facilitated international drug smugglers (notably, collaboration with Panama's General Noriega and Haiti's Colonel Paul, both of whom were subsequently indicted for their drug-related activities). In these cases, U.S. policy resulted from a realpolitik desire to oppose leftist governments, as in Nicaragua, or leftist insurgencies, as in El Salvador, or simply to prop up right-wing, anticommunist dictatorships. The Soviet Union has been equally amoral whenever issues of raw power have been opposed to morality or ideology.

Status Quo Versus Revisionist States

Considerations of realpolitik also seem to influence whether states are satisfied with current circumstances or whether they agitate for change. The former are known as "status quo states," like the United States, which generally seek to keep things as they are. Their wars are fought against those who try to change things, notably aggressors such as Nazi Germany or, more recently, revolutionary nationalist movements. The doctrine of deterrence — which is not limited to the nuclear age, but which nonetheless looms especially large in the calculations of nuclear-armed superpowers, especially the United States — lends itself especially well to states whose primary desire is to prevent change. Thus, deterrence represents a way of preventing another state from becoming aggressive; by its nature, deterrence is most successful when nothing happens. In itself, it is inimical to change.

On the other hand, "revisionist states" are those that typically believe their status is not commensurate with their power and aspirations: Japan in 1905 (on the eve of the Russo-Japanese War) and again in the 1930s and early 1940s, Germany in the 1870s and again in the 1930s. Observers have debated whether the U.S.S.R. in the late twentieth century is a status quo or revisionist state: Under Gorbachev, it first became increasingly revisionist at home (sponsoring numerous political and economic reforms) and status quo abroad (diminishing its support for revolutionary movements and revolutionary governments such as Vietnam and Cuba). By the late 1980s, the U.S.S.R. initiated an unexpected kind of revisionism abroad as well: supporting the liberalization of communist rule, notably in Eastern Europe. The United States, by contrast, seems to have become a seeker of the status quo both at home and abroad.

INTERNAL COHESION

Considerations of realpolitik and raison d'état may lead states to engage in foreign wars so as to consolidate their domestic situation. When external forces threaten states, strong psychological and sociological pressures induce citizens to "rally round the flag," typically ignoring or postponing complaints with the current government so as to present a united front to the enemy. Thus, Jean Bodin, a conceptualizer of state sovereignty, also wrote that "the best way of preserving a state, and guaranteeing it against sedition, rebellion, and civil war is to keep the subjects in amity with one another, and to this end, to find an enemy against whom they can make common cause."[21] Similarly, on the eve of the American Civil War, Secretary of State William Seward urged that President Lincoln consider declaring war on France and Spain, so as to unite the country and preserve the union.

A major reason that Bismarck demanded the French provinces of Alsace and Lorraine as part of the spoils of the Franco-Prussian War was that he knew such a cession would guarantee French hostility, making France a long-standing military enemy. This, Bismarck calculated, would help maintain alertness and unity within the newly established German state.

In George Orwell's *1984*, the world was divided into three megastates, which constantly made war against one another, not to win, but rather to preserve their internal conditions:

> The war, therefore, if we judge it by the standards of previous wars, is merely an imposture. It is like the battles between certain ruminant animals whose horns are set at such an angle that they are incapable of hurting one another. But though it is unreal it is not meaningless. It eats up the surplus of consumable goods, and it helps to preserve the special mental atmosphere that a hierarchical society needs. . . . The war is waged by each ruling group against its own subjects, and the object of the war is not to make or prevent conquests of territory, but to keep the structure of society intact.[22]

Wars can also serve states by providing an outlet for pent-up energy as well as surplus manpower. Discussing the revolutionary wars of France during the 1790s, a noted historian suggested that these wars helped the newly established French government to go

> far towards relieving the social instability that had triggered revolution in the first place. Under the Directory, the mass of young men who had been unable to find satisfactory careers in civil occupations before the revolution were either successfully absorbed into the work force at home or living as soldiers at the expense of neighboring peoples, or else more or less gloriously dead.[23]

In a related vein, on the eve of the Russo-Japanese War, Russian interior minister V. K. Plehve is said to have argued that Russia needed "a little victorious war to stem the tide of revolution." (As it happened, Russia not only lost the war, but also had the revolution: a small, failed one in 1905 and then a successful one in 1917.) Prior to World War I,

Wounded World War I soldiers being withdrawn from the front. Many people in Europe initially welcomed this war; its immense costs became apparent only later. (National Archives of Canada, PA 678)

German conservatives began to tout the merits of a "brisk and breezy" (*frisch und frohlich*) war to curb the growing influence of the Social Democrats.

On the other hand, if wars have consistently been initiated so as to achieve internal cohesion, a correlation should exist between the frequencies of internal and external conflicts; careful studies have not been able to demonstrate any significant statistical relationship between these variables. Moreover, wars initiated in the hope of achieving national unity and minimizing dissension don't always work out that way. If the war is prolonged and costly, citizen dissatisfaction can grow, despite the pressures for conformity that wars typically engender. Major causes for resentment include the burden of added taxes to pay for the war, the mounting toll of casualties, unhappiness with the direction of the war, and especially, anger if the war is lost. Enormous Russian casualties during World War I were very important in precipitating the Bolshevik Revolution of 1917 and popular resentment with the conduct of the Falklands War led to the downfall of General Galtieri's Argentine government in 1982.

On the other hand, the government of Ayatollah Khomeini in Iran was, if anything, strengthened by its bloody war with Iraq, even though the economy was devastated and hundreds of thousands of lives were lost.

Only rarely are moral considerations important in generating unhappiness with a regime's warlike behavior. The Vietnam War was an exception; it proved to be a major disruptive factor in the United States during the 1960s and early 1970s.

Finally, it is worth noting that since warfare requires unity and effective central coordination, states that are internally chaotic and lacking in cohesion may well be especially hesitant to engage in a war that they could end up losing. Following its defeat by Japan in 1905, for example, and having been shaken by an unsuccessful revolution, Russia — as we have seen — was unwilling to risk war with Austria-Hungary when the latter annexed Bosnia and Herzegovina in 1908. By the late 1930s, the two most cohesive states of Europe were Germany and Italy; it seems doubtful that these states launched World War II so as to achieve unity. By contrast, Britain and France appeared fractionated and distracted; hence, they seemed (to Hitler at least) unlikely to resist aggression. When Iraq launched its war with Iran, in 1980, the situation within Iran appeared chaotic, which made the Iranians more vulnerable to outside attack rather than especially likely to initiate war themselves.

ARMS RACES

Short of war itself, an arms race is the most prominent and warlike form of competition between states. Arms races have been defined as "intense competitions between opposed powers or groups of powers, each trying to achieve an advantage in military power by increasing the quantity or improving the quality of its armaments or armed forces."[24] Since 1945, the nuclear arms race between the United States and the Soviet Union has occupied considerable resources and attention; we shall examine it in greater detail in Chapters 12, 14, and 15. As noted previously, however, arms races existed long before the invention of nuclear weapons. Moreover, arms races have long been a major arena for interstate competition, from the city-states of Greece, to competing feudal overlords during the Middle Ages, to modern times. As William James rather cynically put it, "the intensely sharp competitive *preparation* for war by the nations *is the real war*, permanent, unceasing, and the battles are only a sort of public verification of the mastery gained during the 'peace' interval."[25]

Reciprocal anxiety has often fueled arms races, with each side worried that the other was about to pull ahead or was already in the lead. Often, this involved incorrect estimates, which exaggerated the other side's forces. In 1914, for example, German intelligence estimated that the French army had 121,000 more soldiers than the German army; at the same time, the French judged that the German army exceeded the French by 134,000. (Interestingly, both agreed as to the strength of third parties.) During the period 1906 to 1914, when Great Britain and Germany were engaged in a vigorous naval arms race, each of the two states was greatly worried that the other was about to launch a preemptive attack. Such anxiety almost certainly played a part in the actual declaration of World War I. Listen to Edward Grey, British foreign secretary during the decade leading up to World War I:

> Great armaments lead inevitably to war. The increase of armaments . . . produces a consciousness of the strength of other nations and a sense of fear. Fear begets suspicion and distrust and evil imaginings of all sorts, till each Government feels it would be criminal and a betrayal of its country not to take every precaution, while every Government regards the precautions of every other Government as evidence of hostile intent.[26]

Governments, and their citizens, often tend to make what psychologists call the "attribution error," attributing their opponent's behavior to ill will and aggressive designs, while attributing their own behavior (even though it may be objectively comparable to that of the opponent) to a laudable and understandable effort at self-protection.

It can be argued, however, that just as the preWorld War I arms races helped precipitate that conflict, the *failure* of the Western powers — notably

Britain and France—to engage Germany in an arms race may have helped bring about World War II. Hitler appears to have been emboldened by what he saw as the rise of pacifism in western Europe. When Germany first began violating the provisions of the Versailles treaty (which called essentially for the demilitarization of Germany), the democracies were considerably stronger than Germany, yet no response was taken. When Germany reoccupied the Rhineland, again in violation of the treaty, the democracies once again failed to act or even to arm themselves significantly. The German general staff is now known to have been quite apprehensive about these early aggressive moves by Hitler; had the Western allies responded more forcefully, it seems clear that Germany would have backed down, and Hitler's aggressive momentum might have been halted before it gathered steam.

Many factors drive arms races: the financial profits to be made (see Chapter 11), desire for advancement on the part of individuals whose careers depend on success in administering or commanding major new weapons programs, political leaders pandering to bellicose domestic sentiment, as well as interservice rivalry within a state. For example, one of the important factors leading to the U.S. entrance into World War I was Germany's decision to engage in unrestricted submarine warfare, which resulted in the sinking of the civilian ocean liner *Lusitania*, among others. This escalation of the war by Germany was due at least in part to the fact that while the German army was fully engaged on both western and eastern fronts, the German fleet had been inactive while Britain dominated the oceans, including the North Sea. A frustrated Admiral Tirpitz wrote that

> If we come to the end . . . without the fleet having bled and worked, we shall get nothing more for the fleet, and all the scanty money that there may be will be spent on the army. The great efforts of His Majesty the Emperor to make Germany a naval power will have been all in vain.[27]

In all fairness to the arms racers, we should identify one other potential reason for their activities: genuine concern about the security needs of the state. Faced with an uncompromisingly hostile opponent, states have often felt that arming themselves is their only legitimate option. This leads to what has aptly been called the "security dilemma": When states perceive that they must increase their military power so as to achieve security, their rivals feel constrained to do the same (for the same reason). As a result, both sides have entered into a dangerous competitive spiral by which all sides are made less secure. Like a muscle-bound idiot caught in a Chinese finger puzzle, each seeks to resolve its insecurity by pulling hard (acquiring more weapons), which only leads to its being held yet more tightly (even more insecurity when the other responds similarly), which leads to yet more pulling, and so forth.

Pioneer peace researcher Lewis Richardson attempted to create a simple mathematical model for the mutually reinforcing interaction that occurs during an arms race. His equations are as follows:

$$\Delta X = r_x Y - f_x X + g_x$$
$$\Delta Y = r_y X - f_y Y + g_y$$

ΔX and ΔY stand for the changes in military expenditures by each state (X and Y); r is a "reaction coefficient," which indicates the extent to which military spending by one state influences spending by the other. Thus, r_x is the reaction of state X to military spending by Y, and vice versa. If the reaction coefficients are positive, then an action–reaction process ensures that both X and Y will engage in an ever-upward spiral. Other factors are also recognized, however: the f-term is a "fatigue factor," which tends to slow the expenditures of each state as a function of how high those expenditures currently are. For example, f_y is the fatigue factor for state Y, which subtracts from Y's arms race activities in proportion as Y is already spending heavily. Finally, each state is also influenced by a "grievance factor," g_x and g_y, which indicates underlying complaints of each state against the other, independent of the arms race as such.

British historian Herbert Butterfield suggested that perhaps "no state can ever achieve the security it desires without so tipping the balance that it becomes a menace to its neighbors."[28] In the process,

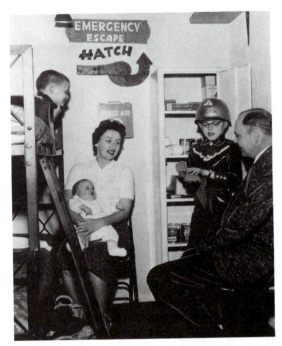

Official U.S. Civil Defense photo from the 1950s, showing a typical family living happily in their home fallout shelter, presumably in the aftermath of a nuclear war. During the prolonged Cold War, the U.S. (and the U.S.S.R.) spent much time and resources preparing for war and not for peace. (Fossil Films and Photos)

ponents of arms races point, in turn, to World War I, when arms races caused the European powers to blunder into an unwanted and unnecessary war.

It has proved virtually impossible to evaluate these propositions, although most attempts to examine the historical record have shown that arms races seem more likely to produce war than to prevent it. For example, one political scientist examined 99 serious international disputes between 1815 and 1965. Of these disputes, 28 had been preceded by an arms race; 71 had not. Of the former, 23 (82 percent) resulted in a war, whereas of the 71 disputes not preceded by an arms race, only 3 (4 percent) resulted in war.[29] Although this study does not prove that arms races cause war, it does suggest that when a serious dispute occurs in conjunction with an ongoing arms race, war is far more likely than when the disputing nations have not also been competing militarily.

And yet, not all arms races have led to war. Many have been resolved peacefully, including the following:

1. Great Britain versus France, navy, 1841–1865

2. Germany versus France, army, 1870s–1890s

3. Great Britain versus France and Russia, navy, 1884–1905

4. Chile versus Argentina, navy, 1890–1902

5. United States versus Great Britain, navy (cruisers), 1920–1930

In case 1, one side simply gave up; in case 2, the competition simply petered out, at least temporarily; case 3 was resolved by an alliance among the racers; case 4 ended with a resolution of the existing boundary dispute; and case 5 (and case 4 as well) ended with an arms limitation treaty.

Many statesmen as well as citizens remain convinced that security often demands strength, and strength often cannot be obtained without an arms race. This theme is described in the famous Latin motto, *si vis paoem, para bellum*, ("if you want peace, prepare for war"). "A wiser rule," according

it becomes a menace to itself. But this has not prevented states from trying.

Do arms races lead to war? One influential point of view (which we have seen reflected in Lord Grey's comments) claims that they do. Another— equally influential, if not more so—maintains just the opposite: By being militarily strong, a state prevents war. Arguing in favor of greater military expenditures, President Reagan, for example, claimed that the United States has never gotten into a war because it was too strong. (This omits the Mexican-American and Spanish-American wars, and perhaps the Vietnam War as well.) Proponents of military strength and arms racing point to the "lessons of Munich," when the prospects of World War II were increased by the failure of the West to answer Germany's strength with strength of its own; opto sociologist William Graham Sumner, "would be to make up your mind soberly what you want, peace or war, and then to get ready for what you want; for what we prepare for is what we shall get."[30]

A FINAL NOTE ON WAR AND STATES

When it comes to the causes of war, states seem to be much more the problem than the solution (although most people would agree that if there is to be a solution, states will have to be a part of that as well—see Part III). Increasingly, states appear to exist for their own benefit, not for the benefit of their citizens. They enter into wars for raisons d'état, and terminate them for the same reasons. If defense is the primary reason for people to associate into those large entities known as states, then what is to be done in the nuclear age, when that relationship has become potentially lethal, and one-sided as well? Nuclear weapons in particular may well exist almost entirely because of the purported realpolitik benefits they confer on states that possess them; it is difficult to argue that they confer security on the individual. Indeed, inhabitants of nonnuclear states such as New Zealand, Australia, and Switzerland are in many ways more secure than citizens of the superpowers.

A glance at the map of the world today reveals few prospects of imminent conquests and significant boundary changes.* Venezuela claims some of Guyana, and Guatemala claims all of Belize, but generally, armies of today have little immediate prospect of going to war against the armies of another state. Mostly, they specialize in internal control, and appear to exist for their own sakes, rather

like the so-called parasitic DNA that doesn't contribute to proteins or cell architecture, but rather exists simply for the purpose of its own replication. At least this gene material, however, does not threaten the life of its host. On the other hand, "The time may be approaching," writes novelist E. L. Doctorow,

> when we will have to choose between two coincident reality systems: the historical human reality of feeling, of thought, of multitudinous expression, of life and love and natural death; or the supra-human statist reality of rigid, ahistorical, censorious and contending political myth structures, which may in our name and from the most barbaric impulses disenfranchise 99 percent of the world's population from even tragic participation in their fate.[31]

With the world in ecological and social crisis, states have largely compounded the problems through increasing violence and militarism. If one is to oppose war, is it also necessary, then, to oppose the state? Can positive peace be achieved within the current system of states? And if so, what about the various positive roles of the state, such as maintaining order, structure, and common purpose? Many of the most important factors affecting people's lives occur on a global scale, and are to a large extent beyond the ability of states to manage. Yet, states tend to monopolize the political arena, resulting also in an impoverishment of the creative imagination when it comes to inspired problem solving.

In the future, states may turn their attention increasingly toward some of these global, state-transcendent problems such as poverty and ecological destruction, as well as the urgent need for worldwide demilitarization. But it seems likely that a narrowly defined sense of realpolitik and the "national interest" will tightly circumscribe the willingness of states to address these problems seriously . . . especially since sovereignty may have to be compromised. As a result, students of Peace Studies can also expect (and perhaps encourage) attempts to go beyond existing state boundaries, seeking alternative and/or additional ways of resolving these issues and establishing a wider human identity.

---

*At the close of World War II, the Polish border was moved to the West, displacing several hundred thousand Germans and adding previously German territory to Poland. Forty-five years later, with the Germanies rushing toward reunification, the Polish government has worried that right-wing nationalist sentiment might seek to regain this territory for Germany.

Study Questions

1. Compare the attitudes of modern liberals and conservatives toward the state.

2. Define "state sovereignty." What connections are there between sovereignty and the work of Hobbes?

3. Describe current cases in which sovereignty has been tacitly ignored, that is, cases in which both the "violator" and the "violated" have found it in their interest to violate state sovereignty, but to do so quietly.

4. What is meant by the state system?

5. Distinguish between a "system analysis" and a "situation analysis" of the cause of war. Choose a recent war, and sketch the details of both kinds of analysis.

6. Make the argument that alliances among states reduce the likelihood of war; make the argument that they increase it.

7. Describe the tension between realpolitik and morality. Indicate your personal sympathies.

8. Distinguish between status quo states and revisionist states. Give some examples.

9. It has been argued that wars sometimes serve the state by increasing internal cohesion. Make this argument, using specific examples. Make the alternative argument, that wars have reduced internal cohesion.

10. What is meant by the "security dilemma"? How does this relate to the question of whether arms races increase the chances of war?

Suggestions for Further Reading

James M. Buchanan. 1975. *The Limits of Liberty: Between Anarchy and Leviathan*. University of Chicago Press: Chicago, IL.

Gwynne Prins (ed.). 1983. *Defended to Death: A Study of the Nuclear Arms Race*. Penguin: New York.

Louis Rene Beres. 1984. *Reason and Realpolitik*. Lexington Books: Lexington, MA.

Robert R. Alford. 1985. *Powers of Theory: Capitalism, the State, and Democracy*. Cambridge University Press: New York.

Leslie Green. 1988. *The Authority of the State*. Oxford University Press: New York.

Source Notes

1. Randolph S. Bourne. 1964. *War and the Intellectuals*. Harper & Row: New York.

2. Quincy Wright. 1964. *A Study of War*. University of Chicago Press: Chicago.

3. Benito Mussolini. 1963. "The Doctrine of Fascism." In J. Sommerville and R. Santoni (eds.), *Social and Political Philosophy*. Anchor: New York.

4. Jean Bodin. 1962. *The Six Books of a Commonweale*. Harvard University Press: Cambridge, MA.

5. Kenneth Waltz. 1959. *Man, the State and War*. Columbia University Press: New York.

6. Augustine. 1950. *The City of God*. Modern Library: New York.

7. V. Gordon Childe. 1936. *Man Makes Himself*. Watts: London.

8. Karl Wittfogel. 1957. *Oriental Despotism*. Yale University Press: New Haven, CT.

9. Michael Howard. 1984. *The Causes of Wars*. Harvard University Press: Cambridge, MA.

10. Raymond Aron. 1954. *The Century of Total War*. Doubleday: Garden City, NY.

11. Hans Morgenthau. 1972. *Politics Among Nations*. Random House: New York.

12. Ibid.

13. Carl von Clausewitz. 1984. *On War*. Princeton University Press: Princeton, NJ.

14. Ibid.

15. Ibid.

16. Quoted in J. E. Dougherty and R. L. Pfaltzgraff. 1981. *Contending Theories of International Relations*. Macmillan: New York.

17. Quoted in S. B. Fay. 1967. *The Origins of the World War*. Free Press: Glendale, IL.

18. Quoted in J. Morley. 1903. *The Life of William Ewart Gladstone*. Macmillan: New York.

19. Ibid.

20. Quoted in G. M. Trevelyan. 1925. *The Life of John Bright*. Houghton Mifflin: Boston.

21. Bodin, *Six Books*.

22. George Orwell. 1984. *1984*. Harcourt Brace Jovanovich: San Diego, CA.

23. William H. McNeill. 1982. *The Pursuit of Power*. University of Chicago Press: Chicago.

24. Hedley Bull. 1965. *The Control of the Arms Race*. Praeger: New York.

25. William James. 1967. *The Writings of William James*. Random House: New York.

26. Edward Grey. 1925. *Twenty-Five Years*. Frederick A. Stokes: New York.

27. Quoted in John G. Stoessinger. 1985. *Why Nations Go to War*. St. Martin's: New York.

28. Herbert Butterfield. 1951. *History and Human Relations*. Macmillan: New York.

29. Michael D. Wallace. 1979. "Arms Races and Escalation." *Journal of Conflict Resolution*, 23: 3–16.

30. William G. Sumner. 1934. *Essays of William Graham Sumner*. Yale University Press: New Haven, CT.

31. E. L. Doctorow. "It's a Cold War World Out There, Class of '83." *The Nation*, July 2, 1983.

10

The Decision-Making Level

The offhand decision of some commonplace mind high in office at a critical moment influences the course of events for a hundred years.
  Thomas Hardy

Even large groups of people are led by much smaller groups, and in many cases, the ultimate decisions of war and peace are made by remarkably few people, and sometimes just one person. In our examination of the causes of war, it is therefore appropriate that we consider decision making at the level of government leaders.

THE ROLE OF LEADERS

There has long been debate over the role of crucial individuals in the causation of history. So-called great man theories maintain that the personality of certain select, major figures has had a determining effect on world events. (Their greatness is often measured by the number of corpses left in their wake.) By contrast, theories of "impersonal forces" claim that most significant events would have happened no matter who was nominally in charge, because they represent the culmination of large ebbs and flows of societies and historical trends, rather than resulting from the actions of a miniscule and self-important minority.

In various writings, but most notably in *War and Peace*, Leo Tolstoy argued the "impersonal forces" theory. He portrayed Napoleon as a bit ridiculous, imagining himself making important decisions such as whether or not to go to war, or how to conduct important battles, whereas according to Tolstoy, major leaders are actually "history's slaves." In discussing the outbreak of war between France and Russia in 1812, Tolstoy's novel proceeds as follows:

> What produced this extraordinary occurrence? What were its causes? The historians tell us with naive assurance that its causes were the wrongs inflicted on the Duke of Oldenburg, the non-observance of the Continental System, the ambition of Napoleon, the firmness of Alexander, the mistakes of the diplomats, and so forth and so on. . . . To us, their descendants who are not historians and who can therefore regard the event with unclouded common sense, an incalculable number of causes present themselves. The deeper we delve in search of these causes, the more of them we find; and each separate cause, or whole series of causes, appears to us equally valid in itself and equally false by its insignificance compared to the magnitude of events, and by its importance to occasion the event. To us the wish or objection of this or that French corporal to serve a second term appears as much a cause as Napoleon's refusal to withdraw his troops beyond the Vistula and to restore the Duchy of Oldenburg; for had he not wished to serve, and had a second, a third and a thousandth corporal and private also refused, there would have been so many less men in Napoleon's arms and the war could not have occurred. . . . And there was no one cause for that occurrence, but it had to occur because it had to! Millions of men, renouncing their human feelings and reason, had to go from West to East to slay their fellows. . . . The actions of Napoleon and Alexander were as little voluntary as the action of any soldier who was drawn into the campaign by lot or by conscription. . . . It was necessary that millions of men in whose hands lay the real power . . . should consent to carry out the will of these weak individuals. . . . To elicit the laws of history we must leave aside kings, ministers and generals, and select for study the homogeneous, infinitesimal elements which influence the masses.[1]

Tolstoy's view that the common people are as responsible as their leaders for war laid the foundation for his conviction that individuals have the opportunity — indeed, the responsibility — to take things into their own hands and refuse to fight.

With regard to its causes, probably no war has been analyzed in greater detail than World War I, because the interweaving factors that culminated in that war were unusually complex, and because so many relevant government documents are available to historians. No single villain (and certainly, no hero) emerges from all this scholarship, and some respected observers have even proposed that somehow, war was "in the air":

> What was in the air by 1914 was a spirit of violent repudiation of the age that can scarcely be accounted for in any objective historical or political terms, but only by a judgment on human character. The nineteenth century had abolished war; but the peace and stability of that world perished because men could hardly bear to live for a century with the kind of world they had made.[2]

This view does not ignore other causes, but it emphasizes the irrational and impersonal:

> No single cause will explain the First World War. But the formal causes — the commercial and colonial rivalries, the cocked war establishments of Europe designed to mobilize, deploy, and conquer by the execution of a single and irreversible general-staff plan, the strident minorities and grandiose nationalisms, the disintegration of the Austro-Hungarian Empire, the colonial rivalries, the rot of Turkey, the instability of the balance of power — all these pale before the fact that Europe in 1914 wanted war and got it.[3]

This debate cannot be resolved by somehow proving that inchoate historical factors, combined with the acquiescence of millions of unnamed citizens, contribute, say, more or less than 50 percent to an ultimate outcome. We should, however, attend to the specific issue of leaders and their decision making, if only because leaders do exist, they do make decisions, and moreover, there is good reason to think that these decisions are important . . . although perhaps not as important as most leaders themselves would like to think.

"Strong" Leaders

In the past, when rulers embodied the political and military power of their group, they clearly played a major role in deciding whether or not to go to war. In "The Education of a Christian Prince," Erasmus urged that

> although a prince ought nowhere to be precipitate in his plans, there is no place for him to be more deliberate and circumspect than in the matter of going to war. Some evils come from one source and others from another, but from war comes the shipwreck of all that is good and from it the sea of all calamities pours out.[4]

The role of individual leaders may well have been unduly glamorized, and they often receive credit — and blame — that they do not entirely deserve. And yet, undeniably, certain individuals, by the force of their personalities and the decisions they made, have had enduring effects on history. Sometimes, they represent the culmination of currents within their societies, and they may also catalyze other events, but there seems little doubt that people like Alexander, Genghis Khan, Charlemagne, Joan of Arc, Napoleon, Bismarck, Hitler, Stalin, de Gaulle, and Mao Ze-dong have acted as lightning rods for popular discontent, and often as precipitators of war; only rarely, we must note, have leaders achieved renown as peacemakers.

On the other hand, when it becomes necessary for a state to accept defeat, a strong leader may be the only person capable of getting the populace to swallow the bitter pill: for better or worse, Marshal Petain played this role in France in 1940, as did Finland's revered Carl Mannerheim in 1944, and France's de Gaulle in granting Algerian independence in 1961. Perhaps the British people were better able to tolerate the postwar dissolution of their empire when it was conducted by Churchill, an avowed proimperialist Tory, just as the warming of Sino-American relations during the Nixon administration was facilitated by the fact that Richard Nixon's reputation as a hard-line anticommunist insulated him against accusations of spinelessness or appeasement.

Many leaders may be moved by the desire to go down in history as a peacemaker. Thus, the dramatic warming of relations between the United States and the U.S.S.R. during the late 1980s must be attributed, at least partly, to a shift in perceptions and goals by President Reagan. It is also equally, if not more, a result of the new leader in the Kremlin; thus, Mikhail Gorbachev, having committed himself to economic and social reforms within the U.S.S.R., sought to forge a less confrontational foreign policy. Insofar as the outcome of such maneuvering results in a lessening of U.S.-Soviet tensions and movement toward arms control and even partial nuclear disarmament, it must be seen as a positive step toward peace, one that almost certainly would not have been taken if any of Gorbachev's more Stalinist rivals had assumed power instead. On the other hand, it seems clear that Ronald Reagan's highly personal and idiosyncratic commitment to Star Wars (known officially as the Strategic Defense Initiative) hindered the prospects of dramatic cuts in U.S.-Soviet strategic nuclear weapons.

Whereas the exaltation of national honor and state power have doubtless been crucial throughout history, these general sentiments seemingly were filtered through the unique personal embodiments of people such as Edward III and Henry V of England in the fourteenth and fifteenth centuries, Philip II and Charles V of Spain in the sixteenth, Charles XII of Sweden and Louis XIV of France in the seventeenth, Russia's Peter the Great and Prussia's Frederick the Great in the eighteenth, Napoleon Bonaparte in France and Britain's Queen Victoria in the nineteenth, and Mussolini in Italy and Hitler in Germany during the twentieth.

The role of individual leaders, and of chance, is perhaps most clearly illustrated by what happened at the end of the Seven Years' War (1756–1763). By 1762, a coalition of France, Austria, and Russia had virtually defeated Prussia's Frederick the Great. But then came an unexpected personal event: the death of Frederick's most implacable enemy, Empress Elizabeth of Russia. She was succeeded on the throne by Peter III, an admirer of Frederick, who proceeded to make peace with the beleaguered Prussian. (Shortly afterward, Peter —

British Prime Minister Winston Churchill (center) inspecting the ruins of Coventry Cathedral in 1941. Churchill's eloquence and dogged energy marked him as one of the great wartime leaders of all time. (The Bettmann Archive)

not "the Great" — was deposed by Catherine, who later became Catherine the Great.)

When Britain stood alone against Nazi Germany, Churchill not only represented British defiance and determination, he also helped generate it with such stirring pronouncements as, "We shall fight on the beaches, we shall fight on the landing grounds, we shall fight in the fields and in the streets, we shall fight in the hills; we will never surrender." And when President Sadat of Egypt went to Israel and ultimately negotiated a historic peace treaty with Israel's Menachem Begin, through the mediating efforts of President Carter, it was a triumph of the courage, vision, and hard work of a few individuals.

In many cases, of course, wars are imposed on their people by the decisions of their leadership. The various wars of succession during the eighteenth century, for example, did not well up from public anger or concern; rather, they were decreed by leaders for "raisons d'état," and obediently entered into by the populace. At other times, charismatic leaders, from Alexander to Hitler, have succeeded in generating wartime enthusiasm (although admittedly, their messages could only flourish in fertile soil). In his war message to the

American people in 1917, President Wilson expressed the oft-spoken distinction between people and their leadership, one that — true or not — has proven especially convenient during war:

> We have no quarrel with the German people. . . . It was not upon their impulse that their government acted. . . . It was a war determined as wars used to be determined upon in the old, unhappy days when people were nowhere consulted by their rulers and wars were provoked and waged in the interest of dynasties or of little groups of ambitious men who were accustomed to use their fellow men as pawns or tools.[5]

"Weak" Leaders

Of course, it is not necessarily true that only strong leaders make for war. The weak personalities of Germany's Kaiser Wilhelm and Russia's Czar Nicholas rendered them unable to hold their general staffs in check; stronger leadership on their part might have prevented the First World War, just as stronger leadership in Britain and France during the 1930s might have averted the Second. (In the former case, such strength would have been needed to restrain those within the country who felt bound to follow predesigned mobilization plans, and who worried excessively about being preempted by the other side; in the latter, strength was needed in restraining those outside the country — notably Hitler and Mussolini.)

The Cuban Missile Crisis — the closest we have ever come to general nuclear war — was brought about in part because John F. Kennedy had been browbeaten by Premier Khrushchev at their 1961 summit meeting in Vienna. The following year, Kennedy was determined that he would not be pushed around again by the Soviet leader; fortunately for the world, Khrushchev had sufficient ego strength (and also, perhaps, insufficient military strength) to back down.

The volatile personality of Egypt's Gamal Abdel Nasser was involved in his decision to close the gulf of Aqaba, which precipitated the disastrous Six Day War with Israel in 1967. Yahya Khan, of Pakistan, couldn't tolerate being cowed by a woman, Indira Gandhi of India; this contributed directly to the India-Pakistan war through which Pakistan was dismembered. Lyndon Johnson also seemed to have been influenced by a macho insistence, as well as perhaps a racist attitude, not to be defeated by Ho Chi Minh. The origins, to say nothing of the continuation, of the war between Iran and Iraq depended in large part on the personal animosity between the two leaders, Saddam Hussein of Iraq and the Ayatollah Khomeini of Iran. The list goes on.

Sometimes, wars result from the overwhelming personal ambition of leaders, something that is hardly limited to modern tyrants or would-be conquerors. Consider this boast from Xerxes, King of Persia in 480 B.C. (and recounted by Herodotus):

> Once let us subdue this people [the Greeks] . . . and we shall extend the Persian territory beyond our borders; for I will pass through Europe from one end to the other, and make of all lands which it contains one country. . . . By this course then we shall bring all mankind under our yoke.[6]

Sometimes, the issue is saving face, in which case leaders are especially likely to precipitate a crisis — or respond aggressively to one — if they are wary of opposition at home. Thus, President Truman, stung by criticism that he had "lost" China, felt he had no choice but to intervene in response to the North Korean invasion; later, he hesitated to restrain General Douglas MacArthur from seeking to unify Korea by conquest in 1950. John F. Kennedy seriously worried that he might be impeached if he did not respond forcefully to the discovery of Soviet missile sites under construction in Cuba. Also in 1962, India's Nehru had stirred up anti-Chinese feeling in India, and when the Chinese resisted Indian territorial encroachments, he had to choose between fighting and losing face; he chose to fight, even though the Chinese had overwhelming logistic advantages and ten times as many troops.

THE ROLE OF VILLAINS

We know almost nothing about what produces personalities that tend toward national leadership, or what distinguishes a peacemaker from a warmonger. Alexander grew up as one of many children in a royal, polygynous household. Contact with his distant father (Philip of Macedon) was rare, and young Alexander apparently had a very intense relationship with his mother, who was ambitious, energetic, demanding, punitive, and rather violent. Perhaps it is not surprising that Alexander's quest for approval included conquering much of the known world before he was thirty-three. On the other hand, Prussia's Frederick — one of many leaders known as "the Great" — had a submissive, ineffectual mother, but a demanding, callous, and rather brutal father (who forced him to witness the beheading of his boyhood friend . . . who may also have been his homosexual lover). In his book *The Anatomy of Human Destructiveness*, psychoanalyst Erich Fromm argued that the early experiences of Hitler and Stalin produced a kind of malignant sadism (Stalin) and necrophilia (Hitler).[7]

In southern Africa during the nineteenth century, one man, known as Shaka, became king of a small group known as the Zulus. By his brilliance, courage, charisma, and ruthlessness, he went from being head of one relatively obscure tribe occupying about 300 square miles to ruling an empire consisting of three hundred tribes and covering 80,000 square miles. Single-handedly, Shaka invented new military tactics of envelopment, a new weapon (the short, broad, stabbing sword to replace the relatively inaccurate thrown spear), and concepts of discipline that changed African tribal warfare from personal duels to sustained campaigns with up to 60,000 participants and 15,000 casualties per battle. Like so many "great men," Shaka may have had some admirable qualities, but peacemaking was not among them. Virtually nothing is known of his early life.

Genghis Khan, Attila the Hun, Tamerlane, Hitler . . . these leaders often appear as villains, and rightly so, insofar as they figured prominently in causing wars that resulted in the deaths of millions. But what of Cecil Rhodes, architect of British imperialism, Adolf Krupp, German weapons manufacturer, J. Robert Oppenheimer and the other American physicists who created the first atomic bombs, or President Truman, who ordered their use, or the bomber crews that dropped them, or the patriotic citizens who paid their taxes in support of the war effort, and so on? The point is that it may be relatively easy to assign villainy to a select number of prominent individuals, but by most measures there is more than enough blame to go around.

Revolutions are often stimulated by the perception that leadership is particularly corrupt or villainous. Even though the new leadership may enjoy wider popular support (at least for a time), however, it may be as bad as, or worse than, what it replaces: Robespierre, for example, was more dreaded than Louis XIV, who was rather mild and fumbling by contrast. And Stalin was far more vicious than the ineffectual Czar Nicholas II. Moreover, heroes in one nation are often perceived as evil-doers in another, and vice versa.

It is often difficult to assign villainy in matters of politics, and especially in war and peace, because supporting arguments often exist for even the most violent and inhumane acts. On the other hand, in certain cases, responsibility and blame seem sufficiently clear that widely accepted moral judgments have been made (see Chapter 17). Other cases seem reasonably clear: After Pol Pot and his Khmer Rouge took power in 1975, at least a million people out of Cambodia's total population of 7 million were killed—anyone with Western connections, training, language, even eyeglasses. Idi Amin, formerly an Army sergeant, took over the Ugandan government in 1971, initiating a reign of terror that is believed to have claimed more than 300,000 lives before Tanzanian troops, supported by Ugandan exiles, drove Amin from power in 1979. (Although order was not restored in Uganda until 1981, the world generally breathed a collective sigh of relief when this "humanitarian intervention" succeeded in removing a true villain.)

It should be emphasized, however, that even villainy—or at least, the extent of villainy—is open to dispute. The traditional interpretation of the causes of World War II, for example, stresses Hitler's aggressive designs plus, in a supporting role, British and French appeasement.[8] But at least one highly esteemed revisionist historian has refused to heap all the blame on Hitler, viewing the Second World War instead as reflecting a continued pattern of German expansionism and militarism traceable

Ugandan president and military dictator Idi Amin in 1975. His destructive reign marked him as one of modern history's "villains." (UPI/Bettmann Newsphotos)

at least to Bismarck.* Also to blame: the unsatisfactory Versailles treaty that terminated the First World War, plus a large dose of faulty calculations both by Hitler and the Western leaders.[9]

Regardless of the specific historical details, there may be some validity to placing substantial responsibility for many and perhaps most wars on a limited number of individuals. This view, however, must reconcile itself with the likelihood that

*We are concerned here with the causes of World War II, not with Nazi atrocities during that war; no reputable scholars have sought to absolve Hitler and his followers from culpability in the murder of millions of Jews, for example.

even with a different cast of major characters, the outcome might have been fundamentally the same! In addition, much blame should also go to what has been called the "military mind," which

> emphasizes the permanence of irrationality, weakness and evil in human affairs. It stresses the supremacy of society over the individual and the importance of order, hierarchy and division of function. It accepts the nation state as the highest form of political organization and recognizes the continuing likelihood of war among nation states. . . . It exalts obedience as the highest virtue of military men. . . . It is, in brief, realistic and conservative.[10]

Not surprisingly, the author of this selection is himself a conservative political scientist. But the first part of his description rings true, regardless of political ideology.

As to the military's preoccupation with "security," to some extent it is only doing its job . . . or at least, what society expects. "If you believe the doctors," wrote England's Lord Salisbury, "nothing is wholesome; if you believe the theologians, nothing is innocent; if you believe the soldiers, nothing is safe." There is, however, a crucial difference between the warnings of doctors, theologians, and soldiers: We are not likely to make ourselves ill if we obey our doctors, or to be damned if we obey our theologians. However, the warnings of soldiers can lead to mistrust, arms races, and war. Let us turn now to the best-known case in which military planning contributed directly to war.

INFLEXIBILITY AND WORLD WAR I

In pre–World War I Europe, the major powers were all heavily armed and mistrustful of one another, especially the states in the Triple Entente (Britain, France, Russia) and the Triple Alliance (Germany, Austria-Hungary, Italy). All sides, moreover, were acutely aware that in the event of war, they had better mobilize their forces quickly; they all felt, as well, that it could be disastrous to mobilize after their opponent had a head start. (In the last major European war, Prussia's overwhelming defeat of France in 1871 was largely due to the prompt and efficient Prussian mobilization.) So, the general staffs of the continental powers in particular had drawn up elaborate and detailed mobilization schedules. For all the concern about the dangers of *not* mobilizing in time, however, military and political leaders seem to have given relatively little thought to the effect of mobilizing prematurely, or to the dangers of being captive of these prearranged war plans. Nervously, each eyed the other.

The Chain Reaction of Mobilization

Thus, in 1914, Austria was threatening to attack Serbia, thereby avenging the murder of the Austrian archduke while also sending a strong signal to Serbian nationalists within the Austrian empire. Russia then mobilized her armed forces in support of Serbia, hoping to dissuade Austria from attacking, but also to be ready in case war came. The czar wanted to mobilize only the four military districts directly facing Austria, but his generals said that was impossible: No plans for partial mobilization existed. "The whole plan of mobilization," explained General Dobrorolski to the czar, "is worked out ahead to its final conclusion and in all its detail . . . once the moment is chosen, everything is settled; there is no going back; it determines mechanically the beginning of war."[11] Thus, total mobilization called for the alerting of troops facing Germany in the northwest as well as Austria in the Balkans. The czar gave in; Russia couldn't mobilize only against Austria; it had to move against Germany, too.

Germany, not surprisingly, mobilized in response. But the Germans too were captives of their own planning. Since shortly after the Franco-Prussian War, German staff officers had been working on a plan for the next war, which, it was assumed, would be something of a nightmare: against both Russia in the east and France in the west. The resulting war plan was based on the assumption that Russia would be the more formidable foe, but would also be slower to mobilize. So, it called for a concentration of forces first against France, to knock it out of the war quickly, and then to turn attention to Russia.

World War I infantrymen marching away from the battlelines while supplies and replacements go the other way. The need to employ large numbers of soldiers and supplies, and to avoid being outdone by the other side, produced a lethal momentum and inflexibility on all sides. (National Archives of Canada, PA 913)

Rigidity of Plans

When word of the Russian mobilization reached the German kaiser, he sought to attack only in the east, thereby avoiding war with France. "That is impossible, Your Majesty," he was told by his chief of staff, General Moltke. "An army of a million cannot be improvised. It would be nothing but a rabble of undisciplined armed men. . . . It is utterly impossible to advance except according to plan."[12] Originally, the unappealing prospect of fighting a war on two fronts had led to the scheme of defeating France first, known as the Schlieffen Plan; once it became official military policy, however, it made precisely this war unavoidable. The Schlieffen Plan also called for attacking France through Belgium. But England had pledged to support Belgian neutrality, so the German attack quickly brought England into the war as well. It also swayed U.S. public opinion, paving the way for American involvement three years later.

In *The Guns of August*, historian Barbara Tuchman describes the momentum of mobilization as follows:

> Once the mobilization button was pushed, the whole vast machinery for calling up, equipping, and

transporting two million men began turning automatically. Reservists went to their designated depots, were issued uniforms, equipment, and arms, formed into companies and companies into battalions, were joined by cavalry, cyclists, artillery, medical units, cook wagons, blacksmith wagons, even postal wagons moved according to prepared railway timetables to concentration points near the frontier where they would be formed into divisions, divisions into corps, and corps into armies ready to advance and fight. One army corps alone—out of the total of 40 in the German forces—required 170 railway cars for officers, 965 for infantry, 2960 for cavalry, 1915 for artillery and supply wagons, 6010 in all, grouped in 140 trains and an equal number again for their supplies. From the moment the order was given, everything was to move at fixed times according to a schedule precise down to the number of train axles that would pass over a given bridge within a given time.[13]

Each side was acutely aware that it would be at a disadvantage if it allowed the other to begin mobilization first. So military planners on each side urged that the other be preempted. But once begun—even if just as a show of strength, or an effort to avoid being left defenseless—the immense momentum of mobilization made it impossible for either side to pull back. Indeed, the tragic inflexibility shown by the belligerents in World War I stands as an important cautionary tale for modern times, when the "mobilization" time for nuclear-armed missiles is measured in minutes. During the Cuban Missile Crisis, in October 1962, President Kennedy expressed the hope that no historian of the future would write a book on "The Missiles of October."

CRISIS DECISION MAKING

Stimulated in particular by the "close call" of the Cuban Missile Crisis of 1962, psychologically minded students of international relations have directed considerable attention to the process whereby decisions are made, focusing on issues of perception and misperception, communication and miscommunication, understandings and misunderstandings, and the effects of crisis conditions and of small-group processes on decision making.

Small Groups

Major governmental decisions, especially regarding war or warlike actions, often are made by small ad hoc groups, that is, groups convened for that specific purpose. During the crisis provoked by the North Korean invasion of South Korea, for example, fourteen people participated in the emergency deliberations of the U.S. government; during the Cuban Missile Crisis, the committee convened by President Kennedy had sixteen members. The Politburo, the core unit of decision making in the Soviet Union, normally consists of fourteen full members. Taking note of this, it has been suggested that the UNESCO charter should be rewritten to read: "Since wars begin in the minds of men in the core decisional groups of the nation-states, it is in the minds of those men that the defenses of peace must be constructed."[14]

The hope is that a group will temper the enthusiasm and impetuosity of a leader. However, studies suggest that the opposite is more likely: Group members tend to egg one another on, reinforcing tendencies present in the most dominant individual(s). Social psychologists have found that risk taking tends to be more pronounced in groups than in individuals, because no one person must (or can) take responsibility for the outcome. And contrary to the widespread belief that "tough" leadership makes would-be aggressors back down, convincing data show that the likelihood of war increases when leaders are willing to accept a high level of risk.[15]

Moreover, the greater the outside threat, the greater the tendency to put up a united front, so as to suppress personal doubts and foster the illusion of unanimity. This tendency is enhanced by the fact that high-level leaders generally surround themselves with "yes men," people who agree with them and who rarely present contrary views. In short, leaders become victims of what social psychologist Irving Janis called "groupthink,"

> a mode of thinking that people engage in when they are deeply involved in a cohesive in-group, when the members' strivings for unanimity override their motivation to realistically appraise alternative courses of action. Groupthink refers to a deterioration of mental efficiency, reality testing, and oral judgment that results from in-group pressures.[16]

Janis also emphasized that groupthink "is likely to result in irrational and dehumanizing actions directed against out-groups."[17] The unavoidable conclusion is that groups may be no more rational than individuals, and often less so.

Following General MacArthur's surprising success in repelling the North Koreans in 1950, the United States made the fateful decision to seek to unify all of Korea by force of arms. (This eventually resulted in Chinese forces crossing the Yalu River into Korean territory, and three years of stalemated war, with hundreds of thousands—perhaps more than a million—additional casualties.) This decision was taken by a small group of American officials, strongly influenced by the charismatic MacArthur's overconfidence. Discussion within the group shared and reinforced an illusion of invulnerability based in part on stereotyping of the enemy—the North Koreans—and the potential enemy—the Chinese. Experts with dissenting views were excluded from the decision-making process.

General Douglas MacArthur (in dark jacket) inspecting the front lines during the Korean War. (UPI/Bettmann Newsphotos)

Excluding Bad News

This situation is worth exploring in more detail: MacArthur's commitment to his goal of destroying the North Koreans made him insensitive to reports that would counsel caution to someone more open-minded. As a result, subordinates — eager to ingratiate themselves with their commander, or at least, to avoid antagonizing him — actually slanted intelligence reports to reinforce this bias.

This is a widespread and dangerous phenomenon in crisis decision making: the fact that the decision may be based on incorrect information, because the information sources have been hesitant to send "bad" news. For example, prior to World War I, Prince Lichnowsky, the German ambassador to Britain, reported (correctly) to the kaiser that Britain was prepared to declare war against Germany; he was alternately disregarded and derided as incompetent. By contrast, the German ambassador to Russia was praised for sending reassuring messages back to Berlin, stating that the czar was not likely to defend Serbia, even while he was noting something very different in his personal notebooks. There are two useful lessons here: (1) When the bearer of bad tidings is likely to fare poorly, he or she may well doctor the message, and (2) people — including state leaders — often exhibit selec-

tive attention, so that, if they are already committed to a course of action, they tend to disregard what they do not want to hear, focusing only on information that confirms their preexisting beliefs. Thus, Stalin actually ordered the execution of a Czech agent who warned in April 1941 (correctly, it turned out) that Nazi Germany was preparing an attack on the U.S.S.R. At the time, Stalin maintained that the spy must be a British provocateur, so convinced was he of British animosity and the reliability of his alliance with Hitler.

Decision-Making Pressures

A crisis may be defined as an unanticipated threat to important values for which the decisions must be made promptly. Decisions made during crises are likely to be especially crucial for issues of war or peace; unfortunately, it is precisely under such conditions — when stress is unusually high — that decision making is most likely to be flawed.

Crisis decision making is likely to have the following characteristics:

1. *Time pressure.* There is frequently a need (or a perceived need) to make decisions quickly.

2. *Heavy responsibility.* Most leaders are aware, some of them acutely aware, of the potential costs in human suffering if their decision results in war.

3. *Faulty and incomplete data.* Intelligence about the potential opponent (motivations, alternative options, strengths and weaknesses) is usually limited and inadequate. Under such conditions, the tendency is to rely on simplistic and often inaccurate stereotypes of the opponent.

4. *Information overload.* Modern decision-makers are typically innundated with large amounts of information, and although much of it may in fact be erroneous, decision-makers typically do not know what information to ignore or believe.

5. *Limited options.* Decision-makers often see themselves as having only a limited range of

potential courses of action (in part, because the stress of the situation itself tends to limit creative problem solving); at the same time, the opponent is seen as enjoying wide latitude.

6. *Short-term over long-term.* Attention tends to be focused on the immediate, short-term effects of a course of action, with relatively little patience for assessing the possible long-term implications. As a result, the overwhelming desire is to act in such a way as to relieve the current, pressing crisis.

7. *Surprise.* Although the situation may not be entirely unexpected, an element of surprise often is involved, so that most crises have to be resolved on the spot, without benefit of preanalyzed scenarios.

8. *Personal stresses.* Decisions of great import often must be made under conditions of sleep deprivation and sometimes under great anxiety, bordering on panic.

All of the above combine to make it especially difficult for leaders — either singly or in small groups — to render intelligent and rational judgments. Writing of the Berlin Crisis of 1961, the Cuban Missile Crisis of 1962, and the U.S.-Soviet tensions raised during the Arab-Israeli Six Day War (1967), former Defense Secretary Robert McNamara noted that

> on each of these occasions lack of information, misinformation, and misjudgments led to confrontation. And in each of them, as the crisis evolved, tensions heightened, emotions rose, and the danger of irrational decisions increased.[18]

Crisis Management

In view of the importance of such situations, a new area of concern, known as "crisis management," has emerged. The goals of crisis management are not only (1) to prevent a crisis from escalating to war, but also (2) to keep the leaders in control of the situation, and (3) to gain maximum advantage, whenever possible, from such crises when they occur. When crises involve the danger of war, especially nuclear war, the elite decision-makers on each side want to appear strong, fear to seem weak, and are eager to gain some advantage over the other that they would not like to see the other achieve over them. Crisis behavior then tends to become an exercise in "competitive risk-taking."[19] The leaders on each side are inclined to engage in "one-upsmanship," hoping to induce the other side to back down, in a situation dangerously reminiscent of the game of chicken (see Chapter 5), whether nuclear weapons are involved or not. For example, a senior aide to President Kennedy recounted that during the Cuban Missile Crisis, former Secretary of State Dean Acheson recommended bombing the Soviet missile sites that had just been revealed in Cuba. When asked what, in his judgment, the Soviets would do in response,

> He replied, "I think they'll knock out our missile bases in Turkey." "What do we do then?" "Under our NATO Treaty, we'd be obligated to knock out a base inside the Soviet Union." "What will they do then?" "Why, then we hope everyone will cool down and want to talk."[20]

Psychological Effects of Repetitive Crises

Even when an individual crisis is resolved peacefully (as in the case of the Cuban missiles), repetitive crises can produce an expectancy of war. For example, during the years immediately preceding the outbreak of World War I, Germany had been embroiled in numerous situations of near-war — with Russia over Austria's annexation of Bosnia and Herzegovina, with Britain and France over Morocco — in addition to a navy race with Britain and an army race with France. Such situations can result in a feeling of fatalism as yet another crisis emerges, or an existing one is painfully prolonged and things appear to be leading slowly but irrevocably toward war. Finally, rationality is replaced by a sense of acceptance of the ensuing, and now inevitable, destruction. Thus, on the eve of the First World War, the kaiser exclaimed, in a fit of pique and resignation, "Even if we are bled to death, England will at least lose India."[21] And when, after an ongoing series of economic and diplomatic confrontations with the United States, the Japanese government secretly decided upon war with the United States, the Japanese war minister commented that "Once in a while it is necessary for one to close one's eyes and jump from the stage of the Kiyomizu Temple"[22] (a renowned suicide spot). Crises, in short, can be psychologically erosive, leaving war as the simplest solution.

On the other hand, in some cases, a crisis terminated short of war has actually served to bring the two sides closer together. In 1898, for example, a small contingent of French troops briefly occupied Fashoda, in the Sudan, contesting the colonial claims of England. The ensuing "Fashoda crisis" generated enormous tension between France and England, nearly leading to war. It turned out, however, that this confrontation marked the high point of Anglo-French colonial rivalry, after which the two states became increasingly allied, leading to the entente of 1904 and subsequent friendship throughout the twentieth century. Similarly, the Cuban Missile Crisis seems to have sobered the leadership of both the United States and the U.S.S.R., leading to a warming of relations the following year, including the signing of the Atmospheric Test-Ban Treaty.

Crises in the Nuclear Age

Prior to World War I, mobilization of the Great Powers was astoundingly fast, given the immense number of men and amount of material involved; but it still required several days. The nuclear age, by contrast, can be described as a state of chronic, low-level crisis; "mobilization" requires mere minutes, and entire wars can be fought within hours. The quick-reaction regime of ballistic missiles has resulted in a chronic crisis mentality in leaders, advisors, and military chiefs. Nuclear strategist Thomas Schelling gives a metaphor:

If I go downstairs to investigate a noise at night, with a gun in my hand, and find myself face to face with a burglar who has a gun in his hand, there is danger of an outcome that neither of us desires. Even if he prefers just to leave quietly, and I wish

him to, there is danger that he may *think* I want to shoot, and shoot first. Worse, there is danger that he may think that I think *he* wants to shoot. And so on.[23]*

In the idealized case, crisis decision making is based on rationality (more correctly, on a particular and — some might argue — rather peculiar kind of rationality). Decision making is seen as a variant of mathematical economics, a process of maximizing the difference between benefits and costs; for obvious reasons, this approach is especially popular among devotees of nuclear deterrence theory. Herman Kahn, for example, developed an elaborate classification of forty-four different rungs of nuclear escalation, beginning with precise, low-intensity options such as "slow-motion counterproperty," moving through "augmented disarming attacks," and culminating in "spasm or insensate war."[24]

The assumption that decision-makers will remain rational during a full-fledged nuclear crisis, carefully picking and choosing among the various nuclear options while the bombs are going off all around, is one of the less credible aspects of modern nuclear strategy. In 1974, Secretary of Defense James Schlesinger testified in Congress about his judgment as to the feasibility of rationally conducting a "limited" nuclear war:

If we were to maintain continued communications with the Soviet leaders during the war, and if we were to describe precisely and meticulously the limited nature of our actions, including the desire to avoid attacking their urban industrial bases . . . in spite of [the claims] that everything must go all out, when the existential circumstances arise, political leaders on both sides will be under powerful pressure to continue to be sensible. . . . Those are the circumstances in which I believe that leaders will be

---

*There are several possible solutions to this dilemma: don't break into people's houses, have a good burglar-alarm system, don't carry guns (or at least, not lethal or accurate guns), announce your intentions as clearly and non-threateningly as possible, etc.

Meeting of the Executive Committee, established to deal with the Cuban Missile Crisis in October 1962. President Kennedy is flanked by Secretary of State Dean Rusk and Secretary of Defense Robert McNamara; Attorney General Robert Kennedy is across the table. (John F Kennedy Library)

rational and prudent. I hope I am not being too optimistic.[25]

Evidence from history and psychology suggests that almost certainly he is.

The Effects of Crises on Rational Decision Making

What must be decided during a crisis? According to one noted political scientist, the tasks include (but are not limited to) the following:

> (a) identify major alternative courses of action; (b) estimate the probable costs and gains of alternative policy choices; (c) distinguish between the possible and the probable; (d) assess the situation from the perspective of other parties; (e) discriminate between relevant and irrelevant information; (f) tolerate ambiguity; (g) resist premature action; and (h) make adjustments to meet real changes in the situation (and, as a corollary, to distinguish real from apparent changes).[26]

There have been numerous cases of crisis decisions made hastily, emotionally, and erroneously. The psychological data are also clear that mild stress tends to facilitate human decision making, but that intense stress is likely to be especially disruptive, resulting in actions that are increasingly irrational. Paradoxically, therefore, during severe crises, good policy decisions become both more important and less likely. Information overload, for example, becomes a substantial problem:

> As the volume of information directed at policymakers rises, the search for information within the communication system will tend to become less thorough, and selectivity in what is read, believed and retained takes on increasing importance. Unpleasant information and that which does not support preconceived beliefs is most likely to fall by the wayside.[27]

Laboratory studies have also shown that as a perceived threat increases, messages sent and received tend to reveal assessments of the situation that are more and more stereotyped and simplistic. There is a corresponding restriction in the range and originality of the options being considered. During real-life international crises, time pressures are often intensified by the use of deadlines and ultimatums. "Nothing clarifies the mind," according to Samuel Johnson, "like the prospect of being hanged in the morning." This may be true, but it also seems likely that nothing fogs the mind like the prospect of making a catastrophic decision, in a crisis environment, right now.

Experimental research has shown that severe stress is particularly likely to impede precisely those decision processes needed during international crises: Verbal and logical performance deteriorates; problem solving becomes more rigid; tolerance for complexity and ambiguity diminishes (this is especially crucial because in the real world of international affairs, issues are rarely laid out in simple "either/or" terms, or even the clean options of a multiple choice exam); errors are more frequent; the focus of attention is reduced, both spatially and temporally; and decision-makers become less able to discriminate the trivial from the crucial. In short, the decision maker finds him- or herself less able to "see" the problem clearly and to respond creatively.

Of course, it remains uncertain whether simulation studies accurately reflect real experiences. But speaking from his own experience in the Kennedy administration, Theodore Sorensen notes that "I saw first-hand, during the long days and nights of the Cuban crisis, how brutally physical and mental fatigue can numb the good sense as well as the senses of normally articulate men."[28] In general, we must concur with Robert Kennedy that the effects of crises on human decision making are largely unpredictable: "That kind of pressure does strange things to a human being, even to brilliant, self-confident, experienced men. For some it brings out cl..aracteristics and strengths that perhaps they never knew they had, and for others the pressure is too overwhelming."[29]

PERCEPTUAL AND COGNITIVE ISSUES

It can be argued that most wars begin in error, since each side generally believes at the outset that it will win . . . or else it wouldn't go to war in the first place. Insofar as this is true, then the process of war itself represents a process of movement, from error, through agony, to a more accurate appraisal of the situation — wars end when both sides agree as to which is the stronger. To be sure, some wars take place because one side is attacked, or perceives the actions of the other side as hostile or threatening, and it may fight back not because it expects to win, but because it sees no viable alternative (for example, Poland, after Germany invaded in 1939, or Finland, after being attacked by the Soviet Union in that same year). But in many other cases, human

error — notably perceptual distortions — appear to play a role in causing war. Thus, Horatio, in Shakespeare's *Hamlet*, relates a tale

> Of carnal, bloody and unnatural acts,
> Of accidental judgments, casual slaughters,
> Of deaths put on by cunning and forced cause,
> And, in this upshot, purposes mistook
> Fall'n on th'inventors' heads.

Insofar as blunders and misperceptions have an important role in the real world as well, we have an obligation to be attuned to these sources of error. "We can never walk surely," noted the British statesman Edmund Burke, "but by being sensible of our blindnesses."

Even in the absence of a crisis, leaders and decision-makers must often labor under some heavy disadvantages, which prevent them from getting a clear, unbiased view of the situation. The result is a range of potential errors, resulting from misperceptions, misunderstandings, or miscalculations. Some of these, such as the tendency to disregard information that does not conform to one's preconceptions, have already been touched upon. There are two major contending theories of perceptual distortion: cognitive theory, which is concerned with errors in the processing of information, and motivational theory, in which the emotional needs of the decision-makers are paramount.[30] In the following review, however, we shall focus on the nature of the misperception rather than its cause.

Inaccurate Perception of Others

History is replete with examples of this phenomenon. Hitler disdained the British as "shopkeepers," and the Russians as "barbarians." The Arabs, who attacked the fledgling state of Israel with five armies in 1948, were highly (and inappropriately) confident of victory over a Jewish nation that was greatly outnumbered and had, in modern times at least, been avowedly nonmilitarist. Conversely, the Israeli armed forces came to suffer from a misconception that Arabs were hopelessly incompetent in military matters; as a result, they nearly lost the 1973 Yom

Kippur War. Five different U.S. presidents misread the nationalist determination of the Vietnamese and their leader, Ho Chi Minh, each convinced that the drive for unification would crumble if only a bit more military pressure was applied. Iraq underestimated the resilience of Khomeini and the Iranians. The list is very long; decision-makers have persistently underestimated their opponents. (Of course, perhaps we only become acutely aware of such errors because the results can be spectacular; when, by contrast, leaders correctly assess a would-be opponent, or overestimate its strength, the resulting inaction doesn't make headlines.)

Decision-makers commonly misjudge the strength of allies as well. U.S. leadership misjudged the power of the shah of Iran, for example, until it was too late. According to one expert on the role of misperceptions in international affairs, American officials were so slow in recognizing the Iranian revolution because it went counter to many preexisting and mutually reinforcing beliefs:

> Not only were the Shah and his regime perceived as strong, but also the specific image was supported by the general belief — based on good historical evidence — that leaders who control large and effective internal security forces were not overthrown by popular protest. These preconceptions were reinforced by several others that were more peculiarly American: the menace to pro-Western governments comes from the left; modernization enjoys the support of the strongest political elements of society, and those who oppose it cannot be serious contenders for power; religious motives and religious movements are peripheral to politics.[31]

As a result, U.S. policy-makers not only misinterpreted events in Iran, but also made highly inappropriate decisions based on those misperceptions. This difficulty was if anything enhanced by the anguish associated with making difficult decisions: The harder it is to make a decision, set a policy, and so on, the greater the resistance to reversing that decision once it has been made.

Many preconceptions are self-serving: Hawks, for example, see an opponent as unrelentingly hostile, so that even conciliatory moves are interpreted as clever maneuvers to make the other side let down its guard . . . thus further proving the correctness of the original impression. Doves, it should be noted, tend to emphasize the role of perceptions, thereby sometimes excusing an unacceptably aggressive act as a consequence of misunderstanding or misperception. These have been called "motivated errors," and include, for example, the tendency among British leaders during the 1930s to underestimate German hostility and simultaneously to overestimate German strategic air power vis-à-vis British cities. This latter view was appealing to the appeasers because it made it all the more important to avoid war with Germany; at the same time, the hawks also found it useful because it reinforced their assertion that Hitler was dangerous and that a military buildup was needed.

Misuse of History

If one or a small number of values dominates policy, perceptions are often modified so as to minimize psychological distress and to provide a congenial view of current events. In addition, there is an understandable yearning to avoid repeating past errors combined with the hope of repeating past successes. Following the Franco-Prussian War, two assumptions were widespread in Europe: (1) The next war would be intense and brief, because (2) a long war would ruin a state's economy. The result was a premium on striking first and decisively; this contributed, in turn, to plans for total mobilization, with now-familiar consequences.

Past successes can also overshadow present realities. For example, Austria's success in annexing Bosnia and Herzegovina led the Central Powers to the (mistaken) belief that history would repeat itself if Austria dealt harshly with Serbia; it did not. Che Guevara's success during the Cuban revolution led him to believe that history would repeat itself in Bolivia; it also did not.

On the other hand, decision-makers have also erred in trying to avoid the mistakes of the past. In the 1930s, statesmen like Britain's well-intentioned Neville Chamberlain, appalled at the senseless and avoidable slaughter of World War I, were convinced that nonbelligerent, far-sighted diplomacy would prevent similar disasters; hence, they tended to favor appeasement.* In the infamous Munich Conference of 1938, Chamberlain acceded to Hitler's demand to annex the Czech Sudetenland; a generation later, those remembering this great mistake and seeking to learn from it were likely to be especially hard-nosed. After Egypt nationalized the Suez Canal in 1955, for example, British prime minister Anthony Eden (one of Churchill's deputies during World War II) was convinced that the West was facing a "second Munich" or a "second Rhineland" unless it responded militarily. (In fact, 1930s-style appeasement probably would have prevented the First World War, and 1914-style intransigence might well have headed off the Second.)

Hitler also misread recent events. When Germany invaded Poland in 1939, Hitler did not expect that Britain and France would honor their commitments and declare war on Germany; after all, just six months earlier, they had refused to go to war over Czechoslovakia, which was militarily more valuable and also more defendable. The supposed "lessons of Munich," learned too late by the West, also contributed to a hardening of Cold War alliances in the nuclear age, in the hope that by making commitments clear, similar outcomes could be avoided. Comparable perceptions have also generated skepticism about arms control and disarmament among most conservatives. A historical metaphor is like a cookie: tasty perhaps, but if squeezed too hard, it crumbles.

Professional "security managers" (members of the military/political establishment) generally give special attention to cases in which aggressive powers were not perceived as such until it was too late. As a result, they are inclined to overestimate the aggressiveness of a potential opponent. For exam-

ple, during the 1870s, Bismarck was largely concerned with maintaining the status quo in Europe; however, because his pre-1871 activities had been so aggressively expansionist, other statesmen put the worse possible light on each of his post-1871 maneuvers. When Argentine forces initially took over the Falkland Islands in 1982, Argentines looked as a historical analogy to the Indian takeover of Goa, a small colonial enclave on the Indian mainland whose loss was quickly accepted (without bloodshed) by the Portuguese government. To the British, however, the relevant metaphor was Hitler and the origins of the Second World War, and they responded, not as Portugal did in 1961, but rather as they wished they had done in 1938.

States like the United States, which have a relatively limited historical experience in world affairs, may be unusually susceptible to drawing inferences from the small number of international events that have been significant for them. And the more recent the event, the more likely it is to be salient in memory, even if it may not be especially relevant: "If generals are prepared to fight the last war, diplomats may be prepared to avoid the last war."[32]

The Double Standard of Hostility

During the Vietnam War, the United States bombed and invaded Cambodia in 1970, claiming that because Cambodia was providing haven and supply routes for the North Vietnamese, it could legally be attacked, even though it was a sovereign, nonbelligerent state. In 1988, however, after Nicaraguan forces had pursued contra rebels to their staging and supply areas inside neighboring Honduras, the Reagan administration decried what it called an "unjustified invasion," and dispatched 3,000 U.S. troops to Honduras. Similarly, the Soviet Union, after denouncing the U.S. role in Vietnam, had no trouble justifying its invasion of Afghanistan. In the late 1950s, when the United States placed medium-range missiles capable of reaching the Soviet Union in Turkey and Great Britain, this was considered (by the United States) to be defensive and justified; but when, shortly afterward, the U.S.S.R. sought to place medium-range missiles

---

*Note that in those days, appeasement referred to reasonable acquiescence, without the very negative connotations it carries today.

capable of reaching the United States in Cuba, this was deemed a dastardly, offensive, and unjustified act . . . and the Kennedy administration was willing to go to the brink of nuclear war in order to get them removed.

The principle sounds absurd, but it is widely followed: When We (the U.S.S.R., the United States, Sierra Leone, whomever) do something, it is acceptable — often laudable — but if They do the exact same thing, it is not. What is involved here, in part, is a profound absence of empathy, a failure to "walk a mile in the other's shoes," to recognize that there is more than one way to look at a problem, and a refusal to consider that the motivations and actions of one side may be perceived in an entirely different light by the other. Historian Herbert Butterfield attributed much of this widespread misperception to what he called "Hobbesian fear":

> You yourself may vividly feel the terrible fear that you have of the other party, but you cannot enter into the other man's counter-fear, or even understand why he should be particularly nervous. For you know that you yourself mean him no harm, and that you want nothing from him save guarantees for your own safety; and it is never possible for you to realize or remember properly that since he cannot see the inside of your mind, he can never have the same assurance of your intentions that you have.[33]

During a 1989 speech at an East–West conference on reducing conventional forces in Europe, Secretary of State James Baker asserted that "Those in the West should be free of the fear that the massive forces under Soviet command might invade them. Those in the East should be free of the fear that armed Soviet intervention . . . would be used again to deny them choice."[34] Fair enough, but an empathetic statesman would also have added something like the following: "Those in the East should be free of the fear that the forces of the West will invade them, as they have so often in the past," and perhaps even that "Those in the West should be free of the fear that their own military forces might precipitate a war, which, although ostensibly fought on their behalf, would destroy them."

Among psychologists, three related theories have sought to explain this tendency to perceive the Other as hostile, while holding the Self blameless:

1. *Ego defense.* A theory of ego defense emphasizes that individuals would find it troublesome to admit that their activities threaten others; hence, they protect their self-images by maintaining their own innocence and insisting on their benevolent intentions. When others then respond aggressively, this is seen as evidence of their hostility, since it couldn't possibly have been evoked by the "good guys." President Eisenhower's secretary of state, John Foster Dulles, once noted that "Khrushchev does not need to be convinced of our good intentions. He knows we are not aggressors and do not threaten the security of the Soviet Union."[35]

2. *Attribution.* Attribution theory suggests that individuals are intensely aware of the various external constraints on their behavior, including economic factors, the need to placate others, and so on. Any threat or actual harm to others is therefore unintended. By contrast, it is much more difficult to empathize with the complex forces acting to produce the behavior of others; hence, such behavior is more likely to be seen as resulting from an oversimplified stereotype, rather than the conflicted, multifactorial process known to operate within oneself and one's group.

3. *Projection.* Projection is the phenomenon in which people take certain unacceptable tendencies of their own and identify them instead in the Other. Finding it painful to recognize nastiness, aggressiveness, and the like in oneself, it is more acceptable to project such internal tendencies onto an opponent, and then criticize them. "How wicked these people must have been," sobbed Hitler, as he observed the demolition of Warsaw, "to make me do this to them."[36]

Whatever the origin, the perception of the Other as hostile has served as a self-fulfilling prophecy: Prior to World War I, for example, German leaders assumed (erroneously) that other statesmen

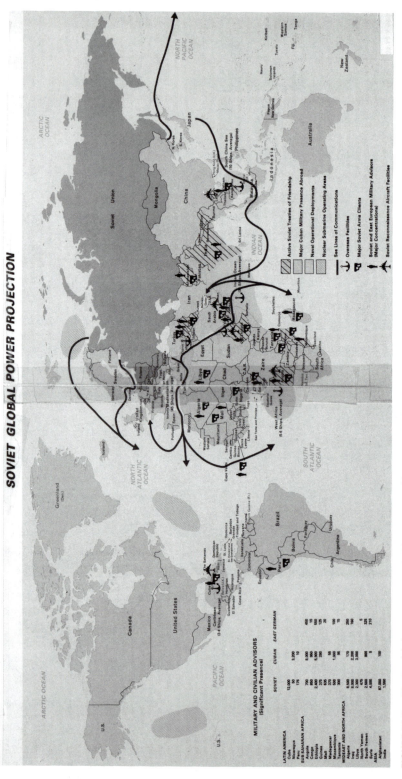

FIGURE 10.1 "Soviet global power projection." (U.S. government publication *Soviet Military Power*)

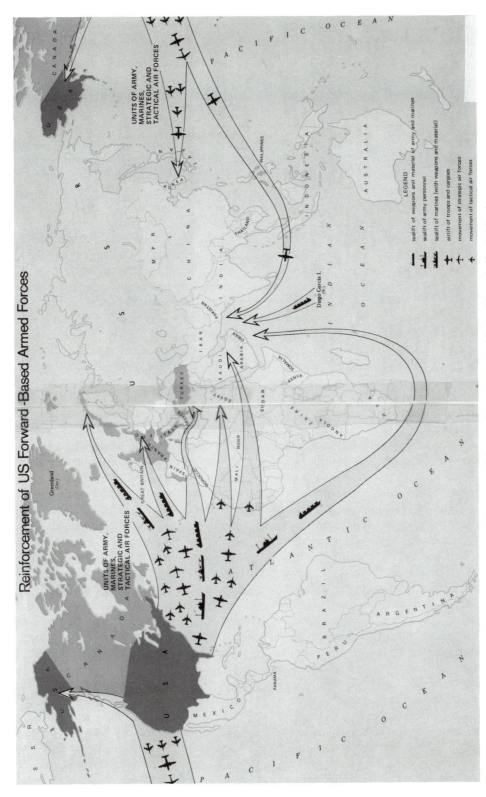

FIGURE 10.2 "Reinforcement of U.S. forward-based armed forces." (English-language Soviet government publication *Whence the Threat to Peace*)

were as willing to go to war in pursuit of their national interest as they themselves were. The result was aggressiveness and hostility, which heightened the anxiety of Germany's neighbors, in turn generating precisely the encirclement Germany had so feared. (During the 1930s, interestingly, advocates of appeasement erred the opposite way, thinking Hitler wanted to *avoid* war as much as they did. Hence, they also made it more likely.)

Not surprisingly, wars fought because of the perception that an opponent is hostile, allied with an enemy, or bent on conquest, make that opponent hostile, allied with an enemy, or bent on conquest. Such wars vindicate the assumptions on which they were based. For example, the Vietnam War was presented to the U.S. public as resulting largely from North Vietnam's invasion of the South; this came to pass after U.S. bombing of the North triggered massive movement of North Vietnamese units into the South. Similarly, Soviet repression of reform efforts in Hungary and Czechoslovakia, out of fear that they were anti-Soviet, served only to heighten anti-Soviet sentiment.

The double standard of hostility prescribes not only that one's own actions are blameless, but also that one's opponents are relentlessly hostile. Prior to the First World War, Austria saw Serbia as populated by devils, the Russian leadership was particularly distrustful of the Austrians, and, while British diplomats were desperately trying to prevent war, the German kaiser wrote on a diplomatic note: "The net has been suddenly thrown over our head, and England sneeringly reaps the most brilliant success of her persistently prosecuted, purely anti-German world policy, against which we have proved ourselves helpless, while she twists the noose of our political fidelity to Austria, as we squirm isolated in the net."[37]

To Israelis, their country is small and isolated; geographically, it is a tiny, vulnerable sliver of land. To Arabs, and especially Palestinians, that same Israeli land area is a dagger wielded by Western imperialists, stabbing right into the midsection of the Arab world. The Sandinistas saw the Reagan administration as an imminent threat to their survival; to President Reagan, Nicaragua ostensibly posed an equally imminent threat to the security of the United States, located as it was merely "two days' drive from Harlingen, Texas."

Miscommunication

Some communication errors come about simply because people speak different languages and experience different cultures. Consider the *mokusatsu* affair. In the early summer of 1945, the Allies, meeting in Potsdam, issued a surrender ultimatum to Japan. The official Japanese response was to *mokusatsu* the ultimatum, which was translated as "ignore." The Truman administration saw this as an outright rejection, whereas in fact, it should more accurately have been rendered as "withhold comment, pending deliberation." It is at least possible that with better communication, atomic bombs would not have been dropped shortly thereafter.

In many other cases, and for diverse reasons, communication may result in what the French call *un dialogue des sourds*, "a dialogue of the deaf." Senders typically assume that if they spend much time and effort designing a message calibrated to convey a particular meaning, the receiver will necessarily understand it. Often, however, "messages" are not read as intended, whereupon warnings are not heeded, and the sender may even blame the receiver (unjustifiably) for intransigence or hostility. President McKinley, in 1898, sent what he thought was a blunt ultimatum concerning Cuba to Spain; the Spanish government erroneously interpreted the message as reassuring. The result, ultimately, was the Spanish-American War.

Numerous miscommunications seem to have taken place in the early stages of the Korean War. In 1950, Secretary of State Acheson testified to Congress that Korea was outside the United States' Pacific defense perimeter; the North Koreans, not understanding that these words were intended more for domestic consumption than as an international signal, felt emboldened to attack the South. Later, when U.S. forces were pushing far north of the 38th parallel (dividing North and South Korea), China sent many signals indicating that it would intervene if U.S. troops continued their military operations near the Chinese border. The U.S., however, simply did not pick up on these warnings. Moreover, in seeking to reassure the Chinese that it did not wish to expand the Korean conflict, the United States referred frequently to a long-standing friendship between the American and Chinese people. At the same time, Chinese authorities had a very different perception of Sino-American relations, viewing the United States with deep distrust, as merely one of many imperialist exploiters of China during the nineteenth century, and more recently, as the inheritor of Japan's goal of an Asian empire.

In 1961, after India had set up military out-posts in contested regions of Ladakh, Chinese troops surrounded them, and then withdrew, without attacking. Indian leaders saw this as a failure of Chinese nerve, and felt encouraged in their adventurism, whereas in fact the Chinese were seeking to send a message demonstrating their resolve and the military untenability of the Indian incursion.

Wishful Thinking

People have a disconcerting habit of hearing what they want to hear, and believing that something is true simply because they dearly wish that it was so. Military leaders are "can do" people; their job entails taking an aggressive, problem-solving approach to their mission. Often, there is no lack of intelligence (defined either as data or IQ), but rather, a reluctance to draw unpleasant conclusions. Prior to the 1962 Sino-Indian War — a stinging defeat for India — Indian leaders blithely assumed that the Chinese leadership was timid, and that their military forces were superior to the Chinese, simply ignoring evidence to the contrary. The same kind of unassailable self-confidence led the United States into the quagmire of Vietnam, confident that there was "light at the end of the tunnel." In 1965, President Johnson was told by his Joint Chiefs of Staff that the communists would be defeated in Vietnam within two years, if only sufficient additional military pressure would be applied. In 1971, the Pakistani leadership, ignoring all evidence that India enjoyed clear superiority, attacked its arch-rival, seeking, unsuccessfully, to destroy the Indian air force on the ground, as Israel had done to Egypt at the onset of the Six Day War in 1967.

When the risks are high, one might expect that an uncompromising, self-critical honesty — if only for selfish benefit — would be well developed. In fact, the opposite occurs at least as frequently: Self-delusion is rampant in the events before a war and in its early stages. Lord Asquith, British prime minister in the early days of World War I, claimed that the War Office "kept three sets of figures: one to mislead the public, another to mislead the Cabinet, and a third to mislead itself." On the eve of their attack on Pearl Harbor, Japanese leaders realized that Japan could only hope to prevail over the United States in a brief and limited war, so they convinced themselves that this is what would probably happen, especially if the United States was sufficiently shocked and crippled militarily at the outset.

Wishful thinking is hardly a recent phenomenon. The defeat of its Armada, in 1588, marked the end of Spain as a global power. Before sailing, one Spanish commander "reasoned" as follows:

> It is well known that we fight in God's cause. So when we meet the English, God will surely arrange matters so that we can grapple and board them, either by sending some strange freak of weather, or more likely, just by depriving the English of their wits. If we come to close quarters, Spanish valor and Spanish steel — and the great mass of soldiers we shall have on board — will make our victory certain. But unless God helps us by making a miracle, the English, who have faster guns and handier ships than ours, and many more long-range guns, and who know their advantage as well as we do, will never close with us at all, but stand aloof and blow us to pieces with their culverins, without our being able to do them any serious hurt. . . . So, we are sailing against England in the confident hope of a miracle.[38]

Of course, military adventures are often launched on something more than the "confident hope of a miracle." Nearly three-quarters of all wars in the last 150 years have been won by the initiator, suggesting some tendency toward accurate planning.

Immediate results of the Japanese surprise attack on the U.S. navy base at Pearl Harbor, Hawaii. The Japanese leadership had hoped to shock the U.S. into agreeing to an early termination of war. (Library of Congress)

However, there have been notable exceptions, including the American Civil War, World War I, World War II, the Korean War, the 1973 Arab-Israeli War, the Falklands War, and the Iran-Iraq War. The United States and the U.S.S.R. allowed themselves to become embroiled in their disastrous Vietnam and Afghanistan wars, each confident of relatively easy victory against a small, impoverished Third World state.*

Overconfidence has often cost states and leaders dearly. In the autumn of 1914, the kaiser promised Germany that its sons would be back "before the leaves had fallen from the trees." Hitler did not even have his quartermasters issue winter uniforms to his troops attacking the Soviet Union, so confident was he that the campaign would be over before winter (as it happened, many German soldiers died of exposure). In fact, most wars have been initiated on a note of optimism; in many cases, this optimism may itself have been a cause of the war. Only rarely have people marched off to war in a mood of grim determination and resignation — those emotions usually come later.

On the other hand, it can be argued that what is unintentional about most wars has not been the

*Not surprisingly, brief interventions by powerful states in much weaker states (such as the United States in Panama in 1989) are more likely to be successful, at least in the short term. The long-term consequences, however, are more difficult to predict.

decision to fight, but the outcome. Wars have often turned out to be longer or costlier than expected at their outset. Above all, they typically result in the defeat of half the participants who expected to win.

The biases of certain leaders may well have contributed to dangerous and costly misperceptions. For example, the two most influential secretaries of state in the period immediately following World War II, Dean Acheson (for President Truman) and John Foster Dulles (for President Eisenhower) were zealously, even rigidly, anticommunist and profoundly distrustful of anything smacking of peaceful relations with the U.S.S.R. But the reader should beware of another potentially erroneous conclusion, namely, that international conflict arises solely from psychological errors and misperceptions: In some cases, negative perceptions are, regrettably, accurate. Conflict may arise not because the adversaries misunderstand each other, but rather because they understand each other all too well. In some ways, Stalin was a monster, and the Soviet state truly dangerous and repressive; it is far from clear that a more conciliatory attitude by the West would have averted the Cold War. Perhaps it would only have whetted a Kremlin appetite for expansion.

And in his day, Neville Chamberlain seemed reasonable in his perception that peace in Europe could be assured if only Hitler was granted what were widely acclaimed to be his legitimate nationalistic ambitions; Winston Churchill, by contrast, was excoriated by critics who thought him irrational, hyper-militaristic, and bedeviled by all the bogeymen of misperception that we have discussed above. Of course, with the wisdom of hindsight we now know that Chamberlain was deceived, and that Churchill saw quite clearly. In short, we must at least admit the possibility that sometimes states and their leaders are nefarious and war-seeking. To see prospects for peace and harmony, to strive for mutual understanding and confidence building is not necessarily to be naive or duped by the other side. But similarly, to be distrustful, to recognize danger, or enmity, is not necessarily to misperceive.

A FINAL NOTE ON DECISION MAKING

The making of war — and of peace — is the responsibility of human beings, typically those who find themselves in a position of political leadership. To some degree, therefore, we are at the mercy of those leaders whose decisions may be crucial for our happiness and survival. We therefore have an interest in maximizing the quality of these decision-makers and of the information available to them. Nonetheless, even with perfect perception of all current issues, decision-makers are necessarily plunging into an uncertain darkness. Some influential members of Spain's aristocratic military tradition felt, in 1898, that a war with the United States was necessary, in order to lose Cuba gracefully; they hadn't counted, however, on losing Puerto Rico and the Philippines too. "The future," writes an eminent historian, "is a land of which there are no maps, and historians err when they describe even the most purposeful statesman as though he were marching down a broad highway with his objective already in sight."[39] How much more important, then, that leaders be as free as possible from emotional and perceptual blinders in making such crucial decisions related to issues of war and peace.

Study Questions

1. Make an argument in favor of the "great man theory" regarding the causes of war. Make an argument against it.

2. Describe the role of personalities in causing, or preventing, war.

3. Describe at least one misperception on the part of the leadership of each major country that ultimately resulted in World War I.

4. What is meant by "groupthink"? What is its relevance to the decision to wage war?

5. Compare crisis decision making in nuclear and conventional conflicts.

6. What are some characteristics of crisis decision making that distinguish it from, say, the decision to buy a particular make and model of automobile?

7. What is the difference between motivated and un-motivated perceptual errors?

8. Was history misused by governmental decision-makers in the period leading up to World War II? Explain.

9. Discuss the possible role of empathy in contributing to better decisions with respect to war and peace.

10. Much misunderstanding in international relations has been caused by what has been called the "mirror image" problem, in which both sides are in fact similar, but see each other as being very different. Elaborate.

Suggestions for Further Reading

Ralph K. White. 1970. *Nobody Wanted War: Misperception in Vietnam and Other Wars*. The Free Press: New York.

Ole Holsti. 1972. *Crisis Escalation War*. McGill-Queen's University Press: Montreal.

Robert Jervis. 1976. *Perception and Misperception in International Politics*. Princeton University Press: Princeton, NJ.

Richard Ned Lebow. 1981. *Between Peace and War*. Johns Hopkins University Press: Baltimore, MD.

Irving Janis. 1982. *Groupthink*. Houghton Mifflin: Boston.

Source Notes

1. Leo Tolstoy. 1942. *War and Peace*. Simon & Schuster: New York.

2. E. Stillman and W. Pfaff. 1964. *The Politics of Hysteria*. Harper & Row: New York.

3. Ibid.

4. Desiderius Erasmus. 1936. *The Education of a Christian Prince*. Columbia University Press: New York.

5. Woodrow Wilson. 1965. *A Day of Dedication*. Macmillan: New York.

6. Herodotus. 1910. *History of Herodotus*. E. P. Dutton: New York.

7. Erich Fromm. 1973. *Anatomy of Human Destructiveness*. Holt, Rinehart and Winston: New York.

8. See, for example, A. Bullock. 1962. *Hitler: A Study in Tyranny*. Harper & Row: New York; W. L. Shirer. 1960. *The Rise and Fall of the Third Reich*. Simon & Schuster: New York.

9. A. J. P. Taylor. 1961. *The Origins of the Second World War*. Atheneum: New York.

10. S. P. Huntington. 1964. *The Soldier and the State*. Vintage: New York.

11. Quoted in John G. Stoessinger. 1985. *Why Nations Go to War*. St. Martin's: New York.

12. Quoted in Stoessinger, *Why*.

13. Barbara Tuchman. 1962. *The Guns of August*. Macmillan: New York.

14. R. A. Falk and S. S. Kim. 1980. *The War System*. Westview: Boulder, CO.

15. Bruce Bueno de Mesquita. 1981. *The War Trap*. Yale University Press: New Haven, CT.

16. I. Janis. 1972. *Victims of Groupthink*. Houghton Mifflin: Boston.

17. Ibid.

18. Robert McNamara. 1986. *Blundering into Disaster*. Pantheon: New York.

19. Thomas Schelling. 1966. *Arms and Influence*. Yale University Press: New Haven, CT.

20. Theodore Sorenson. 1965. *Kennedy*. Harper & Row: New York.

21. Quoted in Stoessinger, *Why*.

22. Quoted in Jerome Frank. 1982. *Sanity and Survival in the Nuclear Age*. Random House: New York.

23. T. C. Schelling. 1960. *The Strategy of Conflict*. Harvard University Press: Cambridge, MA.

24. H. Kahn. 1960. *On Thermonuclear War*. Princeton University Press: Princeton, NJ.

25. James Schlesinger. 1974. Testimony to the Senate Armed Services Committee.

26. Ole R. Holsti. 1971. "Crisis, Stress and Decision-Making." *International Social Science Journal* 23(1).

27. Ibid.

28. T. C. Sorensen. 1964. *Decision-Making in the White House*. Columbia University Press: New York.

29. Quoted in Holsti, "Crisis."

30. See Robert Jervis. 1976. *Perception and Misperception in International Politics*. Princeton University Press: Princeton, NJ; and Richard Ned Lebow. 1981. *Between Peace and War: The Nature of International Crisis*. Johns Hopkins University Press: Baltimore, MD.

31. Robert Jervis. 1985. "Perceiving and Coping with Threat." In R. Jervis, R. N. Lebow, and J. G. Stein (eds.), *Psychology and Deterrence*. Johns Hopkins University Press: Baltimore, MD.

32. R. Jervis. 1968. "Hypotheses on Misperception." *World Politics* 20(3).

33. H. Butterfield. 1951. *History and Human Relations*. Macmillan: New York.

34. Quoted in *The New York Times*, March 7, 1989.

35. Quoted in Frank, *Sanity*.

36. Ibid.

37. Quoted in Stoessinger, *Why*.

38. Quoted in B. and F. Brodie. 1962. *From Crossbow to H-bomb*. Dell: New York.

39. A. J. P. Taylor. 1955. *Bismarck, the Man and the Statesman*. Knopf: New York.

11

The Social and Economic Level

Theories and schools, like microbes and corpuscles, devour one another and by their warfare ensure the continuity of life.
Marcel Proust

Wars are caused not only by individuals, groups, states, and leaders, but also at the broader transnational level of social and economic factors. We shall look first at some of the more strictly social causes, then turn our attention to others in which economic issues figure more prominently. Then, to conclude, we shall briefly examine some of the social and economic effects of war and war preparation.

CONFLICTING IDEOLOGIES

An ideology is a pattern of ideas based upon which social and political actions are explained, justified, and implemented. Ideologies are usually characterized by an intense concentration on certain central propositions, a degree of comprehensiveness and systematization, and often, a feeling of urgency about the need for and desirability of pursuing the favored approach. Ideologies organize information and viewpoints in ways that are generally not amenable to simple refutation. That is, differing ideologies represent patterns of beliefs and assumptions that make up a self-contained thought system, which, once accepted, leads to only one admissable set of conclusions. Ideologies can be organized around religious traditions, or around secular ways of life, such as capitalism, communism, democracy, aristocracy, conservatism, liberalism, or, as we have seen, nationalism. They are typically based on differing fundamental assumptions, and cannot be proved right or wrong. However, they can be powerful engines driving human behavior, and when they conflict, ideologies can contribute to war. Ideologies are not necessarily bad in themselves, however, nor is the word pejorative. However, the term *ideologue* generally conveys negative connotations, indicating someone whose worldview and objectivity is distorted by rigid adherence to a particular, and limiting, ideology.

Because they are deeply held, ideological differences can result in wars of extraordinary brutality, with little or no quarter asked or given. The eighteenth-century wars of monarchical succession, for example, were fought among states that all accepted the same ideologies; hence, they were relatively brief and limited. By contrast, "wars of religion," such as the Crusades and the Thirty Years' War, involved heartfelt ideologies, and were exceptionally bloody. While the United States was fighting its Civil War (1861–1865), an immense tragedy based to some degree on differing ideologies, and in which perhaps 650,000 people died, the Tai ping Rebellion, in which the Tai pings sought unsuccessfully to overthrow the Manchu dynasty, was raging in China. This rebellion, driven by the fanatical zeal of its Chinese Christian leader, resulted in nearly *20 million* fatalities, making it the most destructive civil war in history, and second only to World War II in total deaths.

Marxism, Capitalism, and Fascism

Among Western ideologies, only Marxism has addressed itself specifically to the causes of war and peace, as follows: Capitalism results in two antagonistic classes, the proletariat (workers) and the bourgeois (owners), with the bourgeoisie controlling the repressive machinery of government. War

Karl Marx, founder and chief theoretician of communism. (The Bettmann Archive)

is the external manifestation of this class struggle; war will therefore be abolished when communism has triumphed worldwide. Capitalist ideology, by contrast, states that the potential for happiness and well-being is greatest in a situation of maximum economic and intellectual freedom for individuals. Wars are caused by many factors, but most notably by threats to human freedom, such as those posed by communism.

Although fascist ideology has not been clearly articulated, it can be viewed essentially as a far right-wing, nationalistic/militarist version of capitalism that places great reliance on social rigidity and respect for hierarchy. It glorifies patriotism, the state, and militarism, harking back to a "golden," and typically very sexist, past. Big business and religion typically enjoy a prominent place in fascist states, so long as the former cooperates especially in the production of war material, and so long as the latter espouses doctrines that emphasize obedience to secular authorities (including the promise of heavenly reward in return for patriotism and the meek acceptance of one's lot) and that participate actively in demonizing opponents. Racist appeals have also been important to most fascists, largely to buttress claims about the appropriateness of dominating other peoples and achieving a nation's legitimate "place in the sun."

Ideologies and Wars

Ideologies determine worldviews, and as such, they can lead to perceptions that bring about wars. For example, those who saw the Sandinista government in Nicaragua as a manifestation of international communism were likely to consider it a threat to the peace and stability of the Western Hemisphere, whereas those who saw it as an example of revolutionary nationalism were more likely to recommend accommodation and coexistence . . . maybe even friendship! Rigid ideologues within the communist bloc, similarly, have tended to view reform efforts in Poland or revolutionary movements in Afghanistan as part of a capitalist offensive against socialism and the U.S.S.R., and to recommend a military response.

World War II had definite ideological underpinnings; the Axis powers saw it as a holy war in defense of their nation-states and in opposition to communism, while the West saw it as the equally holy defense of democracy against Nazi Germany and fascist Italy and Japan. In the Atlantic Charter of August 1941, Britain and the United States agreed to "respect the right of all peoples to choose the form of the government under which they will live." They also pledged "to see the sovereign rights and self-government restored to those who have been forcibly deprived of them," and promised to make "no territorial changes that do not accord

with the freely expressed wishes of the peoples concerned." Although similar sentiments were expressed in World War I, that conflict was not really an ideological war . . . until it began. World War I quickly evolved into an ideological conflict, not only to make the world "safe for democracy," but also as the "war to end wars." Before August 1914, however, no one in the United States, Great Britain, or France had proposed war on Germany or Austria-Hungary simply because the Central Powers were autocratic and monarchical; moreover, Russia under the czar (and then in World War II under Stalin) was as undemocratic as any nation on earth. For the Germans, Austrians, and Turks, World War I became an equally ideological conflict in defense of monarchy and—more importantly—their national homelands.

The following is part of the 1917 address by President Woodrow Wilson, in which he requested a congressional declaration of war:

> A steadfast concern for peace can never be maintained except by a partnership of democratic nations. We are glad . . . to fight thus for the ultimate peace of the world and for the liberation of its peoples, the German peoples included; for the rights of nations great and small and the privilege of men everywhere to choose their own way of life and of obedience. . . . America is privileged to spend her blood and her might for the principles that gave her birth and happiness and the peace which she has treasured. . . . The world must be made safe for democracy.[1]

The sentiments are laudable, and doubtless sincere, especially this famous renunciation of narrow self-interest:

> We have no selfish ends to serve. We desire no conquest, no dominion. We seek no indemnities for ourselves, no material compensation for the sacrifices we shall freely make. We are but one of the champions of mankind.[2]

In the modern world, ideologies may make crosscutting demands. For example, although the state of Iran is Islamic, its populace is Persian and not Arab. During the Iran-Iraq War, therefore, many Arabs were forced to choose between their religious ideology (Shiite Islam) and their secular ideology (Arab nationalism). In most cases, they opted for the latter and supported Iraq over Iran.

Many wars, on the other hand, have been non-ideologic: communist Vietnam against communist China in 1979, or right-wing capitalist Great Britain under Margaret Thatcher against right-wing neofascist Argentina under General Galtieri in 1982. And, owing to realpolitik, states that we might expect to be ideologic enemies have become allies instead: communist, atheist China and right-wing, Islamic Pakistan.

DEMOCRACIES AND WAR

Human beings are organized into larger groups according to a variety of shared patterns: geographic proximity, religious affiliation, ethnic and national identity, political and economic system. Often, these patterns are crosscutting: Individuals of differing religions may find themselves within the same nation-state, people in different states may share the same ethnicity, and so on. What role, then, do these differing patterns play in generating war? On the personal level, internal conditions undoubtedly determine (or at least influence) external behavior, but does this principle apply on the level of states?

This question can be approached in many ways. At least partly because the Western states generally pride themselves in being democracies, and because a widespread public perception exists that democracies are more peace-loving, let us focus on the issue of the war-proneness of democratic versus totalitarian states. The facts are a bit disconcerting: Statistically, no significant difference has yet been demonstrated between the war-proneness of democracies and despotisms. Authoritarian Sparta was no more aggressive or expansionist than democratic Athens; similarly, Franco's Spain, Somoza's Nicaragua, and Marcos's Philippines, although dictatorships, were not expansionist. By contrast, during the nineteenth century in particular, the British

and U.S. democracies engaged in expansionist wars. For the United States, these included successful wars against the indigenous native Americans, Mexico, and Spain, as well as the failed War of 1812 against Great Britain. And the British acquired an immense world empire, it has been said, "in a fit of absent-mindedness."

The connection between democracy and war, although counterintuitive, should not be all that surprising. In feudal Europe and Japan, the aristocracy had a monopoly on war. As we have seen, this changed with the spread of firearms, which made a commoner capable of stopping a charging horse and penetrating a nobleman's armor. Today, the military has become a relatively low-level and mercenary occupation in most democratic states. Moreover, the right to keep and bear arms (the Second Amendment to the U.S. Constitution) has been seen as fundamental to democracy.

Total Commitment

Our perception of the peaceableness of democracies may be strongly colored by events in the twentieth century, in which democracies have become "status quo" powers, less likely to initiate wars of aggression. However, the United States in particular has taken on the role of world policeman, thereby becoming embroiled, directly or indirectly, in armed conflicts on every continent but Australia and Antarctica. In addition, democracies have proven to be no less likely than totalitarian states to fight when provoked — and they may be even more fierce in their prosecution of such a war. "A democracy is peace-loving," claimed noted diplomat–historian George Kennan.

> It does not like to go to war. It is slow to rise to provocation. When it has once been provoked to the point where it must grasp the sword, it does not easily forgive its adversary for having produced this situation. The fact of the provocation then becomes itself the issue. Democracy fights in anger — it fights for the very reason that it was forced to go to war. It fights to punish the power that was rash enough and hostile enough to provoke it — to teach that power a

lesson it will not forget, to prevent the thing from happening again. Such a war must be carried to the bitter end.[3]

Conservative politicians in particular have distrusted democracy because of what they saw as its inclination *toward* war. Thus, England's Disraeli maintained that if the British electorate was enlarged, "You will in due season have wars entered into from passion and not from reason."[4] And young Winston Churchill pointed out (correctly) in 1901 that "Democracy is more vindictive than Cabinets. The wars of peoples will be more terrible than the wars of kings."[5]

In the late 1930s, Britain and France made concessions to and claimed friendship with Hitler, yet once war was finally declared — and even while Neville Chamberlain was still prime minister — nothing less than the elimination of the Nazi regime was deemed acceptable. The fearsome energy of popular, total war, once unleashed, makes it very difficult for accommodations to be made. This is at least partly because as losses accumulate, it becomes all the more important to demonstrate that lives and property have not been expended in vain. Political necessity demands a commitment to total victory. During World War I, France sacrificed hundreds of thousands of young men without ever seriously considering a compromise that might allow Germany to retain Alsace (mostly German-speaking) and France to take back Lorraine, whose inhabitants largely identified themselves as French.

A major factor prolonging the Vietnam War was the feeling that, having suffered so many casualties and expended so much money, "we must not stop now." National honour was at stake, as well as the very human reluctance to admit a mistake. For a similar logical fallacy, consider this example (which, because it is less emotionally gripping, allows us to be more objective). The British and French governments continued to spend money on developing the Concorde supersonic transport, even after it was demonstrated to be economically unviable, so that the money already spent would not be seen as wasted. The principle seems to be a general one, even though it is based on faulty logic: Having suffered losses and incurred costs, whether in a war or a financial investment, it is very difficult to back away. Stuck in a hole of their own making, people and governments are liable to dig themselves deeper, rather than climb out and admit error or defeat.

Democracies in Peacetime Versus Wartime

Peace is not a prerequisite for democracy, but democracies clearly function better in times of peace than in times of war. In fact, whereas democracies do not necessarily lead to peace, the tendency may work in reverse: Peace predisposes toward democracy. Certainly, the converse holds: Rights of dissent and due process are often abridged during wars, even within democracies. War requires increased discipline, secrecy, unswerving and unquestioning devotion to the state, and obedience to its authority; all of these are easier to achieve with military governments. In fact, the nurturing of democracy in Great Britain and the United States may have been facilitated by the fact that neither of these nation-states has faced constant military threats. During World War II, by contrast, Churchill and his cabinet held almost dictatorial power; indeed, that war produced a remarkable convergence in the political systems of all participants. There was also widespread suppression of dissent within the United States during World War I, and attempts at similar suppression as the Vietnam War became increasingly unpopular.

It is noteworthy, however, that some democracies nonetheless retain an abiding sense that the military is subordinate to the civilian. In the middle of the Korean War, for example, President Truman was able to fire General MacArthur, the most popular and successful military figure in the country, then at the peak of his powers. Comparable events would be unimaginable in countries lacking a similar democratic tradition. In Panama, for instance, when Panamanian president Eric Delvalle dismissed the military chief, General Manuel Noriega, early in 1988, the military backed Noriega, and

Delvalle himself was forced from office. Similarly, when the civilian president of Haiti, Leslie Managat, sought to fire the military leader, General Henri Namphy, the general led a coup that deposed the president.

Military leaders are specialists in violence. It follows that they should be more willing, even eager, to enter wars. Moreover, they should be able to do so without the prolonged and divisive procedures found in democracies. Nonetheless, as we have seen, no clear data show that democracies are any less war-prone than dictatorships. And in the nuclear age, no formal declaration from Congress is required for World War III to commence. Even without nuclear weapons, however, it can be argued that when it comes to the decision to go to war, democracies are not really democratic at all. The following selection — written by Randolph Bourne in the early days of World War I — conveys a strong sense of despair at and disillusionment with government activities, even in a democracy:

> The Government, with no mandate from the people, without consultation of the people, conducts all the negotiations, the backing and filling, the menaces and explanations, which slowly bring it into collision with some other Government, and gently and irresistibly slides the country into war. For the benefit of proud and haughty citizens, it is fortified with a list of the intolerable insults which have been hurled towards us by the other nations; for the benefit of the liberal and beneficent, it has a convincing set of moral purposes which our going to war will achieve; for the ambitious and aggressive classes, it can gently whisper of a bigger role in the destiny of the world. The result is that, even in those countries where the business of declaring war is theoretically in the hands of representatives of the people, no legislature has ever been known to decline the request of an Executive, which has conducted all foreign affairs in utter privacy and irresponsibility, that it order the nation into battle. Good democrats are wont to feel the crucial difference between a State in which the popular Parliament or Congress declares war. But, put to the stern pragmatic test, the difference is not striking. In the freest of republics as well as in the most tyrannical of Empires, all foreign policy, the diplomatic negotiations which

produce or forestall war, are equally the private property of the Executive part of the Government, and are equally exposed to no check whatever from popular bodies, or the people voting as a mass themselves.

> The moment war is declared, however, the mass of the people, through some spiritual alchemy, become convinced that they have willed and executed the deed themselves. They then with the exception of a few malcontents, proceed to allow themselves to be regimented, coerced, deranged in all the environments of their lives, and turned into a solid manufactory of destruction toward whatever other people may have, in the appointed scheme of things, come within the range of the Government's disapprobation. The citizen throws off his contempt and indifference to Government, identifies himself with its purposes, revives all his military memories and symbols, and the State once more walks, an august presence, through the imaginations of men. Patriotism becomes the dominant feeling, and produces immediately that intense and hopeless confusion between the relations which the individual bears and should bear towards the society of which he is a part.[6]

Noted commentator Walter Lippmann, on the other hand, maintained that democracies are peaceful because of a certain public inertia:

> The rule to which there are few exceptions . . . is that at the critical junctures, when the stakes are high, the prevailing mass opinion will impose what amounts to a veto upon changing the course on which the government is at the time proceeding. Prepare for war in time of peace? No. It is bad to raise taxes, to unbalance the budget, to take men away from their schools or their jobs, to provoke the enemy.[7]

Thus, there appears to be a paradox in the relationship of democracies to war: once provoked, they fight energetically but they prefer to be peaceful. The United States experience during the late twentieth century, however, suggests a troubling variation on this theme; namely, a penchant for brief, successful wars of intervention. Both the 1983 invasion of Grenada and the 1989 invasion of Panama were illegal by most standards of international

U.S. forces involved in the invasion of Panama in 1989. (U.S. Department of Defense)

law, yet they were very successful domestically, boosting the presidential popularity of Ronald Reagan and George Bush, respectively. There is also reason to think that both invasions were motivated, in part, by the perception (accurate, as it turned out) that the presidents in question would benefit politically. Thus the Grenada invasion took place just after the United States was injured and humiliated by the bombing of a United States Marine barracks in Beirut and the Panama invasion occurred when President Bush was being criticized for failing to lend United States support to a previously unsuccessful anti-Noriega coup and for "kowtowing" to the politically repressive Chinese government. The United States military action in Panama effectively countered this supposed "wimp factor" but raised the specter that presidents may seek to offset their political difficulties by engaging in a quick war that is relatively painless (at least for the United States) and popular. So long as public opinion responds favorably to such wars, democracies will be susceptible to them.

Finally, note that whereas democracies are no less war-prone than tyrannies, one fact stands out: They have not made war on other democracies. While the reasons for this are unclear, its significance may be great: A world that seems to be moving toward democracy may thus be more likely to remain at peace. Indeed, beyond whatever domestic benefits democracy may convey, the reluctance of democracies to make war on each other is in itself a powerful reason to encourage — and rejoice in — the spread of democratic government.

Capitalism and War

The relationship between capitalism and war seems similar to that between democracy and war: It was widely thought (except by Marxists) that capitalism would discourage war, since capitalism favors trade over the forcible seizure of land and order over disorder, thereby leaving the bourgeoisie free to maximize profits with a minimal role for national governments. In the nineteenth century, influential sociologists like Herbert Spencer and August Comte, for example, argued that of the two great styles of society — military and industrial — the latter would eventually win. In fact, capitalist-industrial states have generally done well in war, although often the pressure for war has come from other classes than the bourgeoisie. In the nineteenth century, for example, agitation for the War of 1812 and the Civil War came primarily from the agrarian South and West rather than the mercantile East or North. In Britain, liberal merchants and industrialists were less supportive of imperialism than was the landed aristocracy. Japanese militarism was similarly spearheaded by the army and the peasantry rather than the capitalist classes, just as twentieth-century German militarism came primarily from the aristocratic Prussian *Junkers* rather than from the business community.

Capitalists were not even united as to the merits of imperialism. Thus, the theory of "mercantilism" favored economic self-betterment via a favorable balance of trade (accumulating wealth by exporting more than you import). In 1833, Thomas Macaulay expressed the perspective of English mercantilists as follows:

> It would be, on the most selfish view of the case, far better for us that the people of India were well-governed and independent of us, than ill-governed and subject to us; that they were ruled by their own kings, but wearing our broadcloth, and eating with our cutlery, than that they were performing their salaams to English collectors and English magistrates, but were too ignorant to value, or too poor to buy, English manufactures. To trade with civilised men is infinitely more profitable than to govern savages.[8]

POPULATION PRESSURE AND OTHER SOCIAL STRESSES

Some scholars have argued that internal stresses make war more likely, even though the evidence doesn't seem to back this claim. The Vietnam War was clearly associated with an increase in domestic stress within the United States, but just as clearly, this increase was a result of that war rather than a cause of it. No correlations have yet been established between war-proneness and population density, homicides, suicides, alcoholism, or urbanization. The role of population pressure, however, has repeatedly drawn attention.

The simplest claim is that expanding population drives a state to conquest, much as Hitler claimed that his invasion of Poland and the western U.S.S.R. was a result of the German need for *lebensraum* (living space). Japan was, by many standards, overpopulated in the 1930s, when it was also very aggressive; today, however, it is even more crowded, and yet its aggressiveness is limited to foreign trade. Nor is this a recent phenomenon: Between the third and eighth centuries A.D., for example, the population of Europe fell, yet this was a time of Roman imperial wars followed by smaller "barbarian" conquests and the end of the *pax Romana*. Later, the European population was reduced by about one third during the Black Plague (fourteenth century), and yet, this period was characterized by the Hundred Years' War, and an uneasy transition from the religious wars of the Crusaders to feudal wars among opposing lords. Moreover, rapid population growth during the first two centuries A.D. and during the nineteenth century was associated, not with increased war, but rather with the *pax Romana* and *pax Britannica*.

Any correlation between population and war-proneness might, if anything, be counterintuitive: Smaller states have often worried that they were at risk of being attacked by larger, more populous ones (Belgium's fear of France, France's fear of Germany, Germany's fear of Russia, Vietnam's fear of China, Cambodia's fear of Vietnam). In fact, when they are not provoked, larger states seem more inclined to confidence and complacency. Nevertheless, high unemployment and general dissatisfaction, whether in industrial regions or among rural societies where population growth has exceeded available land, can lead to a dangerous kind of national restlessness (although it doesn't invariably do so).

Other, related patterns of war-proneness and war-avoidance have been suggested. For example, the historian Arnold Toynbee proposed that there are cycles of war-weariness, in which the sad and bitter memories of a recent war restrain the populace until this short-term immunity wears off and wars become likely once again; the comparatively peaceful period in Europe following the Napoleonic Wars has been interpreted in this way. Toynbee recounts that during the 1920s, hiking with a knapsack was unpopular, presumably because it conjured up unpleasant military memories. It was, he points out, an ominous sign when knapsacks came back into vogue in the 1930s.[9]

On the other hand, the peace that typically follows a war may simply occur because there is nothing left to fight about, at least for a time. In some cases — when there was something to fight about — wars have followed hard upon one another, with no breathing space. For example, after fighting the Japanese invaders during the early 1940s, the Viet Minh continued battling the French forces that had reoccupied the Republic of Vietnam; then, they fought the Americans. As soon as their devastating war with the Japanese was finished, the Chinese communists resumed, with scarcely a pause, their equally devastating civil war against Chiang Kai-shek's government. If wars lead to exhaustion and therefore peace, we might expect that periods of peace would lead to a lower threshold for war, as the immunizing effect of painful memories wears off. But states like Switzerland or Sweden, which have by now accumulated long histories of peace, do not seem any more war-prone than others, like Afghanistan, Israel, or South Africa, that should rightly be tired of war.

On the other hand, following the Vietnam War, the United States went through a period when it was hesitant to engage in other military adventures; conservatives in particular criticized this "Vietnam syndrome." This did not, however, appear to be a weariness with war in general so much as a determination to avoid "bad wars." And it may be short-lived. (It is also possible that the Soviet Union, following its decidedly unpleasant experience in Afghanistan, has begun to undergo a parallel "Afghanistan syndrome.")

There is also another, rarely articulated yet significant, component of the Vietnam syndrome that is essentially a variant of the childhood notion of "good winner, bad loser." The United States showed itself to be a good winner following World War II; indeed, U.S. economic largesse toward its defeated enemies Germany and Japan contributed to their economic prominence, and led some wags to suggest that the United States won the war but lost the peace. By contrast, the United States has been an extremely bad loser in Vietnam. Having been defeated militarily and politically, the United States has continued to punish Vietnam for its success, encouraging China to support the Khmer Rouge in Cambodia so as to constitute a thorn in

the Vietnamese side, and isolating Vietnam from the world economy, thereby crippling that country's ability to recover from the wounds of their successful war. In the case of Vietnam, the United States lost the war, but by making Vietnam suffer, it hopes somehow to win the peace — or rather, to assuage the pain of defeat by inflicting pain on others.

THE ROLE OF POVERTY

Poverty as a Cause of War

According to classical Marxist thinking, wars are caused by class struggles, including the conflicts within societies as well as those between the upper classes of different societies for control over other countries. An official Soviet publication, *Marxism-Leninism on War and Army*, reads as follows:

> All wars in the past and present, those between exploiter states in pursuit of the selfish interests of the slave owners, feudal lords, and the bourgeoisie, as also the uprisings and wars of the working people against whom they rose when their position had become unbearable and their patience had worn out, all these wars were caused by private ownership relations and the resultant social and class antagonisms in exploiter formations. . . . Wars are a means of rapid enrichment for the capitalists and, hence, a constant travelling companion of capitalism. The system of the exploitation of man by man and the system of the destruction of man by man are two sides of the capitalist order.[10]*

And from the Communist Manifesto: "In proportion as the antagonism between classes within the nation vanishes, the hostility of one nation to another will come to an end."

One doesn't have to be a Marxist, however, to see that poverty can breed dissatisfaction, which, in turn, can lead to war. During the Chinese Revolution, Josue de Castro, later president of the Executive Council of the Food and Agricultural

---

*Note that Soviet Marxism differs from the classical formulations of Marx and Engels; essentially, it is a revisionist orthodoxy based originally on Marx, but more directly on Lenin, Stalin, and Russian nationalism.

Organization (an agency of the United Nations), wrote that

> some people think that Soviet infiltration and material aid are the principal explanation for the victories of the Communists over Chiang Kai-shek's troops. It is my impression that there is a more profound reason. The Communist revolution is winning in China today because, although Chiang Kai-shek has a powerful ally in the United States, the followers of Mao tse-Tung have a still stronger ally. That ally is hunger. . . . The fear of famine has been the great recruiting agent of Mao's armies and the decisive factor in the Chinese civil war has been the strategy of starvation. The successes of Communism in China, in my opinion, are due to the fact that the Communists have promised freedom from the threat of starvation. Starvation is in turn a result of imperialist exploitation of man and the soil. No one can deny that this Chinese hope is an exceedingly natural one, and that its frustration has been nothing less than inhuman.[11]

In 1962, President John F. Kennedy, referring specifically to Latin America, warned that "Those who possess wealth and power in poor nations must accept their own responsibilities. . . . Those who make peaceful revolution impossible will make violent revolution inevitable."[12] In saying this, President Kennedy was echoing an influential liberal view put forth in 1870 by the philosopher T. H. Green:

> The privileged class involuntarily believes and spreads the belief that the interest of the state lies in some extension without, not in improvement within. A suffering class attracts sympathy from without and invites interference with the state that contains it. . . . The source of war between states lies in their incomplete fulfillment of their function; in the fact that there is some defect in the maintenance or reconciliation of rights among their subjects.[13]

Thus, socioeconomic deprivation was a major factor in generating support for Fidel Castro's successful revolt against Cuban dictator Fulgencio Batista in 1959, and for the overthrow of Nicaraguan dictator Anastacio Somoza in 1979. Right-wing violence has also been spawned by difficult eco-

nomic conditions, as witnessed by the (CIA-assisted) overthrow of Chilean president Salvadore Allende, as well as the coming to power of Adolf Hitler during the early 1930s, a time of severe economic stress in Germany. Efforts to "destabilize" a given regime by creating economic and social chaos — as successfully accomplished by the United States in Chile in 1978 and attempted against the Sandinista regime in Nicaragua during the Reagan administration — testify to the widespread assumption that governmental stability can be diminished when a domestic economy is under siege. Between 1882 and 1930, the frequency of lynchings in the American South, for example, correlated with the price of cotton and other indices of economic well-being.[14]

Some of history's most notable revolutions (France in 1789, Russia in 1917, Italy's fascists in 1922, Iran's Islamic revolution in 1979, and Filipino "people power" in 1986) have not involved lengthy civil wars, but rather an array of confusing strikes and mob actions, in which the government lost the ability to control its own armed forces as a result of the disaffection of the people.* In recent times, military governments have been especially likely to fear their own people more than any external enemy; accordingly, police expenditures in developing countries have increased much more rapidly than have expenditures for external military forces. The large "defense" budgets of many Latin American and African countries, in particular, are directed almost entirely against their own populace rather than against some external and threatening enemy.

Poverty and Domestic Unrest

Poverty does not, however, inevitably breed war, or even revolution. The decade preceding the American Revolutionary War (1765–1775), for example, was not a time of poverty and deprivation, but rather of prosperity and expansion; business was

---

*The Russian Revolution ultimately led to a long and bloody civil war, but only after the czarist monarchy had been peacefully overthrown by the Mensheviks, who, in turn, lost power to the Bolsheviks.

booming, and the number of ships in New York Harbor had nearly doubled in a decade. The French Revolution has long been considered a classic case of hunger leading to violence. (Marie Antoinette, having been told that the rioting people wanted bread, is reputed to have responded airily, "Let them eat cake.") According to Alexis de Tocqueville, however, the fury of the French Revolution in fact took place at a time when conditions, although bad, were improving: "It is a singular fact," he wrote, "that this steadily increasing prosperity, far from tranquilizing the population, everywhere promoted a spirit of unrest. . . . Those parts of France in which the improvement in the standard of living was most pronounced were the chief centers of the revolutionary movement."[15] Misery within a country, in short, does not necessarily lead to war. Germany was not belligerent during a period of runaway inflation in 1923, but rather in 1914, at a time of unparalleled prosperity. Hitler may indeed have been aided in his rise to power by the Depression of the early 1930s, but by the time of German expansionism (the late 1930s), prosperity was already growing.

"The revolution of rising expectations," rather than declining conditions, may in fact be especially likely to lead to social violence. Some theorists have proposed, accordingly, that the crucial point at which a society turns violent depends not so much upon objective conditions, but rather on a gap between prevailing conditions and a public *expectation* — that is, when the "want:get ratio" is high.[16] Marxist teachings can, of course, intensify the effect of this gap.

In fourteenth-century England, a bloody rebellion by Wat Tyler and his followers was stimulated by resentment at the high taxes imposed by the government, which sought to pay for the Hundred Years' War in France.* Five centuries before Karl Marx, itinerant priest John Ball, one of the instigators of this uprising, spoke for an angry, resentful underclass:

> My good friends, matters cannot go well in England until all things be held in common; when there shall be neither vassals nor lords; when the lords shall be no more masters than ourselves. . . . For what reason do they hold us in bondage? Are we not all descended from the same parents, Adam and Eve? And what can they show, or what reason can they give, which they should be more masters than ourselves? They are clothed in velvet and rich stuffs, ornamented with ermine and other furs, and we are forced to wear poor clothing. They have wines, spices, and fine bread, while we have only rye and the refuse of the straw; and when we drink, it must be water. They have handsome seats and manors, while we must brave the wind and the rain in our labors in the fields; and it is by our labors that they have wherewithal to support their pomp.[17]

In our own time, Franz Fanon, apostle of anti-colonial revolutionary violence, maintained that "violence is a cleansing force. It frees the native from his inferiority complex and from his despair and inaction; it makes him fearless and restores his self-respect."[18] Che Guevara, revolutionary comrade-in-arms of Cuba's Fidel Castro, asked rhetorically:

> Why does the guerrilla fighter fight? We must come to the inevitable conclusion that the guerrilla fighter is a social reformer, that he takes up arms responding to the angry protest of the people against their oppressors, and that he fights in order to change the social system that keeps all his unarmed brothers in ignominy and misery.[19]

War and Social Change

Civil wars generally occur when a disparity exists between the forces of socioeconomic change and the ability of existing structures to accommodate those changes. Thus, the wars heralding the breakup of the Hapsburg and Ottoman empires occurred when nationalist sentiment could not be satisfied within those existing systems. The idea is, however, a relatively new one: Prior to the late eighteenth century, wars had resulted largely from ambitions for empire and conquest, from dynastic and

---

*Tax collecting at that time must have felt more like robbery than a legitimate civic function: The tax collector demanded money and yet the government offered essentially no services in return.

realpolitik squabbling, from messianic impulses, or for self-defense. There had always been sporadic uprisings, like that of the ill-fated Wat Tyler in England, or before that the Spartacus Revolt in ancient Rome. But with the American Revolution and, even more so, the wars of the French Revolution, organized violence between large armed groups came to be seen as a potential instrument for social change. Nearly two hundred years ago, the newspaper *Patriote Francais* exulted over the coming "expiatory war which is to renew the face of the world and plant the standard of liberty upon the palaces of kings, upon the seraglias of sultans, upon the chateaux of petty feudal tyrants and upon the temples of popes and muftis."[20]

Although economic and social deprivations appear to have been important in unleashing certain rebellions like Wat Tyler's and civil wars such as the Chinese and Cuban revolutions, they seem less likely to produce wars *between* states. In many cases, economic gain was a major motivating factor, especially the prospect of booty obtained by looting the defeated side: The successes of the Macedonians under Alexander, the Huns under Attila, the Mongols under Genghis Khan, or the remarkable advances of the armies of Islam during the seventh and eighth centuries A.D. all seem due at least in part to the lure of direct economic gain. However, these armies were driven not so much by desperation about their personal well-being as by the hope of obtaining yet more booty.

Poverty may drive war in unexpected ways. In 1966, President Johnson sought to justify the presence of so many U.S. troops overseas (including, notably, those in Vietnam at the time). "There are three billion people in the world," he said while reviewing U.S. troops in Korea, "and we have only 200 million of them. We are outnumbered 15 to 1. If might did make right they would sweep over the United States and take what we have. We have what they want."[21] Thus, when it comes to violence between states, poverty may be less influential in motivating the poor than in activating the wealthy through a kind of guilty anxiety.

Truly desperate conditions, more often than not, reduce rather than enhance an army's motivation for fighting. For example, the terrible food, medicine, and supply situation (as well as despair over the high casualties and lack of success on the battlefield), led Russian forces to seek an end to their war against Germany and Austria-Hungary from early 1917 onward, and with even greater determination following the Bolshevik Revolution later that year.

On the other hand, economic conditions can serve as an indirect cause of international war, as other states become nervous at the success of the newly established revolutionary regime. Undoubtedly, the French Revolution was stimulated at least partly by the outright physical hunger of at least some of the French people. In turn, the new republican government was seen as a threat to the established monarchies of Europe, and efforts were therefore made to invade France and suppress that revolution. The resulting French Revolutionary Wars led to the ascension to power of Napoleon Bonaparte, and to the much larger Napoleonic Wars that were to engulf Europe.

Poverty as a Restraint on War

Overall, the correlations between poverty and war are unclear. Poor people are more likely to seek food and land than overseas conquests. In the modern world, impoverished Third World peasants may occasionally pose a threat to their own governments, but not to their wealthy, well-armed neighbors. No one seriously believes that the poor *campesinos* of Mexico, for example, are going to invade the United States.* It can be argued that, if anything, poverty has been more likely to restrain the military adventuring of states than to encourage it. Wars are expensive; it is costly to equip soldiers, navies, and air forces, and to supply them in the field. When England, for example, introduced the world's first nationwide income tax in the early nineteenth century, it was to pay the costs of the Napoleonic Wars. Only rarely has poverty pushed a country to war; more often, leaders have hesitated to make war unless their economies were strong

---

*They are far more likely to do so individually, as illegal immigrants.

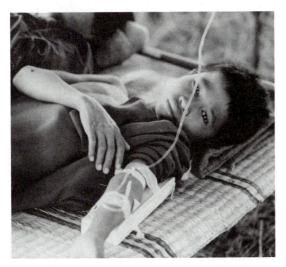

Young malnourished Cambodian boy receiving medical treatment at a refugee camp in Thailand. Poverty and human misery are much more likely to result from war than to cause it. (United Nations/Saw Lwin)

enough to withstand the strain. By contrast, a degree of prosperity can make leadership pushy and dangerously self-confident. (It can also make them relatively happy and "peace-loving"—although highly militarized—like modern-day Switzerland or Sweden.)

Recently, the Soviet Union has publicly recognized that economic factors, rather than provoking war, are more likely to operate against both war-making and war-preparing. In a speech to the assembled diplomatic service of the U.S.S.R. during 1987, Soviet foreign minister Eduard Shevardnadze said:

> The main thing is that the country not incur additional expenses in connection with the need to maintain its defense capacity and protect its legitimate foreign policy interests. This means that we must seek ways to limit and reduce military rivalry, eliminate confrontational features in relations with other states, and suppress conflict and crisis situations.[22]

There is nothing new in national leaders proclaiming their desire to diminish confrontation, especially those with a military dimension (although

some leaders, to be sure, have made a point of seeking confrontation). What is relatively novel here is the expressed linkage of military cautiousness with the economic costs of military preparation.

IMPERIALISM

Imperialism refers to the policy of extending the rule or authority of a country over other, foreign peoples. It has an ancient history, beginning with the first efforts to conquer and subdue a foreign people. The Roman historian Tacitus commented that "Worldwide conquest and the destruction of all rival communities or potentates opened the way to the secure enjoyment of wealth and an overriding appetite for it."[23]

Until the early twentieth century, imperialism was widely accepted and even lauded . . . at least, by the leadership within major imperialist states. At the same time, imperialism may have been a major factor in causing war and suffering, generating not only the direct violence of war but also the indirect violence of colonial oppression. In the late twentieth century, we are well into the postimperialist era, and, suggestions that imperialism causes war therefore may appear outdated. It should be emphasized, however, that imperialism still occupies an important place in Marxist thinking on war; moreover, imperialism itself can be a very resilient force, cropping up in many different forms.

Historical Background

During its heyday, imperialism had many backers, notably among conservatives such as Benjamin Disraeli, Lord Curzon, Rudyard Kipling, and Cecil Rhodes in England, Jules Ferry in France, and Theodore Roosevelt, William McKinley, and other "manifest destiny" supporters in the United States. They argued that imperialism was appropriate because it helped "modernize and Christianize" the savage, benighted people of the Earth, whose improvement and care were "the white man's burden." Moreover, they were generally unapologetic about the value of imperial conquests in providing raw materials for domestic industrial production and overseas markets for manufactured goods, as well as the pride and prestige that befits a Great Power. "The issue is not a mean one," wrote Benjamin Disraeli, Conservative Prime Minister of Great Britain during the 1870s. "It is whether you will be content to be a comfortable England, modeled and molded upon Continental principles, and meeting in due course an inevitable fate, or whether you will be a great country, an imperial country."[24]

But imperialism has had numerous critics as well, especially from the political left. In the early twentieth century, the liberal English economist John Hobson[25] argued forcefully that imperialism was a social and economic wrong, indicating a defect in capitalism. In this view, imperialism results when nations enter the machine economy, with its advanced industrial methods, and manufacturers, merchants, and financiers find it increasingly difficult to dispose profitably of their products. This, in turn, generates pressure for access to undeveloped overseas markets as well as to sources of raw materials.*

Hobson's line of reasoning seemed especially cogent, coming as it did after such events as the Boxer Rebellion and Opium Wars in China, which represented protests against Western economic domination of China and the insistence of the European imperialist powers on opening China to the lucrative opium trade. The major conflict of the eighteenth century, the Seven Years' War (known in North America as the French and Indian War) was in some ways the first world war, brought about by worldwide colonial competition between England and France that extended to India, the Caribbean, the west coast of Africa (over the lucrative slave trade), Canada and the upper Ohio valley, and the Atlantic seaboard. The Crimean and Boer wars, as well as the Moroccan crises of 1905 and 1911, lent further weight to Hobson's critique of imperialism as a cause of war. "As soon as one of our industries

fails to find a market for its products," we read in Anatole France's novel *Penguin Island*, "a war is necessary to open new outlets. . . . In Third Zealand we have killed two-thirds of the inhabitants in order to compel the remainder to buy our umbrellas and braces."[26]

The Leninist View

The most detailed analysis of imperialism was conducted by Lenin, in his book *Imperialism: The Highest Stage of Capitalism*. According to this view, which was strongly influenced by Hobson, imperialism arises from the contradictions inherent in capitalism, and is inevitable as capitalism proceeds:

> Capitalism has concentrated the earth's wealth in the hands of a few states and divided the world up to the last bit. . . . Any further enrichment could take place only . . . as the enrichment of one state at the expense of another. The issue could only be settled by force—and, accordingly, war between the world marauders became inevitable.[27]

Noting the participation of socialists in the First World War, Lenin also argued that war between capitalist states also served "to disunite the workers and fool them with nationalism, to annihilate their vanguards in order to weaken the revolutionary movement of the proletariat."[28] In contrast to the liberal school, Lenin maintained that only revolution—not reform—could undo capitalism's tendency toward imperialism and thus to war. His view became a major part of the neo-Marxist interpretation of the causes of war.

Undoubtedly, imperialism can lead to war between the imperial government and the local population: wars of occupation and conquest (for example, the Maori Wars in New Zealand, the Zulu Wars in southeast Africa, the Indian Wars in the United States), followed in turn by wars of national liberation (for example, the Huk rebellion against the United States in the Philippines, the Mau-Mau rebellion in Kenya, the Algerian war of independence). Dispute centers on the questions of (1) whether capitalist states are necessarily driven to imperialism and (2) whether imperialism has been a primary cause of war between imperial states.

*Hobson also maintained, incidentally, that pressures resulting in imperialism derive largely from inadequate distribution of purchasing power. Therefore, with successful trade unionism and other social reforms, imperialism will no longer pay, he argued, and will disappear.

In Lenin's view, the collapse of capitalism—predicted by Marx—had been delayed because the capitalist states not only had bamboozled the proletariat into fighting the proletariat in other countries, but also had used imperialism to acquire overseas outlets for their surplus goods and financial investments. Lenin applied his thesis in particular to the causes of World War I. By the early twentieth century, essentially the entire world had been carved into colonies or spheres of influence, with Britain's the largest. Germany, on the other hand—although a rising power—had been effectively excluded. In the Leninist view, World War I was fought to determine whether Germany or Britain would be free to loot the world. In the words of one radical historian of that war,

> Each side was defending its imperialist interests by preventing the balance of power from being tipped in favor of its opponents. These imperialist interests were in the last analysis the private interests of finance and monopoly capital, which, through the influence of the plutocracy on governments and public opinion, were identified in the minds of the rulers with "national honor and vital interests." There were, of course, other factors in the situation, and the psychological process by which promoting vested interests . . . is transmuted in men's minds into loyalty to religious, philanthropic, and patriotic ideals is complex and largely unconscious.[29]

Even when states are not directly competing for colonies, they are likely to conflict with other states: intervening on behalf of their own nationals, or competing with local forces or with the nationals of another would-be imperial country, in some Third World arena. Of the frequent U.S. interventions in Latin America, many have occurred on behalf of private U.S. investments, notably those of the United Fruit Company. For example, in 1954, the CIA organized the overthrow of the democratically elected Arbenz government in Guatemala. Arbenz, a leftist, had sought to nationalize United Fruit holdings in his country, distributing them to landless peasants and insisting that the company accept, as fair compensation, the value it had declared for tax purposes, which had been accepted by the pliant, pro-U.S. Guatemalan government that preceded him.

The U.S. obsession with Nicaragua in the 1980s, by contrast, seemed motivated largely by fear of a kind of ideological/social/economic domino effect: If a small, poor state such as Nicaragua were to escape from the U.S. orbit, and to prosper as a consequence, perhaps this would encourage others to do likewise. This interpretation also explains the single-minded U.S. insistence on destroying the Nicaraguan economy, since by this strategy, even if the Sandinistas were not overthrown, their revolution could be discredited if Nicaraguan society could be sufficiently damaged. If nothing else, the suffering of the Nicaraguan people can serve as an object lesson for what could well befall any other client state that might seek to go against the United States.

Reinterpretations of the Leninist View

During the 1960s and 1970s, because imperial powers had dissolved their empires and virtually all former colonies had gained political independence, even while economic dependence continued unabated, traditional Leninist interpretations of Marxism were rethought. Modern neo-imperialism is seen to operate more subtly, not through outright colonial control and only rarely through war. Rather, it typically manipulates the economic, political, and intellectual structures of Third World states, maintaining them in a condition of dependency, by a process that Lord Lugard, British governor of Nigeria, called "indirect rule": control via indigenous ruling classes. For example, consider the role of the United States in Central America, France in West Africa, or Britain in its former colonies in east Africa and the Caribbean. Former colonial masters no longer rule by naked military power; rather, they exercise control over local economies — and often, sources of information as well — typically relying on home-grown political flunkies recruited from the dominant socioeconomic classes (see Chapter 22). The emphasis here is not so much on war as on the structural violence found when one state (and/or one class) dominates another.

Particularly influential in this regard is the Norwegian peace researcher Johan Galtung,[30] who has developed a model in which both the neo-imperial state and the neo-colony are divided into "center" (elites) and "periphery" (peasants and workers). The neo-imperial system involves a connection whereby the center in the neo-imperial state is closely allied with the center in the neo-colony, with antagonism between center and periphery in the neo-colony, and a perceived disharmony of interest between the peripheries in the neo-colony and the neo-imperium. Instead of physical occupation, the imperial state provides limited economic aid, relatively abundant military aid, and intellectual underpinning and legitimacy to a colonial center that actively oppresses its own people, for the benefit of the two centers, both colonial and imperial.

A Rebuttal of the Leninist View

According to economist Walter Rostow, the acquisition of colonies — especially during the nineteenth century — was not warranted by European capital markets, nor by military or strategic considerations, but rather by competition for prestige:

> The competition for colonies was conducted for reasons that were unilaterally rational on neither economic nor military grounds; the competition occurred essentially because competitive nationalism was the rule of the world arena and colonies were an accepted symbol of status and power within the arena.[31]

The question still remains: Regardless of the underlying cause of imperial competition, to what extent did this competition lead to war among the competitors? The issue has not been resolved. In World War I, for example, the prime movers — Austria, Serbia, and Russia — were involved in a relatively straightforward struggle over prestige, territory, power, national self-determination (Serbia), and survival as a state (Austria), not in a competition for overseas possessions or raw materials. Moreover, at least arguably, the common interest in shared trade between, say, Britain and Germany was far greater than the rivalries over international markets and imperial ambition. In addition, overseas businesses may be as much the pawns of governments as their manipulators. Prior to the Russo-Japanese War, for example, private Russian business interests invested money in the timber industry near the Yalu River, in a region under dispute with Japan; apparently, they were put up to it by their government, which sought to use these investments as an excuse to further its own expansionist goals. Economics, in short, may be manipulated by politics, no less than the other way around.

The following arguments have also been raised against the Leninist view that capitalism leads to imperialism, which leads to war:

1. Economic interests do not always determine foreign policy. In some cases, foreign policy even goes against economic interest.

2. Foreign investments do not yield a higher rate of return on investments. In fact, there is growing evidence that nineteenth-century imperialism, at least, nearly always hurt the imperial power economically more than it helped.[32]

3. Although the total investment of major capitalist countries in Third World economies is (and has been) large in absolute numbers, it has always been a very small proportion of the domestic economic investment, typically less than 10 percent. It is very difficult, therefore, to argue that capitalism relies on foreign investments in order to survive.

4. Foreign capital is increasingly being invested in other developed countries, rather than being sunk "imperialistically" into Third World countries. Japanese and Arab oil money, for example, has been invested heavily in the United States, thereby financing the huge U.S. federal deficit. Most Third World countries, moreover, seek to attract such investment.

It is difficult to argue, for example, that participation of the United States in the Vietnam War was economically motivated. Thus, Vietnam's teak, tin, tungsten, and modest off-shore oil deposits pale when measured against the cost of that war as borne just by the United States: 50,000 lives, $150 billion. The stock market fell whenever it appeared that the Vietnam War would be prolonged, further suggesting that it was not good for business.

THE MILITARY-INDUSTRIAL COMPLEX

The link between economics and war nonetheless is instructive, particularly as this connection operates in capitalist societies through the role of money-making and the military-industrial complex. Although the phrase "military-industrial complex" has become especially popular among left-wing critics, it was first introduced by a moderate conservative, President Dwight Eisenhower, in his 1961 farewell address:

> We have been compelled to create a permanent armaments industry of vast proportions. . . . This conjunction of an immense military establishment and a large arms industry is new in the American experience. The total influence — economic, political, even spiritual — is felt in every city, every statehouse, every office of the federal government. . . . In the councils of government, we must guard against the acquisition of unwarranted influence, whether sought or unsought, by the military-industrial complex. The potential for the disastrous rise of misplaced power exists and will persist.[33]

This alliance of military and industry that Eisenhower so decried has now been joined by science, labor, and government, and it is more firmly entrenched than ever.

The military-industrial-science-labor-government complex of the past few decades is not totally new in human experience. Those with a financial and social interest in warmaking have long had a disproportionate influence on the policies of governments. In the days of warrior-kings, they *were* the government. And from ancient times, soldiers were rewarded with a proportion of the spoils of a sacked city. Mercenary armies, by definition, fought for pay and/or a share of the booty. Much of the martial enthusiasm that marked the Moslem conquests of the Middle Ages, for example, has been attributed to the fact that Islamic warriors were fighting not only for their faith but also for their personal enrichment. In the late sixteenth century, Spanish soldiers — fighting the Dutch effort at independence — sacked Antwerp in modern-day Belgium (then the richest city in northern Europe), when Philip II of Spain went bankrupt and could not make good on their back pay.

"The orientation toward war," wrote the economist Joseph Schumpeter, "is mainly fostered by the domestic interests of ruling classes, but also by the influence of all those who stand to gain individually from a war policy, whether economically or socially."[34] From early in the industrial age, the great armaments manufacturers — Krupp in Germany, Vickers and Armstrong in England, Remington and Colt in the United States, and more recently, Dassault in France — all profited when their country went to war. They even profited when other countries went to war, by selling arms to the belligerents . . . often to both sides. Krupp also made a fortune playing one side against the other, for example, developing and selling to the navies of the world a new form of armor plate, then producing and marketing an especially penetrating explosive naval artillery shell, to be followed by yet more "impregnable" armor, and so on. This pattern continues today: Arms sales are currently the number one export for Brazil, France, and Israel. With the exception of Japan, arms comprise a major proportion of the exports of every industrialized state, with the United States and the Soviet Union leading all the others in absolute terms.

Huge amounts of money no doubt are made on armaments, both through domestic weapons programs and in sales to other states. Within the United States, 10 percent of all business derives from military-related production. This figure is much higher for large high-tech industrial corporations such as Lockheed, General Dynamics, Boeing, and Northrup, which in some cases derive 50 percent and more of their profits from military spending. In certain regions, such as California and parts of the Southeast, military spending accounts for upward of one third of all jobs. Influential politicians have often succeeded in bringing extraordinary amounts of military business to their local districts. For example, the Charleston, South Carolina, district of Representative Mendel Rivers, longtime chairman of the House Armed Services Committee, contained an air force base, a marine air station, an army depot, several naval hospitals, and a naval weapons station and supply center, a Polaris submarine base, as well as AVCO, Lockheed, Sikorsky, and GE plants. The military payroll alone in this one congressional district exceeded $2 billion. Not surprisingly, Rivers — who was responsible for overseeing military expenditures — was inclined to see "the Soviet threat" almost everywhere, and to support a high level of military preparedness. Moreover, he was regularly reelected by his appreciative constituents.

During the years preceding World War I, H. H. Muliner, the director of a British shipbuilding firm, announced that he had secret information that Germany had increased its production of battleships; the British public immediately demanded more British battleships, to which Germany responded by increasing its production. Muliner subsequently admitted that it was all a hoax, but the British-German naval race, to which it contributed, continued nevertheless.

During the 1930s, a Senate committee, chaired by Senator Gerald Nye, investigated the charge that U.S. arms manufacturers were responsible for American entry into the First World War. Although the Nye Committee was unable to prove these allegations, the "merchants of death" theory gained credibility. On the other hand, popular pressure in opposition to military spending has also influenced government decisions: Britain and France, for example, found it very difficult to maintain adequate military forces during the early 1930s because of popular antimilitary sentiment, and the United States and the Soviet Union have succeeded in restricting at least certain aspects of their nuclear competition (see Chapter 15).

There is a communist counterpart to the military-industrial complex. Nikita Khrushchev called them the "metal eaters," the alliance of industrial bureaucrats and military leaders in the U.S.S.R. In a society that has long valued heavy industry and national defense over civilian goods, military production receives highest priority. Moreover, in both communist and capitalist states, career advancement within the military is most readily achieved by being associated with some major military building program. In the United States, at least, a kind of "revolving door" operates, whereby senior government officials are recruited by military contractors after their retirement; while in government service,

many of these people (often from industry or the military in the first place) are typically reluctant to alienate the military contractors who are their potential employers after they retire. Nonetheless, it is widely acknowledged, especially in the nuclear age, that whereas preparations for war may be profitable, the fighting of wars is likely to be a losing proposition.

The issue, therefore, is not so much war-profiteering as preparation-profiteering. In limited cases, wars can help stimulate an economy: The Great Depression of the 1930s ended with the onset of World War II. However, peace researcher Lewis Richardson concluded that fewer than one third of wars from 1820 to 1949 were generated by economic causes, and these were limited to small wars rather than large ones. Economics clearly influences military spending levels as well as specific procurement decisions (the purchase of one weapons system over another). Current perceptions are that the profit motive may contribute indirectly to war by supporting arms races and by creating important constituencies with an interest in the maintenance of international tension — which in turn makes it difficult to achieve disarmament or even arms control — but that the military-industrial complex does not directly cause war.

Having considered, albeit briefly, some arguments concerning the economic causes of war, we close this chapter with a quick review of some of the economic *effects* of war, and of preparation for war.

THE ECONOMIC EFFECTS OF WAR

When it comes to the effect of war on a country's economy, not surprisingly, the location of the war is crucial: A war on one's own territory can be devastating; on someone else's, it is much less painful. It can even help a distant economy. The Napoleonic Wars put a special premium on iron, which in turn hurried along Britain's entry into the Industrial Revolution:

> Indigent and underemployed men do not buy cannon and other expensive industrial products. But by putting indigent thousands into the army and navy and then supplying them with the tools of their new

trade, effective demand was displaced from articles of personal consumption towards items useful to big organizations—armies and navies in the first place, but factories, railroads, and other such enterprises in times to come. Moreover, the men who built the new coke-fired blast furnaces in previously desolate regions of Wales and Scotland would probably not have undertaken such risky and expensive investments without an assured market for cannon. At any rate, their initial markets were largely military.[35]

There is another view, however, that war has done little to stimulate industrial progress, whereas industrial progress has done much to stimulate war, and to make it more horrendous when it occurs. Wars rely heavily on the arts of peace: advances in metallurgy, transportation, chemistry, medicine, communication, transportation, mathematics, even food processing and preparation. War is essentially a parasite on civilian economies, taking much and contributing little. Substantial evidence suggests that recent declines in U.S. economic productivity, and increasing trade deficits, are due to the large investment of resources—both human and material—in the military economy. Thus, while the United States produces MX missiles and Trident submarines, we purchase our cameras, VCRs, and increasingly, even our automobiles from Japan.

As for the vaunted "spin-offs" from military technology, if societies really wanted no-stick frying pans, or computer miniaturization, they would have been able to create these things much more rapidly and cheaply by investing directly in such technology. Moreover, military research and development is typically insensitive to cost, while very demanding as to performance; as a result, advanced weaponry tends to be very expensive, but not useful in the civilian marketplace.* Consumers, for example, don't need toasters that will operate at 80 degrees below zero, or megacomputers that can perform

Child collecting rubble with which to build a shelter during the Korean War. For those caught up in it, war is far more likely to be destructive than creative. (United Nations)

Star Wars calculations in nanoseconds; rather, they need reliable, inexpensive items that benefit their lives.

In Third World countries today, wars have contributed nothing positive to the local economy, whereas the physical, economic, and social effects have been horribly destructive. Wars lay waste not only by the direct detonation of weapons, but also through the disruption of economies. It was estimated, for example, that in 1988, after nine years of war, food production in Afghanistan was only about one quarter its prewar levels. And in that same year, Angola spent 60 percent of its government revenues on military forces, defending itself against guerrillas supported by South Africa, Saudi Arabia, and the United States; this impoverished state, which invests only $49 per capita in educating its children, now spends $133 per capita on its military.

In addition, emergency and relief efforts—difficult enough to mount successfully in peacetime—can be lethally disrupted by war. In 1984, Ethiopia was suffering from a serious famine, in which

---

*In many cases, they are not even useful on the battlefield. There are numerous examples of high-tech weapons—such as the Sgt. York Antiaircraft Gun—that do not function as intended (see James Fallows. 1982. *National Defense*. Random House: New York).

hundreds of thousands starved and millions were malnourished. Ethiopia received $534 million from abroad for famine and development aid; at the same time, the government was spending $447 million on military forces to fight its civil wars in Eritrea and Tigre, as well as in the Ogaden. Moreover, relief convoys, conducted by the Red Cross, have been unable to make deliveries of needed food to people in Eritrea and Tigre. The Ethiopian government claims that such convoys could not be adequately guarded, while critics accuse the Ethiopians of withholding food and thereby using it as a weapon against the rebels, and of spending three-quarters of their budget on arms and internal security when poverty and hunger are pressing needs.

Similarly, Mozambique, a region of fertile soil and rich mineral deposits, has been fighting a disastrous civil war since 1975 against South African–backed guerrillas. As of 1988, 6.5 million people out of a total population of 14 million were requiring international food assistance, with 3.2 million getting direct emergency food aid. Malnutrition is rampant, as relief supplies have been destroyed by guerrilla attacks, and once-productive farms in contested regions have reverted to brambles.

Assembly of Pershing II missile components. The production of high-technology weapons employs a relatively small number of highly skilled workers. (Martin Marietta Corporation)

THE EFFECTS OF MILITARY SPENDING

Some people argue that military spending is economically beneficial, providing jobs, permitting federal governments to target areas needing financial investment, and providing demand that can stimulate a lagging economy. On the other hand, most experts agree that in the long run, military spending is economically damaging. (Of course, the primary justification for military spending is not economic, but rather that it supposedly enhances national security; economic arguments are generally seen to be secondary to that more fundamental justification.) Criticisms of military spending as economically detrimental focus on five areas:

1. *Employment.* Although military spending creates jobs, it almost invariably creates fewer jobs than would be generated by the same funds spent for civilian purposes. This is especially true for high-tech military procurement, notably for aerospace and nuclear weapons development and shipbuilding. Such expenditures are capital-intensive — that is, they cost a lot of money, but create relatively few jobs — as opposed to such labor-intensive expenditures as education, health care, and construction.

2. *Inflation.* Military spending is perhaps the most inflationary way for a government to spend money. By using up major resources without producing consumable goods, military spending reduces supply while also increasing demand for raw materials, thereby stimulating inflation in two ways. Moreover, costs tend to rise yet further when the supply of money and credit increases without corresponding increases in productivity. The result

is the classic inflationary process: too much money chasing too few goods.

3. *Deficits*. Governments can obtain military forces only by purchasing them. The immense federal deficits of the Reagan administration, for example, occurred largely because the U.S. government chose to lower taxes while dramatically increasing military expenditures.

4. *Productivity*. Industrial productivity is strongly influenced by the availability of scientists and engineers to provide innovative technologies, and the ability of federal governments to invest in civilian research and development as well as the renovation of aging industrial plants. Military economies tend to dominate scientific and R&D (research and development) activities, thereby robbing the civilian economy. As a result, a strong inverse correlation exists between military spending as a function of GNP and growth in economic productivity: States like Denmark, Canada, and, notably, Japan — which invest in their domestic rather than their military economies — have been growing more rapidly than states like the United States or Great Britain. Only rarely do military innovations yield significant "spin-offs"; certainly, such collateral benefits would be much greater if they were earmarked for civilian purposes.

5. *Unmet social needs*.   Resources spent on the military are not available to be spent in other ways. A "substitution effect" tends to operate whereby expenditures for submarines, missiles, or machine guns, for example, are deleted from money available for hospitals, daycare centers, or schools. One half of 1 percent of one year's world military spending would purchase enough farm equipment, according to the Brandt Commission on North/South issues, to permit the world's low-income countries to reach food sufficiency within a decade. The world's annual military budget in 1987 equaled the total income of the population of the forty-four poorest nations on earth: 2.6 bil-

lion people. Global military expenditures that year reached an all-time high of $1.8 million per minute, at a time when people were dying from hunger-related, preventable diseases at a rate comparable to one Hiroshima bomb every two days. Also in 1987, a United Nations conference on the relationship between military spending and economic development was attended by 128 countries; the United States boycotted this meeting, claiming that disarmament and development are separate issues.

Although military spending is a serious problem in the United States and the Soviet Union (which has recently acknowledged the need to reduce military spending so as to address its inadequate domestic productivity), it is even more acute in many developing countries. In the 1970s, for example, military spending in Africa increased by 6.6 percent per year, while economic growth was only .4 percent. Taken as a proportion of GNP, the military expenditures of the world's richer states have actually declined since 1960, whereas those of the poorer states have increased; countries that cannot meet the basic social needs of their people are now spending a larger proportion of their meager incomes on weapons and soldiers than the richer states spend of their much more abundant income.

"Every gun that is made," said President Eisenhower,

> every warship launched, every rocket fired signifies, in the final sense, a theft from those who hunger and are not fed, those who are cold and are not clothed. The world in arms is not spending money alone. It is spending the sweat of its laborers, the genius of its scientists, the hopes of its children.[36]

A FINAL NOTE ON SOCIAL AND ECONOMIC FACTORS

Wars — and the preparation for wars — take place within a context that goes beyond individuals and their group affiliation. This context includes the diffuse but terribly important factors of ideology and economic condition. There are no simple cause-and-effect relationships in this difficult realm, where conflicting theories abound. (By contrast, there is little doubt about the overall harmful effects of military spending and of war itself.) It is said that one way to distinguish an optimist from a pessimist is by his or her reaction when confronted with a large pile of horse manure: The pessimist is likely to be discouraged, whereas the optimist will conclude that given the evidence, there must be a horse around somewhere. Let us hope that students of Peace Studies will be optimists and continue to search amid various social and economic theories of war for something that might prove useful.

Study Questions

1. Compare Marxist and capitalist ideology with regard to the question of what causes war.

2. Are there any current states in which fascism is the dominant ideology (even though it may not be publicly admitted)? Explain.

3. Compare democracies and dictatorships with regard to their war-proneness.

4. Compare the U.S.S.R. with the United States with regard to tendencies to export their ideologies abroad, by force if necessary.

5. Make a case for the role of population pressure in producing war. Make the alternative case.

6. Make a case for the role of poverty in producing war. Make the alternative case.

7. Describe and support the Marxist theory of imperialism leading to war. Refute this theory.

8. What is meant by "neo-imperialism"?

9. Compare the United States and the U.S.S.R. with respect to their military-industrial complexes.

10. Make the case that war (and/or preparations for war) enhances a state's economy. Make the case that it weakens the economy.

Suggestions for Further Reading

Theodore Gurr. 1970. *Why Men Rebel*. 1970. Princeton University Press: Princeton, NJ.

Kenneth E. Boulding and T. Mukarjee (eds.). 1972. *Economic Imperialism*. University of Michigan Press: Ann Arbor.

Michael Howard. 1978. *War and the Liberal Conscience*. Rutgers University Press: New Brunswick, NJ.

Lloyd Jeffry Dumas. 1986. *The Overburdened Economy*. University of California Press: Berkeley.

Michael Parenti. 1989. *The Sword and the Dollar*. St. Martin's: New York.

Source Notes

1. Woodrow Wilson. 1965. *A Day of Dedication*. Macmillan: New York.

2. Ibid.

3. G. F. Kennan. 1951. *American Diplomacy, 1900–1950*. Little, Brown: Boston.

4. Quoted in M. Howard. 1978. *War and the Liberal Conscience*. Rutgers University Press: New Brunswick, NJ.

5. Ibid.

6. Randolph S. Bourne. 1964. "The State." In *War and the Intellectuals, Collected Essays 1915–1919*. Harper & Row: New York.

7. Walter Lippmann. 1955. *The Public Philosophy*. Little, Brown: Boston.

8. Quoted in Mary Kaldor. 1987. "The World Economy and Militarization." In S. Mendlovitz and R. B. J. Walker (eds.), *Towards a Just World*. Butterworths: London.

9. Arnold J. Toynbee. 1935. *A Study of History*. Oxford University Press: London.

10. *Marxism-Leninism on War and Army (a Soviet View)*. 1974. Soviet Military Thought, No. 2, United States Air Force: Washington, DC.

11. Josue de Castro. 1952. *The Geography of Hunger*. Little, Brown: Boston.

12. T. H. Green. 1986. *Lectures on the Principles of Political Obligation and Other Writings*. Cambridge University Press: Cambridge.

13. Quoted in M. Howard. 1978. *War and the Liberal Conscience*. Rutgers University Press: New Brunswick, NJ.

14. C. Hovland and R. Sears. 1940. "Minor Studies in Aggression, VI: Correlation of Lynchings with Economic Indices." *Journal of Psychology* 9: 301–310.

15. Alexis de Tocqueville. 1955. *The Old Regime and the French Revolution*. Doubleday: New York.

16. T. Gurr. 1970. *Why Men Rebel*. 1970. Princeton University Press: Princeton, NJ.

17. Quoted in Arthur Bryant. 1966. *The Fire and the Rose*. Doubleday: New York.

18. Franz Fanon. 1963. *The Wretched of the Earth*. Grove Press: New York.

19. C. Guevara. 1968. *Guerrilla Warfare*. Monthly Review Press: New York.

20. Quoted in Howard. *Liberal Conscience*.

21. Quoted in John Stoessinger. 1985. *Why Nations Go to War*. St. Martin's: New York.

22. Quoted in the *New York Times*, January 2, 1989.

23. Cornelius Tacitus. 1942. *The Complete Works of Tacitus*. Modern Library: New York.

24. Quoted in Howard. *Liberal Conscience*.

25. John Hobson. 1938. *Imperialism, a Study*. Allen & Unwin: London.

26. Anatole France. 1933. *Penguin Island*. Modern Library: New York.

27. V. Lenin. 1939. *Imperialism: The Highest Stage of Capitalism*. International Publishers: New York.

28. Ibid.

29. K. Zilliacus. 1946. *Mirror of the Past*. Current Books: New York.

30. J. Galtung. 1971. "A Structural Theory of Imperialism." *Journal of Peace Research* 8: 81–117.

31. Walter Rostow. 1960. *The Stages of Economic Growth*. Cambridge University Press: Cambridge.

32. K. E. Boulding and T. Mukarjee (eds.). 1972. *Economic Imperialism*. University of Michigan Press: Ann Arbor.

33. Dwight D. Eisenhower. 1961. *Peace with Justice: Selected Addresses*. Columbia University Press: New York.

34. J. Schumpeter. 1955. *Imperialism and Social Classes*. Meridian: New York.

35. W. H. McNeill. 1982. *The Pursuit of Power*. University of Chicago Press: Chicago.

36. Eisenhower. *Peace with Justice*.

12

The Superpower Level: U.S.–Soviet Rivalry

It may seem melodramatic to say that the U.S. and Russia represent Good and Evil, Light and Darkness, God and the Devil. But if we think of it that way, it helps to clarify our perspective of the world struggle.

Richard M. Nixon

The United States and the Soviet Union have never had a full-fledged war with each other. However, they have been adversaries for most of the twentieth century, and they have organized (or have sought to organize) many of the smaller states into contending camps. Much of the organized violence in the world today is somehow connected — at the level of ideology, political alliance, economic or military aid — with either the United States or the U.S.S.R., or both. In addition, these two states are, for good reasons, known as the two "superpowers": They are by far the two most powerful states, at least as measured by military strength. Moreover, between them, the United States and the U.S.S.R. account for the overwhelming majority of nuclear weapons in the world today. They are also at the cutting edge of an ongoing nuclear arms race. Clearly, the relationship of the United States and the Soviet Union is critical to any consideration of war and its causes, today and tomorrow.

THE ROOTS OF THE COLD WAR

For a time, relations between the United States and Russia were relatively smooth, as when the United States purchased Alaska from the czar's government in the nineteenth century. But from the time of the Bolshevik Revolution in 1917, when the U.S.S.R. was born, the two future superpowers have been locked on a competitive and often antagonistic track. To a large extent, U.S. antagonism began with the Bolshevik Revolution itself: As one of the major bastions of capitalism, the United States government felt itself threatened by a communist ideology that proclaimed itself both at odds with and superior to capitalism.

There were also practical, immediate problems. The United States had entered World War I in the spring of 1917, at which time Russia was playing a major part in fighting Germany. A year later, the fledgling Soviet government elected to make a separate peace with Germany, signing the one-sided Treaty of Brest-Litovsk, which ceded large areas (including the Baltic states of Latvia, Lithuania, and Estonia, and the entire Ukraine) to Germany, and permitted the Central Powers to concentrate their attention on the West. Not surprisingly, this greatly antagonized the Western allies, whereas the Soviets saw their peace with Germany as necessary to save their country, in that the eastern front had become an ongoing disaster. Western forces invaded the Soviet cities of Vladivostok and Archangel in 1918, and a year later—after World War I was over—Allied soldiers landed at Murmansk to assist the anticommunist White forces in their civil war against the Reds. Although the invasion itself was small and ineffectual,* it established a tone of confrontation between the Soviet Union and the West, including the United States.

Early ill will between the U.S.S.R. and the West was accentuated by Lenin's refusal to pay war debts (incurred by the czar's government), and by mutual ideological hostility: fear of communism on the part of the United States and the governments of western Europe, and in Moscow, fear of capitalism. Re-

---

*This episode is almost unknown to Americans. The U.S. contingent was relatively small, 14,000 soldiers, and it suffered "only" 1,000 casualties, although Soviet citizens remain acutely aware of it.

vulsion over the heavy-handed dictatorship of Lenin's successor, Josef Stalin, as well as the bloodshed associated with forced collectivization at that time, cast a further pall over U.S.-Soviet relations. The United States did not even recognize the Soviet government until 1933, and even then, there was continuing antipathy, due partly to Stalin's purges and partly to fears that "international communism" would make inroads into U.S. society. The Great Depression of the 1930s served to radicalize many in the labor movement, and big business, in turn, used fear of communism to gain support in its battles against unionism.

For its part, the Soviet government not only responded to U.S. antagonism, but also continued to espouse a doctrine of worldwide revolution that made U.S. authorities understandably distrustful. As though adherence to the inevitability of socialist triumph was not provocative enough, Lenin established the Comintern, or Communist International, to "give history a push." When, in the 1930s, Hitler made communism a special target of Nazi Germany, Stalin sought to form alliances with Great Britain and France, but was rebuffed. Shortly after the Munich Conference, at which Britain and France sought to appease Hitler rather than confront him, the Soviet government shocked the West by signing a nonaggression pact with Germany. This evoked memories of the Soviet "defection" in 1917, and further reinforced the perception that the U.S.S.R. was hostile and could not be trusted. Moreover, when Hitler invaded Poland in September 1939, Soviet forces also invaded from the east. During the brief Russo-Finnish War (1939–1940), public sentiment strongly supported the valiant but outnumbered Finns; in that war, the Soviets eventually acquired large parts of the Finnish region of Karelia, near the Soviet city of Leningrad. Subsequently, as a result of his pact with Hitler, and his fear of further German advances in Poland and Finland, Stalin annexed the Baltic states of Latvia, Lithuania, and Estonia, which had been ceded to Germany after World War I and then granted independence by the victors. Even though the Baltic states had been controlled by the Russian czars throughout the nineteenth century, this action made the U.S.S.R. appear increasingly aggressive and expansionistic.

In June 1941, Hitler surprised Stalin by attacking the U.S.S.R. By December of that year, the United States had also entered the Second World War, fighting alongside the Soviet Union and the Western allies. However, tensions developed during the war, as the Soviets pressed for the opening of a second, western, front to relieve pressure in the east. This didn't happen until June 1944, with the Normandy landing. (Before this, many Soviets commented ruefully that Churchill and Roosevelt were willing to fight to the last drop of Russian and German blood.)

The Red Army bore the brunt of Germany's onslaught, and eventually rolled back Hitler's empire throughout eastern Europe, so that by the war's end, in 1945, most of the formerly independent states of eastern Europe were in Soviet hands. It should also be pointed out that all of these states had either been German allies—like Hungary, Romania, and Bulgaria—or anti-Soviet for other reasons—like Poland. By contrast, the states of western Europe, which had been liberated by Western armies, had rather different political experiences.

Under the czars, Russia had been a highly secretive, despotic state. Under communism, the Soviet Union has also been highly secretive, and—at least under Stalin—despotic as well. The West has long been puzzled by this enormous country, which Winston Churchill once described as "a riddle wrapped in a mystery inside an enigma."

THE POST–WORLD WAR II PERIOD

When Churchill, Roosevelt, and Stalin met at Yalta, on the Black Sea, in February 1945, they agreed on a division of power in postwar Europe. Not surprisingly, it corresponded broadly to the positions of the various armies at the time of Germany's defeat, some twelve weeks later. Disputes soon arose over the governing of several European countries, with the Western allies pressing for democracy and cap-italism, and Stalin insisting on communist governments that were ultimately to come under Soviet control.

The Red Army established a communist government in Poland, for example, bypassing the Polish government-in-exile located in London, and violating Stalin's earlier promise to permit free and independent elections in that country. In Greece, communist and nationalist/democratic partisans clashed in virtual civil war, although in this case, Stalin withdrew his support for the communists, allowing Britain to install a pro-West government. The pattern of conflict and competition between Stalin and the West was becoming increasingly clear, however. The U.S.S.R., for example, was reluctant to withdraw its troops from northern Iran, finally doing so only after what may have been a nuclear threat from President Harry Truman. The Soviet Union retained a firm hold on the governments of Eastern Europe, however, permitting very little internal political freedom. In some cases (Germany, Austria), this was by agreed partition, while in others (Yugoslavia, Albania) the U.S.S.R. didn't have control at all. Nonetheless, nationalist/democratic sentiments were crushed in other states, notably Poland and, several years later, Czechoslovakia.*

Right-wing politicians saw this as indicating Soviet expansionism, part of a communist plot to conquer the world. Others saw it as a regrettable but understandable response to the painful experiences that the U.S.S.R. historically had with the West, having been invaded by Napoleon in the nineteenth century, and then twice, disastrously, by Germany in the first half of the twentieth century. While conservatives pointed to the "captive nations" of Eastern Europe as part of a Soviet drive

---

*The general pattern appears to be that the U.S.S.R. was able to establish postwar control in those countries that were overrun by the Red Army. By contrast, Yugoslavia and Albania—which had vigorous partisan forces and had essentially liberated themselves—became autonomous.

for world hegemony, liberals and moderates saw "buffer states." Winston Churchill, a conservative who had profoundly distrusted the Soviet Union, even while allied with it, was touring the United States in 1946 when he made a famous speech in which he noted that

> from Stettin in the Baltic to Trieste in the Adriatic an iron curtain has descended across the continent. . . . I do not believe that Soviet Russia desires war. What they desire is the fruits of war and the indefinite expansion of their power and doctrines.[1]

The next year, President Truman initiated the "Truman Doctrine," which provided that the United States would "support free peoples who are resisting attempted subjugation by armed minorities or outside pressure." The Truman Doctrine was stimulated specifically by the communist insurrections in Turkey and Greece, but the Soviets saw it — not incorrectly — as really directed against themselves. Within just two years of the end of the wartime antifascist alliance, Bernard Baruch, financier and long-time advisor to U.S. presidents, announced the status of U.S.-Soviet relations: "Let us not be deceived, today we are in the midst of a cold war."[2]

The Cold War took many forms and involved many events, which can variously be seen as causes of the antagonism or as responses to it. Thus, the Truman Doctrine was quickly followed by the European Recovery Plan — better known as the Marshall Plan, after Secretary of State George Marshall — which channeled financial aid to the war-devastated economies of Western Europe. Americans perceived this program as humanitarian; the Soviet government saw it as directed against the U.S.S.R., a virtual declaration of economic war, intended to bolster Europe against communist influence. In reality, it was both. In his famous "long telegram" to the State Department in Washington, diplomat George Kennan in 1946 had warned that the United States would have to support the states of Europe, and especially, to strengthen their economies, if the United States was to compete successfully with the powerful presence of the Soviet Union in the postwar world.

U.S. air force cargo planes participating in the Berlin Airlift in 1948; after the Soviets closed ground access to West Berlin, that city was supplied, by the United States, by air. (UPI/Bettmann Newsphotos)

For its part, the U.S.S.R. continued to alarm Cold Warriors in the West. Thus, in 1948, the Kremlin engineered a communist coup in previously democratic, socialist Czechoslovakia (a state that had a strong indigenous Communist party). That same year, the Soviets initiated the now-famous Berlin Blockade, with which the U.S.S.R. refused the Western allies access to West Berlin, a partitioned city within the Soviet-dominated sector of Germany. They were outraged by the Allies' plan to unify their sectors by instituting a common currency, fearing that this might lead to the establishment of a new and potentially powerful state (as eventually it did, with the birth of the Federal Republic of Germany, or West Germany). The following year marked the success of Mao Ze-dong's communist forces, which defeated the nationalists in the decades-long Chinese civil war, while to make matters even worse (from the U.S. perspective), the U.S.S.R. exploded its own atomic bomb, ending the U.S. monopoly on nuclear weapons. A year later, in 1950, North Korea invaded South Korea. The Korean War was to drag on for three years, with Chinese and U.S. troops, in addition to Korean forces on each side, heavily engaged.

Communist gains around the world at this time were seen as orchestrated largely from Moscow. Political life in the United States was transformed into a mass of anticommunist recriminations, such as the accusatory "Who lost China?" (The left would respond that China never was ours to lose; nonetheless, international liberalism was very much on the defensive, as it appeared that the Kremlin was making spectacular gains worldwide.) Revolutionary nationalist movements were widespread, with wars of independence fought against such occupying colonial powers as Britain, France, and Holland, each of which had been seriously weakened in World War II. Since the old imperial powers were capitalist, their opponents often rallied around Marxist revolutionaries, sometimes aided directly by Moscow and, to a lesser extent, Beijing. In most cases, however, even though these revolutions were truly nationalist more than ideological, they were seen as additional evidence of Soviet expansionism. Apparently, one of the major driving forces of the Cold War mentality during the postwar period was an American inability to distinguish between worldwide communist subversion and indigenous Third World nationalist movements. (That confusion has continued, and it particularly characterized the policies of the Reagan administration as late as the 1980s.)

Although Stalin's policies must bear a proportion of the blame for the beginning of the Cold War during the late 1940s, the United States engaged in policies and behavior that the U.S.S.R. found provocative as well. A very important policy document, NSC (National Security Council) Report no. 68, concluded that the Soviet Union "seeks to impose its absolute authority over the rest of the world," and it defined the Soviet Union as the primary threat to U.S. security. This document has been a cornerstone of national security policy every since, cementing a stance of U.S.-Soviet hostility. NSC 68 recommended a departure from U.S. policy since 1776: the maintenance, for the first time, of large standing armed forces so as to deter further Soviet expansionism. "Containment" (of the U.S.S.R.) became the byword of U.S. foreign policy during the 1950s. The United States also began increasingly to ally itself with right-wing military dictators, whose "friendship" with the United States was based on a willingness to allow large American economic investments on favorable terms for the investors, as well as a vigorous policy of anticommunism.

The United States also was largely responsible for forming the North Atlantic Treaty Organization (NATO) in 1949. All NATO members are pledged to respond collectively to an attack on any one of them, and NATO was clearly designed to bolster Western Europe against the perceived "Soviet threat." Membership in NATO marked another dramatic departure in U.S. policy: It was the first time the United States had ever committed itself, in a peacetime alliance, to fight on behalf of another country. Although NATO was almost certainly intended as a defensive alliance, the Soviet Union considered it to be threatening, especially after its nemesis, a rearmed West Germany, joined in 1955. Immediately thereafter, the U.S.S.R. responded with its own alliance, the Warsaw Pact,* made up of its Eastern European satellite states.

Interestingly, the leading U.S. conservative at the time of the formation of NATO, Ohio senator Robert Taft, opposed the alliance as "a treaty by which one nation undertakes to arm half the world against the other half." He also predicted that it "means inevitably an arms race," since "if Russia sees itself ringed gradually by so-called defensive arms, from Norway and Denmark to Turkey and Greece . . . it may decide that the arming of Europe, regardless of its present purpose, looks like an attack upon Russia."[3]

The Soviet Union remains the undisputed head of the Warsaw Pact states, as does the United States vis-à-vis NATO; the military commander of NATO, for example, is always an American. However, there is considerable heterogeneity and differences of political will within NATO. Greece and Turkey, for example, have virtually been at war several times, and several NATO states (Canada, Norway, Denmark) do not permit the peacetime deployment of nuclear weapons on their territory; neither does the Warsaw Pact state of Romania. As of the early 1990s, the Soviet Union has agreed to

---

*Officially known as the Warsaw Treaty Organization.

withdraw its forces from Czechoslovakia and, it seems likely, from other Eastern European states as well. Combined with the democratization of what used to be known as the "Soviet bloc," this raises real doubt as to the future of the Warsaw Pact.

U.S.-SOVIET RELATIONS AFTER STALIN

Since the death of Stalin in 1953, U.S.-Soviet relations have been variable, although generally less confrontational than previously. Thus, Nikita Khrushchev initiated a process of "de-Stalinization" in 1956, which included somewhat greater concern for consumer products, tempering Stalin's single-minded obsession with heavy industry. The U.S.S.R. also suffered a notable series of reverses in the post-Stalin era, especially in Third World countries: China switched in the early 1960s from being a Soviet ally to a bitter opponent. The Cuban Missile Crisis, in addition to frightening both sides, was also a bitter defeat for the U.S.S.R. After an unsuccessful coup attempt, literally hundreds of thousands of communists (as well as suspected communists and other minorities such as Chinese and Indians) were slaughtered in Indonesia, and Soviet advisors — along with Soviet influence — were banished from Egypt by President Sadat in the early 1970s. Even Cuba and Vietnam, which seemed to be examples of successful Third World communist revolutions, have become headaches to Moscow, since they require subsidies running into billions of dollars annually. And other Marxist regimes, such as in Somalia, Ethiopia, Mozambique, and Angola, have not been notably receptive to Soviet foreign policy overtures, even while imposing a substantial burden on the U.S.S.R.'s limited treasury.

The 1960s were a time of vigorous competition in various Third World arenas, with the U.S.S.R. assisting left-wing revolutionary movements, and the United States supporting military dictatorships and an array of counterinsurgency actions. As that decade ended, U.S.-Soviet relations came to be dominated by the Vietnam War, and a gradual recognition that some form of nuclear arms control would be necessary.

Beginning with the Nixon administration, and especially under the guidance of National Security Advisor (and then Secretary of State) Henry Kissinger, the United States and the U.S.S.R. entered into a period of accommodation and relative harmony known as "detente." Some critics — notably China — saw detente as an effort at shared hegemony, by which the two superpower imperialists agreed to divide up the planet. Others — mainly from the hawkish right-wing within the United States — saw detente as a misguided effort to appease the U.S.S.R., while the United States was hoodwinked by Soviet protestations of peaceful intent. Yet others — primarily from Western Europe — saw detente as a practical and economic necessity, which would result in a lowering of tensions, a reduced danger of nuclear war, and an opportunity for economic gains through expanded trade.

Detente began to wear thin during the late 1970s, with Cuban and Soviet assistance to Angola and Ethiopia, the overthrow of the American-backed dictators Somoza in Nicaragua and the shah in Iran. In addition, the U.S.S.R. had hoped for economic gains in conjunction with detente, but legislation in the United States (notably the Jackson-Vanik Amendment) tied favorable trading practices to increased emigration by Soviet Jews, a restriction that the Soviets considered to involve unacceptable meddling in their internal affairs. Thus, by the time of the Soviet invasion of Afghanistan in 1979, detente was effectively dead.

THE GORBACHEV ERA

The Reagan years (1981–1989) began with a resurgent Cold War, brought on in part by an American perception that the United States had been bested by the Soviet Union during the late 1970s. Military expenditures and hostile rhetoric skyrocketed, and the U.S.-Soviet competition became both more militarized and more ideological, largely at the initiative of the most right-wing and thoroughly ideological administration in U.S. history. Small, symbolic military adventures were carried out, such as the successful invasion of Grenada, an ill-fated

President Mikhail Gorbachev (left) of the Soviet Union shaking hands with President Ronald Reagan of the United States in 1988. Shortly afterwards, the two exchanged documents bringing about the INF Treaty. (Reuters/Bettmann Newsphotos)

intervention in Beirut, Lebanon, and the bombing of Libya. The nuclear arms race was greatly enlivened, with a resulting dramatic growth in antinuclear peace movements in the United States and Europe. Toward the end of his tenure, however, President Reagan and Soviet General Secretary Gorbachev reached an accommodation concerning Euromissiles, and, by a series of summit meetings and lesser arms control agreements, signaled a return to a policy of detente, though by a different name: "realistic engagement."

This change was due in part to adjustments in the perception of U.S.-Soviet relations on the part of President Reagan, who began looking toward his place in history, and toward the ultimate necessity of peace. But even more, it seems attributable to the Soviet leader, Mikhail Gorbachev, who was committed to achieving internal restructuring ("perestroika") of the Soviet system, both economically and politically, accompanied by greater openness, or "glasnost." Gorbachev recognized that such changes could not occur in a context of U.S.-Soviet antagonism, which tends to produce a closing rather than an opening of Soviet society. Nationalist unrest within the U.S.S.R. demanded attention

that could not simultaneously be focused on tense, competitive international maneuvering. Most important, perhaps, was the almost desperate condition of the Soviet economy, which was stagnant, enmeshed in massive bureaucratic delays, and unable to produce an adequate quantity of quality consumer goods. It has been widely recognized, within the Soviet Union no less than in the capitalist West, that revitalizing the civilian economy requires a reduction in superpower military rivalry, so as to free up scarce resources that are otherwise requisitioned by the economically unproductive military. (It is also possible, although rarely credited in the West, that the Gorbachev government really has been unusually concerned about the danger of war — especially nuclear war — and has sought to reinstitute detente and to cool the arms race so as to make the world safer for everybody.)

In any event, the late 1980s witnessed a remarkable warming in U.S.-Soviet relations, with a proliferation of cultural, scientific, military, and political exchanges, along with an extraordinary series of arms control proposals, including a new-found willingness to permit intrusive verification procedures, often going beyond what the United States finds acceptable (see Chapter 15). At the same time, the U.S.S.R. has reorganized its governmental structure and moved toward instituting genuine democratic political procedures; the newly organized Soviet legislature, for example, has been for the first time the scene of vigorous open political debate and disagreement.

Paralleling these changes, the Soviets have permitted — in fact, encouraged — unheard of liberalization in certain of their Warsaw Pact allies. As of 1989, for example, Poland inaugurated its first noncommunist government since World War II (military and police control remains with the Communist Party, however), and Hungary also began moving rapidly toward an adoption of Western economic and political structures. Hard-line communist regimes have been replaced throughout Eastern Europe, the Berlin Wall — long-time symbol of the Cold War — has essentially been dismantled, and throughout Eastern Europe, the Communist Party has relinquished its previously guaranteed "leading role." Although these changes were spearheaded by local activists in each country, they probably would not have succeeded if Soviet policy under Gorbachev had not permitted it . . . or as in many cases, actually encouraged the process of liberalization and democratization.

As a result of all these changes, the U.S.S.R. now appears much less threatening, even to many devoted anticommunists in the United States. On the other hand, while Europeans have been quick to applaud Soviet liberalization, the Bush administration has been exceptionally cautious about the warming trend in U.S.-Soviet relations. The result has been a vigorous debate within the United States. Liberals and moderates urge that the Gorbachev era represents a golden opportunity, since a reformed, less threatening, and more cooperative Soviet Union would augur well for world peace (defined either negatively or positively). They urge the United States to assist Gorbachev in his program of reforms and liberalization, arguing that if he fails, he could be replaced by hard-line opponents who would be more repressive at home and more dangerous abroad. By contrast, conservatives take a very different view, which is largely responsible for

the United States' resistance to diminishing its military profile:

1. *Economics and careers.* Many people make a lot of money on military expenditures; in addition, numerous careers are staked on the military and on the continued operation of military industries. Furthermore, these individuals tend to be important and influential.

2. *Old habits.* The world view of many people, both in and out of the military-industrial complex, was formed during the long period of U.S.-Soviet rivalry following World War II. Old habits die hard and new realities are often difficult to accept.

3. *Third World intervention.* U.S. military forces are not kept only for possible use against the Soviet Union. They also are intended for intervention in other countries, especially Third World states. Some critics even charge that for some time the real motivation for United States hostility toward the U.S.S.R. has been that it provides a pretext for maintaining such interventionist forces. (According to this view, the United States' strategic nuclear weapons serve to keep the Soviets at bay, thereby providing the United States with a relatively free hand to intervene elsewhere.)

4. *Skepticism.* In all fairness to conservatives, there are some who truly remain skeptical that events in the Soviet Union warrant any reduction in United States military forces. Initially, they doubted that the Soviets were making the unilateral cuts they had announced. This line of argument soon became untenable, with even the CIA acknowledging that the cuts were real and substantial. Conservative skepticism then switched focus, claiming that (a) the Soviets are seeking to trick the United States into letting down its guard, (b) Gorbachev and his reform elements may be only a passing phase, to be replaced by hardline leaders antagonistic to the United States, (c) it is not in the United States' national interest to assist the creation of a stronger, more economically and politically

vibrant Soviet Union that would also be a more formidable opponent, and finally, (d) the goal of the United States should not be "reform" of the Soviet communist system, but its replacement with a capitalist, democratic state. Toward that end, United States hardliners claim that reducing military and other competitive pressures will only make it easier for Soviet communists to deal with their domestic difficulties, thereby helping them to retain power. Hence, conservatives tend to recommend a continuance of political and economic hostility as well as military competition, hoping to pressure the U.S.S.R. toward yet more reforms as well as possibly disbanding its empire and abandoning communism altogether.

An alternative, liberal/moderate view is that Soviet reform will indeed be facilitated by a more cooperative, less militarized international environment but that such reform is in the United States' interest no less than that of the U.S.S.R. and that it should therefore be encouraged and facilitated. Moreover, it is also possible that at least some United States old-line Cold Warriors actually prefer an atmosphere of intense U.S.-Soviet antagonism and they hope to use American political, military, and economic intransigence to help bring this about.

Amid this debate, fundamental uncertainty exists as to what extent the United States can in fact influence Soviet domestic events, although it seems clear that Gorbachev's prestige will increase in proportion as some of his policies—both domestically and internationally—bear fruit. Clearly, however, the United States can play a major role in the reduction of superpower military tensions, something that would greatly benefit both countries. In 1946, George F. Kennan was a major architect of the policy of containment, which he saw largely as strengthening the economies and political will of Western Europe. More than forty years later, Kennan felt that

> whereas in 1946 the military aspect of our relationship with the Soviet Union hardly seemed to come into question at all, today that aspect is obviously of prime importance. But . . . when I say that this military factor is now of prime importance, it is not because I see the Soviet Union as threatening the United States or its allies with armed force. . . . I see the weapons race in which we and they are now involved as a serious threat in its own right, not because of aggressive intentions on either side but because of the compulsions, the suspicions, the anxieties such a competition engenders, and because of the very serious dangers it carries with it of unintended complications—by error, by computer failure, by misread signals, or by mischief deliberately perpetrated by third parties. For all these reasons, there is now indeed a military aspect to the problem of containment, as there was not in 1946; but what most needs to be contained, as I see it, is not so much the Soviet Union as the weapons race itself.[4]

Perhaps the most important point about the recent Gorbachev-inspired shift in U.S.-Soviet relations is its suggestion that the Cold War, in all its manifestations—military, economic, political, ideological—is not something that has been imposed on us by malevolent, uncontrollable forces. Rather, it is largely the result of conscious choices, and accordingly, we are free to make other choices, which could lead us in different directions. With this in mind, we now turn to the question of the nuclear arms race.

A BRIEF HISTORY OF THE NUCLEAR ARMS RACE

The Period of United States Supremacy

The first atomic bombs were produced by the United States in 1945, after an intensive three-year effort known (misleadingly) as the "Manhattan Project." This effort was stimulated largely by fears that Nazi Germany might produce nuclear weapons first. By the end of World War II, the United States had a nuclear monopoly, and proposed what to some people was a uniquely generous option: the Baruch Plan. This plan called for complete United Nations control over all the atomic facilities in the world, including uranium mining, nuclear reactors, and prospective weapons plants. When the Soviet Union rejected the Baruch Plan, this seemed to confirm suspicions about the U.S.S.R.'s implacable hostility. However, the Baruch Plan had stipulated that the United States would relinquish its nuclear weapons only after all other nations had first surrendered control of their facilities. This meant that the Soviets would be forgoing the prospect of ever developing their own nuclear arsenal. The Baruch Plan therefore seemed to them a blueprint for assuring a continuing U.S. monopoly on these fearsome weapons. Moreover, the plan included the possibility of "condign punishment" of any violators, which — although never specified — could have involved the use of nuclear weapons against the U.S.S.R.; and according to the plan, the Soviets would have been unable to veto such actions.

Lacking nuclear weapons in the immediate postwar years, but engaged in a growing tug-of-war with the West, especially the United States, the U.S.S.R. did not demobilize its Red Army to the degree that the Western allies did with their armies. The implicit threat was that if the United States resorted to nuclear weapons, the U.S.S.R. would counter by overrunning Europe with its conventional forces. Many observers in the United States, of course, saw the threat exactly the other way: Nuclear weapons were justified by the need to restrain the Red Army.

The Empire Strikes Back (Or Rather, Catches Up)

In 1949, the U.S.S.R. shocked many in the United States when it exploded its own atomic bombs, and by the mid-1950s, both the United States and the Soviet Union had developed thermonuclear (hydrogen) bombs, as well as long-range strategic bombers. Coming as they did at a high point in the Cold War, and on the heels of the McCarthy-inspired anticommunist hysteria within the United States, these developments generated substantial public anxiety. In 1955, when the Soviets unveiled their new Bear bomber, U.S. analysts estimated that the U.S.S.R. "could" produce several hundred such planes within two years; this much-publicized "bomber gap" never materialized, however, except in favor of the United States, which produced about 500 B-52s and more than 1,500 medium-range B-47s, many of them stationed at bases adjacent to the U.S.S.R.

In 1957, however, the Soviet Union stunned the West by orbiting *Sputnik*, the world's first artificial satellite, launched by a missile that could also carry nuclear weapons to attack Western Europe and (with range extension) the United States. The Gaither Committee, appointed by President Eisenhower to assess this new-found Soviet missile capability, reported that within two years, the U.S.S.R. "could" have 100 missiles ready to attack the United States. The resulting "missile gap" played a role in the election of John F. Kennedy, under whose administration the United States deployed 1,000 solid-fueled Minuteman missiles to replace hundreds of liquid-fueled Atlas and Titan missiles. Significantly, this major escalation in the arms race was not slowed when the new technology of satellite surveillance revealed that the Soviets had never deployed more than a handful of ICBMs. In short, the missile gap — like the bomber gap before it — was actually in favor of the United States.

During the 1960s, the United States began deploying large numbers of SLBMs, as the Polaris and then the Poseidon strategic submarine programs came to fruition. But the Soviets, after backing down during the Cuban Missile Crisis, initiated their own program of military expansion following the ascendancy of Leonid Brezhnev; as a result, Soviet ICBM and SLBM arsenals were greatly expanded by the late 1960s and 1970s, reaching overall nuclear parity with the United States. By certain strictly numerical counts — number of ICBM launchers, number of MIRVed ICBMs, total deliverable megatonnage — the U.S.S.R. had in fact achieved superiority. At the same time, in most qualitative measures — accuracy, reliability, technological sophistication — the United States remained substantially ahead. (Opponents of detente, who advocated increased U.S. military spending in the face of the "Soviet threat," tirelessly emphasized the former considerations, while ignoring the latter.)

The Era of MAD

During the 1950s, when the United States had enjoyed unquestioned nuclear supremacy, its strategic doctrine had emphasized "massive retaliation," or the threat of responding with nuclear weapons to any serious Soviet provocation. By the time the U.S.S.R. had achieved the capacity to devastate the U.S. homeland, however, such a threat began to lack credibility. Accordingly, it was ultimately replaced with the doctrine of Mutually Assured Destruction (or MAD), the notion of deterrence as currently understood: Each side presumably will be deterred from attacking the other by the certainty that the attacker would be destroyed in turn. (This is not so much a thought-out strategy as a simple fact of life in the nuclear age; neither side has the ability, unilaterally, to render MAD obsolete, whether they like it or not, and whether or not they officially enshrine MAD as national strategic doctrine.) Nonetheless, strategic doctrine has continued to emphasize the possibility of gaining some kind of strategic leverage out of nuclear weapons, some realpolitik benefits short of, on the one hand, postponing warfare indefinitely, and on the other, precipitating a worldwide holocaust.

For example, one authority made a telling distinction between accomplishing things by brute force (for example, killing, wounding, taking, forcibly disarming, confining, and so on) and doing so by coercion, that is, by *threatening* to hurt.[5] In the nuclear age, victory is no longer a prerequisite for hurting an opponent, and war — at least, nuclear war — has become less a contest of strength than one of nerve. According to some observers, nerve and determination must be demonstrated not only during crises, but also in the arms race itself, by a willingness to match the opponent, and when necessary, to raise the ante.

The 1970s and 1980s

The 1970s and 1980s had been marked by occasional efforts at controlling the nuclear arms race (see Chapter 15), but even more so by its continuing momentum. The arms race expanded most notably in areas that were not constrained by arms control treaties, and in many cases, the treaties themselves simply established permissible ceilings rather than mandating actual reductions. Both sides developed and deployed warheads that were increasingly accurate, and MIRVed as well. Larger and more threatening land-based ICBMs (the MX for the

United States, the SS-18 for the U.S.S.R.) were accompanied by larger and more threatening strategic submarines (the Trident series for the United States, the Typhoon submarines for the U.S.S.R.), as well as advanced bombers that were increasingly invisible to radar (the B-1 and Stealth bombers for the United States; nothing comparable, yet, for the U.S.S.R.). Highly accurate cruise missiles have also been developed and deployed, capable of being launched from the ground, sea, or air, along with enhanced radiation warheads ("neutron bombs") stored in the United States. Strategic doctrine, in the meantime, has given increased prominence to counterforce (see Chapter 5). Nuclear "modernization" has come to mean the fielding of new and ever more threatening weapons that are capable — at least in theory — of destroying the nuclear weapons of the other superpower.

In Europe, the nuclear arms race was marked by a continuing perception of military inferiority on the part of NATO, or at least the promotion of this view, despite the fact that NATO countries have substantially larger populations and gross national products than the Warsaw Pact countries, as well as distinct advantages in training and in the quality of military hardware. Moreover, the U.S.S.R. has to be concerned with its 4,500-mile hostile border with China as well as the questionable reliability of its Eastern European "allies." Most recently, Soviet willingness to relinquish its hold on Eastern Europe presumably reflects an awareness that (1) the Warsaw Pact was not a reliable alliance, (2) NATO really is not threatening to attack the U.S.S.R., and (3) resources must be spent on the Soviet Union's internal problems. Moreover, the difficulty of "defending" Western Europe with nuclear weapons has long underscored the problem of credibility in the nuclear age: Since the use of nuclear weapons in Europe could only result in the destruction of that densely populated continent, strategies based on recourse to nuclear weapons lack credibility. Or, when credible, they are threatening, not only to the other side but also to the public whom they are ostensibly designed to protect.

This quandary has resulted in the development of neutron weapons, technically known as "enhanced radiation warheads." These are specially

A Trident submarine, the largest and most modern of the U.S. strategic nuclear submarines. (U.S. Department of Defense)

modified thermonuclear explosives that produce relatively less blast and heat, and more immediate radiation; hence, they presumably could be used in densely populated regions such as Europe, since they would be somewhat more likely to destroy enemy forces (notably, tank crews) and somewhat less likely to kill innocent civilians. The hope — ironically — is that by making nuclear war more likely (because the threat of it will be more credible), it will be made less likely. The European people have refused to permit the introduction of neutron weapons onto their continent; they have instead been stockpiled in the United States. Tensions over Euromissiles, at least, were eventually resolved with the INF Treaty (see Chapter 15). With the onrushing liberalization and democratization of Eastern Europe, it appears increasingly unlikely that short-range nuclear weapons — capable of reaching these fledgling democracies — will be modernized. Indeed, their very deployment appears more and more absurd and unnecessary.

Throughout much of the nuclear arms race, observers and participants alike have decried the wasteful expenditure and the growing tensions, while both superpowers have jockeyed for tempo-

rary advantages. The United States has generally led the competition, and has been responsible for most qualitative innovations, whereas the Soviet Union has typically taken about five years to catch up, but has usually done so with the production of vast quantities of armaments. This difference in itself reflects the contrasting socioeconomic systems of the two superpowers. Thus, technological innovation is a U.S. strength, whereas the ability to direct large amounts of government resources is characteristic of centrally planned, communist states. In the United States, various arms manufacturers such as Lockheed, Boeing, General Dynamics, Northrup, and Martin Marietta compete with one another for government contracts, in part by proposing new weaponry and then selling legislators and Pentagon procurement officers on the merits of their latest innovations. By contrast, although some competition exists among the various design and production bureaus within the Soviet Union, production quotas are decreed from the top down, and if anything, innovation is discouraged because bureaucrats are reluctant to stick their necks out by championing something new that might be a disappointment.

CAUSES OF THE NUCLEAR ARMS RACE

What caused the nuclear arms race? And what drives it today? Ideologues of the left or right place the blame squarely on one superpower or the other, not only with respect to the causes of the arms race, but of the Cold War as well. Thus, to right-wingers, the nuclear arms race is a direct function of rabid Soviet expansionism and the aggressive designs of worldwide communism; to those of the far left, American war-mongering and greedy capitalism are entirely to blame. In fact, the actual causes of the nuclear arms race are undoubtedly more complex than either of these "good guy/bad guy" caricatures. These causes can be divided into two general categories, external and internal, of which there are many subcategories.

External Causes

The Search for Superiority.   Although neither side will admit it, each has sought to attain security by becoming superior to the other. Shortly after World War II, when the United States emerged the world's dominant power, publisher Henry Luce proclaimed the beginning of "the American century." It did not last very long. But believers have not given up; the hope remains that with superiority might come the ability to get one's way in the world.* This dream ignores the fact that possessing nuclear weapons has actually contributed remarkably little to a state's influence: It did not prevent the United States from "losing" China, Cuba, Vietnam, Nicaragua, or Iran, nor has it aided the Soviet Union in pacifying Afghanistan or Poland, or in "keeping" Yugoslavia, China, Indonesia, or Egypt. It has been said that trying to make the world work by nuclear weapons is like trying to make a marriage work by dynamite. "What in the name of God is strategic superiority?" asked Henry Kissinger in exaspera-

tion. "What is the significance of it, politically, militarily, operationally, at these levels of numbers? What do you do with it?"[6]

In Charlie Chaplin's film *The Great Dictator*, Hitler and Mussolini are each seated on barber chairs, which can be raised by pumping a handle. They take turns pumping up their own chair, trying to be higher than the other . . . until eventually, they both bump their heads on the ceiling. In the same way, seeking nuclear superiority is a prescription for a never-ending arms race, with no winners. With regard to the nuclear arms race, the question "Who is ahead?" is truly absurd, since in fact, both sides are behind. The real race is not between the two superpowers, but rather between the designers and builders of nuclear weapons and those who would control and eliminate them. In this competition, there is no question who has been winning.

But the quest for the will-o'-the-wisp of nuclear superiority continues, with the Soviets favoring quantitative factors (more ICBMs, more warheads, and so on) and the United States tending toward qualitative ones (such as the Strategic Defense Initiative, or Star Wars) as a way of making a "technological end run" around the U.S.S.R.

Action–Reaction Sequences.   To some extent, the nuclear arms race is not really a "race" at all, in that neither side is going at top speed. If they were, the world would contain literally tens of thousands of missiles and perhaps hundreds of thousands, or even millions, of warheads. Much of what passes for a race is actually a series of actions that lead to reactions, and then to counterreactions, and so forth. Insofar as the United States has initiated most escalations of the nuclear arms race (first atomic bombs, intercontinental bombers, tactical nuclear weapons, SLBMs, MIRVs, cruise missiles, neutron bombs, and so on), it has largely been running a race with itself, especially since innovations are often driven by a supposition of what the Soviets might conceivably be doing, which then must be "countered." Often, action–reaction cycles involve misinterpretation of the other side's activities, but by the time the error is caught, the arms race has been ratcheted up yet another notch or two.

---

*Nuclear superiority is reminiscent of what might be called the dog/car problem: Picture a dog who repeatedly chases cars. One day, he catches one. What does he do with it?

Test-firing of a Titan II ICBM. These missiles were deployed during a period when the United States claimed to be facing a missile gap in favor of the Soviet Union; in truth, however, the United States was far ahead in ballistic missiles at the time. (U.S. Department of Defense)

For example, the buildup in American ICBMs during the early and mid-1960s was partly a response to the feared missile gap in favor of the U.S.S.R., first reported in the late 1950s. This gap was entirely fictitious, but the resulting escalation in U.S. forces stimulated the buildup of Soviet ICBMs in the late 1960s and early 1970s. This in turn led to fears of a "window of vulnerability" — that is, a possible Soviet first strike against U.S. ICBMs — which led to pressure for the MX missile as well as antimissile defense systems.

Similarly, during the 1960s, the Soviets began deploying the so-called Tallinn air defense system near Leningrad. This "action" was thought by the United States to constitute an antimissile system. As such, it threatened the ability of U.S. missiles to retaliate against a Soviet attack, thereby, in theory, undermining deterrence. The U.S. "reaction" was to proceed with MIRVing, so as to assure that, if necessary, at least some warheads would penetrate Soviet defenses. Subsequently, the Tallinn system was revealed to be strictly an antiaircraft weapon, itself a reaction to U.S. superiority in strategic bombers, especially the B-70 and SR-71 strike/reconnaissance aircraft . . . neither of which was ever deployed.

Action–reaction systems cannot be finetuned, because the research and development required for each new weapons system typically takes five to ten years. Thus, certain escalations in the arms race — such as the development of fusion bombs, which occurred in the Soviet Union within six months of their development in the United States — must be attributed to other processes instead. On the other hand, action–reaction sequences can involve drastic and damaging overreactions, as a result of misperceptions as well as the cynical manipulation of information by those with an ulterior motive in stimulating the arms race.

Action–reaction sequences usually are motivated by attempts to counter the weapons of the other side: aircraft giving rise to antiaircraft weapons, submarines to antisubmarine technology, tanks to precision-guided antitank missiles. Not all action–reaction processes, however, are of the weapon–counterweapon type. In many cases, the arms race proceeds by a kind of symmetrical competition: The United States MIRVs its ICBMs, and so the Soviet Union does the same, even though a MIRVed ICBM is no more effective than a single-warhead missile in defending against the opponent's MIRVed ICBM.* What appears to be operating here is not so much logic — except for the ever-present logic of the arms profiteers — as a primitive, viscerally satisfying psychology: If the Warsaw Pact nations field a new kind of armoured tank

---

*There is no defense against an ICBM, whether it is MIRVed or not.

(an action), then the militarily appropriate response might be for NATO to concentrate on antitank missiles (a reaction). Instead, NATO force planners inevitably will fret about the "imbalance" in armoured units, and will be placated only when and if their side gets equal, if not greater, numbers of tanks.

Worst-Case Analyses. Military analysts think of themselves as prudent and conservative. As such, their bias is that, if anything, they should err by overestimating the military capabilities of the other side. Such errors are facilitated by the fact that intelligence data are rarely exact, leaving considerable leeway for interpretation. For instance, the alleged bomber and missile gaps, which greatly fueled the arms race during the 1950s and early 1960s, resulted from poor information combined with worst-case analyses. The same can be said for the supposed spending gap, ABM gap, civil defense gap, and first-strike gap of the late 1970s and early 1980s. Such worst-case analyses can be self-serving, especially when promoted by the military or by the industries that stand to profit from efforts to close these gaps.

To make matters worse, when both sides engage in worst-case analyses, they interact to yield an ever-increasing spiral. Imagine, for example, that country A begins deploying a new kind of ballistic missile submarine, giving it 1,000 deliverable warheads. Country B makes a worst-case assumption that all the missiles carrying these warheads will work correctly, so in planning its defense, it decides to have 1,200 lasers: one laser per warhead, plus an extra 200 because country B has also made the additional worst-case assumption that not only will all of A's missiles work as planned, but 20 percent of its own defending lasers will malfunction. Country A, however, also makes worst-case assumptions: Only a fraction of its 1,000 warheads, it assumes, will function correctly, facing 1,200 lasers of country B, all of which — under worst-case assumptions — will fire perfectly. So, country A reasons that it would only be prudent to build yet more submarines; whereupon country B, reasoning similarly, will build more lasers.

Military analysts, seeking to assess a prospective opponent, like to distinguish between capabilities and intentions. The former refers to what can physically be done, the latter to what the other side actually plans to do. It is often said (on both sides, presumably) that since we cannot know intentions, we must base planning on capabilities. As former Defense Secretary Robert McNamara described it,

> When calculating the force required, we must be conservative in all our estimates of both a potential aggressor's capabilities and his intentions. Security depends upon assuming a worst plausible case, and having the ability to cope with it.[7]

Two additional kinds of worst-case assumptions are linked to such an approach: (1) Capabilities are often not known precisely, so estimators are free to imagine the worst (moreover, they often have a vested interest in exaggerating the threat from the other side); and (2) by focusing only on the weapons themselves, each side implicitly makes an additional and unspoken worst-case assumption concerning intentions, namely, that the other side is planning to attack. And in a world in which each side nervously eyes the other, these assumptions become a self-fulfilling prophecy, one that generates the kind of spiraling arms race and mutually reduced security that it is supposed to prevent. "It is the business of military strategists to prepare for all eventualities," wrote the theologian Reinhold Niebuhr (who was, most emphatically, not a pacifist), "but it is the fatal error of such strategists to create the eventualities for which they must prepare."[8]

In some cases, the arms race has been driven by factors even more insubstantial than overestimates of an adversary — that is, by imagining what the other side might possibly do, some time in the future. Thus, John S. Foster, director of research and engineering at the Defense Department in the Carter administration, testified to Congress that

> We are moving ahead to make sure that, whatever they do, or the possible things we imagine that they might do, we will respond. . . . We see possible threats on the horizon, usually not something the enemy has done, but something we may have thought of ourselves that he might do, and that we must therefore be prepared for.[9]

Options for Intervention.   It can be argued that the nuclear arms race is motivated, not so much by U.S. (or Soviet) desire to ward off a nuclear attack by the other, as by an urge to provide a nuclear shield under which each side can be relatively free to intervene militarily in other states, without fear of being intimidated into quiescence by the other superpower.[10] Thus, of the enormous annual U.S. military expenditures, less than 10 percent go to coastal defense and about 25 percent to nuclear weapons and their delivery systems. The great majority of U.S. military might is designed for "projecting power" overseas. This might not be feasible if the Soviets overawed the United States in nuclear forces, and threatened to respond to U.S. interventionism with the use of their own strategic arsenal. Thus, Eugene Rostow, while director of the Arms Control and Disarmament Agency, argued in favor of building up U.S. nuclear forces so as to regain its previous nuclear superiority over the U.S.S.R.:

> The nuclear weapon is a persuasive influence in all aspects of diplomacy and of conventional war, and in a crisis we could go forward in planning the use of our conventional forces with great freedom precisely because we knew the Soviet Union could not escalate beyond the local level. . . . However as our lead in nuclear power diminished, our capacity to control the escalation of crises diminished correspondingly. So did our capacity to use conventional forces or credibly threaten their use.[11]

Internal Causes

Technology.   Physicist J. Robert Oppenheimer referred to certain concepts in nuclear physics as "technically sweet." From the perspective of the scientist or engineer, working on the cutting edge of the latest in high-tech research can be enormously appealing. And since it is typically much more time-consuming for people to overcome political barriers than technological ones, specialists can generally design and produce a new weapon much more quickly than diplomats can control it. Disarmament or arms control agreements can therefore seem about as earth-shaking as a decision to ban the use of bows and arrows.

Ideally, technological innovations should come at the behest of policy decisions; they should not drive policy. And there is in fact a healthy debate as to which comes first, the "policy chicken" or the "technological egg." Often, technology has presented policymakers with a weapon that subsequently posed a dilemma: Cruise missiles and MIRVing fall into this category, as does the invention of nuclear weapons themselves, which came about before politicians and strategists had even begun to work out the political and strategic implications.

On the other hand, it can be argued that modern technological innovations are not the work of some backyard genius, tinkering on weekends. Rather, they require budgetary decisions and vast expenditures of government money. No amount of technological sweetness can drive a major new arms project unless it is accompanied by political decision-making, especially when research and development costs alone may run into the billions of dollars. In short, without a commitment to create new weapons, it seems unlikely that they would be produced. Under this view, the arms race is like a sailboat race, with governments blowing financial wind into the sails of technology via the military-industrial complex. Without this regular infusion, the arms racers would quickly find themselves becalmed. Such a prospect holds out more hope than the one that emphasizes the autonomous role of technology, because if true, then maybe people and governments are not necessarily doomed to face a continuing onslaught of unwanted Frankenstein's monsters.

The Military-Industrial Complex.   The nuclear arms race, like all arms races, has developed a formidable constituency: military contractors who derive profits from it, workers whose jobs depend on it, politicians who are closely associated with it, scientists whose discoveries promote it (see Chapter 11). The B-1 bomber, for example, had components produced in every state in the country; as a result, this weapon was politically very attractive and difficult to oppose, especially since national politicians vie with one another to bring federal money to their

Lawrence Livermore National Laboratory, in Livermore, California. This multimillion-dollar research and development complex (along with Los Alamos National Laboratory in New Mexico) designs nuclear weapons and other military systems. These two institutions have been influential in blocking a comprehensive test-ban treaty and they—and others—exert strong pressure toward furthering the arms race. (Los Alamos National Laboratory)

home districts. A comparable system exists in the Soviet Union, with careers closely linked to the continuation of current production levels. On the other hand, a centrally planned economy seems unlikely to foster the same competition over profits to be derived from military contracts.

Interservice Rivalries. Representatives of each branch of the military want their units to have the newest and most prestigious weaponry, the largest budgets, the highest "tech." As a result, the various branches find it in their interest to exaggerate the extent to which their counterparts in the other superpower are poised to surpass them, thereby contributing to the phenomenon of "threat inflation." The U.S. Air Force and Navy point to the size of Soviet ICBMs and strategic submarines, respectively, and U.S. Army spokespersons speak darkly of the capability of Soviet tanks and artillery, especially when military appropriations are being debated in Congress. (It can be assumed that something analogous occurs among the Soviet military services as well.)

In addition, rivalry among the services seems almost as intense as the competition between the superpowers. At the end of World War II, for ex-

ample, the U.S. Air Force was established as co-equal with the army and navy. Because of its strategic bombers, it also obtained control of nuclear weapons. The navy—which had been cut out of the nuclear action—argued vigorously against the concept of massive retaliation. Then, navy representatives began pointing to supposed "SAC vulnerability," theoretical calculations showing that Strategic Air Command bases could be vulnerable to a Soviet surprise attack. Not surprisingly, this new concern—combined with a sudden enthusiasm for strategic nuclear bombardment—coincided with plans for the navy's own nuclear weapons delivery system, the Polaris submarine (which, submerged, would be invulnerable).

The air force responded by sponsoring studies at its newly formed RAND Corporation, emphasizing the importance of counterforce, which required accuracy. Whereas the navy's SLBMs were inaccurate, land-based ICBMs (which were air force programs) could be made highly accurate. When it later became clear that SLBMs could also be made highly accurate, the navy too became enamored with counterforce. Meanwhile, the army had to content itself with a newly defined counterinsurgency mission, as well as with the proposed ABM system of the late 1960s and early 1970s, and for-ward-based, battlefield nuclear systems, deployed particularly in Europe.

When President Carter initially canceled the B-1 bomber—to the consternation of the air force—he elected to support the MX missile, es-sentially as a consolation prize. And to no one's surprise, the military service that was most con-vinced of the need for NATO-sponsored Euromis-siles was the army, which had been promised control of the ground-launched cruise missiles and Pershing IIs.

Public Opinion.   Entrenched bureaucratic and ideo-logical forces help maintain the arms race, inde-pendent of the short-term vagaries of public opinion. In the long run, however, democracies can only pursue something as expensive and dangerous as the nuclear arms race when public opinion fun-damentally supports it. Accordingly, the armed forces devote substantial funds to public relations, and governments use current events to whip up support for military spending. For example, the So-viet downing of a Korean airliner in 1983 was used by the Reagan administration to generate congres-sional votes in favor of the MX missile, even though the administration knew that the incident had oc-curred because of a Soviet error rather than overt hostility. Even political liberals have been wary of being branded as "soft on communism" or "soft on defense," and as a result, the nuclear policies of Democratic and Republican administrations have not been notably different.

IDEOLOGIES

The United States and the U.S.S.R. are distin-guished by a variety of ideological differences. Most importantly, the U.S.S.R. is a communist state; the United States is capitalist. The U.S.S.R. is officially atheistic; although religion is permitted, the state is not sympathetic, and has engaged in some forms of persecution. By contrast, although the United States officially espouses the doctrine of separation of church and state, in fact religion plays a relatively

prominent role in public life. The United States is a representative democracy; the U.S.S.R. is a one-party state, although it is becoming increasingly democratic. In the United States, the state promises to refrain from undue restriction of private free-doms; in the U.S.S.R., the state promises to provide a range of social services.

Pragmatism in Soviet Policies

Perhaps most provocative is the Marxist doctrine of class struggle, which predicts and justifies revolu-tionary violence to overthrow capitalism. Leon Trotsky, military commander of the Red forces in the Russian civil war, had been confident that worldwide revolution would follow the success of the Bolshevik Revolution. It is one thing, however, to believe in the ultimate triumph of one's ideology, and quite another to promote its success via warfare. (After all, most Americans believe that ultimately, democracy and free enterprise will triumph.) Furthermore, many Americans have not understood that the Twentieth Communist Party Congress (1963), presided over by Nikita Khru-shchev, rejected the doctrine that war between cap-italist and communist states is inevitable. Current Soviet thinking emphasizes that Lenin's theories were developed when socialism was very weak and capitalism was all-powerful and threatening. ("All events in world politics," Lenin once wrote, "are necessarily concentrated against the Russian Soviet republic."[12]) But the Soviet state now sees itself as having become powerful enough to restrain the capitalists and imperialists from unleashing war.

The U.S.S.R., moreover, has had dreadful ex-periences in recent wars, with more than 20 million deaths in World War II alone; virtually every family in the Soviet Union suffered direct personal losses in that war. By contrast, the United States lost "only" about 350,000 lives, less than one sixtieth of the Soviet level, and in addition, no fighting took place on the U.S. mainland. As a result, the Soviet Union is likely to be, if anything, more war-averse than the United States, and, as far as can be told, even more sensitive to the dangers posed by nuclear weapons.

Despite the attention given to Marxist theory, there is reason to think that pragmatism has always been more important. Stalin, for example, was much more interested in power than in ideology, communist or otherwise. He was able to reach accommodations with democratic Finland, and sought (unsuccessfully) to ally himself with the right-wing Romanian monarchy, because these groups presented themselves as potentially useful; on the other hand, he was, at best, lukewarm about Chinese communists and outright hostile to Yugoslav communists, because these groups refused to do his bidding. For Stalin, communist orthodoxy was a means to an end, that end being the power of the Soviet state. At the same time, his opponents in the United States—who took Leninist ideology more seriously than he did—tried to interpret Soviet actions in terms of that doctrine. To some extent, this has continued to the present day, in which Soviet leadership, although much less ruthless than Stalin, has become no less pragmatic and, if anything, even less ideological.

After a period of relative stagnation under Leonid Brezhnev, followed by the very brief leaderships of Yuri Andropov and Constantin Chernenko, Mikhail Gorbachev came to power in 1985, embarking upon a policy of both "perestroika" (restructuring) and "glasnost" (openness). There have also been notable changes in ideology, building upon Khrushchev's earlier revisionism. According to traditional Marxist-Leninist doctrine, global peace will come only after the capitalist system is destroyed. According to Gorbachev, however, the danger of nuclear war has given all people, regardless of political ideology, a "real, not speculative and remote, common human interest"[13] in survival. Ideological, political, and economic competition between East and West will continue, but "it can and must be kept within a framework of peaceful competition which necessarily envisages cooperation."[14] Class competition—the foundation of Marxist theory—has now reached an "objective limit" that has destroyed the "cause and effect relationship between war and revolution."[15] And the old dialectic of class conflicts and war is to be sup-

planted by "a new dialectic of the common human and class interests and principles in our modern age."[16] The change, if real, could hardly be more dramatic, or more important.

Revolution

Nonetheless, communism is an ideology not only of sharing and utopian classlessness, but also of revolution. Revolution and violence were widely acknowledged to be the means of achieving the communist end, and as Lenin is reported to have commented, "you can't make a revolution wearing white gloves." U.S. opposition to communism as a system has been combined, often uncritically, with fear of communist-inspired revolution, and from its inception, Bolshevism (at least in the United States) was confused with unacceptable revolutionary violence.

It should be noted that the United States also has a revolutionary heritage. Included in the Declaration of Independence is the concept that, among various "self-evident" truths, people have certain inalienable rights, and that

> to secure these rights, governments are instituted among men, deriving their just power from the consent of the governed; that whenever any form of government becomes destructive of these ends, it is the right of the people to alter or to abolish it, and to institute new government, laying its foundation on such principles, and organizing its powers in such form as to them shall seem most likely to effect their safety and happiness.

A subsequent passage goes even farther, and affirms that, when governments behave unacceptably, it is not only the people's right, but also "their duty, to throw off such government." The United States has therefore faced a quandary (although one that has rarely been debated in front of the electorate): On the one hand, it is allied with most of the former colonial powers—Britain, France, Germany, Belgium, Holland, Portugal, Japan—and has had colonial holdings itself. The United States nonetheless prides itself on favoring self-determination and democracy. And yet, the U.S.S.R. has typically become allied with anticolonial nationalism, and the United States, with maintaining the status quo, often with the help of right-wing despots.

Leading up to what was our own war of independence, note this prorevolutionary oratory from Patrick Henry, rhetoric that is not only part of the cultural background of the United States, but also a vivid statement of what, in some people's minds, has become transformed into "better dead than Red":

> Gentlemen may cry peace, peace—but there is no peace. Is life so dear, or peace so sweet, as to be purchased at the price of chains and slavery? I know not what course others may take, but as for me, give me liberty or give me death.[17]

Within the United States, liberals in particular have had to make difficult choices between espousing the virtues of peace and the merits of freedom. Conservatives are generally more eager to claim support for the latter. In a world of nuclear weapons, however, we need to distinguish between the willingness to fight and risk one's own death and the willingness to bring about the deaths of everyone.

Ideological Self-Justification

The issues of freedom and its defense are important, however, because the working belief of certain influential U.S. ideologues is that communism equates with slavery, and moreover, that communism is—perhaps uniquely—a fundamentally immoral and illegal doctrine that espouses the use of force and violence. Hence, military actions against communism are seen as necessarily defensive, preventative, and justified, both legally and morally. Communist doctrine can, however, be considered less provocative than capitalist/democratic doctrine, in that orthodox Marxism sees communism as a historical inevitability, with capitalism being a predictable stage through which society will pass on the way to a world free of classes, and thus, free of war. "Our aim," wrote Lenin, "is to achieve a socialist system of society, which, by eliminating the division of mankind into classes, by eliminating all exploitation of man by man and nation by nation, will inevitably eliminate the very possibility of war."[18] Just as feudalism gave way to capitalism, capitalism can be expected to give way, eventually, to communism. The use of force, accordingly, might speed things along, but it will not change history significantly. By contrast, whereas communism sees capitalism as a necessary evil, although a transitional one, capitalism is prone to see communism as an unnecessary evil, and hence something that should be expunged.

In its own way, the United States is no less aggressively ideologic than the U.S.S.R. As an immigrant nation, the United States does not find its identity in ethnicity, or even in shared historical experience, so much as in shared values and dedication to those values. American society owes its cohesion to a kind of nineteenth-century liberal creed: freedom, democracy, and capitalism. The United States has also had its own version of messianic ideology, the determination that it has something uniquely wonderful to offer everyone else. John Winthrop, eventually governor of the Massachusetts Bay colony, wrote in 1630 that "We must consider that we shall be as a city upon the hill. The eyes of all people are upon us."[19] With its developing qualities of religious freedom, entrepreneurial economic success, representative democracy, abolition of hereditary aristocracy, and attainment of political independence, the United States came to think that it had a mission (perhaps divinely inspired) to share its system with the rest of the benighted world.

On occasion, U.S. ambitions have not differed significantly from the ardent and expansionistic communism of Lenin's war minister Trotsky, who so alarmed the West. Thus, Woodrow Wilson sought to "make the world safe for democracy," a phrase that sounded benign enough to most Americans. But imagine the U.S. response to a Soviet declaration that the U.S.S.R. was dedicated to "making the world safe for communism," especially if this accompanied a declaration of war. In his war

John Foster Dulles, Secretary of State during much of the Eisenhower Administration, conferring with President Eisenhower (left). Dulles was one of the most uncompromising proponents of the Cold War during the 1950s. (Dwight D. Eisenhower Library)

message of 1917, Wilson added: "We have no selfish ends to serve. We desire no conquest, no dominion. We seek no indemnities for ourselves, no material compensation for the sacrifices we shall freely make. We are but one of the champions of mankind."[20]

John Foster Dulles (secretary of state under Dwight Eisenhower) unblushingly divided the world into good (the United States and its allies) and bad (the U.S.S.R. and its allies), leaving no room for neutrals, which were considered immoral because of their failure to choose between good and bad. The American ideological crusade may have reached its peak during the presidency of Ronald Reagan, who unabashedly called the U.S.S.R. an "evil empire," and the "focus of evil in the modern world," and who saw virtually every dispute and indication of international dissatisfaction as proof of Soviet meddling. At the same time, a strain of realpolitik, if not real accommodation, has persisted, reflected in various efforts at arms control (see Chapter 15), as well as the policy of detente initiated by Henry Kissinger and Richard Nixon and rekindled in the remarkable warming of U.S.-Soviet relations during the final years of the Reagan administration.

The assumptions of communism and of democratic capitalism — in addition to the fervor with which they are espoused — make their ideologies especially troublesome, resembling religious fundamentalism in their universalism (confidence that the ideology can apply anywhere, to anyone) and singularism (certainty that each is the only acceptable solution). A particular challenge to Peace Studies, therefore, is to articulate alternative visions for the world, involving some mixture of the two prevalent secular ideologies, or maybe entirely different systems.

Ideology Versus Realpolitik

Finally, there is another way of viewing the fundamental U.S.-Soviet competition: that it is not really ideologic at all, but rather, a realpolitik result of the nation-state system. Thus, conflicting ideologies have not prevented a Sino-American rapprochment, just as shared ideology did not prevent war between (communist) China and Vietnam, or between (right-wing capitalist) El Salvador and Honduras. Perhaps the announced ideologies are merely so much window dressing, covering and seeking to justify what is after all the same kind of "Big Power" competition that has occurred in one form or another for hundreds of years. Since 1945, the world has had two notable Big Powers, but in many ways these two states have jockeyed for position just like their predecessors, whose immediate motivation was especially religious (the Thirty Years' War), or colonial (the Seven Years' War), or over the role of monarchies and nationalism (the Napoleonic Wars). Given that the United States and the Soviet Union are today the two superpowers, perhaps it is not surprising that they have found something to quarrel about, and that they have claimed that this quarrel has profound moral implications.

Continuation of the Vietnam War, for example, was sold to the American people as a moral crusade against international communism. And yet, in a secret memorandum within the Defense Department, the U.S. goals in Vietnam were spelled out as follows: "70 percent — to avoid a humiliating U.S. defeat; 20 percent — to keep South Vietnamese territory from Chinese hands; 10 percent — to permit the people of South Vietnam to enjoy a better, freer way of life."[21]

Imagine that the United States and the U.S.S.R. adhered not to communism and capitalism/democracy, but rather to a different pair of ideologies, perhaps wholly compatible ones. Their post-1945 behavior still might not have been substantially different from what has occurred, with each side laying claim to areas that its armies "liberated," and each side seeking advantages over the other (such as the support of uncommitted countries), as well as various other forms of competition including even an arms race. In short, maybe a large part of the U.S.-Soviet dispute isn't really about ideology at all, but rather about two large, powerful, and competitive states that have not yet learned how to tolerate each other's presence.

INTERVENTIONISM

Mirror Images?

Each side in the superpower rivalry is intensely aware of the military interventions conducted by the other, typically describing these as proof of the other's aggressive, expansionist, and untrustworthy nature. Similarly, each sees its own interventions as laudable, defensive, and at worst, forced by the aggressive designs of others. For example, in 1965, the United States sent 25,000 marines to the Dominican Republic to foil an effort to restore the presidency of democratically elected Juan Bosch, who had previously been ousted in a right-wing military coup. Bosch had been the first popularly elected Dominican leader following decades of tyranny under the U.S.-backed dictator Rafael Trujillo. The Soviet Union expressed outrage at this American intervention in the affairs of another sovereign state . . . which had essentially been a U.S. satellite and was kept that way by military force.

Three years later, the U.S.S.R. invaded Czechoslovakia, to prevent the liberalization of communism in that country . . . which had essentially been a Soviet satellite and was kept that way by military force. Just as President Johnson was said to fear "another Castro" in the Dominican Republic, the Soviet leadership was worried about "another Tito" (the independent-minded nationalist leader of Yugoslavia) in Prague. Not surprisingly, the United States expressed outrage at the Soviet action, and U.S. officials made self-righteous speeches criticizing superpower interventionism and supporting the sovereignty of other states, just as Soviet officials had denounced the U.S. intervention in the Dominican Republic.

The U.S. citizenry is accustomed to thinking of the Soviet Union as having brutally invaded its neighbors and suppressing dissent; in fact, they have done just that, notably in Hungary, Czechoslovakia, and Afghanistan. We are less familiar with another perspective, which suggests that the United States has been no less inclined to seek to impose its will on others. Americans warn of the dangers of "Finlandization," the process whereby a smaller, weaker neighbor of the U.S.S.R. feels constrained to avoid any foreign policy that might antagonize its neighbor. They don't think very much, however, about "Canadization."* They rightly criticize the Soviet Union for annexing the Baltic states, for example, but rarely blame the United States for dismembering Mexico in the nineteenth century, annexing what became California, Arizona, New Mexico, and ultimately, Texas.

As long ago as 1927, widely respected political commentator Walter Lippmann (not considered to have been radical or even left-leaning) wrote:

> All the world thinks of the United States today as an empire, except the people of the United States. We

---

*Imagine, for example, the likely U.S. response if Canada — ostensibly an independent, sovereign state — decided to make bases available for Soviet medium-range nuclear missiles.

shrink from the world "empire," and insist that it should not be used to describe the dominion we exercise from Alaska to the Philippines, from Cuba to Panama, and beyond. We feel that there ought to be some other name for the civilizing work which we do so reluctantly in these backward countries.[22]

Realpolitik Rears Its Head

To some extent, both superpowers carry out the "civilizing work" of interventionism in pursuit of their ideological goals. Even more so, the major motivation is undoubtedly realpolitik: economic and political power. In the early 1960s, when the U.S. military budget was about $50 billion (it is now about $300 billion), an aide to Defense Secretary McNamara commented:

> How much do we really need for the defense of the United States of America? The maximum for the defense of our shore is one billion dollars. So all the rest of our defense budget relates to what we regard as our responsibilities as a world power.[23]

In a 1975 speech, Henry Kissinger gave voice to the peculiarly American certainty that on its shoulders lies the responsibility to police the world: "We cannot escape the fundamental reality that it is the United States, alone among the free nations of the world, that is capable of — and therefore responsible for — maintaining the global balance against those who would seek hegemony."[24]

As a result of the "Vietnam syndrome," efforts to maintain this "global balance" have involved an increasing emphasis on so-called low-intensity conflicts, notably counterinsurgency efforts in countries such as El Salvador and Nicaragua, as well as the active support — and in some cases, the outright creation — of insurgencies in Nicaragua, Afghanistan, Angola, and, to a lesser extent, Cambodia. Such conflicts are less visible to the voting public than outright traditional warfare, and since they involve the livelihoods — and lives — of inhabitants of other lands, they are less likely to provoke domestic controversy. On the other hand, they are not cheap: In 1987 alone, the United States sent $660 million in military aid to the Afghan *mujahedeen,*

and between 1981 and 1986, $1.7 billion to El Salvador, 74 percent of which was in direct or indirect support of that government's war efforts. The CIA and National Security Council each have budgets that are significantly higher than that of the U.S. State Department.

There have been very few direct military confrontations between the United States and the Soviet Union. And yet, as former Canadian prime minister Pierre Trudeau noted, the superpowers "breathe an atmosphere common to themselves, and share a global perception according to which even remote events can threaten their interests or their associates."[25] As a result, both superpowers think nothing of defying the ostensible sovereignty of Third World states whenever they consider that such intervention is in their own national interest. As a result, they have often confronted each other competitively in the Third World, typically using local forces — or occasionally, mercenaries — as proxies. A pastoral letter from the Catholic bishops of Nicaragua complained in 1984 that

> foreign powers are taking advantage of our situation to promote economic and ideological exploitation. They view us as adjuncts to their own power, without respect for our persons, our history, our culture and our right to determine our own destiny.[26]

The results, as in Nicaragua, are often bloody and destructive. Advocates of such policies typically justify them as "supporting democracy" (the U.S. line) or "providing fraternal assistance to fellow socialists" (the Soviet claim). Former Defense Secretary Caspar Weinberger, at least, was more direct when he criticized the "pernicious sophistries of those who wish to construe these wars as the efforts of sovereign people to pursue their own destinies and as such, no business of our own."[27]

On the U.S. side, indigenous dissatisfactions and aspirations have consistently been seen through an ideological lens that shows all internal discontent as part of the larger U.S.-Soviet competition. The result has been a continuing pattern of heavy-handed intervention in Third World societies, often involving the sponsorship of vicious dictators as

Young, hungry Palestinian boy is about to be fed at a refugee camp. Both the U.S. and the U.S.S.R. emphasize military aid in their "foreign assistance" programs, which are far more influenced by East–West competition than by recipients' need. (United Nations)

long as they claim to be anticommunist. Thus, during his 1984 presidential debate with Walter Mondale, President Reagan justified continuing support for Ferdinand Marcos in the Philippines by claiming that the only alternative to his oppressive dictatorship would be a communist takeover (the success of Corazon Aquino just two years later proved otherwise). Political conservatives have similarly justified continuing support for apartheid in South Africa by maintaining that full rights for blacks would somehow result in a Soviet-sponsored takeover.

Things have changed little since Hans Morgenthau, in an article accusing the United States of being "repression's friend," observed that

with unfailing consistency, we have since the end of the Second World War intervened on behalf of conservative and fascist repression against revolution and radical reform. In an age when societies are in a revolutionary or prerevolutionary stage, we have become the foremost counterrevolutionary status quo power on earth. Such a policy can only lead to . . . disaster.[28]

Both superpowers also try to remake Third World economies in their image. A 1986 publication of the Agency for International Development (AID), a government agency that oversees U.S. economic aid abroad, included this message from President Reagan: "We already know what works: private ownership, the freedom to innovate, reliance on market forces, and faith in the strength and inventiveness of the individual citizen." Foreign aid generally, economic as well as military, has been used by both superpowers to bend others to their will. In 1985, for example, AID held up food shipments to Kenya for several months until the Kenyan government agreed to let the private sector see to its distribution. On the other hand, foreign assistance may fail: Billions of U.S. dollars did not save the shah of Iran, or Ferdinand Marcos of the Philippines, and after investing heavily in Egypt—including construction of the multi-million dollar Aswan Dam—Soviet influence in Egypt was abruptly terminated in the early 1970s.

The superpowers also seek to intervene in each other's internal affairs (in addition to spying, which is done, but denied, by both). Thus, the United States has severely criticized the Soviet Union for denying "human rights" to its citizens, by which the critics especially mean political pluralism, freedom of expression, and freedom to emigrate. Soviet government spokespersons respond by berating the United States for what they see as failures in "human rights," as shown by unemployment, racism, poverty, and extreme disparities in wealth and opportunity. Americans point to their freedom of expression; Soviets point to their free health care and education and subsidized food and housing. In the Soviet view, society has an obligation to provide what have been called "positive rights," including the "right" to an education, to medical care, to a job, and so on. By contrast, the U.S. perspective emphasizes a governmental duty to provide "negative rights," guarantees as to what the government will *not* do: abridge freedom of speech, the press, or religion, or the opportunity for entrepreneurs to try to make a profit in their own way, with minimal interference by the authorities (see Chapter 20).

At present, Soviet leaders find it easier than their Western counterparts to admit that such elements are provocative to the other side. State sovereignty dictates that the internal affairs of one superpower are not legitimate concerns for the other. But in fact, much of the two superpower's hostility derives from distrust of each other's political and social system. It would be a boost for peace if each side could seek to restrain the unpleasant excesses of its own system. For the Soviets, this means Stalinism, with its political and intellectual repression, and occasional resort to state-sponsored terror; for the United States, it is a kind of neo-fascism, combining Big Business with Big Religion and hyperpatriotism, along with high levels of unemployment, homelessness, racism, and the perpetuation of privilege.

Although some people in the United States—notably extreme conservatives—maintain that the United States is best served when the U.S.S.R. is relatively backward, poor, and dissatisfied, most recognize that prospects for peace will increase with a moderate and reforming Soviet Union, one that permits the exercise of increasing personal freedoms. By the same token, continued evolution of the United States toward a more caring and socially conscious society seems likely to be welcomed by our Soviet counterparts as suggesting that Uncle Sam is something other than a rapacious imperialist and heartless industrialist, with a boot firmly planted on the neck of the proletariat.

Finally, the resolution of U.S.-Soviet issues can only be helped by attention to one single, overriding fact, as emphasized by George Kennan: "There is no issue at stake in our political relations with the Soviet Union—no hope, no fear, nothing to which we aspire, nothing we would like to avoid—which could conceivably be worth a nuclear war."[29]

A FINAL NOTE ON THE SUPERPOWER RIVALRY

Of all the potential causes of war, those involving the superpowers are undoubtedly the most dangerous. French social philosopher Raymond Aron once suggested that the Cold War is founded on the impossibility of peace and the improbability of war. The overriding task for Peace Studies is to make war as improbable as possible, and to help identify conditions that will make peace not only possible, but also likely, not only between the U.S. and the U.S.S.R., but also among all people.

Study Questions

1. To what extent was the Cold War foreshadowed in U.S.-Soviet relations from 1918 until World War II?

2. Who is to "blame" for the Cold War that followed World War II? Support your argument.

3. What was meant by "containment"? How did it influence foreign policy?

4. Define *detente*. What did it achieve, and what caused its demise by the late 1970s?

5. Describe the phenomenon of "threat inflation" as it influenced the nuclear arms race.

6. Distinguish internal and external causes of the arms race. In what ways are these connected?

7. What is the relationship between action–reaction sequences and worst-case scenarios?

8. Interservice rivalries have had an influence on the importance that the U.S. Air Force and the Navy have attributed to counterforce. Explain.

9. Conflicting ideologies have fueled the superpower rivalry, and yet, in some ways the United States and the U.S.S.R. have acted in ways similar to the eighteenth-century Great Powers, which were not separated by ideological differences. Explain.

10. Should the United States seek to support the liberalization of Soviet society undertaken by Mikhail Gorbachev? Why or why not?

Suggestions for Further Reading

George F. Kennan. 1982. *The Nuclear Delusion: Soviet-American Relations in the Atomic Age*. Pantheon: New York.

Mark Garrison and Abbott Gleason (eds.). 1985. *Shared Destiny: Fifty Years of Soviet-American Relations*. Beacon Press: Boston.

Stephen F. Cohen. 1986. *Sovieticus: American Perceptions and Soviet Realities*. Norton: New York.

Daniel Nelson and Roger B. Anderson (eds.). 1988. *Soviet-American Relations*. Scholarly Resources Books: Wilmington, DE.

Padma Desai. 1989. *Perestroika in Perspective*. Princeton University Press: Princeton, NJ.

Source Notes

1. Winston Churchill. 1948. *The Sinews of Peace: Post-War Speeches*. Houghton Mifflin: Boston.

2. Quoted in Margaret L. Coit. 1957. *Mr. Baruch*. Houghton Mifflin: Boston.

3. Speech by Senator Robert A. Taft, Eighty-First Congress, first session.

4. George F. Kennan. 1987. "Containment Then and Now." *Foreign Affairs*, 65: 885–890.

5. Thomas C. Schelling. 1966. *Arms and Influence*. Yale University Press: New Haven, CT.

6. Quoted in Lawrence Freedman. 1981. *The Evolution of Nuclear Strategy*. St. Martin's: New York.

7. Robert McNamara. 1968. *The Essence of Security*. Harper & Row: New York.

8. Quoted in Alan Geyer. 1982. *The Idea of Disarmament!* Brethren Press: Elgin, IL.

9. Quoted in Freedman. *Evolution*.

10. Joseph Gerson (ed.). 1986. *The Deadly Connection: Nuclear War and U.S. Intervention*. New Society Publishers: Philadelphia.

11. Quoted in Michael Parenti. 1989. *The Sword and the Dollar*. St. Martin's: New York.

12. Quoted in R. W. Clark. 1988. *Lenin, The Man Behind the Mask*. Faber: London.

13. Mikhail Gorbachev. 1987. *Perestroika: New Thinking for Our Country and the World*. Harper & Row: New York.

14. Ibid.

15. Ibid.

16. Ibid.

17. Quoted in Robert D. Meade. 1969. *Patrick Henry: Patriot in the Making*. Lippincott: Philadelphia, PA.

18. Quoted in P. H. Vigor. 1975. *The Soviet View of War, Peace and Neutrality*. Routledge & Kegan Paul: London.

19. Quoted in Robert C. Black. 1966. *The Younger John Winthrop*. Columbia University Press: New York.

20. Woodrow Wilson. 1965. *A Day of Dedication*. Macmillan: New York.

21. 1971. *The Pentagon Papers*. Quadrangle: New York.

22. Walter Lippmann. 1927. *Men of Destiny*. Macmillan: New York.

23. Quoted in Geyer. *Idea*.

24. Quoted in G. Cleva. 1989. *Henry Kissinger and the American Approach to Foreign Policy*. Associated University Presses: Cranbury, NJ.

25. Pierre Elliot Trudeau. 1983. "Reflections of Peace and Security." *Vital Speeches* 50: 100.

26. Reported in the *Washington Post*, May 12, 1986.

27. Speech given at Ft. McNair, Washington, DC, January 14, 1986.

28. *The New York Times*, October 10, 1974.

29. George Kennan. 1982. *The Nuclear Delusion*. Pantheon: New York.

Unidentified Chinese man standing in front of a column of tanks headed for Tiananmen Square in 1989. He stopped their advance and pleaded for an end to the killing; eventually, he was pulled away by bystanders and the tanks continued on their way. (Bettman Archive)

III

Building "Negative Peace"— *(THE AVOIDANCE OF WAR)*

We have now taken a tour through the causes of war. Specialists in war and its immense complexity may complain that our sojourn was altogether too brief and superficial; specialists in peace, on the other hand, may complain that it was too detailed, and that our focus should be elsewhere . . . on peace. My own feeling is that the avoidance of war — that is, the building of "negative peace" — is too important to be left to the professionals in government, strategic studies, international relations, political science, or any combination of these disciplines. At the same time, the establishment of "positive peace" is also too important to be left to whimsical dreams, on the one hand, or to the tumult of the streets, on the other. Similarly, it is too important to be sacrificed by insufficient attention to the prevention of war.

Throughout history, people have recognized the absurdity and horror of war, even as they have engaged in it. There has been no shortage of proposed solutions to the problems posed by war. The simplest solution, perhaps, can be derived from the "war on drugs": Just say No. But as in that other "war," this turns out to be no solution at all. Although seemingly straightforward moral judgments and outright condemnation undeniably are appealing, most nations have been no more able to go "cold turkey" on war than individuals have on drugs.

Mark Twain once noted that it was easy to stop smoking . . . he had done it many times. Similarly, it has been easy to prevent war — many different solutions have been proposed, and some of them have even been implemented (to varying degrees).

Perhaps these solutions are not sufficiently innovative, or forward-thinking, or creative. And others may not be practical or altogether feasible. Perhaps the problem is that no one solution has been pushed hard and far enough. Or perhaps war is still with us because these various solutions have not been attempted in the right combination, or with the right variation or nuance. Perhaps they actually are working, only slowly, so that peace — like President Herbert Hoover's claim about prosperity during the Great Depression — is just around the corner. On the other hand, perhaps they have not and will not, so that something else will be needed. If so, let us hope that by reviewing the distilled wisdom of humanity's efforts to prevent war, we can at least save peacemakers of the future from repeating the errors of the past. And maybe, we can inspire greater efforts, and achieve greater success, in the days to come.

"War is waged," wrote St. Augustine, "so that peace may prevail. . . . But it is a greater glory to slay war with a word than people with a sword, and to gain peace by means of peace and not by means of war."[1] In the following six chapters, we shall examine efforts to gain peace by means of peace. It is no easy quest. As General Omar Bradley put it:

The problem of peaceful accommodation in the world is infinitely more difficult than the conquest of space, infinitely more complex than a trip to the moon. . . . If I am sometimes discouraged, it is not by the magnitude of the problem, but by our colossal indifference to it. I am unable to understand why . . . we do not make greater, more diligent and more imaginative use of reason and human intelligence in seeking an accord and compromise which will make it possible for mankind to control the atom and banish it as an instrument of war.[2]

His words apply equally well to the more general problem of war itself, conventional no less than nuclear. What, then, does human reason and intelligence have to offer by way of preventing war and creating peace?

"There is no way to peace," wrote the great pacifist A. J. Muste, "peace is the way." But if we are to follow it, the way to peace must at least be discerned, even if dimly. And like the blind men and the causes of war, the causes of peace are also multifaceted. Most likely, just as no one body part defines an elephant, there is no one way to peace but rather many ways . . . some of which might lead down blind alleys, some to dangerous cliffs, and others to yet more paths, each with additional branching points and an unending series of twists and turns. In Part III, we shall walk a short way down some of the most prominent of these paths.

13

Diplomacy, Negotiations, and Conflict Resolution

We have met the enemy and he is us.
   Pogo

Disagreements must be settled, not by force, not by deceit or trickery, but rather in the only manner which is worthy of the dignity of man, i.e., by a mutual assessment of the reasons on both sides of the dispute, by a mature and objective investigation of the situation, and by an equitable reconciliation of differences of opinion.
   Pope John XXIII

One way of gaining peace "by means of peace and not by means of war" is for the contending sides in a dispute to reach a mutually acceptable agreement among themselves. When such agreements or understandings are obtained among states, we say that "diplomacy" has taken place; it may be defined as "the art of resolving disputes between states by highly skilled communication between the trained representatives of governments."[1] The people who practice this art are known as diplomats. (Of course, there is a less positive view of diplomats that defines them as "honest men sent abroad to lie for their country."[2])

Peace researcher Anatol Rapaport has made a useful distinction between fights, games, and debates.[3] In a fight, the intent is to defeat the opponent, sometimes even to destroy him or her. Rules may exist, as in a prizefight, but they may also be ignored, as in a street fight or a particularly vicious war, and in any event, the actual fight is likely to be violent. In a game, by contrast, each side tries to outwit the opponent, playing strictly within the rules. And in a debate, the goal is to persuade the opponent of the justice or correctness of one's cause. The process of conflict resolution, ideally, is closest to a debate, just as wars are fights, although with some aspects of a game as well. However, even diplomacy and negotiations involve the elaborate rules of complex games, not uncommonly backed up by the threat of fighting as well.

Although ways of fighting have changed through history, the basic techniques of negotiations scarcely have. At their most contentious, negotiators have two things they can offer: threats and promises. (As we shall see, an important recent insight adds a third option, a shared willingness to identify the problem and engage in creative problem solving.) Conflict resolution can be backed up by varying degrees of goodwill or ill will, and based on a continuum from blind trust to iron-clad verification and/or arm-twisting. Negotiations, however, can succeed only if a set of outcomes exists that each party prefers to reaching no agreement. Whereas the participants in a dispute (especially if they are governments) occasionally engage in negotiations just to appear virtuous, there is good reason to think that, in most cases at least, a negotiated settlement is preferred—at least in theory—over either a failure to agree or the use of violence to force an outcome. The trick is to find a peaceful settlement that will be acceptable to all sides.

In the course of seeking to achieve agreements and resolve disputes short of violence, the contending parties typically try to obtain the most favorable outcome possible for their side. The process of give-and-take, and the strategies for succeeding—in reaching an agreement, and also getting the best outcome—involves skill at negotiating. This applies both to the governments in question and, frequently, to third parties who are called in to help the disputants reach an agreement. Techniques for successful negotiations therefore can contribute greatly to the peaceful resolution of conflicts. And finally, in our search for various routes toward peace, we must ultimately consider the phenomenon of conflict resolution more generally, not only in the international sphere, but also with respect to domestic antagonisms, examining interpersonal as well as intrapsychic efforts at resolving conflict.

It is important to realize how often we negotiate solutions to conflict, typically on the interpersonal level. Disagreements among siblings over who gets to sit in a given chair, or within families over what television program to watch, or between co-workers over whether or not to have an office party, or between landlord and tenant over repairs and rent—these disputes are nearly always resolved, and in most cases short of violence. This fact highlights the many routes available for dealing with conflict; it is something we do every day. And yet, one of the most pervasive myths of our current culture of militarism is that war and preparation for war are natural, unavoidable phenomena, whereas peace and preparation for peace are hopelessly unrealistic activities. We are surrounded with subliminal messages to the effect that peacemaking is an impossible dream, whereas warmaking—or at best, deterrence—is the only reality. Hence, it is important to affirm and make visible the peacemaking that happens all around us, most of the time. It is only when individual peacemaking takes place at the highest government level that it receives society's attention.

SUMMITRY

In ancient times, leaders were themselves renowned warriors, and sometimes, they would meet person-to-person, to settle their disputes via individual combat. On occasion, at least according to folklore, champions would be selected, one from each side, to fight it out: The classic example is David versus Goliath. More recently, leaders have tended to be political figures, and in their meetings have sought to help establish or cement relationships, or to engage personally in a resolution of disputes between their countries (while also playing to their domestic constituencies).

When the leaders of two major groups meet, this is referred to as a summit meeting. There have been many; for example, Nixon's meeting with Mao Ze-dong in 1972 was especially dramatic, as was Egyptian president Sadat's journey to Jerusalem and his meeting with Israeli prime minister Begin. In both these cases, the states involved had previously been bitter enemies, so antagonistic, in fact, that they were not even communicating with each

President Eisenhower (left) and Soviet Premier Khrushchev at Camp David, Md., just before their summit meeting in 1955. (Dwight D. Eisenhower Library)

perhaps improving the international atmosphere, but offering few if any specific changes, and thereby often disappointing those who had hoped for more. The 1955 summit meeting between Nikita Khrushchev and Dwight Eisenhower falls into this category, as does the 1985 meeting between Mikhail Gorbachev and Ronald Reagan in Geneva. At other times, minor progress has been achieved, largely by signing agreements that diplomats had laboriously worked out in advance: the 1972 summit between Richard Nixon and Leonid Brezhnev, for example, at which the SALT I agreement was signed, or the 1987 meeting in Washington, DC, between Mikhail Gorbachev and Ronald Reagan at which the INF agreement was signed.

It should be pointed out, however, that summit meetings occasionally have made things worse, resulting either in feelings of ill will or in dangerous misjudgments by one or both parties. An example of the former is the 1986 summit meeting between Gorbachev and Reagan in Reykjavik, Iceland, which terminated in animosity and subsequent claims by each side that the other misunderstood and/or misrepresented what had transpired. Similarly, a summit meeting between John F. Kennedy and Nikita Khrushchev in Vienna in 1961 apparently was a personal embarrassment for the younger, less experienced American, and it may have led to Khrushchev's inaccurate estimation that the U.S. president could be pushed around (thus setting the stage for the Cuban Missile Crisis the following year). It may also have contributed to Kennedy's determination that he would be especially tough in the future.

Summit meetings notwithstanding, it is not even necessarily true that closer relations and greater communication among world leaders will make war less likely. Kaiser Wilhelm of Germany and Czar Nicholas of Russia, for example, were first cousins, and on the very eve of World War I were exchanging telegrams signed "Willy" and "Nicky"! Summit meetings and personal relationships, in short, can be helpful, but they can also cause problems, depending on the issues and the personal dynamics between the leaders, or provide only an illusion of warmth and understanding.

other. Hence, the mere fact that political leaders were meeting together and talking amicably sent a powerful signal about the possibilities of peaceful coexistence.

Often, however, the term *summit* is reserved for meetings between the two most elevated leaders, those of the two superpowers, the United States and the U.S.S.R. Here, too, it is widely thought that if only the leaders could meet and talk over their disagreements, as intelligent and concerned human beings, then peace would result. Unfortunately, no legitimate reasons exist for believing this. In some cases, summit meetings have been merely cosmetic,

Summit meeting between President John F. Kennedy and Soviet Premier Nikita Khrushchev in Vienna, in 1961. Soviet Foreign Minister Andrei Gromyko is at the far right. (John F Kennedy Library)

A BRIEF HISTORY OF DIPLOMACY

In the past, diplomats were drawn from the same social and economic class (upper), and they spoke the same language, not only figuratively but also literally (French). Although monarchs throughout history have sent ambassadors to the courts of other rulers, it is generally agreed that the current system of diplomatic protocol was established by Cardinal Richelieu, chief minister—some would say, chief manipulator—of the early seventeenth-century French king Louis XIII.

The peculiar stiffness and formality of official diplomatic discourse and protocol have evolved over many years, so as to enhance precision of communication and, whenever possible, reduce the chances that personalities will interfere with formal and serious communication between governments. Historically, ambassadors were the personal repre-

sentatives of one sovereign to the court of another, and that polite fiction is still maintained, even in the case of democracies: Upon their arrival, ambassadors typically present their credentials to the head of state of the host country. In modern times, electronic communication has largely superceded the functions of the individual diplomat when it comes to the establishment of important international agreements, but as we shall see, the role of person-to-person contact, even at the highest levels, remains important.

Ironically, states communicate with one another least frequently and least clearly during war ... precisely when such communication is likely to be the most important. At such times, and occasionally when interactions become severely strained during peacetime, diplomatic relations are broken off, and each state recalls its ambassador. Otherwise, officials are available to correct possible misunderstandings, clarify positions, and, when all else fails, simply to buy time, perhaps in the hope that tensions will eventually ease. As we shall see, diplomacy has failed in many cases; however, there have also been successes.

Some Diplomatic Successes in Averting War

In 1987, Indian military exercises near the Pakistan border alarmed the Pakistanis, whose forces were mobilized in response. Soon, over 300,000 armed men were facing one another across a border that had known substantial violence in the past. Tensions gradually eased, however, due to urgent diplomatic exchanges between the two sides; among other things, both agreed (verbally) to refrain from attacks against the other's nuclear facilities. Also in 1987, Greece and Turkey exchanged threats over Turkish plans to prospect for oil near several islands in the eastern Aegean that were under Greek ownership but very close to the Turkish mainland. Like India and Pakistan, these two states also had a long history of antagonism and warfare. (Greece was long dominated by Turkey, as part of the Ottoman empire, and more recently, the two states had engaged in threats as well as fighting over the fate of Greek and Turkish ethnic nationals on the island of Cyprus.) Once again, tensions were gradually cooled, at least in part because both sides feared to antagonize their NATO ally, the United States, and face a possible cutoff in military aid.

And in 1987, five Central American countries (Costa Rica, El Salvador, Nicaragua, Honduras, and Guatemala) agreed to a peace accord, designed largely by Costa Rican president Oscar Arias, that called for (1) elimination of all restrictions on political dissent, (2) political amnesty for rebels, (3) national elections under international supervision, (4) a negotiated cease-fire between national governments and all rebel groups, (5) each country forbidding the use of its territory to rebels seeking the overthrow of other countries, and (6) a cutoff in aid provided by outside countries to insurgent groups (that is, the United States to the Nicaraguan contras, the U.S.S.R. to the Salvadoran FMLN). As of this writing, it remains uncertain whether this so-called Arias Plan will be successful; the desirability of this agreement, however, plus the difficulty of implementing it, gives a sense of why diplomacy is so desirable, yet so difficult. On the strength of his efforts, Arias was awarded the 1987 Nobel Peace Prize.

Some Diplomatic Failures

Sometimes, diplomats make things worse. They are human beings, after all, and as such, fallible. Moreover, although it is hoped that direct, personal interactions can reduce the likelihood that nations will resort to force in order to settle their differences, such interactions also provide the opportunity for interpersonal hostility. Perceived slights among rulers and diplomats have, on occasion, endangered the peace. Late in the seventeenth century, for example, France and Spain nearly went to war after a coach in which the Spanish ambassador to England was riding cut in front of the French ambassador on a London street. And in 1819, the dey (ruling official) of Algiers, angered about the failure of the French government to make good on a debt, struck the French consul three times with a flyswatter. This insult precipitated a naval blockade by the French, and ultimately served as an excuse for what became the long-time occupation of Algeria.

Even at its best, diplomacy breeds a certain deviousness and social artifice that most people find laughable, if not downright unpleasant. During the protracted negotiations leading to the Treaty of Paris after Napoleon's defeat, Metternich was told that the Russian ambassador had died. The story has it that he responded, "Ah, is that true? I wonder what he meant by that."[4]

Efforts at diplomatic clarification sometimes backfire, making things worse. For example, in late July 1914, Sir Edward Grey, the British foreign secretary, warned Kaiser Wilhelm that if a general war occurred, Britain would enter it on the side of France and Russia. Rather than deter Germany (as Grey had intended), this was seen as a threat, which made Wilhelm more belligerent, convinced of a plot against him by the Triple Entente. Similarly, at

Secretary of State Dean Acheson (right) conferring with President Harry Truman. (National Park Services/Abbie Rowe, courtesy Harry S. Truman Library)

almost precisely the same time, the German chancellor, Bethmann-Hollweg, sent the following diplomatic message to Sazonov, the Russian foreign minister: "Kindly call M. Sazonov's serious attention to the fact that further continuation of Russian mobilization measures would force us to mobilize and in that case European war could scarcely be prevented."[5] This only made Sazonov and the Russian government more intransigent, convinced that Germany was aiming at sovereignty in the Balkans, including control of the Dardanelles.

Sometimes, statements by diplomats, intended for domestic consumption, have had serious international repercussions. In 1950, for example, Secretary of State Dean Acheson gave a speech in which he outlined the United States' "defense perimeter" in the Pacific; this zone appeared to exclude Korea, which gave the North Korean government the false impression that the United States would not forcibly resist an invasion of South Korea.

The prospect of a negotiated settlement is nearly always a desirable one, especially if the alternative is war. However, war sometimes can intensify even while diplomats are striving to bring the fighting to a close, as each side seeks gains on the battlefield that might influence the ultimate peace

settlement. Middle East diplomats noticed that the proposals put forward by Count Bernadotte, the first UN negotiator sent to help settle the 1948 war, closely reflected the immediate battlefield situation; as a result, both sides paid less attention to him and put more effort into achieving military gains so as to influence the negotiations in their favor. And during the closing stages of the Iran-Iraq War, in late autumn of 1988, Iraqi forces initiated several major offensives, hoping to improve Iraq's bargaining position. Similar intensification of war-fighting took place about the time that serious peace negotiations were under way in Panmunjom, Korea, in 1953. For this reason, it is generally recommended that the first step in negotiating peace be to establish an immediate cease-fire.

On occasion, diplomacy has even been consciously employed by leaders eager to initiate war. The most famous example of this was the Ems telegram, which, as we saw in Chapter 10, was craftily abbreviated by Bismarck to make it appear to the French that Kaiser Wilhelm had snubbed the French ambassador. In Bismarck's own words, he "waved a red flag in front of the Gallic bull."[6] The bull charged, as Bismarck had calculated, and ran into a Prussian steel wall in the ensuing Franco-Prussian War. In this case, Bismarck could simply have declared war on France, but he wanted to goad the French into appearing to be the aggressor, in order to assure the cooperation of the independent south German states of Bavaria, Wurtemberg, Baden, and Hesse, and also to prevent other states (notably Russia and Austria-Hungary) from aiding France. In this case, then, diplomacy was used to create war, and to isolate one side. Before the United States had declared itself a belligerent in World War I, German diplomacy attempted to induce Mexico to go to war against its northern neighbor, promising the return of territory that the United States had annexed following the Mexican-American War. But Mexico never took the bait, and when the "Zimmerman telegram," which contained this inflammatory offer, was made public, it succeeded only in further alienating U.S. public opinion toward Germany.

Classically, European diplomacy served to make peace in ways that avoided excessive humiliation of the loser, so as not to foment grievances that would lead promptly to additional war. Some territory would be transfered, fortresses would be surrendered and frontiers adjusted, indemnities might be required, and reparations might be exacted, but no one demanded crippling concessions. For example, following the Peace of Utrecht in 1714, France and her neighbors ceased fighting any major battles over the succession to the Spanish and English thrones. The peace in Europe was basically kept for the next few decades by this diplomatic style of mutual concessions and avoidance of humiliation, combined with respect for one another's vital interests.

More recently, however, especially with national wars replacing sovereign's wars, concessions have often caused lasting resentment, which in turn has sowed the seeds of subsequent wars. Thus, France's loss of Alsace and Lorraine during the Franco-Prussian War — and its national fervor for reclaiming these lost regions — did much to bring about World War I. The German anger and humiliation associated with the Treaty of Versailles (which ended that war) led in part to World War II. By contrast, the diplomatic settlements at the end of World War II, although imperfect, have had greater staying power.

Diplomacy of this sort, however, is not so much an alternative to war, or a means of avoiding it, as an adjunct to national hostilities. As one critic puts it:

> Diplomacy is a disguised war, in which States seek to gain by barter and intrigue, by the cleverness of wits, the objectives which they would have to gain more clumsily by means of war. Diplomacy is used while the States are recuperating from conflicts in which they have exhausted themselves. It is the wheedling and the bargaining of the worn-out bullies as they rise from the ground and slowly restore their strength to begin fighting again. If diplomacy had been a moral equivalent for war, a higher stage in human progress, an inestimable means of making words prevail instead of blows, militarism would have broken down and given place to it. But since it is a mere temporary substitute, a mere appearance of war's energy under another form, a surrogate effect is almost exactly proportioned to the armed force behind it. When it fails, the recourse is immediate to the military technique whose thinly veiled arm it has been.[7]

Let us therefore turn now to the relationship between diplomacy and military force.

DIPLOMACY AND MILITARY FORCE

According to one view, diplomacy is only as effective as the military power available to each side, the threats that underwrite courteous diplomatic interchanges. "Diplomacy without armaments," according to Frederick the Great, "is like music without instruments."

There have been many cases of diplomatic intimidation, some successful, some not. During the late 1930s, Hitler bluffed and bullied the Western democracies into successive territorial concessions — occupation of the Ruhr Valley, union with Austria, dismemberment and annexation of Czechoslovakia — because Germany had become militarily powerful, and Britain and France, remembering the pointless devastation of World War I, were eager to avoid a repetition. On the other hand, during the early 1980s, the U.S.S.R. sought to intimidate NATO into refusing to deploy Euromissiles by threatening, in the event of war in Europe, nuclear retaliation against any state that accepted them. However, this attempt to back up diplomacy with the threat of armed force backfired. By making itself appear more belligerent, the Soviet Union reinforced the arguments of those who proclaimed the need for the Euromissiles in the first place. Subsequently, these missiles were removed via bilateral U.S.-Soviet negotiations.

Arguing for the legitimacy — indeed, the necessity — of connecting diplomacy with "realism" (that is, military force), Hans Morgenthau stated:

> Diplomacy must determine its objectives in the light of the power actually and potentially available for the pursuit of these objectives. Diplomacy must assess the objectives of other nations and the power actually and potentially available for the pursuit of these objectives. Diplomacy must determine to what extent these different objectives are compatible with each other. Diplomacy must employ the means suited to the pursuit of its objectives. Failure in any one of these tasks may jeopardize the success of foreign policy and with it the peace of the world.[8]

Otto von Bismarck, the nineteenth-century chancellor of Prussia and architect of German unification, was hardly a pacifist. Yet, while he freely employed military force, he also understood its limitations. During the Austro-Prussian War, for example, the Austrians were badly defeated at the battle of Koniggratz, far more soundly than anyone had expected. At this point, political pressure quickly developed within Prussia for a wider victory over Austria, including the dismemberment of the Austrian empire itself. But Bismarck insisted on limiting Prussian demands to the provinces of Schleswig and Holstein, thereby preventing a wider war, with France and possibly Russia and Britain. As the arch-diplomat Metternich once put it, "Diplomacy is the art of avoiding the appearance of victory."[9]

In contrast to Bismarck's sensitivity to the dangers of pushing one's victories too far, General Douglas MacArthur and President Harry Truman were insensitive to the costs of similarly pressing the North Koreans and Chinese. After a surprise landing of U.S. forces at Inchon had resulted in dramatic gains in the autumn of 1950, UN (mostly U.S.) troops advanced far into North Korea. This action led to large-scale Chinese involvement and massive bloodshed on both sides, ending three years later in a stalemated situation . . . which could have been achieved with much less suffering had the Western leaders been more far-sighted. The lesson of Koniggratz — that military restraint can often lead to greater diplomatic and long-term success — had not been learned.

Another kind of bargaining, has, on the other hand, occasionally been useful in diminishing levels of violence. Often termed "tacit bargaining," this involves reaching agreements without actually spelling out the terms of the understanding. Because threats are strongly implied in such tacit bargains, they have most commonly taken place in close association with conditions of war or other organized violence. For example, during the Korean War, a tacit bargain existed on both sides: The Chinese would refrain from attacking U.S. aircraft carriers, supply lines, and bases in Japan, and the United States would not bomb North Korean supply lines in China. In the Middle East today, there is another tacit bargain: Israel will not flaunt its secret stockpile of nuclear weapons, and the Arab states will not call attention to them. To some extent, this understanding serves the interests of both sides, in that the Israelis would rather not acknowledge their nuclear capability, and the Arab states would rather not have to respond publicly to its existence. Neither the Korean War nor the Mideast nuclear examples are particularly satisfying to students of peace, however, since they both involve at best a kind of stand-off (the Mideast), and at worst the legitimization of violence (Korea). Skilled diplomats and negotiators generally hope for better.

RULES AND GOALS OF DIPLOMACY

In *Poetry and Truth*, the German poet Goethe wrote, "If I had to choose between justice and disorder on the one hand, and injustice and order, on the other, I would always choose the latter."[10] Many others — notably Metternich in the nineteenth century, and Henry Kissinger, the twentieth-century's best-known adherent to the teachings of Metternich — have followed suit and made stability a goal in itself. Diplomacy, in such hands, should not necessarily be seen as an unalloyed good in itself, since regrettable goals, not just stability but also repression and other forms of injustice, can be achieved through diplomacy. Diplomacy and techniques of negotiation in general are of interest in Peace Studies insofar as they represent nonviolent ways of resolving conflict short of overt violence. It is a different question, however, whether the end result of diplomacy, or other forms of conflict resolution, result in a better world.

Hans Morgenthau, whom we have already encountered as the twentieth century's most influential advocate of realpolitik in international relations, proposed nine rules for diplomacy, which, he hoped, would help states resolve conflicts short of war while also pursuing their own self-interest in international affairs. Morgenthau's rules may be summarized as follows:[11]

1. Do not be a crusader. Avoid "nationalistic universalism," the insistence that the goals of one's own nation warrant being the universal goals of all. As nineteenth-century French foreign minister Talleyrand put it, *pas trop de zele* ("not too much zeal"). A recent case of excessive zeal was the assistance provided by National Security Council aides to the contra rebels in Nicaragua, even at the cost of illegal activities and, ultimately, great harm to U.S. influence and prestige.

2. Employ a narrow definition of vital national interests, namely, the survival and maintenance of socioeconomic well-being. Morgenthau emphasized that in the nuclear age, states cannot afford to go to war — or to risk going to war — for anything short of their most supreme security interests. This implies, among other things, a substantial winding down of international treaty commitments. (Peace advocates may also want to question whether any interests are so "supreme" as to justify nuclear war.)

3. Be willing to compromise on all national interests that are not truly vital. During negotiations leading to the INF Treaty, the Soviet Union

made a remarkable compromise, agreeing to destroy significantly more missiles than the United States.

4. Try to see the other side's point of view, recognizing that the opponent will also have vital national interests and should not be pushed into compromising them.

5. Distinguish between what is real and what is illusory; do not allow considerations of honor, credibility, or prestige to override issues of real national security.

6. Never paint yourself into a corner; always retain avenues of retreat (or advance).

7. Do not allow an ally (especially a vulnerable one) to make decisions for you; as a corollary, do not allow yourself to be drawn into someone else's fight.

8. Always keep military factors subordinate to political ones. Remember that military planners know "nothing of that patient, intricate, and subtle maneuvering of diplomacy, whose main purpose is to avoid the absolutes of victory and defeat and meet the other side in negotiated compromise."[12]

9. "Neither surrender to popular passions nor disregard them."[13]

Following Napoleon's defeat in 1815, the European world entered into a period of relative stability, based in large part on the system of mutually respectful concessions established by the victors at the Congress of Vienna. Some of this "success" was because all the major players accepted the agreed system as legitimate, and everyone felt about equally rewarded and equally slighted by the outcome. As Henry Kissinger put it:

> Since absolute security for one power means absolute insecurity for all the others, it is obtainable only through conquest, never as part of a legitimate settlement. An international settlement which is accepted and not imposed will therefore always appear *somewhat* unjust to any one of its components. Paradoxically, the generality of this dissatisfaction is a condition of stability, because were any

one power *totally* satisfied, all others would have to be *totally* dissatisfied and a revolutionary situation would ensue. The foundation of a stable order is a *relative* security—and therefore the *relative* insecurity—of its members. Its stability reflects, not the absence of unsatisfied claims, but the absence of a grievance of such magnitude that redress will be sought in overturning the settlement rather than through an adjustment within its framework.[14]

In contrast to Morgenthau's conception of value-free diplomacy is the notion that issues of right and wrong lie at the heart of international disputes. Unfortunately, states generally find it easier to look dispassionately at conflicts in which they are not themselves embroiled; once physically involved, the process of moralizing often becomes intense, leaving only victory as a tolerable outcome. President Woodrow Wilson had urged the participants of World War I to seek a "peace without victory" and "a peace between equals" . . . until the United States entered that war. Then, even the American Peace Society declared that "This is not a war of territory, of trade routes or of commercial concerns, but of eternal principles. There can be no end of war until after the collapse of the existing German government."[15]

Historically, many of the crucial aspects of diplomacy have been carried out largely in secret. Secrecy was subsequently blamed, by many, for the errors and miscalculations that led to World War I, and President Wilson accordingly called for "open covenants openly arrived at." On the other hand, although secret diplomacy sounds inherently unpalatable, especially to a democratic society, it remains true that when conducted in public, diplomatic negotiating isn't conducive to compromise. Each side fears appearing soft, or a dupe, and is inclined to play to domestic public opinion, making arguments and advancing proposals that may be politically popular, even if it knows that other solutions may be fairer, and even more desirable. So, there is much to be said for diplomacy that is carried out not so much "in secret" as under a mutual understanding that not every offer and counteroffer will be leaked to the waiting world.

TRACK II DIPLOMACY

Since the late 1970s, there has been growing interest in what has been called Track II diplomacy, also sometimes known as unofficial or "encounter group" diplomacy. Track II diplomacy is unofficial in that it need not involve formal negotiations between representatives of different states; rather, it takes place in the course of relatively informal interactions among representatives of opposing groups, helping to lay the social and political groundwork needed in order for government leaders to act. It also can represent a way of solving problems independent of the nation-states themselves.

In Track II diplomacy, people are brought together, typically in the presence of an experienced third party or facilitator, for the purpose of achieving mutual understanding, exploring their commonalities as well as differences, and establishing interpersonal relationships despite the political disagreements between their "home" groups. This has been attempted, often with remarkable success, with groups of Catholics and Protestants from Northern Ireland, Greek and Turkish Cypriots, and Israelis and Palestinians. Typically, the individuals in question are relatively influential in their communities: doctors, lawyers, professors, journalists, midlevel politicians, and military officers. Success is never guaranteed, and typically, substantial distrust is evident. Numerous minor incidents occur, especially at the outset. Over time, however, most of these "encounter groups" have produced very positive results.

The most dramatic example of Track II techniques employed successfully at the highest levels of government occurred during the Camp David meetings in 1977. Hosted by President Jimmy Carter, who served as the facilitator, Israel's Menachem Begin and Egypt's Anwar Sadat spent thirteen days at the rustic presidential retreat in Maryland. The meetings took place without the formalities, protocols, and rigid negotiating procedures characteristic of traditional summit meetings or bargaining sessions. Rather, there was no formal agenda, no intrusive press, and—perhaps as a

Egyptian President Sadat (left), U.S. President Jimmy Carter (middle), and Israeli Prime Minister Begin during their informal conference at Camp David, Md., in 1978. (Jimmy Carter Presidential Library)

result — some highly emotional interchanges. Although the Camp David meetings did not solve all the problems in the Mideast, or even all areas of Egyptian-Israeli dispute, they did turn out to be highly productive.

Interestingly, just as the meetings were about to end, apparently in failure because of Prime Minister Begin's refusal to sign any accord, a breakthrough occurred. At Begin's request, President Carter was autographing photographs of the three Camp David participants, to be given to Begin's grandchildren. Carter personalized his autograph, dedicating each photo to one of Begin's grandchildren by name. Then, as Carter recalled,

> I handed him the photographs. He took them and thanked me. Then he happened to look down and saw that his granddaughter's name was on the top one. He spoke it aloud and then looked at each photograph individually, repeating the name of the grandchild I had written on it. His lips trembled and tears welled up in his eyes. He told me a little about each child and especially about one who seemed to be his favorite. We were both emotional

as we talked quietly for a few moments about grandchildren and about war.[16]

Shortly afterward, Begin indicated his willingness to sign the accords, and the Camp David "process" ended on a strong — even euphoric — note of accommodation, agreement, and mutual respect. Regrettably, a similar Track II approach was not attempted for the Egyptian and Israeli advisors and midlevel leaders at Camp David; their involvement in and commitment to the Camp David process would presumably have been greater had they been included as well. Nor has the process been repeated. The Camp David experience does, however, hint at the possibilities when individuals come together on a personal level, with time, goodwill, a skillful facilitator — and, perhaps, some luck — on their side.

THIRD-PARTY INVOLVEMENT

Consider a married couple who have been squabbling over how to divide household chores. Left to themselves, they may be unable to reach agreement, in part because each individual sees only his or her viewpoint. Moreover, each may hesitate to give in, even partially, for fear that any concession might be seen as an admission that he or she has a weaker case. Similar deadlocks can occur in other situations of conflict, such as disputes between labor and management. In such cases, disagreements between contending parties — whether individuals, organizations, or states — are sometimes more readily resolved if a third party is brought into the process. For domestic disputes, marital counselors may be helpful; for labor disputes, trained mediators or arbitrators, often provided by the government, may help resolve matters. A similar process can apply to international disputes.

An outside expert may be called in to help clarify the issues, resolve misunderstandings, and suggest areas of compromise and common ground. A third party — unbiased and trusted by both sides — can sometimes help reach agreements for which everyone may be grateful, but which (for a variety of reasons) neither party could suggest, or even accept if it was proposed by the other. Imagine, for example, that two adjacent states are disputing the location of the border in a 100-mile-wide strip of land between them. If state A proposes placing the border right down the middle, giving 50 miles to each side, then state B might use this "opening" to bargain further, "splitting the difference" between them, and proposing a border so that B gets 75 miles and A gets 25 miles. In such a case, the side that first proposes a compromise finds itself at a disadvantage. One obvious solution, therefore, is for a third state, C, to propose independently that A and B agree to 50 miles for each. (Unfortunately, international disputes are rarely this simple, given historical backgrounds, social factors, political passions, military alliances, and economic considerations, as well as geographic factors such as marshes, rivers, mountains, and so on.) It is also important to bear in mind that disputes always occur on at least two levels: the specific issue under dispute, and also the underlying question of who wins, who is more powerful, and what this portends for subsequent interactions.

The Functions of Go-Betweens

Third parties can be helpful to disputants in several specific ways. First, they can serve as go-betweens, providing what is known as their "good offices." This may simply involve making a meeting place available, on neutral ground. Thus, a long-standing dispute between Austria and Italy over control of the Tyrol, a German-speaking region, formerly Austrian but since World War I part of Italy, was resolved in 1969 through negotiations held in Denmark. The neutral states of Austria and, particularly, Switzerland have often made themselves available as sites for international dispute-settlement; when in doubt, international diplomats meet in Geneva.

During the Falklands/Malvinas War, the United States considered itself an ally of both Argentina and Great Britain, and Secretary of State Alexander Haig accordingly sought to interpose himself between the two sides, offering to act as an

"honest broker." His efforts were unsuccessful, despite numerous trans-Atlantic flights, in part because the United States was perceived to be more supportive of Britain. Similarly, Henry Kissinger engaged in vigorous "shuttle diplomacy" between Israel and her Arab neighbors during the early and mid-1970s; again, he was seen (accurately) as more supportive of Israel.

As of the late 1980s, the Arab governments — except for Egypt — do not officially recognize the state of Israel, thereby making it especially important for third parties to provide a means of communication between them. Of course, when the third party is a high-ranking representative of a major power, he or she presumably does not merely act as a messenger, but also can engage in various forms of arm-twisting, such as threatening to cut off economic or military aid unless some proposed compromises are accepted. (This suggests why some forms of diplomacy are best conducted in secret: It may be politically unacceptable, for example, for a state to appear to knuckle under to such pressure, although it may be better for everyone concerned if it does so.)

In 1967, Greece and Turkey — both U.S. allies and NATO members — were threatening to go to war over Cyprus. The U.S. emissary, Cyrus Vance, eventually succeeded in persuading both sides to step down their military preparations and accept an expanded role for the United Nations peacekeeping force already on that island. Soviet premier Kosygin was similarly successful in inducing India and Pakistan to terminate their second Kashmir War (1966), in part by secret arm-twisting.

Third parties, if they have the respect of the contenders, can also serve a valuable role as "factfinders," ascertaining, for example, whether or not a disputed border was crossed, how many political prisoners are held in specified jails, how large the military forces involved are, or what the economic situation in a particular region is. International organizations, notably the UN, have been especially helpful in this respect (see Chapter 16), establishing various "commissions of inquiry" to evaluate conflicting claims. In certain cases, basic facts are in dispute (for example, the number of Warsaw Pact troops in Europe), but in others, the disagreement is not over numbers or other data, but rather over values—not over what is true, but what is right.

Mediation and Arbitration

Aside from providing a place to meet, facilitating communication, finding facts, and occasionally, twisting a few arms, third parties can fulfill two basic diplomatic functions: mediation and arbitration. Mediators make suggestions that might be agreeable to both sides. Like marriage counselors, mediators try to resolve disputes, but adherence to their suggestions is entirely voluntary. By contrast, in the case of arbitration, both sides agree in advance to accept the independent judgment of the arbitrator. Because mediation involves less of a threat to sovereignty, it represents a less radical, and more often acceptable option to contending states. A third procedure, adjudication, which involves making decisions with reference to international law (see Chapter 17), sometimes is employed as well.

The use of mediation and arbitration to settle disputes is hardly a modern phenomenon. They were especially common in Europe during the late Middle Ages, from about the thirteenth to the fifteenth centuries. Apparently, this period of successful third-party involvement was due to several factors, one or two of which might be replicated today: Family ties among political leaders were frequent (not uncommonly, heads of state were cousins or even closer); the economic costs of war were widely recognized to be exceptionally high, and local treasuries often teetered on the edge of bankruptcy. Finally, a powerful third party was available to aid in the settling of disputes, namely, the Catholic church and its emissaries.

One advantage of mediation and arbitration is that a third party can sometimes succeed in fashioning a solution that both contending parties find acceptable, but neither would be willing to propose, for fear of being seen as too conciliatory and, thus, weak. Opposing governments often face a dilemma: Even when a compromise is feasible, both sides want to project an image of power. Accord-

ingly, the mediator or arbitrator can suggest something that, privately, both sides want but that neither is willing to propose. President Theodore Roosevelt won a Nobel Peace Prize for his successful mediation between Russia and Japan, which ended the Russo-Japanese War. During the Geneva Conference of 1955—which ended the French occupation of Indochina—Britain, China, and the Soviet Union mediated between France and the Viet Minh. In this case, as with many others, it can certainly be argued that mediation did not resolve the dispute, but only postponed it. Five years after Soviet premier Kosygin's successful mediation between India and Pakistan, war broke out between these two countries (although this time the issue was Bangladesh). And, at least in the eyes of the North Vietnamese, and many in the South as well, the United States essentially replaced France as colonial occupier of Indochina, leading to another destructive war. But even some apparent failures may sometimes be helpful; as Winston Churchill once noted, "Jaw, jaw, jaw is better than war, war, war." Sometimes, moreover, there can be a real advantage in postponing war, if, over time, passions cool and peaceful solutions eventually become possible. And sometimes, of course, mediation is altogether successful. During the 1980s, for example, the Vatican successfully interceded between Argentina and Chile, defusing a border dispute that threatened to escalate into war.

With respect to arbitration, one of the best-known cases is the so-called *Alabama* claim. This arose after a Confederate warship was purchased (illegally) in Britain, a neutral country, during the U.S. Civil War. When the U.S. government subsequently demanded reparations for the damage done to U.S. shipping by the *Alabama* and other, similar ships, both sides consented to arbitration in 1872. An independent panel eventually awarded the U.S. more than $15 million in damages, which Britain paid, thereby lowering tensions between the two countries. In fact, the now-close relationship between Britain and the United States is considered to have begun with this successful arbitration.

In 1965, India and Pakistan nearly went to war over a 35,000-square-mile salt marsh known as the

Rann of Kutch. Britain mediated this dispute, getting the two sides to agree to arbitration. A three-member panel was set up, with one member nominated by India, one by Pakistan, and one by the UN secretary general. A decision was made, to which both sides have subsequently abided (when the two countries later went to war, it was for other reasons). Since their peace treaty calling for a return of the Sinai to Egypt in exchange for recognition of Israel, the two countries continued to dispute ownership of a small but valuable stretch of beachfront on the Red Sea. They finally agreed to arbitration, and in 1988, a panel awarded most of this property to Egypt. Because of its status and reputation for impartiality, the United Nations has often been asked to mediate or arbitrate disputes among states: UN mediators have been very active, for example, in arranging for the Soviet withdrawal from Afghanistan and in working toward a settlement in the disputed region of Western Sahara (see Chapter 16).

NEGOTIATING TECHNIQUES FOR RESOLVING CONFLICT

Numerous techniques are available to arbitrators. One promising example is the so-called last best offer. Imagine two sides disagreeing over the amount of money to be paid for ownership of a disputed island. Rather than making offers and counteroffers, each side is told to give the arbitrator its last best offer, from which the arbitrator will choose the one that seems the most fair. The arbitrator cannot decide to split the difference, since this would only encourage each side to be intransigent. In the last best offer technique, by contrast, each side is nudged to be as conciliatory as possible, in hopes that its offer will be the one accepted.

Resolution Versus Dominance

In 1964, an American policy analyst wrote an influential book entitled *How Nations Negotiate*. This work revealed two common attitudes, especially prominent and persistent among Cold Warriors even today (the author went on to become a senior Defense Department official in the Reagan admin-

istration). For one, it dealt almost exclusively with U.S.-Soviet negotiations, criticizing the Soviets for their misdeeds, and U.S. negotiators for not being tough enough. And for another, it was entirely concerned with the question of besting the other side. It concluded as follows:

> And a good negotiator should be patient—though not primarily in order to sit in Geneva for months at a time hearing the opponent repeat speeches and repeating his own. He should be patient in working for seemingly lost causes, because by doing so he may slowly change the opponent's views and objectives. He should be patient to live with conflict and uncertainty and know that he may have succeeded even if (or precisely because) his negotiations failed. Above all, he must maintain the will to win.[17]

This view would still be endorsed by the majority of diplomats and negotiators today. However, if negotiations are to help resolve conflict, rather than become arenas for yet more conflict, another perspective is needed. This new perspective views negotiations as a means whereby contending parties seek to resolve their differences, not to prevail over each other. It suggests that to be fruitful, negotiations must be seen as non-zero-sum solutions, interactions in which state A's gain is not necessarily balanced by state B's loss, or vice versa. It aims to achieve "win-win" solutions in which all sides are better off than they were before.

Compromise

The most obvious, and in some cases the most common, negotiating technique is to compromise, that is, to reach an agreement that acknowledges the demands of both sides. There are, however, several disadvantages to this method. For one thing, a compromise may leave both sides dissatisfied. In some cases, this may actually be desirable, so that a "fair" decision may be defined—only somewhat tongue in cheek—as one that leaves everyone equally unhappy. But one side's claim may in fact be just, and the other's unjust; in such a case, a compromise simply rewards the unjust side while penalizing the just one. Compromise assumes that both contenders are equally worthy, so that "splitting the difference" between them will produce a fair settle-

Biography

Roger Fisher

Roger Fisher is an acknowledged authority on international law and negotiations. Born in Illinois, he served with the U.S. Army Air Force during World War II, and then attended Harvard Law School, where he is now Williston Professor of Law and Director of the Harvard Negotiation Project, which he founded. He has specialized in ways to improve the theory and practice of negotiation, along with other nonviolent means of resolving interpersonal and international differences. His books include *Getting Together: Building Relationships as We Negotiate*, and *Getting to YES: Negotiating Agreement Without Giving In*. Other writings include *Improving Compliance with International Law* and *International Conflict for Beginners*.

Roger Fisher was also originator and executive editor of two acclaimed public television series: "The Advocates," and "Arabs and Israelis." He has received numerous honors — including the Szilard Peace Prize — and serves on the Board of Directors of the Council for a Livable World and the Overseas Development Council. He is also an active member of numerous organizations dedicated to improving international cooperation and understanding. He is especially noted for combining a high degree of scholarly expertise with commitment to nonviolent conflict resolution, and for the ability to convey ideas and possibilities in an understandable, down-to-earth style.

---

ment. But what if state A arbitrarily insists that it is entitled to impose a 50 percent tariff upon all imports from state B, but refuses to allow B to tax its imports? Clearly a "compromise" that allows a 25 percent tariff would not be fair or acceptable . . . at least, not to state B.

In certain cases, however, one side can "win," without the other "losing." For example, Franco-German relations have been bedeviled through the first half of the twentieth century by a dispute over ownership of the Saar region, a rich industrial sector of the Rhineland. Following World War I, occupation and mining rights to the Saar were ceded to France; French control was reasserted after World War II. But the region's population was (and still is) overwhelmingly German, and the governments in Paris and Bonn eventually cooperated to resolve this issue: After a plebiscite in 1955, France permitted the Saar to rejoin West Germany. This negotiated agreement, in which France ostensibly "lost," served everyone well, since it proved to be a cornerstone for subsequent Franco-German cooperation and friendship.

Positional Versus Integrative Bargaining

Compromises are often the outcome of what has been called "positional bargaining," in which each side stakes out a position, and then holds to it. Positional bargaining clearly does not encourage flexibility and reasonable stances or attitudes; rather, intransigence is rewarded, and willingness to compromise (or even to suggest compromise) is penalized. Thus, in positional bargaining, the participants are rewarded for staking out a "hard" position and sticking to it, and penalized, in turn, for being "soft." As a result, "good" bargainers are those who remain relatively intransigent — that is, who make it difficult or unlikely that an agreement will be reached. Fortunately, there is a third way, known as "integrative bargaining"[18] or "principled negotiating."[19] Table 13.1 will help clarify the differences between positional bargaining, with its "hard" and "soft" approaches, and principled negotiating.

Integrative or principled bargaining tries, among other things, to separate the actual dispute

TABLE 13.1   Approaches to Bargaining[20]

Hard	Soft	Principled
participants are adversaries	participants are friends	participants are problem solvers
the goal is victory	the goal is an agreement	the goal is a wise outcome
demand concessions to maintain the relationship	make concessions to cultivate the relationship	separate the people from the problem
be hard on the problem and on the people	be soft on the people and on the problem	be soft on the people, hard on the problem
distrust others	trust others	proceed independently of trust
dig in to your position	change your position easily	focus on interests, not positions
make threats	make offers	explore interests
mislead as to your bottom line	disclose your bottom line	avoid having a bottom line
demand one-sided gains as the price of agreement	accept one-sided losses as the price of agreement	invent options for mutual benefit
search for the one solution *you* will accept	search for the one solution *they* will accept	develop multiple options to choose from; choose later
insist on your position	insist on agreement	insist on objective criteria
try to win a contest of wills	try to avoid a contest of wills	try to reach an agreement based on interests, not wills
apply pressure	avoid pressure	yield to principle, not pressure; reason and be open to reasons

from the underlying interests of each side. The goal is to focus on the latter, and avoid getting bogged down in the former. As negotiators Roger Fisher and William Ury recount, consider the story of two sisters who quarreled over an orange; they decided, finally, to compromise, each getting one half. One sister than proceeded to squeeze her half for juice while the other used the peel from her portion to flavor a cake. By compromising—an old and honorable solution—they overlooked the integrative solution of giving one all the peel, and the other all the juice.

Or imagine that two states disagree over a boundary. The real dispute may not be over territory as such, but rather one state's desire for access to certain transportation routes, and the other state's concern that granting such access would diminish its military security. In such a case, integrative bargaining would seek to identify the under-

lying issues and solve them directly, perhaps reaching an understanding in which the needs of both sides are integrated into one solution: access to the desired transportation routes, for an agreed annual fee, along with a bilateral treaty specifying strict limitations on the nature of the vehicles or number of personnel permitted to travel along them.

Numerous tactics may be employed by negotiators seeking to bridge differences between contending sides. They include such things as focusing on the shared interests of all parties rather than the demands as such, diminishing the role of personalities (that is, separating the people from the problem), and "fractionating" the conflict. This is analogous to medical triage—that is, separating a dispute into intractable components and resolvable components, then working on the latter. This tactic can also contribute to the important process of "confidence-building," which increases the probability that more difficult issues will be solved in the future.* Having made some degree of progress, by building on the easier cases, the disputants are likely to be all the more energetic and optimistic about achieving additional success, and, perhaps, less likely to resort to violence in the event of failure.

Certain disputes — such as the story of the oranges — have a high "integrative potential" in that they inherently lend themselves to agreements that leave all parties entirely satisfied. Other cases are more difficult, as when, for example, buyer and seller disagree over the price of a house. Even here, however, there is room for integrative agreements: modifications in the interest rate, the date of occupancy, the amount of principle to be paid off by certain dates, and so on. In such cases, it may be possible to integrate the interests of both sides, essentially by reaching agreement on other dimensions aside from those initially in dispute (in this case, the purchase price).

Methods of Integrative Bargaining

Let us now examine five different methods[21] by which integrative agreements might be reached, taking as an example a hypothetical dispute between a husband and wife over where to spend their two-week vacation: The wife wants to go to the seashore, the husband to the mountains. One solution is to compromise, and spend one week at each; they would like, however, to find some more satisfactory settlement.

Expanding the Pie.   Sometimes, solutions can be achieved by increasing the amount of a resource in short supply. Perhaps the couple could arrange to take four weeks of vacation, thereby spending two weeks at each location. This is not as utopian as it may seem, since expanding the pie need not necessarily involve getting something for nothing. Thus, if they value their vacation enough, it might be possible, for example, to work overtime during the rest of the year so as to pay for it. For such solutions to work, however, each party must not find the other's preferred outcome to be aversive; that is, it could work if each objects to the other's preference not because of something inherent in the choice itself, but rather because it prevents him or her from doing the other. Specifically the husband must be able to tolerate going to the seashore, and the wife to the mountains. Solutions of this sort are largely based on efforts to help each side get what it wants, and to do so by increasing the amount of a limited resource (time, money, land, people, security, hard currency, and so on).

Nonspecific Compensation.   In this case, one party "gives in," but is repaid in some other way. The husband, for example, may agree to go to the seashore, but only if he is relieved of housecleaning chores for the next four months. By extension, a country may permit a neighbor to flood its markets with exported goods, if the exporting country agrees to continue providing a certain number of jobs for citizens of the importing country. Solutions of this sort require information about what is particularly valued by both parties, and what one party may be able (and willing) to provide to another, in return for getting its way. An important factor is whether some form of compensation exists that may be of low cost to the donor and high value to the recipient: Perhaps the wife doesn't particularly mind doing the husband's share of the housecleaning, at least for a few months, and perhaps the exporting country actually needs the labor skills of the importer.

Logrolling.   If both parties differ on issues within the main ones under dispute, and if they differ in their priorities regarding these issues, then the possibility exists for creative "logrolling," which is, in a sense, a variant of nonspecific compensation. For example, perhaps the husband–wife disagreement over vacations also involves differences of opinion

---

*In fact, students of international relations have become increasingly interested in enumerating possible confidence-building measures (CBMs) as better than ICBMs at keeping the peace.

about the preferred accommodations. Let us say that the wife favors simple, rustic beach cottages, whereas the husband is looking forward to an elegant mountain resort. Perhaps, then, the husband will be quite happy going to the seashore, so long as the wife agrees that they stay in an elegant seaside resort (or alternatively, maybe a rustic cabin — desired by the wife — in the mountains — preferred by the husband). For solutions based on logrolling to be developed, it helps to identify potential concessions, and especially to ask, "Are some of my low-priority issues of high priority to the other party?" or vice versa.

Cost-Cutting. Solutions based on cost-cutting are those in which one party essentially succeeds in "winning," but the costs to the other party are reduced or eliminated. Thus, cost-cutting solutions are more one-sided than those discussed above, but they are nonetheless feasible and potentially stable, if the side that "gives in" truly does not suffer any disadvantage from the agreement. In the case of the husband–wife vacation dispute, perhaps the husband had resisted going to the seashore because he feared being lonely and isolated while his wife was wind-surfing; in this case, a cost-cutting solution — and one that could be entirely satisfactory to the husband — might be for the couple to agree to go to the seashore, but to do so along with some of their friends, who could provide company for the husband.

Cost-cutting differs from nonspecific compensation in that it involves a kind of "specific compensation," a particular kind of recompense directed toward one of the parties, but not really compensation for a painful outcome so much as a way of making the settlement agreeable for the "loser." For cost-cutting to be successful, there must be clarity as to the reasons either side opposes the desires of the other, and an openness (especially on the part of the side giving in) to considering ways in which it might be possible to give in without really losing.

Bridging. Bridging occurs when the two parties agree to a solution in which neither side wins or loses, but rather both agree to a different option

from the ones each originally favored. This solution must address the primary interests that actually underlie the specific issues in dispute. Thus, if the husband wanted to go to the mountains so as to hike, and the wife wanted to go to the seashore for the sun, perhaps it would be possible to find a beach resort near hiking trails (or a vacation site where the mountains are dry and sunny). Successful bridging requires that the parties refocus their negotiations from an insistence on their *positions* to an examination of their underlying *interests*. Why are they pushing for their particular position? Is there some alternative outcome that would meet their actual needs? Is it really the mountains, or the seashore, that they want, or do they simply provide a means of achieving some other goal?

A fundamental principle underlying all of these diverse solutions is that perceived conflicts of interest may be illusory; in many cases, it is possible to obtain good agreements (that is, solutions that are beneficial to both sides) without either party having to give in, without there being a winner and a loser, and — most important for our purposes — without violence. Moreover, because such solutions respect the fundamental interests of each side, they also avoid instilling resentment, which so often serves as the seeds of violence in the future.

ADDITIONAL NEGOTIATING TECHNIQUES

Apparently trivial details can become surprisingly influential in the negotiating process. In some cases, for example, attention to the physical arrangement of participants may be important. Thus, it can even be helpful to seat the contenders on the same side of a table — opposite the negotiator, whose job is to articulate the disagreement — thereby literally facing the problem together, rather than contentiously facing each other. This sometimes encourages both sides to cooperate rather than compete, to concentrate on defining the problem and then solving it, rather than defeating each other. In other cases, a wise conflict resolver will simply ignore uncooperative statements, rather than allowing them to derail an agreement; during the Cuban Missile Crisis, the

The Yalta Conference in 1945. Seated are, from the left, British Prime Minister Winston Churchill, U.S. President Franklin Roosevelt, and Soviet Premier Josef Stalin. The Yalta Conference arranged for the postwar division of Europe into Western and Eastern spheres of influence. (UPI/Bettmann Newsphotos)

U.S. government received two communications from Soviet premier Khrushchev, one conciliatory and the other contentious. At Robert Kennedy's suggestion, the United States simply ignored the latter and responded to the former.

Clarity is generally a virtue; in some cases, negotiated agreements come unraveled or become a source of irritation when they are interpreted differently by the different parties. For example, Britain and the United States believed that at the Yalta Conference toward the end of World War II, the Soviet Union had agreed to allow a pluralistic democracy in postwar Poland. Soviet diplomats (and some U.S. participants as well), on the other hand, recalled the event differently. It is also possible, however, that if the expectations and intentions of each side had been spelled out in detail, an even greater falling out would have occurred. Part of the

negotiator's art may therefore include recourse to equivocal and imprecise language. Nobel Prize–winning Canadian diplomat Lester Pearson put it this way:

> I know that there have been occasions, and I have been concerned with one or two, when, as the lesser of two evils, words were used in recording the results of negotiations or discussions whose value lay precisely in the fact that they were imprecise, that they could be interpreted somewhat freely and therefore could be used not so much to record agreement as to conceal a disagreement which it was desired to play down and which, it was hoped, would disappear in time.[22]

In order to avoid misunderstandings, a negotiator can request that each side state, as clearly as it can, the arguments of the other. This can help

Admiral Nomura, representing the government of Japan during an official mission to the United States, just prior to the surprise attack on Pearl Harbor. (Library of Congress)

build empathy, a deeper awareness and appreciation of the other's perspective, and of the constraints felt by the other. (Remember that in serious disputes, each side is often intensely aware of the limitations on its own behavior, while considering that the opponent has great latitude; failure to reach agreement then seems fairly attributed to the other's intransigence.)

Adequate empathy can lead to another helpful exercise, the "yesable proposition,"[23] in which each party to a dispute is asked to consider formulating a proposition that the other side is likely to accept. This represents a subtle but important shift. In most cases, each side makes demands — indeed, the

nature of the negotiating process encourages them to do so — that tend to be outrageous and unacceptable. In the search for yesable propositions, both sides are more likely to uncover shared interests, based on which a mutually acceptable outcome might become clear. Famed negotiator Roger Fisher, for example, recounted that he once asked Egyptian president Nasser and Israeli premier Golda Meir what they wanted from the other that the other could conceivably agree to; neither had seriously considered this question.

In the course of seeking an agreement, it can be helpful to make proposals through an intermediary — often a low-ranking one — so that they can be disowned if the other side rejects it out of hand. This avoids the embarrassment that could result from acrimony and ridicule; by having the capability of denying that any such opening was ever made, either side may be more willing to make an initial attempt. For example, during the Cuban Missile Crisis, Premier Khrushchev chose a low-ranking Soviet embassy official to convey his proposal: removal of Soviet missiles from Cuba in return for a U.S. pledge not to invade that island. In addition, this message was sent to a news broadcaster rather than directly to U.S. officials.

Additional suggestions include the following: Avoid ultimatums, do not impugn the motives of the other side, try to keep from playing to the crowds, be flexible but not spineless, avoid *ad hominem* (personal) attacks, avoid nonnegotiable ploys, and do not be so desperate for agreement that you sacrifice future peace for short-term palliatives. In his inauguration address, President John Kennedy said, "We shall not negotiate out of fear, but we shall never fear to negotiate." The second part sounds just fine, but it is not at all clear why we or anyone else should refrain from negotiating out of fear. It is precisely when fear is greatest — fear that a conflict situation might get out of hand — that serious and creative negotiations are most needed. Ideally, of course, the process would have begun long before a difficult situation became a tense, fear-inducing crisis.

What counts, in the long run, is reaching agreements without either side giving in, or resorting to violence. Sometimes, it may be possible, even desirable, to "paper over" disagreements so as to buy time for new events to unfold, or for old disputes to grow stale. And of course, there is no guarantee that all disputes can be resolved by negotiations. A positive outcome, for example, requires a degree of goodwill and a genuine desire to reach an agreement. It also requires willingness to "bargain in good faith," and there have been cases in which good faith was not shown. For example, the Soviet government in 1939 was openly negotiating with Britain and France for a mutual defense pact against Nazi Germany, while at the same time se-

cretly organizing the now-infamous nonaggression pact that briefly allied Stalin with Hitler, and paved the way for Germany's invasion of Poland. Similarly, Japanese diplomats were negotiating with their U.S. counterparts on December 7, 1941, when Japanese forces attacked Pearl Harbor. And when, in 1955, Soviet negotiators accepted U.S. disarmament proposals, complete with international verification procedures, the U.S. delegation put a "reservation" on those proposals . . . in other words, having been accepted, they were withdrawn!

Nonetheless, there is good reason to believe that such cases are exceptions. The desire for honest, nonviolent resolution of conflicts is, if anything, stronger and more widespread today than at any time in the past. In addition, other factors — domestic opinion, international law, international organizations, the shared costs of violence — combine to make nonviolent conflict resolution an attractive alternative to the use of force, so long as the participants (including the mediator if there is one) are both skillful and persistent.

A FINAL NOTE ON CONFLICT RESOLUTION

Ultimately, belief in the feasibility of nonviolent conflict resolution — whether by diplomacy or negotiation, between two parties or with the assistance of a mediator or arbitrator — is just that, an exercise of faith: faith in the underlying goodwill of people, and in their fundamental rationality. Such faith may or may not be warranted. Certainly, the human species, personally as well as collectively, has long displayed a penchant for irrational acts. But skeptics might consider that the alternative — war — is usually no more rational. And moreover, if it seems unrealistic to rely on the rationality of one's opponents, bear in mind that the fundamental peace-keeping strategy of the nuclear age — deterrence — relies precisely on a hefty dose of rationality and mutual dependence. How much better, therefore, to apply such negotiating tactics to the pursuit of conflict resolution rather than conflict prolongation or, worse yet, violence as the final arbiter of disputes.

Study Questions

1. Describe some pros and cons of summit meetings.

2. Identify some factors common to diplomatic successes in averting war.

3. Identify some factors common to diplomatic failures in averting war.

4. It is important for diplomacy to be sensitive to issues beyond the immediate prospects of military defeat or victory. Explain.

5. Make a case for value-free diplomacy. Do the same for value-oriented diplomacy.

6. What is meant by Track II diplomacy? Describe some advantages and disadvantages.

7. Distinguish between mediation and arbitration, and give some examples of each.

8. What are some pros and cons of secret diplomacy?

9. Distinguish between positional bargaining and principled negotiation. Give examples of each.

10. Choose examples other than those in this chapter, and use them to illustrate these various negotiating techniques: expanding the pie, nonspecific compensation, logrolling, cost-cutting, and bridging.

Suggestions for Further Reading

Harold Nicholson. 1955. *Diplomacy*. Oxford University Press: New York.

Fred Charles Ikle. 1964. *How Nations Negotiate*. Harper & Row: New York.

John Burton. 1969. *Conflict and Communication*. Macmillan: London.

Roger Fisher and William Ury. 1981. *Getting to YES*. Houghton Mifflin: Boston.

D. G. Pruitt. 1981. *Negotiation Behavior*. Academic Press: New York.

Source Notes for Part III

1. St. Augustine. 1950. *The City of God*. Modern Library: New York.

2. Quoted in Alan Geyer. 1982. *The Idea of Disarmament!* Brethren Press: Elgin, IL.

Source Notes for Chapter 13

1. David Zielger. 1977. *War, Peace, and International Politics*. Little, Brown: Boston.

2. Attributed to British ambassador Sir Henry Wonnon, by Harold Nicholson. 1955. *Diplomacy*. Oxford University Press: New York.

3. A. Rapoport. 1974. *Fights, Games and Debates*. University of Michigan Press: Ann Arbor, MI.

4. Quoted in Nicholson. *Diplomacy*.

5. Quoted in John Stoessinger. 1985. *Why Nations Go to War*. St. Martin's: New York.

6. Quoted in Stoessinger. *Why*.

7. Randolph S. Bourne. 1964. *War and the Intellectuals, Collected Essays, 1915–1919*. Harper & Row: New York.

8. Hans Morgenthau. 1978. *Politics Among Nations*. Knopf: New York.

9. Quoted in Nicholson. *Diplomacy*.

10. J. W. von Goethe. 1930. *Poetry and Truth from My Own Life*. G. Bell: London.

11. Morgenthau. *Politics*.

12. Ibid.

13. Ibid.

14. Henry Kissinger. 1957. *A World Restored*. Houghton Mifflin: Boston.

15. Quoted in Michael Howard. *War and the Liberal Conscience*. Harvard University Press: Cambridge, MA.

16. Jimmy Carter. 1982. *Keeping Faith*. Bantam Books: New York.

17. Fred Charles Ikle. 1964. *How Nations Negotiate*. Harper & Row: New York.

18. R. E. Walton and A. B. McKersie. 1965. *A Behavioral Theory of Labor Negotiations*. McGraw-Hill: New York.

19. R. Fisher and W. Ury. 1981. *Getting to YES*. Houghton Mifflin: Boston.

20. Modified slightly from Fisher and Ury. *Getting to YES*.

21. Derived from Dean G. Pruitt. 1983. "Achieving Integrative Agreements in Negotiation." In M. H. Bazerman and R. J. Lewicki (eds.), *Negotiating in Organizations*. Sage Publications: Beverly Hills, CA

and from J. Galtung. 1980. "The Middle East Under Social Conflict." *Essays in Peace Research*, vol. 5. Christian Ejlers: Copenhagen.

22. Lester B. Pearson. 1949. *Diplomacy in the Nuclear Age*. Harvard University Press: Cambridge, MA.

23. R. Fisher. 1969. *International Conflict for Beginners*. Harper & Row: New York.

14

Peace Through Strength?

Have you walked up and down upon the earth lately? I have; and I have examined Man's wonderful inventions. And I tell you that in the arts of life man invents nothing but in the arts of death he outdoes Nature herself, and produces by chemistry and machinery all the slaughtered, of plague, pestilence, and famine . . . when he goes out to slay, he carries a marvel of mechanism that lets loose at the touch of his finger all the hidden molecular energies, and leaves the javelin, the arrow, the blow-pipe of his fathers far behind. In the arts of peace Man is a bungler. . . . His heart is in his weapons. . . . Man measures his strength by his destructiveness.

the Devil, in George Bernard Shaw's *Man and Superman*

Most people point to military strength as an important — often the most important — way of maintaining peace. The slogan of the Strategic Air Command forthrightly proclaims, "Peace Is Our Profession."* Not surprisingly, however, advocates of Peace Studies generally look askance at the traditional reliance on military force to maintain peace, viewing armed force as part of the problem, not the solution.

Like it or not, and agree with it or not, "peace through strength" is probably the most politically potent and influential concept of war-prevention in the twentieth century. It is also probably the most perilous. It is a viewpoint against which Peace Studies must struggle. Whether or not it "works" in maintaining peace, peace through strength undoubtedly "works" in another sense: It directs the expenditure of vast quantities of national treasure, and virtually all major governments adhere to its precepts. The major challenge for Peace Studies is to break away from the existing war system — which

---

*Below this sign at SAC headquarters, someone had recently scrawled, "Mass Murder Is Our Specialty"!

Aerial view of the Pentagon, home of the U.S. Department of Defense and "home base" for those who believe in "peace through strength." (U.S. Department of Defense)

includes reliance on peace through strength — and seek to establish a viable ecology of peace whose strength does not derive from violence or the threat of violence. Hence, some professional students of peace may even object to including a chapter on peace through strength in a text such as this. But any modification of current policies would be enriched by an understanding of the background of our current system, and the assumptions under which, in large part, it currently operates. And if students of peace are not to be dismissed as incurably romantic or hopelessly uninformed, it behooves them to understand the arguments, if only so as to refute them.

The motto "Peace Through Strength" is a modern version of the Latin *vis paoem, para bellum* (if you want peace, prepare for war). It has been taken as axiomatic by entire generations of conservative politicians and military leaders. In all fairness to them, we should at least consider that this perspective may be more than a rationalization for the maintenance of large and threatening armed forces, sought for other reasons that are rarely acknowledged (economic gain, career benefits, distracting

the populace, or satisfying one's own psychological needs to feel potent and powerful, to have clearly defined enemies, and so on). There have been, and still are, people who sincerely believe that the only way to achieve peace is by the ability and willingness to employ military force. In this chapter, we shall briefly examine their arguments.

BALANCE OF POWER

Generally, a "balance of power" is obtained when the primary contending states are roughly equal in their military strength. Thus, balance of power is intimately associated with the assumptions of peace through strength, as shown in this observation by Henry Kissinger:

> Throughout history the political influence of nations has been roughly correlative to their military power. While states might differ in the moral worth and prestige of their institutions, diplomatic skill could augment but never substitute for military strength. In the final reckoning weakness has invariably tempted aggression and impotence brings abdication of policy in its train. . . . The balance of power has in fact been the precondition for peace.[1]

How Balance of Power Works

In its traditional usage, balance of power involves a tacit agreement among governments that power will be distributed among the various states so as to prevent any one from becoming so strong as to threaten the others. Thus, it relies fundamentally on deterrence, the expectation that a would-be aggressor will refrain from attacking opponents who are more powerful than itself, or who are capable of inflicting unacceptable damage if they are attacked. In the late twentieth century, balance of power has come to refer specifically to the relative military and economic strength of the United States and the U.S.S.R.; hence, adherence to balance of power implies a continuing arms race, or possibly, mutual agreements to keep the system stable by keeping the mutual threat balanced and equal. Before that, however, especially during the eighteenth and nineteenth centuries, balance of power referred less to arms races than to a constantly shifting system of alliances whereby states arranged themselves to keep any one state from becoming too powerful. When they occurred, wars were fought for limited objectives rather than universal, crusading goals. Balance of power also represented an extreme of realpolitik, in that states were expected to shift alliances readily, looking out only for their own interests.

Balance of power considerations may sometimes have prevented war. For example, Prussia threatened Switzerland with war over the disputed Neuchatel region in 1856; although Prussia was much stronger than Switzerland, the Prussian king, Frederick William, backed down, largely because he feared antagonizing Britain and France, which would have seen Prussian success as a threat to the delicate continental balance. Just as we can never conclude with certainty that nuclear deterrence has prevented a specific war, we also cannot know with confidence when (or if) balance of power considerations inhibited states from going to war. In many cases, however, a state's willingness to disrupt the balance has precipitated war with other states, who sought to preserve it; for example, Germany's invasion of neutral Belgium in the early days of World War I led Britain to enter that war. Speaking in Parliament at that time, British foreign secretary Edward Grey argued that

> if, in a crisis like this, we run away from those obligations of honour and interest as regards the Belgian Treaty [promising British support for Belgian neutrality], I doubt whether, whatever material force we might have at the end, it would be of very much value in face of the respect we should have lost. And I do not believe, whether a great Power stands outside this war or not, it is going to be in a position at the end of it to exert its superior strength . . . to prevent the whole of the West of Europe opposite to us — if that had been the result of the war — falling under the domination of a single Power.[2]

Great Britain as "Balancer"

During the 1930s, Winston Churchill sought to rally Britain against the growing might of Nazi Germany. He pointed out that for centuries English foreign policy had been to ally itself with the weaker powers in Europe, in opposition to the stronger, so

as to prevent the emergence of any threat to English security:

> For four hundred years the foreign policy of England has been to oppose the strongest, most aggressive, most dominating Power on the Continent. . . . We always took the harder course, joined with the less strong Powers, made a combination among them, and thus defeated and frustrated the Continental military tyrant whoever he was, whatever nation he led.[3]

Thus, when Spain was strong and threatening, England fought Spain (defeating the Armada in 1588). Then, when France under Louis XIV appeared capable of dominating Europe, England joined military alliances against it, and again when Napoleon came to power. Indeed, for much of its history prior to the twentieth century, England saw itself as the "balancer" in world affairs, and some historians claim that the *pax Britannica* was due to Britain's success in preventing any one state from becoming dangerously powerful. In part because of its relative invulnerability as an island nation with the world's most powerful navy, Britain felt safe enough to refrain from keeping a large army, which in turn made it less menacing to others. And because of its prior unsuccessful attempts to conquer France, Britain had no serious continental ambitions. Moreover, British success in enriching itself via its overseas colonies left it free to pursue a relatively peaceful policy in Europe, which in turn may have given balance of power a relatively good name . . . probably better than it deserved.

In a passage described by Arnold Toynbee as "excruciatingly complacent,"[4] historian Edward Gibbon wrote:

> The balance of power will continue to fluctuate, and the prosperity of our own or the neighboring kingdoms may be alternately exalted and depressed; but these partial events cannot essentially injure our general state of happiness, the system of arts, and laws, and manners, which so advantageously distinguish, above the rest of mankind, the Europeans and their colonies. . . . In peace, the progress of knowledge and industry is accelerated by the emulation of so many active rivals: in war, the European forces are exercised by temperate and undecisive contests.[5]

Shifting Alliances

For hundreds of years, European alliances shifted rapidly. In 1740, for example, during the first of Frederick the Great's wars, England and Austria were allied against France and Prussia; within a few years, following the so-called Great Diplomatic Revolution in 1756, France began to fear Prussia more than Austria, whereas England continued to distrust its traditional rival, France, so the new lineup became England and Prussia versus Austria and France. Even lesser states were affected. During the first of Frederick the Great's wars for Silesia (1740–1743), for example, Saxony was allied with France, Prussia, and Bavaria against Austria, England, and Hanover; during the second war for Silesia (1744–1745), Saxony switched and allied with its three former enemies; by the Seven Years' War (1756–1763), which might also be called the third war for Silesia, Saxony found itself allied with Austria, Russia, and France against Prussia, Hanover, and England.*

Although England was the most notable practitioner of balance of power politics, such efforts were not unique to England, or even to Europe. During the Thirty Years' War, France (a Catholic country) sided with Protestant Scandinavia and the Low countries (Belgium and the Netherlands) out of fear that Hapsburg power (Austria and Spain) would grow too great if the Catholics won. This conflict, often described as a "war of religion," was thus a "balance of power war" as well. To take a more recent example, following India's success in partitioning Pakistan in 1971, the government of Ceylon (now Sri Lanka) moved to improve economic and military cooperation with the United States, as a counterweight to the recent enhancement of Indian strength. More recently yet, the primary anxiety of the United States, the U.S.S.R., and most Arab states concerning the Iran-Iraq War was

not the bloodshed and destruction of the war itself, but rather that the winner would emerge as the predominant power in the Persian Gulf region. Hence, assistance tended to flow to whichever side was losing.

The "Entente Cordiale," linking Britain and France in 1904, was due to shared fear of Germany; during the 1970s, the United States and Chinese entered into a comparable improvement in relations between old enemies, this time based on a shared fear of the Soviet Union. Not surprisingly, the state left out of such alliances is also likely to be fearful. In addition, when states jockey ceaselessly with one another, and obsessively count and weigh one another for signs of a relative increase or decrease in power, wars may result. Such anxieties lead to concerns such as the "domino theory," in which one side (sometimes both!) worry that the other is progressively gaining territory and strength. For example, after the Korean War, advocates of the domino theory worried that other regions in Asia were likely to fall to the communists, like a row of toppling dominoes: the islands of Quemoy and Matsu in 1958, Vietnam and the rest of Southeast Asia, including Thailand and Burma, in the 1960s and 1970s.

Following World War II, the United States and the Soviet Union emerged as the two dominant states of the world: a "bipolar" balance of power, with each state seeking to buttress its position by establishing competing alliances and courting the favor of Third World countries. By the early 1990s, that situation appears to be changing once again, with the emergence of China, Japan, and an increasingly united Western Europe creating a "multipolar" balance.† Some authorities claim that multipolar systems are more stable and less warlike than bipolar systems, because they involve (1) more cross-cutting loyalties, (2) less anxious attention directed to any one state by another, and (3) recognition that increased

---

*It is not necessarily important that students be able to recount these arcane historical maneuverings. Rather, they are recounted here simply to make a point: Alliances have shifted wildly in pursuit of balance of power.

†The liberalization of Eastern Europe opens the possibility that all of Europe will someday be unified as a single political and economic power source.

armaments by one state (an incipient arms race) has less impact on the security of any other state. On the other hand, equally competent authorities point out that satisfactory balances may be more difficult to achieve with the many different actors of a multipolar system, and also that the greater diversity of interests and demands provides more opportunities for conflict. It appears increasingly clear, in any event, that the two superpowers no longer exercise decisive influence ("hegemony") in world affairs.

PROBLEMS WITH BALANCE OF POWER

Advocates of balance of power often assume and sometimes assert that such a balance deters war. It remains uncertain, however, whether wars are more or less likely during conditions of balance. Thus, the Peloponnesian War presumably would not have occurred if Athens and Sparta were not so close in strength as to constitute a threat to each other; similarly for the early Punic Wars between Rome and Carthage. During the *pax Romana*, on the other hand, Rome was supreme; there was no balance of power, yet there was comparative peace. The Soviet Union and Mongolia have not fought any wars, nor have the U.S.S.R. and Bulgaria, in part because of the *imbalance* of power in these cases; similarly — in recent years — for the United States and its neighbors, Canada and Mexico.

The Promotion of War

Wars often occur when rival states disagree as to their relative strength; they end when both sides agree. The war itself terminates disagreement: The stronger state is acknowledged by having won, and the weaker by having lost. Looking at the distribution of power at the end of wars, we can conclude that indecisive wars, which resulted in a relative balance of forces, were more likely to result in another war shortly thereafter, whereas cases of decisive victory led more frequently to periods of peace.[6] Thus, the War of the Polish Succession, an inconclusive struggle between Austria and France,

was followed five years later by the War of the Austrian Succession, which was also largely ineffectual, and which gave rise eventually to the destructive Seven Years' War. Even that conflict was equivocal (England won overseas, but was stalemated in Europe), and eventually led to the French Revolutionary Wars (1792–1802), which left England dominant overseas but France ascendant on the continent. Finally, it took the Napoleonic Wars to defeat France soundly, creating not a balance of power but an imbalance, and thereby ushering in an extended period of relative peace.

It is true that during the heydays of balance of power, a coalition of European states regularly took the field against whatever ruler seemed about to establish hegemony: against the Hapsburgs in the late sixteenth and again in the early seventeenth centuries, against the French in the late seventeenth and again in the early nineteenth centuries (first Louis XIV and then Napoleon), and against Germany and its allies in World Wars I and II. And perhaps balance of power "worked," in that it prevented domination by a single state, and likely tyranny as well. Rather than prevent war, however, balance of power may well have promoted it. After all, the underlying goal of balance of power is not to deter war, but rather to preserve the balance, and thus national sovereignty and the system of states of which the balance is composed. Sometimes, it operates via war. Accordingly, standard liberal doctrine has long maintained that wars are caused by arms races, the military-industrial complex, misunderstandings and misperceptions, secret diplomacy, *and* balance of power.

Slight Imbalances in Power

Evidence also suggests that wars tend to break out when a slight imbalance exists, especially when one side has grown rapidly, but has not yet reached the power of its opponent. In this situation, the reigning power feels threatened that the balance is about to tip against it, sometimes calculating that war now is preferable to waiting for the upstart to gain yet more strength. States actively committed to a balance of power, in short, have an incentive to attack their neighbors whenever they perceive an adverse shift in that balance. Whether that attack is justified as preventive (to forestall gradual change and eventual war) or preemptive (jumping the gun to short-circuit an attack that is considered imminent), states find themselves impelled to jump through a "window of opportunity" and begin a war, lest it become a "window of vulnerability" through which they are attacked. This occurred to Germany, for example, in 1914. In July of that year, General von Moltke, the German chief of staff, wrote that

> basically, Russia is not at the moment ready for war. Nor do France or England want war now. In a few years, on all reasonable assumptions, Russia will be ready. By then it will overwhelm us with the number of its troops; its Baltic fleet and strategic railways will have been constructed. Our own group will in the meantime have become much weaker.[7]

This situation is exacerbated by the widespread assumption that the offense has the advantage (true of nuclear war but not conventional war, in which, it is widely agreed, the offense needs a 2:1 to 3:1 advantage in order to be successful, especially against prepared defenses). It also contributed to the Israeli decision to attack Egypt and Syria in 1967, when Israeli officials calculated that the Arab states, though gaining power, were still weak enough to be defeated.

Balance of power theories also contain an important and often unstated assumption. Given the opportunity, a stronger state will attack a weaker one. This, presumably, is why imbalances in strength must be prevented. Although numerous cases of such aggression have taken place (for example, China attacking Vietnam in 1979, the U.S.S.R. attacking Finland in 1939, Italy attacking Ethiopia — then known as Abyssinia — in 1934), the world nonetheless abounds in unbalanced power relationships, many of them even involving neighboring countries, which have not resulted in war. We do not see headlines such as "Brazil Did Not Invade Uruguay Today." The fact that power imbalances do not necessarily produce war has not, however, diminished the cogency of the concept.

Additional Problems

The reliance on balance of power to prevent war presents other difficulties as well, several of which have been touched on in previous discussions.

Increased Involvement in Wars. When and if war breaks out in a balance of power system, a larger number of states likely will be involved, since governments will have been allying themselves with one side or the other. World Wars I and II, for example, were made even worse by the fact that so many different countries were involved. By contrast, even though various states took sides during the Iran-Iraq War (Syria and China aiding Iran; Arabia, Jordan, and Egypt aiding Iraq), that war did not spread to other parts of the Middle East because the noncombatants took pains to remove themselves from the actual fighting. This occurred in part because they counted on the United States and the Soviet Union to maintain a rough balance in the Middle East, largely by using their influence to prevent a decisive victor from emerging. In short, the Iran-Iraq War was limited to two states because it was not really a balance of power war.

Instability. The relative balance is never static, leading to constant anxieties and adjustments, some of which may generate instability as well as stability. (Balance of power thus resembles deterrence, not only in some of its underlying assumptions, but also in some of its liabilities.) Similarly, it is debatable whether one pattern of balance is more stable than others, and thus preferable. Bipolar systems, for example, appear to produce fewer but more prolonged wars. Multipolarity, on the other hand, might be more stable because it reduces the tension between two major antagonists; yet evidence also indicates that it produces more wars (because there are more potential irritants, and a larger number of troublemakers within the system).

The Balance Backfire. Efforts to upset the balance, on the part of an ambitious ruler or state, may readily succeed and lead to war. For example, when Louis XIV tried to establish his grandson on the throne of Spain, the fear of excessive Bourbon power on the part of other states led to the War of the Spanish Succession. Similarly, two centuries later, French objections to Bismarck's efforts to set a German prince on the throne of Spain contributed greatly to the outbreak of the Franco-Prussian War. The Soviet Union was widely perceived to be upsetting the nuclear balance when it attempted to place nuclear missiles in Cuba in 1962; from the Soviet perspective, the United States had upset that balance several years earlier by placing missiles in Turkey and Great Britain. In any case, the Soviet response, and the subsequent U.S. reaction, precipitated the Cuban Missile Crisis, which nearly led to nuclear war. This suggests that, while a state may be tempted to produce an *imbalance* in its favor, such actions may backfire, generating a crisis on the other side, and possibly leading to war.

"What is essential to understand here," wrote former Defense Secretary Robert McNamara,

> is that the Soviet Union and the United States mutually influence one another's strategic plans. Whatever their intentions or our intentions, actions — or even realistically potential actions — on either side relating to the buildup of nuclear forces necessarily trigger reactions on the other side. It is precisely this action–reaction phenomenon that fuels an arms race.[8]

And it is precisely anxiety about the perceived impact of these actions, or reactions, on the balance of power that makes government leaders take these steps, and their opponents' steps, so seriously.

Military Alliances. The existence of a supposed balance based on military alliances may give a false sense of security, leading in turn to undue aggressiveness, as with Austria's harsh and uncompromising ultimatum to Serbia in 1914, after having received assurances of support from the German government. George Washington expressed a fundamental distrust when, in his farewell address, he urged the United States to avoid "entangling alliances." Of course, it should be pointed out that alliances — crucially important to any balance of power system — do not always promote war, either.

NATO forces on maneuvers in Europe. According to its supporters, NATO has helped keep the peace in Europe since World War II. (U.S. Department of Defense)

It can be argued that NATO, balanced by the Warsaw Pact states, has promoted the peace and stability of Europe since World War II. Immediately prior to World War I, Kaiser Wilhelm sought to restrain his Austrian ally from attacking Serbia; had he succeeded, textbooks such as this might now be extolling the benefits of balanced alliances in preventing war! The fact remains, however, that military alliances have often led to war, with the major participants sometimes drawn in through the actions of their proxies, and out of fear that inaction would mean a loss of national honor (today referred to as "credibility").

Consider, for example, the Seven Years' War (1756–1763), a conflict that was in many ways the first world war, being fought on virtually every continent and at sea: the Caribbean, Cuba, eastern North America, Austria, off the French coast, the Philippines, India, the Mediterranean, Spain, Portugal, and West Africa. It involved primarily England versus France, but also drew in Prussia versus Austria, Russia, Saxony, Hanover, and Sweden. Later, Spain joined with France, and Portugal joined with England.

Neither England nor France wanted this war, and both sought to keep their conflict limited to North America, even though by modern standards, everything unfolded in slow motion: Three years passed between the first hostilities and declarations of general war, and almost another year went by before serious fighting actually commenced (all of which shows that events can "spin out of control" even without the time pressures of split-second decision making). Preceded by a lengthy "cold war" between England and France, the Seven Years' War began as a proxy war in a distant theater, with a dispute about the Ohio Territory in North America. Each side thought it was acting defensively. Moreover, neither side considered its North American colonies worth fighting over in themselves. French Canada was costing France more than was returned to the national treasury, and the English considered their American colonists to be impudent, obstreperous liabilities rather than assets. But as a competitive and mutually aggressive sequence developed, both England and France identified their national interests increasingly with the outcome of the growing confrontation, and the fate of their proxy forces. With national honor at stake, each side's perception of the other's goals narrowed and hardened over time; actions intended to be deterrent were instead perceived to be compellent, and were rejected as improper and excessive. Hence, to give in would have been to "send the wrong signal" and endanger the precious balance.

COLLECTIVE SECURITY

Closely related to balance of power, but nonetheless distinct from it, is the concept of "collective security." In systems of collective security, states promise to refrain from using force against other members of the "collective," except that they agree to band together against any member who attacks any other within the group. Collective security differs from balance of power in that it relies on the participation of each state as an individual, nonaligned entity, as opposed to involving unstable, constantly shifting alliances. Note that NATO and the Warsaw Pact are not examples of collective security, since they are predicated on mutual defense against a potential aggressor from *outside* each alliance, whereas collective security pacts are specifically directed at defense against any aggression from *within* the pact. Early in its history, some statesmen hoped that NATO might exemplify collective security, and include the Soviet Union, for example, among its members. However, the system of post–World War II alliances has degenerated from collective security to "selective security," a series of bilateral and regional arrangements that — notably in the case of NATO and the Warsaw Pact — have set themselves up as competing, opposed alliances.

The now-defunct League of Nations was an effort at collective security, and various regional organizations — the Arab League, the Organization for African Unity, the Organization of American States (comprising most states of the Western Hemisphere) — involve aspects of collective security as well. (We shall examine these in greater detail in Chapter 16, along with the most important of such organizations, the United Nations.)

Among the advantages of collective security is that, by agreement, any aggression will be forcefully opposed. By contrast, in balance of power systems, a would-be aggressor might attempt something, calculating that so long as the other participants considered that the balance (from their perspective) was not adversely affected, a relatively small power grab might be successful. Thus, no major European state protested when Prussia annexed the previously Danish provinces of Schleswig and Holstein during the mid-nineteenth century, and similarly, no leader seriously considered preventing Bismarck from grabbing Alsace and Lorraine from France as spoils of the Franco-Prussian War a few years later. Everyone recognized that the balance of power was shifting toward Germany, but the imbalance was not considered so great at the time as to warrant war.*

---

*As we have seen, in the Austro-Prussian War, Bismarck wisely refrained from defeating Austria too badly, so as not to upset the European balance and thereby arouse the antagonism of the other European states.

Another advantage of collective security over balance of power is that under a balance of power system, a power grab by one state might occasionally meet with an enthusiastic response by another, thereby adding fuel to the fire. For example, during the mid-eighteenth century, Frederick the Great of Prussia was able to initiate several wars aimed at detaching the province of Silesia from Austria and annexing it to Prussia. He was successful in part because (at least in the early Silesian wars) France sided with Prussia, seeing Frederick's power grab as beneficial to French interests, since it would weaken France's greatest rival on the continent, Austria. (In fact, in two of these Silesian wars, France and Austria ended up fighting long after Prussia and Austria had made peace.)

There have, however, been problems with collective security, some of which we shall take up in Chapter 16. For now, let us point out that collective security agreements are only as good as the will of the participants to abide by them. Given the extreme destructiveness of war, states may be understandably reluctant to meet their treaty obligations, especially if their populace does not strongly support the military action that is called for. And given the social and economic interdependence of modern states, even responses short of war — boycotts, trade embargoes, and so on — may cause real hardship, thereby making political leaders hesitant to take such steps.

Also, collective security arrangements, when they involve small states with large and powerful friends, can give rise to highly destructive and interminable wars. Left to themselves, for example, the war between North and South Korea would almost certainly have ended quickly, one way or another. But as it happened, the United States and China became deeply involved, thereby greatly prolonging and intensifying the conflict. The same process occurred in the struggle between North and South Vietnam and between the contra rebels and the government of Nicaragua. The Middle East is kept simmering, if not boiling, in part by assistance provided by the United States and the Soviet Union, primarily to the Israelis and the Arabs, respectively. By contrast, the wars between India and Pakistan, and India and China, were decisive, in part because they were fought without significant involvement of allies on either side.

It is almost certain, moreover, that without U.S. aid, the contras could not have mounted serious opposition to the Sandinistas. Indeed, with the cutoff in military assistance in 1988, the contras quickly folded. By contrast, serious revolutionary movements, with widespread indigenous support, have not been dependent on outside assistance. Thus, without Soviet aid, the communist Kabul government in Afghanistan would almost certainly have been quickly toppled by the rebel *mujahedeen*. Leftist rebels in El Salvador have not required massive aid from the Soviet bloc in order to mount a continuing challenge to the repressive and unresponsive government in that country.

In addition, "allies" sometimes attack each other. The Soviet Union invaded its ally, Afghanistan, in 1979, ousting Hafizullah Amin, the leader they had previously supported, and installing Babrak Kamal, who was eventually replaced by yet another Afghan of Soviet choosing. And the U.S.S.R. has invaded its Warsaw Pact "allies" Hungary (1956) and Czechoslovakia (1968) when those states threatened to become too independent in their ideology and socioeconomic policies. Likewise, the United States has invaded various states of the Western Hemisphere on numerous occasions, most notably the Dominican Republic (1965). It can even be argued that in recent years, the United States has been less restrained in employing violence in its "backyard" (Central America and the Caribbean) than the Soviet Union has in its (Eastern Europe).

NATIONAL SECURITY VIA MILITARY FORCE

Given the uncertainties of maintaining peace through balance of power or collective security, it is not surprising that many government leaders opt for going it alone — not necessarily avoiding alliances, but rather placing their primary emphasis on being sufficiently strong to deter war by the military power of the state, standing by itself. Just as balance of power and collective security systems depend ultimately on a contest of strength, the doctrine of peace through strength is similarly committed to military force.

Richard Perle, the very hawkish assistant secretary of defense during the Reagan administration, once said, "Those who believe that the way to maintain peace is by being weak are over and over again shown by history to be wrong."[9] Here, the political right wing is in agreement with the far left. Mao Zedong wrote that "we do not desire war, but war can only be abolished through war — in order to get rid of the gun, we must first grasp it in hand."[10] In fact, the lessons of history are more equivocal. Diplomatic historian George Kennan suggests that "modern history offers no example of the cultivation by rival powers of armed force on a huge scale that did not in the end lead to an outbreak of hostilities. And there is no reason to believe that we are greater, or wiser, than our ancestors."[11] Moreover, there is every reason to believe that, in the nuclear age, the consequences of hostilities would be far more severe than they have ever been in the past.

As we have seen, strong states are far more likely than weak ones to be involved in wars, especially if the weak ones maintain a position of neutrality, and even more so if their "weakness" is really a refusal to provoke or threaten others. Thus, Switzerland and Sweden have been war-free for centuries, and although they are far weaker than the adjacent larger, more belligerent countries, they are militarily rather strong. In other cases, small, weak countries have been conquered or absorbed by their more powerful neighbors: Latvia, Lithuania, and Estonia were annexed by the Soviet Union just prior to World War II, the kingdom of Hawaii was incorporated into the United States, and the Portuguese enclave of Goa was swallowed up by India.

Military Strength and Failure

The notion that one is better off being strong than weak has a certain primitive logic, yet overwhelming military strength has often resulted in failure: the United States, for example, was victorious in essentially every engagement of the Vietnam War. The world's strongest military power dropped 8 million tons of bombs (making more than 20 million craters), and nearly 400,000 tons of napalm, killing approximately 2.2 million Vietnamese, Cambodians, and Laotians, maiming and wounding about 3.2 million more, and leaving more than 14 million homeless . . . and yet was "defeated." Israel is more than a match for all her Arab neighbors combined, and is infinitely more powerful — militarily — than the largely unarmed Palestinians inhabiting the West Bank and Gaza . . . and yet, Israeli security (and even control of the occupied territories) is by no means assured. Similarly, the Soviet Union was, and still is, enormously more powerful than the Afghan rebels who eventually compelled it to retreat. And, as with the United States in Vietnam, the Soviets, although almost always victorious on the battlefield, were defeated in their ambitions.*

This paradox — that military force, even military victory, does not necessarily lead ultimately to success or even security — holds especially with respect to nuclear weapons. Thus, ironically, the inhabitants of the two strongest powers the world has ever known, the United States and the Soviet Union, are probably less safe than people living in smaller, less armed states, like New Zealand or Belize, whose weaponry does not provoke an opponent to arm and threaten in return. Part of the irony lies in the fact that by committing a state's existence to military success, leaders paradoxically place the state's security in the hands of its opponents. Writing about the Cuban Missile Crisis, Robert Kennedy stated, "We all agreed in the end that if the Russians were ready to go to nuclear war over Cuba, they were ready to go to nuclear war, and that was that."[12] In short, it was up to the Soviets to choose war or peace; having committed itself to a show of force, the U.S. leadership was willing to abrogate

---

*Pyrrhus was a king in ancient Greece. During the third century B.C., he lost nearly all his men in the battle of Asculum. The Romans, however, had been defeated; upon being congratulated for his victory, Pyrrhus replied, "One more such victory and we are utterly undone." Hence, the phrase a "Pyrrhic victory."

Water-filled craters made by 750-lb bombs, dropped by U.S. B-52 bombers during the Vietnam War. (U.S. Department of Defense)

any further decision making. At this point, one must ask whether war is really the continuation of politics by other means, or rather the abandonment of politics, and of humanity, in favor of mass violence.

Security Through Superiority

Government leaders typically argue that their prime responsibility is the maintenance of national security, a concept that is often invoked but rarely scrutinized. It is relatively easy to equate strength with safety, and weakness with vulnerability and danger. Fearing to be seen as too weak, too accommodating, too easily pushed around, government leaders are prone to use threats of military force in efforts to coerce an opponent, or to inhibit further adventuring. Sometimes, this works; other times, the bluff is called. The Soviet invasion of Afghanistan in 1979 was interpreted by the United States as a "grave threat to the free movement of Middle Eastern oil," (and also to the reelection of President Jimmy Carter). The result was the so-called Carter

Doctrine, whereby "any attempt by any outside force to gain control of the Persian gulf region will be regarded as an assault on the vital interests of the United States. It will be repelled by use of any means necessary, including military force."[13] With the benefit of hindsight, we can now conclude that the U.S.S.R. was in fact not seeking control of the Persian Gulf or of Mideast oil. It is also possible, of course, that U.S. saber-rattling discouraged such ambitions . . . or that under other circumstances, it could have raised tensions and provoked incidents not otherwise likely to come about.

During times of international tension, participants tend to be especially aware that the other is aggressive, dangerous, and likely to probe for weakness, being deterred only by strength. In the early days of the Korean War, and again during the Cuban Missile Crisis, White House aides argued that the Soviets were following the Leninist maxim, "If you strike steel, pull back; if you strike mush, keep going." So, better to meet the enemy with steel than with mush. And of course, so long as both sides do this, they can justify their policies by pointing to the other side's policies, and the other side's steel as well. And by a kind of self-referential logic, both sides would be correct.

This argument readily leads to an insistence on being more powerful than the opponent, to maintain what President Reagan called a "margin of safety" (that is, superiority) over the opponent. In his famous "Iron Curtain" speech in 1946, Winston Churchill argued not for a military balance between the West and the Soviet Union, but for superiority: "The old doctrine of a balance of power* is unsound. We cannot afford, if we can help it, to work on narrow margins, offering temptations to a trial of strength."[14] Similar thinking motivated the massive U.S. increases in military forces, including nuclear programs, during the Reagan administration.

The inherent logic of such a policy crumbles when one considers its role in generating the security dilemma. Nonetheless, such thinking has long dominated the national security managers of many states. Through much of the nineteenth century, for example, Britain proclaimed the "two-power standard," by which the Royal Navy ought always to be at least equal, and preferably superior, to the combined navies of the next two most powerful states. This was considered necessary in order to guarantee British national security. The British sought absolute security, but as Henry Kissinger has put it, "The desire of one power for absolute security means absolute insecurity for all the others."[15]

Hence, it is not surprising that the British and German naval establishments competed vigorously during the first decade or so of the twentieth century, or that the tension generated by this competition contributed to the outbreak of World War I. This Anglo-German arms race also exemplifies another difficulty in trying to achieve peace through strength: the fact that new manifestations of "strength" can undermine a state's preexisting se-

curity. For example, the Royal Navy was quite far ahead of its German counterpart when the British Admiralty introduced a new class of extra large, heavily armed and armoured battleships, known as "Dreadnaughts," after the name of the first such ship. At a stroke, this act — which was the logical culmination of a policy of seeking to maintain peace through strength — made much of its own Royal Navy obsolete, and forced Britain to engage in a more intense competition with Germany (which also began building its own Dreadnaughts).

Something similar has happened repeatedly in the nuclear arms race, with the United States, consistently the leader and innovator, introducing new delivery systems or warheads, only to find the Soviet Union following suit, after which both sides have been less secure than they were before the escalation. For example, the United States, seeking to exploit its long-standing technological advantage, introduced MIRVing in the early 1970s, which resulted in a large U.S. lead in number of deliverable warheads — even though the United States actually fielded fewer ICBMs than the Soviets. But when the U.S.S.R. caught up, and began MIRVing its large SS-17, SS-18, and SS-19 missiles, this innovation backfired and produced a less stable balance than had existed before. (By the late 1980s, some U.S. policymakers were attempting to reverse this trend by going back to single-warhead missiles, such as the so-called Midgetman.)

Military Interpretations of National Security

Another, more general problem derives from employing a strictly military interpretation of "national security." One authority notes that the only definition of national security he has seen appeared in a dictionary prepared for the Joint Chiefs of Staff: "a. a military or defense advantage over any foreign nation or group of nations, or b. a favorable foreign relations position, or c. a defense posture capable of successfully resisting hostile or destructive action from within or without, overt or covert."[16] According to this approach, widely shared among government policymakers, national security is a very scarce commodity, obtained via a zero-sum game:

---

*Here, Churchill is referring to the relative strength of the West versus the U.S.S.R., not to the historical concept of balance of power.

the more one side gets of it, the less there is for the other. Furthermore, it is measured entirely in units of military strength. Such a mind-set suggests three rejoinders:

1. Military strength is often a two-edged sword, evoking less rather than more security. This security dilemma arises because states, trying to increase their security via military forces and alliances, succeed only in making other states less secure . . . which, in turn, respond militarily themselves, as a result of which everyone is less secure. The United States may well offer the most dramatic example: After pioneering the development of the "ultimate weapon," and leading in virtually every dimension of the ensuing arms race, the United States is less secure today than at any previous time in its history. After all, surrounded by two great oceans and happy Canada to the north and hapless Mexico to the south, the United States has never had to worry seriously about invasion by a foreign power. But because of the very nature of the nuclear age, there is much reason to worry about "national security," and personal security as well.

2. The tendency is to think of security as an exclusive, competitive accomplishment: Security for me can only be purchased at the cost of insecurity for you. In fact, however, national security can be a positive-sum game, in which both sides win. Indeed, in the nuclear age — when each side has the capacity to destroy the other — national security can only be achieved via *mutual* security. The United States, for example, is only as secure as the U.S.S.R., and vice versa. Insofar as either is insecure, the other is threatened.

3. In their quest for "national security," government leaders may — intentionally or unintentionally — actually create "enemies" so as to justify their continuing position of power and authority within their own society. In addition to producing a situation of reduced security (see rejoinder 1, above), which presumably is

unintentional, leaders who create enemies can also facilitate the social and economic exploitation of their own populace, a process that is likely to be wholly intended, although rarely identified as such.

For example, during the latter stages of the Roman republic, the populace was wantonly exploited and pillaged, by its own leadership, in the name of "security." Enemies were created to justify ruinously high taxes, the appropriation of private holdings, and the abridgment of personal liberties. Economist Joseph Schumpeter unsparingly criticized "that policy which pretends to aspire to peace but unerringly generates war, the policy of continual preparation for war, the policy of meddlesome interventionism." He went on to describe these excesses on the part of Rome's rulers:

> There was no corner of the known world where some interest was not alleged to be in danger or under actual attack. If the interests were not Roman, they were those of Rome's allies; and if Rome had no allies, then allies would be invented. When it was utterly impossible to contrive such an interest — why, then it was the national honor that had been insulted. The fight was always invested with an aura of legality. Rome was always being attacked by evil-minded neighbors, always fighting for a breathing space. The whole world was pervaded by a host of enemies, and it was manifestly Rome's duty to guard against their undubitably aggressive designs. They were enemies only waiting to fall on the Roman people.[17]

"Meddlesome interventionism" is not limited to the ancient past; it is also with us today, as many inhabitants of the Third World can attest. And moreover, much of the U.S.-Soviet competition, especially in the nuclear arena, can be seen as a consequence of warnings by those who see enemies everywhere. "Our government has kept us in a perpetual state of fear," said General Douglas MacArthur, "kept us in a continual stampede of patriotic fervor — with a cry of a grave national emergency. Always there has been some terrible evil at home or some monstrous foreign power that was going to gobble us up."[18]

Other National Security Considerations

Finally, although there is definitely a military dimension to national security, it must be emphasized that national security cannot be measured by military parameters alone. It is also a function of economic strength, political cohesiveness, social equity, and environmental soundness. National security is diminished if the populace is inadequately housed or fed, or when medical care is insufficient. For a state to neglect its own people in pursuit of "national security" is very much like a person destroying his or her house in order to obtain materials with which to build a fence around the devastated shell.

In this respect, one historian has developed the influential thesis that great powers tend to rise and then fall in a predictable cycle, as their world ambitions make excessive demands on their domestic productivity:

> A nation projects military power according to its economic resources but eventually the high cost of maintaining political supremacy weakens the economic base. Great powers in decline respond by spending more on defence and weaken themselves further by directing essential revenues away from productive investment.[19]

This argument points to the rise and fall, in turn, of Hapsburg Spain and the British empire, and then suggests that we look critically at whether the United States is about to experience a similar decline. The United States devotes approximately 7 percent of its GNP to military expenditures, and the U.S.S.R. invests about the same absolute amount; given that the Soviet economy is only about one half as powerful, this translates into twice the financial strain, or approximately 14 percent of the GNP. By contrast, only about 1 percent of the Japanese GNP is spent on its military; not coincidentally, Japan has become an economic titan, while the relative position of the United States and U.S.S.R. has declined. It may also be notable that 10 percent of Japanese government investment in research and development goes into military products; the analogous figure for the United States is a whopping 75 percent. The Japanese are pioneers in developing and marketing VCRs, automobiles, cameras, and so

Parisians cheering U.S. armed forces that liberated Paris from the Germans in 1944. National security is most often defined in military terms; increasingly, however, other dimensions are being recognized. (Library of Congress)

forth, which they sell to the world economy, and as a result enjoy an enormous financial surplus. The United States makes MX missiles, which cost immense sums, but can only be purchased, collectively, by the U.S. taxpayers, contributing ultimately to inflation, to the burgeoning trade deficit, and to the national debt.

"The problem in defense," wrote President Eisenhower in 1953, "is how far you can go without destroying from within what you are trying to defend from without."[20]

BARGAINING CHIPS

"We arm to parley," said Winston Churchill, and indeed, political leaders have long maintained that one of the benefits of armaments is that they provide leverage in disarmament or arms control negotiations with the other side (see Chapter 15).

Generally, whenever two sides agree to divest themselves of weaponry (something that happens very rarely), or to refrain mutually from acquiring certain military forces — either by qualitative or quantitative restrictions — both sides are expected to forgo something comparable. If one side is militarily weak, and the other strong, then what incentive is there for the latter to build down? One answer is for both sides to be comparably strong at the outset of any serious disarmament discussions.

This idea has many supporters, especially in the nuclear age. Thus, when the United States had an overwhelming lead over the Soviet Union during the first two decades of the nuclear arms race, the United States predictably advanced numerous "disarmament" proposals that essentially involved either a "halt in place" or equal reductions and restrictions on both sides, which would have frozen the U.S. advantage. Just as predictably, the U.S.S.R. consistently rejected these initiatives, instead proposing wide-ranging and equally unrealistic cuts, which the United States, not surprisingly, rejected as well. Only when the Soviets achieved nuclear parity with the United States, in the late 1960s, did serious, joint efforts at nuclear arms control gather momentum.

Proponents of the "bargaining chip" justification for armaments also point to several episodes in which bargaining from strength may have been helpful. For one, the United States and the Soviet Union reached agreement on the Anti-Ballistic Missile (ABM) Treaty in 1972 only after the United States went ahead with plans to deploy an ABM system of its own, to match the ABM weapons already deployed by the Soviets. For another, the Intermediate Nuclear Forces (INF) Treaty, by which the United States and the U.S.S.R. agreed to eliminate all intermediate-range, land-based nuclear missiles in Europe, was reached only after the United States and NATO had persevered in deploying ground-launched cruise and Pershing II ballistic missiles, in response to the Soviet deployment of SS-20 missiles several years before.

It is further argued, accordingly, that the United States must proceed with "modernization" of its nuclear arsenal — including Trident II submarine-launched missiles, Stealth bombers, addi-

tional MX missiles, and rapid development and deployment of the Strategic Defense Initiative (SDI, more popularly known as Star Wars) — if it is to have any hope of reaching agreement with the Soviets on further and more significant mutual cuts, this time in strategic weaponry.

On the other hand, these cases are ambiguous. Both sides agreed to the ABM Treaty, not because the other had begun deploying ABM systems, but rather because both sides recognized that an effective defense against ballistic missiles was simply not possible. Within a few months after it was completed, for example, the sole U.S. ABM system, near the Minuteman missile base at Grand Forks, North Dakota, was abandoned. Moreover, it was argued — in the early 1970s with respect to ABM systems, just as in the late 1980s with respect to SDI — that competition over strategic defenses would simply generate more offensive countermeasures by the other side, and end up adding yet another layer to the spiraling arms race.

Regarding the INF Treaty, it has been pointed out that the major factor leading to Soviet acceptance of asymmetric cuts was a dramatic change in the U.S.S.R.'s leadership. The ascension to power of Mikhail Gorbachev resulted in a decision to defuse military competition with the United States so as to focus Soviet attention and resources on domestic development. Insofar as this is so, then, as former Senator Gary Hart put it, crediting the INF Treaty to U.S. armaments is like a rooster taking credit for the dawn.

In addition, most of the time the weapons that are justified as bargaining chips are never cashed in. Rather, they develop a powerful constituency — civilian contractors who build them, military commanders who deploy and command them, politicians in whose district they are constructed and/or sited — and so they insidiously become part of the arsenal, whether needed or not. Cruise missiles, for example, were initially justified as bargaining chips for the SALT I negotiations, and Trident submarines and the MX missile as bargaining chips for SALT II. We wound up without any SALT II treaty, but with both Trident and the MX.

Finally, conservatives who advise against diminishing U.S. military expenditures now that the

Cold War is winding down, allege that the United States' military buildup during the Reagan administration successfully pressured the Soviet leadership into a more conciliatory stance.* While this is possible, another interpretation—equally if not more plausible—is that the Soviet policy shift took place *despite* the United States' military buildup. Thus, military pressure most commonly undercuts the conciliators on the opposing side and leads to a corresponding military buildup in return. If the military had been in charge of negotiating the Montreal Protocols, for example, which established standards for ozone protection (see Chapter 21), we might all be stockpiling chlorofluorocarbons as bargaining chips.

APPEASEMENT, PROVOCATION, AND DETERRENCE

Just as doves point to the dangers of overarming and of provocation, referring especially to the lessons of World War I, hawks point to the dangers of underarming and of appeasement, citing specifically the lessons of Munich and World War II. The Soviet experience during World War II, in which they suffered a massive surprise attack by German forces in June 1941, was matched by the traumatic U.S. experience of a surprise attack by Japan at Pearl Harbor in December of that same year. Whether these historical examples have much relevance in the nuclear age, however, is questionable. Thus, whereas in the past, leaders worried about being attacked by surprise and rendered unable to respond, the greater danger today may well be "responding to" an attack that never happened. Probably the most likely scenario for a nuclear war is for it to occur by accident or false alarm (especially during conditions of crisis). Closely related are the threatening qualities of these weapons—especially their accuracy and short flight times—which generate considerable anxiety in the opponent that might itself precipitate war. This represents a special case of the security dilemma, in that, seeking to deter adversaries, one can wind up provoking them instead.

World Wars I and II

This dilemma is certainly not entirely unique to the nuclear age. In the decade before World War I, for example, both German and British naval leaders worried that the other side might be planning a preemptive attack on their fleet. And as we have seen, one of the driving forces behind the actual declarations of war by Germany and Russia in 1914 was anxiety over the consequences of allowing the opponent to mobilize first. A would-be defender, seeking to achieve peace via strength, must walk a narrow line between, on the one hand, provoking the war it wants to prevent (the experience of both sides in World War I), and on the other, failing to prevent war by being perceived as too weak or lacking in resolve (the "Munich syndrome" in 1938, or Britain vis-à-vis Argentina in 1982).

In 1914, British foreign secretary Sir Edward Grey announced that "Britain probably would be unable to stand aside" if war came to Europe; a clearer statement of intent to stand by France if war came to Europe might have made Germany more hesitant. Similarly, France had a treaty with Czechoslovakia in 1938, committing the French nation to come to Czechoslovakia's defense. But France had vacillated when Germany remilitarized the Rhineland (in defiance of the Versailles treaty) and annexed Austria; thus, Hitler was convinced that France would find some way to weasel out of its obligation to Prague. He was right. He thought the same thing about his attack on Poland, but that time he was wrong.

The Nuclear Age

Supporters of peace through strength like to point to the fact that no U.S.-Soviet war has taken place in the nuclear age, a claim that cannot reasonably be assessed. Perhaps peace has prevailed between the two superpowers because they have no quarrel that would justify fighting a terribly destructive war, or even a conventional one. It is not at all clear,

---

*And that, by extension, more pressure will generate yet more Soviet concessions.

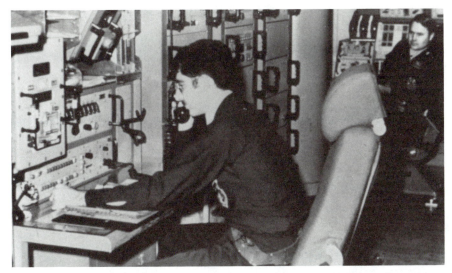

Missile launch officers at their consoles, which control ICBMs in their underground silos. Hair-trigger alerts make accidental nuclear war more likely and it can be argued that nuclear weapons themselves generate anxiety and may increase, rather than decrease, the chances of war. (U.S. Department of Defense)

for example, that the Soviet leadership has been itching to invade Western Europe, and has been restrained only by NATO's nuclear arsenal. Such post facto arguments—especially negative ones, purporting to show why something has *not* happened—are, in fact, impossible to prove.*

In addition, in the context of world events, the four decades since World War II is not really all that long. More than twenty years separated World Wars I and II; before that, there were more than forty years of peace between the end of the Franco-Prussian War and World War I; and fifty-five years had elapsed since the previous major war, which ended with Napoleon's defeat at Waterloo in 1815. the point is that periods of peace are not unheard of, even in war-prone Europe. And furthermore, in each case, when peace ended and the next war began, it was fought with the weapons available at that

time . . . which for the next major war would include nuclear weapons.

In short, it may be premature to congratulate ourselves, or our nuclear weapons, for keeping the peace. The story is told about the man who sprayed perfume on his lawn every morning. When his perplexed neighbor asked about this strange behavior, the man replied "I do it to keep the elephants away." The neighbor protested, "But there aren't any elephants within ten thousand miles of here." Whereupon the man announced, triumphantly, "You see, it works!"

There is also a logical fallacy at work here: If nuclear weapons had failed to keep the peace, and we had a nuclear war, then there would be no one around to argue about their effectiveness as peacekeepers. Moreover, while the post-1945 U.S.-Soviet peace may have been achieved "through strength," it may also have occurred *in spite of* the provocations of deterrence rather than because of them. Thus, the presence of nuclear weapons on hair-trigger alert capable of reaching each other's homeland certainly makes both sides nervous and edgy. Although in the 1962 Cuban Missile Crisis, the two

*If a dog barks in the night, we might be able to say with confidence that it did so "because" someone walked by. If it does not bark, however, we may never know "why."

sides refrained from active hostilities apparently because of the unacceptable costs of nuclear war, the crisis itself was brought about because of the provocative nature of the weapons.

Beyond this, there have been many cases in which the possession of strong military forces — including nuclear weapons — has not deterred war. The Chinese, Cuban, Iranian, and Nicaraguan revolutions all took place despite the fact that the United States was allied to the governments in power, and had nuclear weapons. Similarly, the United States lost the Vietnam War, just as the U.S.S.R. lost in Afghanistan, although both countries were not only only nuclear-armed, but also much stronger, militarily, than their opponents. It was a nuclear-armed United States that "lost" China in 1949, and a nuclear-armed Soviet Union that "lost" China once again, in the early 1960s.* Moreover, Argentina was not deterred from attacking the Falklands/Malvinas, even though Britain is a nuclear state and Argentina is not. Deterrence has failed in other, nonnuclear contexts as well: between Iran and Iraq, and many times between Israel and her neighbors.

As we have seen, the nuclear arms race in particular has been criticized as a kind of action–reaction sequence, in which an action by one side leads to a reaction by the other, which leads, in turn, to yet another action. Closely related are "worst-case analyses," in which the military establishment of each side — seeking to be prudent — assumes the worst of the other's capabilities and intentions. The result is a process of "threat inflation," in which each side takes an alarmist view of the threat that the other poses, and as a result, overreacts, thereby further escalating the competition and nervousness on both sides. "The worse aspect of this development," wrote Albert Einstein, "lies in its apparently inexorable character. Each step appears as the inevitable consequence of the one that went before, and at the end, looming ever nearer, lies universal annihilation."[21]

---

*It may seem odd that a nation of nearly a billion people can have been so frequently misplaced.

THE USE AND ABUSE OF THREATS

The most extreme example of attempted peace through strength is the nuclear arms race. Arguments in its favor rely, as we have seen, on the concept of deterrence, and the presumption that in the absence of immense destructive power, the United States would be susceptible to attack, blackmail, and/or domination. Supposedly, we are to be made safe by nuclear weapons. It may not be the best of all imaginable worlds, we are told, but perhaps it is the best of all realistically possible worlds, in that it keeps our enemy — international communism — at bay. As we read in Shakespeare's *Henry IV*, Act I, "Out of this nettle, danger, we pluck this flower, safety." And as Winston Churchill proposed, referring specifically to nuclear deterrence, "Safety will be the steady child of terror, and survival, the twin brother of annihilation."[22]

Fear, Stubbornness, and Opportunity

When we seek to maintain peace via nuclear weapons, we basically rely on the effectiveness of threats. Thomas Schelling[23] distinguished between "compellent" and "deterrent" threats. The former are more aggressive, forcing the opponent to *do* something, surrender something of value, and so on; the latter are intended simply to *prevent* something, to dissuade the opponent from acting in a way that the threatener finds undesirable, such as deterring aggression by or subversion of another state. Schelling also pointed out that force can be used for its punishment or shock effect, aside from its military usefulness: Sherman's march through Georgia, General Sheridan's genocidal tactics against the Comanches, German use of V-1 and V-2 weapons against Britain in World War II, or the atomic bombing of Hiroshima and Nagasaki.[24] States also tend to employ force when they see a need to shore up their credibility.

It may be that deterrence — especially nuclear deterrence — has made the superpowers cautious in their provocations of each other. However, deterrence in general has also encouraged a kind of "competitive risk-taking," in which the bolder, tougher, more violence-prone player appears likely to win: Mussolini was more willing to incur risks to ensure that his side (Franco and the fascists) was victorious in the Spanish civil war, and Ho Chi Minh and his followers were more willing to undergo risks — and suffer losses — so as to be victorious in Vietnam. But when two sides collide, each determined to be the tougher, peace through strength succumbs to war through stubborness, as with World War I.

Moreover, a cogent argument can be made that when they are debating whether or not to go to war, political leaders do not necessarily follow the expectations of deterrence theory, which assumes that states regularly assess their potential prospects vis-à-vis one another, and are likely to leap through any "windows of vulnerability" that might reveal themselves. Thus, military weakness relative to another state is assumed to invite attack, whereas strength deters it. But as we have seen, wars have been precipitated much more often by *fear* (that the other side is stronger, or — even more often — that it will shortly become stronger) than by overconfidence. It is now widely recognized that the Soviet invasion of Afghanistan was not brought about by a breakdown in traditional deterrence. The U.S.S.R. did not suddenly realize, in December of 1979, that it was stronger than Afghanistan, and then proceed to attack. Deterrence didn't "fail" in this case. Rather, it never existed: The U.S.S.R. did not invade Afghanistan because it felt strong, but because it felt weak, threatened by the prospect of a hostile Islamic state on its southern border.

By the same token, the U.S. invasion of Vietnam did not occur because the United States had suddenly developed, or become aware of, its ability to use military forces successfully in Southeast Asia. Deterrence between the United States and Vietnam did not break down, at least not in the sense that deterrence theorists typically assume. The United States did not wish to conquer and occupy Southeast Asia with military force. Rather, the U.S. government feared (correctly, as it turned out) that the anticommunist government in South Vietnam would be unable to withstand the existing challenges from the North and from its own dissatisfied people. The United States was motivated much more by fear of communism ("losing" Vietnam as we had "lost" China and Cuba, and had almost

"lost" South Korea) than by dreams of conquest on the Asian mainland.

Abundant evidence also suggests that states are more likely to be influenced by their own internal political needs than by their objective military strength vis-à-vis an opponent. Thus, Argentina clearly was militarily inferior to Great Britain when it attacked the Falkland Islands in 1982, just as India clearly was militarily inferior to China when it provoked the brief and (for India) disastrous Sino-Indian War over the disputed Himalayan region of Ladakh in 1962. (It is also noteworthy that in both these cases, the unsuccessful attacker was not deterred by the fact that the "victim" possessed nuclear weapons.)

Concern About Image

Deterrence theory and the assumptions of peace through strength can also have a pernicious effect. Nuclear deterrence in particular depends on a mutually threatening posture, as each side seeks to impress the other with its toughness and willingness to use nuclear weapons if provoked. Thus, conflicts that may in themselves be of no intrinsic consequence for either side, and that often occur far from the borders of either superpower, become imbued with a peculiar significance: indicating the credibility, reliability, toughness, and hence, the security of one side (or both). It then becomes vital to intervene in virtually any struggle, just to prove that "we" will not be pushovers, and to ensure that our "national will" is not about to be doubted, or tested, again in the future.

For example, a 1988 report entitled *Discriminate Deterrence*, and authored by the Commission on Integrated Long-Term Strategy (which included Reagan administration Deputy Defense Secretary Fred Ikle and other notable Cold War architects such as Albert Wohlstetter and Zbigniew Brzezinski), noted that

> nearly all the armed conflicts of the past forty years have occurred in what is vaguely referred to as the Third World. . . . These conflicts are obviously less threatening than any Soviet-American war would be, yet they have had and will have an adverse cumulative effect on U.S. access to critical regions, on

American credibility among allies and friends, and on American self-confidence. If this cumulative effect cannot be checked or reversed in the future, it will gradually undermine America's ability to defend its interests in the most vital regions, such as the Persian Gulf, the Mediterranean and the Western Pacific.[25]

We have already noted that concern about avoiding the image of the United States as a "pitiful, helpless giant" served as a major motivator for U.S. perseverence in the Vietnam War.

Finally, we must note that reliance on threats may also lead to a false estimate of the other's threshold, which can be dangerous in the extreme if both sides engage in a game of nuclear chicken, each determined that the other must be the one to swerve. When General Douglas MacArthur—no shrinking violet when it came to the application of military force—addressed the Philippine Parliament in 1961, he noted that

> global war has become a Frankenstein to destroy both sides. No longer is it a weapon of adventure—the short cut to international power. If you lose, you are annihilated. If you win, you stand only to lose. No longer does it possess even the chance of the winner of a duel. It contains now only the germs of double suicide.[26]

THE PRISONER'S DILEMMA

Advocates of peace through strength often maintain that states have no choice: They must maintain and even increase their armaments—as well as a credible threat to use them if called upon to do so—because if they relied less on military force, they would be at the mercy of another state that continued to arm heavily. Hence, each may find itself forced into a warlike posture that neither wants, but both are unable to escape. This situation has long been recognized, and modeled mathematically, as the so-called Prisoner's Dilemma. Analyses based on the Prisoner's Dilemma have a prominent place in mathematical game theory, strategic analysis, and even studies in social psychology that attempt to model arms races and various competitive interactions. Understanding this system is therefore important, not only for the light it might shed on threats, competition, and the problems of cooperation, but also for what it reveals about the mind-set of people whose opinions are influential in shaping major decisions about the arms race.

In its original formulation, the Prisoner's Dilemma is as follows: Imagine two prisoners, apprehended by the police and accused of collaborating in a bank robbery. The prosecutor's goal is to get both prisoners to plead guilty. He separates the two—keeping each in a different cell, allowing no communication between them—and makes each prisoner the following offer: "If you and your partner insist on pleading not guilty, I do not have enough evidence to convict either of you of bank robbery, but you will both be found guilty on a lesser charge, say, illegal possession of a weapon, and you will both be sentenced to a year in jail. If both of you plead guilty, then you will each face a severe sentence, five years in jail. On the other hand, if one of you cooperates with me and pleads guilty to the robbery charge, thereby implicating the other, then this will give me enough evidence to convict the other prisoner, and the government will reward you for your assistance by letting you go free while your partner will then be sentenced to forty years behind bars. But if you do not cooperate and your partner does, then you get the forty years, and he goes free."

These options are shown in the "payoff matrix" in Figure 14.1, in which each individual can choose between two courses of action—pleading guilty or pleading not guilty. The payoffs to individual 1 are shown within the matrix (the payoffs to individual 2 are symmetrical). Thus, if individual 1 pleads guilty, he gets five years in jail if individual 2 also pleads guilty (payoff a). If individual 1 pleads guilty and individual 2 pleads not guilty, then individual 1 gets to go free (payoff b).

Under these conditions, each prisoner faces a cruel dilemma. Both would do best—just one year in jail—if they cooperated with each other and stuck to their plea of not guilty (payoff d for both). However, each one fears what the other might do, reasoning as follows: "My partner might plead either guilty or not guilty. If he pleads guilty, then I

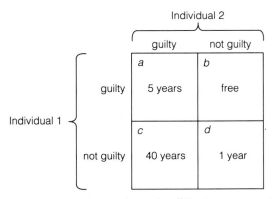

FIGURE 14.1   Prisoner's Dilemma Payoff Matrix

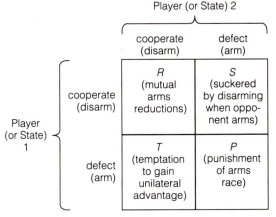

FIGURE 14.2   Payoff Matrix for Players or States. The indicated payoffs are those received by player (or state) 1; the payoffs for 2 are reciprocal.

can either plead guilty or not guilty. If I do the former, I get five years; if I do the latter, I get forty years. So clearly my best choice is to plead guilty. On the other hand, if my partner pleads not guilty, then my best choice still is to plead guilty, because then I get to go free rather than spend a year in jail."

As a result, the prisoner finds himself forced to plead guilty out of fear that the other will double-cross him and plead not guilty. And of course, prisoner 2, reasoning identically, comes to the same conclusion. The ironic result of this process is that both prisoners plead guilty and spend five years in jail (payoff *a*), because each fears that otherwise,

he might end up with forty years (payoff *c*), whereas they could have gotten a far better joint payoff (*a*), if they had only figured out some way of cooperating.

In general terms, the Prisoner's Dilemma is considered a model for the evolution of cooperation versus competition. In this simplified system, players (or states) have two options, call them "cooperate" (or disarm) versus "defect" (or arm). The matrix in Figure 14.2 shows the various payoffs: If both players cooperate, then both receive the payoff *R*, the reward for cooperation; if both defect, then both receive the payoff *P*, the punishment of mutual competition; if one defects and the other cooperates, then the defector receives *T*, the temptation to defect; and the one who cooperates (disarms) while the other takes advantage of the situation receives *S*, the sucker's payoff.

Basically, a Prisoner's Dilemma occurs when the payoffs are in the following relationship: $T > R > P > S$. In this case, the players are each tempted to get *T*, and fearful of getting stuck with *S*, and so, they wind up getting *P* (a punishing arms race) when the best mutual payoff would have been *R*, the reward for cooperation or mutual restraint.

The Prisoner's Dilemma is a useful way of modeling the dilemma of thinking that one must be "nasty" for fear that anyone who is "nice" is at the mercy of others who persevere in being nasty. On the other hand, it may well be unduly pessimistic, in that it assumes only two choices, whereas in reality, individuals or states have a variety of options. They can try a mix of strategies: disarm in one respect, build up in another, delay a modernization program, and so forth. The Prisoner's Dilemma model also assumes that there is no interaction between the players; in fact, however, government leaders can be in constant communication, sending signals and doing things that may be more, or less, reassuring or anxiety-provoking. The simplified model also requires that there be only one payoff, and that everything depend on that; in reality, states interact many times in succession, and they can vary their behavior depending on what happened the previous time. And if both sides have an interest in generating a sequence of cooperative interactions, then cooperative outcomes can yield the highest payoff.[27]

In short, the Prisoner's Dilemma can be useful in clarifying our thinking, and indeed, variants of it are used extensively by analysts in the promilitary intellectual community, where the mathematical theory of "games" is taken quite seriously. It should be remembered, however, that such an approach carries many hidden assumptions, and that individuals — and states — must avoid becoming prisoners of their own narrow-minded dilemmas.

NONPROVOCATIVE DEFENSE

Finally, having considered the major traditional doctrines related to peace through strength, and found them wanting, let us turn to another concept, one more likely to commend itself to military-minded seekers after peace. It is variously known as "defensive defense," "nonoffensive defensive," "alternative defense," "transarmament," or "nonprovocative defense." This approach seeks to make war less likely through a substantial restructuring of strategic planning and the actual disposition of forces. Thus, although most countries describe their military as "defense" forces, they almost always have a large offensive component, which leads, in turn, to the widespread "security dilemma." By contrast, under a regime of nonprovocative defense, states would emphasize weapons that are unambiguously defensive, and would reconfigure their forces so as not to threaten other states. The goal would be to establish a regime in which defense dominated offense, in which states felt secure in their ability to repel an aggressor, but insecure in their ability to aggress successfully upon another.

The idea is not altogether new. In 1912, French socialist Jean Jaures proposed a nationwide civilian militia, with six months' training and reserve availability for twenty-five to thirty years. This militia would not constitute a standing army, and would therefore not be available for overseas adventures, but it would be eminently suitable for defending borders. For his suggestion, Jaures was vilified as a pro-German traitor, and eventually assassinated.

If nonprovocative defense had been tried, it might well have enabled Europe to avoid war in 1914. During the 1930s, Basil Liddell Hart — one of Britain's foremost military historians and strategists — proposed that peace could be maintained if military forces were redesigned to assure that defense had primacy over offense. Essentially, the idea was that states would become like medieval knights, with invulnerable armor and puny swords: "The idealist may regret to see men going about in armour, but the realist can perceive that the process is innocuous, if still expensive. And gradually the humour of it may become apparent, thus leading to it being discarded."[28]

How It Would Work

After languishing for several decades, the concept of nonprovocative defense has been resurrected once more, given special impetus by the illogic of seeking security via nuclear weapons, as well as the mutually threatening and expensive military stalemate between NATO and the Warsaw Pact states in Europe. Numerous groups have sprouted, especially in Europe but in the United States as well, promoting the concept of making war obsolete by restricting military forces to a nonprovocative, strictly defensive posture. More specifically, tanks would be prohibited, and antitank defenses permitted; bombers would be prohibited, and antiaircraft batteries and short-range fighter–interceptors permitted; heavily armored mechanized forces would be prohibited; and lightly armed, mobile infantry units permitted; supplies would be prepositioned, and defensive networks constructed throughout the countryside. Such arrangements are not suitable for attack, but can help compose a formidable defense.

U.S. military thinking has not been especially receptive to nonprovocative defense. By contrast, the Soviet leadership has shown substantial interest in what it calls "reasonable sufficiency." Writing in *Pravda*, Gorbachev called for "such a structure of the armed forces of a state that they would be sufficient to repulse a possible aggression but would not be sufficient for the conduct of offensive actions."[29]

One difficulty with implementing nonprovocative defense is the potential difficulty of

Swiss Army forces on training maneuvers. The Swiss Army is a notable example of armed neutrality and nonprovocative defense. (Office of the Defense, Military, Naval and Air Attache, Embassy of Switzerland)

distinguishing unambiguously between defensive and offensive forces. Fighter aircraft, for example, can be used to supplement offensive operations, as well as to defend against invaders. Armored personnel carriers can be either aggressive or defensive, as can destroyers and even submarines. Even fixed defensive fortifications can serve the offense: The Siegfried Line, built by Germany along its border with France, made it less likely that France would assist its Polish ally while the Nazis made war in the east. In other cases, however, the distinction is more clear-cut: Minefields and immobile tank-traps are unambiguously defensive, while nuclear weapons are offensive (even if they ostensibly provide deterrence).

Moreover, nonprovocative defense would require a massive change in doctrine. Both NATO and the Warsaw Pact states, for example, would have to abandon their current plans for "forward-based defense," "deep strikes," and the like — tactics that call for "defending" their respective alliances by carrying the fight deep into the opposing territory. Both sides would concentrate instead on a "defense in depth," emphasizing small mobile units trained to mount defensive operations, if necessary deep within their own borders. In addition, states such as the United States, Britain, France, and (increasingly) the Soviet Union have deployed military forces that are capable of "projecting power" far from their shores. These forces — aircraft carriers, long-range fighter–bombers, mobile artillery, amphibious assault units — are not used for defending one's own borders; rather, their purpose is overwhelmingly to intervene (or threaten to intervene) in other countries, generally far from home, and most often in the Third World. So, nonprovocative defense would require that states forgo such activities.

Prospects and Current Examples

The prospects, although cloudy, are not altogether bleak. The idea of confining each state's "defense forces" to real defense, thereby making war less likely, reducing tensions, and saving money to boot, has an undeniable practical appeal. (It must be

Biography

Randall Forsberg

Randall Forsberg is widely credited as being the "mother" of the Nuclear Freeze movement. From 1968 to 1974, she worked at the Stockholm International Peace Research Institute (SIPRI), studying worldwide military and development programs. From 1973 until 1982 she served as consultant for a highly regarded series of estimates of United States and Soviet strategic weapons, appearing in SIPRI's annual yearbook of *World Armaments and Disarmament*. In 1979, she coauthored an important, critical study of military spending and strategy, *The Price of Defense*, reissued in 1982 under the title *Winding Down*. She has taught at Boston University and has participated in the Harvard Program on Science and International Affairs.

In 1980 Ms. Forsberg founded the Institute for Defense and Disarmament Studies in Brookline, Massachusetts, which she continues to direct. That same year, she wrote the four-page "Call to Halt the Nuclear Arms Race," which launched the national Nuclear Weapons Freeze Campaign and became its manifesto. She established numerous pro-freeze organizations, lectured widely, and in 1983 was awarded a MacArthur Foundation Fellowship.

In recent years, Randall Forsberg has turned her attention to long-term policy options that involve limiting military forces to strictly defensive roles. She organized an international Alternative Defense Working Group in 1986, and in 1987 launched a major East-West Conventional Force Study to analyze NATO and Warsaw Pact needs and propose feasible strategies for mutual reductions.

emphasized that nonprovocative defense would not offer any less defense than current military postures; in fact, by being less threatening to would-be opponents, it should reduce the probability of armed hostilities, thereby providing much more defense.) In addition, unlike most arms control or disarmament proposals, the transition to nonprovocative defense does not require complex bilateral or multilateral negotiated agreements; any state that wishes to can make the shift unilaterally.

And several have already done so. A number of countries, notably the European states that practice "armed neutrality," are living, practical examples of successful nonprovocative defense. For example, Switzerland requires that all men between 20 and 50 years of age participate in a civilian militia. They keep their guns, ammunition, and uniforms at home, giving the Swiss the option of mustering an impressive force of more than 600,000, within forty-eight hours. The Swiss army empha-

sizes antiaircraft systems, tank-traps, and antitank defenses, as well as a high degree of mobility, keyed to the mountainous Swiss homeland. Supplies have been cached throughout the country; thousands of strategic demolition points have been identified and prewired, so as to slow any invader; and the Swiss Air Force features short-range fighter–interceptors, deliberately excluding long-range heavy bombers. The net result is a robust military capability, but one oriented toward deterrence by dissuasion rather than by threat.*

---

*Switzerland has also kept itself at peace by other, strictly nonmilitary policies. Thus, the country has made itself useful to other states, as a banking center, source of international programs (such as the Red Cross), and site of international conferences. Switzerland has also maintained a posture of rather strict neutrality.

Yugoslavia is another country that achieves military security by making potential aggression against it very costly, rather than by threatening its neighbors. Yugoslavian strategic planning was based in part on its ultimately successful partisan warfare against Nazi Germany; it employs a substantial fallback capacity for unrelenting guerrilla warfare, as well as a "general people's defense" involving a large proportion of the population in a wide range of highly organized defensive activities. Military forces are decentralized and well dispersed, rendering them unsuitable for invading another country, but well designed for defending their own. Also, the Yugoslav national constitution contains a "no surrender" clause, thereby giving any potential invader pause because it suggests that victory will not be easily achieved. The virtual certainty that a population will resist, stubbornly refusing to give in, itself sends a strong cautionary message to any would-be aggressor. In fact, Yugoslavia's impressive and multilayered defensive capacities may well have enabled that country to withdraw from Stalin's control after World War II. Sweden is yet another example of a modern state that has achieved a kind of peace through strength, by emphasizing truly defensive and nonprovocative strategies.*

A FINAL NOTE ON PEACE THROUGH STRENGTH

In today's world, the pursuit of security clearly must be deepened (beyond military strength) and widened (beyond national security). Specifically, security must be identified to encompass economic, political, social, and environmental considerations, and can no longer be achieved independent of others — that is, real security must be mutual, or better yet, global. In 1956, when he was being urged to initiate a major new program of military expenditures to bolster U.S. "national security" in the face of the latest (greatly exaggerated) descriptions of the Soviet military threat, President Dwight Eisenhower wrote as follows:

> I have spent my life in the study of military strength as a deterrent to war, and in the character of military armaments necessary to win a war. The study of the first of these questions is still profitable, but we are rapidly getting to the point that no war can be won. War implies a contest; when you get to the point that contest is no longer involved and the outlook comes close to destruction of the enemy and suicide for ourselves — an outlook that neither side can ignore — then arguments as to the exact amount of available strength as compared to somebody else's are no longer the vital issues. When we get to the point, as we one day will, that both sides know that in any outbreak of general hostilities, regardless of the element of surprise, destruction will be both reciprocal and complete, possibly we will have sense enough to meet at the conference table with the understanding that the era of armaments has ended and the human race must conform its actions to this truth or die.[30]

With this in mind, let us turn now to the issues of disarmament and arms control.

Study Questions

1. What is the relationship between balance of power and peace through strength?

2. Agree or disagree with the motto *vis paccem, para bellum*.

3. In the nuclear age, balance of power has taken on a different meaning from its conception in the eighteenth and nineteenth centuries, when Great Britain was acknowledged to be the "balancer." Explain this difference.

4. What are some disadvantages of balance of power systems? Some advantages?

5. What is meant by collective security? Compare it with balance of power.

---

*To a degree not shown by any other country, Sweden has also sought to enhance its own security by promoting disarmament — especially nuclear disarmament — as a major issue on the world agenda. Thus, Swedish politicians have long been prominent in disarmament efforts, and the Swedish government funds what is probably the preeminent peace institute, the Stockholm International Peace Research Institute (or SIPRI).

6. Discuss the relative merits and demerits of defining national security in strictly military terms.

7. It may be said that the Prisoner's (singular) Dilemma should be rewritten as the Prisoners' (plural) Dilemma. Explain the significance of this difference.

8. Discuss the use of "bargaining chips" in seeking to obtain peace through strength.

9. Support the argument that nuclear deterrence has kept the peace since 1945. Make the contrary argument.

10. If the United States and the U.S.S.R. essentially terminate the Cold War between them, what does this portend for "meddlesome interventionism" in the Third World?

Suggestions for Further Reading

Inis L. Claude. 1962. *Power and International Relations*. Random House: New York.

Ludwig Dehio. 1962. *The Precarious Balance: Four Centuries of the European Power Struggle*. Knopf: New York.

Thomas Schelling. 1966. *Arms and Influence*. Yale University Press: New Haven, CT.

Alan Ned Sabrosky (ed.). 1985. *Polarity and War*. Westview Press: Boulder, CO.

Paul M. Kennedy. 1987. *The Rise and Fall of the Great Powers: Economic Change and Military Conflict 1500–2000*. Harper & Row: New York.

Source Notes

1. Henry Kissinger. 1979. *White House Years*. Little, Brown: Boston.

2. Quoted in J. Stoessinger. 1985. *Why Nations Go to War*. St. Martin's: New York.

3. Winston Churchill. 1948. *The Gathering Storm*. Houghton Mifflin: Boston.

4. Arnold J. Toynbee. 1935. *A Study of History*. Oxford University Press: London.

5. Edward Gibbon. 1782 (1932). *The Decline and Fall of the Roman Empire*. The Modern Library: New York.

6. Geoffrey Blainey. 1973. *The Causes of War*. Free Press: New York.

7. Quoted in Richard Ned Lebow. 1981. *Between Peace and War*. Johns Hopkins University Press: Baltimore, MD.

8. Robert S. McNamara. 1968. *The Essence of Security*. Harper & Row: New York.

9. Quoted in the *New York Times*, August 16, 1987.

10. Mao Ze-dong. 1971. *Mao Tse-tung: An Anthology of His Writings*. New American Library: New York.

11. George F. Kennan. 1982. *The Nuclear Delusion*. Pantheon: New York.

12. Robert Kennedy. 1969. *Thirteen Days*. Norton: New York.

13. Jimmy Carter, State of the Union Address, January 1980.

14. Winston Churchill. 1948. *The Sinews of Peace: Postwar Speeches*. Houghton Mifflin: Boston.

15. H. Kissinger. 1964. *A World Restored*. Grosset & Dunlop: New York.

16. Quoted in Richard Barnet. 1988. "Reflections: Rethinking National Strategy." *The New Yorker*, March 21, pp. 104–115.

17. Joseph Schumpeter. 1955. "The Sociology of Imperialism," in *Two Essays by Joseph Schumpeter*. Meridian Books: New York.

18. Douglas MacArthur. 1965. *A Soldier Speaks*. Praeger: New York.

19. Paul M. Kennedy. 1987. *The Rise and Fall of the Great Powers: Economic Change and Military Conflict 1500–2000*. Harper & Row: New York.

20. Dwight D. Eisenhower. 1981. *The Eisenhower Diaries*. Norton: New York.

21. Albert Einstein. 1960. *Einstein On Peace*. Simon & Schuster: New York.

22. Winston Churchill. 1948. *The Sinews of Peace: Post-War Speeches*. Houghton Mifflin: Boston.

23. Thomas Schelling. 1960. *The Strategy of Conflict*. Harvard University Press: Cambridge, MA.

24. Thomas Schelling. 1966. *Arms and Influence*. Yale University Press: New Haven, CT.

25. Commission on Integrated Long-Term Strategy. 1988. *Discriminate Deterrence*. Government Printing Office: Washington, DC.

26. Quoted in Ralph E. Lapp. 1962. *Kill and Overkill: The Strategy of Annihilation*. Basic Books: New York.

27. Robert Axelrod. 1984. *The Evolution of Cooperation*. Basic Books: New York.

28. Basil Liddell Hart. 1965. *Memoirs*. Cassell: London.

29. M. Gorbachev. 1987. "The Reality and Guarantees of a Secure World." *Pravda*, September 17.

30. Excerpted from a letter from Dwight D. Eisenhower to Richard L. Simon, April 4, 1956.

15

Disarmament and Arms Control

No one — not even the most ardent advocate of disarmament — claims that doing away with weapons will solve the problem of war. So long as the underlying causes of personal, group, and state instability remain, and so long as human beings possess the capacity and inclination to resort to violence under certain circumstances, war will continue to haunt us. Nonetheless, advocates of peace often favor getting rid of certain weapons, or at least, exercising strict control over the ones remaining. In this chapter, we shall therefore examine some aspects of disarmament and its close cousin, arms control.

DISARMAMENT ISSUES

The philosopher Martin Buber[1] once noted that a revolution can succeed only if it has already happened — that is, from the ground up, by infiltrating the basic cultural and intellectual underpinnings of a society. If true, then disarmament among states can only take place after sufficient grass-roots, popular support for doing away with weapons has been established. There is doubtless some validity to this, since nearly all actions by governments — and especially something so radical as serious disarmament — depend for their success ultimately on the consent of the people. (This is even true, although less obviously so, in totalitarian societies; witness, for example, the enormous amount of effort expended by the governments of Hitler and Stalin to propagandize their own citizenry.) "People in the long run are going to do more to promote peace than are governments," observed President Dwight Eisenhower. "Indeed, I think that people want peace so much that one of these days governments had better get out of their way and let them have it."[2] On the other hand, the fact that public opinion may overwhelmingly favor something — especially if that something is in the direction of disarmament — does not in any way guarantee that governments will go along. A recent example is the nuclear freeze movement of the early 1980s; in its heyday, more than 80 percent of the American people favored a bilateral U.S.-Soviet freeze on the production, testing, and deployment of nuclear weapons and delivery systems. But nothing of the sort happened.

The "Futility" of Disarmament

It has long been argued that "men do not fight because they have arms; rather, they have arms because they insist on fighting." Advocates of this view point to the futility of disarming Germany following World War I, emphasizing that the first step toward building a more peaceful world must be political — and by extension, psychological, economic, social, and so on — not military. Disarmament, they maintain, will follow when trust is sufficient, when recourse to violence is delegitimized, and when areas of disagreement are effectively diminished or abolished altogether. This point of view carries much weight, and is particularly relevant in its emphasis on the importance of making fundamental changes in underlying conditions and attitudes, as well as its recognition of the limitations of merely cosmetic arms agreements. Among states no less than among individuals, disarmament alone is not sufficient to guarantee

peace: You can cut off people's arms, but if they hate enough, then they will start biting one another.

By the same token, the claim that disarmament must come last, not first, can be used as a subtle way of defeating feasible and potentially useful proposals. It may be a case of letting the best be the enemy of the good. Moreover, a strong case can be made that certain kinds of armaments in themselves engender distrust and hostility. Nuclear weapons in particular seem to fit this category: It is difficult to think well of anyone who is armed to the teeth and possesses the ability to devastate your country, and who persists in fielding yet more weapons. Superpowers such as the United States and the Soviet Union are widely assumed to require superweapons because their enmity is so great. But what if the logic of that assumption is backwards, and the possession of superweapons has *created* superenemies? In that case, good disarmament agreements — carefully negotiated, verified, and complied with — can help overcome suspicion and generate confidence and goodwill.

For example, the Rush-Bagot Treaty of 1817, which arranged for the demilitarization of the U.S.-Canadian border, helped set the stage for persistently good relations between these two North American neighbors. This was no mere cosmetic treaty. It called, among other things, for a 3,000-mile unfortified border, and for the actual dismantling of a number of naval vessels, which had been built on the Great Lakes and were too large to be sailed out. It is also worth noting that this agreement was reached only two years after the United States and Britain — then governing Canada — had fought a war, including several naval battles on the Great Lakes. Looking at U.S.-Canadian relations today, we blithely take peace for granted, but at the time of the Rush-Bagot Treaty, things were much different. And the treaty itself did not immediately lead to peace; rather, distrust and several near wars characterized the ensuing several decades. Undeniably, however, in this case a serious disarmament agreement eventually helped create real peace. If threatening naval vessels had been allowed to continue patrolling the Great Lakes, and if military fortifications had been constructed along the U.S.-

Peace Arch located at the U.S.–Canadian border at Blaine, Washington. All of this border is demilitarized. (Blaine Peace Arch State Park, Washington)

Canadian border, U.S.-Canadian relations might have evolved quite differently.

On the other hand, in some cases, disarmament — especially unilateral disarmament — has led to war. Following the 1979 Iranian revolution, that country's military was allowed to decline drastically: Many officers were killed, technicians were discharged, and equipment was allowed to deteriorate. Several billion dollars' worth of military purchases from abroad were canceled. And a year later, an emboldened Iraq attacked its old rival. (This example speaks more to the dangers of unilateral and unplanned disarmament than to disarmament generally.)

In other cases, disarmament has been imposed on one side, typically the loser in a war, by the victor. The shame and anger associated with the forced disarmament of Germany after World War I apparently contributed to the rise of Nazi militarism during the 1930s. Disarmament of a sort was also imposed on Japan after World War II, includ-

ing Article IX of their constitution, which states that "land, sea, and air forces, as well as other war potential, will never be maintained." But just five years later, when the United States became embroiled in the Korean War, it insisted that Japan form a National Police Reserve Force of 75,000 men, which has since been expanded to a powerful "Self-Defense Force" of more than 300,000 men, equipped with tanks, artillery, and naval vessels. Remilitarization of Japan has been a U.S. priority, not a Japanese one.

The Role of Governments

The Rush-Bagot Treaty was a case in which disarmament was achieved from the "top down," by governments arranging mutual agreements among themselves. Although such initiatives are rare, in the overwhelming majority of cases in which disarmament has been sponsored in this way, the populace has gone along. In short to paraphrase Buber, in some cases, revolutions can be made to happen, especially if they are revolutions in the behavior of governments themselves.*

Some critics allege, however, that disarmament agreements are necessarily valueless because, in times of war or severe crisis, they will be violated. Even if we assume that with the outbreak of war, states will produce armaments as rapidly as possible, we should note that we have come a long way from biblical weaponry, when swords could supposedly be beaten into pruning hooks, and then back again at a moment's notice. As armaments grow more sophisticated, the "production lag" between the decision to make weapons and their actual production also increases. Even during World War I, for example, when the United States had been gearing up for war production for about a year prior to the actual declaration of war in April 1917, significant quantities of U.S.-built war material

---

*In all fairness to Buber, we should note that he was a pacifist, and did not advocate that governments should wait until their citizens clamor for disarmament before moving in that direction.

(other than raw explosives) did not begin to arrive in Europe until the following spring. Furthermore, prior to its entry into that war, the United States was not party to any disarmament agreement that restricted its freedom to construct plants necessary for arms production. With such restrictions, disarmament "breakouts" would be even more difficult and time-consuming—hence, perhaps, less likely. Moreover, modern warfare requires relatively large numbers of highly trained personnel; if the numbers and skill levels of such people were significantly diminished by prior international agreement, the production lag would be greater yet. And presumably, the more difficult it is to rearm, the less the temptation to do so.

The "Communist Threat"

In general, peace advocates tend to support disarmament efforts, although more and more, it is recognized that disarmament alone will not be sufficient to establish a peaceful world. Furthermore, public campaigns that have focused on limited aspects of disarmament—a ban on above-ground testing, a nuclear freeze, halts in the deployment of particular systems such as the MX missile or anti-satellite weapons, and so on—have tended to be excessively narrow in their appeal, and have left their followers frustrated and directionless when such campaigns failed . . . or even if they succeeded. On the other hand, advocates of peace through strength, drawn largely from the political right wing, almost universally oppose disarmament, viewing it with distrust and alarm. Disarmament is equated with communist propaganda, or even direct subversion.

In fact, the Soviet government established the Third Communist International, or Comintern, in 1919 in an effort to "give history a push," by subverting and interfering in the affairs of various Western countries. But these efforts were never successful, which is why Stalin disbanded the Comintern in 1943. Today, it can safely be concluded that prodisarmament sentiment in the Western democracies reflects a legitimate grass-roots yearning.

For many, "peace is patriotic," and so is disarmament. In fact, some efforts, like the nuclear freeze campaign of the early 1980s, were so unstructured and essentially spontaneous as to be virtually leaderless. In part, they were reactions to the unbridled militarism of the Reagan administration from 1981 to 1985. And they have almost invariably called for disarmament on the Soviet side as well as by the United States. Nonetheless, the antiwar and prodisarmament movement still has to contend with varying degrees of "red-baiting," the accusation that by opposing U.S. or NATO armaments and the West's aggressive military policy, upstanding citizens are, consciously or unconsciously, acting in the interest of world communism. And for many people, fear of the Soviet Union (or of world communism) is far greater than fear of nuclear war; for such individuals, weaponry equals strength and security, even if in fact we are endangered by the weapons themselves.

Fear of the Unknown

Archbishop Raymond Hunthausen of Seattle once noted:

> I am struck by how much more terrified we Americans often are by talk of disarmament than by the march to nuclear war. We whose nuclear arms terrify millions around the globe are terrified by the thought of being without them.[3]

After all, we have had abundant experience with weapons, and virtually none with disarmament. And even though our weapons have often "gone off in our faces," at least they represent a known quantity, and we have some feeling about what it is like to entrust our future to them. By contrast, entrusting our future to a disarmed world seems a much more dangerous leap into the unknown. In this vein, General Omar Bradley observed:

> Admittedly, the problem of peaceful accommodation in the world is infinitely more difficult than the conquest of space, infinitely more complex than a trip to the moon. . . . If I am sometimes discouraged, it is not by the magnitude of the problem, but

Afghan refugees gathered to receive food at Pashawar, Pakistan. Warfare in Afghanistan not only caused massive destruction and millions of refugees, it also used up a very large percentage of the Afghan government's resources, which might otherwise have been available for development. (United Nations/John Isaac)

by our colossal indifference to it. I am unable to understand why — if we are willing to trust in reason as a restraint on the use of a ready-made ready-to-fire bomb — we do not make greater, more diligent and more imaginative use of reason and human intelligence in seeking an accord and compromise which will make it possible for mankind to control the atom and banish it as an instrument of war.[4]

It is indeed ironic — as well as a major block to progress in disarmament — that a weapon-free world is often considered more dangerous than a weapon-filled one. In addition to anxiety about disarmament as a goal, however, many people also worry about dangers en route to a disarmed world. Thus, it is often claimed that in any disarmament proceedings, democracies are necessarily at a disadvantage relative to totalitarian states, since the latter speak with one voice, and the former with many. Moreover, totalitarian states are better able to keep secrets and, possibly, to cheat on agreements after they have been made. Disarmament supporters counter by pointing out that the strength of democracy lies in its pluralism, and accordingly, it doesn't serve U.S. or Western interests for their governments to emulate Soviet-style repression. In fact, in the case of many disarmament proposals, the United States, not the U.S.S.R., tends to be more reluctant, and appears to need an extra push. If it were the other way around, then the prospects for a successful peace movement would be less than they are today, since U.S. citizens can do relatively little to influence Soviet government policy, but quite a lot to influence their own. And for those who complain that peace movement pressure is unfairly applied only to the U.S. government (that is, "tell it to the Russians"): As U.S. citizens, we are most responsible for the actions of our own government, which — because of our political system — is, to our great good fortune, susceptible to citizen involvement and pressure.

Disarmament and World Development

The desirability of disarmament is also influenced by the connection between disarmament and development, especially in Third World countries. A tiny fraction of the military budgets now consumed by the superpowers could fund major programs of public health, agriculture, and education, greatly bettering and extending the lives of millions of people. The most immediate environmental threats to our planet could be overcome with the investment of less than one quarter of what the superpowers spend on their military competition. And the superpowers are not the only countries that invest heavily in armaments; Third World states, especially in Africa and the Middle East, typically spend an even higher proportion of their GNP on military forces. And not only are these countries among the lowest in educational and health expenditures per capita, they also are plagued with illiteracy, disease, and severe environmental deterioration. Accordingly, some degree of disarmament may well be a prerequisite for positive world development.

Others maintain that military strength is required for national security, which in turn is required for development. Some also argue that perhaps a special kind of development — oriented toward human and environmental needs — must *precede* disarmament. The U.S. government refused to send any representatives to a 1987 UN-sponsored conference on development and disarmament held in Nairobi, Kenya, which was attended by more than 120 countries. The position of the U.S. government was that disarmament and development bear "no necessary or logical relationship" to each other, and moreover, that there is no reason to expect that savings — if any — generated by future disarmament would be redirected toward Third World development.

Finally, it must be emphasized that nuclear weapons have introduced a new urgency to disarmament. Nuclear weapons pose an overwhelming and unique threat, to national, human, and planetary survival. Disarmament has long been an attractive idea, even in a world dominated by musket and cannon; since 1945, we have all been living under what President John Kennedy called a "nuclear Sword of Damocles," making it not just desirable, but essential, that these weapons be controlled and ultimately eliminated. As difficult as it will be to achieve, nuclear disarmament in the short run may well be more necessary than complete disarmament, if only because the world could survive conventional warfare, whereas it might not survive a nuclear war. There is a risk here as well, that by banning or even restricting nuclear weapons, we might "make the world safe for conventional war," an outcome that no one wants. But it might be a risk worth taking.

DIFFERENT VISIONS OF DISARMAMENT

There have been many different visions of disarmament. Perhaps the simplest is General and Complete Disarmament, or GCD (General = all countries; Complete = all weapons). Not surprisingly, there are problems here, one of which is how to define a weapon. Dynamite, for example, can make an effective weapon, but it is also used for legitimate commercial purposes such as mining or demolition. What about firearms? Citizens of the United States, for example, jealously guard their "right to keep and bear arms," as guaranteed by the Second Amendment of the Bill of Rights; in most Soviet-bloc countries, by contrast, private firearms are prohibited. Other, less sweeping disarmament measures have been considered as well.

Maintenance of National Security Capabilities

A less ambitious goal was proposed by President Woodrow Wilson in his Fourteen Points, which he recommended for worldwide consideration at the end of World War I. Wilson called for national disarmament "to the lowest point consistent with domestic safety." This suggests that states would be allowed to retain police forces, but nothing capable of threatening other states. A police force adequate for China, however, might be quite threatening to Korea or Vietnam. And a Soviet police force could threaten Bulgaria. At the Versailles Conference, Wilson's proposal was watered down to "the reduction of national armaments to the lowest point consistent with *national* safety," [italics added] terminology that allows for a wide variety of interpretations. A state like Poland, for example, located on the wide plains of Europe and surrounded by large and potentially threatening neighbors, would seem to require a larger military force than does Switzerland, which has many mountain barriers. And the United States, with friendly neighbors north and south, and oceans east and west, would appear to need relatively little military force . . . unless (as has been the case for most of the twentieth century) it considers that its national "safety" requires a military presence — via bases, advisors, and/or intervention — in countries overseas.

Selective Disarmament

Another possibility is to disarm selectively, focusing on offensive weapons. This was the goal of the Geneva Disarmament Conference of 1932; it failed because of an inability to reach general agreement on exactly which weapons are defensive, and which are offensive (states typically define their own armaments as defensive, and those of their opponents as offensive). When the United States ended its occupation of South Korea in 1949, it removed its airplanes and tanks, seeking to ensure that South Korea would not be emboldened to attack the North. One result was that the North, instead, attacked the South, which found it very difficult to mount an effective defense after being deprived of these "offensive" weapons.[5]

The Superpowers.   Probably the most popular version of selective or qualitative disarmament reflects the enthusiasm that each superpower has for disarmament of the other, but not for itself. Moreover, it has been argued that the United States and the U.S.S.R. essentially collude in creating a "duopoly," whereby the two superpowers exclude others from being major players on the world stage. For example, Swedish disarmament expert and Nobel Peace Prize winner Alva Myrdal charged that "between their outwardly often fierce disagreements . . . there has always been a secret and undeclared collusion between the superpowers. Neither of them has wanted to be restrained by effective disarmament measures."[6] Myrdal noted that "military competition results in an ever-increasing superiority — militarily and technologically — of the already overstrong superpowers, thus sharpening the discrimination against all lesser powers."[7] Therefore, one kind of selective disarmament likely to be especially attractive to the superpowers is anything directed toward diminishing the power of states other than themselves.

Ballistic Missile Defense.   Recently, the U.S. government has been seeking to develop and deploy a "defensive" shield (Star Wars, or the Strategic Defense Initiative) against Soviet nuclear missiles. The Soviets, however, as well as critics within the United States, point out that such a development could be offensive, if paired with a U.S. first strike. Let us grant that neither side would be able to defend against a determined first strike by the other. Suppose, however, that a surprise U.S. attack eliminated a large proportion of Soviet missiles. A Star Wars system, incapable of defending against a Soviet first strike, nonetheless could, in theory, be effective against the "ragged retaliation" that would take place if the U.S.S.R. sought to fire back with its limited remaining forces. In short, a Star Wars "defensive" system — even one of limited effectiveness — might encourage its possessor to strike first, confident that the victim could not retaliate effectively. A system described as defensive could therefore also appear offensive, and thus, very provocative, to an opponent.

abc Weapons.   Even without a full-fledged adoption of nonprovocative defense (see Chapter 14), the possibility exists for mutually agreed restrictions on obviously offensive weapons, such as bombers, motorized artillery, and the like. Perhaps the greatest prospects — as well as the greatest need — for selective disarmament concern atomic, biological, and chemical weapons (the so-called abc weapons), because of the unique threats they pose. In addition, nuclear weapons — especially when combined with fast and highly accurate delivery systems such as the MX missile, the Trident II (D-5) missile, or the Soviet SS-18 — are unusual in that they generate their own instability by arousing fears of a preemptive strike. This fact gives selective disarmament agreements an incalculable potential value. Later in this chapter, we shall look at some of the efforts in this direction.

Military Budgets. Reductions and restrictions in military budgets have often been discussed. Not surprisingly, problems have arisen as well. If all states are restricted to a maximum total expenditure, then the same total national defense would be purchased for, say, Luxembourg, which has a small border and few enemies, as for the U.S.S.R., which has an immense border and much greater legitimate need for defense. But if larger states are permitted larger military budgets (such as an agreed-upon percentage of population, or of the GNP), then they might pose a threat to smaller ones. In addition, real difficulties are involved in determining the actual military expenditures of most states, notably the U.S.S.R., which has never published reliable figures.* Even the budget for the U.S. Department of Defense is misleading: It does not include the costs of nuclear bombs and warheads, for example, which are listed in the Department of Energy budget.

Proportional Limitations. As we shall see, agreement was reached in the past over the relative proportions of certain naval vessels to be permitted the major powers, with set ratios allotted for each state. Similarly, various numerical restrictions have been established in the past for certain kinds of strategic nuclear weapons. However, considerations of prestige have made it difficult for states to accept smaller forces than their rivals. And a further problem remains: How shall these proportions be allocated? If by population, then, again, larger states will receive larger forces, thereby constituting a greater threat to their neighbors. During the Geneva Conferences in the 1920s and 1930s, for example, France requested force allotments that would make up for the fact that its traditional rival, Germany, had a larger population and industrial capacity. Not surprisingly, Germany disagreed. Yet another problem concerns the question of alliances. During the Euromissile negotiations in the early 1980s, the Soviet Union emphasized that since the nuclear forces of Britain and France (not to mention China) were directed against the U.S.S.R., it should be permitted to maintain forces that equaled those of all NATO countries combined, and not just those of the United States.

Weapon-Free Zones. The idea here is to agree on the elimination of weapons within a designated geographic area. For example, under the Treaty of Tlatelolco (named for a suburb of Mexico City), most of the states of the Western Hemisphere agreed not to develop or deploy nuclear weapons. Similar suggestions, especially for nuclear-free zones, have been made for Africa, the Middle East, the Balkans, and Scandinavia. Agreement to forgo all weapons within a designated zone, or even just those of a certain type, can help diminish anxiety that a local rival is seeking to gain superiority. Consequently, such agreements could diminish pressure to push ahead with armaments that — when matched by the opponent — would ultimately diminish the security of all concerned. Thus, they offer the prospect of escaping from the Prisoner's Dilemma (see Chapter 14).

Another type of disarmament agreement, similar to the establishment of a weapons-free zone, results when all parties agree to the neutralization of a particular country. Following World War II, for example, the victorious allies occupied Austria. By the Austrian State Treaty of 1955, all sides agreed to end that military occupation, signing an accord whereby the state of Austria was essentially demilitarized and pledged to East–West neutrality.

---

*After long insisting on an absurdly low figure for their budget, the U.S.S.R. published a more realistic figure of $120 billion for 1989.

A BRIEF HISTORY OF DISARMAMENT

Self-Serving Plans

Governments have on occasion tried to reduce armaments, and sometimes they have even succeeded, but the history of such efforts is largely one of failure. In 1766, Austria proposed a bilateral arms reduction to Prussia's Frederick; he refused. In 1787, France and Britain agreed to a short-lived freeze in naval construction. Financial considerations often have been important in prompting disarmament efforts. In 1816, after the Napoleonic Wars, Czar Alexander led an (unsuccessful) effort to save governmental funds via multilateral disarmament. Later, Czar Nicholas II convened the first Hague Peace Conference in 1899, once again in an effort to stave off an arms race that threatened to lead to bankruptcy. But political motivations — especially the desire to appear peace-loving — have also been important. After taking office in 1981, for example, President Reagan showed himself to be not only uninterested in disarmament, but downright antagonistic. Later, the U.S. government begrudgingly entered into arms negotiations with the Soviet Union, almost certainly as a response to mounting political pressure, both within the United States and in Europe.

Other practical concerns have motivated past disarmament efforts as well. In the nineteenth century, for example, Czar Nicholas was particularly worried about Russia's inability to compete successfully with Germany. Self-interest — especially the hope of gaining some advantage over other states — has loomed large at all disarmament conferences. Thus, participants at the Hague Peace Conferences of 1899 and 1907 were unable to reach agreement on any arms reduction, largely because various states typically proposed a halt or moratorium in areas in which they were ahead, thereby seeking to freeze that advantage.

For example, when Nicholas II suggested a freeze on all military budgets in 1899, Russia already had the largest army in Europe; a freeze would have perpetuated that imbalance. Churchill proposed a naval building "holiday" to the Germans, from 1912 to 1914, when Britain was ahead, especially in battleships. Immediately following World War II, the United States advanced the Baruch Plan, which would have required that all states surrender the capability of producing their own nuclear weapons, *after which* the United States would place its nuclear facilities under international supervision. This would have left the United States the only state with the knowledge and ability to produce nuclear weapons in the future. The Soviets countered with a plan whereby the United States would dispose of its nuclear facilities first, after which other states would join in (and the U.S.S.R., as a vast and secretive society, would have had a greater opportunity to cheat if it sought to do so). In short, disarmament negotiations and conferences have often served as a forum for advancing the interests of each state and prosecuting interstate rivalries, rather than as a means of diminishing those rivalries.*

Between World Wars I and II, Britain and the United States, the great naval powers, sought to abolish submarines (which were threats to the preeminence of their surface fleets), but to keep battleships and cruisers. France, a traditional land power, fought restrictions on tanks and heavy artillery. In recent nuclear arms negotiations, the Soviet Union has tried to restrict cruise missiles, forward-basing of nuclear forces, and most new technological developments in the arms race, all areas in which the United States retains a lead. The United States, in turn, has urged reductions in large-throw-weight ICBMs (where the Soviets are ahead), while

---

*There is a fable that describes a disarmament conference held among the animals. The eagle, eying the bull, recommends that all horns be cut off. The bull, looking at the tiger, suggests that sharp teeth and claws should be pulled. The tiger, sizing up the elephant, urges that tusks be filed down. The elephant, concerned about the eagle, insists that all would be well if only wings and beaks were clipped. Then the bear, speaking in tones of sweetness and reason, spoke up, "Come now, my friends, let us abandon these half-way measures and agree to abolish all weapons, and simply resolve any disagreements with a great, friendly hug."[8]

The U.S.S. *New Jersey* launching a Tomahawk sea-launched cruise missile, one of the weapons in which the U.S. holds a substantial technological lead over the U.S.S.R.; not surprisingly, the U.S. strenuously resists any treaty restrictions concerning these missiles. (U.S. Department of Defense)

zealously protecting bombers and submarine-based missiles (where the United States is particularly strong). The U.S.S.R. has sought restrictions on SDI/Star Wars as a precondition for any START (Strategic Arms Reduction Talks) agreement, while the United States has, with equal vehemence, sought to protect that program, and to achieve unilateral cuts on Soviet heavy armor in Europe.*

Germany disarmed briefly after World Wars I and II, as did Japan after World War II. But in these cases, the victors simply imposed disarmament on the losers; there is no evidence that the people of Germany and Japan suddenly came to appreciate the merits of disarmament. Shortly afterward, the United States was instrumental in encouraging its new ally, West Germany, to rearm during the 1950s,

---

*In late 1989, the U.S.S.R. agreed to drop its insistence that a START treaty be linked to U.S. guarantees to abide by the ABM Treaty.

and eventually to join NATO, much to the dismay of the U.S.S.R. And throughout the 1980s, U.S. government officials urged Japan to devote a larger share of its national budget to their military forces. (By tradition, since World War II, this had always been less than 1 percent of its GNP, and according to its postwar constitution, Japan is pledged never to maintain offensive military forces.)

Unsuccessful Attempts

Some attempts at renouncing war by treaty have been notably unsuccessful. By the early 1920s, the Treaty of Versailles appeared to be unraveling, with Germany refusing to pay its obligatory World War I reparations and France responding by sending troops to occupy Germany's Ruhr Valley. The German foreign minister then organized a peace conference involving the major European powers, hoping to head off the establishment of a new anti-German alliance. At a major meeting in Locarno, Italy, numerous agreements were reached, including demilitarization of the Rhineland, and a mutual defense treaty linking France to both Poland and Czechoslovakia. Enthusiasm ran high for the abolition of war altogether, and shortly thereafter, French foreign minister Aristide Briand proposed to U.S. Secretary of State Frank Kellogg that, on the tenth anniversary of the U.S. entry into World War I, France and the United States sign an agreement outlawing war between the two states.

The U.S. government responded with unexpected enthusiasm, urging that the proposed instrument be expanded to a worldwide renunciation of "war as an instrument of national policy," in addition to further agreement that "the settlement or solution of all international disputes or conflicts . . . shall never be sought except by peaceful means." There were some caveats, however: France insisted that the agreement, known eventually as the Kellogg-Briand Pact, apply only to "wars of aggression," and Britain reserved the right to intervene militarily in "certain regions of the world, the welfare and integrity of which constitute a special and vital interest for our peace and safety" (meaning primarily her colonies). Kellogg-Briand was not really a disarmament plan, but rather a sweeping, multilateral agreement to renounce war and to settle disputes by peaceful means.

Unfortunately, the Kellogg-Briand Pact was utterly unenforceable, and — along with the "Spirit of Locarno" — may ultimately have done more harm than good, since it gave a false sense of security to states that were already peace-loving, and set up a smokescreen behind which aggressive states were able to pursue their ambitions. Indeed, the Kellogg-Briand Pact has become a prototype of meaningless and often misleading "statements of principle." One such statement, redolent with hope but bereft of any specifics, was the McCloy-Zorin Agreement (1961), by which the United States and the U.S.S.R. agreed to multilateral negotiations that would ostensibly lead to the design and implementation of general and complete disarmament, in concert with a standing UN peacekeeping force. On the other hand, such agreements may be important in affirming a widespread yearning for dramatic reductions in armaments; violations of the Kellogg-Briand Pact were also used against former Nazi officials in the Nuremberg Trials, after World War II (see Chapter 17).

Modest Successes

There have, in addition, been some modest examples of successful nonnuclear disarmament. The Washington Naval Conference resulted in a 1922 treaty that caused the United States, Britain, and Japan to scrap 40 percent of their capital ships (battleships and aircraft carriers). Remaining capital ships for the United States, Britain, Japan, France, and Italy were fixed in a ratio of 5:5:3:1.67:1.67. By this agreement, Britain, weakened by World War I, finally agreed to abrogate its policy of naval superiority, although the United States actually made the largest material concessions. A decade later, in the London Naval Treaty of 1930, these limits, including restrictions on total tonnage, were extended to cruisers. At this second conference, the major powers were unable to reach agreement on limiting de-

stroyers and submarines, however, and France and Italy did not sign at all. The Italians had demanded naval parity with the French, who found this unacceptable. Japanese militarists also chafed under their restrictions, and Japan renounced both treaties in 1934 when a new, more nationalist government came into power.

Despite their ultimate failure, these agreements probably helped diminish tensions during the years immediately following World War I, as well as postponing the economic stress of a costly naval arms race during that period. But they may also have contributed to the rise of Japanese extremism, as well as impeding attempts by Britain and America to keep up with the naval threat that Japan eventually posed. The actual disarmament achieved by the Washington Naval Treaty was due in large part to the audacious proposals put forth by U.S. Secretary of State Charles Evans Hughes; it must be accounted a success (although admittedly a short-lived one) in terms of the weapons eliminated, but clearly not an unambiguous triumph for the disarmament process. If nothing else, however, it demonstrated at least the possibility of some kind of disarmament, in some cases.

But consider the Anglo-German Naval Agreement of 1935, a bilateral understanding between Britain and Germany that set some modest restraints on new naval vessels on both sides. Britain gained a guarantee that its traditional naval superiority would be maintained, but at the cost of legitimizing German rearmament, which might otherwise have been seen more clearly as violating the Treaty of Versailles.

This checkered history has led to a rather jaded view of disarmament proposals, one that is — unfortunately — justified in most cases. "The most persistent objective of any nation's disarmament policy," writes one authority,

> is that of demonstrating to opinion at home and abroad that efforts are being made towards disarmament, and that the reason why no agreement is arrived at lies in the policies of other nations, not in its own. The more radical and grandiose a disarmament proposal, the more it will satisfy this objective.

Proposals which are radical and grandiose, moreover, are advanced in the knowledge that they will be rejected, and are an indication that the policy of the power advancing them is not directed towards disarmament.[9]

There have been many well-meaning attempts at establishing GCD. All of them, however, have been failures, usually resulting — at best — in certain minor restrictions, such as the elimination of expanding ("dum-dum") bullets, or prohibitions against the use of poison gas. When Albert Einstein was asked his opinion of the Geneva disarmament conference of 1926, he responded:

> What would you think about a meeting of a town council which is concerned because an increasing number of people are knifed to death each night in drunken brawls, and which proceeds to discuss just how long and how sharp shall be the knife that the inhabitants of the city may be permitted to carry?[10]

At another such conference, in 1931, great excitement arose when it was found that several Afghans were present. The conference organizers were delighted that the idea of disarmament had spread so far and was being so widely accepted. But when asked why they were attending, the Afghans replied, "If these nations really are going to disarm themselves, perhaps we can pick up some weapons cheaply."[11]

ARMS CONTROL

In the aftermath of World War II — which was widely seen not only as a "good war," but also as one that was hastened by the West's reluctance to arm adequately in the 1930s — public enthusiasm for disarmament waned significantly. The two emerging superpowers each proposed plans for disarmament, but these were almost certainly a mixture of propaganda ploys and efforts to achieve a unilateral advantage over the other. By the late 1950s, governments began to turn their attention from disarmament to a more modest and attainable goal, especially as regards nuclear weapons, namely, "arms control."

There were many reasons for this shift. Following Stalin's death, the Cold War thawed somewhat. Improvements in technology permitted verification with higher confidence, especially by satellite surveillance. The ongoing arms race had heightened citizen anxiety, and pushed the West in particular to recognize the growing dangers posed by radioactive fallout from above-ground nuclear testing. And finally, with their acquisition of ICBMs and a growing nuclear arsenal, the Soviet Union began to achieve essential parity with the United States, thereby permitting both superpowers to negotiate seriously, from a position of more or less equivalent strength.*

To dovish critics, arms control is a mere smokescreen, a thinly veiled excuse for continuing the arms race, while quieting the public with claims that "progress" is being made. Moreover, arms controllers are concerned with managing and stabilizing the arms race; disarmers, by contrast, do not seek to stabilize the arms race, but rather, to *destabilize* it, and end it altogether. To hawkish critics, it should be added, arms control is only somewhat more acceptable than disarmament (which is utterly anathema); it is a snare and a delusion whereby a nation allows itself to be outmaneuvered by its adversary. If one is opposed to any agreement on arms limitation, or at least to any agreement that applies equally to all sides, then, not surprisingly, any such agreement is perceived as damaging to national security. This opposition is typically based on the presumption that the other side is untrustworthy and will inevitably cheat, and also on a determination to settle only for victory — or, in the case of an arms race, remaining continually ahead. To some extent, a free-for-all arms race, unfettered by international agreements, also smacks of the economic free market so beloved by political conservatives.

---

*It has been said that there are two rules for negotiators: Don't negotiate when you are behind, and don't negotiate when you are ahead. Hence, the best opportunity for progress comes when two sides are functionally equal.

We have considered some of the nefarious goals of arms control: gain a unilateral advantage either by ending competition when you are ahead or by steering competition into an area of one's advantage; establish a duopoly that effectively subjugates other states; create the false impression of progress, thereby quieting domestic dissatisfaction. The legitimate goals of arms control are as follows:

1. *Reduce the likelihood that war will break out, by removing some of the more threatening situations or weapons.* For example, World War I might have been averted if some agreement could have been reached that dampened competition for early mobilization on both sides. During the 1980s, many people considered that the Euromissiles (especially NATO's Pershing IIs and the Warsaw Pact's SS-20s) were unnecessarily provocative and thus destabilizing: With their high accuracy and short flight-time, they constituted a destabilizing first-strike threat. Hence, their removal by the INF Treaty may substantially diminish the chance of nuclear war. A similar argument applies to the accurate and highly MIRVed strategic ICBMs of both superpowers, and especially to the Trident D-5 missile, soon to be deployed by the U.S. Navy.

2. *Prevent competition that could be not only destabilizing but also financially ruinous.* The Washington and London Naval treaties were in fact arms control or partial disarmament agreements, which temporarily precluded some aspects of naval competition among the Great Powers. The ABM Treaty of 1972, by which the United States and the Soviet Union agreed not to develop or deploy significant antimissile weapons, was (and still is) especially attractive because it headed off a strategically futile and economically intolerable spiral of competition between the offensive and defensive weapons of each side. The likelihood is that such competition would otherwise lead to offensive countermeasures (to overcome the defensive missiles), defensive counter-countermeasures, offensive counter-counter-countermeasures,

Test-firing of a Pershing II missile. (U.S. Department of Defense)

and so on. In addition, active competition of this sort must necessarily create an environment of mutual distrust and anxiety, which could lead not only to "arms race instability" (a spiraling increase in military competition) but also to "crisis instability" (a situation in which an international crisis leads one or both sides to attempt a first strike, fearing that war is inevitable and that it is better to strike first than to be the victim).

3. *Create an environment of increasing trust and confidence.* By reaching agreements — even over trivial issues — contending parties can progressively gain greater confidence in each other, as they become increasingly familiar with their counterparts, comfortable with their motivations, and thus, more willing to engage in serious agreements in the future. Of course, this also presupposes that the participants are

well meaning, and that the agreements in question will be adhered to. Otherwise, such agreements can backfire. The Soviet Union, for example, constructed a radar facility near the town of Krasnoyarsk, which appeared to be in violation of the ABM Treaty; this angered U.S. officials, and was used by right-wing hawks to discredit the sincerity of the U.S.S.R., as well as the entire arms control process.* Similarly, the United States has engaged in questionable procedures in upgrading radars in Greenland and Britain, and has pushed for deployment of some sort of Star Wars/SDI program, which would absolutely violate the ABM Treaty.

The vast majority of arms control agreements have nonetheless been lived up to, on both sides, and this has, on balance, created a climate of trust that is favorable to yet more progress. Furthermore, agreements themselves sometimes establish mechanisms for airing and resolving grievances: the SALT I Interim Agreement, for example, created a Standing Consultative Commission (SCC), which was able to resolve numerous Soviet and U.S. accusations of noncompliance. Regrettably, the Reagan administration refused to employ the SCC for this purpose, using it instead as merely a public forum for accusations and recriminations. On the other hand, the INF Treaty may have contributed toward warmer U.S.-Soviet relations, in which gradual nuclear disarmament may become increasingly acceptable if the process is allowed to gather momentum.

4. *In the event that war does break out, arms control can still be helpful if, because of preexisting arms control agreements, the war is less destructive than it otherwise would have been.* The major powers appear to have destroyed biological warfare agents, for example, following an international agreement in 1972. The banning of dum-dum bullets has helped, in a small way, to make war more "humane." (One danger

here is that in making war less destructive, it might also be rendered more tolerable, and therefore, a more acceptable instrument of national policy; after all, nuclear deterrence rests on the proposition that by making the costs of war *in*tolerable, it will be prevented.)

NUCLEAR WEAPONS TREATIES

Many arms control treaties have been signed since 1945, most of them related in some way to nuclear weapons. Although the list of treaties is long, however, it is not impressive because there has been a tendency to restrict only those activities that neither side was interesting in pursuing anyhow. The momentum and danger has continued virtually unabated. Arguably, the real arms race has not been between the United States and the U.S.S.R., but rather between the builders of nuclear arms and those who would restrict these weapons. If so, there is no question who is winning: The arms race has been largely a victory for the builders. But there have been some successes for the controllers, and we turn now to them. We shall not attempt a complete overview of arms control treaties and accomplishments, but rather a brief summary of some salient points, by grouping these treaties into logical categories.

Geographic Treaties

The Antarctic Treaty (1959) essentially demilitarized the Antarctic continent. The Outer Space Treaty (1967) banned "weapons of mass destruction" from orbit and from celestial bodies. The Sea-Bed Treaty (1971) prohibited the implanting of such weapons on the ocean floor. These treaties have been successful and uncontroversial; critics contend, however, that they restricted armaments of a kind and in a place where states had not been contemplating military activity in any event . . . kind of like banning weapons from Saturn.

Test-Ban Treaties

The Partial Test-Ban Treaty, or PTBT (1963), capped many years of public protest against rising levels of worldwide fallout from atmospheric

---

*In late 1989, the U.S.S.R. acknowledged the violation and announced that this facility will be dismantled.

nuclear tests. In this treaty, signatories agreed to refrain from atmospheric, outer space, or underseas testing of nuclear weapons. However, testing was not stopped altogether; attempts to perfect existing warheads and to develop new ones have continued, with testing moved to underground sites. The governments of China and France, moreover, refused to sign the PTBT, and persisted in testing aboveground (China) and beneath the ocean (France).

A Threshold Test Ban Treaty, restricting testing to 150 kilotons (more than ten times the Hiroshima explosion) was signed in 1974, but has never been ratified by the U.S. Senate. The same applies to the 1976 Peaceful Nuclear Explosions Treaty, which applies these limits to "peaceful" as well as warlike explosions. Critics argue that these limits are so high as to be meaningless, and thus that these two treaties are shams; in addition, it can be maintained that no nuclear tests are peaceful. We should note that at the time of the PTBT, the real goal of most antitesting advocates was a Comprehensive Test-Ban Treaty (CTBT), which would constrain all nuclear testing, underground as well as above-ground. Prior to the Reagan presidency, a CTBT had been the announced goal of all U.S. administrations since that of Dwight Eisenhower. That goal still remains elusive, despite the fact that in 1986, the U.S.S.R. initiated a unilateral eighteen-month moratorium in such testing. The United States has stubbornly refused to go along, claiming that (1) such a ban could not be satisfactorily verified, and that even if it could, continued testing is needed to (2) assure the reliability of the existing nuclear arsenal, and (3) enable the development of the next generation of "Star Wars" weapons such as the X-ray laser.

Most seismologists, however, agree that a CTBT would be verifiable, especially if it involved a series of on-site monitoring stations (to which the U.S.S.R. has agreed). As to arsenal reliability, CTBT supporters argue that this can be ensured by nonnuclear testing of warhead components. Moreover, some decrease in reliability would have the beneficial effect of rendering each side less confident about its ability to conduct a successful first strike (and also, less concerned that the opponent might be contemplating the same action), while also retaining enough uncertainty for successful deterrence. This is because very high reliability would be required for a first strike, but not for deterrence; it would be awkward at best to attack the other side with malfunctioning warheads that go "Thump" against their silos, leaving the opponent armed and, presumably, rather peeved. By contrast, retaliation against an attacker's cities with only a fraction of the victim's remaining arsenal would still be devastating.

Mutual Understandings and Improvements in Communication

The "Hot Line" agreement (1963) established an emergency communications link between Washington and the Kremlin. In 1987, this was updated and modernized, with the addition of satellite links and so-called crisis control centers in each capital. In the Nuclear Accidents Agreement (1971), the two superpowers agreed to notify each other in the event of accidental or unauthorized nuclear detonations, and a High Seas Agreement (1972) sought to establish rules of conduct to minimize the chances of oceanic collisions and misunderstandings during naval maneuvers.

In 1975, NATO, the Warsaw Pact countries, and most other European states agreed to the final act of the Conference on Security and Cooperation in Europe (better known as the Helsinki Accords), which essentially ratified the post–World War II map of Europe, and also arranged for advance notification of large military exercises. In 1986, procedures for such notification were further established (for example, one-year notification for maneuvers involving 40,000–75,000 troops, two-year notification for those involving more than 75,000, and so on). In addition, potentially important new precedents were created by the agreement that NATO and Warsaw Pact observers could inspect certain military activities on each other's soil.

Nonnuclear Weapons

The Biological Weapons Convention (1972) committed the United States and U.S.S.R. to refraining from developing, producing, or stockpiling biological weapons (primarily viruses and bacteria).

Chemical weapons, however, are not included, nor are chemical toxins such as botulinus, the cause of the disease botulism, or the various fungal agents that the United States has accused the U.S.S.R. of using in Afghanistan and Kampuchea. (Nongovernmental biologists are now agreed, however, that "yellow rain," once thought to be caused by Soviet use of chemical warfare materials, was in fact a red herring, the feces of tropical bees.) The Environmental Modification Convention (1977) prohibited the alteration of the environment, including the climate, of an adversary.

NATO and Warsaw Pact representatives have been negotiating fruitlessly, since 1973, at the Mutual and Balanced Force Reduction talks, which are aimed at achieving reductions in conventional forces in Europe. These talks, renamed the talks on Conventional Stability in Europe, have been stalled over several issues. For one, the United States and the U.S.S.R. disagree over current troop levels in Europe, with the United States claiming there are more Warsaw Pact troops than the U.S.S.R. acknowledges. The West wants reductions *to* equal levels; the Soviets want reductions *of* equal amounts ... which the West claims will result in unequal numbers. In addition, the West claims that the Warsaw Pact states have an unacceptable lead in conventional forces; the Soviets — and many in the West as well — point out that NATO actually has larger total manpower, much greater economic strength, more modern equipment, and superior training. However, it is generally agreed that the Warsaw Pact states enjoy a notable lead in tanks and mechanized artillery. Under Mikhail Gorbachev, the Soviets have agreed to the principle of asymmetrical reductions, which might hold out the promise, at long last, for some conventional demilitarization in Europe, especially if the West would be willing to accept some trade-offs, such as reductions in NATO's naval and tactical aircraft superiority in return for reductions in Warsaw Pact tanks. With the apparent crumbling of Warsaw Pact political solidarity in 1989–1990, it seems that the two contending alliances are ripe for substantial conventional cuts, especially because the new East European governments have begun pressing for the removal of Soviet troops from their soil, while the Warsaw Pact itself is clearly less under Soviet control and thus less threatening to the West.

As of 1990, the two sides have agreed, in principle, to the maintenance of 195,000 troops in Central Europe, plus an additional 35,000 U.S. troops along NATO's periphery. From one perspective, this arrangement represents a remarkable asymmetric concession by the U.S.S.R., acknowledging that whereas Soviet troops are largely unwanted by their "hosts," U.S. troops are requested by theirs. From another viewpoint, peace activists might object that having to maintain such forces is actually a disadvantage to the United States.

Strategic Nuclear Weapons

SALT I. The first set of Strategic Arms Limitation Talks, or SALT I, resulted in an Interim Agreement (1972) that established numerical limits for each side's guided-missile submarines, submarine-launched missiles, and ICBMs. It granted the Soviets higher numbers in these categories, to compensate for the U.S. lead in MIRVing, submarine systems, strategic bombers, and in the fact that U.S. "forward-based systems" in Europe (such as F-111 bombers) could reach the U.S.S.R., whereas the Soviets had no counterparts. Later, the Vladivostok Accords (1974) set equal numerical limits for strategic launch vehicles, for MIRVing, and for anti-missile systems.

SALT II. SALT II, negotiated through the 1970s, and signed (1979) but never ratified by the U.S. Senate, called for greater detail in numerical limits: restrictions on the number of MIRVed ICBMs, as well as on the various permissible combinations of bombers with and without cruise missiles, and of MIRVed SLBMs. It also established restrictions on the amount of MIRVing permitted, on the development and testing of new missiles, and on reload capacity and other fine points. SALT II fell victim to domestic U.S. politics (it was strongly opposed by an influential right-wing group, The Committee on the Present Danger, and by Ronald Reagan, both before and after he became president).

Jimmy Carter and Leonid Brezhnev signing the SALT II Treaty. (Jimmy Carter Presidential Library)

START. Under the Reagan administration, the United States unilaterally breached the terms of SALT II in 1986, although both sides have continued to observe its general outlines. After delaying more than a year, President Reagan belatedly began negotiations on a replacement, known as START (for Strategic Arms Reduction Talks). Critics maintained that these talks were begun with no serious expectation of success, but only to quiet the U.S. peace movement. The Soviet Union has proposed substantial cuts in warhead numbers, by as much as 50 percent, and the United States has agreed to such cuts, in principle. By the late 1980s, although agreement had been reached on many details, the major stumbling block was Star Wars/SDI. The United States insisted on retaining the right to develop and, if possible, deploy some kind of strategic defense system, whereas the Soviets insisted that both sides live up to the terms of the ABM Treaty. Then the U.S.S.R. dropped this requirement, which should pave the way to a START Treaty.

The ABM Treaty. The Anti-Ballistic Missile (ABM) Treaty, signed in 1972, was part of SALT I. It was a watershed in strategic doctrine in that both sides essentially pledged themselves to mutually assured

destruction: Nuclear deterrence between the United States and the U.S.S.R. would be based on the mutual vulnerability of each state. Both sides committed themselves to maintain only two ABM sites (reduced by the Vladivostok Accords to one site each), and to refrain from developing, testing, or deploying mobile ABM systems or components based on land, at sea, in the air, or in space. Research, however, was permitted. Although both sides have continued to abide by this treaty, it is under attack, especially by U.S. plans to develop, test, and deploy Star Wars/SDI.

Future Prospects. The possibility exists, nonetheless, for substantial progress in strategic nuclear forces, especially if some compromise can be reached regarding Star Wars/SDI and cruise missiles (in both areas, the United States holds a substantial technological lead). The superpowers have moved seriously toward negotiating a 50 percent reduction in ballistic missiles. Prospects are relatively bright, as well, for a comprehensive test-ban treaty (CTBT); the technology to verify a CTBT appears to be adequate, and the Soviets are eager for it. Such an agreement would diminish some of the innovative momentum of the arms race, while also diminishing fears of a first strike, as arsenals became somewhat less reliable than before. The sticking point here is political will on the part of the United States. Similarly, a treaty banning the testing and deployment of antisatellite weapons would contribute to crisis stability, and appears quite feasible, along with a monitored cutoff in the production of plutonium. Like plutonium, tritium is a man-made substance, but unlike plutonium, whose half-life is 26,000 years, tritium's half-life is only about 12 years. Since tritium is important in boosting the yield of bombs and warheads, it has been suggested that a negotiated halt in tritium production would be an effective way of achieving a kind of prompt nuclear disarmament via technological obsolescence, as the tritium in existing bombs and warheads simply "winds down."

Another feasible and exciting prospect that could lead to substantial dismantling of strategic nuclear arsenals is known as "minimum deterrence." Under this concept, each superpower would maintain only those nuclear weapons that are minimally necessary to assure that nuclear weapons would not be used against it. Consider that a single Trident submarine equipped with C-4 missiles contains 24 missiles × 8 warheads per missile = 192 independently targeted warheads, each many times the power of the bomb that destroyed Hiroshima. Accordingly, few such submarines are needed to guarantee that the Soviet Union, for example, would not attack the United States. Supporters of minimal deterrence point out that the overwhelming mass of both superpower arsenals is thus unnecessary, and indeed, provocative. Movement toward a world of minimum deterrence would require that each side forgo such strategies as "extended deterrence," "escalation dominance," and "limited nuclear wars," each of which requires the presence of extensive nuclear arsenals. Rather than constituting a sacrifice, however, these changes in themselves would probably make the world a safer place.

Euromissiles

In the late 1970s, the Soviet Union began replacing its aged intermediate-range, ground-based missiles in Europe with SS-20s: mobile, MIRVed weapons with expanded range and improved accuracy.

NATO responded with the "two-track" policy of seeking to deploy ground-launched cruise missiles and Pershing II ballistic missiles, while also pursuing a negotiated agreement by which the Soviets would reduce or eliminate their SS-20s. These Euromissiles — particularly the Pershing IIs — were especially controversial because their great accuracy and short flight time threatened to precipitate nuclear war by accident. In addition, there was virtual agreement that their real significance was political, as a show of strength and resolve on the part of NATO, rather than military, since their targets could be covered equally well by strategic weapons based in the United States or on submarines. The European peace movement generated widespread protests against deployment, and numerous negotiating options were considered. In the end, the proposed NATO Euromissiles were deployed, and the Soviets and Americans finally agreed to the so-called zero option: no intermediate range missiles, on either side. Eventually, a "zero-zero option" was agreed upon, which removed shorter-range missiles as well. The INF Treaty thus covers all Euromissiles with ranges of 500 to 5,000 kilometers.

The original zero option was proposed by the Reagan administration largely as a way of silencing the European peace movement; no one seriously expected that the U.S.S.R. would accept, since this meant destroying substantially more Soviet than U.S. missiles. When the Soviets agreed, the U.S. side began pointing to the shorter-range missiles, where the U.S.S.R. had a monopoly; the U.S.S.R. quickly agreed to destroy these as well, unilaterally, and U.S. negotiators — to the apparent surprise of their own government and the consternation of right-wing hawks — agreed to go along. Despite the vigorous anti-Euromissile sentiment in Western Europe, once the GLCMs and Pershing IIs had been deployed, many conservative government leaders considered their removal to be unacceptable "disarmament," even though the Soviets were removing theirs as well, and more of them, to boot. The resulting INF Treaty also included unprecedented on-site inspections, whereby Soviet and U.S. personnel have been stationed at factories and munitions depots, to assure that the terms of the treaty are followed in the future.

In the wake of the INF Treaty, conservatives (notably in the United States and British governments) have urged that NATO deploy additional, modernized, short-range nuclear missiles, to "take up the slack." The West German government, on whose soil these weapons would be deployed, has objected. With the democratic upheavals in Eastern Europe, such modernization* seems very unlikely, especially because these weapons would be targeted against the fledgling democracies of Poland, Czechoslovakia, Hungary, and — especially — East Germany, which is soon to be part of a unified Germany.

NATO Versus the Warsaw Pact

Following World War II, Europe was divided along political/economic/ideological lines, with the boundaries essentially determined by the position of the Allied armies when hostilities ceased. As the Cold War developed and intensified, Europe became increasingly fractured and frozen into two rival camps, composed of competing, heavily armed states. Europe, previously a major battleground, became the major theater for Cold War conflict. Shorter-range, tactical nuclear weapons were introduced, along with formidable conventional arsenals, including tens of thousands of tanks and artillery pieces, and hundreds of thousands of troops.

The ascension to power of Mikhail Gorbachev in 1985 has been marked not only by *perestroika* (restructuring of the Soviet bureaucracy, economy, and political system) and *glasnost* (increased tolerance of dissent and honesty in news reporting and communications), but also by a dramatic change in U.S.-Soviet relations. This has included an extraordinary series of unilateral arms control/disarmament initiatives on the part of the U.S.S.R. Most of these have been directed toward reducing NATO and Warsaw Pact military forces in Europe, and thus, diminishing the threat of surprise invasion or military/political coercion.

Specifically, in late 1988, the Soviets announced the following unilateral reductions:

- the elimination of 500,000 troops from their total military forces

- the elimination of 10,000 tanks, 8,500 artillery, and 800 combat aircraft, including six tank divisions in Eastern Europe

- the removal of 500 short-range nuclear warheads

- a public announcement of the Soviet military budget for the first time ($120 billion) and a reduction in that budget by more than 14 percent

- a halt in the production of enriched uranium and a reduction in the production of weapons-grade plutonium

The Soviets have also been urging negotiations on eliminating short-range nuclear missiles in Europe. The United States, by contrast, maintains that such missiles will be needed, into "the forseeable future." Under considerable pressure from other NATO countries, however, President Bush has advanced a plan whereby NATO and Warsaw Pact forces in Europe will be considerably reduced — even beyond the levels proposed by the U.S.S.R. — and has also agreed to include helicopters and combat aircraft, on which the United States has traditionally refused to negotiate. A policy was also established whereby reductions in short-range nuclear missiles would be considered only if success was achieved in negotiating reductions in conventional forces. The U.S. argument is that nuclear forces will be needed so long as the Warsaw Pact states enjoy an advantage in conventional forces.

Despite the potential difficulties involved in achieving major reductions, many analysts — even some of the most hawkish, who have long been very skeptical of Soviet intentions — have begun to consider that an opportunity may be at hand for ending the Cold War. It appears that much of the impetus for doing so currently lies with the U.S.S.R., and most of the reluctance emanates from the United States, whose leadership is very cautious about

---

*In the judgment of many, such "modernization" is indistinguishable from escalation.

accepting a dramatic reduction in superpower arsenals, and even, it seems, in the tone of U.S.-Soviet hostility. Essentially, the postwar world has long been organized by the Cold War, and substantial changes in that relationship — although clearly in the wind — take time, largely because they require changes in that most complicated of processes: human thinking and feeling.

PITFALLS OF ARMS CONTROL AGREEMENTS

It sometimes seems as though the threat of weaponry can be ended via treaties and appropriate negotiated agreements. But even if we leave aside the problem of underlying hostilities, numerous pitfalls lurk along the road of negotiated arms control.

Numerical Obsessions

Treaties involve things that can be counted, which in turn gives inordinate importance to quantitative as opposed to qualitative factors. For example, given the current levels of nuclear destruction available to both superpowers, an actual count of warheads or missiles can be misleading and distracting, especially since imbalances in specific weapons systems make it possible for partisans on either side to point selectively to certain measures, thereby making it seem that their side is unacceptably far behind. By focusing on the need for nuclear parity, excessive "bean counting" tends to discourage interest in nuclear "sufficiency," in which states would assess what they need for their legitimate defense needs, rather than seeking to match their opponent in every category.

The United States and the U.S.S.R., for example, are huge political, social, economic, and military systems, with vastly different strengths and weaknesses. If each side insists on strict numerical equality in every category in which it is behind, while insisting that it remain ahead in areas of its advantage, then no agreement can ever be reached. The United States has an advantage, for example, in strategic bombers and cruise missiles; the Soviets have more ICBMs. The two states also differ geographically in fundamental and important ways. For example, U.S. submarines enjoy unimpeded access

to the major oceans; by contrast, Soviet submarines must run a gauntlet of NATO sensing apparatuses and antisubmarine devices. Also, Soviet land forces can be seen as posing a direct invasion threat to Europe, while by contrast, the United States is at a disadvantage, forced to ferry supplies and additional troops across the Atlantic Ocean. At the same time, however, its geography also means that the U.S.S.R. can be attacked by NATO forces, forward-based in Europe. In such cases, insistence on strict numerical equality can become a way of avoiding resolution of differences.

Slowness

Negotiations are almost always slow. It took three years to agree on SALT I, seven years for SALT II, and another seven years for the INF Treaty. Moreover, for reasons of pride and ideology, new presidents tend to discard what their predecessors have accomplished, insisting on starting fresh. It is also inherently more difficult to reach the political consensus needed to ban or even restrict a weapon than to meet the engineering requirements of designing and constructing it; as a result, by the time negotiators finally do ban a weapon, it may be virtually obsolete, while new weapons are being planned and produced. (On the other hand, when the political will to do so exists, agreements can be made quickly; the PTBT, for example, was negotiated in a matter of weeks.)

"Leveling Up"

It is easy to decide to build more weapons; such decisions are *unilateral*. It is much more difficult, by contrast, to decide on a *bilateral* or *multilateral* halt, or even a ceiling, because such decisions must be made in concert with others. States also tend to be reluctant to destroy expensive weapons that have already been deployed, even if they are unnecessary or provocative. So, rather than accept a limit below one's current level, negotiators are inclined to agree on the level of the side that is currently highest. Often, treaty limits are even set above those of either side, whereupon they become production goals, stimulating the arms race rather than damping it.

The "Balloon Principle"

Whenever some weapon is constrained, states tend to focus their efforts on another, unconstrained system, which then expands, like a balloon that is squeezed in one place and pops out somewhere else. For example, after the PTBT was ratified, the rate of nuclear testing—now moved underground—actually *increased*. After SALT I, which did not restrict the number of warheads per missile, the strategic arsenals of each side increased dramatically, as both sides proceeded with MIRVing. The INF Treaty may well result in increased "modernization" of some conventional forces in Europe, as well as additional nuclear systems such as aircraft-launched ballistic missiles and sea- and air-launched cruise missiles.

Bargaining Chips

It is widely held that bargaining should proceed from a "position of strength," that is, lots of weapons. At a time, for example, when even its advocates agreed that the MX missile was not supportable on its merits, the MX was promoted (and ultimately approved) as a way of buttressing the ongoing strategic arms negotiations. We have seen how weapons, originally justified as bargaining chips, tend to be retained when the negotiations fail. It has even been suggested that governments may begin negotiations so as to build support for the procurement of weapons, ostensibly as bargaining chips. President Reagan and his supporters have credited NATO's Euromissile deployment for the success of the INF Treaty. In fact, while NATO's steadfastness in deploying its Euromissiles likely contributed to Soviet willingness to eliminate their SS-20 missiles, the major factor appears to have been the ascension to power of Mikhail Gorbachev, who pledged himself to diminishing the U.S.S.R.'s military/economic competition with the United States.

National governments also sometimes find themselves having to bargain with their own military-industrial leadership, whereupon weapons become bargaining chips within governments instead of between them. For example, the vast increase in underground testing that followed the PTBT took place because President Kennedy had to agree to it

President Richard Nixon and Soviet leader Leonid Brezhnev shaking hands after signing the SALT I Treaty. (U.S. Arms Control and Disarmament Agency)

in order to garner support within the Joint Chiefs of Staff for the PTBT. Similarly, President Nixon purchased military support for SALT I by vigorously backing the MIRVing program, and President Carter had to support the Trident and MX programs in return for SALT II . . . which was never even ratified.

Linkage

Arms control skeptics often claim that agreements should be held hostage, "linked" to other aspects of Soviet behavior.* In particular, they urge that agreements not be reached unless the U.S.S.R. improves its human rights record, by permitting unlimited emigration of Jews and others, relaxing restrictions

---

*Presumably, Soviet hard-liners also argue symmetrically, insisting that agreements be linked to United States restraint in aiding the anticommunist rebels in Afghanistan, for example.

on freedom of expression, and the like. This line of reasoning suggests that arms treaties are favors that the United States extends to the Soviet Union, whereas in fact, if they are of any value, it is as positive-sum-game developments that are beneficial to both sides. Moreover, as President Kennedy pointed out:

> A sea wall is not needed when the seas are calm. Sound disarmament agreements, deeply rooted in mankind's mutual interest in survival, must serve as a bulwark against the tidal waves of war and its destructiveness. Let no one, then, say that we cannot arrive at such agreements in troubled times, for it is then that their need is greatest.[12]

In fact, SALT I was concluded during the Vietnam War . . . although the Soviet invasion of Czechoslovakia delayed the initial negotiations a full year. The Soviet invasion of Afghanistan, on the other hand, contributed to the U.S. failure to ratify SALT II. It is also worth noting that when, as part of the U.S.S.R.'s liberalization program in the late 1980s, large numbers of Soviet citizens were permitted to emigrate (as they and the United States had long been requesting), the United States was unwilling to accept all those wanting to enter.*

Legitimizing the Arms Race

Only very rarely (the INF Treaty, the ABM Treaty) have treaties actually stopped serious weapons competition. More often, they have gone along with prevailing trends, in effect ratifying the arms race itself, and providing government leaders with a touchstone by which they can assure their citizenry that military actions — even escalations — are consistent with treaty obligations. Rather than getting out in front of the arms race and slowing it down,

---

*This suggests the old proverb, "Beware of what you wish for, because it might come true!" U.S. immigration policy presented would-be Soviet emigrés with a Catch-22: They were welcome in the United States so long as they were being persecuted in their home country and unable to emigrate. Once they were permitted to leave, however, then by definition they were no longer being persecuted, and hence, no longer eligible for admission.

arms control agreements have tended to run alongside, on a parallel track, waving at it, and sometimes even egging it on. The presence of arms control agreements also allows leaders to claim that they are pursuing an end to the arms race, while actually managing and channeling it.

False Confidence

By the end of the Reagan administration, nuclear weapons had become so unpopular that their very legitimacy began, finally, to be seriously questioned. In the past, popular revulsion at these weapons has come largely from signs that governments were not sincere about trying to restrain or abolish them. By providing occasional arms control "successes," all the while ensuring that the nuclear weapons regime remains fundamentally undiminished, governments may succeed in quieting public opposition while essentially maintaining the very dangerous status quo. Thus, with the ratification of the PTBT in 1963, an upsurge in antinuclear sentiment largely subsided; the arms race — or at least, nuclear testing — had dropped out of sight and, for most people, out of mind. As we have seen, however, the rate of nuclear tests actually increased. Similarly, the INF Treaty of 1987 largely quieted the previously vibrant European antinuclear movement, even though it resulted in the removal of only a very small fraction of the world's nuclear weapons.

Hawks, by contrast, tend to worry that arms control agreements produce a false sense of confidence in the other direction. Thus, Reagan administration Assistant Secretary of Defense Richard Perle worried that "democracies will not sacrifice to protect their security in the absence of a sense of danger. And every time we create the impression that we and the Soviets are cooperating and moderating the competition, we diminish that sense of apprehension."[13]

BENEFITS OF ARMS CONTROL AGREEMENTS

We live in a real world, not an ideal one, an incontrovertible fact that is regularly used to justify the presence of armed forces. It also helps explain why efforts to control these armed forces have so often been frustrated. And, most important, it may well explain why these efforts are so important, despite their disappointments. Especially in the nuclear age, enormous risks are involved in permitting an uncontrolled arms race; hence, we must identify non-zero-sum-game solutions to our shared dilemma, since nothing less than survival is at stake. "We have a choice between the quick and the dead," said Bernard Baruch, addressing the UN in 1946.

> Behind the black portent of the new atomic age lies a hope which, seized upon with faith, can work out salvation. If we fail, then we have damned every man to be the slave of fear. Let us not deceive ourselves: we must elect world peace or world destruction.[14]

In that choice, arms control and continued efforts at disarmament apparently will play a crucial role. Good agreements can inhibit wasteful competition (the ABM Treaty), reduce worldwide pollution (the PTBT), diminish the chances of accidental war (the Hot Line), and help set the stage for further reductions (the INF Treaty). In his farewell address, President Eisenhower emphasized that

> the conference table, though scarred by many past frustrations, cannot be abandoned for the certain agony of the battlefield. Disarmament, with mutual honor and confidence, is a continuing imperative. Together we must learn how to compose differences not with arms but with intellect and decent purpose.[15]

VERIFICATION

Successful arms control (and disarmament as well) must rely on something more than trust. Specifically, compliance must be verifiable. The Soviet Union, with its traditionally closed and secretive society, has historically been averse to on-site verification, which it has long considered unacceptably intrusive and a license for spying. So, just as the Soviets once cynically pressed for widespread (and unverifiable) disarmament schemes, U.S. authorities — no less cynically — would insist on iron-clad verification procedures that they knew would be vetoed by the Soviets. Verification is not simply an excuse for avoiding arms control or disarmament, however, it is also important in its own right. No

one can seriously expect that either side will tolerate substantial cuts in its own arsenal unless it can be confident that the other side is abiding by its share of such agreements. (Let us assume that certain reductions — even if made unilaterally — do not diminish a state's security. Thus, so long as thousands of warheads remain in the superpower arsenals, it won't matter if either side squirrels away a few hundred more than are called for in a build-down agreement. Even in this case, verification may well be helpful, and perhaps necessary, if the reductions are to be acceptable to the hard-liners on each side.)

Techniques

A useful distinction can be made between "absolute" or legalistic verification, by which *any* violation will be detected with absolute certainty, and "functional" or realistic verification, by which some violations may be missed, but any that could be of strategic significance will be detected. With the advent of spy satellites and other detection techniques, functional verification can generally be assured; insistence on absolute verification, by contrast, is tantamount to insistence on no agreement at all.

A variety of verification procedures are available. Most treaties provide for verification by "national technical means," which refers to a variety of long-range reconnaissance procedures that do not directly intrude on the side being monitored. Of these, satellite observation is the most powerful and important; increased sensitivity and sophistication of satellite monitoring have led some enthusiasts to claim that U.S. spy satellites such as the "Big Bird" can read the license plates in Moscow's Red Square. Although this may be an exaggeration, technical advances currently permit ground resolution of as little as twelve inches. Infrared imaging can even penetrate cloud cover and detect changes in work patterns inside factories. Serious suggestions have also been put forward, notably by France, for an International Satellite Monitoring Agency, administered by the United Nations, which would provide accurate and unbiased data on arms-related activities worldwide.

Unmanned seismic monitoring station operating in upstate New York. Seismologists estimate that a limited number of monitoring stations could effectively police a low-threshold or comprehensive test-ban treaty. (Sandia National Laboratory)

Even without such a development, however, governments have additional sources of information. Radar, for example, provides for accurate detection, tracking, and monitoring of missile tests, thereby assessing compliance with treaty restrictions. Seismic instrumentation has become so sensitive that nuclear explosions as small as one kiloton reportedly can be distinguished from natural events such as earthquakes; this appears to hold even for so-called decoupled explosions, detonated in sites designed to absorb the blast effects. An array of tamper-proof black boxes, installed on each side's territory, could reassure each side that the other is not conducting nuclear tests. A private organization, the National Resources Defense Council, has been engaged in an unprecedented series of seismological exchanges with Soviet scientists, in which the ability of each side to monitor the other's nuclear tests has been confirmed. National technical means for verification also include the capability of electronic signal interception, whereby each side listens in on the communications of the other. Every

radio broadcast in the U.S.S.R. is monitored, for example; this includes not only regularly scheduled broadcasting but also governmental communications of all sorts. Taken together, these various capabilities are important not only in the information they provide, but also in their potentially deterrent effect. Thus, neither side can be confident that its activities will not be detected by the other, after which the other side would be free to renounce its adherence to the violated agreement.

Prospects for the Future

We may also assume that the current verification regime — impressive as it may be — represents only a small fraction of the information potentially available to interested parties. Thus, in a substantially disarmed world, it is probable that a large fraction of military budgets, now devoted to the procuring of weapons and the maintenance of large armed forces, would instead be devoted to improved verification capabilities. Detection would replace destruction as the major goal of each side's "national security" apparatus. With such a motivation, verification procedures will, if anything, become more precise and reliable. It must be emphasized, however, that ultimately, adherence to arms control or disarmament treaties depends not so much on the capacity for verification as on the political will of each party — that is, on the fact that such treaties must be in the interests of the countries involved. Insofar as that is true, and recognized as such, the temptation to cheat will be greatly diminished.

Since the mid-1980s, the Soviet position on verification has changed dramatically. In fact, during deliberations regarding the INF Treaty, the Soviets were more willing to accept on-site inspections than was the United States. It is also worth noting that verification is far easier in cases of an across-the-board freeze, or the absolute prohibition of certain kinds of tests or of an entire weapon system, than when constantly shifting levels must be monitored. This may add additional impetus and feasibility to broader, more sweeping attempts at serious arms control and disarmament than we have yet seen. Certainly, in the early 1990s, we seem to be approaching an unusual conjunction of need (both strategically and economically) and feasibility (political climate plus the delegitimization of war in general and nuclear war in particular).

ECONOMIC CONVERSION

The economies of both the United States and the Soviet Union are heavily militarized. (Other states, notably Israel, Iraq, South Africa, North and South Korea, are even more so, as measured by the proportion of GNP devoted to military purposes.) Converting such economies from military to civilian functions poses special challenges as well as opportunities. The apparent end of the Cold War has stimulated wide debate over how to spend the anticipated, but thus far elusive, "peace dividend." Major contenders include a tax cut, reducing the deficit, and funding domestic needs. Regardless of the outcome, it seems clear that economic conversion must also have a place on the national agenda.

Challenges

For one thing, as previously noted (see Chapter 11), large military expenditures tend to create their own constituency, which in turn makes disarmament — and even arms control — politically difficult. When big corporations and their many employees make large amounts of money based on current market demands, the result is powerful pressure to continue business as usual. Moreover, whole regions now rely on military spending, and many politicians attribute their election and reelection to success in bringing some of the Pentagon "bacon" home to their constituents. Disarmament — even if it is partial — can thus appear to threaten the livelihoods of many people. Not only do economic factors make disarmament politically unattractive to many government leaders, but the reality is that large-scale demilitarization of an economy would in fact require a major overhaul, in some cases generating real hardships.

Opportunities

On the other hand, as we have also noted (see Chapter 11), military spending is, on balance, more hurtful than helpful to a national economy. In the long run — and aside from its major benefit in diminishing the likelihood of war — restructuring from a military to a civilian economy offers the promise of (1) reducing inflation, (2) increasing employment, (3) lowering the deficit, (4) improving productivity, and (5) freeing up resources (human as well as financial) for needed social programs. While pessimists may choose to bemoan the problems posed by economic conversion, it is equally valid — the Peace Studies perspective would say, more so — to consider economic conversion as a wonderful opportunity yielding a potential "disarmament dividend" that is yet another reason for moving toward a demilitarization of security.

Economic conversion has been achieved in the past. Following World War II, the U.S. military budget plummeted from nearly $76 billion in 1945 to less than $19 billion in 1946 and barely $12 billion in 1947. As part of this postwar demobilization, the armed forces went from 11 million troops in 1945 to 2 million two years later, yet unemployment never exceeded 4 percent during this period. Currently, the U.S. military budget hovers at the $300 billion mark.* There are 2.2 million troops in the armed forces, a million civilians employed by the Department of Defense, and 3.3 million industrial and service workers providing various military goods and services. If anything, however, this understates the total structure of the U.S. military economy. For example, we must also include a large proportion of the budgets and employees of the Department of the Energy (which produces nuclear bombs and warheads), NASA (since a large part of the space program is military), Veterans Affairs, and so on. More than one third of the aircraft industry, and more than one half of communications equipment and shipbuilding, is devoted to military products. Engineers, scientists, and program managers are disproportionately represented in today's military economy.

---

*On closer examination the Bush administration's proposed "cuts" in the military budget of $180 billion turn out to be a promise to refrain from requesting that much *additional* money and no real cuts at all.

Skeptics point out that successful post–World War II conversion in the United States was based in part on conditions that would not be repeated in the event of comparable conversion today. For example, many women who had been recruited into the work force during the war returned home to raise families, thus making room in the work force for demobilized servicemen. In addition, a large pent-up consumer demand accumulated during the war years, when new automobiles, for example, were not being produced, since factories had retooled to make jeeps, tanks, and military trucks. On the other hand, the U.S. economy is far larger today than it was forty-five years ago, and the number of people to be "demobilized" is far smaller. If substantial government expenditures are ever redirected away from the military, these funds will not simply evaporate; rather, they will be available for use in other areas (except for any proportion left unspent, to diminish the federal deficit). And such expenditures actually produce more jobs, per dollar spent, than does military spending. Moreover, national and global needs are immense: funding for education, health, renewable energy, pollution abatement, housing, and public transportation; rebuilding roads, bridges, and structures; retooling the industrial base for the production of fundamental consumer goods; reconstructing our blighted cities; reforestation and other types of land reclamation; providing drug treatment and rehabilitation; establishing more humane penal institutions, and so on. Literally billions of dollars and millions of workers would be released as resources were redirected from destructive to constructive projects. Only a stunted imagination would consider this a calamity to be avoided rather than an opportunity to be embraced.

Conversion Planning

Estimates show that most people employed in today's military-industrial complex could be retrained for productive work in the domestic economy within about six months. Mid- and upper-level managers and engineers would require somewhat more extensive retraining, since they have generally specialized in making narrowly focused, cost-insensitive products, rigidly defined within certain bureaucratic guidelines. In short, they are accustomed to pleasing the Pentagon, not the public. But there is no reason to think that this cannot be changed. Within the Defense Department, the United States already maintains an Office of Economic Adjustment, concerned with helping local communities mitigate the effects of plant and base closings. Such work could readily be expanded on a national scale. Some industries and labor unions have (in most cases begrudgingly) begun making contingency plans for converting their activities to domestic and civilian purposes, although peace groups have thus far done the bulk of the work. Careful conversion planning could yield several pay offs: (1) In the event of a transition from a military to a nonmilitary economy, dislocation would be greatly reduced; and (2) the existence of realistic, mutually beneficial plans would make the disarmament process itself more feasible politically.

Other states have had practical experience — nearly always positive — with conversion. A notable example is China, which in 1985 eliminated fully one quarter of its army — a million troops — and began restructuring its military-industrial capacity to produce additional domestic goods. Of the output of China's 30,000 "military" factories, 20 percent currently goes to domestic products; this is expected to increase to 50 percent within ten years. Substantial additional benefits already have been reaped, especially as the Chinese have begun addressing their pressing environmental problems (see Chapter 21). It is arguable whether centrally planned economies such as China's or the Soviet Union's can achieve economic conversion more readily than free enterprise systems such as the United States or Great Britain. It seems likely that the former would be more capable of making the necessary top-down decision, whereas the latter, because of their more vibrant economies, would be better situated to carry it out productively.

Economic conversion is especially important as a practical nuts-and-bolts consequence of disarmament, as well as a necessary prerequisite for real movement in that direction. Some people argue, however, that a fresh approach will also be necessary if we are to avoid the disadvantages and disappointments of traditional arms control. With this in mind, we briefly consider an important and promising strategy: GRIT.

GRIT

Psychologist Charles Osgood[16] proposed a practical means whereby states might achieve substantial progress in reducing tensions as well as the level of armaments. He called it GRIT, for "Graduated and Reciprocated Initiatives in Tension reduction." The idea is quite simple: Just as individuals, or states, increase tension by a series of unilateral escalations, they also can proceed down the "tension ladder" by a series of unilateral initiatives in the opposite direction. Arguments between two people, for example, often escalate through a series of annoyances, insults, and affronts to each other, with increasing distrust and animosity. However, people also often "make up," and this generally requires a reaching out from one to the other; that is, it begins with some sort of unilateral initiative.

Comparable initiatives can be applied to international affairs, quite possibly with comparable results. These initiatives are not to be confused with appeasement. Rather, Osgood points out that when individuals, or states, make conciliatory gestures, substantial pressure builds up in favor of matching gestures from the other side. It is possible — even likely — that the initial phases of GRIT will encounter skepticism. Over time, however, assuming that the initiatives are maintained and (better yet) intensified, powerful psychological and social pressure build up to reciprocate . . . which, in turn, contributes to a process of mutual tension reduction that can be as real as the process of tension escalation that preceded it. Osgood recommends that a national policy of GRIT follow certain basic rules:

1. Each step should be small, so that the initiator does not at any time run risks with its military security.

2. Each step(s) in question should be taken in the interest of reducing armaments and defusing tension; steps should not be accompanied by threats or efforts at coercion . . . which tend to harden the opposition.

3. Each initiative should be publicly announced, and carried out with maximum publicity.

4. Each action should be real and meaningful, not something that would be done in any case, like retiring an obsolete weapons system.

5. The GRIT initiatives should be continued, and if necessary repeated several times, in the hope of generating a like response. If it fails, a GRIT strategy can always be abandoned, with little loss and no diminution to national security.

The United States and the U.S.S.R. apparently used a GRIT-like strategy of progressive mutual disengagement to defuse a highly tense situation during the Berlin crisis, when U.S. and Soviet tanks were literally facing each other. President John Kennedy was aware of GRIT in the summer of 1963, when he initiated a series of outreaches to the U.S.S.R., beginning with the announcement that the United States would stop atmospheric testing, and not resume unless the Soviets did so first. Premier Khrushchev responded positively and announced a decrease in production rates for strategic bombers. The Soviets agreed to permit UN supervision of an ongoing military conflict in Yemen; the United States, in turn, agreed to allow Hungarian government representatives, excluded since the 1956 Soviet invasion, to assume full status at the UN. Within weeks, there was the Hot Line agreement, a large wheat sale, the PTBT, and a dramatic lowering of East–West tensions. (The Soviets liked the interaction so much that they coined their own phrase to describe it, "the policy of mutual example.") President Nixon also used GRIT successfully when he announced a unilateral halt to the production of biological weapons in 1969, which led eventually to a major treaty.

On the other hand, GRIT has not always succeeded. When the Soviets unilaterally suspended all nuclear testing in 1986, and continued their self-imposed moratorium for eighteen months, the United States steadfastly refused to show similar restraint. However, the possibility remains for substantial GRIT-like initiatives in the future. If there is anything good to be said about having an arsenal of about 30,000 nuclear weapons, it is that major

President Kennedy signing the Partial Test Ban Treaty in 1963; a GRIT-like process led up to this agreement. (John F. Kennedy Library)

reductions could be initiated without compromising national security. And of course, GRIT need not be restricted to nuclear weapons; it should be equally effective in reducing tensions in various regional conflicts, improving economic and cultural relationships, and so on. A useful exercise would be to consider what each side could do, or stop doing, that would be especially appreciated by the other, and at little cost to itself. Such actions could be the foundation of a GRIT-ty effort at reducing tensions and, possibly, establishing the foundation for meaningful disarmament.

A FINAL NOTE ON DISARMAMENT AND ARMS CONTROL

In 1981, when he received the Albert Einstein Peace Prize, diplomat/historian George F. Kennan assessed the nuclear arms race as follows:

> We have gone on piling weapon upon weapon, missile upon missile, new levels of destructiveness upon old ones. We have done this helplessly, almost involuntarily: like the victims of some sort of hypnotism, like men in a dream, like lemmings heading for the sea, like the children of Hamlin marching blindly along behind their Pied Piper. And the result is that today we have achieved, we and the Russians together, in the creation of these devices and their means of delivery, levels of redundancy of such grotesque dimensions as to defy rational understanding.[17]

He then proposed an immediate across-the-board 50 percent cut in superpower nuclear weapons stockpiles, to be followed by further reductions of two-thirds. Kennan concluded as follows, in words that might apply not only to his own suggestion, but to disarmament proposals more generally:

> We are confronted here, my friends, with two courses. At the end of the one lies hope — faint hope, if you will, uncertain hope, hope surrounded with dangers, if you insist. At the end of the other lies, so far as I am able to see, no hope at all. Can there

be—in the light of our duty not just to ourselves (for we are all going to die sooner or later) but of our duty to our own kind, our duty to the continuity of the generations, our duty to the great experiment of civilized life on this rare and rich and marvelous planet—can there be, in the light of these claims on our loyalty, any question as to which course we should adopt?[18]

Disarmament is a long-standing, traditional value, to which—like Mom and apple pie—many people pay lip service, yet efforts at disarmament typically bog down when it comes to the specifics of implementation. The devil, it is said, is in the details. Nonetheless, we should remember that human beings have used weapons and war to resolve their differences for thousands of years; it is not reasonable to expect that such ancient habits will be overturned easily, in a matter of years, or even decades. And whereas the goal of absolute disarmament may seem unattainable, short-term setbacks in the struggle to attain that goal should not blind us to the benefits to be obtained from various accomplishments along the way. Most of all, we must recognize that disarmament is a *process*, not an *event*, more a way of progressing than a finished masterpiece to be unveiled to the admiring world with a grand "voila!" Like perfect grace, total disarmament may never be achieved, but that doesn't diminish its worth as a goal, or rather, as a route toward possible salvation.

Study Questions

1. Discuss some possible disadvantages of disarmament.

2. Distinguish between "top-down" and "grass-roots" movements for disarmament.

3. What are some advantages and disadvantages of "selective disarmament"?

4. What, in your opinion, have been the most important disarmament and/or arms control agreements since World War II? Why?

5. What can we learn from the disarmament efforts that occurred during the 1920s and 1930s?

6. Distinguish between arms control and disarmament. What are some similarities?

7. Place the various post–World War II arms control treaties and agreements in categories different than those presented in this chapter.

8. What are some disadvantages of nuclear arms control agreements? Be specific.

9. Identify a military or military-industrial facility near you; suggest possible opportunities for economic conversion.

10. How does GRIT differ from traditional strategies used in obtaining negotiated agreements?

Suggestions for Further Reading

Charles Osgood. 1961. *An Alternative to War or Surrender*. University of Illinois Press: Urbana.

Burns Weston (ed.). 1984. *Toward Nuclear Disarmament and Global Security*. Westview Press: Boulder, CO.

Suzanne Gordon and Dave McFadden (eds.). 1984. *Economic Conversion*. Ballinger: Boston.

Allan S. Krass. 1985. *Verification: How Much Is Enough?* Lexington Books: Lexington, MA.

Harry B. Hollins, Averill L. Powers, and Mark Sommer. 1989. *The Conquest of War*. Westview Press: Boulder, CO.

Source Notes

1. Martin Buber. 1958. *Paths in Utopia*. Beacon Press: Boston.

2. Dwight D. Eisenhower. 1984. *Ike's Letters to a Friend*. University Press of Kansas: Lawrence.

3. Speech by Raymond G. Hunthausen at Pacific Lutheran University, Tacoma, Washington, June 12, 1981.

4. Speech by General Omar Bradley, reprinted in *The Washington Post*, April 3, 1983.

5. David Ziegler. 1977. *War, Peace, and International Politics*. Little, Brown: Boston.

6. A. Myrdal. 1976. *The Game of Disarmament: How the United States and Russia Run the Arms Race*. Pantheon: New York.

7. Ibid.

8. Salvador de Madariaga. 1929. *Disarmament*. Coward McCann: New York.

9. Hedley Bull. 1965. *The Control of the Arms Race*. Praeger: New York.

10. Albert Einstein. 1960. *Einstein on Peace*. Simon & Schuster: New York.

11. Quoted in M. Howard. 1978. *War and the Liberal Conscience*. Rutgers University Press: New Brunswick, NJ.

12. Quoted in A. Geyer. 1982. *The Idea of Disarmament!* The Brethren Press: Elgin, IL.

13. Quoted in Robert Scheer. 1982. *With Enough Shovels*. Random House: New York.

14. Quoted in Margaret L. Coit. 1957. *Mr. Baruch*. Houghton Mifflin: Boston.

15. Dwight D. Eisenhower. 1961. *Peace With Justice: Selected Addresses*. Columbia University Press: New York.

16. Charles Osgood. 1961. *An Alternative to War or Surrender*. University of Illinois Press: Urbana.

17. Reprinted in George F. Kennan. 1981. *The Nuclear Delusion*. Pantheon: New York.

18. Ibid.

16

International Organizations

Conflict situations can be resolved in two basic ways, contrasting options that peace researcher Kenneth Boulding called "associative" and "disassociative."[1] The latter involves reliance on military strength and political separation, based on the notion that "good fences make good neighbors." Associative solutions, on the other hand, represent efforts to tear down walls, to join together. As we have seen, prominent among the causes of war is the existence of feisty, sovereign states that are, by definition, disassociative relative to one another. Their very existence is also a major obstacle to disarmament and even arms control. In Chapters 17, 18, and 19, we shall examine strongly associative solutions that go beyond the current state-centered world system and look toward larger patterns of integration: international law, world government, and ethical and religious norms. But first, in this chapter, we shall consider moderately associative possibilities, ways of ameliorating—although not eliminating—the often troublesome role of states. We start with the League of Nations, since its failures have much to teach us.

THE LEAGUE OF NATIONS

Since the early nineteenth century, serious wars have led to concerted (and ultimately unsuccessful) efforts to avoid further ones. The Concert of Europe, established in 1815 after the defeat of Napoleon, represented the first attempt to implement a system whereby states would seek to prevent war by meeting regularly, during peacetime, to consider threats to the peace. The Crimean War, similarly, gave rise to the Paris Peace Congress of 1856; and as the Concert system was breaking down (as it finally did in World War I), the European states at last began — at the Hague Conferences of 1899 and 1907 — to consider rules for the mandatory arbitration of disputes.

A Brief History of the League

Civilians and leaders alike were shocked and sobered by World War I. One result was the League of Nations, a notable, although unsuccessful, effort to transcend some of the problems of state sovereignty and to produce a war-free world. World War I was the most disastrous war in the Western world up to that time, and the old balance of power system (see Chapter 14) was widely blamed for that conflict; hence, balance of power as a way of maintaining the peace was discredited in its aftermath. President Woodrow Wilson argued cogently that wars would continue so long as states had to be responsible for their own defense. To prevent states from forming competing groups, each arming and plotting against the other, he urged the establishment of a League of Nations, which all states would join, and which would function by "collective security" (see Chapter 14).

Structure and Function. Under the terms of the League, formally inaugurated in 1920, states retained their sovereignty in domestic affairs and in virtually all foreign dealings as well. However, as part of its Covenant (constitution), members pledged to refrain from the use of force against any other state, and to submit any disputes to arbitration or an investigation by the League Council. The League Council, similar to the Security Council of the United Nations, had the Great Powers as permanent members, as well as a varying number of additional rotating members; it was to be the League's primary peacekeeping agency. In Article 16 of the League Covenant, signatories pledged:

> Should any Member of the League resort to war . . . it shall ipso facto [by this fact] be deemed to have committed an act of war against all other Members of the League, which hereby undertake immediately to subject it to the severance of all trade or financial relations, . . . and the prevention of all financial, commercial or personal intercourse between the nationals of the Covenant-breaking State and the nationals of any other State, whether a Member of the League or not.

In addition, the League Council was authorized to recommend to member states that specific military forces be raised and employed against the violator. The hope was that by virtue of their membership in the League of Nations, all states would obtain an equal measure of security, which in turn would remove any temptation for alliances. Any aggressor would also be deterred by the prospect of having to face the collective might of all other League members. The consequence of aggression having been made clear, it was further expected that secret diplomacy would be unnecessary, and would be replaced by "open covenants openly arrived at."

Although President Wilson was the intellectual father of the League of Nations, the United States never joined, because the U.S. Senate refused to ratify League membership. In the aftermath of World War I, isolationist sentiment in the United States prevailed over internationalism. Germany did not join until 1926, and it withdrew in 1933 when the League refused to lift the arms restrictions imposed earlier on Germany by the Treaty of Versailles. The Soviet Union did not join until 1934, by which time the League's authority had already been severely undermined by its inability to act decisively following Japan's conquest of Manchuria (see below).

Early Challenges. During its first decade, the League functioned reasonably well, largely because there were no world-shaking crises. It successfully ended fighting, for example, between Bulgaria and Greece in 1925, and between Lithuania and Poland in 1927. In 1932, Bolivia and Paraguay went to war over a disputed border region known as the Gran Chaco; an arms embargo against both states, organized by the League, contributed — although not decisively — to resolution of that conflict. Later, however, when disputes arose involving powerful states, the League proved woefully ineffective.

Throughout the 1920s, Manchuria had been nominally under Chinese political control, but in fact it was economically exploited by Japan, which also controlled Korea. In response to growing militant nationalist sentiment, Japan invaded Manchuria in 1931, using a small railroad explosion (most likely initiated by the Japanese themselves) as a pretext. The League protested, asking Japan to withdraw, but the Japanese ignored the League's objections and proceeded to set up the puppet state of "Manchukuo." The League also set up a Commission of Inquiry, which took nearly one and a half years to issue a final report (in 1933) that found Japan clearly guilty of unprovoked and unjustified aggression. However, the collective security provisions of the League's Covenant were not invoked, because of the legal nicety that Japan had not formally declared war. The only result, therefore, was moral condemnation and League refusal to recognize the legitimacy of the conquest; that is, currency and postage stamps from Manchukuo would not be accepted by other states. Japan thereupon withdrew from the League of Nations.

The Abyssinian Crisis.   The major crisis, however, and the one that led most directly to the collapse of League authority and, ultimately, the organization itself, was the Italian invasion of Abyssinia (now Ethiopia). Italy, which already occupied Eritrea (since incorporated into Ethiopia, and the source of current civil warfare), had long coveted Ethiopia to the south. Under the fascist dictator Benito Mussolini, Italy nurtured dreams of reestablishing the glory that had been Rome, beginning with colonial conquests in Africa. In 1934, with Italian forces in Eritrea obviously preparing to invade, Ethiopian king Haile Selassie appealed to the League of Na-

tions for assistance. But no action followed, since no aggression had yet taken place.

When the Italian invasion actually occurred, a year later, the League immediately condemned Italy as an aggressor, and voted to apply a full range of economic sanctions . . . except for those related to oil importation, which alone would have crippled the Italian war effort. Moreover, the Suez Canal was not closed to Italian shipping, and no military action was taken — or even seriously considered — against Italy. Because neither Japan, Germany, nor the United States belonged to the League, economic sanctions were unavailing; furthermore, by trading with Italy, these states, the United States in particular, could easily have defeated any oil embargo, while also enriching themselves in the process. The overwhelming "community of power" that Wilson had envisioned to oppose any aggressor simply did not materialize. Italy completed its conquest of Ethiopia, and Haile Selassie's 1936 appearance before the League of Nations, as an exile, served to emphasize the cowardice and failure of that organization.

Postmortem on the League

It is important to understand why the League of Nations failed, not simply for the sake of history, but because these factors shed light on the difficulties of keeping peace via international cooperation. No one cause can be identified as being responsible for the failure of the League; rather, a series of factors combined to doom it.

Nonsupport from Major States.   The League depended on the support of the major states. Although it acted effectively in the case of minor conflicts, it was unable to enforce its will against stronger powers. No clear-cut international peacekeeping force existed, nor was there any reliable mechanism for recruiting one if need be. The Soviet Union, as a Pacific power, might have become involved in the Manchuria invasion, but it was convulsed at the time with Stalin's purges. The United States was not a League member. Britain had sufficient naval forces to "project power" into either

Italian troops, machine guns slung over their backs, advance to take up positions during their attack on Abyssinia (Ethiopia) during 1935. (UPI/Bettmann Newsphotos)

Manchuria or Ethiopia, but was more concerned instead with protecting itself from a growing German threat.

U.S. Refusal to Join.   The United States never joined the League. Not only did this deprive the League of U.S. input, such as the possibility of U.S. support for military intervention against an aggressor, it also meant the United States could serve as "strikebreaker," foiling any attempts at economic sanctions against such an aggressor, even if the League mustered the will to attempt it. Eventually, Germany and Japan also left the League, making the prospects of economic sanctions even less credible.

Lack of Interest in Remote Conflicts.   For collective security to be successful, it was necessary for all members to agree that "peace is indivisible," that is, that a threat to the peace of any nation — no matter how small or seemingly insignificant — was a threat to themselves. But when conflicts are seen as remote and not significantly affecting the security interests of other states, governments have traditionally been hesitant to commit themselves to the economic costs — and even more so, to military adventures — that might preserve the peace or restore the *status*

quo ante (the preexisting situation) in some far-off land such as Manchuria or Ethiopia. Shortly after India gained independence from Britain, for example, Indian troops invaded the province of Hyderabad, forcing it to join the new state. Hyderabad called for international assistance, but none was forthcoming from the League's successor, the United Nations, largely because Hyderabad was entirely surrounded by Indian territory, and its fate seemed relevant only to itself and India, not to the rest of the world.

British prime minister Neville Chamberlain was roundly criticized (especially with the advantage of 20/20 hindsight) for having urged Great Britain not to assist Czechoslovakia in its 1938 Sudetenland crisis with Germany. At the time, he maintained that it was a "quarrel in a faraway country between people of whom we know nothing."[2] And yet, if indifference is dangerous, interventionism is not much beloved either. What, in fact, are the legitimate boundaries of governmental concern? Or — more narrowly — of national security? The U.S.S.R. evidently figured that its security required a notably unpeaceful intervention in Hungary in 1956, and again in Czechoslovakia in 1968. In 1962, the United States stayed out of hostilities between India and China, but almost went to nuclear war over Soviet missiles in Cuba. And where, today, is the real U.S. frontier? In Western Europe? Korea? Nicaragua?

Selfish Collusion.   Closely related to the problems of indifference and interventionism is that of selfish collusion. Once states start acting in what they consider to be their own selfish national interest, systems of collective security begin breaking down. This was most dramatically shown in the case of Italy's invasion of Ethiopia. At that time, Britain and France hoped to obtain an alliance with Mussolini, or at the least, to keep Italy from joining forces with Germany. Several years after the League's inaction in Ethiopia, it was revealed that Britain, and especially France, had actually conducted secret negotiations with the Italian government, in which they sought to win over Mussolini by promising Italy a free hand in gobbling up Ethiopia. The result? The Italian people became united behind their leader's successful expansionist policies, Mussolini was emboldened by League inaction to attempt further aggression, and the League of Nations became a laughingstock, powerless to contain the massive aggression that was eventually unleashed against Britain and France themselves. And Mussolini allied himself with Hitler after all.

Confusion over the Nature of Aggression.   There have long been problems in defining aggression. Clearly, the ritual declaration of war is insufficient, as shown by the absurdity of the claim that Japan did not violate the League's Covenant in 1931 since it did not technically declare war on Manchuria. One definition frequently employed is "violation of territorial integrity and political independence," but even this leads to difficult and confusing cases. For example, consider the Six Days War in 1967, when Israel attacked her Arab neighbors. At first glance, this appears to have been a clear-cut case of Israeli aggression, involving as it did a violation of the territorial integrity of Egypt's Sinai Peninsula, Syria's Golan Heights, and Jordan's proprietorship of Jerusalem. Clearly, Israel "started it." Just prior to the Israeli attack, however, Egyptian president Nas-

ser had closed an international waterway, the Straits of Tiran, to Israeli shipping, thereby blockading Israel's use of the important port of Aqaba. And such a blockade has itself traditionally been considered an act of war. (For their part, the Egyptians claimed that the Straits were in Egyptian territorial waters.) As to the Golan Heights, Israel argued that this region had been used by Syria to violate Israel's territorial integrity and Israel also claimed ancient, biblical rights to Jerusalem. Nasser, in turn, had announced previously that the very existence of the state of Israel was an act of aggression against the Arab people.

Some other examples: Was it aggression when the United States sent troops into South Vietnam, given that this action was at the request of the legally recognized government there? And what about the Soviet troops sent to Afghanistan, in response to a similar request by the legally recognized Afghan government? What about the U.S.-sponsored mining of Managua harbor in 1984, which was most assuredly against the wishes of the legally constituted and recognized Nicaraguan government? Or the sending of military advisors and munitions to revolutionary movements in a foreign country (Angola, Nicaragua, Afghanistan, Cambodia, and so on)?

When India swallowed up the tiny Portuguese enclave of Goa, in 1961, virtually no international protests were raised, in part because India argued that it was not initiating aggressive war, but rather acting to help erase one manifestation of a great injustice: European colonialism. Whereas in some cases, questions of definition appear to be mere quibbling over technicalities, in others, they reflect real uncertainty as to what constitutes aggression, and therefore, what response—if any—is appropriate.

A BRIEF HISTORY OF THE UNITED NATIONS

As World War II drew to a close, the victorious Allies—once again traumatized by war, and disillusioned at the failure of the state system to prevent it—decided once more to establish an international body that would work toward the abolition of war.

They also hoped that this new organization, known as the United Nations, would avoid some of the pitfalls that had doomed the League of Nations. The idea developed in part from the Atlantic Charter, signed in 1941 by Winston Churchill and Franklin Roosevelt, by which the two leaders committed themselves to a postwar world devoted to economic cooperation and eventual disarmament. The formal idea of an international organization for preserving world peace was approved by Roosevelt, Churchill, and Stalin during a conference in Tehran in 1943. Specific plans for such an organization were drawn up at the Dumbarton Oaks Conference, outside Washington, in late 1944.

It was agreed that all governments would be welcome, with membership in a large General Assembly, but that primary enforcement power would rest with a Security Council, with the United States, the Soviet Union, Britain, France, and China as permanent members. Finally, in the spring of 1945, delegates from fifty countries met in San Francisco at the United Nations Conference on International Organization, which actually established a Charter for the United Nations. The Preamble to that Charter* reads as follows:

> **We the peoples of the United Nations** determined to save succeeding generations from the scourge of war, which twice in our lifetime has brought untold sorrow to mankind, and
> to reaffirm faith in fundamental human rights, in the dignity and worth of the human person, in the equal rights of men and women and of nations large and small, and
> to establish conditions under which justice and respect for the obligations arising from treaties and other sources of international law can be maintained, and
> to promote social progress and better standards of life in larger freedom, **and for these ends**
> to practice tolerance and live together in peace with one another as good neighbors, and
> to unite our strength to maintain international peace and security, and to ensure, by the acceptance of

principles and the institution of methods, that armed force shall not be used, save in the common interest, and to employ international machinery for the promotion of the economic and social advancement of all peoples,
> **have resolved to combine our efforts to accomplish these aims**.

The United Nations first formally convened in 1946, in London; it moved to its present location, by the East River in New York City, in 1952.

The UN's Basic Structure

The United Nations differed from its predecessor, the League of Nations, in several significant ways. For one, whereas the United States remained aloof from the League, it became a charter member, and in many ways, the single most important actor, in the UN. For another, the United Nations, unlike the League of Nations, was constituted so as to have many other important functions beyond those dealing strictly with the avoidance or termination of wars. A branch of the UN, the Economic and Social Council, was established, with many specialized agencies concerned with various economic, educational, health, scientific, and social issues — such as the Food and Agriculture Organization, the World Health Organization, the World Bank and International Monetary Fund, and UNICEF and UNESCO, as well as lesser-known organizations such as the International Civil Aviation Organization, the International Telecommunication Union, and the World Meteorological Organization. The major organs of the UN, and their prime missions, are as follows:

- the Security Council — issues of war and peace

- the General Assembly — the main parliamentary, budget, and decision-making organ

- the Economic and Social Council — quality of life worldwide

- the International Court of Justice (also known as the World Court), located at The Hague, Netherlands — adjudication of international legal disputes

---

*Jan Christian Smuts, of South Africa, is generally credited with drafting this Preamble.

Headquarters of the United Nations in New York City. (United Nations/Yutaka Nagata)

- the Trusteeship Council — established to oversee the eventual independence of regions that, in the immediate postwar period, were not self-governing or had been colonies of Germany, Italy, or Japan

- the Secretariat — essentially the executive organ of the UN, led by one individual, designated the Secretary-General

The UN and the State System

To understand the United Nations and assess its actual and potential contributions to peace, it is important to realize what it is *not*. Thus, it is not a world government, or even an effort at establishing one. It does not offer an alternative to state sovereignty; in fact, the UN was established with a number of guidelines to assure that, if anything, state sovereignty supercedes it. Accordingly, although the UN often proclaims high-minded goals and resolutions, the decisions and actions taken by the UN are not above the national interests of the states that compose it. It is not a substitute or cure-all for the current state system; rather, it is in large part a *reflection* of that system; a mirror, not a panacea. It is not a solution to problems of personal aggressiveness, poor decision-making, nationalism, oppression, or the Cold War. It is limited to the actions of states, and can solve only problems that those states want to solve, in ways that are approved by the member states themselves. Whatever our disappointments in how it has functioned, we cannot fairly say that the UN has failed its member states; rather, if there has been failure, it is the states that have failed the UN.

Shortly after the UN was founded, it became apparent that the United States and the Soviet Union were not going to cooperate very much, if at all. In fact, the Cold War quickly began in earnest. In the early years after the UN's founding, the United States had a number of friends and allies in the General Assembly, and thus was able to use the United Nations essentially to prosecute its side of the Cold War; the U.S.S.R., in turn, was isolated, and forced to use its veto in the Security Council on numerous occasions. However, UN membership expanded rapidly, due largely to an influx of newly independent former colonies. In 1946, the UN had only 55 members; by 1960, it had 99; and by 1982, 157. By the late 1950s the United States could no longer count on an automatic two-thirds majority in the General Assembly, as most of the new states considered themselves nonaligned, and in 1966, the United States cast its first veto in the Security Council. For decades, while the United States refused to recognize the communist government of China, the Chinese had been excluded from the United Nations. By 1971, however, a watershed was reached when — over U.S. objections — mainland China was seated in place of Taiwan. Security Council operations had earlier ceased to be a means whereby the United States prosecuted the Cold War, and the UN entered more clearly into a phase of limited peacekeeping and peacemaking.

Attitudes Toward the UN

Conservatives in the United States have long been uncomfortable with the United Nations, seeing it as — at minimum — an infringement on national sovereignty. "Get the U.S. out of the UN," read bumper stickers and the occasional roadside sign, "and get the UN out of the U.S." As Third World states have become a numerical majority in the UN, right-wing opposition to it has intensified. Annoyance with the organization has been especially fueled by the fact that every state has only one vote in the General Assembly, no matter how insignificant it may be or how despotically governed. Moreover, the UN has voted for numerous resolutions that many Americans have found disagreeable, such as one stating that Zionism (worldwide support for the establishment of Israel) is a "form of racism." And the UN tends to embrace concerns that conservatives generally oppose, namely disarmament, economic and social equality, environmental protection, and women's rights.

During the 1980s, the Reagan administration was especially upset with the UN's prodisarmament and pro-PLO stances, and the fact that it did not always endorse U.S. foreign policy objectives. In response, the U.S. has also lagged behind in paying its UN dues, resulting in a continuing series of financial crises.

From a Peace Studies perspective, the major failing of the United Nations has been its inability to achieve global disarmament, to prevent wars, and to end those wars that it could not prevent. On the other hand, the UN offers a vision of superordinate goals: the coming-together of sovereign states because of a commitment — albeit sometimes a modest one — to planetary concerns. It may also help legitimize the idea of world government (see Chapter 18). In the meantime, the United Nations does good work in bettering the social, economic, educational, medical, scientific, and cultural condition of humanity. This is desirable in itself, and it also helps create conditions more conducive to "positive peace." In addition, the UN has had some (admittedly limited) success in acting directly to make peace and to keep it. Let us turn now to an overview of the UN's record in this respect.

PEACEMAKING EFFORTS OF THE UNITED NATIONS

Hopes for what the UN might accomplish have passed through several stages. In the initial aftermath of World War II, it was hoped that the grand alliance that defeated Germany and Japan would hold together, and that the major powers, acting in concert, would fashion a truly functional system of collective security. The Security Council was empowered to identify an aggressor, and then to request that various member states provide military force as necessary to enforce the peace. To keep disagreements from escalating, and possibly even becoming causes of war between them, the permanent members of the Security Council were each given veto power over any such decision; this meant, in effect, that the UN would be paralyzed if any one of its major members opposed a given action. Although this feature has often prevented UN involvement in many cases where it might have been helpful, the Security Council veto has also acted as a circuit breaker, preventing the system from overloading and possibly blowing itself apart when it faced situations that were especially contentious. As a result, however, the UN has also been virtually powerless to resolve disputes in which any of the permanent members believed they had a high stake. On the other hand, the UN has been able to function much longer than its predecessor, the League of Nations, and — especially in issues involving the lesser states — more effectively as well. The following examples illustrate the diversity of armed disputes in which the UN has been involved.

Indonesia

Indonesia had been a Dutch colony for hundreds of years, and was occupied by the Japanese during World War II. In 1947, severe fighting broke out between Indonesian nationalists and The Netherlands, which sought to reestablish and retain colonial control. The UN Security Council called for a truce, which was ignored. Nearly six months later, in 1948, a committee appointed by the Security Council persuaded the combatants to sign a cease-fire; later that year, however, The Netherlands renounced the UN-sponsored agreement, and fighting resumed. But the Council eventually approved a plan calling for an independent Indonesia, and established another commission that successfully arranged another cease-fire and brought the combatants together once again, this time for a peace conference that ultimately approved independence for Indonesia in December 1949. In the 1960s, fighting broke out once more between Indonesian forces and Dutch occupiers of West New Guinea. UN secretary-general U Thant arranged for temporary Indonesian control, followed eventually by elections, which gave Indonesia sovereignty over West New Guinea (Irian).

The UN did not prevent war in Indonesia. Moreover, it is questionable whether the UN even brought the war to a significantly earlier conclusion. The Netherlands turned to the UN largely because the Dutch were unable to defeat the Indonesian nationalists. The UN served mainly as a useful intermediary and, to some extent, a face-saving way

for decolonization (probably inevitable in any event) to proceed. In other, similar, cases, however, such as the struggle between Algeria and France — in which 10 percent of the Algerian populace perished before ultimately winning their independence — the UN played essentially no part whatever.

India/Pakistan

India and Pakistan went to war in 1947 over Kashmir. After more than a year's effort, a UN commission in 1949 got both sides to agree on a cease-fire line, and to permit the people of Kashmir to vote on their preference for affiliation with one state or the other. The two sides could not agree on troop withdrawals, however, and the promised vote never took place. When fighting broke out again between India and Pakistan in 1965, Kashmir was once more at issue. The Security Council demanded that both sides withdraw to the 1949 line, and after meetings with Secretary-General U Thant, a cease-fire was finally arranged. Two UN observer groups were sent to enforce this cease-fire, and in 1966, with Soviet mediation (and, perhaps, some armtwisting), both states agreed to refrain from settling their dispute by force; the issue itself has not yet been resolved, and the UN observers have remained in place.

Korea

When World War II ended, Soviet troops occupied Korea north of the 38th parallel, with U.S. troops controlling the South. A UN commission sought, unsuccessfully, to find ways to unite the country. In June 1950, North Korean forces penetrated deep into the South, leading to U.S. intervention. Meanwhile, the Security Council identified the North as the aggressor, and voted for UN members to send troops to assist the South, designating the U.S. military leadership as commanding UN forces in Korea. This vote occurred because the Soviet delegation was boycotting Security Council meetings to protest the UN's refusal to seat a delegation from communist China, which had recently replaced the Nationalist Chinese government after a

Soldiers and flags of some of the armed forces that fought in Korea from 1950 to 1953. From left, Australia, the United States, South Korea, the United Kingdom, and the Philippines. The UN flag is in the middle. (United Nations/U.S. Army)

long, bloody civil war. Hence, the Soviets were unable to veto Security Council proceedings.

There were, at the time, sixty UN members; of these, sixteen sent troops and forty-one sent supplies. However, the United States contributed over 95 percent of both supplies and troops, as well as providing virtually all the commanders and making most major decisions. In fact, the so-called police action in Korea by UN forces was essentially a ratification by the UN of a military policy that the United States had already initiated unilaterally. When the Chinese then entered the Korean conflict in October 1950, with UN forces deep in North Korean territory, the Security Council met to discuss further action. By now, however, the Soviet delegate had returned, and it vetoed any proposed military response. The United States reacted by taking up the matter in the General Assembly, which passed a "Uniting for Peace" resolution, stating that when the Security Council was unable to act in repelling armed aggression, the General Assembly had the right to call on member states to do so. The U.S.S.R. denounced this move as a subversion of the

Security Council's powers, but the UN, by this strategy, continued its active involvement in the Korean War until China and the United Nations (really, the United States) signed a cease-fire agreement in 1953. No peace treaty has yet been signed.

Korea was by far the major case in which UN forces were used directly to repel an aggressor. In the case of Korea, the UN was in a sense functioning closer to what the original designers of the world organization had in mind . . . except for the fact that it was acting largely on behalf of one superpower (the United States) and against the interests of another (the U.S.S.R.). This occurred in part because many governments feared that failure to act on North Korea's invasion of the South would doom the UN to irrelevance, like the League of Nations before it. But the UN also acted because of the Soviet tactical error in boycotting Security Council proceedings. This has not happened since, and it seems unlikely that, as currently constituted, the UN will again find itself fighting in contests so directly involving the military forces of either superpower.

The Arab-Israeli Wars

Over Arab opposition, the General Assembly approved a British plan in 1947 that divided Palestine into a Jewish and an Arab state, with Jerusalem to be governed under UN auspices. When Israel was declared an independent state in 1948, it was invaded by armies from Egypt, Syria, Lebanon, Iraq, and Transjordan (now Jordan). The General Assembly and Security Council tried in vain to stop the fighting; a Swedish diplomat, sent to the Middle East as a potential mediator, was assassinated by Jewish extremists. Eventually, Ralph Bunche (a U.S. diplomat and UN mediator) established an armistice in 1949, for which he received a Nobel Peace Prize. Bunche met with representatives of the Arabs and Israelis on the island of Rhodes (because the Arabs did not extend diplomatic recognition to Israel, Bunche had to shuttle messages between different floors of a hotel in order to hammer out a written agreement). However, the issue had been resolved not so much by UN diplomacy as by force of arms — that is, by the effective defeat of the Arab armies in the field. Indeed, the underlying issues were not resolved.

When the fighting was over, Israel had expanded its borders over those earlier approved by the UN, and hundreds of thousands of Arab refugees (known as Palestinians) fled to neighboring Arab states, where they remain today, stateless, largely unassimilated, and demanding a homeland. A continuing UN truce organization failed to make progress in settling these difficulties during the early 1950s. By 1956, Egypt had blockaded Israeli shipping in the Gulf of Aqaba, and nationalized the Suez Canal, whereupon Britain and France, in coordination with Israel, invaded Egypt, and captured the Sinai Peninsula as well as the Suez Canal. Not surprisingly, Britain and France vetoed action by the Security Council; the General Assembly then called for a cease-fire, which was finally achieved several months later. In this case, UN pressure was relatively unimportant, however: Britain and France were largely pushed to withdraw by the vigorous opposition of their close ally, the United States. But the General Assembly did arrange for UN troops to guard the border between Egypt and Israel, which agreed to pull back to the 1949 cease-fire line.

This new UN presence, the United Nations Emergency Force (UNEF) represented a very important and innovative step, first proposed by Canada's Lester Pearson (for which he won a Nobel Peace Prize) and administered by Secretary-General Dag Hammarskjöld: a new system that came to be known as "peacekeeping." The idea was not to favor either side, but to enforce the peace by interposing a lightly armed UN presence between the belligerents. By what Hammarskjöld called "preventive diplomacy," UN peacekeepers could help to patrol and maintain otherwise shaky cease-fires; at minimum, this would at least prevent further bloodshed. At maximum, it could gain time and help create conditions under which creative diplomacy might help resolve the conflict. In Hammarskjöld's conception — which has been retained ever since — the UN would seek to isolate local conflicts from superpower involvement. Peacekeepers, for example, would be recruited largely from nonaligned states.

The Arab-Israeli conflict, however, has remained largely intractable. The 1956 cease-fire did not hold, and by 1967, Egyptian president Nasser demanded that the UNEF withdraw from the Sinai. (Israel never permitted UNEF forces to patrol its territory.) As tension mounted, Israel again attacked its Arab neighbors in the Six Days War. The Security Council unsuccessfully called on Israel to give up the territory it gained in that conflict (notably the West Bank, formerly part of Jordan) in return for security guarantees. Following the 1973 October War in which Arab states attacked Israel, the belligerents agreed to another separation of forces, to be supervised by two new UN peacekeeping units, which still remain in place.

Lebanon has also been a hot spot for UN peacekeepers. The Security Council, in 1958, sent observers to investigate Christian Lebanese claims that Syria and Egypt were fomenting revolution among its Moslem population. As disruption increased, the United States sent 10,000 troops. Israeli forces later invaded southern Lebanon in 1978, in response to terrorists attacks emanating from PLO (Palestinian Liberation Organization) bases

A Norwegian soldier serving with the UN Interim Force in Lebanon (UNIFIL) surveying a region in Southern Lebanon in 1978. (United Nations / J. K. Isaac)

near the Israeli border, after which another UN peacekeeping force was established there as well. However, UNIFIL (United Nations Interim Forces in Lebanon) could not prevent continued terrorist provocations, or the second Israeli invasion of Leb- anon, in 1982.

The Congo

After fifty-five years of Belgian rule, the Congo (now Zaire) became independent in 1960. How- ever, Belgium had done virtually nothing to estab- lish a well-trained and educated indigenous civil service, so that, when it withdrew, chaos ensued. Belgian troops then returned, ostensibly to keep order, but in the opinion of many, to reclaim their colonial hold on the country. Meanwhile, stability in the Congo — and perhaps, much of the rest of central Africa — was further threatened by the at- tempted secession of mineral-rich Katanga Prov- ince, which also received assistance from European mercenaries. At the request of the Congolese lead- ership (who themselves were bitterly divided on most issues), the Security Council sent UN forces to the Congo.

At its peak, the Congo operation was a substan- tial military commitment, involving 20,000 men and including fighter aircraft. The Soviet Union believed that the UN was aiding the forces of right-

wing politician Joseph Kasavubu rather than the Soviet choice, left-wing Patrice Lumumba.* When the U.S.S.R. vetoed subsequent UN actions in the Congo, operations were — as in the case of Korea — authorized by the General Assembly. The Katanga rebellion was eventually ended, and a stable (right- wing military dictatorship) Congolese government was established, whereupon the UN forces finally withdrew in 1964. The Soviet Union, disapproving the actions of the UN in the Congo, refused to pay its share of the costs, as did France as well.

Cyprus

Cyprus became an independent republic in 1960, following a period of British rule. Its population was about 80 percent Greek and 20 percent Turk- ish, and nationalist passions were the cause of fre- quent small-scale violence. In late 1963, the Cypriot leader, Archbishop Makarios (an ethnic Greek), suspended certain rights of Turkish Cypriots. Tur- key sent a fleet to the island, and Cyprus appealed to the Security Council for aid. A UN peacekeeping force was dispatched to Cyprus; it helped prevent violence between Greeks and Turks and still re- mains. However, fighting broke out again in 1974, when a coup by ardent pro-Greek nationalists re- sulted in a full-scale invasion by Turkish forces. Eventually, the Security Council negotiated a cease- fire, but only after Turkey had seized more than one third of the island, which remains effectively parti- tioned today.

FUNCTIONS OF THE UNITED NATIONS

The UN's ability to serve as an active peacemaker and peacekeeper has been severely limited. For one thing, member states have never been able to agree on maintaining an independent UN force with

---

*Lumumba was in fact subsequently arrested and assas- sinated, and the Zaire government has been a right- wing military dictatorship ever since. The Soviets, meanwhile, established Patrice Lumumba University in Moscow, devoted to the education of aspiring Third World leaders.

sufficient military strength and political independence to deter would-be adversaries. Trygve Lie, the first secretary-general, tried several times to establish a uniformed "UN Legion," but was unable to achieve consensus among the permanent Security Council members. Financial troubles have also been serious and ongoing, further restricting the UN's effectiveness. In addition, there has been disagreement — and some inconsistency — among states as to what the role of the UN ought to be. Thus, the UN took no action in Nigeria from 1967 to 1970, when the Ibo people sought to secede and establish an independent state of Biafra. In that conflict, most African states argued that the UN should refrain from becoming involved because the Nigerian civil war was a domestic matter. At the same time, many African states believe the UN should be more actively engaged in opposing apartheid in South Africa, which is also a domestic matter.* The Nigerian civil war was terribly bloody and destructive (and led to perhaps 2 million deaths). But Ibo success in their secessionist effort might have had repercussions in other African states, many of which are also made up of diverse ethnic groups. By contrast, most African states are united in their opposition to the racist policies of the Republic of South Africa.

In the case of many large-scale conflicts, the UN was uninvolved or impotent, reduced to making futile pleas for peace, or — worse yet — failing even to make any statement at all. For example, when Pakistan brutally crushed the attempt by East Pakistan to secede in 1971, UN intervention was rejected by the Pakistani government, which made the familiar claim that the issue was entirely an internal, domestic affair. Later, after perhaps 3 million people had been killed and India went to war with Pakistan, ultimately establishing the new state of Bangladesh, India also rejected the prospect of UN involvement. The UN briefly discussed, but stayed out of, the Vietnamese invasion of Cam-

bodia, which overthrew the murderous, pro-Chinese government of Pol Pot; and the UN again failed to act during the subsequent Chinese "punishment" of Vietnam in 1979. In response to the Iranian hostage crisis of 1979–1980, the Security Council toothlessly requested that Iran release the U.S. hostages, but the U.S.S.R. vetoed a recommendation for economic sanctions. The UN also did essentially nothing to end the Vietnam War or the Ogaden and Eritrea/Tigre secessionist wars in Ethiopia. The Tanzanian invasion of Uganda that deposed dictator Idi Amin, in 1980, never even made it to the Security Council's agenda, nor did Libya's invasion of Chad several years after that.

Peacekeeping Forces

On the other hand, the fact that the UN hasn't prevented or stopped all wars does not mean that it has not been effective and useful in certain cases. Peacekeeping troops — lightly armed, blue-helmeted "soldiers without enemies" — serve as valuable buffers between contending forces, especially from the eastern Mediterranean to the Indian subcontinent. They have also been important in monitoring compliance with cease-fires, supervising disengagement lines, maintaining "no man's lands" between belligerents, and so forth. When neutral forces are interposed between opponents, suspicious events are less likely to be misinterpreted as a provocation, and intentional provocations themselves are less likely. Since 1948, fourteen peacekeeping operations altogether have been conducted, most frequently in the Middle East. UN operations in the Golan Heights have been notably successful. This elevated region along the Israeli-Syrian border has great strategic value, since it constitutes a high spot from which one can look down on either Damascus or Jerusalem. Under UN supervision, the Golan Heights has been effectively demilitarized, thereby removing it as a bone of contention between Israel and Syria.

UN officials believe that the role of peacekeeping forces will grow in the future; it is anticipated, for example, that a force of about 7,000 will be sent to monitor and maintain a truce in Namibia and Angola, while other contingents are planned for the

---

*It is claimed that because of its institutionalized racial injustice, South Africa's existence as a sovereign state is illegitimate; the Ibo people claimed similarly, however, that Nigeria's racial injustice toward them delegitimized Nigerian sovereignty as well.

A United Nations General Assembly meeting. Every state gets one vote in the General Assembly. Under current peacekeeping policies, UN forces are recruited from the smaller states for disputes not involving the major powers. (United Nations / Milton Grant)

Western Sahara, and to observe and monitor cease-fires, troop withdrawals, and prisoner exchanges along the Iran-Iraq border and in Afghanistan. In 1988, the UN's peacekeeping forces were awarded a well-deserved Nobel Peace Prize for their extensive and courageous efforts.

Third-Party Mediation

UN mediators have occasionally served as valuable third parties, helping belligerents to reach acceptable and face-saving agreements (see Chapter 13). Secretary-General Javier Perez de Cuellar and other UN diplomats were instrumental in working out the plan whereby Soviet troops began leaving Afghanistan in 1988; the secretary-general and his deputies also served as intermediaries, helping to achieve a long-awaited cease-fire in the Iran-Iraq War that

same year. And in 1988, Dean Rusk—U.S. secretary of state during the Cuban Missile Crisis twenty-six years before—revealed that President Kennedy had prepared a memo to be proposed by Secretary-General U Thant in the event the United States and the Soviet Union appeared irreconcilably headed toward war. The memo suggested a "compromise" that the U.S. government had already decided would be acceptable . . . but only if it came from a disinterested third party, not the Soviet Union. The compromise—that the United States would remove its land-based missiles from Turkey in return for the Soviets dismantling their Cuban missiles—proved unnecessary, since Premier Khrushchev subsequently agreed to Kennedy's terms. It does, however, show the value of a respected and disinterested third party. (Even if the UN had prevented only one nuclear war—and done nothing else—

this would have been more than enough to justify its existence!)

The UN has in fact met with some success in preventing the escalation of hostilities, and sometimes, in helping to terminate them. This is quite different, however, from preventing war. Admittedly, in many cases, the UN has only been "effective" after the guns have spoken, and/or after depleted treasuries and popular sentiment have forced governments to seek some kind of settlement as a result. A peacekeeping regime, on the other hand, helps produce an atmosphere of calm, in which a just and peaceful solution can be negotiated. But even peacekeeping has its drawbacks as well. While it may save lives at the time, it may also help perpetuate a crisis, by reducing the urgency of reaching a political solution. By taking the edge off a conflict, in a sense it prolongs that situation, making it more tolerable, and even part of the way of life in the affected region.

Forum for Debate

Nonetheless, peacekeeping is acknowledged to be an overall plus, and the UN remains important, beyond its function as a debating society. In the words of one observer, the UN "has become indispensable before it has become effective."[3] It should be noted, incidentally, that even debating societies can be very useful, providing an opportunity for government representatives to meet one another and exchange views, often removed from the glare of publicity. In addition, there have been cases — and doubtless will be others in the future — in which governments believed their people demanded a vigorous response, but one short of war. When its citizenry is outraged by some international event, a state may feel pressed to show its people that it is doing something . . . whereas, in fact, peace is best served by doing nothing. In such cases, the UN provides an opportunity for states to meet their adversarial obligations symbolically rather than through bloodshed. For example, U.S. authorities judged (no doubt correctly) that it would be unwise to intervene militarily when the Soviet Union invaded Hungary in 1956. So, its delegates roundly condemned the Soviets in the UN, thereby satisfying American public opinion that the U.S. government strongly supported the Hungarians. The Soviets had comparable opportunities to score debating points and satisfy their domestic constituencies when the United States unilaterally dispatched troops to Lebanon in 1958, and to the Dominican Republic in 1965. Similarly, Arab delegates get to castigate Israel regularly, attacking the Jewish state verbally while their armies generally refrain from doing so militarily.

Focus on Lesser States

Observers acknowledge that the UN has moved away from its original function of providing collective security, and toward the job of peacekeeping, working not only to defuse potential violence, but also to reduce the likelihood that the superpowers might intervene. Originally, it had been hoped that concerted military action by the major powers would keep the peace. Now, we find the UN operating under an opposite assumption: that peace will be enhanced specifically by excluding the major powers from crises, and by recruiting peacekeepers from smaller, neutral states. Secretary-General Dag Hammarskjöld admitted in 1961 that the UN could not intervene successfully in cases of superpower rivalry, such as disputes over Berlin, or regarding nuclear weapons. But it could work, he maintained, to localize disputes in which the superpowers did not have an overriding interest. By bringing in the small powers, the UN's preventive diplomacy keeps the superpowers out, thereby averting a major confrontation, while also working to defuse local crises. In Hammarskjöld's words, the job of the UN was "not to bring mankind to Heaven, but rather, to save it from Hell."[4]

Constraints on the Use of Force

In theory, the UN has the authority, through its Charter, to raise military forces and interject them into a conflict, without the permission of the conflicting parties. Article 42 authorizes the Security Council to call for military operations against aggressors, and Article 43 calls on member states to provide such forces as requested. Moreover, Article 39 of the UN Charter says that the Security Council shall

> determine the existence of any threat to the peace, breach of the peace, or act of aggression and shall make recommendations, or decide what measure shall be taken . . . to maintain international peace and security. . . . Such action may include demonstrations, blockade, and other operations by air, sea, or land forces of Members of the United Nations.

Note that a buildup of forces, an oppressive social system, or even the ascension to power of a militaristic government could legitimately be defined as a "threat to the peace." In theory, therefore, the UN has substantial discretionary powers for the use of force. In practice, however, it has been very cautious.

Not only has it generally kept out of superpower affairs, the UN has studiously avoided involvement in most civil wars as well. It is worth noting that if the UN was to take its original mandate literally, and squash any "threat to peace," then in the process it might well be squelching hopes for national liberation on the part of Eritreans, Kurds, Basques, Afghans, Salvadorans, and so on. For better or worse, the UN operates under numerous constraints.

This seeming weakness of the United Nations actually reflects a weakness of the world system as a whole: the fact that it is divided into contending and sovereign states, which nearly always evaluate a policy based on national interests rather than international benefit. For example, when white supremacists unilaterally declared Rhodesia independent from Britain in 1967 and proceeded to establish a racist state along the lines of South Africa, the UN responded by imposing economic sanctions. The United States reluctantly went along, but only after announcing its own unilateral decision: It reserved the right to keep trading in commodities that had previously been exchanged between the two countries (officials in Washington wanted to assure that the United States could continue to import Rhodesian chromium, necessary for making steel alloys used in military manufacture).

Of course, in redefining its UN obligation so as to conform to its perceived domestic needs, the United States made a mockery of the attempted UN sanctions. Forced to decide between the ethics of international obligations and the practicalities of national interest, narrowly defined, the United States — like virtually every UN member faced with similar choices — opted for the latter.

Sensitivity to State Sovereignty

The UN attempts to be sensitive to issues of national sovereignty, trying not to force choices between allegiance to the state on the one hand, and to the world body on the other. For example, since the Korean War and the controversial Congo intervention, prospective host countries have had the option of forbidding any UN peacekeeping presence; the UN can only send observers into a country if it is specifically invited to do so. And the UN withdraws its forces whenever the host country so requests (as happened in Egypt in 1967). "The umbrella was removed," complained Israeli diplomat Abba Eban, "at the precise moment when it began to rain."[5] As a result of such sensitivity to matters of state sovereignty, the UN has been less muscular than it might otherwise be, but it has also been able to persevere in a changing world of jealous and strong-minded states. This kind of flexibility and adaptability has served it well, and kept it around for those cases in which it has been able to make its mark.

As we have seen, the framers of the UN Charter had hoped that the major powers would stand united against aggression, and that upon them would fall the responsibility for maintaining peace and order. The UN was thus ill-equipped to deal with the major East–West schism that developed. The competing superpowers, not surprisingly, have elected to handle their own controversies by themselves (for example, the Berlin and Cuban Missile crises, or the strategic arms and INF negotiations, in which the UN had essentially no part). Similarly, the superpowers vigorously rebuff what they see as UN interference in their own foreign policy goals; the United States did not consult with the UN before sending troops to the Dominican Republic in 1965, or to Grenada in 1983. And if tensions should rise between Poland and the Soviet Union, it seems unlikely that a UN force will be interposing itself along the Soviet-Polish border, just as we can be confident that the U.S.S.R. would veto any attempt to make sure that the Red Army does not once again invade Hungary. At the same time, the UN has become more and more a forum for the tension between the industrialized, wealthy north, and the impoverished, dissatisfied south. To some extent, the various economic and social agencies of the UN also help redress this imbalance.

REGIONAL ORGANIZATIONS

Although the UN has largely failed as an organ of collective security, numerous smaller, regional organizations have been established that attempt to provide this function. In examining this approach, also known as "regionalism," we do not include the establishment of entities such as NATO, the Warsaw Pact, SEATO, or CENTO. These military alliances have been directed outward against potential aggressors, and are not intended as collective security organizations, designed to protect all members against an aggressor from within the region. Regional organizations include the Organization of African Unity (OAU), the Organization of American States (OAS), the Association of East Asian Nations (ASEAN), and the Arab League. In some cases, these organizations have helped maintain the peace. Although these are not strictly collective security systems, they at least provide for third-party pressure to be brought against member states that might otherwise go to war.

For example, when Kuwait received its independence from Britain in 1961, Iraq claimed sovereignty over the new, oil-rich ministate. Kuwait received admission into the Arab League, which sent a force of several thousand troops (especially from Egypt and Saudi Arabia) to supplant British forces that had been requested by the fledgling Kuwaiti government, and Iraq thereupon backed

down. In 1960, the OAS was able to resolve accusations by Venezuela that the Dominican Republic was employing political subversion against it. When the "Soccer War" broke out between El Salvador and Honduras in 1969, the OAS was able to arrange a cease-fire, and to provide independent observers to supervise its implementation. Early in 1979, the OAS severely criticized and isolated the government of Nicaraguan dictator Anastacio Somoza; this may have contributed to his ouster less than a year later. Ten years later, after an obviously fraudulent election in Panama, the OAS roundly condemned Panamanian military leader Manuel Noriega, thereby officially serving notice that U.S. displeasure with Noriega was shared by virtually all of the governments of the Western Hemisphere; this provided additional pressure toward his removal. However, the OAS vigorously disapproved of the U.S. invasion of Panama in 1989; like other regional organizations, it favors multilateral rather than unilateral acts.

The OAU, for its part, has helped facilitate the settlement of border disputes between Morocco and Algeria, and among Kenya, Somalia, and Ethiopia, as well as coordinating African opposition to South African apartheid. (Critics, of course, view this latter activity as provoking violence rather than fostering peace; supporters emphasize that peace in Africa requires an end to apartheid and its structural violence.) In other cases, regional alliances have sought United Nations assistance; the UN was called in, for example, after the British Commonwealth of Nations couldn't solve the India-Pakistan disputes over Kashmir and Bangladesh. It should be noted, by the way, that the UN Charter explicitly endorses regional peacekeeping organizations.

On balance, however, regionalism has not been especially successful, generally for the same reasons that the UN has been limited in its peacemaking: State sovereignty restricts its effectiveness. In addition, regional organizations have often become vehicles for superpower domination. OAS members, for example, were largely coerced by the United States into supporting sanctions against Castro's Cuba, and approving the U.S. invasion of Grenada.

During the 1982 Falklands/Malvinas War, the OAS largely stood by Argentina, out of regional and anticolonial loyalty; yet it was fractionated because the English-speaking Caribbean states sympathized with Britain.

FUNCTIONALISM AND FUNCTIONAL AGENCIES

When we think of the possible role of worldwide international organizations such as the United Nations — or even regional organizations such as the OAS or the OAU — in promoting peace, we are inclined to think about disarmament conferences and such relatively direct measures as peacekeeping and mediating. But according to advocates of another approach — "functionalism" — the long-term prospects for peace are enhanced even more by other, humanitarian activities that cut across state and national borders.[6]

Functionalism can best be understood by reference to the so-called functional agencies, such as the World Health Organization (WHO), Food and Agriculture Organization (FAO), and International Postal Union (IPU), which are typically given short shrift in discussions of the UN. The aims of these organizations do not include the establishment or maintenance of peace as such, but rather such goals as eradicating malaria, providing protein to growing children, and seeing to the fair exchange of international mail. In the view of its proponents, functionalism represents a way of deemphasizing the role of states, and even to some extent undermining their authority. As one political scientist has emphasized,[7] functionalism pins its hopes on a three-pronged attack on war:

1. By reducing human misery, as by eradicating diseases, developing new strains of food crops, disseminating technological know-how, promoting literacy, and so forth, it is hoped that war will be made less likely.

2. By showing that institutions other than the state can attend to human needs — sometimes much better than the states do — it is hoped that state sovereignty will gradually be undermined.

3. By providing opportunities for interactions across political borders, it is hoped that mutual understanding, tolerance, and respect will be enhanced.

It is difficult to evaluate the success, or the future prospects, of functionalism. Although conventional wisdom holds that misery leads to war, as we have noted (see Chapter 11), no clear evidence supports this claim, at least with regard to international war. And prosperity, at least, often seems to have made violence more likely, not less, in that strong and wealthy states, flushed with self-confidence, may be more inclined to engage in military adventures while weaker ones tend to be more cautious. On the other hand, making a better life for people might well decrease the chances of rebellions and civil wars. And certainly, the humanitarian goals of functionalism are worthwhile in themselves, regardless of whether they result in fewer wars.

When it comes to undermining the authority of states, functionalism may be on stronger footing. Thus, social scientists emphasize the so-called social contract, whereby loyalty of citizens to the state is supposed to result from a kind of exchange: The state provides certain benefits to the populace, and in return, the people support the state by, for example, going to war when told to do so. But if inoculations are provided by doctors from the WHO, or new tractors by technicians from the FAO, or literacy programs by teachers from UNESCO, the state's claim to the loyalty and gratitude of its citizens quite possibly might be eroded in subtle ways. Within a domestic society, individuals have many cross-cutting loyalties: They may be members of the PTA, a trade union, a garden club, and also a particular church. This prevents any one group from becoming dominant, and leads to a general sense of social solidarity. Perhaps something of this sort can be achieved internationally. In this context, the hope of functionalists is that

> man can be weaned away from his loyalty to the nation-state by the experience of fruitful international cooperation; that international organizations arranged according to the requirements of the task could increase welfare rewards to individuals

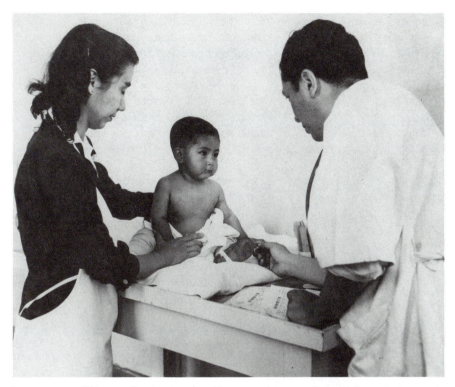

Luis, a one-year old Peruvian boy, being examined by a WHO physician in the town of Vegueta. Functionalists hope that by providing services of this sort, the prospects of peace will be enhanced in several ways. (United Nations)

beyond the level obtainable within the state; that the rewards would be greater if the organization worked, where necessary across national frontiers. . . . Individuals and groups could begin to learn the benefits of cooperation and would be increasingly involved in an international cooperative ethos, creating interdependencies, pushing for further integration, undermining the most important bases of the nation-state.[8]

Enthusiasts of this approach should be cautioned, however, that states have historically insisted that loyalty to them supercedes other affiliations: social, political, intellectual, emotional, economic. They have obtained the cooperation, and often the lives, of their subjects while providing very little in return. Czarist Russia, for example, interacted with the great majority of the impover-

ished Russian people only to collect taxes and induct their sons into the army; yet, the system worked effectively for centuries. States jealously guard their sovereignty, and seem unlikely to permit functionalist activities that subvert the loyalty of their citizens. One factor impeding a worldwide campaign against AIDS, for example, has been the refusal of certain African states even to admit that they have a problem, for fear that it will result in the loss of international prestige and tourist dollars.

Nonetheless, by accepting the authority of certain functional agencies, states are in fact accepting certain limitations on their sovereignty, which is probably a healthy step. For example, the use of airspace and sea lanes is now increasingly governed by decisions made by the International Civil Aeronautics Organization and the International

Maritime Consultative Organization, respectively. In these areas, might no longer makes right, nor can a given state follow its own rules and procedures, without regard to others. To cite another example, in international telecommunications, the best frequencies are not simply preempted by the most powerful broadcasters; rather, it is universally recognized that to be legitimate, broadcasting frequencies must be allocated by the International Telecommunication Union.

Finally, simple common sense suggests that communication and interaction would be beneficial. The nineteenth-century British statesman Richard Cobden advocated "as little intercourse as possible between Governments, as much connection as possible between the nations [that is, peoples] of the world."[9] And in his now-famous correspondence with Albert Einstein, Sigmund Freud opined that "anything that creates emotional ties between human beings must inevitably counteract war. . . . Everything that leads to important shared action creates such common feelings."[10] Again, however, we caution that most wars have occurred between neighbors, who often know each other quite well. The cultural affiliation between Japan and China did not prevent wars between them; neither did the fact that the Irish and English speak the same language. Along with contact often comes resentment. In addition, relations between the United States and Canada, which are otherwise very close, are strained by Canadian irritation at U.S. domination of the communications industry — radio, television, books, and magazines — which tends to make the smaller state a cultural colony of the larger.

Perhaps no single strategy or policy will ultimately serve to banish war; nevertheless, hope remains for the functionalist approach as one of many promising avenues to peace. Functionalism can also include processes beyond those of the designated functional agencies. Cooperative projects, for example, have long been proposed as ways of cementing relationships. President Eisenhower suggested the construction of several nuclear reactors in the Mideast, for example, to be operated by the International Atomic Energy Agency (another functional

unit of the UN), and designed to provide electricity and fresh water to Arabs and Israelis alike. During the height of detente, between 1972 and 1974, the United States and the U.S.S.R. signed ten cooperative agreements, resulting in a range of cultural exchanges as well as more than a hundred joint projects, in medical research, agriculture, environmental protection, ocean research, environmental protection, and the like. In 1975, the United States and the U.S.S.R. cooperated in the Apollo–Soyuz Test Project, which linked spacecraft from the two superpowers. The event was televised to millions.

With the revival of the Cold War in the 1980s, most of these cooperative efforts were terminated, though many were resurrected in the closing months of the Reagan administration, when relations warmed up once again. In these cases, cooperation apparently was more a result than a cause of improving relations. Nonetheless, the possibility always exists that positive experiences among individuals will lead to a snowballing, positive feedback effect, which in turn can lead to improved relations at the official level. In this regard, substantial gains could be realized from sister city relationships, or even international pen pals, each of which can serve to break down the political/geographic/ideological barriers between states. When the Soviet republic of Armenia was devastated by an earthquake in December 1988, a substantial humanitarian response was evoked in other countries, including the United States; this must have served — if only in a small way — to enhance goodwill between the people involved, and ultimately, perhaps, between the governments as well.

It has been suggested that a more dramatic shared threat — such as an invasion from outer space — might be needed to get the two superpowers to put their antagonism and mistrust aside. In the meantime, others have proposed a joint U.S.-Soviet attempt to send a manned mission to Mars. It also remains to be seen whether it might be possible to initiate joint projects involving cooperation between Greek and Turk, Israeli and Arab, Tamil and Sinhalese, and so on. And even if "successful," it is uncertain whether and how much such endeavors will actually contribute to peace.

IGOs, NGOs, TNOs, AND MNCs

States also can cooperate at the functional level in other, more formal ways, such as by forming so-called intergovernmental organizations (IGOs), like the Organization of Petroleum Exporting Countries (OPEC*). If, as Mao said, power once grew out of the barrel of a gun, it also grows out of a barrel of oil: The oil revenues of the Middle East OPEC members in 1970 totaled $4 billion; in 1974, following price increases by the oil cartel, the figure was $60 billion. International cartels can be effective in raising certain prices; although this helps states exporting these commodities, it often hurts other states, which have to pay more for the products in question. Moreover, increases in international prices do not always help the poor, even in exporting countries; for example, unroasted coffee rose from 60¢ per pound in the mid-1970s to over $3 per pound in the late 1970s. As a result, the price to growers rose from 9¢ per pound to 14¢ per pound, which did not even keep up with inflation. And the pay raise to laborers was even less. The OPEC oil embargo of 1973 was particularly painful to oil-poor developing countries, whose economic growth was strangled by having to pay increased prices for petroleum. In short, no clear evidence exists that monopoly cartels by producers, or exporters, or importers, will further world peace, except perhaps indirectly by weakening the traditional state-centered world system. In fact, they seem as likely to foster war, by generating intolerance, resentment, and further inequities of wealth.

Another notable IGO is the European Coal and Steel Community (ECSC), established in 1950 to integrate the industrial economies of West Germany, France, Italy, and the Benelux countries (Belgium, The Netherlands, and Luxembourg). By 1958, the ECSC had evolved into a larger, more integrated entity, the European Economic Community, also known as the Common Market. It now consists of twelve members, with a total population and GNP exceeding that of the United States. Current plans call for the elimination of all trading and transportation barriers throughout most of Western Europe by 1992. This process of transnational integration could ultimately lead to a common monetary system, and even a political union, a kind of United States of Europe.

Finally, connections across international borders do not require the direct action of governments. There are many different kinds of nongovernmental organizations (NGOs† — also known as transnational organizations, or TNOs). These include many religions (the Roman Catholic church, the Society of Friends) and other groups whose affiliations cut across political boundaries, such as the Rotary Clubs International, the International Physicians for the Prevention of Nuclear War (winner of the 1986 Nobel Peace Prize), CARE, the International Olympic Committee, Amnesty International, and a wide array of scientific, educational, business, and other professional organizations. The number of NGOs has been increasing rapidly, from 176 in 1909 to more than 18,000 in 1988. Some of these groups seek as part of their agenda to break down the traditional barriers between states; for example, European Nuclear Disarmament (END) endeavors to overcome the postwar division of Europe into pro-American and pro-Soviet alliances. Most commonly, however, the various NGOs simply go about their affairs, which, as it happens, are best served by cutting across state boundaries. They are subtly, benevolently, subversive of state authority. Whereas an international organization

---

*Saudi Arabia, Kuwait, Iraq, Libya, Oman, Qatar, United Arab emirates, Iran, Algeria, Nigeria, Gabon, Venezuela, Ecuador, and Indonesia compose OPEC.

†Johan Galtung has pointed out that the phrase *nongovernmental organizations* is regrettable, since by defining such organizations with respect to governments, it gives too much importance to the latter; analogously, consider replacing "governments" with "nonpeople organizations"! In place of NGOs, therefore, Galtung suggests using "interpeople organizations," or some equivalent phrase.

requires *accord* among nations, the transnational organization requires *access* to nations. . . . The restraints on an international organization are largely internal, stemming from the need to produce consensus among its members. The restraints on a transnational organization are largely external, stemming from its need to gain operating authority in different sovereign states. International organizations embody the principle of national sovereignty; transnational organizations try to ignore it.[11]

One of the most important transnational phenomena of the late twentieth century is the emergence of powerful multinational corporations (MNCs). Such companies as General Motors, Ford, Exxon, General Electric, Shell Oil, and CIBA/GEIGY typically have major commercial operations spread through various states, particularly in the First and Third Worlds. (Increasingly, the multinationals are gaining footholds in Second World — communist — states as well, as witnessed by the activities of Pepsi-Cola in China, and Occidental Petroleum in the U.S.S.R.) Great controversy surrounds the role of multinational corporations. On the one hand, given the size of these businesses — many of which have annual earnings larger than the GNP of a midsized country — they should be powerful actors on behalf of transnational integration. And since profitable operations generally require a smooth international environment, the influential multinationals seemingly would act to reduce the probability of war, pouring their financial resources like oil on troubled waters. Furthermore, it can be argued that by entrapping different countries in a web of economic interdependence, multinational corporations make war less likely, exemplifying a kind of absent-minded functionalism — although one that is oriented toward profits instead of good deeds.

On the other hand, war has in the past been precipitated by economic entanglements; for example, during the 1930s, Japan was dependent on the United States for oil and iron ore, and this dependence led to competition, resentment, and fear that the United States intended to strangle further Japanese expansion . . . which in turn contributed

to the Japanese decision to attack Pearl Harbor in 1941. As to the multinationals themselves, their pursuit of profits rather than peace can sometimes involve the fomenting of disorder, via revolution or coup (for example, Kennecott Copper and ITT in Chile, in 1973) or counterrevolution (for example, the influence of United Fruit in inducing the United States, through the CIA, to overthrow the democratically elected Arbenz government in Guatemala in 1954).

In 1935, the U.S. Marine Corps commandant, General Smedley Butler, offered this remarkable first-person testimony to the role of multinational corporations in generating military intervention:

> I spent 33 years in the Marines, most of my time being a high-class muscle man for big business, for Wall Street and the bankers. In short, I was a racketeer for capitalism. I helped purify Nicaragua for the international banking house of Brown Brothers in 1910–1912. I helped make Mexico and especially Tampico safe for American oil interests in 1914. I brought light to the Dominican Republic for American sugar interests in 1916. I helped make Haiti and Cuba a decent place for the National City [Bank] boys to collect revenue in. I helped in the rape of half a dozen Central American republics for the benefit of Wall Street. In China in 1927 I helped to see to it that Standard Oil went its way unmolested.
>
> I had a swell racket. I was rewarded with honors, medals, promotions. I might have given Al Capone a few hints. The best he could do was to operate a racket in three city districts. The Marines operated on three continents.[12]

The U.S. defense secretary during the Eisenhower administration once proclaimed, "What is good for General Motors is good for the country." In many cases, government officials have apparently acted on this presumption, engaging military forces worldwide in support of various multinational corporations, especially in the Third World. There is nothing unique about this. The British East India Corporation, for example, was one of the guiding forces behind English colonial expansion during the eighteenth and nineteenth centuries, just as the

Hudson's Bay Company and the large railroads (such as Union Pacific) helped motivate the decidedly unpeaceful expansion of Canada and the United States throughout North America.

Furthermore, although the multinationals do provide jobs in their host country, they also extract resources, paying the lowest possible prices for raw materials as well as labor. In the process, they contribute to the long-term environmental degradation of host (that is, exploited) countries, while also keeping these countries economically and often politically dependent on the multinational corporation. The resulting *dependencia* relationship (from the Spanish word for dependency) has been seen as a kind of neo-colonialism that brings economic and social enslavement, and not prosperity and peace (more on this problem in Chapter 22).

A FINAL NOTE ON INTERNATIONAL ORGANIZATIONS

Although their record has not been perfect, there is much to applaud in the activities of international organizations. Some of these—notably the United Nations—promote human and planetary betterment in numerous ways, including but not limited to the keeping of "negative peace." They also represent a partial step in the progression from individualism through nationalism to globalism, a transition that may well be essential if we are ever to give peace a realistic chance. As such, international organizations can be seen as possible halfway houses toward the establishment and solidification of international law (see Chapter 17), and perhaps even world government (see Chapter 18).

Study Questions

1. What can be learned from the failure of the League of Nations?

2. How did the League of Nations have difficulty dealing with realpolitik among states? To what extent is this true of the United Nations as well?

3. Explain why efforts at international peacekeeping or collective security often have difficulty over the question of how to define aggression.

4. In what way were the original hopes of the framers of the United Nations frustrated by the Cold War?

5. In what way does the UN differ from a world government? Does it have any similarities?

6. What is meant by peacekeeping, and how does it differ from collective security? What is the role of the superpowers in peacekeeping, and why?

7. What can be learned from the specific cases of UN intervention (Cyprus, the Congo, Kashmir, and so on) beyond simple historical information?

8. How are the world's regional organizations similar to the UN? How are they different?

9. Define functionalism, and describe its underlying premises, as well as its weaknesses.

10. Sketch the dubious effect of multinational corporations on the maintenance of peace.

Suggestions for Further Reading

D. Mitrany. 1966. *A Working Peace System*. Quadrangle: Chicago.

Inis Claude, Jr. 1971. *Swords into Plowshares: The Problems and Progress of International Organizations*. Random House: New York.

Larry Fabian. 1971. *Soldiers Without Enemies*. Brookings Institution: Washington, DC.

Indar Rikhye, Michael Harbottle, and Bjorn Effe. 1974. *The Thin Blue Line: International Peacekeeping and Its Future*. Yale University Press: New Haven, CT.

Leroy Bennett. 1980. *International Organizations: Principles and Issues*. Prentice-Hall: Englewood Cliffs, NJ.

Source Notes

1. Kenneth E. Boulding. 1978. *Stable Peace*. University of Texas Press: Austin.

2. Quoted in David Dilks. 1984. *Neville Chamberlain*. Cambridge University Press: New York.

3. Quoted in H. Hollins, A. L. Powers, and Mark Sommer. 1989. *The Conquest of War*. Westview Press: Boulder, CO.

4. Dag Hammarskjöld. 1962. *Servant of Peace.* Harper & Row: New York.

5. Quoted in Robert St. John. 1972. *Eban.* Doubleday: Garden City, New York.

6. See, for example, D. Mitrany. 1966. *A Working Peace System.* Quadrangle: Chicago.

7. Inis Claude, Jr. 1971. *Swords into Plowshares.* Random House: New York.

8. Paul Taylor. Introduction to Mitrany. *Functional Theory.*

9. Quoted in M. Howard. 1978. *War and the Liberal Conscience.* Rutgers University Press: New Brunswick, NJ.

10. Albert Einstein. 1960. *Einstein on Peace.* Simon and Schuster: New York.

11. Samuel P. Huntington. 1973. "Transnational Organizations in World Politics." *World Politics,* April, p. 333.

12. General Smedley Butler. Article in *Common Sense,* November, 1935.

17

International Law

The international community should support a system of laws to regularize international relations and maintain the peace in the same manner that law governs national order.

Pope John Paul II

Schemes for ending war — for creating negative peace and, ultimately, positive peace as well — often founder at the level of states. By zealously guarding their sovereignty, states undermine, or at best diminish, the authority and effectiveness of international organizations such as the United Nations. Even when these organizations operate in a manner that recognizes the primacy of state sovereignty, an unavoidable tension arises between a state-centered world system and one organized around different fundamental values. By providing a unit around which dangerous and misleading notions such as peace through strength can congeal, nationalism and state-centeredness legitimize the use of violence in settling disputes. By emphasizing the similarities and often suggesting some kind of superiority on the part of each group of people, and cutting them off from others, the current political divisions of our planet make prospects for disarmament seem terribly difficult, perhaps impossible. By rewarding those who behave violently — so long as such violence, or the threat of violence, is successful — our current world system works strongly against peaceful ethical or religious resolutions of conflict. And by fractionating the people of the world, our current political organization makes it very difficult to deal effectively with problems that cross traditional borders and that require global solutions. In a sense, we already have a transient sort of nuclear war avoidance, supposedly operating via deterrence, while lesser Third World wars go on, often encouraged by the superpowers. This is a kind of "peace system," and according to "realists," the best that could be devised. Others, especially those interested in Peace Studies, are looking for something better.

In short, many people are becoming increasingly aware that our current state-centric system is part of the problem, and that we must move beyond the nation-state to find the solution. In this chapter, we shall consider some of the directions that such a quest might take. All governments operate by laws, the rules of behavior that specify what is permissible and, more commonly, what is not. Even in our current system of separate states, a legal framework undergirds the relationship of states to one another. It is known as international law, and will be reviewed in this chapter. Then, in Chapter 18, we address the question of world government, a dream (for some, a nightmare) that constitutes a frontal assault on state sovereignty itself.

THE SOURCES OF INTERNATIONAL LAW

We are all familiar with domestic law, with its prohibitions against violent crimes such as murder, robbery, and assault, as well as with the way it regulates the nonviolent conduct of daily living, from the flow of traffic to the affairs of business and the standards of acceptable conduct in private and public life. Less familiar, by contrast, is international law, the acknowledged principles that guide the interactions between states, and that sets limits upon what is and what is not permissible. People live within societies, not between them, so we have done far more to encourage *intra*national law than *inter*national law. And yet, international law does exist; in fact, the current body of international law is very large. Just as most daily life among individuals within a society is peaceful, most interactions among states on the world scene is also peaceful,

in accord with expectations, and thus, in a sense, "legal."

Unlike domestic law, which in the United States is codified in constitutions and amendments, as well as in the specific laws passed by federal, state, and municipal law-making bodies, the body of international law is relatively chaotic, spread over history and generated in many different ways. There are four major sources of international law: (1) classical writings that have become widely accepted, (2) custom, (3) treaties, and (4) the rulings of international courts.

Classical Writings

In the sixteenth century, the Spanish legal scholar Francisco de Victoria developed the thesis that war must be morally justifiable, and could not simply be fought over differences of religion or for the glory of a ruler. He also maintained that soldiers were not obliged to fight in unjust wars, even if so commanded by their king. But the best-known and most influential example of classical international law is found in the work of the Dutch legal scholar Hugo Grotius. In his treatise *On the Law of War and Peace* (1625), Grotius maintained that there was a fundamental "natural law," which transcended that of nations, and which emanated from the fact that people were ultimately members of the same community. Grotius argued strongly for the sovereignty of individual states, within their own realms. From this, he concluded that states must avoid interference in the internal affairs of other states. Grotius pointed to the agreements that states have made among themselves, and that have proved to be durable: peace treaties, decisions as to the allocation of fishing and navigation rights, commonly accepted boundaries, and so on. The Grotian tradition thus derives the legitimacy of international law from the legitimacy of states themselves. But it goes further in seeking to derive principles whereby the behavior of one state toward another can be regulated, arguing that "natural right" must govern the interactions among states, and that this supercedes the authority of the states themselves. As Grotius saw it (and subsequent international law has affirmed), international "society" exists, which requires certain norms of conduct among states, including rules governing what is acceptable during war itself. For Grotius, war was not a breakdown in the law of nations, but rather a special condition to which law still applied.

One of the earliest and most effective examples of international law in action was the battle against international piracy, during the sixteenth through eighteenth centuries. It was widely agreed at the time — even by England and France, for example, which were bitter enemies and which often outfitted or tacitly supported pirates against each other — that all states had jurisdiction over acts of piracy on the high seas; this unanimity of states permitted concerted and successful action. Note, however, that pirates were apprehended by the military forces of individual sovereign states, and tried by domestic courts, rather than by some international legal body.

The term *international law* first appeared in 1783, with the publication of Jeremy Bentham's *Principles of International Law*. Accordingly, it is worth emphasizing that, whatever its shortcomings, nearly all our progress in international law has taken place in just a few hundred years; in fact, things have really gathered steam in the last fifty years. We might therefore be on the threshold of dramatic new developments.

Custom

Custom is one of the most important and least appreciated sources of international law. For example, consider the "rules of diplomatic protocol," whereby diplomats from one country are considered immune to arrest or detention in another. Clearly, these "rules" are in the interest of all countries, since, if the representatives of opposing states could legally be harrassed, communication between states could quickly cease, to the disadvantage of all sides. Diplomats occasionally are expelled from a host country, usually for "activities incompatible with their diplomatic status" (that is, for spying), in which case some of the other side's diplomats typically are expelled in retaliation. But

normally — that is, customarily, and thus by international law — diplomats are allowed substantial leeway, including the ability to communicate freely and secretly with their home government, as well as guarantees of their safety. (The strength of this presumption is shown by the outrage when it is violated, as when U.S. diplomats were held hostage in Iran in 1979–1980.)

Another example of international law derived from custom — or perhaps we should say "in the process of being derived," because it is currently in flux — relates to the concept of the "common heritage of mankind" (CHOM). This increasingly important notion has figured in such accords as the Law of the Sea and Antarctic Treaties and the Montreal Protocols, directed at reducing the production of chemicals implicated in the depletion of the ozone layer. According to CHOM, the fact that certain entities such as the ocean bed, Antarctica, or the ozone transcend state sovereignty does not mean that individuals or states are therefore free to exploit or despoil them as they wish. Rather, as part of the common heritage of mankind, these things (and presumably, others as well) are entitled to protection under international law. At present, CHOM is of uncertain but growing status as an established principle of international law. It also exemplifies the important principle that international law, no less than domestic law, must be flexible and responsive to changes in accepted standards.

Treaties

International treaties are analogous to contracts among individuals. And of course, there have been many treaties, covering not only the termination of wars, but also agreements about boundaries, fishing and navigation rights, and mutually agreed restrictions as to permissible actions during war. Treaties are not always honored, but in the vast majority of cases, they have been. Backing away from treaty obligations results in a substantial loss of face, and once branded a treaty-breaker, a state may not be able to establish useful, reliable relationships with other states. Through treaties as well as customary practice, international law provides "rules

The Peace Palace at The Hague, Netherlands, headquarters of the International Court of Justice. (United Nations)

of the road" by which international interaction, beneficial to each side, can be conducted. As a result, states have a strong interest in abiding by them.

Courts

Finally, international law — just like domestic law — requires courts to hear disputed cases and render decisions. The first example of an international court was the Central American Court of Justice, established by treaty in 1908 by five Central American republics. During its ten-year lifespan, this pioneering court heard ten cases; in one, it resolved a dispute in which Honduras, El Salvador, and Guatemala teetered on the edge of war. The European Community has established a Court of Justice, which hears disputes arising from treaties among Common Market states; in addition, the European Court of Human Rights, at Strasbourg, hears human rights cases involving citizens from any of its twenty-one member states.

Best known and most important, however, is the International Court of Justice (formerly the Permanent Court of International Justice, during its tenure under the League of Nations), located at The Hague, Netherlands, and administered by the UN. Also known as the World Court, this institution consists of a rotating membership of world jurists. It issues decisions about international law that are generally considered authoritative, although typically unenforceable. The verdict on international courts is thus mixed. On the one hand, states are gradually becoming accustomed to letting go of enough sovereignty to settle disputes in court instead of in combat. On the other, adherence to the dictates of the World Court is entirely "consensual" — it is up to the consent of those involved — whereas adherence to domestic law is obligatory. Imagine a community in which accused lawbreakers could only be brought to trial if they agreed that the laws applied to them; further, imagine that they could then decide whether or not to abide by the ruling of the courts!

ENFORCEMENT OF INTERNATIONAL LAW

The major problem with international law, therefore, aside from its diffuseness, is enforcement. Because enforcement provisions are generally lacking, some people contend that international "law" is not, strictly speaking, law at all, but rather, a set of acknowledged customs, or norms of behavior. The importance of norms alone should not be underestimated; in fact, most human behavior is conducted according to widely shared norms, not law itself. Nonetheless, domestic law is the last resort (short of violence, which domestic law typically prohibits), and law is effective at least in part because if worst comes to worst, and a lawbreaker is apprehended and found guilty of violating the law, he or she can be held accountable, suffering fines, prison terms, and the like. In the case of domestic law, individuals acknowledge (whether overtly or not) that they are subordinate to the state and its machinery of enforcement: the police, court bailiffs, the national guard, and so on. When it comes to relations among states, by contrast, the "individuals" insist on their sovereignty; they most emphatically do not recognize that any authority supercedes their own. If individual people behaved this way, domestic law could not effectively regulate their behavior. The major problem with international law, therefore, is that individual states insist on a kind of latitude that they would never allow their own citizens.

Let us briefly consider the role of sanctions (punishments for noncompliance) in law more generally. There are three primary incentives for obeying any law, domestic or international: self-interest, duty, and coercion. For example, most individuals stop at red lights not because they fear getting a traffic ticket, but rather because they know that otherwise, they are more likely to have an accident. Rules may therefore be followed out of purely utilitarian concerns, in this case, interest in one's own personal safety. Laws provide a way of regulating human conduct, for the benefit of all: You can proceed with reasonable safety through an intersection when your light is green, because you know that opposing traffic has a red light, and you have some confidence that other drivers will respect this law, just as you do.

In addition, individuals may follow the law because they feel themselves duty-bound to contribute toward an orderly society that functions with respect for authority. As members of society, who benefit from it, individuals assume a responsibility toward it. That is, some are influenced by normative considerations, or a kind of Kantian categorical imperative to do what is right and good for its own sake. And finally, some people are induced to be law-abiding by fear that "violators may be prosecuted" and forced to succumb to the state's authority if they are found guilty. Although the role of such coercive factors cannot be denied, coercion is not the only reason why most people obey the law. And similarly, the absence of such coercion does not invalidate international law, or render it toothless.

States have numerous incentives, both positive and negative, for abiding by their legal obligations to other states. If a state defects from its legal obligations, adversaries may well retaliate, one's friends and allies are liable to disapprove, and world opinion is likely to be strongly negative, leading to ostracism and possible economic, political, and cultural sanctions. Moreover, governments themselves have a strong stake in their own legitimacy, and — even in totalitarian states — adherence to law is funda-

mental to such legitimacy. Furthermore, according to one authority on international law, enforcement per se is less important in inducing compliance in any law — domestic or international — than is the aura that surrounds all law:

> The weakness of international law lies deeper than any mere question of sanctions. It is not the existence of a police force that makes a system of law strong and respected, but the strength of the law that makes it possible for a police force to be effectively organized. The imperative character of law is felt so strongly within a highly civilized state that national law has developed a machinery of enforcement which generally works smoothly, though never so smoothly as to make breaches impossible. If the imperative character of international law were equally strongly felt, the institution of definite international sanctions would easily follow.[1]

THE CONFLICT WITH STATE SOVEREIGNTY

It simply isn't true that all is anarchy in the international arena, any more than it is true that all is peaceful in the domestic sphere: More than one quarter of all wars, for example, are civil wars. States generally obey the law — out of a combined sense of duty and self-interest — even though coercive sanctions, as understood in domestic law, are absent. States engage in nonviolent commerce — exchange of tourists, diplomats, ideas, trade — according to certain regulations, and usually with goodwill and amity. Moreover, states usually do not enter into treaties unless they intend to abide by them, and they only acquiesce with customary norms of behavior when they anticipate that over the long run, they will benefit by doing so. At the same time, however, they typically cling to various aspects of sovereignty. Most treaties — notably those involving nuclear weapons — include a provision permitting signatories to withdraw within a set period of time, typically three or six months, if their "supreme national interests" are jeopardized. And who makes this decision? The state itself.

We have defined states as those political entities that are granted a monopoly of legitimate violence within their borders. When they engage in what they claim is lawful violence outside their borders, states typically maintain that (1) they are acting in self-defense (the U.S.S.R. in World War II, Israel in the Six Day War), (2) they are fulfilling treaty obligations (France and Britain in World War II), (3) they are intervening on the side of legitimate authority (the United States in Vietnam, the U.S.S.R. in Afghanistan), (4) the situation is anarchic and lacks a legitimate authority (the UN in the Congo), or (5) the conflict is within the realm of international obligations (the UN in Korea). In short, state sovereignty continues to reign, although a semblance of international law is generally invoked as well. States have been especially hesitant, however, to circumscribe their day-to-day authority. It is significant that whereas the Hague Conferences produced a few halting restrictions on the waging of war, they were unable to establish any significant binding rules for peace.

States are also selective when it comes to accepting the jurisdiction of the International Court of Justice, a process known as "adjudication." Adjudication is similar to arbitration (see Chapter 13) in that the decision of the third party is binding. The only difference is that in adjudication, the decision is based on international law, rather than made by an arbitrator. The Soviet Union, for example, has historically refused to submit disputes to this body, although in late 1988, the Soviet government announced that it was reconsidering this policy, and was willing to accept a greater role for the International Court. The United States has been no better, despite the fact that in 1946, it formally agreed to submit all of its international disputes to the International Court of Justice. At that time, the U.S. Senate attached an amendment, known as the Connally Reservation, stipulating that the Court would not have authority over any disputes that "are essentially within the domestic jurisdiction of the United States of America as determined by the United States of America." With this loophole, the United States is free to "determine" that any dispute is essentially within its domestic jurisdiction, thereby avoiding international adjudication whenever it wishes.

This stance is not unusual. France, for example, refuses to acknowledge the jurisdiction of the World Court (or anyone else, for that matter) when it comes to the testing of nuclear weapons in the Pacific, despite complaints of international illegality from New Zealand, Australia, and other Pacific states. Similarly, when the World Court ruled against the United States and in favor of Nicaragua in a case deriving from U.S. mining of Nicaraguan harbors during 1983 and 1984, the United States simply shrugged aside this verdict, claiming that in this instance it did not recognize the authority of the Court.

In the early twentieth century, two lesser-known cases of international disputes, both involving the United States and Mexico, revealed the impotence of international law in the face of state power. One case concerned the so-called Chamizal Tract. The Rio Grande had long served as the boundary between these two states, but a flood in that river transferred about 600 acres from the Mexican side to the U.S. side. The two states eventually agreed to arbitration, by a legal commission established for the purpose. Although this commission found in favor of Mexico in 1911, the United States refused to abide by its decision until 1967. William H. Taft, who was president in 1911, later spoke to the New York Peace Society in support of a plan to *require* arbitration of international disputes:

> But the query is made: "How will judgments of such a court be enforced; what will be the sanction of their execution?" I am very little concerned about that. After we have gotten the cases into court and decided and the judgments embodied in a solemn declaration of a court [are] thus established, few nations will care to face the condemnation of international public opinion and disobey the judgment.[3]

Three years after the U.S.–Mexico land dispute, the two countries became embroiled in another controversy, when some U.S. sailors were detained by Mexican revolutionaries. The United States demanded their release and an apology; they got the former but not the latter, whereupon U.S. troops proceeded to capture and hold the entire Mexican city of Vera Cruz. (The Mexican authorities promptly apologized, whereupon the U.S. forces withdrew.) Thus, when the United States felt offended, it acted unilaterally and violently by seizing Vera Cruz, rather than seeking recourse to international law. By contrast, when Mexico — a much weaker state — appealed to international law in the case of the Chamizal Tract, the United States, despite President Taft's assertions to the contrary, ignored the ruling for more than fifty years.

LAW, POWER, AND CHANGE

Law is an important part of modern human life; some would even say that it is crucial to civilization. Despite concerns about enforcement — and anxiety when, as in the case of international law, enforcement powers are lacking — law is in many ways the antithesis of rule by brute force. Might does not make right; law does (or better yet, it reflects what is right). As a result, most good, decent people are presumed to be "law-abiding," and in fact, rule by law is almost inevitably seen as preferable to rule by force. We should also be aware, however, that law can be an instrument of oppression. Laws are made by those in power, and as such, they serve to perpetuate that power, and to prevent change. Thus, laws — international as well as domestic — serve best in a conservative environment. Third World and revolutionary states often point out that international laws were established by Western powers in support of their domination. The clearest example might well be the Treaty of Tordesillas (1494), following Columbus's "discovery" of the New World, whereby the pope "legally" divided that world into Spanish and Portuguese domains . . . without any regard for the people already living there.

Similarly, Western international law relies heavily on the basic principle of *pacta sunt servanda* ("treaties should be honored"). But consider cases in which a puppet ruler, propped up by a colonial power, signs a treaty granting economic privileges to that power; if an indigenous, representative government eventually replaces the colonial authorities, should the new government be obliged to fulfill those obligations? For example, rights to the Suez Canal were originally "negotiated" with a British-installed government in Egypt. Similarly, the U.S.

Aerial view of Guantanamo Bay naval base. This base is operated by the United States in Cuba under a treaty negotiated before Fidel Castro came to power. (U.S. Department of Defense)

naval base at Guantanamo, in Cuba, was established following an agreement reached with the U.S.-backed Batista dictatorship, which was overthrown in the Cuban Revolution.

Not surprisingly, Third World and, to a lesser extent, communist states in general are often inclined to repudiate *pacta sunt servanda*, and to rely instead on an opposing doctrine, which is also recognized under law: *rebus sic stantibus* ("circumstances have changed"). The principle states that international laws must be living documents, subject to modification and, if necessary, annulment, whenever conditions become substantially different from those existing when an agreement or treaty was reached. In addition, agreements made by illegitimate authority, or under duress — like contracts signed with a gun at one's head — are not generally considered valid.

International law must be flexible, if only because of the march of technology. For several centuries, for example, ever since a Dutch ruling in 1737, "territorial waters" have been considered to extend three miles from shore; this distance was based on the effective range of shore-based cannons. Now, new guidelines are being sought, with controversy fueled by disagreement among states, especially between the exploiters and the exploited. The former, particularly the developed industrialized states with relatively little shoreline (such as Britain and Japan) argue for narrow territorial waters, while those with extensive coastal waters (like Brazil and Burma), which seek to protect their fishing industry from foreign fleets, argue for a 200-mile limit.

These issues were partly resolved by the Law of the Sea Treaty, completed after decades of wrangling. This treaty also arranged for mechanisms of dispute resolution, waste disposal, and navigation procedures, but under the Reagan administration, the United States refused to sign, maintaining that the treaty's call for an intergovernmental body to supervise mining on the deep-sea bed constituted "international socialism." This also highlights once again the susceptibility of international law to asserted claims of state sovereignty, as well as the growing pressure of north/south cleavages.

HIDDEN STRENGTHS OF INTERNATIONAL LAW

Governmental Respect for Law

Yet, governments do not routinely flout the law, not even their own domestic statutes, over which they have complete control. In most democratic countries, governments accede to legal decisions, even those that go against them. Citizens of the United States, for example, often take for granted the fact that in many cases, they can, if they wish, bring legal action against their own government. And if the courts — which are themselves organs of the government — rule against the government, citizens can receive compensation or other redress for their grievances, even though governments, not the courts, have the strong-arm potential of enforcing

their will. This emphasizes the primacy of law over force. For example, following a strike during the Korean War — an action that supposedly threatened U.S. war production at a critical time — President Truman sought to nationalize the U.S. steel industry. The Supreme Court, however, overruled this action, whereupon the government obeyed the law, albeit reluctantly. Because democratic governments have a long-range interest in settling disputes amicably, that supercedes any short-term interest in winning a given dispute, they tend to abide by legal rulings, even those that they dislike.

In international affairs, as we have seen, major powers are less likely to abide by international laws (except when dealing with admittedly trivial cases, like the Chamizal Tract), unless the opponents are so balanced that the potential costs of losing a case are less than those of further wrangling, and possibly war. For example, in 1960, Nicaragua complied with an order from the International Court of Justice to cede certain territory to neighboring Honduras, as agreed to in an arbitration proceeding conducted in 1906 by the king of Spain, Alfonso XIII. The consequences of a possible war, as well as the loss of prestige that would have come from defying the World Court, combined to pressure Nicaragua into abiding by this decision, while also providing an excuse for doing so. Thus, although some Nicaraguan nationalists opposed giving up the land, the government was able to do so by referring to Nicaragua's obligation under international law and by placing the responsibility on a prestigious third party.

Tacit Acceptance and Expectation

International law often appears weaker than it really is, however. This is because violations, when they occur, are often sensational and dramatic, whereas compliance is taken for granted. When domestic law is broken by individuals, only rarely are we moved to question the appropriateness of the law itself, and never to doubt the existence of such law. But a different standard seems to be applied to international law. When states violate international law, they may or may not be condemned by public opinion, but almost invariably, the law itself is called into question, and the purported weakness of international law is once again lamented. Just as we are not told about the vast majority of people who obey domestic law every day, we do not see news stories proclaiming that "Paraguay today complied with its treaty obligations regarding its border with Bolivia, and therefore, no invasion took place."

Virtually the entire civilized world was shocked, by contrast, when Chancellor Theobald von Bethmann-Hollweg justified the German invasion of Belgium in the early days of World War I by describing the international guarantee of Belgian neutrality as a "mere scrap of paper" that could readily be torn up. On the one hand, this announcement — and even more so, the brutal invasion itself — showed the truth of the chancellor's assertion: Belgian neutrality was in fact "only" an international agreement, lacking any guarantee and incapable, by itself, of keeping the invading German divisions out. On the other hand, the level of international outrage showed that international law, even when it lacks explicit means of enforcement, has undeniable effects on public perception. (In addition, we should note that the immediate reason for Britain entering the war against Germany was the German violation of Belgian neutrality; so, in a sense, international treaty law was ultimately enforced in this case. Had Germany respected the law, it might have won the war.)

The Law of War

War — the violent resolution of conflict — can be seen as the antithesis of law, whose goal after all is the ordering of relations without recourse to violence. Cicero first wrote that *inter arma silent legis* ("in war the law is silent"). This is taken to mean that the justifiability of any given war is outside the purview of international law, since states are sovereign authorities unto themselves, and free to make war or not, as they choose. Under this view, since there is no higher authority than a state, no one can claim that a state is making war unlawfully. "For as long as men and women have talked about war," writes a modern authority on moral and political philosophy,

> they have talked about it in terms of right and wrong. And for almost as long, some among them have derided such talk, called it a charade, insisted that war lies beyond (or beneath) moral judgment. War is a world apart, where life itself is at stake, where human nature is reduced to its elemental forms, where self-interest and necessity prevail. Here men and women do what they must to save themselves and their communities, and morality and law have no place.[3]

Nonetheless, a body of law is widely thought to apply to states under conditions of war. War itself can even be defined as "the legal condition which equally permits two or more hostile groups to carry on a conflict by armed force."[4] Therefore — at least according to some experts — war represents a highly formalized interval during which violence may legitimately be practiced between two opposing groups. Enough agreement exists within the community of nations that belligerents and neutrals alike recognize the existence of certain accepted standards: "Although war manifests the weakness of the community of nations, it also manifests the existence of that community."[5]

THE NUREMBERG PRINCIPLES

States that are party to international treaties may find themselves subject, even against their will, to the legal restraints of these treaties. The losers in World War II, for example, were tried — and many were convicted — for having waged aggressive war in defiance of their obligations under the Kellogg-Briand Treaty (see Chapter 15). These trials, conducted in the German city of Nuremberg, were unique in developing the legal doctrine that individuals are personally liable to criminal prosecution for crimes against international law. This includes illegal resort to war as well as violations of accepted restraints as to appropriate conduct during war,

Nazi woman doctor pleads "not guilty" at the Nuremberg War Crimes Trials. (UPI/Bettmann)

notably the treatment of prisoners and the waging of genocide. Thus, the chief Allied prosecutor at Nuremberg wrote that

> war consists largely of acts that would be criminal if performed in time of peace — killing, wounding, kidnapping, destroying or carrying off other people's property. Such conduct is not regarded as criminal if it takes place in the course of war, because the state of war lays a blanket of immunity over the warriors. . . . But the area of immunity is not unlimited and its boundaries are marked by the laws of war.[6]

It should also be pointed out, however, that critics objected to these proceedings, claiming that the Nuremberg Trials were simply examples of "victors' justice," and not concerned with genuine international law. Nevertheless, the so-called Nuremberg Principles have served as a benchmark in efforts to introduce humane and reasoned limits to acceptable wartime behavior. Thus, the interna-

tional military tribunal that convened in Nuremberg specified a series of international crimes. Article 6 of the Nuremberg Charter identified the following:

1. Crimes against the peace, namely planning, preparation, initiation or waging of a war of aggression, or a war in violation of international treaties, agreements or assurances, or participation in a common plan or conspiracy for the accomplishment of any of the foregoing.

2. Crimes against humanity, namely murder, extermination, enslavement, deportation, and other inhumane acts committed against any civilian population, before or during the war, or persecutions on political, racial or religious grounds . . . whether or not in violation of the domestic law of the country where perpetrated.

3. War crimes, namely, violations of the laws or customs of war. Such violations shall include, but not be limited to, murder, ill-treatment or deportation to slave labor or for any other purpose of civilian population of or in occupied territory, murder or ill-treatment of prisoners of war or persons on the seas, killing of hostages, plunder of public or private property, wanton destruction of cities, towns or villages, or devastation not justified by military necessity.

Article 7 specified that "the official position of defendants, whether as Heads of State or responsible officials of Government departments, shall not be considered as freeing them from their responsibility or mitigating their punishment." And according to Article 8, "the fact that the defendant acted pursuant to orders of this Government or of a superior shall not free him from responsibility."

Whereas the German defendants at Nuremberg were tried for crimes they had committed in violation of international law, a series of lesser-known trials were also conducted in Tokyo, of Japanese officials accused in large part of crimes of *omission* — that is, illegal failure to act. For example, Koko Hirota, Japanese foreign minister from 1932 to 1937, failed to insist on an end to Japanese atrocities against civilian Chinese during the "rape of Nanking," and General Tomoyuki Yamashita,

Lieutenant William Calley (right) leaving a preliminary court martial hearing at which he was charged with murder in connection with the shooting deaths of 102 South Vietnamese civilians, including women and children, at the village of My Lai. (UPI/ Bettmann Newsphotos)

commander of Japanese troops in the Philippines, was found guilty of failing to restrain the troops under his command when they committed atrocities against Filipinos as well as U.S. prisoners of war. Several decades later, when U.S. army lieutenant William Calley was tried and found guilty for his role in the My Lai massacre during the Vietnam War, it marked the first time a state had accused one of its own soldiers of war crimes. Calley's highest-ranking commanding officers were not tried, however, despite the fact that parallels can be drawn between the actions of General William Westmoreland (U.S. military commander in Vietnam) and General Yamashita, and between Secretary of State Dean Rusk, Secretary of Defense Robert McNamara, and indeed, Presidents Johnson and Nixon, and Minister Hirota. So again, whereas international laws exist, and have been enforced, such enforcement has been highly selective.

The treaties that were violated by the Nuremberg defendants, originating from the Geneva and Hague Conventions, specified limitations on such actions as naval or aerial bombardment. But they also made allowances for "military necessity," which can be stretched to permit nearly any act in wartime, however outrageous. Similarly, even the toothless Kellogg-Briand Treaty was interpreted by many as permitting "wars of self-defense," as does the current UN Charter: Article 51 grants states the "inherent right of individual or collective self defense." Self-defense would clearly justify Poland's short-lived response in seeking to resist the German invasion in 1939, but what about France's response, namely, declaring war on Germany (France was treaty-bound to help defend Poland)? And what about the Israeli invasion of Egypt in 1967, in which Israel clearly struck first, but in which it was argued that Egyptian behavior constituted a real provocation as well as an imminent threat that justified a "preemptive" attack by Israel? Similarly, the "Brezhnev Doctrine," by which the U.S.S.R. justified its invasion of Czechoslovakia, was described as laudable pan-socialist self-defense against Western-inspired counterrevolutionaries. And the "Reagan Doctrine," under which the United States has assisted right-wing revolutionaries in Marxist states such as Angola or Afghanistan, has also been described by its supporters as providing aid to people seeking to defend themselves. Apologists for wars of self-defense and self-determination have thus far always been able to find loopholes in international treaties large enough to drive an army through.

In short, when states consider that their security interests require it, violations of international law have occurred, and can be expected to continue. Many scholars argue that the nuclear arms race itself runs counter to international law, because it involves preparations for genocide. It seems likely, however, that if nuclear weapons are to be abolished, it will be for reasons other than their "illegality."

A FINAL NOTE ON INTERNATIONAL LAW

International law has many imperfections. It appears to have exerted some useful restraints in some cases, while being woefully inadequate in others. The major powers give it less credence than do the

U.S. B-52 dropping bombs on North Vietnam, a country with which the United States was not legally at war. (U.S. Department of Defense)

lesser states, in part because the former have recourse to their military strength, whereas the latter must depend on the rule of law to offer them the possibility of a "level playing field" in contests with larger, stronger opponents. Some authorities recommend only a modest role for international law in the future, avoiding "the Charybdis of subservience to state ambitions and the Scylla of excessive pretensions of restraint," and recognizing that "it is the interest of international law itself to put states' consciences neither to sleep nor to torture."[7] Another view holds that international law is a beginning, something on which to build a world without boundaries, or at least, one in which the sanctity of state sovereignty is greatly curtailed in the interest of human survival as well as quality of life.

Study Questions

1. It has been said that, to the extent that law is law, it is not international, and to the extent that it is international, it is not law. Explain.

2. Describe the major sources of international law, giving one example of each.

3. How does the question of enforcement in international law differ from that of domestic law? How is it similar?

4. Are there any weaknesses in international law other than the problem of enforcement? Describe them.

5. What are meant by the Nuremberg Principles? What relevance, if any, do they have today?

6. Describe cases in which state sovereignty and international law have conflicted, and state sovereignty has won.

7. Describe cases in which state sovereignty and international law have conflicted, and international law has won.

8. There is a tendency for Third World countries to take a different view of international law than that held by the developed states. Explain.

9. In what sense can international law be a conservative, even reactionary force?

10. How do states protect themselves against what they see as excessive loss of sovereignty with regard to international law?

Suggestions for Further Reading

Richard A. Falk. 1968. *Legal Order in a Violent World.* Princeton University Press: Princeton, NJ.

Michael Barton Akehurst. 1977. *A Modern Introduction to International Law.* Allen & Unwin: London.

Burns H. Weston, Richard A. Falk, and Anthony D'Amato (eds.). 1980. *International Law and World Order.* West: St. Paul, MN.

Francis Anthony Bayle. 1985. *World Politics and International Law.* Duke University Press: Durham, NC.

Gerhard Von Glahen. 1986. *Law Among Nations.* Collier Macmillan: London.

Source Notes

1. J. L. Brierly. 1949. *The Law of Nations.* Oxford University Press: New York.

2. William Howard Taft. 1914. *The United States and Peace.* C. Scribner's Sons: New York.

3. Michael Walzer. 1977. *Just and Unjust Wars.* Basic Books: New York.

4. Quincy Wright. 1964. *A Study of War.* University of Chicago Press: Chicago.

5. Ibid.

6. Telford Taylor. 1970. *Nuremberg and Vietnam.* Quadrangle: Chicago.

7. Stanley Hoffmann. 1971. "International Law and the Control of Force." In K. Deutsch and S. Hoffmann (eds.), *The Relevance of International Law.* Anchor Books: New York.

18

World Government

I have long believed the only way peace can be achieved is through World Government.
Jawaharlal Nehru

As we approach the end of the twentieth century, most of the problems afflicting our planet and our species clearly transcend the boundaries of the nation-state: pollution, poverty, overpopulation, racism, resource shortages, hunger, injustice (see Chapters 20–22 for more detail). When the Soviet nuclear plant at Chernobyl experienced a catastrophic accident in 1986, for example, radioactive contaminants were deposited throughout much of the world. Wind patterns and fallout do not respect national boundaries. Neither does global warming due to increasing atmospheric levels of carbon dioxide and other chemicals, known as the greenhouse effect. And of course, governments and states constitute the major units of war.

THE NEED FOR WORLD GOVERNMENT

Ever since the Tower of Babel, people have been plagued by their own political disunity. A potential solution, proposed in one form or another for literally thousands of years, has been to erase the existing political boundaries, and to replace them with government structures at the largest, most inclusive level—namely, world government. This suggestion has been raised most urgently with regard to war and its prevention, since, when it comes to war, nation-states have been only reluctantly and haltingly part of the solution (see, for example, Chapter 15). In the eyes of many, they are part of the problem (see, for example, Chapter 9). And for some, they are virtually the whole problem (see, for example, Chapter 14). Warmaking has fractured the human community along ideological, social, and geopolitical lines. The prevention of war, accordingly, may well require that this community be reforged on a global scale. Similarly, the achievement of justice, ecological wholeness, and economic fairness may well require structures of coordination and a recognition of unity that demands nothing less than a global revolution, albeit a nonviolent one. In short, it may well be necessary to rethink and rebuild the world. Self-styled "realists" scoff at the prospects for world government. But it is worth considering whether they are in fact being realistic at all in assuming that the current world system can—or should—go on indefinitely. This chapter is therefore offered, unblushingly, as an admitted exercise in idealism plus exhortation, but based on global needs that are altogether real.

The shortcomings of the world political system have been readily apparent through the greater part of modern history. But these weaknesses are even more obvious in the nuclear age, in which nationalist passions and the jockeyings of states literally threaten an end to the entire human experiment. People have long looked for alternatives to the nation-state system; not surprisingly, in an age of diminishing resources, shrinking distances, and ever more devastating weaponry, advocates of world government speak with a particular urgency.

In the medieval world, the typical European owed allegiance to his or her feudal lord, who in turn may have been subject to the secular authority of the Holy Roman Emperor and the religious power of the pope. At least in theory, the world was integrated in a roughly pyramidal power structure. Then came the so-called Wars of Religion, culminating with the Thirty Years' War and the signing, in 1648, of the Treaty of Westphalia, which inau-

gurated the state system that was eventually extended into the modern pattern of nation-states. For citizens in pre-Westphalian, medieval times, concerns were overwhelmingly bounded by day-to-day events taking place in local surroundings: the happenings in local fields, woods, nearby towns, and the closest castle with its protector (or oppressor) nobility. The Westphalian world expanded the allegiance of state and national subjects to include lands and people more distant than one's immediate surroundings. In addition, technological advances, especially in transportation and communication, made it unavoidable that individuals be involved with other places and other people beyond their closest neighbors.

Continuing this line of thinking, it can be argued that we now live in a post-Westphalian world, one in which the state or nation-state system is as obsolete as its feudal antecedents. Our mounting problems, notably pollution, poverty, resource depletion, and the destructive effects of war—especially nuclear war—supercede the old, traditional political boundaries. They have made it imperative that we think as planetary citizens. The world, in short, has become functionally integrated, even while it remains politically fragmented.

The appeal of world government basically rests on the assumption that superior authorities ought to be able to force quarreling subordinates to refrain from violence, to respect larger, common interests, and to solve their disputes in some other way. When two individuals disagree about something, they are expected to settle the dispute in a law-abiding manner; they are not supposed to go "outside the law" and start shooting at each other. Settling disputes by a duel, popular in previous centuries, is analogous to nation-states settling disputes by war. The former has been universally outlawed;* the latter has not. Or rather, not yet. Similarly, individual households are not "sovereign." They do not have the right to dump toxic chemicals

---

*Actually, duelling is still legal, under certain circumstances, in Uruguay.

Large mushroom cloud produced by a thermonuclear explosion in the multimegaton range. The possibility of worldwide nuclear war gives a special urgency to the issue of world government. (U.S. Department of Defense)

A BRIEF HISTORY OF PLANS FOR WORLD GOVERNMENT

Many proposals have been advanced for world government of one sort or another. Most of the early suggestions advocated the dominance of one ruler or superstate. For example, Dante, in *De monarchia* (1310), suggested a universal empire with a single ruler, who would guarantee peace. Early in the seventeenth century, the duke of Sully, Maximilien de Bethune, proposed a "Grand Design" for European peace, involving a council consisting of representatives from all European states. In 1623, the French monk Emeric Crucé developed a proposal calling for a universal world structure, including not only Europe but also India, China, the kingdoms of Africa, and representatives of the pope and the Jews.

The Seventeenth and Eighteenth Centuries

By the seventeenth and eighteenth centuries, there had been a flourishing of proposals designed to establish some form of worldwide political restraints on warmaking. William Penn, in 1693, wrote an *Essay Toward the Present and Future Peace of Europe*, which included the suggestion of a general parliament with military force to compel observance of its decrees. A similar plan was advocated in 1710 by John Bellers, calling for the division of Europe into 100 equal provinces, each of which would send a representative to a central senate, as well as contributing an equal number of military forces to a common central army. In 1713, the Abbé de Saint-Pierre, in his *Project for Perpetual Peace*, called for a "Senate of Europe" made up of twenty-four representatives, including one from each European state, a plan that received much attention, and criticism as well. Voltaire, for example, noted that the states in question would overwhelmingly be monarchies, and maintained that for peace to be preserved, democracy was necessary . . . and at that time, democracy was unthinkable as a practical matter, just like world government itself.

Notable among such proposals, in addition to the efforts of William Penn, (*Essay Towards the*

into "their" stream, thereby poisoning their neighbors' water supplies; why, then, should "sovereign" states be permitted to do this?

International organizations such as the UN, as we have seen, offer frameworks for transcending political boundaries (see Chapter 16), but they operate within the present system of sovereign states, which are free to disagree, overrule, or simply ignore these organizations if they choose. These same limitations also apply to international law (see Chapter 17), although here, once again, some of the fundamental ingredients for transcending state sovereignty are present. What is missing is the ability of a larger authority to impose restraints on the states themselves. Whatever their underlying causes, wars take place because no higher authority exists to prevent them. In modern times, the parts (states) claim to be greater than the whole (Earth). With a world government, this would change: States would be prohibited from imposing themselves on their neighbors, whether economically, ecologically, or militarily, just as domestic governments now prevent individuals from overstepping their bounds or settling their disagreements by duels, and just as federal governments keep the peace among their provinces or smaller, constituent republics.

Present and Future Peace of Europe, 1693), Saint-Pierre (*Project to Make Peace Perpetual,* 1713), and Jeremy Bentham (*Plan for an Universal and Perpetual Peace,* 1789), was one advanced by the French philosopher and novelist Jean-Jacques Rousseau (1712–1778). In his *Discourse on the Origin of Inequality,* Rousseau concluded that ownership of private property was the underlying cause of war; he therefore proposed that to achieve world peace, it would be necessary to abolish private property worldwide. His work, in turn, leads to an interesting — if currently unanswerable — question: If war is a result of a specific form of social organization, is this reason to condemn the society, or to justify certain wars? Thus, many theorists have argued that the defense of property is a legitimate reason for war.

Probably the most notable design for a potentially workable form of world government was put forth by the great German philosopher Immanuel Kant. In his short but wide-ranging book entitled *Perpetual Peace* (1795), Kant made the first major effort to focus specifically on the dangers of arms races and armaments, rather than just proposing yet another kind of world parliament. He also argued that, in spite of the evil of which human beings are capable, the continuing cultural progress of humanity will enable them to use reason and logic to act increasingly on behalf of moral perfection. Consistent with the philosophy of the Enlightenment, Kant maintained that ethical and intellectual truth exists independent of time, place, and matter, and that this truth is binding on all people because our rational capacities transcend day-to-day circumstances and permit us to grasp certain fixed principles.

Kant's views should be contrasted with those of Thomas Hobbes, who, 150 years earlier, had emphasized that perceptions are individual and personal, rather than universal, and that, because of this, individual perspectives are bound to diverge, so that agreement among different and contending agents requires enforcement by fear and physical power. Whereas Hobbes's emphasis on conflicting interests served to justify the existence of a powerful political state, Kant was concerned with preventing the excesses of state power, especially when states interact violently with one another. He proposed a worldwide organization that would be bound by international law and composed of a federation of free states. His work reflected a growing tendency toward what may be called "optimistic internationalism" among peace theorists and devotees of world government. (It may also have been discouraging to many that, shortly after Kant's book appeared, the Napoleonic Wars convulsed Europe.)

Whereas Thomas Hobbes had argued that war is our "natural" situation, the French political philosopher Montesquieu, in his *Spirit of Laws* (1748), maintained that the blame lay not in human nature, but squarely on the system of political states:

> As soon as man enters a state of society he loses the sense of his own weakness; equality ceases, and then commences the state of war. Each particular society begins to feel its strength, whence arises a state of war between different nations.[1]

He shared this belief with Rousseau, who argued that war could be prevented only by severing the bonds by which the state held people together: "It is only after he is a citizen," noted Rousseau, "that he becomes a soldier."[2] Rousseau also maintained that "conquering princes make war at least as much on their subjects as on their enemies," and that "all the business of kings . . . is concerned with two objects alone; to extend their rule abroad or make it more absolute at home."[3] Hence, the enemy was not only the political state, but most especially the institution of monarchism.

Immanuel Kant also identified the state as the prime war-causing culprit, but rather than focus on the problem posed by the state's very existence, Kant located the blame in what he called the "lawlessness" of how states interact with one another:

> We look with deep contempt upon the way primitive peoples are attached to their lawless liberty — a liberty which enables them to fight incessantly rather than subject themselves to the restraint of law established even by themselves; in short, to prefer wild

A view of Chums Camp, outside of Cairo, where some members of the Canadian, Finnish, and Polish battalions making up the United Nations Emergency Force (UNEF) stayed while supervising an Egyptian–Israeli cease fire. State sovereignty is preserved during such United Nations operations; on the other hand, the close coordination of detachments from different countries carries with it the aura of world government. (United Nations/Y. Nagata)

freedom to a reasonable one. We regard such an attitude as raw, uncivilized, and an animalistic degradation of humanity — so, one should think, civilized peoples (each united in a state) would hasten to get away from such a reprehensible situation as soon as possible. Instead, each *state* insists upon seeing the essence of its majesty (for popular majesty is an absurd expression) in this, that it is not subject to any external coercion.[4]

For Kant, then, some form of "external coercion" was necessary in order to establish peace between states.

The Early Twentieth Century

The nineteenth century was not notable for serious proposals concerning world government, at least in part because the post-Napoleonic Concert of Europe did a reasonable job of keeping the peace. After World War I, and the subsequent failure of

the League of Nations, however, there was a flurry of renewed interest in a world union, led by groups such as the United World Federalists. In fact, some tension has arisen between supporters of the United Nations and world federalists who believe that international organizations of this sort tend to enhance state authority rather than transcend it. Some argue that, so long as international organizations are structured around the preservation of state sovereignty, they are not so much stepping stones to world government as threats and impediments to its implementation.

In 1950, a serious proposal surfaced, which, had it been acted upon, would have produced the world's first truly supranational army. The suggestion was for a European Defense Community (EDC), to integrate the armed forces of France, Italy, Benelux, and West Germany (which at that time was demilitarized). The plan would have

Delegates voting during a meeting of the UN Security Council. Under the Clark/Sohn Plan — and unlike the present UN system — no state would hold a veto power. (United Nations/S. Lwin)

established identical transnational military uniforms, a common pay scale, and a thoroughly integrated command structure. It was approved by all the national parliaments except for France, which feared German rearmament; as it happened, Germany was rearmed anyhow — by the United States — and it quickly became a mainstay of NATO. Although the EDC scheme was put forth on behalf of the Cold War, not world government, it signaled real movement toward transcending traditional patterns of state sovereignty.

The Clark/Sohn Plan

The most elaborate and detailed scheme for world government was developed by legal scholars Grenville Clark and Louis Sohn.[5] It basically called for transforming the UN into a world peacekeeping unit, whereby states would retain their sovereignty *except* in matters of disarmament (which would be mandatory) and war (which would be prohibited). Clark and Sohn proposed to increase the power of the General Assembly and to change its voting procedures, making decision making largely proportional to population. Under the Clark/Sohn plan, the four largest countries (China, India, the U.S.S.R., and the United States) would have thirty votes each, the next eight largest would have fifteen votes each, and so on. An Executive Council would be authorized to intervene militarily worldwide, so as to prevent war. Unlike the present Security Council, however, no states would hold veto power, although a clear majority (twelve of seventeen members) would be required to approve any armed action, and this vote would have to include a majority of the largest states. An Inspection Commission would assure that disarmament is total; after a two-year census of each country's military forces, it would supervise 10 percent annual reductions, across the board. A World Peace Force, under UN auspices, would consist of from 200,000 to 600,000 professional volunteers, initially using supplies and weapons obtained as the member states disarmed themselves. Nuclear weapons would not normally be supplied to this force, but they could be obtained if needed — from a Nuclear Energy Authority — to deter the use or threatened use of nuclear weapons by any state that kept a small cache.

The Clark/Sohn plan, although wonderfully detailed and specific about its goal, does not offer any suggestions as to the means of achieving this goal, of getting from "here" to "there." It does illustrate, however, that there is no shortage of precise ideas about possible future world governments. Another suggestion, for example, has called for vesting war–peace decisions within the General Assembly, but modifying the requirements for passing a major vote by specifying that such a vote must include two-thirds of the states of the world, as well as two-thirds of the population of the world, and two-thirds of the contributors to the UN budget. Such a "binding triad" would thus include most of the countries, most of the people, and most of the world's economic/military/political strength. Accordingly, such an arrangement would be more legitimate than the current situation, in the sense that resolutions now can be passed by states that represent only a small fraction of world population or actual power, or blocked in the Security Council by another minority, one that possesses power but may lack population or moral legitimacy. Clearly, the current situation does not encourage respect for the world body, especially among the powerful states that might be outvoted. Whatever the strengths or weaknesses of the "binding triad" proposal, or of the Clark/Sohn plan, or others, the point is that world government has not been stymied by a shortage of good ideas, but rather by a lack of political will.

WOMP and Others

Other suggestions have also been drawn together by the World Order Model Project (WOMP), which represents a pioneering effort to design potential futures for the planet. International legal authority Richard Falk emphasizes that there are three primary approaches to world order: (1) Maintain the system as it now is (a conservative option), (2) reform it (traditional liberalism), or (3) transform it (a more radical approach). We might add a fourth, namely, return it to what it used to be — a reactionary or, occasionally, counterrevolutionary approach.

Falk makes a strong case for the third option, a radical transformation of the current world system.[6] For example, he has developed a scheme for a "preferred World Polity," consisting of a three-chambered General Assembly, and equipped with a World Security System, which will be prepared to maintain the peace, by military force if need be. Falk's system emphasizes the need to serve three other values beyond the prevention of large-scale collective violence: (1) the maximization of social and economic well-being, (2) the achievement of fundamental human rights and social justice, and (3) the rehabilitation and maintenance of ecological quality and wholeness. He further identifies three eras of social change: (1) an era devoted to consciousness-raising, whereby people are helped to understand that the current world system is simply unable to achieve the basic security — defined broadly — that everyone needs; (2) an era of political mobilization and change, in which governments commit themselves to the transition to a new world order; and (3) the transition itself, which will involve coordinated disarmament of states along with the buildup of new world structures.

Finally, hard-headed visionaries like peace researcher Johan Galtung have emphasized the desirability of establishing "many small societies, more of them and smaller than the countries in today's world. [Because] only in smaller societies can the distance between the ruler and ruled be small enough to permit self-expression to everybody, and only with smaller societies can large-scale hegemonial [that is, predatory and violent] tendencies be avoided."[7] Such decentralization is to some extent at odds with the prospects of a transnational enforcement agency, which Galtung also accepts. But he places himself clearly in the nonviolent camp by emphasizing that his proposed centralized world authority would influence local events, not so much by force or the threat of force, as by "remunerative power":

> I see a world central authority as having enormous resources for constructive use at its disposal, which means capital, goods and know-how. The authority

Biography

Richard A. Falk

Richard A. Falk is one of the premier advocates of international law and one of the most important students of world order. He has taught at Princeton University since 1961, where he currently is Milbank Professor of International Law and Practice, and serves in the Center of International Studies. Professor Falk has written and edited several dozen books on international issues from a world order perspective. These include *This Endangered Planet: Prospects and Proposals for Human Survival, A Study of Future Worlds, The Promise of World Order,* and *The Revitalization of International Law.*

In collaboration with Saul Mendlovitz, Richard Falk launched the World Order Models Project (WOMP), which has sought to identify possible ways of reinventing the world political system. He has been an antiwar activist, involved in the environmental movement, and active in various human rights causes. He has participated in the Permanent People's Tribunal since its inception and has worked over the years with scholars from around the world on the project "Peace and Global Transformation," sponsored by the United Nations University.

Professor Falk has been an especially eloquent voice questioning the legitimacy of states as repositories of military and political authority, and supporting "people power."

---

should be able to disburse all three where they are needed . . . but there could also be above-normal renumeration to those who comply particularly well with the international norms. In short, I am thinking of a system of positive sanctions much more than negative sanctions, for the simple reasons that the latter do not seem to work as an instrument of compliance and the former are at the same time vehicles of global development.[8]

THE PROS AND CONS OF WORLD GOVERNMENT

Despite the attractiveness of the idea of world government, the fact is that people—once they are organized into relatively large units—have generally shown far more eagerness for splitting off than for joining together. There have been virtually no examples of the successful merging of states.* (The union of North and South Vietnam might be one such case, although it was only achieved via appalling violence—and despite substantial resistance, at least some of it from the South Vietnamese themselves.) At one time, Egypt and Syria attempted a peaceful merger, establishing the United Arab Republic (UAR), but that union was quickly disbanded. When consolidation does occur, a smaller unit is typically swallowed up by a larger, often against its will: Tibet was incorporated into China, Goa into India, the Baltic states into the U.S.S.R. Furthermore, much of the tension in the world today is generated specifically by regions desiring not to submerge their identity, but rather to *separate* themselves from control by a larger whole: Northern Ireland, French Canada, the Tamils of Sri Lanka, and so on.

The Maintenance of Peace

The argument for peacefulness under world government is derived largely from analogy: Since domestic governments enforce peace (for example, between New York and Pennsylvania in the United States), or attempt to do so (as between Armenia and Azerbaijan in the U.S.S.R.), a world government would presumably do the same, treating nation-states much as municipal governments now treat their citizens, or as federal governments now treat their subordinate provinces or constituent republics. But analogies do not always hold. Moreover, federal governments do not always create or maintain peace: Civil wars are common, and often

---

*The reunification of Germany may be an exception; significantly, however, the "two Germanies" were one prior to 1945.

highly destructive when they occur. Europe during the nineteenth century, for example, was composed of feisty, sovereign states, while the United States was a single, ostensibly united country. And yet, the war casualties suffered by the "United" States during its civil war (about 600,000) were almost precisely equal in number to those suffered by Europe during the entire century from 1815 to 1913. Perhaps if they were not held forcibly within the Soviet Union, for example, the independent states of Armenia and Azerbaijan would be freer to work out their ethnic conflicts in peace (or, alternatively, maybe they would go to war).

The Danger of Oppression

To some people, the prospect of a world government is truly frightening. If large political units tend to be unresponsive to the needs of their citizens, and are sometimes downright oppressive, imagine the danger inherent in government by a worldwide "superstate," with the power to enforce its decrees on everyone. (The Clark/Sohn plan carefully ensured that the armed forces of several countries, combined, would exceed those of the world force, thereby hedging against centralized despotism.) But why, critics ask, should we expect better government from a world authority than we now get from national governments? And, it is worth noting, only a minority of states today live under real democracy. So what, if anything, guarantees that a world government will not be a worldwide tyranny? Most of us want to have our cake and eat it too: peace *and* freedom, international order *and* national sovereignty. But perhaps these goals are conflicting. If so, and if we have to choose, which is preferable? Or perhaps we can hope for a compromise, maybe along the lines of the Clark/Sohn plan, something that places restrictions on the state's ability to make war, but without impinging on other aspects of domestic life.

This may be easier said than done, however. For one thing, powerful states are not interested in world government; actually, they are not just uninterested but vigorously opposed, since world government would require that they give up some of the influence and power that they exercise today. It might also make them subject to certain basic principles of equality and fairness, from which they are at present largely exempt. In some cases — notably the United States — state sovereignty combined with military/economic/scientific/political might has been a means of achieving and maintaining inequitable access to the world's riches. What if, having surrendered its military autonomy, the United States was faced with a demand from the underdeveloped states that it cease consuming scarce resources and polluting the planet out of proportion to its population, or that it redistribute its wealth? Would world government mean that we would have to share? If so, many U.S. citizens might prefer autonomy and gluttony, even at the risk of eventual war.

Critics of world government also point to what they see as an inconsistency. World government is supposed to be necessary because the ferocious Hobbesian world of independent nation-states is simply too violent and irresponsible to continue unchecked. But then, advocates of dramatic change turn right around and assert that such fierce competitions and vicious inclinations can be rendered peaceful by a kind of world government modeled after the ideals of John Locke and other nineteenth-century liberals: a limited, mild, and democratic authority based largely upon mutual consent. Such a "Lockean" government might indeed be more palatable than its "Hobbesian" alternative, but if the problem is so grave, a mild-mannered world government might simply be inadequate. As one authority notes, "It would be better to recognize that in so far as this is a Hobbesian world, it is likely to require a Hobbesian government."[9] The problem is that a Hobbesian government is likely to be very unpleasant. And it would be even more unpleasant — and more difficult to reform — if its resources and authority were global rather than merely national in scale.

On the other hand, there is no reason why a functioning world government could not allow current national governments to continue exercising complete autonomy and sovereignty in their internal affairs. In fact, it may be that the issue is posed incorrectly: Rather than worrying about what national governments would have to surrender, perhaps we should focus on what they would be gaining. World government could then be viewed not so much as requiring us to give up something that we now have (state sovereignty and the ability to threaten and wage offensive war), but rather offering us the opportunity to gain something that we now lack and desperately need (the extension of the peaceful rule of law to international affairs, and with it, a massive increase in national security).

As for the criticism that world government would deprive states of one of the most important perquisites of state sovereignty — deciding whether or not to go to war — it is sobering to realize that such independence as the nation-states now cherish is in part illusory. The Soviet Union, for example, had no choice about entering World War II; when it was attacked by Germany in June 1941, it was forced to respond. Where was Soviet sovereignty when Adolf Hitler and the German General Staff decided, unilaterally, to initiate war? Similarly, the United States was propelled into World War II not so much by a declaration of war by the U.S. House of Representatives as by decisions made by the Imperial War Council in Tokyo.

Limitations in Power

It is often (and to some extent, accurately) said that the current international system of state sovereignty is essentially one of anarchy, and that the fruit of such anarchy is war. The antidote for anarchy is authority, but any authority with worldwide reach and substantial coercive powers might be excessively strong and, thus, repressive. On the other hand, there might be an opposite danger, namely, the risk that a global authority could be too weak to maintain adequate order. When the state loses respect and power — which could happen to a "world-state" as well — the doors are open to chaos, violence, and social disruption, and then to fascist appeals for structure and "traditional values." For example, in 1919, Italian poet–agitator Gabriele D'Annunzio and his followers occupied the city of Rijeka in Yugoslavia, holding it for sixteen chaotic months, while government authorities in both Yu-

goslavia and Italy tried unsuccessfully to establish public order. More recently, there is fear that with the decline of rigid Communist party authority in Europe, and even possibly in the Soviet Union, old ethnic animosities may erupt in violence, as between Hungarian and Romanian, Serb and Albanian (in Yugoslavia), Armenian and Azerbaijani, or Turk and Uzbek (in the U.S.S.R.).

Again, advocates of world government emphasize that any viable world authority would require clear enforcement powers, but these powers would also be carefully circumscribed and limited. Like the U.S. federal government, rights not specifically granted to the world authority would be reserved for its constituent states. After all, in our private lives, we cherish certain personal rights while also accepting restrictions on them: One person's freedom to swing his or her arm ends, for example, where someone else's nose begins. Under world government, nation-states would have to accept just two restrictions circumscribing their freedom (1) to maintain armed forces and (2) to behave aggressively against other states.

Similarly, there need be no anxiety that world government would necessarily mean the homogenization of national identities. Within the United States, Florida is still recognizably distinct from Alaska, and Maine from Arizona, just as national cultures within the U.S.S.R. range from Baltic seaports and industrialism to seminomadic Islamic pastoralism. As Israeli prime minister Golda Meir once pointed out: "Internationalism doesn't mean the end of individual nations. Orchestras don't mean the end of violins."[10]

THE DREAM OF WORLD GOVERNMENT: A WASTE OF TIME?

There is one other potential problem of world government, however, one rarely confronted by peace advocates: namely that by focusing on it, devotees may lose touch with the world and its serious problems as they now exist. Or, they may simply be ignored by the self-styled "realists" who run today's states and, by extension, the world. Lost in dreams of a utopia, hungering after what may turn out to be nothing more than "globaloney," students of world government run the risk of being marginalized, considered irrelevant to "serious" discourse on issues of war and peace.* If advocates of Peace Studies withdraw into musings over ideal but impractical solutions to real problems, they essentially relinquish the reins of power to those willing to deal instead with current reality. And time itself is critical, since world government will certainly not happen tomorrow, while wars are happening today. Even Freud, who supported the idea of world government, also warned about unrealistic dreams that "conjure up an ugly picture of mills which grind so slowly that, before the flour is ready, men are dead of hunger."[11]

But no serious student of peace or devotee of world government recommends putting all of our eggs in the one distant basket of global political union. It is not necessary to choose between nuclear arms control and world government, or between peace in Central America and global disarmament, or between ecological harmony and transnational thinking and acting. In addition, even while we need to engage ourselves in immediate, practical, pressing issues, shouldn't we also focus on ultimate goals, even if they seem — at the moment — to exceed our grasp? Can serious students of world peace ignore the need for major structural change, or the importance of planning not just for tomorrow but also for the more distant future? As General Omar Bradley once pointed out, "It is time we steered by the stars and not by the lights of each passing ship."[12] Isn't this a "realistic" agenda as well?

Accordingly, we might ask the self-styled realists — the practical, hard-headed men (and they largely are *men*) who operate the levers of governmental power — if it is truly realistic to believe that the state system, with its divisions and contradictions, its history of repetitive warfare and state-centered selfishness, can be relied upon to keep the peace and create a decent and humane planet into

the indefinite future? Clearly, world government is unlikely to be perfect, but in view of the imperfections of the current state system, it could hardly be worse, or more dangerous, than our current plight. The dangers of a world with some form of centralized, war-suppressing government pale in contrast to the dangers of a world without it.

According to historian Arnold Toynbee, "war has proved to have been the proximate [immediate] cause of the breakdown of every civilization which is known for certain to have broken down."[13] And another noted historian — not considered especially radical in his views — concluded a masterly survey of the role of armed force and technology in human society by recommending that all but a token number of nuclear warheads must ultimately be dismantled, with a monopoly of atomic weaponry to reside in a "global sovereign power."

> Nothing less radical than this seems in the least likely to suffice. Even in such a world, the clash of arms would not cease as long as human beings hate, love, and fear one another and form into groups whose cohesion and survival is expressed in and supported by mutual rivalry. But an empire of the earth could be expected to limit violence by preventing other groups from arming themselves so elaborately as to endanger the sovereign's easy superiority. War in such a world would therefore sink back to proportions familiar in the preindustrial past. Outbreaks of terrorism, guerrilla action and banditry would continue to give expression to human frustration and anger. But organized war as the twentieth century has known it would disappear.
>
> The alternative appears to be sudden and total annihilation of the human species. When and whether a transition will be made from a system of states to an empire of the earth is the gravest question humanity confronts. The answer can only come with time.[14]

THE PROSPECTS FOR WORLD GOVERNMENT

Despite its flaws, dangers, and difficulties, world government may well be essential. However, just because something is desirable — even necessary — does not mean that it will come to pass. A drowning person may *need* a life preserver, just as we may need world government, but necessity does not create

---

*As already discussed, it is because of a similar concern that the author of this textbook has elected to devote somewhat more attention to war than many specialists in Peace Studies might prefer.

miracles, and people sometimes drown. Thus, it is not sufficient simply to state that world government is a prerequisite for long-term survival, especially in the nuclear age. Maybe we will not survive.

Commitment to States

The pressures against world government are strong. People retain a deep loyalty to their nation-states, and also a powerful distrust of large centralized systems. In addition, like so many proposals for dramatic reform (for example, disarmament) the "devil is in the details." How do we get from here to there? In 1713, as we have seen, the French Abbé de Saint-Pierre proposed his pan-European Union, complete with a Senate of Peace, which would have authority over military forces sufficient to compel any recalcitrant ruler to submit to the will of the larger unit. Interestingly, the French foreign minister at the time, André Fleury, did not question the desirability of such a system, but he pointed out to Saint-Pierre: "You have forgotten an essential article, that of dispatching missionaries to touch the hearts of princes and to persuade them to enter into your views."[15] Jean-Jacques Rousseau also applauded the scheme, but called it an "absurd dream," since sovereigns would never agree that their shared interest in peace supercedes their personal interest in power.

For government leaders to agree to a world government would be equivalent to slaveholders banding together to outlaw slavery. But slavery has in fact been outlawed worldwide, sometimes (notably in the United States) only after much bloodshed. It might also be worthwhile to examine in greater detail how certain nation-states (such as Sweden, Holland, Portugal, and Spain) have made a seemingly healthy transition from world power to relative insignificance. This might serve not only to prepare the United States for the possibility of future decline in a world of continuing nation-states, but also perhaps to suggest how the state system itself might be afforded lesser prominence and perhaps eventually eased out of existence.

At present, neither East nor West seems any more prone to relinquish sovereignty and embrace world government; both are made up of fiercely

A wounded Canadian and wounded German soldier light each other's cigarette in the mud of Passchendaele, one of the bloodiest World War I battlefields. A crucial question facing a would-be world government is whether people are capable of recognizing their common humanity, transcending patterns of hostility. (National Archives of Canada, PA 3683)

independent states. Tradition in the capitalist West tends to be deeply suspicious of large and powerful governments, and is particularly jealous about guarding political freedom. And whereas Marxist theory calls for the eventual "withering away" of the state, communist states do not appear to be any more receptive to the idea of world government. When the state is taken to embody the needs and aspiration of its citizens — as is especially true of both communist and fascist systems — there is little reason to surrender the state's power. Even "peace groups" are described as unnecessary in most communist states, since the state itself is purported to be everybody's collective "peace group." Traditionally, the political right wing has engaged in relatively more militaristic, flag-waving patriotism, while accusing the left of being part of, or duped by, an "international communist conspiracy" (see Chapter 3). However, the heyday of socialist internationalism, as we have seen, was in the late nineteenth and early twentieth centuries; in recent decades, leftists adhered to their own nation-state almost as much

Biography

Kenneth E. Boulding

Kenneth E. Boulding is one of the most distinguished and prolific scholars of international peace. Born in Liverpool, England, in 1910, he was educated at Oxford and the University of Chicago. Professor Boulding has lived in the United States since 1937, and is currently Distinguished Professor of Economics, Emeritus, at the University of Colorado, where he has taught since 1967. He is also Project Director for the Program of Research on Political and Economic Change. While at the University of Michigan, Professor Boulding cofounded the highly influential *Journal of Conflict Resolution* in 1957 and the University of Michigan's Center for Research on Conflict Resolution.

Professor Boulding also helped organize the International Peace Research Association (1965) and was instrumental in establishing the Consortium on Peace Research, Education, and Development (COPRED) in 1970. He has been president of the Peace Research Society and visiting professor at numerous universities. He has written countless technical articles and numerous books, including *Conflict and Defense, International Systems: Peace, Conflict Resolution and Politics, Stable Peace, Human Betterment, The World as a Total System,* and *Three Faces of Power.* He has also been elected president of the American Association for the Advancement of Science.

Kenneth Boulding's wife, sociologist Elise Boulding, is a highly respected peace scholar in her own right, a distinguished professor at Dartmouth College, Secretary-General of the International Peace Research Association, and a noted authority on nongovernmental organizations.

---

as have partisans of the political right. And in much of the Third World, militant nationalism is even more pronounced than in the industrialized West or East.

Beyond the issue of whether government leaders are capable of divesting themselves of the power that comes with state sovereignty, is the question of whether most human beings have sufficient flexibility and generosity of spirit to embrace world citizenship over comparatively narrow national concerns. More than forty years ago, peace researcher Kenneth Boulding, attending a meeting on the world community, commented as follows:

> The person I cannot get out of my mind these days is the young man who dropped the first atomic bomb. I suppose he is a nice young man . . . yet the odd thing is that, if he had been ordered to go and drop it on Milwaukee, he almost certainly would have refused. . . . Because he was asked to drop it on Hiroshima, he not only consented but he became something of a hero for it. . . . Of course, I don't quite see the distinction between dropping it on Milwaukee and dropping it on Hiroshima. The difference is a "we" difference. The people of Milwaukee, though we don't know any of them, are "we," and the people of Hiroshima are "they," and the great psychological problem is how to make everybody "we," at least in some small degree. The degree need be only extremely small. I don't think we have to love our neighbor with any degree of affection. All that is necessary to create the psychological foundations of a world society is that people in Maine should feel the same degree of responsibility toward the people of Japan or Chile or Indo-China as they feel toward California. That is pretty small, really, but it is apparently enough to create the United States.[16]

Examples of a Wider Identity

Although we do not know whether people are capable of considering themselves part of a united planet, the prospects may not be all that bleak. The United States of America, for example, is a very diverse country, made up of Caucasians, blacks, native Americans, Orientals, Catholics, Protestants, Jews — and yet, despite some prejudice, the country as a whole enjoys a reasonable degree of coherence. Although cynics may say that U.S. citizens are united by a shared fear of "the other" — Chinese, Soviet, or Cuban communists, the Sandinistas of Nicaragua, Libyan terrorists, Islamic fundamentalists — the United States also derives unity from a shared cultural and social identity, a shared history, and shared ideals. Certainly, the human species is capable of establishing even wider affiliations than between Maine and California, if such affiliations are encouraged from birth, and reiterated by teaching, symbols, slogans, and a range of appeals, to emotion as well as reason. Such active propagandizing in favor of world citizenship may well be necessary, but it would hardly be unique: We are all subjected to vast amounts of pronational and prostate propaganda at the present time. A psychology of world citizenship might indeed be attainable, and without anything qualitatively different from what now passes for laudable patriotic teachings.

Take another example: People calling themselves "Germans" and "French" have long been at each other's throats, via their respective governments, the nation-states we identify as Germany and France. And yet, quite near these perennially warring states, several million very "French" people live — and have lived for centuries — peacefully with about three times as many equally "German" people. The difference is that in the former case, a sovereign state of Germany has confronted an equally sovereign France, whereas in the latter, "French" and "German" have submerged warmaking authority in the sovereignty of a third shared entity, known as Switzerland.* Similarly, English and Irish, Italian and Austrian, Vietnamese and Chinese, Arab and Jew, all have waged brutal wars against each other across the globe . . . but as citizens of the United States of America, they submit themselves to a common identity, and live together peaceably, at least for the most part. Clearly, it can be done.

---

*Switzerland also contains a third large subpopulation that is Italian-speaking.

THE CASE OF THE UNITED STATES OF AMERICA

Consider once again the present United States of America. When California, for example, has a dispute with Arizona regarding water rights, the two governments do not call up their militias and fight it out. The "law of force" is subordinated to the "force of law," and both sides submit arguments, if need be, to the U.S. Supreme Court. Then, they abide by the ruling. The states of the United States do not walk about like gunslingers from the Wild West, revolvers on their hips, ready to settle disputes by the fastest draw. Rather, just as individuals submit themselves to the rule of municipal law, the states submit themselves to the authority of the federal government . . . at least in certain carefully circumscribed areas, including the resolution of disputes among them.

Following the Revolutionary War, the United States under the Articles of Confederation was a loose amalgamation of states, headed toward disaster because of its virtual anarchy: Maryland and Delaware fought an undeclared "oyster war" over fishing rights to the Potomac River; nine states had navies of their own; state militias were separate and distinct armies; seven of the states even printed their own currency; New York placed a tariff on wood from Connecticut and on butter from New Jersey; Boston was boycotting grain from Rhode Island; various states imposed taxes on shipping from other states; and so on. Things were a mess, just as they are in the world today.

With the writing of the U.S. Constitution, however, a strong federal system was created, out of whole cloth. Advocates of world government point to this transition that gave birth to the United States of America as "the great rehearsal" for world federalism, a transition that the world system can also make if and when the need is widely recognized.[17] Skeptics argue that the early American states were already homogeneous in culture and tradition, in language and ethnic background, unlike the world states of today. But in fact, there was substantial diversity in the 1780s: Catholics were denied the vote in Rhode Island, and the Catholic priesthood was itself illegal in Massachusetts, whereas Pennsylvania and Delaware were proud of their religious diversity. As just noted, no common system of taxation, currency, or trade existed, and interstate travel was often blocked by local restrictions. Moreover, the southern states practiced slavery, cherishing it as an essential part of their way of life, while majority opinion in the northern states was opposed to slaveholding.

Just as some people today fear a potential world superstate, the delegates to the Constitutional Convention also feared to establish a potential despotic dictatorship. Yet, the framers of the Constitution recognized as well that the current situation could not continue, and so they successfully designed a workable federal union, one that preserved the rights of states to regulate their internal affairs, while establishing a strong federal system capable of creating unity and ensuring the peace. They did this by establishing a careful, democratic system of checks and balances. At present, the states of Europe, with all their similarities, and recognizing all the obvious benefits of federation, have moved only haltingly toward a very limited and fragile form of union. But the reality of what the United States accomplished — in the face of grave doubts — suggests the magnitude of what can be achieved. The problem in 1787 was for people to learn to think nationally, rather than locally about the United States. Now, the problem is for people to learn to think internationally, about the planet, rather than nationally.

Must world government wait then until humanity has achieved a higher level of spiritual development? It is true that the "founding fathers" are currently revered in the United States, but they were human beings, just like us. It is also true that the U.S. Constitution was not perfect (although it was certainly better than what preceded it). Moreover, no one in the late eighteenth century claimed that a strong federal government could not be enacted until all the inhabitants of North America had first become saints.

TOWARD WORLD GOVERNMENT?

Several transgovernmental movements have sought to go beyond the current state system by establishing links that intentionally defy the present political boundaries; the European nuclear disarmament movement, which consciously strives to move "beyond the blocs" separating East and West in Europe, is one example. A number of international tribunals have worked toward delegitimizing certain warlike actions of states, trying to apply principles of international law (see Chapter 17), even though such proceedings have lacked enforcement capability. For example, the Russell Tribunal in the 1960s excoriated the U.S. role in Vietnam; in 1982, another tribunal of international legal experts heard testimony and condemned the current nuclear weapons regime at a meeting held, fittingly, in Nuremberg. The MacBride Commission in Britain investigated Israel's 1982 invasion of Lebanon, and pronounced it a violation of international law. Such tribunals and peace movements generally are unpopular with the governments of nation-states, because they seek to restrict warmaking capacity, and also because they represent a budding transnational sensitivity, which undermines state authority more generally.

If these activities truly threaten the current system of state sovereignty, they exemplify the important sociological principle that "If men define situations as real, they are real in their consequences."[18] If we define ourselves as bound irreversibly to the current state system, then we are so bound, by a kind of self-fulfilling prophecy. But the more we look beyond the states — and the more we find when we do so — then the more we may find ourselves liberated. One of the healthiest and most difficult mental exercises involves taking a fresh look at ourselves and at the world. For example, consider our literal image of the globe and our place on it: We inevitably place north at the top and south at the bottom. Given our bias that "up" is better than "down," this puts North America comfortably "above" South America, just as it puts Europe above Africa. And yet, such a view is purely a matter of convention. It is every bit as correct geographically — and for the purpose of shaking things up, very useful as well — to reverse things, as in Figure 18.1, which shows the Western Hemisphere with south as "up" and north as "down." The change in perspective can be startling, however, and it suggests that other mental habits may also be arbitrary

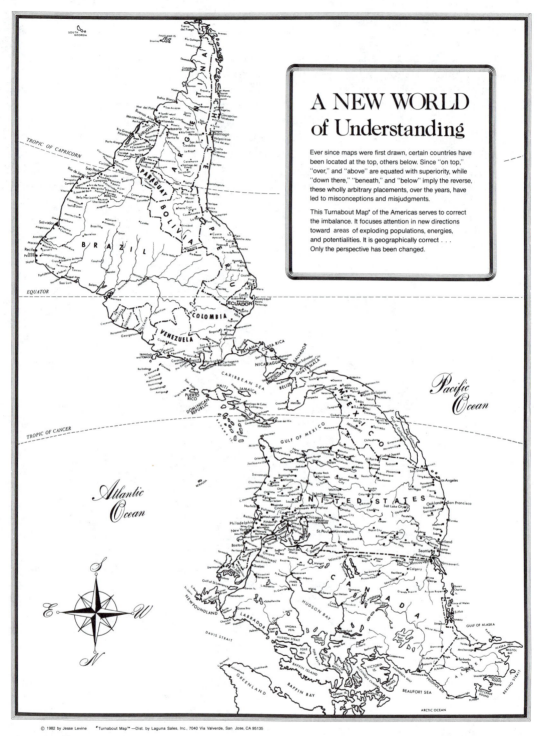

FIGURE 18.1 Turnabout Map of the Americas. Copyright Jesse Levine, 1982. Map available from Laguna Sales, 7040 Via Valverde, San Jose, CA 95135.

A session of the Advisory Board of the International Research and Training Institute for the Advancement of Women, meeting in Havana, Cuba. This Institute, under the auspices of the UN Economic and Social Council, aims at improving the economic and social status of women worldwide and is one of the many examples of "planetary conferences." (United Nations/Milton Grant)

and equally changeable — such as the frequent assumption that nation-states are immutable and forever sovereign in matters of peace and war. Indeed, one of the things that keeps us prisoners of the state system is our inability to envision alternatives to it. Two futures are easy to imagine: this world ending with the "bang" of nuclear war, or with the "whimper" of continued degradation (ecological, social) plus ongoing conventional wars. Both of these are plausible but undesirable extrapolations of the status quo. World government — in whatever specific form — offers a potential third way.

Recent decades have also seen a proliferation of planetary conferences, reflecting and dramatizing the fact that as advances in communication and transportation make the world "smaller," the costs and responsibilities of technology — no less than its benefits — require attention on a global scale. Thus, there has been a World Population Conference in Bucharest, a World Food Conference in Rome, and gatherings to discuss problems of pollution, the

world status of women, the fight against racism and against AIDS, the linkages between disarmament and development, and so on. We can expect that the problems of global warming, ozone depletion, and rain forest protection will soon be receiving comparable international attention. With or without world government, worldwide problems clearly cannot be solved by governments remaining stiffly within their traditional state boundaries.

Not surprisingly, most new social movements tend to be either local, community-based, or region-centered (and thus, below the level of the state), or transnational and global (above the level of the state). Moreover, states themselves have already begun to surrender certain aspects of sovereignty, as we have seen in the case of certain international organizations, as well as in the general acknowledgment of — if not universal obedience to — international law. Perhaps this is a foot in the door. Or perhaps it simply reflects a cynical strategy by the states themselves: Give up a few insignificant crumbs, while at the same time remain as unwilling as ever to permit any meaningful challenge to their authority. But more subtly, many nation-states have already surrendered some aspects of their autonomy: the United States government, for example, is not "free" to declare war on Canada. A kind of *de facto* (in fact) restriction of state sovereignty has thus already come into effect, even though it is not yet *de jure* (in law). And even now, with no true apparatus of world government in place, the nuclear weapons of France, Great Britain, and the United States do not directly threaten one another. Conventional war is even unthinkable between certain long-time rivals such as Britain and France, Holland and Britain, Turkey and the Soviet Union, France and West Germany, and Japan and the United States. Kenneth Boulding refers to the appearance of "zones of peace," which

> probably began in Scandinavia after the Napoleonic Wars between Sweden and Denmark, spread to North America about 1870, to Western Europe, Japan, Australia and New Zealand after the Second World War. Now we have a great triangle of stable peace, stretching roughly from Australia to Japan, across North America, to Finland, with about eighteen countries which have no plans whatever to go to war with each other. This has happened without much planning or even understanding.[19]

As we have seen, interest in world government tends to increase after major world wars: notably World Wars I and II in this century. Just as community pressure for a traffic light on a dangerous corner often does not peak until a child is killed at the intersection, perhaps another major war, or a close call, will be necessary for people to rise up and demand a reworking of state sovereignty. In the meanwhile, it should be emphasized that "futurism" need not be limited to technological panaceas and derring-do, a world of organ transplants, cyborgs, and Star Wars. It can also include moving beyond the state.

It is also important not to discount the role of vision and visionaries. Before we can ever establish a better world, we must first imagine it. This is not to deny the importance of dealing with the world

as it is. It simply emphasizes that to understand current realities is not necessarily to accept them as god-given, engraved in stone, immune to challenge and to change. The world system of states, no matter how firmly entrenched, is nothing more than a human creation, and a relatively recent one at that. There is no reason to think that it is so perfect, or so powerful, as to be a permanent part of the human condition. "The dogmas of the quiet past," wrote Abraham Lincoln, "are inadequate to the stormy present. We must think anew and act anew."[20] Only if we think, plan, dream, and act for a future world that is better than today's or yesterday's can we have any hope of attaining such a future.

A FINAL NOTE ON WORLD GOVERNMENT

Let us conclude with one of the premier theorists and advocates of a new future world order, Richard Falk:

> The present situation is confusing. The state and the state system possess a declining functional capacity and legitimacy, while obscuring this decline behind an intensifying reliance on internal violence and international war-making. Looked at in one way, statism is on the way out, in another, it is stronger than ever. More and more, various civil societies are experiencing disillusionment with facets of the old ways, but have yet to comprehend the feasibility of full-fledged alternatives. Our task is to join in the work of converting this societal disillusionment into creative social action to overcome the menace and begin to fulfill the promise contained in our situation. Never has the dual reality of danger and opportunity been more deeply grounded in the historical situation than it is at present.[21]

In Part IV, we shall examine some of the issues and options involved in the establishment of "positive peace" in a world grown not only increasingly endangered, but also increasingly interdependent. But first, we complement our discussion in this chapter of worldwide political transcendence by exploring one more avenue for the building of "negative peace," namely, ethical and religious traditions, by which many people have already transcended traditional state boundaries.

Study Questions

1. What are the reasons — if any — for thinking that the state system is especially inappropriate to meeting the needs of the present day?

2. What common patterns can be identified in the history of suggestions for world government?

3. It can be said that proponents of world government base their argument on the Hobbesian nature of the state system, then abandon a Hobbesian viewpoint with regard to the actions of a suggested world government. Explain.

4. Discuss various regional movements, especially in Europe, that in some ways are moving toward world government.

5. Describe some strengths and weaknesses of the Clark/Sohn plan.

6. In what ways does it seem appropriate to draw analogies between federal governments and a proposed world government?

7. Why is the idea of a world government frightening to some people?

8. Assess the realistic prospects for world government.

9. What are some useful parallels between the early history of the United States and the possible eventual establishment of world government? What are some important differences?

10. In what ways is state sovereignty already diminished in the modern world?

Suggestions for Further Reading

Grenville Clark and Louis Sohn. 1966. *World Peace Through World Law: Two Alternative Plans.* Harvard University Press: Cambridge, MA.

Roger W. Cobb. 1970. *International Community.* Holt, Rinehart & Winston: New York.

Richard A. Falk. 1975. *A Study of Future Worlds.* Free Press: New York.

Johan Galtung. 1980. *The True Worlds: A Transnational Perspective.* Free Press: New York.

James Dilloway. 1986. *Is World Order Evolving?* Pergamon Press: New York.

Source Notes

1. Charles L. des Montesquieu. 1949. *The Spirit of Laws.* Hafner: New York.

2. Jean-Jacques Rousseau. 1974. *The Essential Rousseau.* New American Library: New York.

3. Ibid.

4. Immanuel Kant. 1939. *Perpetual Peace.* Columbia University Press: New York.

5. Grenville Clark and Louis B. Sohn. 1960. *World Peace Through World Law.* Harvard University Press: Cambridge, MA.

6. Richard A. Falk. 1975. *A Study of Future Worlds.* Free Press: New York.

7. Johan Galtung. 1980. *The True Worlds: A Transnational Perspective.* Free Press: New York.

8. Ibid.

9. In I. Claude, Jr. 1971. *Swords into Plowshares*, 4th ed. Random House: New York.

10. Golda Meir. 1973. *Golda Meir Speaks Out.* Weidenfeld and Nicolson: London.

11. Sigmund Freud. 1953. *Civilization, War and Death.* Hogarth Press: London.

12. Omar N. Bradley. 1983. *A General's Life.* Simon & Schuster: New York.

13. Arnold Toynbee. 1950. *War and Civilization.* Oxford University Press: New York.

14. William H. McNeill. 1982. *The Pursuit of Power.* University of Chicago Press: Chicago.

15. Quoted in F. Schuman. 1958. *International Politics: The Western State System and the World Community.* McGraw-Hill: New York.

16. Kenneth E. Boulding. 1948. "Discussion of World Economic Contacts." In Q. Wright (ed.), *The World Community.* University of Chicago Press: Chicago.

17. Carl van Doren. 1948. *The Great Rehearsal*. Viking: New York.

18. W. I. Thomas. 1928. *The Child in America*. Knopf: New York.

19. Kenneth E. Boulding. 1987. "Peace and the Evolutionary Process." In R. Vayrynen (ed.), *The Quest For Peace*. Sage: Beverly Hills, CA.

20. Abraham Lincoln. 1907. *Speeches and Letters of Abraham Lincoln*. Dutton: New York.

21. Richard A. Falk. "The State System and Contemporary Social Movements." In S. H. Mendlovitz and R. B. J. Walker (eds.), *Towards a Just World Peace*. Butterworths: London.

19

Ethical and Religious Perspectives

The God of peace is never glorified by human violence.
Thomas Merton

War involves killing, one of the most drastic actions a person can take. Killing another human being, except by accident, in self-defense, or out of insanity, is universally condemned — unless done during war, in which case it is not only permitted but applauded. In fact, in war, particularly good killers are often accorded high honors. Not surprisingly, therefore, war has received substantial attention from ethicists and theologians. However, the relationship between moral teaching and war has long been ambiguous; advocates of peace have often derived inspiration and strength from such teachings, even while the war-prone have turned to religious and moral authorities (sometimes the same ones!) to support their arguments as well.

A concerted nationwide and planetary opposition to war may ultimately derive considerable impetus from ethical and religious sources; nonetheless, ethics and religion have also fueled much warfare in the past, and may continue to do so in the future. Although we turn to religious and ethical traditions with hope, in fact the world's organized moral systems historically have been more likely to support militarism than to oppose it. Sometimes, as we shall see, religious authorities

Buddhist monks participating in an antinuclear demonstration. (United Nations/Milton Grant)

have been among the primary cheerleaders for war-making; at other times, their stance has been passive acquiescence. In czarist Russia, for example, Russian Orthodox priests traditionally said a funeral mass for peasants when they were inducted into the army. Most commonly, religious and ethical values were limited to self-protective and self-serving doctrines, such as immunity for the clergy and attempted reassurance for the soldiery and endangered civilians. The following inscription (loosely translated) is commonly seen even today on houses in the various small villages of Bavaria; "Saint Florian, protect our town, pass by my house, burn others down"!

On the other hand, religious and ethical concerns must be central to the establishment of peace—moral decisions cannot be avoided. There was, after all, virtually nothing scientifically or technically wrong with Auschwitz, Dachau, or the bombing of Dresden or Hiroshima (the latter, especially, was a major scientific and technical achievement). Criticism, or condemnation, must come—if at all—in moral terms. In the modern

world, religion in particular has been transformative: Islam in postshah Iran, Catholicism in Poland, Episcopal bishop Desmond Tutu and others fighting apartheid in South Africa, not to mention the role of Protestant Christianity in fueling the civil rights movement in the American South during the 1960s, as well as the impact of numerous churches in opposing the war in Vietnam, and nuclear weapons during the 1980s.

Warfare is typically overlain with numerous rules and elaborate structures of right and wrong. Fundamentally, however, it represents an inversion of one of the most basic precepts of social life: Thou Shalt Not Kill. Hence, it carries an inherent moral dilemma. (This, incidentally, may also be why war is so often the midwife of social change. Having broken out of the prescriptions of what is permissible and what is not, situations of war occasionally open up new possibilities for rearranging the social order.) Any serious turnabout in fundamental attitudes regarding the acceptability of war will almost certainly involve ethical and religious formulations; conversely, no such turnabout will be possible if it is not somehow anchored in ethical and/or religious precepts. This, plus the support now provided by ethics and religion to peace workers and war boosters alike, makes it all the more important that students of peace pay close attention to these issues.

WAR AND GENERAL ETHICS

As we shall see, the mainstream of ethical and religious thought typically condones war in particular cases; occasionally, as in fascist doctrine, war is even embraced with great enthusiasm. But when considering war in general, human ethical judgment by and large is critical. Approval — when it comes (and sooner or later, it usually does) — is largely restricted to specific wars in which people are confronted with particular conflicts and identifiable enemies who typically are also perceived as threats. One might argue that the specifics are what count: Just as there is no such thing as "war" taken in the abstract, but rather specific wars, it avails nothing if moralists condemn war in general but lend their approval to each particular war as it comes along. But this conclusion omits a potentially important characteristic of moral thought: a continuing predisposition *against* violence and killing. This fundamental and often unspoken precept may contribute importantly to the eventual delegitimization of war that is a goal of Peace Studies.

Presumption Against War

Like the presumption of innocence in legal proceedings, a widespread moral orientation presumes that the way of peace is better than the way of war. For war to be justified, therefore, in a world that prides itself on possessing moral values, the burden of proof must lie on those who would make war. This applies even to clear-cut aggressors, who often seek to justify their actions by appeals (however spurious) to moral authority. For example, after Cyrus of Persia conquered Babylon in the sixth century B.C., he commissioned a poem arguing that the actions of the Babylonian king Nabuna'id had of-fended Marduk, patron god of Babylon. In turn, Marduk had sought out Cyrus, and helped him to his deserved victory, which included, among other things, sacking the city.

According to the philosopher Immanuel Kant, war involves an inevitable moral descent. It deprives the enemy of that respect which is fundamentally due to all persons by virtue of their humanity. Kant emphasized that we should treat people as *ends*, whereas war often requires the combatants to see each other as mere *means*, as objects, numbers, or targets. Frequently, commanders even treat their own soldiers as cannon fodder. This underlying depersonalization runs counter to deep-seated moral precepts, hence the widespread need, even on the part of aggressors like Cyrus, to justify their actions in moral terms.

In addition, nearly everyone recognizes that might does not make right. When trial by combat became legal in Burgundy in A.D. 501, the clergy objected, whereupon King Gundobald replied: "Is it not true that the event of national wars and private combats is directed by the judgment of God, and that his providence awards the victory to the juster cause?"[1] Times have changed, and dramatically so; thus, no modern state currently condones the settling of private disputes by combat between the contending individuals. When state or national disputes are settled by war, however, it is analogous to settling personal disputes by individual combat, with the outcome presumably a function of strength, not of merit. Hence, such procedures are difficult to justify.

The most dramatic and famous exception to traditional moral doctrine occurred in the ancient Athenian campaign against the island of Melos. The Melians favored Sparta during the Peloponnesian War, but sought to stay neutral since they were geographically close to Athens, which was far stronger than tiny Melos. After a lengthy siege, the Athenians delivered an ultimatum to the inhabitants of Melos: Surrender and be enslaved, or be destroyed. When the Melians protested the unfairness of this choice, arguing that they had not given Athens any cause for such violence, the Athenian spokesman answered in a speech renowned for its brutal honesty: "Right only comes into question when there is a balance of power, while it is Might that determines what the strong extort and the weak concede."[2] The strong do what they will; the weak endure what they must. Ultimately, all Melian males were killed, and the women and children taken as slaves.

The openness of Athenian disregard for morality is testimony to the virtually universal presumption that, in essentially all wars, blame is heaped on the opponent. It is almost unheard of for a belligerent to announce: "We have decided to make war on our neighbor, not because of any misdeeds on their part, or for any righteous cause, but because we desire to plunder their resources, settle on their territory, enhance our prestige, enrich our arms manufacturers, provide amusement and occupation for our dissatisfied young men, and/or deflect domestic criticism." Rather, even when the aggressive design is transparent, the other side is almost always blamed; such convenient fictions provide a shred of moral legitimacy to which the populace may cling and behind which the leadership may hide.

Blaming the Other Side

Wars are often preceded by attempts to emphasize the perfidy of the other side, or if necessary, to create "incidents" that make the war more acceptable. Many historians suspect, for example, that the sinking of the U.S. battleship *Maine* was either an accident or a deliberate provocation, initiated by persons hoping to goad the United States into declaring war on Spain in 1898. Just prior to its declaration of war in 1914, Austria tried to stir up anger at Serbia for allegedly having cooperated in the murder of the heir to the Austrian throne. Similarly, Hitler repeatedly claimed that ethnic Germans within Czechoslovakia and Poland were being criminally maltreated, and prior to the invasion of 1939, German forces even staged a phony "attack," ostensibly by Polish troops against a German radio station near the border. The Gulf of Tonkin incident (1964) was essentially manufactured by President Johnson as a ploy — successful at the time — to paint North Vietnam as an aggressor against the United States, and to get Congress to approve direct U.S. military intervention in the conflict in Southeast Asia.

Government leaders are only rarely as direct as the Athenians confronting Melos. In addition to setting up justifications, often phony ones, statesmen almost invariably describe their wars as being moral, often moral crusades. Thus, for the United States, the Vietnam War was a crusade to defend the democrats of Saigon against the butchers from Hanoi, just as the murderous contras in Nicaragua were likened by President Reagan to the American Founding Fathers; for Hitler, expansion of the Third Reich was required to save the world from Jews and communists; for the Soviet Union, interventionism was justified to protect the human rights of Afghans (especially the women, oppressed by Moslem fundamentalism), and to liberate Hungary from the horrors of counterrevolution; for China, occupation of Tibet was explained as necessary to banish Tibetan feudalism; for India, the long-sought goal of dismembering Pakistan was clothed in the high moral purpose of aiding the persecuted Bengalis in East Pakistan. And so it has gone.

On the other hand, we should not be unduly cynical about the flexibility of ethical outrage. It is all too easy to criticize the ease with which moral indignation is aroused in support of organized killing. After all, politics is a difficult and messy occupation, and nowhere is it more difficult or messier than when it comes to decisions about war. In the view of some authorities, such as Reinhold Niebuhr, the necessity for tough, practical choice and action transforms politics into nothing less than tragedy: "Politics will, to the end of history, be an area where conscience and power meet, where the ethical and coercive factors of human life will interpenetrate and work out their tentative and uneasy compromises."[3] For Hans Morgenthau, politics also has unavoidable and often painful moral implications:

> To act successfully, that is, according to the rules of the political art, is political wisdom. To know with despair that the political act is inevitably evil, and to act nevertheless, is moral courage. To choose among several expedient actions the least evil one is

moral judgment. In the combination of political wisdom, moral courage and moral judgment, man reconciles his political nature with his moral destiny.[4]

An alternative view, however, is that, especially when it comes to issues of war and peace, death and life, there is no room for compromises or moral equivocation. Under such circumstances, it is not enough to choose the lesser of two evils. One must choose what is right.

Utilitarian Versus Absolutist Ethics

This raises the important distinction between *utilitarian* and *absolutist* ethics. The former (also sometimes called "consequentialist") places particular value on the balance of benefits and costs associated with any act. Ethicist Michael Walzer, in his influential book, *Just and Unjust Wars*, argued that only aggression can justify war. He defined aggression as the "use of force or imminent threat of force by one state against the political sovereignty or territorial integrity of another," further asserting that "once the aggressor state has been militarily repulsed, it can also be punished."[5] The goal of such punishment is to deter others, to exact legitimate retribution, and to restrain or reform the aggressor, as is done with respect to criminals in civil life. Walzer echoes the beliefs of other utilitarian ethicists when he states:

> The domestic maxim is, punish crime to prevent violence; its international analogue is, punish aggression to prevent war. Whether the state as a whole or only particular persons are the proper objects of punishment is a harder question. . . . But the implication of the paradigm is clear: if states are members of international society, the subjects of rights, they must also be (somehow) the objects of punishment.[6]

Critics claim that such ethics can have tragic effects, especially if mass violence can be justified by such verbal niceties as the definition of "aggression," or the legitimate limits to "punishment." Once the door is opened to official sanctions for violence, they argue, consequentialist or utilitarian ethics can rapidly become apologies for mass murder; the deliberate killing of civilians, for example,

can be deemed permissible if enough can be gained by it. The alternative, absolutist ethics, would include such stances as absolute pacifism. In this extreme view, no killing is permissible, no matter what good is achieved, or what evil is averted thereby. (To be consistent, absolute support for destroying one's opponent should also logically be included here, but absolute ethics of this sort are rarely encountered in modern times.)

Our primary interest is to assess the contributions of religious and ethical precepts to the establishment of peace. Nonetheless, an accurate portrayal requires that we first examine the ambiguity of their roles, starting with some of the ways in which religion has disturbed the peace, rather than promoted it.

RELIGIOUS SUPPORT FOR WAR

We have already seen that religious intolerance has led to many wars throughout history; in addition, religions have contributed to warfare directly, by their own internal demands and expectations.

Judeo-Christianity

Judeo-Christian doctrines are contradictory with respect to war. Thus, the ancient Israelites were notable warriors, and indeed, the Old Testament is replete with bloody accounts of the so-called commanded wars, in which God urged his people to destroy others: "When the Lord your God has given them over to you, and you defeat them, then you must utterly destroy them; you shall make no covenant with them, and show no mercy to them."[7] For several thousand years, however, after the domination of Judaism by the Romans, Jewish tradition emphasized pacifism, only to experience a renewed warlike ethos in association with the founding of the state of Israel and in the aftermath of the Holocaust of the late 1930s and early 1940s, when approximately 6 million European Jews were slaughtered. Today, the Israeli army (technically known as the Israeli Defense Forces) is widely considered the most effective fighting force in the world.

Islamism, Hinduism, and Buddhism

Other religious traditions—less important in the United States but influential worldwide—have also displayed a positive attitude toward war. Best known among these is the *jihad*, or holy war, among Moslems, in which fallen warriors are considered to be guaranteed entry into heaven. Hinduism, as we shall see in Chapter 23, contributed to Gandhian nonviolence, but it also had a rigorous military tradition. The great Hindu texts emphasize the duty of devout Hindus to fight even for a cause with which they may disagree. Thus, Bhisma, hero of the *Mahabharata*, fought on behalf of the reigning government, even though he recognized the other side as more just. And in the *Bhagavad Gita*, the hero Arjuna is enjoined to kill even his friends and relatives, if his duty so demands. Moreover, battle is seen as a kind of divine, selfless action (*karma yoga*), and Arjuna, the man and warrior, is advised by Krishna, the warrior–god, to cease all personal striving: "Be thou merely the means of my work."[8]

Peace has long been a central doctrine for Buddhism, like Christianity, but specific war resistance as a self-concious Buddhist goal has historically been rare. Notable exceptions were the United Buddhist church in Vietnam and elsewhere in Indochina, especially after the early 1960s, when many Buddhists committed self-immolation (suicide by burning themselves) as a means of personal protest against the killing during the Vietnam War.

Christianity

Christianity has a complex relationship to war. Although many of its founding principles emphasize pacifism, turning the other cheek, and loving one's neighbor, Christianity (along with Islamism, Hinduism, and Shintoism, the predominant religious tradition of Japan) constituted one of the great warrior religions of history. There is a fundamental Christian ambiguity toward war, reflected in the attitude toward the cross. On the one hand, it is supposed to be the ultimate symbol of peace and love, something with which to replace violence and sin. On the other hand, the cross has long been seen

Marine Corps chaplain holding a prayer breakfast for the troops. (U.S. Department of Defense)

as a new and more effective sword with which to smite the forces of evil. Thus, Saint Paul warned, "If thou dost what is evil, fear, for not without reason does it [government] carry the sword. For it is God's minister, an avenger to execute wrath on him who does evil."[9]

Christianity was the eventual heir to the dying Roman empire, and as such, many of its early wars were unsuccessful, but fought with increasing fervor. The "Holy War" tradition in Christianity is a direct descendant of the commanded wars of the Old Testament, and was especially potent during the Middle Ages, most dramatically during the Crusades. Saint Bernard of Clairvaux, in the twelfth century, delivered the following sermon in support of Christian efforts to drive Moslems from Palestine:

> A new sort of army has appeared. . . . It fights a double war; first, the war of the flesh and blood against enemies; second, the war of the spirit against Satan and vice. . . . The soldier of Christ kills with safety; he dies with more safety still. He serves Christ when he kills. He serves himself when he is killed.[10]

And *The Song of Roland*, one of the early western European masterpieces of poetry and adventure, glorified war against Islam. On the battlefields, dead Moslems are carted off by Satan to hell, whereas dead Christian warriors are escorted reverently into heaven. (Few such distinctions are made by the great Hindu war epic, the *Mahabharata*, or in Greek accounts such as the *Iliad*). In *The Song of Roland*, an archbishop tells Roland's outnumbered fighters,

> Soon, very soon we all are marked to die,
> None of us here will see tomorrow's light;
> One thing there is I promise you outright:
> To you stand open the gates of Paradise,
> There with the holy sweet Innocents to bide.[11]

In 1215, the Catholic church took the important steps of forbidding participation of priests or bishops in trials by combat. God, it was decided, was not concerned with such demeaning matters; nonetheless, the tendency to see wars in terms of divine judgment and retribution continued, in part as a carryover from the time when various Old Testament prophets warned that the sinning city of Babylon would be punished by God, via war. From the sixteenth to eighteenth centuries, Christians continued a similar perspective; war was widely seen as "God's beadle," chastising the ungodly and the sinners, those who were insufficiently devout and righteous.

It may also be possible that, to some extent, war was seen as curiously attractive precisely because it satisfied a guilt-ridden need for punishment, something that has also long been prominent in Christian tradition. For example, the General Court of Massachusetts declared in 1675 that war with the Indians was brought about because the Puritans had ignored previous warnings from God, and that, therefore, "God hath heightened our calamity, and given commission to the barbarous heathen to rise up against us, and to become a smart rod and severe scourge to us."[12] And so, although war was widely perceived as undesirable and punishing, it was also considered to have been ordained by God. Thus, under certain circumstances (that

is, when the clergy approved), war was a legitimate endeavor for Christians. Not only did war represent God's vengeance on the wicked, it could serve as a hair-shirt, a kind of penance for the warmaker, a chastisement for people who had been backsliding, who needed its miseries to remind them of their wickedness and smallness, and of God's almighty power.

At other times, religious zealotry served to legitimize the conquest of nonbelievers. "Conversion by the sword" was a notable stimulus for the adoption of Islam from A.D. 700 to 1450, but was also prominent among Christian warmakers. During the sixteenth century, for example, each Spanish conquistador was required to carry a copy of the *Requerimento*, and to read it to the South American Indians (often inaudibly and in Spanish, which their opponents did not understand) just before each battle, thereby absolving themselves of any responsibility for the slaughter they were about to inflict. This tract insisted that the Indians accept the sovereignty of the king of Spain and the pope; otherwise, they would be subject to enslavement, the loss of property, and punishment as traitors to man and god: "The resultant deaths and damages shall be your fault, and not the monarch's, or mine, or my fellow soldiers'."[13] Even as recently as 1914, the bishop of London urged his countrymen to

> kill Germans — kill them, not for the sake of killing, but to save the world, to kill the good as well as the bad, to kill the young men as well as the old, to kill those who have shown kindness to our wounded as well as those fiends who crucified the Canadian Sergeant [a widely publicized anti-German war myth of the time]. . . . As I have said a thousand times, I look upon it as a war for purity, I look upon everyone who dies in it as a martyr.[14]

And of course, German priests and ministers were simultaneously reassuring their countrymen, *Gott mit uns* ("God is with us"). Warfare is bad enough; when religious zealousness adds absolute certainty of one's righteousness, then it becomes even worse. "Men never do evil so completely and cheerfully," noted Pascal, "as when they do it from religious conviction."[15]

RELIGIOUS SUPPORT FOR THE STATUS QUO

In addition to serving as cheerleaders for war, religious traditions and leaders have also been accused of hindering human freedom by serving as a bulwark in favor of the status quo. Christian doctrine in particular has been criticized for legitimating the oppression of women, blacks, and the impoverished. The faithful often have been called upon to support law and order (frequent code words for government-sponsored repression), as a way of keeping human sinfulness under control. In short, religion has long served to keep people submissive, weak, and accepting of their oppression. Not surprisingly, therefore, communist doctrine generally has been antagonistic to organized religion. Consider the following by Karl Marx:

> The social principles of Christianity justified the slavery of antiquity, glorified the serfdom of the Middle Ages, and equally know, when necessary, how to defend the oppression of the proletariat. . . . The social principles of Christianity preach the necessity of a ruling and an oppressed class, and all they have for the latter is the pious wish the former will be charitable. . . . The social principles of Christianity declare all vile acts of the oppressors against the oppressed to be either the just punishment of original sin and other sins or trials that the Lord in his infinite wisdom imposes on those redeemed. The social principles of Christianity preach cowardice, self-contempt, abasement, submission, humility. . . . The social principles of Christianity are cringing, but the proletariat is revolutionary. So much for the social principles of Christianity.[16]

In fact, Christian doctrine is not inevitably on the side of entrenched power and consistently opposed to social betterment. "Liberation theology," which originated in Latin America, proclaims a vigorously *social* gospel, emphasizing the social sensitivities of Christ, and the need for the modern-day Catholic church to align itself on the side of the poor, the despised, and the disenfranchised. The General Conference of Latin-American Bishops, in Puebla, Mexico, in 1979, issued a statement that includes the following:

> From the heart of Latin America, a cry rises to the heavens ever louder and more imperative. It is the cry of a people who suffer and who demand justice, freedom, and respect for the fundamental rights of man. . . . In [the people's] pain and anxiety, the Church discerns a situation of social sin, of a magnitude all the greater because it occurs in countries which call themselves Catholic and have the capacity to change. . . . We identify, as the most devastating and humiliating scourge, the situation of inhuman poverty in which millions of Latin Americans live, with starvation wages, unemployment and underemployment, malnutrition, infant mortality, lack of adequate housing, health problems, and labor unrest.[17]

CHRISTIAN "REALISM" AND THE JUST WAR DOCTRINE

To some extent, each Christian church has its own tradition with respect to war; often, in fact, the same church has differing, conflicting approaches. Thus, there are pacifist Baptists and Baptist marines, nonviolent Lutherans and Lutheran paratroopers. Undoubtedly, the most carefully enunciated and influential Christian doctrine with respect to war has been a middle-of-the-road approach known as the "Just War" doctrine.

Certainly, there is nothing new in seeking to provide moral underpinnings for the initiation and conduct of war. The Romans and Greeks developed carefully reasoned rationales for their wars, and two thousand years earlier, the Code of Hammurabi, the earliest written set of legal regulations, begins with the statement that Hammurabi (a Babylonian leader) seeks to "establish justice in the earth, to destroy the base and the wicked, and to hold back the strong from oppressing the feeble . . . and to illuminate the land."

The Late Roman Empire

Substantial evidence suggests that the early Christian church was pacifist; indeed, pacifism seems to have constituted a major distinction between early Christianity and both the warlike Roman empire and the equally violence-prone Old Testament Jewish tradition (the latter included the Zealots, Jewish terrorists and assassins who sought to coerce Roman withdrawal from ancient Palestine). Many early Christian martyrs died for refusing service in the Roman legions. By the fourth century A.D., the secular fortunes of Christianity improved, and with the conversion of the Roman emperor Constantine, Christianity became the official religion of the Roman state. Almost overnight, Christianity went from a minority and prophetic movement to the prime defender of government and society. Its transformation was such that soon only Christians were permitted to serve in the Roman army.* And when the Roman empire was threatened by "godless barbarians" such as the Goths, Vandals, and Huns, Christianity quickly developed a more practical and accepting view of organized violence, a middle ground between the bloodthirsty commanded wars of the Old Testament and the uncompromising pacifism of the early Gospels. The result was a series of careful rules by which a Christian could engage in a "just war."

The Augustinian View

Major contributions to Just War doctrine can be found in the writings of medieval secularists such as DeVittoria, Suarez, and Grotius, as well as the work of Saint Thomas Aquinas. The prime mover, however, was Saint Augustine, bishop of Hippo, in the fourth century A.D. Augustine was primarily concerned with justifying Christian participation in the defense of Rome. In *The City of God*, Augustine wrote that "it is the wrong-doing of the opposing party which compels the wise man to wage just wars" and that "war with the hope of peace everlasting" to follow was preferable to "captivity without any thought of deliverance."[18] It has even been reported that when the Persians called for their opponents to surrender, the greatly outnumbered Greeks responded as follows, more than a thousand years before the development of Just War doctrine:

"A slave's life thou understandest, but, never having tasted liberty, thou canst not tell whether it be sweet or no. Ah! Hadst thou known what freedom is, thou wouldst have bidden us fight for it."[19]

To Augustine, and the large tradition of "Christian realism" that followed him, peace was "tranquility in order."[20] Augustine thus prefigured the tension between the devotees of order (often represented in modern times by the political right wing) and justice (typically represented by the political left). In any event, in the Augustinian view, peace often requires violence against evil-doers, and the soldier who goes to war in defense of right — and order — does not violate the commandment against killing. "They who have waged war in obedience to the divine command, or in conformity with His laws," Augustine wrote in *The City of God*, "have represented in their persons the public justice or the wisdom of government, and in this capacity have put to death wicked men; such persons have by no means violated the commandment: Thou shalt not kill."[21]

War, in Augustine's view, must be based ultimately on "Christian charity," that is, the defense of a neighbor who has been unjustly attacked. Nonetheless, a Christian was expected to go to war, if at all, with a heavy heart, and only after carefully examining his conscience, because the presumption was at all times supposed to be in favor of peace. Thus, Augustine emphasized that when the Christian goes to war, he must do so with anguish and deep regret. Whereas the City of God is founded on an act of loving grace, the City of Man, in Augustine's view, is founded on war: "Whatever part of the city of the world raises the standard of war, it seeks to be lord of the world: in fact, it is enthralled in its own wickedness."[22] Since evil exists, the Christian is supposedly obliged to struggle against it. Much debate has arisen, however, over whether this is really a necessity, a permission, or an excuse. In certain hotly contested cases, wars themselves seem to be the greater immorality. Opposition to the Vietnam War in the United States, for example, was fueled by a passionate sense that this war was unjust in its origins, and also unjustly fought. The "Call to Resist Illegitimate Authority," issued in

---

*Many Christians, Catholic as well as Protestant, do not realize that it was in the context of taking up secular — especially war-related — burdens that the Catholic church became the *Roman* Catholic church.

1969, during the height of antiwar sentiment, asserted that "every free man has a legal right and a moral duty to exert every effort to end this war."[23] This raises the painful but unavoidable question of personal responsibility, which is especially acute when society is perceived to be prosecuting an immoral war.

There are, in a sense, two kinds of tragedies: (1) what we might call Greek tragedy, the "tragedy of necessity," in which the tragic outcome was unavoidable, and the observer might be moved to say, "What a pity it had to be this way," and (2) what we might call rational tragedy, the "tragedy of possibility," leading to the conclusion, "What a pity it was this way when it might have been otherwise." The view of so-called Christian realists, who maintain that participation in war is necessitated by the imperfect, sinning nature of human beings, is closer to the former. According to one influential political scientist/theologian, Christian religious faith "ought to persuade us that political controversies are always conflicts between sinners and not between righteous men and sinners. It ought to mitigate the self-righteousness which is an inevitable concomitant of all human conflict."[24]

Thus, if faced with a choice between two courses of action, we like to assume that one is more ethical and allows our honor to remain intact. But what if either choice presents us with evil? What if there truly is a moral dead end? If the world operates this way, then it really is a tragic realm, but nonetheless one in which people — as thinking creatures — are obliged to struggle in their search for moral uprightness.

Jus ad Bellum and Jus in Bello

There are two major components to Just War doctrine. The first refers to the justification of engaging in a particular war — known by its Latin phrase, *jus ad bellum*, or the justice *of* a war — and spells out the requirements that must be met in order for a Christian to identify a particular war as appropriate. The second major component of Just War doctrine is *jus in bello*, or justice *in* a war. Whereas *jus ad bellum* concerns whether or not a war ought to

be fought, the rules by which a choice is made between war and peace, *jus in bello* deals with the manner in which such a war may be engaged, the rules for conducting any given war. Thus, a just war (one that meets *ad bellum* criteria) may be fought unjustly (if it fails to accord with *in bello* restraints); and similarly, an unjust war can be prosecuted justly.

The generally acknowledged criteria for *jus ad bellum* are as follows:

1. *Last resort.* War must not be entered into with undue haste or unseemly enthusiasm, but rather only if all other means of resolution have been explored and found inadequate.

2. *Legitimate authority.* The decision to go to war cannot be made by disgruntled individuals or self-appointed groups; it must come from duly constituted governmental authority.

3. *Right intention and just cause.* War is unacceptable if it is motivated by aggression or even revenge; it must be consistent with Christian charity and/or self-defense. (Interestingly, Augustine specifically excluded self-defense, arguing that it was acceptable only to wage war in defense of *others*.)

4. *Chance of success.* Futile resistance cannot be justified; only when there is reasonable chance of an acceptable outcome may the Christian consider that a war is justifiable.

5. *Goal of peace.* Looking ahead to the conclusion of the war, it must be possible to envision a peace that is preferable to the situation that would prevail if the war was not fought.

Conditions 3–5 are sometimes summarized as the "principle of proportionality," which states that for a war to be just, its overall moral benefits must exceed its costs. Thus, the principle of proportionality recognizes that war is inherently evil, and that therefore it can only be justified if it leads to an even greater overall good. In practice, once a state's leadership decides upon war, the overwhelming majority of its religious figures almost always pronounce it to be just, whereupon the average citizen or soldier goes along. But at the same time, the requirements for *jus ad bellum* arguments provide — at least in theory — a yardstick whereby mainstream Christians can personally evaluate the legitimacy of a state's call to arms.

In Bello Restraints

Once a war is underway, it can, in Just War doctrine, be fought justly or unjustly. The generally acknowledged *in bello* restraints can be summarized in two principles: "double effect" and "discrimination." The principle of double effect is a specific application of the *ad bellum* doctrine of proportionality, described above. Just as wars can be interpreted to have good and bad overall effects, the principle of double effect states that specific *in bello* actions — those taken during a war — typically have two effects: a "good" effect in bringing the war to a successful conclusion and a "bad" effect in causing pain, death, and destruction to combatants, and often noncombatants as well. According to the principle of double effect, therefore, such actions as bombings and invasions can only be countenanced if the good effect outweighs the bad. Military means and the cost of a war must be proportional to a moral end and its presumed benefits.

The second component of *in bello* restraints, the principle of discrimination, is synonymous with "noncombatant immunity," and states that civilians must not be the direct, intentional object of military attack. This principle recognizes that civilians will often be killed during hostilities, but the direct targeting of noncombatants is prohibited. In practice, however, the principle of discrimination further acknowledges that noncombatants will often be targeted "indirectly," and such activities, so long as they are ostensibly inadvertent, are generally condoned. For example, when strategic bombardment seeks either to destroy war-production facilities or to defeat the other side's morale, as in the firebombing of German and Japanese cities during World War II, the practical effect has been the massacre of tens of thousands of noncombatants.

Various attempts have been made to establish *in bello* restraints in the conduct of war. The medi-

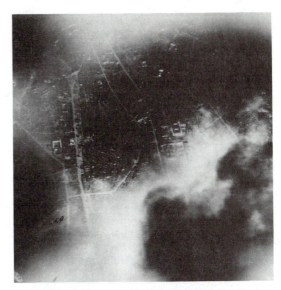

The city of Tokyo burning, after a (conventional) firebombing in the spring of 1945. (USAF Photographic Collection, National Air and Space Museum, Smithsonian Institution)

eval "Truce of God" defined certain days as unacceptable for fighting, and the "Peace of God" prohibited direct attack against certain persons: travelers, merchants, clergy, and farmers. The Code of Chivalry established rules concerning who may fight with whom, and regarding the treatment of prisoners (that is, if they were members of the nobility). The Second Lateran Council, in 1215, even banned the use of certain weapons, notably the crossbow. Significantly, however, these prohibitions applied only to use *against* Christians; the crossbow could still be employed against Moslems, as during the Crusades. But even this prohibition eventually faltered; in fact, to this point, no weapons have been effectively banned because their use was judged immoral. (One possibility concerns chemical weapons, which, although used widely during World War I, were also universally condemned and hardly employed at all in World War II. On the other hand, this restraint may have been more a function of deterrence than of moral considerations, since each side knew that the other was capable of retaliating with comparable weapons. Moreover, chemical weapons have been used during the 1980s, notably by the Iraqis against the Iranians as well as Kurdish rebels in northern Iraq.)

Despite the stereotypical view of war as mercilessly ravaging a countryside, in fact soldiers often obeyed certain rules. Private property, for example, was frequently respected, so long as it belonged to noncombatants. Thus, in 1793, Austria paid rent for the Dutch fields in which its army camped, and in 1794, when Austrian troops could not pay to hire ferries that would have carried them to safety across the Rhine River, they surrendered rather than commandeer the needed boats.

Violations of Noncombatant Immunity

Perhaps the most notable feature of *in bello* restraint, however, and its most tragic failures, involve violations of noncombatant immunity, a trend that has been increasing. For example, although military casualties were roughly comparable during World Wars I and II, civilian casualties were substantially higher in the latter. This seems due to two factors: (1) the greater involvement of entire populations in a nationwide war effort, thereby blurring the distinction between military and civilian, and (2) the invention of increasingly more destructive and less discriminating weapons, most of which also operate at great distance. Nuclear weapons represent a culmination of this trend.

Strategic bombing of cities became increasingly frequent during World War II. There had been great public outcry at the fascist bombing of Guernica during the Spanish civil war, the Japanese bombing of Chinese cities such as Nanking, and the German bombing of Rotterdam and Warsaw. By the time of the London "blitz" and eventual Allied bombing of civilian populations in Germany and Japan, however, countercity warfare was virtually taken for granted. Night bombing was safer than daytime raids for the attacking side, but was substantially less accurate than bombing by day; hence, it was virtually impossible to conduct precision attacks on specific, military targets or even on war industries. Rather, whole cities became the targets. Tens of thousands of civilians died in the nighttime

firebombings of Dresden, Hamburg, Tokyo, and Osaka. Munitions were specifically designed to increase the probability of creating firestorms, and bombing patterns were employed to create a ring of fire, trapping civilians within.

Lewis Mumford denounced the resulting saturation bombing of civilian targets as "unconditional moral surrender to Hitler,"[25] and David Lilienthal, later the first chairman of the Atomic Energy Commission, warned, "The fences are gone. And it was we, the civilized, who have pushed standardless conduct to its ultimate."[26] Others, of course, argued that strategic bombing in general, and the atomic bombing of Hiroshima and Nagasaki in particular, was morally justified under the doctrine of double effect, claiming that the good effect (the supposed hastening of the end of the war) overrode the bad (the killing of hundreds of thousands of civilians). But in fact, moral standards were not abandoned altogether. It is interesting to note that a plaque in Westminster Abbey commemorates the RAF pilots of Fighter Command who died defending Britain against German bombers, whereas there is no comparable recognition of the (equally brave) fliers of Bomber Command who died while raining destruction on German cities.

It is noteworthy that such considerations as noncombatant immunity have been influential even in the misrepresentations associated with war. Typically, each side will accuse the other of causing civilian casualties. President Truman even described the first atomic target, Hiroshima, as "an important military base," whereas it definitely was not. (By late summer of 1945, U.S. bombers had been striking targets throughout Japan at will; all targets of military significance had already been attacked, most of them many times.) Rather, Hiroshima was chosen specifically because it was an intact city, and as such, capable of providing a clear demonstration of atomic destruction.

Another moral justification for overriding the principle of noncombatant immunity argues that such immunity is a dangerous and misleading nicety that makes war seem civilized, and therefore, acceptable. Why, we might ask, is it considered an atrocity to throw a human being into a fire, but a legitimate military activity to throw fire on a human being? The firebombing of Dresden took place during the last days of the war, when its outcome was already a foregone conclusion, and when the city itself was swollen with thousands of refugees and in the middle of a children's carnival. Commenting on the presumed immorality of the Dresden firebombing, a British RAF official maintained that it is

> not so much this or the other means of making war that is immoral or inhuman. What is immoral is war itself. Once the full-scale war has broken out it can never be humanized or civilized, and if one side attempted to do so it would most likely be defeated. So long as we resort to war to settle differences between nations, so long will we have to endure the horrors, barbarities, and excesses war brings with it. That, to me, is the lesson of Dresden.[27]

In the early nineteenth century, the Prussian military theorist Karl von Clausewitz had also argued against the concept of restraints in war:

> He who uses force unsparingly, without reference against the bloodshed involved, must obtain a superiority if his adversary uses less vigour in its application. . . . To introduce into a philosophy of war a principle of moderation would be an absurdity. War is an act of violence pushed to its utmost bounds.[28]

And yet, the horrors of unrestricted warfare are so great that perhaps we should be grateful for whatever *in bello* restraints the human mind can conceive and agree to, no matter how imperfect, or how frequently violated in practice.

RELIGIOUS PACIFISM

Holy wars and Just War doctrine both constitute important aspects of Christian ethics applied to warfare, but neither is unique to Christianity. Holy wars trace their ancestry to the warlike traditions of the Old Testament, and Just War doctrine is essentially a reworking of Greco-Roman ethics. It is in the doctrine of pacifism that Christianity makes its most notably distinct contribution to religious eth-

ics and warfare. In many ways, Christianity marked the advent of organized pacifism, at least in the sense of doctrinal refusal to participate in military service.

The Second Commandment tells us to love our neighbor as ourselves, but the New Testament, especially the Gospel according to Saint John, goes further, enjoining followers to love their *enemy*, and actively to return good for evil. Among modern Christian churches, the historic "peace churches," including the Society of Friends (Quakers), Mennonites, and the Church of the Brethren, are notable for their literal adherence to pacifist doctrines as enunciated, for example, in Christ's Sermon on the Mount:

> You have heard that they were told, "An eye for an eye and a tooth for a tooth." But I tell you not to resist injury, but if anyone strikes you on your right cheek, turn the other to him too; and if anyone wants to sue you for your shirt, let him have your coat too. And if anyone forces you to go one mile, go two miles with him. . . . You have heard that they were told, "You must love your neighbor and hate your enemy." But I tell you, love your enemies and pray for your persecutors, so that you may show yourselves true sons of your Father in heaven, for he makes the sun rise on the bad and good alike, and makes the rain fall on the upright and the wrongdoers.[29]

Pacifist traditions also have been retained as minority views within mainstream churches, including the Catholic, via such organizations as Pax Christi. The Fellowship of Reconciliation (FOR) is an ecumenical effort to unite and coordinate religious pacifists of all faiths. In addition to opposing the military policies of their states, pacifists refuse personal participation in wars, most directly by resisting conscription. They often practice tax resistance as well, which frequently takes the form of refusing to pay the proportion of national taxes that goes toward the military. Many governments, including that of the United States, have reluctantly accepted the legitimacy of conscientious objectors, so long as some form of alternative service is provided; on the other hand, war resisters have traditionally been persecuted and sometimes killed, and in most Soviet-bloc states they have often been imprisoned for their views.

Many pacifists agree with G. K. Chesterton's sardonic observation that "the Christian ideal has not been tried and found wanting. It has been found difficult and left untried."[30] Mennonite theologian John Howard Yoder is one who tries:

> Christians whose loyalty to the Prince of Peace puts them out of step with today's nationalistic world, because of a willingness to love their nation's friends but not to hate the nation's enemies, are not unrealistic dreamers who think that by their objections all wars will end. The unrealistic dreamers are rather the soldiers who think that they can put an end to wars by preparing for just one more. . . . Christians love their enemies not because they think the enemies are wonderful people, nor because they believe that love is sure to conquer those enemies. They do not love their enemies because they fail to respect their native land or its rulers; nor because they are unconcerned for the safety of their neighbors; nor because another political or economic system may be favored. The Christian loves his or her enemies because God does, and God commands His followers to do so; that is the only reason, and that is enough.[31]

Religious pacifists such as Yoder emphasize that people were created in God's image, and that Christ died for all humanity. Hence, they maintain that the Christian has no choice: He or she must follow Christ's injunctions and example, refusing to do violence against others, especially if this might entail taking another's life — regardless of what the secular authorities might demand.

During World War II, Joseph Goebbels — the minister of propaganda in Nazi Germany — suggested to German religious leaders: "You are at liberty to seek your salvation as you understand it, provided you do nothing to change the social order."[32] Similarly, the Russian Orthodox church is permitted to operate freely in the Soviet Union, so long as it does not concern itself with the orthodoxies of communism as it is practiced in the U.S.S.R. The traditionally comfortable relationship between secular power and the Roman Catholic church in

Latin America has seriously been challenged only in the last two decades, as "liberation theology" — which maintains that the church has an obligation to seek social justice — has gained influence. Likewise, when the Roman Catholic bishops of the United States took a strong stand against nuclear weapons in their pastoral letter of 1983, government officials and journalists began questioning whether it was legitimate for organized religion to speak out on the burning issues of the day.

NUCLEAR ETHICS

Although considerable debate exists regarding religious and ethical approaches to war, when it comes to *nuclear* war, the issues are somewhat more clear-cut. Most authorities agree, for example, that a nuclear war could never meet the criteria for a just war. Noncombatant immunity could not be maintained, although some hawkish ethicists argue that civilians might legitimately be killed in such a war so long as they were not targeted directly (a proposition that becomes ludicrous when we realize, for example, that the "military target" rationale has resulted in plans for approximately sixty warheads to be directed at Moscow alone). More than twenty years ago, the Second Vatican Council concluded that "any act of war aimed indiscriminately at the destruction of entire cities or of extensive areas along with their populations is a crime against God and man itself. It merits unequivocal and unhesitating condemnation."[33] In their pastoral letter in 1983, the American Catholic bishops added that "this condemnation, in our judgment, applies even to the retaliatory use of weapons striking enemy cities after our own have already been struck."[34]

And it is difficult to imagine what kind of "good effect" could balance the "bad effect" of killing millions of people, possibly hundreds of millions, and maybe even threatening the continuation of life on Earth. Moreover, nuclear war would seem to fail each of the various *ad bellum* considerations listed previously. The U.S. Catholic bishops concluded that "our No to nuclear war must, in the end, be definitive and decisive."[35]

Corpse of a young boy incinerated in the atomic bombing of Nagasaki. Tens of thousands of noncombatants died at Hiroshima and Nagasaki. (United Nations)

This rejection of nuclear war is not limited to Catholic, or even Christian, teachings alone. Peace researcher Johan Galtung gave this impassioned plea for all religions and all ethical creeds to unite in opposition to worldwide holocaust:

Certain very particular human beings have arrogated to themselves the right to attack the very work of creation, of the Creator — as seen by the monotheistic religions. In terms of the occidental religions, based on the Old Testament, it suffices to read the very opening of the bible, Genesis, to see what this desertification means: it means cancelling most of the work that God did on the second day of creation (the plants), the fifth day of creation (the fishes and the birds), the sixth day of creation (animals and human beings). It would leave us with an inanimate earth, except for the microorganisms. However, God did not imagine a world filled with radioactive dust and ashes because he had, according to Genesis, a more forward looking perspective for his act of creation. These latter day anti-creators not only push the act of creation back, but also try to make their action irreversible, sealing it with radioactivity.

It is at this point that one might ask a question, using a mild understatement: *who gave them the right to do this?* Who gave them the right to engage in the enactment and preparation of such crimes, such extreme blasphemy against the Yahveh of the Jews, the God of the Christians and the Allah of the Muslims? Who gave them the right to cancel the whole setting within which the complex cycles of transmigration and rebirth, believed in by Hindus and Buddhists, go on? Who gave them the right to tamper with and destroy the very essence of that dialectic of nature that Daoism is about? Who gave them the right not only to plan genocide, but also to destroy the whole social setting with its structure and culture, however imperfect, that constitute the very essence of humanist faith? In short, who gave them the right to plan for such cosmic crimes, to set themselves up as anti-gods?

Answer: Nobody did. They came into this largely because they drifted into it, prisoners of the paradigms of pre-nuclear thinking, not quite seeing where they were heading. And yet if there were any justice in the world the whole universe should somehow rally against them, showing very clearly that on the one side there are the nuclear planning groups, West and East, plus some cockroaches and micro-organisms; and on the other side all the rest of us. All the rest of us, human beings with all our imperfections, of all genders and ages, classes, nations and races; of all religions and a-religions and anti-religions. It should make all of us rise together with animals and plants, with air and water, minerals and the sun and the moon and the stars against those who threaten our universe. More particularly, it should make all religions and religious officials stand up as one body against this supreme act of blasphemy, monotheistic, polytheistic, pan-theistic, anti-theistic and a-theistic creeds alike, plainly stating the truth that this is totally, utterly unacceptable.[36]

ETHICS AND NUCLEAR DETERRENCE

Although there is general (but by no means universal) agreement that nuclear war would be profoundly immoral, much debate surrounds the question of whether nuclear *deterrence* is equally unacceptable. The question is, can a country legitimately threaten something that would be immoral if carried out? Protestant ethicist Paul Ramsey uses this metaphor to describe the dilemma:

> Suppose that one Labor Day weekend no one was killed or maimed on the highways, and that the reason for the remarkable restraint placed on the recklessness of automobile drivers was that suddenly every one of them discovered that he was driving with a baby tied to his front bumper! That would be no way to regulate traffic even if it succeeds in regulating it perfectly, since such a system makes innocent human lives the direct object of attack and uses them as a mere means for restraining the drivers of automobiles.[37]

Ramsey's point, asserted by most ethical (as well as legal) teaching, is that moral error lies first in the intention to do wrong, and only later in the act itself. This is why intended wrong (such as homicide) is considered more serious than accidental wrong (such as manslaughter), and doing the right thing for the wrong reason is considered an ethical transgression. To rework Ramsey's metaphor, imag-

ine society decreeing that in the event of murder, punishment would befall not only the murderer, but all his friends and relatives as well. This would clearly be an unethical system, *even if it worked*.

Nonetheless, Ramsey ends up defending the legitimacy of nuclear deterrence, so long as it is limited to counterforce targeting. He admits that an adversary might be restrained by fears of collateral effects — the practical awareness that nuclear retaliation, even if ostensibly aimed at military targets only, would cause enormous destruction to the country at large. But so long as this is a by-product of the intended, discriminate targeting, apologists for nuclear deterrence deem it acceptable.

Others accept nuclear deterrence because they concede that sometimes it is necessary to commit an evil (threatening nuclear war) in order to prevent a greater one (war itself, and/or communist domination of the United States). On the other hand, the paradox remains that only by making credible threats can nuclear deterrence possibly work, and only by "meaning" these threats — that is, deploying weapons and planning strategies that are intended to be used — can they be effective. So, the effectiveness of deterrence varies directly with the likelihood that if one's bluff is called, nuclear war will follow.

The American Catholic bishops, in their 1983 letter, are unequivocal in rejecting any use of nuclear weapons:

> We do not perceive any situation in which the deliberate initiation of nuclear warfare, on however restricted a scale, can be morally justified. Non-nuclear attacks by another state must be resisted by other than nuclear means. Therefore, a serious moral obligation exists to develop non-nuclear defensive strategies as rapidly as possible.[38]

In spite of this sentiment, the bishops wind up with a strictly conditional *acceptance* of nuclear deterrence, echoing the judgment of Pope John Paul II, who said in a speech at Hiroshima that "in current conditions, deterrence based on balance, certainly not as an end in itself but as a step on the way toward a progressive disarmament, may still be judged morally acceptable."[39] As time goes on, however, ethicists may well ask whether deterrence is truly being used as a step toward disarmament or as an end in itself, and also as a means of justifying yet more weaponry (for example, "modernization" justified as a means of "enhancing deterrence"). Thus, the United Methodist Council of Bishops went further than their Catholic counterparts, and refused to condone nuclear deterrence:

> The moral case for nuclear deterrence, even as an interim ethic, has been undermined by unrelenting arms escalation. Deterrence no longer serves, if it ever did, as a strategy that facilitates disarmament. . . . Deterrence must no longer receive the churches' blessing, even as a temporary warrant for the maintenance of nuclear weapons.[40]

Supporters argue that nuclear weapons are moral and acceptable because they preserve the essential values of Western, Christian civilization. The conservative columnist George Will, for example, writes that "it is reckless to decree that any use, even any possession is necesarily a larger evil than the long night of centuries that would follow the extinguishing of Western cultural values by armed totalitarianism."[41] Moreover, they do not discount the possibility that limited nuclear wars could be fought, and even won . . . which, if true, would diminish the ethical onus of fighting such wars, and of preparing for them.

On the other hand, opponents maintain that nuclear weapons are themselves profoundly immoral, and that willingness to employ these weapons is simply unacceptable. In the words of diplomat/historian George Kennan,

> The readiness to use nuclear weapons against other human beings — against people whom we do not know, whom we have never seen, and whose guilt or innocence is not for us to establish — and in doing so to place in jeopardy the natural structure upon which all civilization rests, as though the safety and the perceived interests of our own generation were more important than everything that has ever taken place or could take place in civilization; this is nothing less than a presumption, a blasphemy, an indignity — an indignity of monstrous dimensions — offered to God![42]

A FINAL NOTE ON ETHICS AND RELIGION

It remains uncertain whether ethical and religious precepts and leaders will ultimately lead the way toward the abolition of war and the establishment of peace. Absolute prohibitions — against killing, for example — have rarely been followed with absolute fidelity. And given that human beings have so often used moral or religious certainty as a justification for repression, intolerance, and cruelty, there is some reason to be distrustful of any form of moral absolutism. On the other hand, at the stage of human history when the very survival of the human experiment hangs in the balance, total revulsion against organized violence (especially the use of nuclear weapons) may be an absolute necessity as well as a realistic hope.

Having completed our review of "negative peace" — that is, prospects and proposals for preventing war — let us bear in mind that in the long run, such prevention will be a shallow victory if it does not include the establishment of positive peace as well. Hence, in Part IV, we turn from war to peace, just as we hope that someday, the world will.

Study Questions

1. War involves killing. How is this reconciled with the widespread ethical imperative: Thou Shalt Not Kill?

2. Even in the declaration of war, governments are often at pains to make it appear that they are going to war reluctantly, and under provocation. Explain the significance of this, and give examples.

3. Distinguish between utilitarian and absolutist ethics.

4. Has religion been, on balance, supportive of war or critical, seeking to exercise restraint? Justify your answer.

5. Discuss the relationship between nuclear war and the Just War doctrine.

6. What are some of the major dilemmas in seeking to develop a moral argument in support of nuclear deterrence? What about conventional deterrence?

7. What are some arguments in favor of *jus in bello* restraints? Against?

8. Choose a recent war or armed conflict, and analyze it in terms of the usual *jus ad bellum* criteria.

9. To what extent is religious pacifism a recent phenomenon?

10. Describe, or develop, some nonreligious ethical precepts pertaining to war.

Suggestions for Further Reading

Paul Ramsey. 1968. *The Just War.* Scribner: New York.

Michael Walzer. *Just and Unjust Wars.* 1977. Basic Books: New York.

James Douglass. 1980. *Lightning East to West.* Sunburst Press: Portland, OR.

James Turner Johnson. 1984. *Can Modern War Be Just?* Yale University Press: New Haven, CT.

Robert L. Holmes. 1989. *On War and Morality.* Princeton University Press: Princeton, NJ.

Source Notes

1. Quoted in James Aho. 1981. *Religious Mythology and the Art of War.* Greenwood Press: Westport, CT.

2. Quoted in Bernard W. Henderson. 1927. *The Great War Between Athens and Sparta.* Macmillan: London.

3. Reinhold Niebuhr. 1932. *Moral Men and Immoral Society.* Scribner: New York.

4. Hans Morgenthau. 1960. *Politics Among Nations.* Knopf: New York.

5. Michael Walzer. *Just and Unjust Wars.* 1977. Basic Books: New York.

6. Ibid.

7. Deut. 7:2, King James Version.

8. *The Bhagavad Gita.* 1985. (E. Easwaran, trans.) Nilgiri Press: Petaluma, CA.

9. Rom. 13:4, King James Version.

10. Saint Bernard of Clairvaux. 1980. *Sermons.* Slatkine Reprints: Geneva, Switzerland.

11. D. Sayers (trans.). 1957. *The Song of Roland.* Penguin: Hammondsworth, Great Britain.

12. Quoted in Aho. *Religious.*

13. Quoted in Jean Descola. 1957. *The Conquistadors.* Viking: New York.

14. Roland Bainton. 1960. *Christian Attitudes Toward War and Peace.* Abingdon Press: Nashville, TN.

15. Blaise Pascal. 1954. *Pensées.* Dutton: New York.

16. Karl Marx. 1964. *On Religion.* Schocken: New York.

17. Quoted in Penny Lernoux. *Cry of the People.* Penguin: New York.

18. Saint Augustine. 1950. *The City of God.* Modern Library: New York.

19. Herodotus. 1964. *Selections.* University of Oklahoma Press: Norman.

20. Saint Augustine. *The City of God.*

21. Ibid.

22. Ibid.

23. Quoted in John C. Pratt (ed.). 1984. *Vietnam Voices.* Penguin: New York.

24. Reinhold Niebuhr. 1969. *Christianity and Power Politics.* Archon Books: Hamden, CT.

25. Lewis Mumford. 1970. *The Pentagon of Power.* Harcourt Brace Jovanovich: New York.

26. Quoted in Gregg Herken. 1964. *The Winning Weapon.* Random House: New York.

27. Quoted in D. Irving. 1963. *The Destruction of Dresden.* Holt, Rinehart & Winston: New York.

28. Karl von Clausewitz. 1976. *On War.* Princeton University Press: Princeton, NJ.

29. Matt. 5:38–46, King James Version.

30. Quoted in D. Attwater. 1947. *Modern Christian Revolutionaries.* Devin-Adair: New York.

31. John Howard Yoder. 1982. "Living the Disarmed Life: Christ's Strategy for Peace." In J. Wallis (ed.), *Waging Peace.* Harper & Row: New York.

32. Quoted in Jacques Ellul. 1970. *The Technological Society.* Knopf: New York.

33. Vatican Council, second. 1966. *The Vatican Council and Christian Unity.* Harper & Row: New York.

34. National Conference of Catholic Bishops on War and Peace. 1983. *The Challenge of Peace: God's Promise and Our Response.* United States Catholic Conference: Washington, DC.

35. Ibid.

36. Johan Galtung. 1984. *There Are Alternatives!* Dufour Editions: Chester Springs, PA.

37. Paul Ramsey. 1968. *The Just War.* Scribner: New York.

38. National Conference of Catholic Bishops. *The Challenge of Peace.*

39. Ibid.

40. United Methodist Council of Bishops. 1986. *In Defense of Creation: The Nuclear Crisis and a Just Peace.* Graded Press: Nashville, TN.

41. George F. Will. 1986. *The Morning After.* Free Press: New York.

42. George F. Kennan. 1982. "A Christian's View of the Arms Race." *Theology Today* 39, 2.

Young girls in Afghanistan obtaining pure water from a newly installed pump. Afghanistan has a history of severe seasonal drought, a potentially severe problem that can — and must — be corrected in a world of positive peace. (UNICEF/T. S. Satyan)

IV

Building "Positive Peace"

Introducing some sanity into the question of nuclear weapons and nuclear war is a necessary but insufficient condition for the establishment of peace. The same can be said about the control — even the abolition — of war itself: A world without war (nuclear or conventional) is certainly to be desired, but even this would not really produce a world at peace. In short, it is not enough to be against something, namely, war. We need to be in favor of something as well, and that something must be positive and affirmative, namely, peace. Of necessity, therefore, the positive peace toward which Peace Studies strives must be part of a broader, deeper effort to rethink the relationship of human beings to one another and to their shared planet. "As soon as the simple distinction between war and peace is abandoned," write two authorities on peace and contemporary social movements,

> thinking about peace necessarily becomes integrated into much broader currents of political thought and practice. Indeed, it hardly seems possible to think seriously about political life in the modern world without some understanding of the way the characteristic forms of contemporary violence challenge so many of our inherited assumptions about what it means to be human, and how

we ought to act towards each other. Peace is neither a technical policy problem, nor an easy utopian aspiration. It is a challenge both to prevailing structures of power and to our understanding of what it now means to engage in political life.[1]

The field of Peace Studies is unusual not only in its cross-disciplinary approach to the understanding and prevention of war, but also in its efforts to envision and help establish a desirable and attainable peace. But if war seems difficult to define — as evidenced by disagreement about the role of formal declarations, number of casualties, nature of the combatants, level of violence, and so on — peace can be even more elusive. Nonetheless, the outlines of a just and sustainable peace can be sketched, recognizing that in a world not only beset with violence, but also *reliant* on violence and on the structures of violence, efforts toward such a peace may be not only visionary, but also radical, even revolutionary.

As this world enters the final decade of the twentieth century, it is becoming increasingly clear that the East–West political and military competition is outdated and dangerous, and also irrelevant to the fundamental needs and pressing issues of human beings on the third planet from the sun. Cold Warriors seem more and more to be dinosaurs, formidable but dated, moving clumsily and even stupidly across a rapidly changing landscape. We must end such militarized competition, but we must not stop there. As we survey the issue of positive peace, it will become apparent that the East–West dispute that has so preoccupied the post–World War II world must give way to North–South issues: human rights, poverty, the environment, and fundamental principles of nonviolence in politics and in personal life.

As we have seen, much importance has been attributed to so-called Just War doctrine. The conditions for a "just peace" are no less strenuous, or important. Cultural items originating in the West often have spread to the Third World; this is true not only for superficial things like rock and roll or blue jeans, but also for important conceptual trends such as Marxism, nationalism, and Christianity. (To be sure, Third World phenomena are occasionally reflected in the West as well.) In any event, the antinuclear movement was unusual in being primarily limited to the West, evoking very little resonance in the Third World. For many in the West (at least, those who are relatively affluent and well educated), hope for a peaceful world is equated with nuclear disarmament, whereas for many in the Third World, it is reflected in aspirations for human rights, national autonomy, and economic well-being. For a growing number (including not only affluent Western peace activists but also large numbers of Third World inhabitants), it entails achieving a viable relationship with the natural environment as well. And peace, for such people, seems incomplete unless it also centers around these concerns. A dialectic is thus established: future war (something to avoid) and present peace, defined broadly (something to achieve).

Not that Third World people are indifferent to war as an immediate problem; far from it. Indeed, in many cases the problems of violence are so pressing and immediate that they leave virtually no political space for other concerns. In the Middle East, violent disputes between Arab and Israeli, and between fundamentalists and modernizers, make it difficult, and seemingly almost irrelevant, to question the adequacy or long-term future of traditional politics, the role of the state, and the like. Africa, beset with starvation, racial and ethnic hatreds, acute indebtedness, displaced persons, and drastic ecological destruction, seems unlikely to prioritize a concern about questions of global war. China and South America are overwhelmingly involved with issues of democracy, development, and population pressures. Once again, the social and political imagination of activists tends to be constrained by immediate, concrete, and pressing worries. This is not to say that the situation is hopeless; rather, it is heterogeneous. Third World concerns tend to differ from those of the northern industrialized countries, to be more clearly rooted in the problems of violence, both direct and structural.

Peace scholar Richard Falk has identified an alliterative five-dimensional program of peace goals for the 1990s,[2] to which we can add a sixth: (1) denuclearization (including less reliance on civilian nuclear power, (2) demilitarization, (3) depolarization (moderating the U.S.-Soviet geopolitical rivalry), (4) development, (5) democratization, and (6) deep respect for the natural environment.

This menu helps us confront a major dilemma concerning positive peace. Whereas the absence of war is relatively easy to define — but still susceptible to dispute — reasonable people are even more likely to disagree about what constitutes a desirable condition of positive peace. It reminds us of the "car–canine" problem noted previously: Imagine a dog that has spent years barking and running after cars. Then one day it catches one. What does it do with it? What would devotees of peace do with the world if they had the opportunity?

Before we begin, a quick note on intellectual boundaries and actual continuity: In many cases, the material in previous chapters was arbitrarily separated simply because of the necessities of producing a book. Thus, the discussion of personal motivations for war (Chapter 6) was intimately connected to the phenomenon of decision making (Chapter 10), although they occupied different chapters. Similarly, the material on international law (Chapter 17) in some ways belonged rightfully in our discussion of world government (Chapter 18). This dilemma — the necessity of taking up in a linear order matters that are recursive and interconnected — recurs with even greater force in Chapters 20–24. Social justice and human rights, for example, cannot adequately be addressed without considering environmental soundness (taken up in the succeeding chapter) or economic well-being (taken up in the one after that). And population growth, included in the chapter on planetary economics, could as well have been discussed in the chapter on the world environment. An understanding of our ecological crisis also requires awareness of personal as well as social and economic victimization; the many dimensions of economic "development" are only revealed by awareness of environmental despoliation, as well as the fundamental issues of human (as well as nonhuman) rights. But rather than complain about the difficulty of treating such intimately connected material in separate chapters, let us note the connectedness, and learn from it.

20

Human Rights

Injustice anywhere is an affront to justice everywhere.
Martin Luther King, Jr.

Like Mark Twain's celebrated remark about the weather, we can say that many people talk about human rights, but relatively few do anything about it. And yet, the issue is very serious: A great many human beings are denied some of the most basic human rights. Nearly one half the world's people are denied democratic freedoms and participation; about one third face severe restrictions on their right to own property; over one half of Asia and black Africa do not have access to safe water; jails are filled with political prisoners, many of them held without trial and victimized by torture; child labor is widespread; women are often deprived of the economic, social, and political rights that men take for granted; many workers are not only non-unionized, but prohibited even from forming unions; the right of conscientious objection to military service is not recognized in most countries; censorship is widespread; many millions of people are illiterate, chronically sick, without adequate shelter, and just plain hungry. Human rights, it seems, are more honored in the breach than the reality. Nonetheless, concern with such rights has, if anything, been growing in recent years. Real progress is being made, and more yet can be anticipated.

A BRIEF HISTORY OF HUMAN RIGHTS

It is tempting to claim that human rights are as old as the human species, but in truth, this is not so. Even if human rights themselves are God-given, inalienable, and fundamental, the conception of human rights as such — and respect for them — is relatively new. Individuals may possess rights and privileges, but these have traditionally been considered the province of society, to be bestowed or revoked by the larger unit (band, tribe, village, city, state) at will. In virtually all societies, for virtually all of human history, ultimate value derived from the social order, not the individual. Hence, an individual human being could not claim entitlement to very much, if anything, simply because he or she existed as a human being.

Human Rights in the Ancient World

In ancient Babylon, the Code of Hammurabi provided legal protections against torture and mutilation — but only for the aristocracy. In ancient Rome, certain rights were also guaranteed — for example, no condemnation or torture without a trial — but only for Roman citizens. Rights were conferred or withheld by the larger social unit, according to its judgment or whim, and not because certain basic rights were thought to be shared by all human beings.

Certain key phrases, such as "inherent dignity" and "personal worth," have popped up throughout history, later to be expanded into the concept of universal human rights. But these were few and far between. According to Judeo-Christian tradition, for example, Adam and Eve were created in God's image, and by implication, so were their descendants; this opens the door to the suggestion that each individual has a divine spark, a personal worth . . . and accordingly, certain rights simply by virtue of his or her humanity. And in fact, most of the early glimmerings of human rights are couched in religious terms. In Sophocles' *Antigone* (422 B.C.), the tyrant King Creon is told, "All your strength is weakness itself against the immortal, unrecorded law of God,"[1] and about this law, "Not of today or yesterday its force. It springs eternal: no

man knows its birth."[2] Presumably, no man (or woman) can deny its legitimacy either. But here, the focus was on family obligations — in Antigone's case, to bury her dead brother — which ultimately are owed to God. This is quite different from any obligations that society might owe to each person.

Ancient Judaism recognized some concepts that we might identify today as "human rights": limitations on slavery, protection of women from arbitrary assault, universal education, equitable distribution of land, and certain restrictions on conduct during war. Note, however, that these are not so much rights as *duties*, which are owed to God. And they applied, predominantly, only to male Israelites. The Koran, likewise, enjoined generosity toward the poor, sharing of property, and fair treatment of slaves, but once again, the emphasis is clear: Recipients have no *right* to such benefits; rather, the givers owe it as a *duty* to God, in return for which they increase their chances of gaining personal salvation. By the same token, the early Christians refused laws that, in their view, transgressed holy law, notably Roman idolatry, the bearing of arms, and the supposed divinity of rulers. It was never argued, however, that they had a human *right* to defy Rome, but rather that they had a religious obligation to do so.

The Enlightenment and the Western View

The Magna Carta represented a milestone of sorts, but not really in human rights; it was actually a set of baronial restrictions on the power of the English king in his dealings with the nobility, requiring due process and adherence to ancient custom. It was not until the Enlightenment, particularly in Europe, that the concept of universal human rights for all people first gained prominence. It had existed before, but primarily as a smattering of isolated thought rather than a consistent, widespread trend.

According to this new perspective, a body of human rights exists that are intrinsic and not provable; they stem ultimately from the natural order of things, not from the laws of society or from human logic. Hence, this approach derives human rights from what is called "natural law," with its implication that such rights are established by an authority even higher than that of governments. Heraclitus (about 500 B.C.) wrote that "all human laws are nourished by one, which is divine. For it governs as far as it will, and is sufficient for all, and more than enough."[3] And Aristotle, in his *Ethics*, advanced the notion that "of political justice, part is natural, part legal — natural, that which everywhere has the same force and does not exist by people's thinking this or that."[4] When the natural law viewpoint reappeared during the Enlightenment, it was used especially to counter claims that kings ruled with absolute authority and by divine right. Finally, by the seventeenth and eighteenth centuries, the concept crystalized that people possess inherent rights, and that it is society's job to *recognize* these preexisting rights, not to create them.

Select elements of traditional cultures support the concept of human rights as wide-ranging and universally derived. Confucius, for example, argued that "within the four seas all men are brothers,"[5] and Buddhists believe in "compassion for every living creature." The idea of human rights as currently understood, however, is largely a Western tradition, deriving especially from the work of John Locke and John Stuart Mill. Locke maintained that the fundamental human right was the right to property, the primary one being the right to the secure ownership of one's own body; civil and political rights flowed, in his view, from this. And Mill strove to identify a set of rights not covered by the state. Thus, there is some truth to the criticism that Western human rights advocates may occasionally be guilty of moral arrogance, seeking to export their own rather culture-bound ideas, especially their emphasis on civil/political freedom.

It should also be emphasized that Western political thought is not limited to individualism and human rights; rather, it coexists with respect for — and often, virtual worship of — the state. According to influential theorists such as Hegel and Herder, rights are enlarged and created for individuals only through the actions of the state. And for orthodox Marxists, value derives only from the social order; in Marxist analysis, individual rights do not exist unless they are explicitly granted by society. Although communist societies are supposedly designed to maximize the benefits of every person, the "rights" of each individual come to naught if they run counter to the greater good of society as a whole. Individuals can expect to receive benefits from a community only insofar as they participate in it, and further its goals. And as we shall see, even today — with ever-increasing agreement on the meaning and desirability of human rights — there continues to be substantial disagreement as to priorities.

Human Rights in the Twentieth Century

Internationally, there was very little concern with human rights until quite recently, after World War II. Despite the Enlightenment, despite capitalism's emphasis on individual property rights, and despite democracy's emphasis on individual political rights, as a practical matter, state sovereignty has long superceded human rights. When the worldwide state system was established in the mid-seventeenth century, governments agreed — ostensibly in the interest of world peace — not to concern themselves very much with how other governments treated their own citizens. Within its own boundaries, each state was supreme and could do as it wished.

Gradually, however, human rights law developed, initially out of concern for protecting persons during armed conflict. The Geneva Convention of 1864, for example, sought to establish standards for treatment of wounded soldiers and of prisoners. (It is ironic that war — the most inhumane of situations — should have led to the first organized recognition of shared humanitarian values.) The International Committee of the Red Cross is a notable nongovernmental organization long concerned with international human rights; it was organized by a group of Swiss citizens, involved in the 1864 Geneva Conference. The Red Cross remains active today, seeking especially to assure fair treatment of people during armed conflict; it has also participated in several modifications and revisions of the Geneva Convention, most recently in 1977.

Following World War I, there was widespread recognition that one cause of that conflict had been

Red Cross personnel providing aid to battlefield casualties during World War II. (Red Cross)

the denial of national rights within large empires such as Austria's. Hence, human rights received explicit attention from the League of Nations, which emphasized that the rights of minorities must be respected by larger federal governments. Labor rights — the right to organize and to decent working conditions and wages, and restrictions on child labor — were the focus of the International Labor Organization, which later functioned within the United Nations.* Opposition to slavery catalyzed numerous early human rights organizations, such as the Anti-Slavery League. (Most Americans do not realize that in many countries, slavery was only abolished during the 1950s; some claim that it is still being practiced today, in Mauritania and Pakistan.)

Organized, worldwide concern for human rights did not really coalesce until after World War II, perhaps in part as a reaction to the devastating

denials of rights that occurred in association with that conflict. In the aftermath of the Nazi Holocaust most especially, the world's conscience was finally activated — partly out of regret for those who had suffered, and partly, too, out of enlightened self-interest. Martin Niemoeller put it memorably:

> First they came for the Jews and I did not speak out — because I was not a Jew. Then they came for the communists and I did not speak out — because I was not a communist. Then they came for the trade unionists and I did not speak out — because I was not a trade unionist. Then they came for me — and there was no one left to speak out for me.[6]†

In recent decades, the world's people have begun to speak out for themselves and for human rights of every sort. Before we review some of the legal protections, conventions, and treaties that have

---

*And also won a Nobel Peace Prize.

†In fact, Pastor Niemoeller himself became a victim of the Nazis.

resulted, let us consider the question of what is meant by human rights, and how they have come to be asserted.

THE POLITICAL PHILOSOPHY OF HUMAN RIGHTS

Human rights implies a new way of viewing the relationship of governments and their peoples, whereby governance is intended to enhance the dignity of human beings, not exploit them. With this in mind, let us examine three major political philosophies of human rights, each of which is divisible into two branches.

Liberalism

In traditional liberal thought, human rights exist not only because of their contribution to human dignity, but also because human beings, themselves, naturally possess such rights. "The object of any obligation," wrote the philosopher Simone Weil,

> in the realm of human affairs, is always the human being as such. There exists an obligation towards every human being for the sole reason that he or she is a human being, without any other condition requiring to be fulfilled, and even without any recognition of such obligation on the part of the individual concerned.[7]

In Jefferson's phrase, people have certain "inalienable rights" that may not be denied. The liberal view of human rights thus corresponds to the "natural law" perspective. One of the great classical liberals, John Locke, argued that civil law, to be valid, must be tested against this "natural law," which is the ultimate arbiter of justice. And when the framers of the Declaration of Independence complained of a "long train of abuses and usurpations" on the part of King George III, it was precisely natural law that they believed was being abused and usurped.

Another liberal theory of human rights derives from "utilitarianism," especially the works of John Stuart Mill and Jeremy Bentham. The idea here is that society should value whatever is utilitarian, or useful, in maximizing human happiness and free-

dom. The best-known motto of utilitarianism is "the greatest good for the greatest number," although individual freedom and equality are recognized as well, so as to prevent tyranny by the majority. Social betterment is to be achieved through equality and maximum personal liberty.

Both the natural law and utilitarian approaches are aspects of "classical liberalism," and the United States is a good example of classical liberalism in action. The social democracies, such as Sweden, are also constructed along liberal lines, but with a stronger dose of egalitarianism. Thus, while the classical liberalism of the United States stresses equal civil and political rights, with freedom of socioeconomic competition, egalitarian liberalism such as Sweden's (and to a lesser extent, Canada's and Australia's), places greater emphasis on a right to minimum socioeconomic standards as well.

Conservatism

Traditional conservatism is rarely articulated today with respect to human rights, because it is in large part a philosophy of unequal rights and privileges, and as such, difficult to defend in an avowedly egalitarian age. But the unspoken tenets of conservatism are nonetheless influential in actual practice. Classical conservatism can be said to have originated with Plato, who argued in *The Republic* that all people are not equal, and that the best form of government is therefore not democracy, but rule by a philosopher–king. This belief in unequal rights underpins many right-wing governments, from the "classical conservatism" of the military juntas that ruled Brazil and Greece, as well as the various U.S.-sponsored Central American governments (Guatemala, Honduras, Panama), to the neo-fascist dictatorships that arose in Chile and Paraguay, where rights were reserved only for the most powerful.*

---

*As of this writing, Chilean dictator Pinochet has finally stepped down after losing a binding referendum; General Alfredo Stroessner, long-time Paraguayan military dictator, was deposed in a coup in 1989, and, although his successors promise democratic elections, the prospects are dim.

Group-Oriented Philosophies

Finally, there is a third branch of human rights philosophy, which, for want of a better term, might be called "group-oriented." Like liberalism and conservatism, it can be subdivided into two branches, Marxist and nationalist. For Karl Marx, individuals were not independent actors; rather, they were controlled by economic forces, pawns in a relentless class struggle. In the Marxist view, the liberal emphasis on individual rights is therefore misplaced, a bourgeois luxury, form without substance. Instead, rights are conferred by society, and they should belong exclusively to the proletariat (the working class). Such an approach leads automatically to an embrace of socioeconomic rights and material equality, with a downplaying of civil/political rights. Thus, in Marxist societies, freedom of speech and opinion are permitted insofar as they do not conflict with the stated goals of group advancement and welfare. The state, and not the working class, typically becomes paramount.

In the past, some sporadic efforts have been made to link the Marxist emphasis on socioeconomic rights with the classical liberal concern for personal freedom, notably, the attempt to establish "socialism with a human face" in Czechoslovakia in 1968 (an effort at socialist liberalism that was crushed by Soviet tanks). However, in the late 1980s, *glasnost* (political and intellectual openness) and *perestroika* (economic restructuring) have led to substantial democratic reforms as well as movement toward a market economy in the U.S.S.R. and Eastern Europe, and China as well (the Soviet Union has moved further with respect to civil/political rights, and China in economic freedoms).*

The second version of group-oriented human rights has a leftist flavor, but is not, strictly speaking, Marxist. It originates instead in the experience of national liberation movements, and places special emphasis on the right to national self-determination and economic development, from which all other rights are then derived. Believers in the human right to national self-determination downplay the individual as well as the social class, although they remain committed to equal rights. Emphasis instead is on the rights of a national grouping. This approach lay behind the "Universal Declaration of the Rights of Peoples," which grew out of a meeting of highly regarded, nongovernmental Third World spokespersons in 1976. The first three articles in this thirty-article document read as follows:

1. Every people has the right to existence.
2. Every people has the right to the respect of its national and cultural identity.
3. Every people has the right to retain peaceful possession of its territory and to return to it if it is expelled.

Other enumerated rights include the right of "every people" to break free from colonial, foreign, or racist domination; to control its own natural wealth and resources; to choose its own economic, social, and political system; and to speak its own language. The emphasis on "people's rights" clearly distinguishes this approach from the Western focus on "individual rights."

Nationalist group-oriented regimes are found in many Third World states, such as Algeria and Zimbabwe, which are often leftist, but rarely communist. Tanzanian president Julius Nyerere was one of the most articulate spokespersons for the nationalist group-oriented point of view:

> For what do we mean when we talk of freedom? First, there is national freedom; that is, the ability of the citizens of Tanzania to determine their own future, and to govern themselves without interference from non-Tanzanians. Second, there is freedom from hunger, disease, and poverty. And third, there is personal freedom for the individual; that is, his right to live in dignity and equality with all others, his right to freedom of speech.[8]

---

*Efforts — spearheaded by students — to achieve greater civil/political rights in China precipitated a violent crackdown by the military in June, 1989. Nonetheless, China continues to pursue a vigorous policy of economic liberalization, notably the encouragement of free market reforms.

The difference between this viewpoint and the others (classical and egalitarian liberal, classical and neo-fascist conservative, Marxist group-oriented) is more one of emphasis than of absolutes. But the "rights" associated with individual competition — so dear to the liberal conception of human rights — are devalued. "The important thing for us," explains Nyerere, "is the extent to which we succeed in preventing the exploitation of one man by another, and in spreading the concept of working together cooperatively for the common good instead of competitively for individual private gain."[9]

Choosing the Appropriate Philosophy

Not surprisingly, there is substantial debate over which human rights model is most appropriate for any given country. Both major contending systems — capitalism based on classical liberal principles and Marxism based on a particular group-oriented philosophy — contain within themselves deep structures of oppression. Thus, although Marxism explicitly claims that the state will eventually disappear, the fact remains that Marxist state structures have shown no tendency to do so; in fact, they have become notably oppressive in their own right. Even more than liberal capitalist states, Marxist governments have tended to be super-states, abusing power via ossified bureaucratic structures that have been generally insensitive to personal civil and political liberties. (It should also be pointed out, however, that liberal capitalist democracies have been persistently antagonistic toward the revolutionary Marxist states; this, in turn, has lent some credibility to the latter's claim that state power must be maintained to guard against counterrevolution.)

On the other hand, the supposedly minimal state envisioned by liberal philosophers and established especially in northern Europe and North America, has fared scarcely, if at all, better. These states primarily were concerned with establishing a balance between the various political powers of the government, and between governments and the people. Social and economic "rights" were treated as secondary, as capitalist/democratic societies relied on market mechanisms and an ethos of individual competition. Only begrudgingly have the capitalist/democratic states recognized a social responsibility toward their populace. As Richard Falk suggests,

> Built into the capitalist ethos is an acceptance of inequality, exploitation, and hierarchy, as well as the continuous struggle for power within and among states, necessitating a police system within the state and a war system within the global realm, realities consistent with the maintenance of oppressive structures at all levels of social intercourse.[10]

On balance, capitalist democracies give insufficient attention to socioeconomic rights, while socialist governments take inadequate account of civil/political ones. Recent evidence suggests that economic development is more rapid under capitalism; but relatively little benefit from such development actually reaches the poorest citizens (see Chapter 22). At the same time, some evidence indicates that — with the exception of a few stubborn Stalinist-style diehard governments, such as in North Korea — socialist states are recognizing the need to be more respectful of civil/political rights. Even as these words are being written (in late 1989), democracy has begun blooming in Poland and Hungary, with movement toward dramatic political reforms in East Germany and Czechoslovakia as well. It seems unlikely, however, that Eastern Europe, any more than any other world region, will be politically homogeneous. Perhaps, the optimum system differs for different societies, depending on their historical experience and current situation. Ultimately, however, the goal remains to cultivate (or if need be, create) a nonoppressive system, maximally supportive of human dignity and human rights.

WHAT ARE HUMAN RIGHTS?

After doing much to spark the American Revolution, Thomas Paine went to France at the time of the French Revolution. There, he is said to have had the following conversation with Benjamin Franklin, U.S. ambassador to France. "Wherever liberty is," said Franklin, "there is my country." To which Paine replied, "Wherever liberty is *not*, there is mine." Despite their seeming disagreement, Paine and Franklin were united in espousing the same basic view of human rights, the one that is most readily identified by citizens of the United States even today: personal liberty.

Personal Liberty Versus Socioeconomic Rights

Even personal liberty is not unidimensional. It involves many things, notably, physical freedom from torture, unjust imprisonment, and execution, as well as intellectual freedom to speak, write, and worship, and various political freedoms, including the right to peaceful assembly, to freedom of association, and to vote by secret ballot. Numerous other human rights have also been identified and proposed, including what have been called "socioeconomic rights," such as the right to work and to decent housing, education, medical care, and food. To some extent, the United States and the rest of the First World (developed capitalist states) associate human rights with the first category, whereas the Second World (communist states) and Third World (impoverished undeveloped or "developing" states) give greater weight to the second. Those who are wealthy and privileged characteristically favor maximum freedom (especially, freedom of economic competition) and a minimal role for government, which, at least in the United States, often leads in turn to opposition to the "welfare state" or resistance to affirmative action plans. Those lacking in wealth and power are typically more in need of laws and specified rights, to be assured by society. Hence, Western governments tend to describe socioeconomic rights as not really "human rights" at all, but rather, goals or aspirations for society.

As we shall see, human rights can be characterized in many ways, although a global consensus has been developing that incorporates not only the traditional American concern with political liberty, but also the Second and Third World concern with socioeconomic rights, as well as additional values that are difficult to pigeonhole. Many other rights are also asserted — states' rights, consumer rights — but to suggest that something is a "human right" is

Child receiving a meal at a refugee camp in Jordan. Third World peoples tend to emphasize socioeconomic rights — such as a right to food — as being no less important than such civil–political rights as freedom of expression or the right to vote. (United Nations / J. Isaac)

to claim something particularly fundamental and weighty, and should not be done lightly.

Cyrus Vance, secretary of state during the Carter administration, gave the following useful categorization of human rights from the U.S. perspective:

First, there is the right to be free from governmental violation of the integrity of the person. Such violations include torture; cruel, inhuman, or degrading treatment or punishment; and arbitrary arrest or imprisonment. And they include denial of fair public trial and invasion of the home. Second, there is the right to the fulfillment of such vital needs as food, shelter, health care, and education. We recognize that the fulfillment of this right will depend, in part, upon the stage of a nation's economic development. But we also know that this right can be violated by a government's action or inaction — for example through corrupt official processes which divert resources to an elite at the expense of the needy or through indifference to the plight of the poor. Third, there is the right to enjoy civil and political liberties: freedom of thought, of religion, of assembly; freedom of speech; freedom of movement both within and outside one's own country; freedom to take part in government.[11]

This listing, although useful and authoritative, omits certain other categories of rights that many people consider important, such as the right to security from mass destruction or to a safe natural environment. One simple categorization parallels the famous French motto, "liberty, equality, fraternity": (1) political and intellectual rights, (2) economic and social rights, and (3) the right to peace and to a safe natural environment. Of these, the first (liberty) is the most widely accepted; the second (equality) remains controversial, especially in the United States; and the third (fraternity) is the most unsettled — and for some, unsettling — of all.

Citizens of the United States need to recognize the importance that large numbers of people, especially in the Second and Third Worlds, attribute to socioeconomic rights. In the words of Leopold Senghor, former president of Senegal, "human rights begin with breakfast."[12] Without such an awareness, relatively well-off Westerners too quickly sneer at the poor "rights" records of other countries, oblivious to their own shortcomings in the eyes of others. In addition, once we recognize the validity of socioeconomic rights, then governments such as Libya under Qaddafi or Cuba under Castro — which to many in the West are failures in the civil/political sphere because of their lack of representative government, widespread censorship, and torture and abuse of political prisoners — can be recognized as effective, even admirable, in other domains, such as public health or literacy. (This is not to claim that success in some dimensions of human rights cancels outrages in another; rather, it helps permit a more balanced perception of systems that might otherwise seem unidimensionally evil, and whose high level of domestic acceptance would otherwise be difficult for Americans to understand.) Thus, in an effort to identify basic human rights, Richard Falk has proposed the following:

1. *Basic human needs:* the rights of individuals and groups to food, housing, health, and education; the duty of governments to satisfy these rights, taking into account resource constraints and natural disasters (e.g., drought, flood);

2. *Basic decencies:* the rights of individuals and groups to be protected against genocide, torture, arbitrary arrest, detention, and execution, or their threat; the duty of peoples and governments and their officials to establish an atmosphere wherein these rights can be securely realized, including the protection of the society against para-governmental violence of various kinds (e.g., "death squads"), taking into account constraints on governmental capabilities and the threats and tactics relied upon by enemies of the state;

3. *Participatory rights:* the rights of individuals and groups to participate in the processes that control their lives, including choice of political leadership, of job, of place of residence, or cultural activity and orientation; the duty of peoples and governments to uphold these rights in ways that provide individuals and groups with opportunities to lead meaningful lives, including the freedom to participate in procedures for the shaping and execution of norms;

4. *Security rights:* the rights of individuals and groups (including those of unborn generations) to be reasonably secure about their prospects of minimal physical well-being and survival; the duty of governments and peoples to uphold this right by working to achieve sustainable forms of national and ecological security;

5. *Humane governance:* the rights of individuals and groups to live in societies and a world that realizes the rights depicted in 1–4; the duty of individuals, groups, governments, and institutions to work toward this end.[13]

The Rights of Categories of People

We have thus far focused on the various rights themselves (civil, political, social, economic, and so on), rather than on the categories of people in whom such rights are supposed to inhere. But these categories are in many cases so important that, by themselves, they constitute major areas of concern. Women's rights is one example. Women comprise more than 50 percent of the world's population, and yet they are without doubt an oppressed group. For centuries, women have suffered from patriarchal social structures that devalue their personhood and deny many of their basic human rights. This includes a diverse array of abuses, such as footbinding in precommunist China, the forced seclusion and isolation of women in certain modern-day Hindu and Moslem societies, sexual mutilation as currently practiced on millions of young women in several African societies, polygamy, restricted or nonexistent choice as to marriage, and—even in ostensibly "liberated" societies such as those of the United States and Great Britain—greatly restricted economic and professional opportunities along with underrepresentation in political life.

Other groups also deserve attention. There are about 200 million indigenous people worldwide, representing national majorities in such states as Guatemala and Bolivia, and small minorities in such states as Brazil, Australia, and the United States. Regardless of their numbers, indigenous people are generally in dire straits, sometimes—as in Guatemala or Brazil—being subjected to outright genocide. In other cases, they are severely maltreated, and/or they enjoy dramatically fewer opportunities and privileges than their nonnative counterparts. Australian aborigines are the most imprisoned people on Earth, with an incarceration rate sixteen times that of the Caucasian population; the life expectancy of Mayan Indians in Guatemala is eleven years shorter than that of the nonindigenous population; the average per capita income of native Americans is one half that of the rest of the U.S. population; large dams have devastated the homelands of indigenous peoples in Canada, Brazil, Norway, the Philippines, and India, depriving them of an arguably crucial human right: to live in their ancestral homelands. And this is but a partial list.

Other groups can also be identified as having particular human rights claims and vulnerabilities: the mentally ill, children, the homeless, racial minorities, the handicapped, convicts, unskilled

Andean woman and child in Southern Peru. Indigenous people such as these are typically very poor and often subjected to numerous violations of their human rights, including forced relocation and even genocide. (Tim Johnson)

workers, migrant laborers, refugees, political dissidents, the elderly, and so on. Ideally, human rights such as civil freedoms, economic opportunity, protection from mass destruction, and the right to a safe and clean environment will be equally shared by all people. In practice, these rights must often be defended most vigilantly for those groups that have thus far been the most victimized.

Some Areas of Controversy

In many cases, the distinctions between, say, civil/political rights and socioeconomic ones may be arbitrary. The right to free speech, to vote, or to be free from torture (examples of the former) are clearly different than the right to eat or to work (examples of the latter). But what about the right to form a trade union—is that civil/political or socioeconomic? And what about the right to an education? As we shall see, human rights and "development" policy frequently intersect in the realm of "basic human needs" (see Chapter 22). The list is endless, and yet, this does not mean that the issue of rights is meaningless, or unimportant. Nor does it mean that real and meaningful progress cannot be made.

It seems unavoidable that various rights will conflict. In a famous opinion, U.S. Supreme Court justice Oliver Wendell Holmes concluded that the right to free speech did not extend to yelling "Fire" in a crowded theater. The "right" to a drug-free environment may conflict with the "rights" to privacy, just as the "right" of Third World people to healthy babies has already been found to conflict with the "right" of the Nestlé company to market substandard infant formula. In Islamic states, women's "rights" are often subordinated to the "rights" of people to practice the religion of their choice. A woman's "right" to control her own body, including an abortion if she desires, runs contrary to a fetus's "right" to life; the "right" of religious freedom can conflict with a child's "right" to necessary medical care, as when fundamentalist parents refuse life-saving treatment for their child; the public's "right" to safe air travel appears to have triumphed over individual "rights" not to be searched without a warrant; and the list goes on.

There are other contentious issues as well, such as which human rights, if any, should have priority. As we have seen, poor countries and Marxists typically argue for the primacy of socioeconomic rights, whereas rich countries claim that civil/political rights are fundamental. A case can be made in either direction: A well-educated, well-fed populace is best-equipped, perhaps, to take part in meaningful elections. Thus, many Third World leaders maintain that their people are not "yet" ready for participatory democracy. On the other hand, perhaps civil and political liberties are a prerequisite to establishing a viable economy and social system. In addition, as we have seen, countries with a painful experience of colonial domination are likely to espouse a doctrine of group-oriented rights.

However they are sliced, many human rights are essentially claims against the authority of governments. As such, they are freedoms *from* — guarantees that governments will refrain from behaving badly toward their own people. These can be distinguished from freedoms *to* — the asserted obligations of society to help its members to achieve a better life. This distinction somewhat parallels the one between negative and positive peace — between those rights asserted *against* governments (no war, no intrusions into personal freedom) and those expected *of* them (establish positive peace, provide for basic human needs). In most cases, the first category (negative rights) seems easier for governments to achieve; certain states may simply lack the resources to make substantial improvements in socioeconomic conditions, but they all can stop torturing, murdering, and otherwise oppressing their people.

Although human rights constitute a diverse and sometimes confusing array of causes, from peace, women's rights, environmental protection, and penal reform, to national independence, they share a common humanizing focus, placing individuals at the center of public policy. "The goal of human rights advocacy," writes one authority, "is to insist that the power, security, and economic well-being of states and their ruling elites be accompanied by concern for the average citizen and/or the least well-off in political and economic terms."[14]

THE LEGAL STATUS OF HUMAN RIGHTS

Explicit statements of human rights are most clearly associated with various international agreements, nearly all of which have been developed since the Second World War, and which derive their legal status from international law (see Chapter 17).

UN-Related Agreements

In assessing the legal status of human rights, the UN Charter represents a useful starting point. Its major reference to human rights appears in Article 55:

> With a view to the creation of conditions of stability and well-being which are necessary for peaceful and

friendly relations among nations based on respect for the principle of equal rights and self-determination of peoples, the United Nations shall promote: a. higher standards of living, full employment, and conditions of economic and social progress and development; b. solutions of international economic, social, health, and related problems, and international cultural and educational cooperation; and c. universal respect for, and observance of, human rights and fundamental freedoms for all without distinction as to race, sex, language, or religion.

But if the UN Charter serves as a constitution, it lacks a bill of rights, specifying which human rights are to be "respected" and "observed." This was accomplished largely by the UN-sponsored Universal Declaration of Human Rights (UDHR), passed unanimously in 1948. Thus, after the UN Charter endorsed human rights, the Universal Declaration went ahead and enumerated them. The United States was a major contributor to the UDHR; much of its impetus came from Eleanor Roosevelt, widow of the late U.S. president. The UDHR consists of thirty articles, of which the first twenty-one are primarily civil/political, prohibiting torture and arbitrary arrest, and guaranteeing freedom of assembly, religion, speech, emigration, and even the right to vote by secret ballot. The remaining articles are concerned with socioeconomic and cultural rights, including the right to work, to an "adequate" standard of living, to an education, and to some form of social security, and even specifying the right to vacations with pay.

The Universal Declaration is not technically binding in the sense of an international treaty; it is a recommendation only, and makes no provisions for enforcement. Nonetheless, it has had substantial impact on thinking worldwide. The UDHR is widely respected, and has legitimated concern with human rights; it has even been incorporated into many national constitutions. To some degree, it has become part of customary international law; accordingly, many judicial scholars argue that it has the literal force of law, although it is often violated. (It should be noted that customary law is more universal and more durable than treaty law.)

Numerous worldwide legal instruments have built upon the Charter and the UDHR, including an array of covenants, conventions, treaties, and declarations, of diverse legal meaning, but all helping to define further the concept of human rights. Of these, the most important are the 1948 Convention on the Prevention and Punishment of the Crime of Genocide (only belatedly ratified by the United States), and the 1965 International Convention on the Elimination of All Forms of Racial Discrimination (which the United States has not ratified). There have also been two UN human rights covenants — the International Covenant on Civil and Political Rights, and the International Covenant on Economic, Social, and Cultural Rights — signed in 1966, and entered into force in 1977, when they were ratified by a sufficient number of national governments (but again, not by the United States). There have also been two 1977 Geneva Protocols on Armed Conflict, both of them controversial and not universally in force, in addition to various instruments concerned with specified rights, such as those of refugees and children, as well as denunciations of apartheid and numerous declarations that are less formal in character. Meetings such as the UN World Conference on Women, held in Nairobi, Kenya, in 1985, also help spotlight the question of women's rights.

People dispute precisely what obligations member states undertake when, in the UN Charter, they agree to "promote universal respect for and observance" of human rights. Nonetheless, an underlying consensus has emerged. The accepted phrase is that governments have no business engaging in a "consistent pattern of gross violations of human rights." Thus, isolated incidents are unlikely to generate worldwide outrage. By contrast, "gross violations" — that is, serious, recurring acts — merit condemnation and, ultimately, such actions as censure, economic boycott, and possibly even military intervention. Abuses of this sort could include widespread torture, mass arrests and imprisonment without trial, genocide, and vicious policies of racial segregation and debasement, such as apartheid in the Republic of South Africa.

Mrs. Eleanor Roosevelt holding an English-language copy of the Universal Declaration of Human Rights.
(United Nations)

Regional Approaches

Several regional approaches to human rights also are noteworthy. The most effective of these operates in Western Europe, where the European Court of Human Rights (located in Strasbourg, France) has rendered authoritative decisions based on the European Convention on Human Rights, which entered into legal force in 1953. Eighteen European states currently allow this supranational court to rule on petitions brought by individual citizens against the states themselves. These cases are largely concerned with civil/political rights, and are notable in that individuals — even those who are currently in prison — can bring their grievances directly to be heard. Prison authorities, for example, are prohibited from blocking or censoring their correspondence in any way. In all cases so far, the Western European countries have abided by the judgments of the European Court. Although these states are all democracies, it is also worth pointing out that they, too, have been found guilty of violating human rights on occasion (for example, Britain torturing detainees in Northern Ireland, France bombing an antinuclear Greenpeace protest boat). Unfortunately, no other world region enjoys international judicial protection of human rights of the sort currently operating in Western Europe.

In the Western Hemisphere, an Inter-American Commission for Human Rights has been established, whose legal basis is found in the human rights provisions of the Organization of American States. The Inter-American Commission has had limited success in some instances, but Latin America has also been rife with human rights abuses, especially with respect to treatment of indigenous Indian peoples. To complicate matters, Latin American states operate under two conflicting traditions:

a long history of democracy, in many cases beginning with their own independence in the early nineteenth century, but also national policy that often favors wealthy industrialists, the land-owning aristocracy, the military, and conservative branches of the clergy.*

Both the Organization of African States and the Arab League have human rights legal machinery in place (the OAU's African Charter on Individual and Peoples Rights, as of 1987, and the Arab League's Permanent Arab Commission on Human Rights, which began in 1968). However, the African Charter is relatively weak, especially on the issue of individual liberties, and the Arab Commission is similarly unassertive on most sensitive issues involving criticism of the internal policies of member states. Significantly, the most active human rights work by these groups involves opposition to human rights abuses by nonmember states: South African apartheid, and the treatment of Palestinians within the Israeli-occupied West Bank and Gaza, respectively.

The Helsinki Accord

Finally, one of the more influential—and to some extent, surprising—human rights instruments has been the Helsinki Accord, signed at the conclusion of the Conference on Security and Cooperation in Europe, in 1975. Although it is, strictly speaking, a diplomatic agreement rather than law, it has had important human rights consequences, especially in the Soviet Union and Eastern Europe. The first two parts of the accord are concerned with political and economic issues, notably affirming the post–World War II geopolitical boundaries of Europe.

The Marxist states were especially eager for this, wanting particularly to establish the legitimacy of divided Germany, of current Polish borders, and so on. In return, they agreed to the accord's third "basket," by which the thirty-five signatory states promised the following: to permit the freer flow of ideas across national boundaries, to facilitate the reuniting of families separated by East–West borders, and to work on behalf of human rights for their own citizens. Specifically acknowledged was "the universal significance of human rights and fundamental freedoms." Participating states vowed to respect "freedom of thought, conscience, religion or belief," and to facilitate the "effective exercise of civil, political, economic, social, cultural and other rights and freedoms, all of which derive from the inherent dignity of the human person and are essential for his free and full development." Progress toward these ends is evaluated in regularly scheduled international review conferences, at which these phrases used to be brandished against the Soviet Union and its client states in Eastern Europe.

In addition, a variety of nongovernmental organizations, under the rubric of "Helsinki Watch," have been established to monitor the status of and trends in human rights within the signatory states, especially the relatively repressive regimes of the East. Whereas some of these groups were themselves repressed, such as the Czech-based "Charter 77," there can be no doubt that they have succeeded in discomfiting certain regimes by publicizing human rights abuses. Without the legitimacy afforded to human rights activists by instruments such as the Helsinki Accord, states clearly would feel less constrained in their human rights abuses.

In short, while it is easy to criticize the existing human rights structure worldwide—especially because it lacks enforcement capability—we must recognize the importance of public opinion and governmental self-consciousness with respect to their behavior. Actions once seen as private—those pertaining to domestic affairs—are increasingly recognized as being of general, transnational interest. Furthermore, in a world with ever-improving communication and transportation, even

---

*An important thrust of Latin American catholicism is "liberation theology," which seeks to align the church with the aspirations of the underprivileged. It should be emphasized, however, that this is a relatively recent development, one that is in the minority and very much embattled, both within the church hierarchy and by right-wing Latin American governments and the military.

Biography

Aryeh Neier

Aryeh Neier's first name means "lion" in Hebrew, and he has indeed been a fierce defender of civil liberties and human rights. He was born in Berlin in 1937; his family subsequently emigrated to the United States where he attended Cornell University. Aryeh Neier served from 1963 until 1978 with the American Civil Liberties Union (ACLU), the last eight years as its national executive director. During that time, he took strong stands against police abuse, in favor of the separation of church and state, in opposition to the harassment of antiwar protestors (including a prominent case involving Dr. Benjamin Spock), and at all times in favor of civil liberties. Under Neier's leadership, the ACLU also defended the rights of the Ku Klux Klan and American Nazi party to hold gatherings, explaining that "the freedom denied them today could be denied to us tomorrow." In part because of Mr. Neier's energetic efforts, the ACLU vigorously opposed the death penalty and supported affirmative action as well as urging the availability of abortion on demand.

After leaving the ACLU, Aryeh Neier served for several years as Director of the New York Institute for the Humanities, before becoming Executive Director of Human Rights Watch, an umbrella organization that acts as a watchdog for human rights violations around the world. (Mr. Neier points out, however, that "being a watchdog is sitting back and waiting for some intruder to violate someone's civil liberties. We have to be a good deal of a hounddog.") Human Rights Watch includes the following organizations: Africa Watch, Americas Watch, Asia Watch, Helsinki Watch, and Middle East Watch. It is nonpartisan and has achieved an excellent reputation for its determined efforts in defense of individual human rights, regardless of whether the violating governments are left- or right-wing oriented. Mr. Neier has written several books, including *Only Judgment* and *Defending My Enemy*, and has authored more than 300 articles, including pieces in major magazines and newspapers.

---

speech-making and rhetoric, to some extent, constitutes action. Consciousness is raised, and even brutal, repressive governments such as South Africa have shown themselves sensitive to their image in the world community. Human rights commissions and reports, as well as private organizations and determined individuals, even when lacking strict implementation authority, can be effective in shining the light of publicity into dark, dank, evil places . . . and when this happens, vile perpetrators (and their practices) are likely to scurry away.

At the same time, caution is in order. As we have noted previously, states jealously guard their sovereignty, and are usually at pains to protect their freedom of action when it comes to human rights.

Thus, in Article 12 of the 1966 International Covenant on Civil and Political Rights, we learn that "the above-mentioned rights shall not be subject to any restrictions except those which are provided by law, are necessary to protect national security, public order . . . public health or morals of the rights and freedoms of others." With such immense loopholes, states keep themselves legally unfettered in cases where human rights violations are consistent with rigorously defended national policy. And frequently, international treaties specify that human rights may in fact be violated under certain circumstances, namely an "emergency threatening the life of the nation." Let us therefore turn to the question of state authority versus human rights.

HUMAN RIGHTS AND THE STATE

As of the late 1980s, some halting progress had been made as national courts began ruling to enforce international norms with respect to human rights. For example, in a celebrated legal case, *Filartiga v. Pena*, a U.S. court ruled in 1980 that politically inspired torture and murder were so clearly prohibited by international agreements on human rights that the United States had jurisdiction to prosecute a Paraguayan national for events occurring within Paraguay. As controversial as this and other cases have been, there is nothing new about governments criticizing human rights abuses in other states. Governments have long found it quite easy to complain loudly about the actions of other governments — especially those with which they are not allied — while turning a blind eye to their own misbehavior. The real crunch between states and human rights concerns the degree to which a state is willing to forgo part of its own sovereignty and permit its own human rights practices to be the subject of international scrutiny, judgment, and influence . . . if not control.

Third World Resistance to Western Intervention

Although Western nationals often assume that Third World people would necessarily applaud their actions on behalf of worldwide human rights, sometimes the response from the Third World is less than enthusiastic. Partly, this is because of the moral arrogance with which the primarily Western concept of human rights is exported to other societies. Partly, it is because Third World people remain very aware of Western imperialism and the fact that, in the past, the promotion of human rights was used as a moral pretext for colonial conquest, as in, for example, bringing an end to "barbarous" practices such as the Indian custom of *suttee* (burning the widow of a deceased man), or female infanticide. In addition, many Third World countries are intensely committed to socioeconomic rights, and they believe — rightly or wrongly — that progress in this respect may require a strong governmental authority, exerting some restrictions on civil and political rights.

Following World War II, more than eighty former colonies won their political freedom, liberating more than one billion people in the world's most massive transfer of political power. But national independence does not necessarily guarantee the rights of individuals. In some cases, quite the opposite takes place, especially when the newly established government is less than firmly entrenched; threats to the security of the nation serve as a handy excuse for denying individual rights, and in fact, many newly independent countries are politically insecure, for a variety of reasons. Accordingly, Third World states tend to be run by dictatorial, often military, governments, which can be especially repressive of human rights.

The Primacy of State Sovereignty

But the greatest underlying conflict between human rights and the state is one that is characteristic of virtually all governments, whether in the First, Second, or Third World. This derives from the very nature of state sovereignty and the fact that a call for human rights is generally a claim on behalf of individuals *against* the state. Whether demanding that states refrain from mistreating their people (negative rights), or that they commit themselves more aggressively to their betterment (positive rights), claimants for human rights typically push governments in directions they would not otherwise choose to go. International standards of human rights represent assaults on state power and sovereignty by restricting what a state can do (and sometimes, telling it what to do), even within its own borders. Even the legalisms of a given state, if they are viewed as violations of human rights, may be considered invalid by the international human rights community; for example, the South African apartheid laws are not acknowledged as legitimate, despite the fact that they have been duly passed by that country's legislative parliament.

Paradoxically, a concern for human rights may actually enhance state sovereignty. States that, by and large, adhere to international standards of human rights (the Western democracies generally) experience a higher level of legitimacy and security than do those that routinely trample upon them. No serious observer of the United States, Western Europe, Australia, or Japan genuinely worries that any of these governments will be overthrown by coup or revolution . . . unlike the fate of other states whose leaders abused human rights, such as Marcos in the Philippines, the shah of Iran, Duvalier in Haiti, Somoza in Nicaragua, Batista in Cuba, or Ceausescu in Romania.

The Role of Politics

Governments often are asked to report on the status of human rights within their own borders. It can be argued, however, that leaving states to report on their own human rights situation is like having the fox report on the status of the chickens; the U.S.S.R., for example, regularly reports that there are no violations of human rights within that country — after all, it is said, human rights are protected by the Soviet constitution. Assessment by outside experts, including dissidents, is generally much more critical as well as credible.

The UN also has played politics with human rights. Thus, the UN Human Rights Commission generally has been most willing to criticize pariah states such as Israel and South Africa. On the other hand, organizations such as the Red Cross, the International Labor Organization, UNESCO, UNICEF, FAO, WHO, and the High Commission on Refugees have done much to improve human rights within offending states. Private, nongovernmental organizations, notably Amnesty International (which won a Nobel Peace Prize in 1977) have sometimes been effective in improving conditions for specific political prisoners, and on many occasions, even winning their release. But such groups have typically focused on specific cases, avoiding the more troublesome, general issue of state sovereignty versus human rights.

The view of classical liberalism has long been that the individual — linked to freedom and equality — is the ultimate end of government policy, and that the individual must never be a mere means to state security. In 1978, President Jimmy Carter proclaimed that "there is one belief above all others that has made us what we are. This is the belief that the rights of the individual inherently stand higher than the claims or demands of the State."[15] And a few years before, Henry Kissinger at least paid lip service to this ideal when he noted, "The precious common heritage of our Western Hemisphere is the conviction that human beings are the subjects, not the objects, of public policy; that citizens must not become mere instruments of the state."[16] Nonetheless, states traditionally value themselves more than their component citizens; beyond this, states commonly have trampled wantonly on human rights, especially the human rights of citizens of other states. This occurs either directly, by military intervention and economic pressure, or indirectly, by supporting repressive regimes.

The Problem of Enforcement

Faced with the awesome, sovereign power of states, the international human rights regime can seem woefully inadequate, based as it is on mere legalisms or exhortations, and devoid of enforcement mechanisms. But legal systems always have difficulty controlling powerful actors — labor unions in Britain, for example, or large corporations in the United States. And ultimately, most of them rely on voluntary compliance. Some states have in fact complied voluntarily with international human rights norms, largely to achieve international legitimacy as well as to avoid ostracism.

Frustration with the rights-denying policies of states occasionally spills over into efforts to transcend the authority of states. Although lacking in legal authority, individuals of high moral and international standing have on occasion gathered together to fill what they see as a vacuum in the protection of human rights. So-called people's tribunals have periodically convened to draw attention to various human rights abuses. Most notable of these was the Russell Tribunal, which roundly criticized U.S. policy during the Vietnam War. The League for the Rights of Peoples, established in Rome in 1976, has held numerous sessions, evaluating repression under Marcos in the Philippines, offering a retrospective on Turkish genocide against

Armenians from 1915 to 1916, and criticizing Brazil's behavior toward its indigenous Amazonian population, Indonesia's strong-arm tactics in East Timor, U.S. intervention in Central America, and Soviet intervention in Afghanistan, as well as questioning the legitimacy of nuclear weapons. Such actions are of uncertain effectiveness, but they do attract a degree of public attention, while also serving to undercut the presumption that only state-centered approaches are relevant in dealing with violations of human rights.

New Approaches to the Problem

An approach that emphasizes human rights represents a fundamentally new way of thinking about human dignity and world politics, reflecting as it does the determination that states must meet certain standards, both in their own domestic affairs and in their international relations. Even today, after several decades of vigorous prohuman rights advocacy, states typically act with primary regard to their power and perceived national interests, rather than according to the ideals of human rights. There is, as a result, the constant danger that concern for human rights will be sacrificed on the altar of state sovereignty, expediency, and realpolitik.

Human rights advocacy involves a different perspective from which to view the human condition and the goals of society and politics — as citizens of a larger community than individual states or nation-states. As opposed to the relatively narrow focus of states, concern with superordinate human rights requires that political barriers be transcended, in the search for human dignity on the widest possible scale. With this in mind, let us now turn to the special case of human rights policy in the United States.

HUMAN RIGHTS POLICY AND THE UNITED STATES

The United States thinks of itself as being especially supportive of human rights. After all, as the Declaration of Independence states:

> We hold these truths to be self-evident, that all men are created equal, that they are endowed by their

Creator with certain inalienable Rights, that among these are Life, Liberty and the pursuit of Happiness. That to secure these rights, Governments are instituted among Men, deriving their just powers from the consent of the governed.

The right to "Life" included the right to self-defense and protection against unwarranted attack and unjust government; the right to "Liberty" included freedom of speech, public association, and religion, and freedom to establish a government of one's own choosing; the right to "pursuit of Happiness" included the right to own property and to enjoy the fruits of one's labor. Subsequently, the U.S. Constitution was amended to include a much-cherished Bill of Rights, which specifically guarantees freedom of religion, speech, the press, peaceable assembly and the right to petition the government for redress of grievances, the right to keep and bear arms, freedom from unwarranted search and seizure and from self-incrimination, the right to a fair and speedy trial, and protection against excessive bail.

On the other hand, the early United States was not exactly a paragon of human rights: Slavery was practiced in the South, and women were denied the vote. Even today, racial discrimination is widespread, and the United States still has not passed an equal rights amendment explicitly guaranteeing equal rights for and legal protection to women, including such basic concepts as equal pay for equal work. Moreover, the world frequently views the United States as a repressive opponent of human rights, rather than the white knight on horseback, defending individual freedoms that U.S. citizens typically consider it to be. This is especially true with regard to United States military intervention in Vietnam and Central America, its long-standing association with a large array of oppressive right-wing dictatorships, its economic exploitation of many Third World countries, its coddling of apartheid in South Africa, its tacit support for Israeli oppression of Palestinians in the Occupied Territories, and its vigorous initiation and furtherance of the nuclear arms race. In addition, the United States has pursued a rather intolerant, single-minded sponsorship of free enterprise capitalism as the sole acceptable solution to the world's ills, while urging civil and political liberties and, at the same time, opposing most efforts at promulgating socioeconomic rights.

Messianic Zeal

One of the more pernicious doctrines under which human rights have been, and continue to be, violated is the notion that one's ideas are so good, so pure, and so correct, that anything is justified in pursuit of them. (To some degree, this is a consequence of the notion that "the end justifies the means," which Gandhi found so repugnant; see Chapter 23.) Totalitarian states, fascist and communist alike, have justified violent repression of their own population in the name of a "greater good," either the glory of the fatherland (fascist) or the dictatorship of the proletariat (communist). And the United States has not been immune to a dose of messianic ideology beginning relatively early in its history. In 1848, the government of Austria complained that the United States, by supporting Hungarian independence, was violating "the principle of nonintervention." Secretary of State Daniel Webster expressed a widespread U.S. view when he responded (more than a little self-righteously),

> Well-known circumstances in their history, indeed their whole history, have made the United States the representatives of purely popular principles of government. In this light they now stand before the world. . . . They could not, if they desired it, suppress either the thoughts or the hopes which arise in men's minds, in other countries from contemplating their successful example of free government.[17]

A century later, National Security Council directive number 68, issued in 1950 at the dawn of the Cold War, noted that "the integrity of our system will not be jeopardized by any measures, covert or overt, violent or nonviolent, which serve the purposes of frustrating the Kremlin design." This directive has never been rescinded; in effect, it gives the U.S. government license to intervene — both domestically and overseas — in ways destructive of human rights (psychological, political, and economic,

to say nothing of arranging for assassinations and various forms of social destabilization), so long as such activities are aimed at "frustrating" the Soviet Union. The result has included a range of interventions abroad, as well as the toppling of governments, attempts (on several occasions) to assassinate Fidel Castro, and apparent collaboration in the murder of Vietnam's Diem, the Congo's Lumumba, and Chile's Allende.

To some degree, concern with human rights has long motivated U.S. foreign policy, and at least some of this concern seems to have been genuine. On the other hand, outrage at the mistreatment of people by occupying governments has also served to help justify wars of colonial expansion on our part: the Mexican-American and Spanish-American wars are notable examples from the nineteenth century, just as the U.S. intervention in Vietnam was propagandized, in part, by alleged abuses on the part of the Vietcong and North Vietnamese.

As noted previously, the U.S. concern with human rights sometimes has a messianic quality, as when President Jimmy Carter said, "Because we are free, we can never be indifferent to the fate of freedom elsewhere."[18] And the U.S. entry into both World Wars I and II was facilitated by the argument that both wars were in defense of liberty and democracy. Nonetheless, U.S. foreign policy has not always been directly influenced by concern about human rights in other countries. Of greater importance has been concern for U.S. power and U.S. profit. When democratically elected leftist governments threatened to diminish their predecessors' anticommunist zeal, and/or when such governments threatened to restrict the profits of United States companies abroad, the United States intervened to replace them with others, as in Guatemala, Iran, and Chile. Typically, the human rights records of these new governments were far worse than their predecessors'.

Despite its avowed commitment to human rights as part of American democratic ideology, the truth is that U.S. human rights policy was influenced largely by traditional self-serving Great Power concerns. Shortly before the outbreak of World War II, for example, the U.S. government

Vietnamese "boat people" arriving at a processing center in Indonesia. Such refugees are typically unwanted by most countries, including the United States, and their human rights are often violated. (United Nations High Commission of Refugees/R. Burrows)

refused to permit the immigration of tens of thousands of German Jews, attempting to flee growing Nazi persecution. Influenced in part by anti-Semitism, as well as by concern for the economic and social stresses such an influx might produce, the United States chose to adhere strictly to its narrowly written laws governing immigration and naturalization, rather than to a broader conception of human rights. To a certain extent, the Truman administration initially supported human rights, through the UN charter and the UDHR, but as the Cold War heated up, human rights was subsumed into the more encompassing goal of a foreign policy based on anticommunism and containment of the Soviet Union. This, in turn, produced alliances with a large number of repressive governments, who were said to constitute part of the "free world," regardless of the degree of their own human rights violations, so long as they professed anticommunism. The United States, accordingly, made friends with fascists such as Spain's Franco and Portugal's

Salazar, supported the neo-fascist Greek military junta from 1967 to 1974, despite its record of torture and illegal detention, and also cozied up to dictatorships in South Korea, Taiwan, Saudi Arabia, Morocco, the Philippines, and throughout much of Latin America.

Kissinger and Detente

By the end of the Vietnam War, a gradual shift became detectable in United States attitudes vis-à-vis human rights. Global containment of communism no longer seemed legitimate as the sole basis for foreign policy, and human rights began to emerge as a concern in their own right. Nonetheless, during the 1970s, especially under the influence of Henry Kissinger (first as national security advisor and then as secretary of state), U.S. policy sought to draw the Soviet Union and the People's Republic of China into a modern-day Congress of Vienna, stabilizing the international system via detente. This involved increased trade, nuclear arms control agreements, and a reduced focus on human rights violations. Kissinger was of the "realist" school of international relations, which holds that considerations of power and raison d'état supercede moral issues such as human rights. These were thought to belong within the domestic jurisdiction of states, especially if raising such issues would interfere with sought-after accommodations with the Soviet Union. As a result, U.S. policy downplayed Soviet treatment of dissidents and "refuseniks" (those, predominantly Jews, seeking unsuccessfully to emigrate from the U.S.S.R.). The United States also looked the other way when it came to most human rights abuses worldwide, whether they were in Pakistan, Haiti, Nicaragua, Guatemala, Paraguay, Chile, Zaire, Uganda, Liberia, or elsewhere.

The Carter Reemphasis

With the election of Jimmy Carter, however, the situation changed dramatically. The U.S. public had grown tired of the abuses of power and the "imperial presidency," and was eager for a more activist and moral policy, founded on respect for and promulgation of human rights. Under Carter, hu-

President Jimmy Carter speaking at the United Nations, announcing a renewed U.S. emphasis on human rights. (Jimmy Carter Presidential Library)

man rights achieved a saliency not seen before, or since. Speaking at the United Nations, President Carter announced that "no member of the United Nations can claim that mistreatment of its citizens is solely its own business."[19] And he made it clear that he referred not only to civil/political rights, but also to the "unwarranted deprivation" of the poor. Legislation was passed that predicated economic aid on certain human rights standards on the part of the recipients, and the State Department initiated a new assistant secretaryship for human rights. (Further legislation ensured that economic assistance could be continued if such assistance was judged primarily to benefit needy people within the recipient countries.)

However, concern about human rights also remained selective: The government opposed abuses in countries that were not strategically important to the United States (such as Nicaragua, Uruguay, and the Dominican Republic), while ignoring those in more important countries, such as Saudi Arabia, Iran, and the Philippines. Toward the end of the Carter administration, U.S. foreign policy turned from human rights advocacy to a resumption of aggressive competition with the Soviet Union. (The U.S. government also continued providing equipment and training in repression and "interrogation

techniques" — that is, torture — notably at the Inter-American Police Academy in Panama, and then, more ambitiously, at the International Police Academy in Washington, DC.)

Reaganism and Anticommunist Tunnel Vision

Just as the Carter administration's support of a human rights policy was in part a reaction against the Nixon–Kissinger downgrading of human rights, the Reagan administration (especially during its first term) moved once more away from human rights as a centerpiece of national policy. This shift represented a conscious response to the right wing's claim that under Carter, the United States had been pursuing its ideals at the expense of its interests. Under Reagan, socioeconomic rights were essentially ignored, as were human rights violations by right-wing, anticommunist, military dictatorships. Human rights were equated with civil/political rights, and human rights policy was essentially collapsed once more into global anticommunism. Rights violations were only considered significant if they were conducted by socialist states; otherwise, they were downplayed. Nicaragua's human rights record, under the Sandinistas, was considered deplorable; far worse abuses, by pro-U.S. governments in El Salvador, Guatemala, and Honduras, were ignored. Jeanne Kirkpatrick, U.S. ambassador to the United Nations, enunciated a distinction between "authoritarian" governments (friendly to the United States) and "totalitarian" ones (friendly to Moscow). The former were considered capable of change, whereas the latter were not; abuses of human rights were tolerated or ignored among the former, and severely criticized among the latter. In short, the human rights policy of the United States became characterized by selective outrage.

Terrorism, for example, was denounced when conducted by nongovernmental, anti-Western organizations. By contrast, state-sponsored terror — when carried out by anticommunist U.S. allies — evoked only a feeble protest, if that. For example, although the United States did not directly condone the notorious right-wing "death squads" that have assassinated literally thousands of labor activists, community organizers, and priests in Guatemala,

Honduras, and, notably, El Salvador, such activities have, at best, only briefly interrupted the flow of U.S. military aid to these countries.

Relations with South Africa also became less critical and confrontational, with limited economic sanctions imposed only when forced by Congress. The South African government has compiled one of the world's worst human rights records, with institutionalized racism that explicitly denies democracy to people of color, that arrests and detains its opponents — including young children — without trial, and that has conducted forced deportation, relocating hundreds of thousands of blacks to so-called homelands, which are in fact ecologically devastated regions considered worthless by the white minority. Nonetheless, the U.S. government has practiced — and still prefers — a policy of "constructive engagement" vis-à-vis South Africa; this is supposed to be less obtrusive, and ultimately more effective, than outright opposition. Critics, on the other hand, contend that it is an excuse for nonengagement, or worse yet, collusion with an offensive, illegitimate regime, out of a realpolitik concern for South African strategic minerals and/or an "unrealpolitik" fear that communism is the only alternative to white rule.

Realpolitik Returns

Toward the end of the Reagan presidency, U.S. policy once more began to reflect human rights themes, albeit still selectively. Once it became obvious that the local population would no longer tolerate repressive dictators — in the Philippines, Haiti, South Korea, Chile — the United States grudgingly withdrew its support. Despots, in short, were dumped when they became a liability, but only then. Violators of human rights, it was found, did not make for stable allies, and yet the basic inclination persists. "Given a choice between the extreme left and the extreme right," wrote one specialist in international human rights,

> Washington will choose the extreme right every time: there will be no immediate security threat to the U.S.; and the regime will be sympathetic toward American businesses. More to the point, however, is

that Washington has helped inflict this Hobbesian choice on itself. The U.S. has largely ignored gross violations of human rights in places like El Salvador and Guatemala; in the name of security the U.S. has looked the other way while right-wing governments literally exterminated moderate reformers. Those not killed were driven into further, frequently leftist, rebellion because of the absence of prospect for peaceful reform.[20]

On the other hand, considerations of realpolitik have sometimes led to a tendency to underplay human rights violations on the part of Marxist states as well. Thus, when the Chinese government ruthlessly violated the human rights of thousands of prodemocracy demonstrators in Peking's Tiananmen Square in 1989, Richard Nixon and Henry Kissinger both argued for a tolerant and noncritical U.S. response, maintaining (although not in so many words) that the Sino-American strategic relationship against the U.S.S.R. was more important than the lives and liberties of a few thousand students. And President Bush successfully resisted public and congressional calls for a tough response.

Clearly, there are two horns to the dilemma of human rights and U.S. foreign policy: on the one hand, a real sympathy for human rights (especially the civil/political kind), and on the other, a felt need to respond to narrower concerns of national security, geopolitical maneuvering, state power, and profit. But there is also room for hope, since these objectives need not necessarily always be in conflict.

HUMAN RIGHTS AND THE COLD WAR

As we have seen, despite a historical sensitivity to human rights, and a public fondness for human rights rhetoric and causes, human rights policy in the United States since World War II has typically been subordinated to the East–West conflict. (Prior to World War II, no true human rights policy existed.) In fact, support for human rights has, in some right-wing quarters, become a code word for anticommunism; attempts have been made, for example, to "link" nuclear arms agreements to Soviet domestic political reform . . . in the expectation that the latter will never come to pass, thereby dooming the former as well. The effect has been to block movement toward arms control while intensifying the Cold War. A more moderate view, by contrast, also holds that support for human rights requires vehement anticommunism, backed up by large military forces.

The Soviet Union has in fact been a major violator of human rights, and many Americans accordingly believe that in order to support political freedom in, say, Poland, the Ukraine, or the Baltic states, the United States must take an antagonistic, hardline stance vis-à-vis the U.S.S.R. It seems more likely, however, that the correlation works the other way: When pressured — politically, economically, or militarily — repressive regimes tend to become more repressive; by contrast, when they feel comfortable, relaxed, and not threatened, they tend to open up political and economic space among their population. Jewish emigration from the Soviet Union, for example, skyrocketed during detente in the early to mid-1970s. With the renewal of the Cold War in the late Carter and early to mid-Reagan years, the U.S.S.R. permitted very few dissidents to leave the country; then, with the improvement of U.S.-Soviet relations in the late 1980s, Jewish emigration again rose dramatically, reaching such numbers that the Bush administration began restricting entry.

According to its apologists, Soviet domination and repression of human rights in Eastern Europe since World War II has been justified as a necessary protection against the West, notably the United States. Similarly, United States domination and repression of human rights in Central America has been justified by the specter of Soviet-sponsored revolution. Undoubtedly, the Cold War itself has served to generate substantial human rights abuses, independent of whatever the inclinations of either superpower might have been. With the apparent crumbling of the Cold War in the Gorbachev and post-Reagan era, human rights may improve worldwide. It is noteworthy, for example, that the wave of political freedom in Hungary, Poland, East Germany, and Czechoslovakia came about in the context of substantial thawing of the Cold War.

Although Eastern European activists have typically favored an aggressive U.S. military posture, to force concessions from the Soviets, it seems likely that an atmosphere of U.S.-Soviet military and political confrontations would have worked strongly against such openings as have occurred.

If both superpowers cease viewing smaller states through the lens of Cold War competition, they might find themselves tolerating greater political, economic, and social pluralism. Hence, nuclear and conventional arms reductions might themselves lead toward an improvement in human rights. Some peace and human rights groups are thus beginning to see that they have a common agenda, that, by and large, repression goes hand in hand with militarization, just as human rights is linked to demilitarization and disarmament. The superpower competition has enabled each side to use the other's repressive and militaristic actions to justify its own; a strategy of peace *and* justice might help break this cycle of mutual reinforcement.

HUMAN RIGHTS AND PEACE

Human rights and peace are inextricably connected, in several ways. First, the denial of human rights is itself a denial of peace. A world in which there is no armed conflict, but in which fundamental human rights are thwarted, could not in any meaningful sense be considered peaceful. Speaking at the United Nations, Pope John Paul II explicitly linked human rights and war:

> The Universal Declaration of Human Rights has struck a real blow against the many deep roots of war since the spirit of war in its basic primordial meaning springs up . . . where the inalienable rights of men are violated. This is a new and deeply relevant vision of the cause of peace. One that goes deeper and is more radical.[21]

The pope's perspective applies to socioeconomic rights no less than civil/political ones. As one Scandinavian peace researcher has noted, "Whether a child dies in infancy due to poverty and consequent malnutrition and lack of hygiene, or if it grows up and at a later stage is executed as a political opponent, the society in which this happens must be considered hostile to human rights."[22] And, we might add, to peace as well.

Second, there appears to be a connection between the way a state treats its own population and its inclinations toward other states. As Franklin Roosevelt put it, "We in this nation still believe that it [self-determination] should be predicated on certain freedoms which we think are essential everywhere. We know that we ourselves will never be wholly safe at home unless other governments recognize such freedoms."[23] Secretary of State George Marshall suggested similarly that "governments which systematically disregard the rights of their own people are not likely to respect the rights of other nations and other people and are likely to seek their objectives by coercion and force in the international field."[24] And in fact, democratic states have never made war against other democracies. (On the other hand, not all dictatorships are aggressive: fascist Spain stayed neutral during World War II, and neither neo-fascist Paraguay nor neo-Stalinist Albania have been international aggressors.)

"The most serious defect of a 'closed' society," according to famed Soviet dissident Andrei Sakharov,

> is the total lack of democratic control over the upper echelons of the party and government in their conduct of domestic affairs, and foreign policy. The latter is especially dangerous, for here we are talking about the finger poised on the nuclear button. The "closed" nature of our society is intrinsically related to the question of civil and political rights. The human rights issue, therefore, is not simply a moral one, but also a paramount, practical ingredient of international trust and security.[25]

To some extent, the foreign policies of states reflect their domestic inclinations. A Soviet Union that denies political freedoms at home is unlikely to be especially respectful of such freedoms within its satellites. And similarly, the relative disinterest of the United States in promoting economic justice at home is paralleled by U.S. opposition to the New International Economic Order (see Chapter 22) abroad.

Third, a denial of human rights can provoke breaches of the peace, if other states become in-

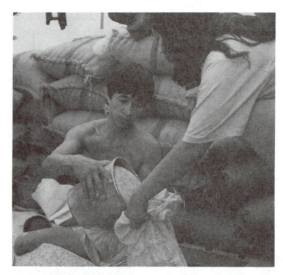

Cambodian refugees receiving supplies at a food distribution camp in Thailand. The official reason for the Vietnamese invasion of Cambodia in 1978 was the gross violations of human rights on the part of the Khmer Rouge government within that country. (United Nations High Commission on Refugees / A. Hollmann)

volved. Humanitarian intervention of this sort may be legal; certainly, there is ample precedent in the classical writings of international law. In Grotius' seventeenth-century *Law of War and Peace*, he questions "whether a war for the subjects of another [is] just, for the purpose of defending them from injuries inflicted by their ruler."[26] Grotius acknowledges that "certainly it is undoubted that ever since civil societies were formed, the ruler each claimed some especial right over his own subjects."[27] But he concludes that "if a wrong be manifest . . . if a tyrant . . . practices atrocities toward his subjects, which no just man can approve, the right of human social connection is not cut off in such a case."[28]

A century later, in Vattel's *The Law of Nations*, we read that "nations have obligations to produce welfare and happiness in other states. In the event of civil war, for example, states must aid the party which seems to have justice on its side or protect an unfortunate people from an unjust tyrant."[29] Great Britain, France, and Russia intervened in 1827 when Turkey had been using especially inhumane means to put down Greek aspirations for independence, and the world cheered. U.S. intervention in the Cuban civil war of 1898 was intended, according to the congressional resolution at the time, to put an end to "the abhorrent conditions which have existed for more than three years in the island of Cuba; have shocked the moral sense of the people of the United States, and have been a disgrace to Christian civilization."

On the other hand, claims of humanitarian intervention have often been used as an excuse for aggression (of which the Spanish-American War may well be an example). Hitler claimed that dismemberment of Czechoslovakia and, later, the invasion of Poland were warranted to stop the persecution of both countries' German-speaking minorities. Vietnam invaded Cambodia ostensibly to oust the genocidal Khmer Rouge regime, and the United States explained its invasion of Grenada at least partly as a response to human rights violations on that Caribbean island. Violations of Nicaraguan human rights have also been cited by the United States as justification for its efforts to overthrow the Sandinista government. (No comparable justifications were ever used by the United States to overthrow rightist regimes, including the Somoza dictatorship, which was far more abusive of human rights, or the government of El Salvador, which receives $1.5 million a day in U.S. aid, despite a human rights record that is among the worst in the Western Hemisphere.)

Finally, one of the widely recognized human rights — specified in the first articles of both 1966 human rights conventions — is that of national self-determination. Abuses of this right often lead directly to war, especially civil war (see Chapter 4), which makes this issue a difficult one. The pursuit of human rights may in fact lead more to violence than to peace, since human rights often are won by struggle and confrontation. Furthermore, it is not obvious whether all claims for national self-determination are worthy of success: Should there be independent states of Tigre, Eritrea, Kurdistan, Baluchistan, Armenia? What about the Baltic states? Or Basques, Welsh, Scots, Quebecois, and native Americans? For its part, the UN Security Council has determined that, at least in certain cases, such as anticolonial struggles, a continuing denial of human rights constitutes a formal threat to international peace (this was applied to Zimbabwe, Namibia, and South Africa).

In summary, the connection between human rights and peace is complex and multifaceted. It is useful to claim that human rights contribute to peace, but the most fundamental connection may well be that such claims encourage adherence to human rights, for their own sake, regardless of whether this actually promotes peace as narrowly defined.

THE FUTURE

An Ongoing Issue

What of the future? Several things can be said with confidence. The first is that the question of human rights will continue to demand attention on the international agenda. Decades of totalitarian Soviet-backed rule evidently have done nothing to dampen the yearning for freedom in Eastern Europe. Concern for human rights is so widespread, resonating so deeply as a fundamental aspiration of most human beings, that governments will be forced to pay attention . . . even though in many cases (perhaps most) they would rather not. And progress has in fact been made, and not only among Marxist states. The following states, for example, have implemented substantial civil/political rights despite having also had a history of despotic rule: India, Botswana, Costa Rica, Malaysia, Senegal, Venezuela. And other states, despite considerable poverty, have made strides in providing widespread socioeconomic rights: South Korea, Sri Lanka, Taiwan.

Competing Conceptions

A second safe conclusion is that the question of human rights will continue to be controversial, with different conceptions competing with one another, while the very notion of human rights competes with the basic inclination of states to engage in amoral, realpolitik maneuverings. The dilemma may be profound. Consider these realpolitik questions, for example, from the perspective of a government leader. What should a state do when confronted with this choice: It desires a particular strategic relationship with another state, but that other state engages in human rights abuses? Which should be sacrificed, national strategy or a commitment to human rights? American philosopher Reinhold Niebuhr argued that "group relations can never be as ethical as those which characterize individual relations."[30] And, he asked rhetorically, "How can [society] eliminate social injustice by methods which offer some fair opportunity of abolishing what is evil in our present society, without destroying what is worth preserving in it, and without running the risk of substituting new abuses and injustices in the place of those abolished?"[31] Similar thinking has also inspired Marxist leaders to rationalize the power politics by which their states generally function, as well as their failure to "wither away," as Marx had originally promised. Niccolò Machiavelli, in *The Prince*, wrote that "a man who wishes to make a profession of goodness in everything must necessarily come to grief among so many who are not good."[32] This may have been largely an excuse, justifying a ruler's amorality, but it also expressed a genuine dilemma.*

Perhaps, on the other hand, the "natural law" school is correct, and support of human rights is simply the right thing to do, period, regardless of its practical consequences. Consider this observation from German philosopher Karl Jaspers, who addressed himself to the question of "metaphysical guilt," following the Holocaust. Jaspers wrote:

> There exists a solidarity among men as human beings that makes each co-responsible for every wrong and every injustice in the world, especially for crimes committed in his presence or with his knowledge. If I fail to do whatever I can to prevent them, I too am guilty.[33]

There is yet another possibility, a way station between the amorality of realpolitik and the absolutism of morality for its own sake. Some argue that power (or at least, security) can readily be reconciled with human rights. "To claim the traditional rights of man is to claim, among other things, both security *and* liberty," writes one observer of the human rights scene.

> Security is not something which is at odds with human rights, because it is itself a human right; it is nothing other than the right to life restated. The security of the individual is bound up with the security of the community; the private enjoyment of the right depends upon the common enjoyment of the right. The demand for liberty and security is not the demand for two things which can only with difficulty be balanced or reconciled; it is a demand for two things which naturally belong together. Part of the traditional Western faith in freedom is a belief that a free country is *safer* than an unfree country. History gives us good ground for continuing to think that this belief is true.[34]

There is much evidence to support this view. After all, the United States has found that brutal, oppressive regimes—Somoza in Nicaragua, the shah in Iran, Marcos in the Philippines—do not make reliable allies. And the U.S.S.R. appears to be acknowledging something similar: that in the long run, its own national security may be enhanced, not diminished, by allowing human rights to flourish within its satellites as well as its own borders. Former Secretary of State Cyrus Vance echoed this sentiment when he observed: "We pursue our human rights objectives, not only because they are right, but because we have a stake in the stability that comes when people can express their hopes and find their futures freely. Our ideals and our interests coincide."[35]

Promoting Human Rights

It is difficult to imagine exactly what a U.S. foreign policy would be if it was organized primarily around the promotion of human rights worldwide. However, the following specific actions, which have already been taken at different times in support of human rights, suggest the benefits to be gained from a continuation, to say nothing of an expansion, of such policies:

- *Subtle diplomacy.* Quiet, persistent pressure raised with offending governments has the

---

*We shall encounter a related dilemma, known as the "tragedy of the commons," when we consider environmental issues, in the next chapter.

advantage that the government in question need not worry about losing face if and when abuses are corrected. A disadvantage, beyond the high chance of being ignored, is that a government may claim that it is employing subtle diplomacy while it is actually doing nothing.

- *Public statements.* This involves drawing world attention to specific abuses and to governments that violate human rights. It may involve publicly dissociating one's own government from the unacceptable behavior of another. Human rights compliance can be promoted by publicizing violations through the publication of reports conducted by respected, impartial investigative commissions; especially in a world climate committed to human rights, most governments seek to avoid the embarrassment that comes with being branded a violator of these rights.

- *Symbolic acts.* Sending support to dissidents, either by words, by contact with opposition figures, or by otherwise indicating disapproval of abuses, is a way of emphasizing to both the offending government and its people that human rights violations are noticed and rejected.

- *Cultural penalties.* By isolating offenders at international cultural events, including athletic contests and other exchanges, such governments are made to feel like pariahs. Although it is easy to scoff at such minimal "penalties," pride and the universal desire to be accepted enhance the impact of such actions.

- *Economic penalties.* Applying trade embargoes, renouncing investment in the offending country, refusing development loans and other forms of foreign aid—these actions can hurt the economy of offending countries, thereby putting pressure (often on the more wealthy and influential citizens) to modify policies and/or oust the government. Both cultural and economic penalties have been applied, with uncertain success, to the Republic of South Africa. Opponents of this strategy argue that it is likely to hurt the poorest and most defense-

less citizens, in South Africa's case, blacks who are already oppressed. Supporters point to the extreme discomfort such policies have already generated among apartheid leaders as an indication that they are having an effect.* Private corporations, which frequently profit from foreign investment in offending countries, typically oppose such economic sanctions, either unsuccessfully, as in the case of South Africa, or successfully, as happened in Rhodesia.

- *Immigration.* Human rights activists, dissidents, and those being deprived of their human rights can be permitted to enter the United States. In the recent past, the "right" of immigration has been applied quite selectively, facilitating immigration by people fleeing leftist countries whose human rights policies the United States wishes to criticize, while making it very difficult for refugees from rightist countries that are allied to the United States, and whose human rights policies it is inclined to ignore or whitewash.

- *Legal approaches.* International law can be applied more vigorously, by indicting violators of human rights overseas, just as people involved in the international drug trade have occasionally been indicted and, when possible, extradited for trial.

- *Multilateral approaches.* The United States can commit itself to the various human rights organizations now active worldwide, especially the United Nations Commission on Human Rights. There are many other possibilities, such as the regular publication of a UN-sponsored catalog of human rights abuses, to be subject to international scrutiny. Regimes with disproportionately large military spending generally tend to be the worst human rights abusers (and it can also be argued that such

---

*The release of anti-apartheid leader Nelson Mandela, after twenty-seven years in jail, was almost certainly spurred by economic sanctions — passed by the U.S. Congress over President Reagan's veto.

spending takes precedence over socioeconomic rights). Thus, the ratio of military to domestic national spending could be publicized for each state, and governments regularly expected to explain and justify their priorities.

- *Destabilization and belligerency.* The United States has actively sought to destabilize the governments of certain countries — for example, Nicaragua — at least in part, we are told, for their human rights abuses. This remains an option, although of questionable legality or morality, unless the abuses are sufficiently flagrant, and unless the policy is applied even-handedly to all regimes, regardless of ideology. Certainly, the human rights abuses of Nazi Germany and imperial Japan were influential in the U.S. decision to make war upon them, although these abuses actually became more serious after war was declared. The Tanzanian invasion of Uganda, which ultimately toppled the government of Idi Amin, won widespread support because that regime's human rights record was particularly atrocious.

Both U.S. and Soviet national security have been undermined, not by excessive attention to human rights, but by insufficient concern. In the case of the United States, this is largely a matter of foreign policy, whereby the U.S. government has aligned itself with oppressive, unjust regimes whose unpopularity has reflected poorly on the sponsor country as well. In the U.S.S.R.'s case, the failing has been essentially at home; the Soviet government faces a continuing crisis of legitimacy, based largely on the fact that governments, to be credible, must treat their people fairly. Accordingly, and especially under the reforming influence of Mikhail Gorbachev, Marxist governments are beginning to admit that individual rights exist even when they are not in conformity with the Communist party line. In the short run, attention to human rights can be destabilizing, as the Soviet leadership is finding out. In the short run, repression can clamp a lid on a boiling pot of unmet human rights; but in the long run, political stability — either within a state or between states — can only be constructed by turning down the heat. Thus, it can be argued, human rights ultimately are not only compatible with security (of individuals and governments), but are necessary for it.

A FINAL NOTE ON HUMAN RIGHTS

We conclude our discussion of human rights with an account by Jerome Shestack, a long-time human rights activist. Shestack recognizes the extraordinarily difficult and seemingly hopeless task of securing human rights worldwide, in the face of human cruelty, frailty, misunderstandings, and the power of states. He conjures up the Greek myth of Sisyphus, who was condemned to spend eternity pushing a boulder up a hill, only to have it roll back again just as he reached the top. Sisyphus' task is absurd, and yet — echoing the existential philosopher Albert Camus — Shestack points out that

> Sisyphus may turn out to be a more enduring hero than Hercules. For if, as Camus taught, life itself is absurd, Sisyphus represents the only triumph possible over that absurdity. In his constancy to reach that summit, even with failure preordained, Sisyphus demonstrated that the human spirit is indomitable and that dedication to a higher goal is in itself man's reason for living. . . . The realities of the world may foredoom a great part of the struggle and make most of the effort seem abysmal. Yet, the very struggle itself takes on symbolic meaning, enhancing human dignity. And when all is said and done, there is no other humane course to pursue.[36]

Study Questions

1. To what extent can human rights be seen as including most of the social/political agenda of a peace activist?

2. What is meant by the "natural law" approach to human rights? Compare this with the "positivist" approach, which states that rights are those specified in law.

3. Comment on the observation that human rights are a primarily Western idea, and that it is inappropriate to apply it to non-Western cultures.

4. Compare liberal and conservative views of human rights. Compare Marxist and Third World nationalist views.

5. Why does the United States tend to be less supportive of socioeconomic rights than of civil/political rights?

6. Trace the status of human rights in international law, as opposed to international exhortation.

7. Human rights often conflict with issues of state sovereignty. Explain.

8. U.S. foreign policy espouses human rights, but has often subordinated concern for human rights to pursuit of anticommunism. Is this true? Is it desirable?

9. Discuss the relationship between human rights and negative peace.

10. What should states do when support for human rights appears to conflict with "national security"?

Suggestions for Further Reading

Alice H. Henkin. 1979. *Human Dignity: The Internationalization of Human Rights*. Oceana Publications: Dobbs Ferry, NY.

Penny Lernoux. 1982. *Cry of the People*. Penguin: New York.

R. J. Vincent. 1986. *Human Rights and International Relations*. Cambridge University Press: New York.

Richard P. Claude and Burns Weston (eds.). 1989. *Human Rights in the International Community*. The University of Pennsylvania Press: Philadelphia.

David P. Forsythe. 1989. *Human Rights and World Politics*. University of Nebraska Press: Lincoln.

Source Notes for Part IV

1. R. B. J. Walker and Saul Mendlovitz. 1987. "Peace, Politics and Contemporary Social Movements." In *Towards a Just World Peace*. Butterworths: London.

2. Richard Falk. 1987. "The Global Promise of Social Movements." In Walker and Mendlovitz *Towards a Just World Peace*.

Source Notes for Chapter 20

1. Sophocles. 1973. *Antigone*. (R. Braun, trans.) Oxford University Press: New York.

2. Ibid.

3. Heraclitus. 1987. *Fragments*. (T. M. Robinson, trans.) University of Toronto Press: Toronto.

4. Aristotle. 1943. *Aristotle's Ethics for English Readers*. (H. Rackham, trans.) B. Blackwell: Oxford, U.K.

5. Confucius. 1983. *The Analects*. Chinese University Press: Hong Kong.

6. Quoted in J. Bentley. 1984. *Martin Niemoeller*. Free Press: New York.

7. Simone Weil. 1952. *The Need for Roots*. Putnam: New York.

8. Julius Nyerere. 1973. *Freedom and Development*. Oxford University Press: London.

9. Julius Nyerere. 1968. *Freedom and Socialism*. Oxford University Press: London.

10. Richard Falk. 1979. "Comparative Protection of Human Rights in Capitalist and Socialist Third World Countries." *Universal Human Rights*: 1.

11. Cyrus Vance. Law Day address at the University of Georgia, 1977.

12. Quoted in David P. Forsythe. 1989. *Human Rights & World Politics*. University of Nebraska Press: Lincoln.

13. Falk. "Comparative Protection."

14. Forsythe. *Human Rights*.

15. Jimmy Carter, Department of State news release, January 4, 1978.

16. Henry Kissinger, Department of State news release, June 8, 1976.

17. Quoted in Abraham Sirkin. 1979. "Elements of a United States Human Rights Strategy." In A. H. Henkin (ed.), *Human Dignity*. Aspen Institute for Humanistic Studies: New York.

18. Inaugural address, January 1977.

19. Quoted in Forsythe, *Human Rights*.

20. Forsythe. *Human Rights*.

21. Address to the UN General Assembly, October 3, 1979.

22. Asborn Eide. 1977. *Human Rights in the World Society*. Norwegian Peace Research Institute: Oslo.

23. Quoted in Vernon Van Dyke. 1970. *Human Rights, the United States and World Community*. Oxford University Press: New York.

24. Ibid.

25. Andrei Sakharov. 1980. "A Sick Society." *The New York Times*, January 23.

26. Hugo Grotius. 1901. *The Law of War and Peace* (A. C. Campbell, trans.) M. W. Dunne: London.

27. Ibid.

28. Ibid.

29. Emmerich de Vattel. 1883. *The Law of Nations*. T. & J. W. Johnson: Philadelphia.

30. Reinhold Niebuhr. 1932. *Moral Man and Immoral Society*. Scribner: New York.

31. Ibid.

32. Niccolò Machiavelli. 1985. *The Prince* (H. Mansfield, trans.). University of Chicago Press: Chicago.

33. Quoted in Louis Rene Beres. 1984. *Reason and Realpolitik*. Lexington Books: Lexington, MA.

34. Maurice Cranston. 1973. *What Are Human Rights?* Bodley Head: London.

35. Testimony to the Senate Committee on Foreign Relations, 1980.

36. Jerome J. Shestack. 1978. "Sisyphus Endures: The International Human Rights NGOs." *New York Law School Law Review* 24 (1): 89–124.

21

Ecological Wholeness

When we see land as a community to which we belong, we may begin to use it with love and respect.
  Aldo Leopold

The word *ecology* derives from the Greek *oikos*, meaning house. Defined broadly, it refers to the interrelations between living things and their environment — which includes other living things (plants, animals, microorganisms), as well as inanimate objects or elements such as climate, rock, water, and air. Despite dreams of space travel and the colonization of other planets, the fact remains that human beings have only one home, and good planets are hard to find. The planet Earth is also the home of millions of other species, all of them intimately connected to one another and, ultimately, to ourselves.

THE GROWING ENVIRONMENTAL AWARENESS

Environmental awareness has emerged fitfully over many centuries. Within the United States, it began to achieve widespread public attention by the second third of the twentieth century, with anxiety about air and water pollution, the effects of persistent pesticides such as DDT (cogently described in Rachel Carson's influential book, *Silent Spring*), and concern about human overpopulation (forcefully argued in Paul Ehrlich's *The Population Bomb*). With nationwide observance of Earth Day in April 1970, it appeared that the environmental movement had come of age.

An additional milestone was the study *Limits to Growth*, which argued that economic and population growth, widely taken for granted as desirable and inevitable, are in fact undesirable and unsustainable. For a time, this perspective was seen by many social activists as a distraction from legitimate socioeconomic needs, and even, in some cases, as a plot to ensure continued Third World underdevelopment. Now, people working closely with Third World social movements are increasingly convinced that environmental/ecological/resource concerns are at the heart of their struggle. In addition, concern for indigenous people — their culture, livelihood, and integrity — requires recognition of their place in the complex web of natural ecosystems. The web of life has been fraying; peace requires that it be rewoven, or at least allowed to regenerate on its own.

The 1980s

By the 1980s, ecological awareness had been raised substantially in the United States — reflected to some extent in legislation as well as public attitudes — but the environment itself continued to deteriorate, at least in part because of the policies of the Reagan administration, which valued short-term economic growth over consideration for the environment. In addition, as part of their strong commitment to free enterprise, most political conservatives are opposed to strong government intervention on behalf of the environment, preferring to leave the free market as unregulated as possible.

Yet, in spite of the growth of the political conservatism of the 1980s, environmental concern has become widespread. The Green parties of Europe have made increasingly strong showings within several countries, including elections to the European Parliament. By the end of the 1980s, the environment was once again back on the front pages, following a series of environmental disasters. For

example, a very serious three-month heat wave and drought in the summer of 1988 reduced U.S. grain harvests by nearly one third, and gave cogency to worries about greenhouse warming. Fires ravaged the American West, including Yellowstone National Park. The earth's protective ozone layer was shown to be fraying, perhaps dangerously. Nuclear accidents at Three Mile Island in the United States (1979) and Chernobyl in the U.S.S.R. (1986), combined with the revelation that U.S. nuclear weapons plants had secretly and recklessly fouled thousands of acres with radioactive waste, all served to tarnish the image of nuclear power as an energy panacea. Waste disposal, along with toxic contamination, came to be recognized as a worldwide problem. The destruction of forest lands led to increases in flooding. In Africa, swarms of locusts devastated farm- and grasslands, and soil became increasingly degraded there and elsewhere. The tropical rain forests have dwindled alarmingly, and the world's wildlife has been besieged, with many well-known species (giant pandas, tigers, rhinos, even elephants) as well as a host of lesser species pushed to the verge of extinction. In addition, the human population surged well over 5 billion. To some degree, even politicians who have made careers fighting the East–West Cold War have begun to consider the need for all human beings to cooperate in protecting the environment of the only planet we have.

The Environment and National Security

In the final analysis, a world at peace must be one in which all living things experience themselves as being "at home." This does not require a state of perfect, unchanging harmony; indeed, our planet has never known an extended period of utter balance, static immobility, or unchanging equilibrium. A world in equilibrium, however, must be distinguished from one in stagnation. Life itself reflects a condition of change, consumption, synthesis, metabolism, locomotion, reproduction, competition, evolution. But life has also depended upon a kind of fundamental, underlying stability, at least in the longer run — that is, measured in hundreds,

African elephants at a watering hole. These magnificent creatures, once abundant, are now in danger of extinction. (H. Dublin)

thousands, even millions of years. In recent years, some of the crucial relationships between the world's species, and between those species and their environments, have become increasingly tenuous, and this in turn has begun to threaten the quality of life, both human and nonhuman, on our planet. It also threatens to undermine the integrity of our fundamental life-support systems: the air we breathe, the water we drink, the food we eat, as well as the diverse fabric of life that provides emotional and spiritual sustenance.

One of the most important — and overdue — shifts in human thinking noticeable in the beginning of the 1990s is the growing realization that national security must be defined in broader terms than the strictly military. As our planet becomes increasingly interconnected politically, economically, and socially, and also increasingly endangered, the health, well-being, and security of every individual becomes inseparable from the health, well-being, and security of the Earth itself. In his famous "strategy of peace" speech, delivered in 1963, President Kennedy noted that

> we are devoting massive sums of money to weapons, that could be better devoted to combating ignorance, poverty and disease.... We all inhabit this same small planet. We all breathe the same air. We all cherish our children's future. And we are all mortal.[1]

Our connectedness — to one another and to other forms of life — is rapidly emerging as something beyond mere rhetoric or metaphor. In the growing numbers of species pushed to extinction, growing numbers of people feel a sense of foreboding for the human future. In the looming threats to clean air, clean water, and the integrity of the Earth's atmosphere, and in an era of diminishing resources, people are recognizing threats to their own well-being that are as real as any military threat emanating from an armed opponent. Some maintain, as well, that human beings have an obligation to be something other than a generalized predatory and destructive species. There is a need, they claim, for wise stewardship over the planet's wild creatures and wild places, not just for our own benefit, but as a moral and ethical imperative. Others see the connection between despoiled, depleted, and polluted lands and human misery. It is becoming increasingly clear that we cannot make "peace" until we make peace with our planetary environment. It will not be easy, but in responding — albeit belatedly — to the various pressing environmental threats, we at least will not be running the risk of anything like the "security dilemma," in which military "preparedness" actually threatens to bring about the danger it is intended to surmount. Environmental sensitivity and protection seems likely to be a "win–win" proposition, although, as we shall see, some economic, social, and political conflicts have yet to be faced. In any case, environmental concerns, once considered an indulgence of the rich, are increasingly recognized as fundamental to a decent life for everybody.

In the absence of dramatic environmental disasters, public attention rarely focuses on the continuing plight of a silently deteriorating planet. Many of the most serious and adverse environmental effects (climate change, resource depletion, accumulated pollution, species extinction) will not become grossly apparent until the year 2000 or later; paradoxically, if we wait until then, we may well have foreclosed on the opportunity to intervene effectively. As with the prevention of nuclear war, the prevention of ecological disaster requires that we intervene *before* the catastrophe actually takes place, and effective responses have become impossible. Thus, in this chapter, we shall briefly review what has aptly been called our "ecological crisis." We are confronted with so many pressing environmental issues that we can only hint at some of the most important, conveying the flavor of the problems, while also pointing toward solutions.

THE TRAGEDY OF THE COMMONS

A model — first described in a scientific article by the ecologist Garrett Hardin[2] — helps us understand one of the major factors underlying environmental problems. The model considers a situation that long existed in Britain, in which some grassland was privately owned, and another part, the "commons," was common property of the community at large. Various citizens owned sheep, which they could graze on their own private lands or on the public commons. It was well known that overgrazing was harmful to the productivity of the grassland, and so, shepherds generally avoided overgrazing their own property. However, they treated the commons differently: The shepherds recognized that a healthy commons was of benefit to everyone, but each one also reasoned that if he refrained from grazing his sheep on the commons, then others would doubtless take advantage of this restraint, and fatten their sheep on the public lands. As a result, tendencies to be prudent and ecologically minded were suppressed because individual sheep-owners reasoned that if they did not take advantage of the commons, then surely someone else would. In short, if the commons was going to be degraded anyhow, they might as well be the ones who benefited from it. The result was deterioration of the commons, until it was no longer fit to support sheep, or shepherds.

The tragedy of the commons, then, is that individuals (and corporations) — each seeking to gain private benefit — find themselves engaging in behavior that is to the disadvantage of everyone. It can also be generalized to other difficulties, whenever short-term selfish benefit conflicts with long-term public good. For example, a factory-owner who uses the atmosphere as a public sewer may reap a selfish benefit; after all, even if his effluents pollute the air, the cost is borne more or less equally by everyone who breathes, whereas the factory-owner personally is saved the expense of having to install pollution-control devices. The same thinking applies to the overuse of scarce resources. Recycling may be inconvenient, and, in fact, individuals may find it easier simply to throw their garbage away, or to use more than their share of scarce commodities. This is because they may derive some personal gain or convenience from doing so, whereas the cost—in overcrowded dump sites or worldwide resource shortages—is a diffuse and general one. Besides, if they don't abuse the environment, then surely someone else will anyhow (this is just what the sheep-owners told themselves about the commons).

The tragedy of the commons has global dimensions: Scandinavian forests and lakes suffer from acid rain because of the effluents of English smokestacks, while Britain reaps the immediate economic benefit. Japan has defied international outcry while hunting the world's great whales to the verge of extinction. Brazil seeks to benefit economically from the Amazon rain forest, even though such "benefit" requires that it be destroyed, to the ultimate detriment of everyone.

CLEAN AIR AND CLEAN WATER

Our modern way of life produces large amounts of by-products, many of which are quite toxic. Pesticides and herbicides, for example, are applied in huge quantities, especially as part of high-tech agriculture, resulting in dangerous contamination of rivers and groundwater. Heavy fertilizer use provides an excess of nutrients, leading to unpleasant and sometimes toxic algae blooms. Industrial processes release vast quantities of poisons into the air and water. For many years, the atmosphere, fresh waters (especially rivers), and the oceans have been considered to be publicly owned, and thus suitable places for disposing of all manner of unwanted substances. Automobiles spew out vast quantities of additional air pollutants, as do power generation and the widespread, large-scale burning of forests and grasslands, especially in the Third World.

The combustion of coal and oil releases hundreds of millions of tons of nitrogen and sulfur oxides into the atmosphere, and these in turn produce photochemical smog at lower elevations. They also combine chemically with water to produce acid rain, which in turn has been destroying the

Pulp and paper mill smokestack, Thunder Bay, Ontario, Canada. Air pollution contributes greatly to acid rain, which destroys forests and lakes. (Greenpeace/J. H. Arcure)

natural life of lakes, ponds, rivers, and streams. Heavy metals—notably aluminum, cadmium, lead, mercury, and zinc—are also toxic, even in small quantities. Of the tens of thousands of chemicals widely used and often carelessly spread across and disposed of in our environment, medical evidence is available for the effects of barely 20 percent. Yet, the consequences of such disregard are likely to be serious, even though they are often diffuse, and therefore have not generated the sort of outrage that would ensue if a clear cause-and-effect relationship could be established between polluter and victim. The American Lung Association estimates, for example, that air pollution alone is responsible for $40 billion worth of annual damage, counting medical expenses as well as damage to crops and buildings. And this is just in the United States, where air quality standards are among the highest in the world.

Even though industrialization generates much air and water pollution, the wealthier countries ironically tend to have cleaner air and water, on average, than the poorer ones. Since pollution control devices may be costly, they are often unattainable for countries that are already poor. Environmental protection has thus become a luxury that most Third World countries cannot afford . . . although, in the long run, they cannot afford *not* to protect their environments. At present, however, transnational corporations have been establishing factories in such countries, where poverty and politically pliant leadership have resulted in minimal standards of environmental protection. The air quality in Mexico City, Manila, or Bombay, for example, is among the worst on earth, and major rivers in such regions often are little more than open sewers.

The problem is not altogether intractable, however. Some lakes and rivers have been cleaned up. Integrated pest management (IPM) offers hope of getting off the treadmill whereby pesticide/herbicide use leads to resistant pests, which in turn necessitates yet more toxic substances, which further pollute the environment while killing off natural predators (birds, beneficial insects) and producing pests that are yet more resistant to the poisons. IPM involves the use of crop rotation, natural pest con-

trols, organic fertilization, and a greater sensitivity to the land and its needs, rather than attempts to overpower nature via technology.

Industrial pollution can also be diminished greatly, not only by end-of-the-pipe treatment of effluents, but also by reducing the waste stream itself. A modest tax on carbon and other emissions can go far toward stimulating conservation and pollution reductions, although domestic industries doubtless would object vigorously, complaining that such a tax inhibited their ability to compete internationally. Therefore, innovations of this sort would probably be most acceptable if adopted by many states simultaneously (thereby getting around the tragedy of the commons).

The world does not have to wallow in its own toxic waste, polluting its air and water, and poisoning those—especially the poor—who cannot afford to live in safer, cleaner environments. Ultimately, in a resource-limited world, it must also be recognized that pollution equals wastage: Mercury belongs in thermometers, not in fish; sulfur belongs in matches and pharmaceutical drugs, not as sulfuric acid in dead lakes; and so on. Furthermore, the direct costs associated with health care, depleted fisheries and forests, and so on make environmental protection good economics as well as good planetary hygiene and good aesthetics. Thus, a thorough cleanup of air and water has practical underpinnings as well as an ethical side.

On the positive side, signs point to increasing international cooperation, along with growing public awareness of the problem. In 1979, the UN sponsored a Convention of Long-Range Transboundary Air Pollution, signed by thirty-five European and North American countries. Part of the pact was a Protocol on the Reduction of Sulfur Emissions, signed by twenty-one countries in 1985. The next year, ten of the signatories had met the goal of 30 percent reductions, set for 1993, and four had committed themselves to cutting fully 70 percent. A similar agreement, freezing nitrogen emissions at their 1987 level, was signed in 1988.

Although progress has been spotty toward establishing a widely recognized Law of the Sea, hope still exists for such an agreement, which would not only regulate the exploitation of the ocean's resources, but also limit the amount of oceanic pollution to be allowed. A comparable Law of the Atmosphere can also be hoped for, along with the United States ratifying the Law of the Sea.

SOLID WASTE DISPOSAL

Although the problem of solid waste disposal involves little that is particularly dramatic or exciting, it is nonetheless very real and not likely to go away. The problem has, moreover, been increasing. Unlike so many other environmental issues, which are general and often diffuse threats that frequently cannot easily be seen or grasped, the problem of solid waste is immediate and tangible, even if inelegant. It is made up of innumerable *things*, many of which we confront in our daily lives, such as old tin cans, plastic packaging, and glass bottles.

Landfill

During the Second World War, Americans reused and recycled large amounts of material, including metals, cardboard, newspapers, and rubber. Afterward, we embarked on a massively wasteful splurge, not only becoming enthralled with our relatively healthy consumer economy, but developing a "throwaway" consumer culture as well. Unfortunately, there never really was an "away." Garbage always winds up somewhere: in abandoned gravel pits, wetlands being filled in, the oceans, or the air (when solid waste is burned). The passage of the Clean Air Act, quickly followed by the Clear Water Act, banned such easy "disposal" methods; however, this only meant a movement back to land-based disposal, on the "commons" of sanitary landfills.

By the late 1980s, however, it was becoming apparent that such landfills were not adequate solutions, because of three main crises, the three c's of solid waste disposal: (1) contamination, (2) capacity, and (3) cost. Toxic materials leach from buried garbage into rainwater, and then into groundwater and streams, creating major hazards to drinking supplies. Even high-temperature incineration releases contaminated ash into the air.

Landfills themselves have become overcrowded, leading to anticipated municipal crises in the 1990s, as cities and counties simply run out of space to put their trash. This crisis has been intensified by the so-called NIMBY syndrome — Not In My Back Yard. Local residents band together to prevent the siting of landfills or incinerators near their homes; as with the tragedy of the commons, people are willing to place burdens — of capacity or of contamination — on the air, water, or land that we all "own" in common, so long as the cost is spread out. This means that, in the long run, everyone suffers, especially the environment, while individual constituencies (polluting industries, governments, and individual citizens) are very reluctant to pay the costs.

Those costs have become increasingly apparent, however, as when medical waste — including used needles — washed ashore on East Coast beaches, or when the *Pelicano*, a freighter carrying 14,000 tons of toxic incinerator ash, spent two years seeking a home for its unpleasant cargo. Eventually, 4,000 tons were deposited off a beach in Haiti, and the rest at undisclosed locations. In itself, the saga of the *Pelicano* dramatizes not only the growing problem of solid waste disposal, but also one of its more troubling socioeconomic dimensions: the tendency for rich countries to use poor countries as international garbage dumps. States such as Haiti and others such as the Cameroons, desperately poor and suffering staggering balance-of-payments deficits, have been willing — for a fee — to accept toxic garbage that the wealthier countries reject within their own boundaries. As a result, the rich states essentially are exporting contamination, death, and disease, and many poor countries believe they have no choice but to accept the arrangement.

Recycling, Reclamation, and Conservation

The amount of solid waste produced by the United States alone is staggering: about 160 million tons per year, or nearly one ton per capita. We annually discard 16 billion disposable diapers, 1.6 billion plastic pens, 2 billion razor blades, and 200 million car and truck tires. In 1986, Americans spent more money on throwaway packaging than was earned by all the country's farmers. (Certain synthetic materials, notably plastics, are highly resistant to bacterial decomposition processes, and thus are virtually permanent.) Whereas Western Europe recycles 30 percent of its trash, and resource-poor Japan 50 percent, the United States recycles less than 10 percent. Although these figures certainly reflect poorly on the United States, they also contain the hopeful message that there is much room for improvement, well within our technological capacities: Germany, for example, currently burns 30 percent of its waste to provide heat energy, the United States only 6 percent. Such "cogeneration" offers the promise of killing two birds with one stone: reducing the solid waste stream while also easing the depletion of fossil fuel reserves such as coal and oil.

Similarly, aggressive recycling programs would not only diminish the problem of trash disposal, but also permit the recovery of resources — many of them nonrenewable — that would otherwise be lost. There is much wisdom in the old expression, "Waste not, want not." Thus, a sustainable world economy will ultimately require a transition, from "extractive industries" that essentially mine the planet's resources, to those that emphasize the recycling of existing materials. To some degree, this process has already begun. In Italy, Spain, and Argentina, for example, more than half the steel produced annually is generated from recycled scrap. Aluminum is the most energy-intensive commercially produced metal; the recycling of aluminum, on the other hand, requires only one twentieth the energy required to produce it from bauxite ore. The waste stream from a single mid-sized American city contains more aluminum than a small bauxite mine, more copper than a mid-sized copper smelter, and more wood than a fair-sized stand of timber.

One question is how to mine such a mother lode. Another is how to help make recycled materials economically attractive. Yet another is how to motivate consumers to cooperate with recycling, by changing their behavior toward packaging and by willingly separating different kinds of recyclables.

And finally, there is the question of how the world's various resources, many of them limited and nonrenewable, are to be allocated among different countries and different people. The meaning of "have" and "have-not" countries, for example, may have to be reconsidered. Thus, the United States already relies on foreign sources for 100 percent of its platinum, chromium, strontium, and mica; for more than 90 percent of its manganese, tantalum, cobalt, and aluminum; and for 50 percent or more of twelve other key minerals, many of them having military applications. Financial power (backed up by military and political influence) has long been sufficient to give wealthy "have-not" countries access to resources they lack. In the long run, however, some transition toward "commodity power" and a seller's market in natural resources seems inevitable, although it can be greatly slowed by effective recycling, reclamation, and conservation.

The Problem of Government Subsidization

Few Americans realize the degree to which their present patterns of wasteful resource use are actually subsidized by government policy. For example, when the federal government grants loans for power plant construction and pollution abatement equipment, this not only places additional demands on the public treasury (another kind of commons), but also obscures the true costs of processing materials. In 1984 alone, the U.S. government provided $44 billion in subsidies to the energy industry, while during a ten-year period, the U.S. Forest Service took in $2 billion less in timber sales than it expended making such sales profitable and attractive to the timber industry (for example, by constructing logging roads). Interestingly, the same people who argue that the market should be left as the ultimate arbiter of what is or is not efficient also support large, hidden government underwriting of major industries, notably nuclear energy production. If energy, wood, and other products were sold instead at their true cost, this alone would go far toward encouraging a more conservation-oriented economy. Such a pricing structure also would include the cost of disposing of the waste, cleaning up water and air pollution, remunerating those who suffer ill effects because of the production process, and so on.

Nuclear Waste

Finally, one of the most pernicious problems of waste disposal is that of nuclear energy. Despite the claims of the nuclear power industry, military contractors, and the government, civilian nuclear power is not "clean," nor is military nuclear production. In the United States alone, more than 100 commercial reactors plus a handful of weapons reactors (as well as several hundred naval power plants) produce an average of 30 metric tons of high-level nuclear waste per reactor per year. Containment of this material is a big headache: 149 underground storage tanks are located in Hanford, Washington, alone, of which almost one third have been confirmed as leaking or strongly suspect. As a result, two-thirds of that 570 square mile federal site is now seriously contaminated; it takes about six years for radiation in the groundwater to reach the Columbia River, which provides drinking water for numerous downstream communities. Major leaks have also been identified at the Savannah River Plant in South Carolina, and at Fernald, Ohio, among others.

Nuclear waste can be "low level," such as contaminated clothing, in which case it is often buried in landfills, or "high level," the actual products of nuclear reactors. In the latter case, these radioactive materials will be with us for a very long time; the half-time of plutonium, for example, is 26,000 years. Certain procedures are being actively investigated, and seem to offer limited promise, such as "vitrification," in which nuclear waste is essentially turned into solid glass. Nonetheless, the search for safe means of disposal is a major unsolved dilemma — the site in Nevada chosen as a national nuclear waste repository may be geologically unstable. Although more than 400 nuclear power plants are operating worldwide, not a single long-term waste disposal system is in place. It may simply

not be possible to guarantee the integrity of wastes and their storage sites over the toxic lifespan of the materials in question. The magnitude of the challenge is apparent when we recall that many nuclear materials will remain life-threatening for many times longer than human civilization has thus far existed on this planet. The task is to provide reliable storage over timespans that are not only historical, but geological, in scope. Some experts have concluded that the United States (and other countries) may well end up with large "national sacrifice zones" that are contaminated forever.

THE GREENHOUSE EFFECT

Since the middle of the twentieth century, scientists have warned that human technology and economic "progress" have been disrupting the worldwide carbon cycle, one of many fundamental processes on which life on Earth depends. Then came the 1980s, in which the five warmest years of the past century all occurred during the same decade. Although such events could, at least in theory, be due to chance alone, it suddenly became increasingly apparent — even to indifferent citizens, antagonistic industrialists, resistant planners, and short-sighted politicians — that the "greenhouse effect" might constitute a grave threat to the planet.

The greenhouse effect occurs as follows: Energy from the sun warms the Earth. This energy is most familiar to people as visible light. However, the Earth then radiates heat back, largely in the form of infrared radiation. This is readily absorbed by the atmosphere, much of it by so-called greenhouse gases, notably carbon dioxide. If not for this atmospheric absorption of heat reradiated by the Earth, the planet would become cold and lifeless. But as the quantity of these gases has been increasing, the atmosphere has apparently become a heat sink, absorbing so much warmth that the Earth's climate has begun to change. This process is known as the greenhouse effect because a very similar principle keeps greenhouses substantially warmer than their surroundings, relying in this case on the structural characteristics of glass rather than the chemical properties of carbon dioxide: Light passes easily through the glass of a greenhouse, but the reradiated infrared light is trapped inside.

Throughout geological time, carbon levels in the atmosphere do not seem to have fluctuated dramatically. Under natural conditions, carbon is released into the atmosphere as a result of the respiration of animals and the burning or decomposition of organic materials. Similarly, carbon is taken from the atmosphere and "fixed" in the bodies of plants via photosynthesis. With the coming of the Industrial Revolution, this cycle became unbalanced, with much more carbon being released into the atmosphere than is being fixed by plants. The combustion of fossil fuels (coal and oil) has been especially responsible, but the burning of forests and grasslands has also added substantially to the atmosphere's carbon load. About two-thirds of the planet's excess carbon comes from fossil fuels (notably automobiles and trucks, power generation, and the workings of industry), with about one third coming from burning and rotting vegetation (especially savannah fires in Africa and burning of the Amazon rain forest in South America). In addition, the steady destruction of the world's forests (for fuelwood, and to clear land for cultivation and/or grazing) not only adds carbon dioxide directly, but also destroys the major vehicle by which carbon is naturally removed from the atmosphere.

In the late 1800s, carbon dioxide levels were about 280 parts per million (ppm). In 1989, this figure had increased to 350 ppm, and by the year 2050, it could be 500–700 ppm. Such carbon dioxide levels could easily result in an increase in world temperatures of 3 to 9 degrees Fahrenheit by the year 2050. This change may sound small, but for comparison, consider that when average temperatures were only about 9 degrees colder than they are today, the world experienced an Ice Age. The worldwide temperature increase due to the greenhouse effect would represent a rate of climate change 100 times faster than at any time in history, and the results could well be catastrophic.

Already, the pace of global change has been increasing: from one degree per 500 years prior to the Industrial Revolution to the current rate of one degree per 100 years, tending toward one degree per decade. If this continues, agriculture will be profoundly disrupted, large numbers of species will die, and accompanying droughts (because of higher evaporation rates) will add to the calamity. And as the oceans expand because of the higher temperatures, and some melting occurs in the polar ice caps, sea levels will rise, causing potentially devastating floods to low-lying terrain. (Much of the world's population lives in coastal areas, and many great cities are at sea level, including Los Angeles, San Francisco, and Manila, and nearly the entire country of Bangladesh.)

Carbon dioxide is not the only greenhouse gas. Others include nitrogen oxides, methane (from landfills, termite mounds, the digestive processes of cattle), and chlorofluorocarbons (CFCs, also implicated in the destruction of the ozone layer). Per molecule, in fact, these chemicals are far more heat-absorbing than CO_2; however, they are much less abundant.

Although the greenhouse effect apparently cannot be reversed, it can be ameliorated, essentially buying time for future generations. One practical solution involves a triad of actions: (1) renewable energy sources (wind, solar, and so on), (2) strict conservation, and (3) reforestation. Other possibilities might include a tax on carbon emissions to exert economic pressure for the development and use of noncarbon energy sources. We don't know the exact dimensions of the greenhouse threat, but such uncertainty has never stopped human beings when it came to other threats, such as that posed by international aggression (for example, mobilizing against Germany or Japan in the 1940s, or during the Cold War that followed). The threat posed by the greenhouse effect may be every bit as great, or greater. Thus far, however, our response has been much more restrained. During its first year in office, the Bush administration even doctored a government-sponsored technical report, so as to make it appear that there is greater uncertainty as to the causes of greenhouse warming, and thus, less need for a national response.

The major culprits—that is, the major carbon emitters—are the United States, the Soviet Union, and China. However, any state, once it becomes heavily industrialized or highly dependent on coal (such as China) will contribute much more than its share to the Earth's carbon load. At a conference on the world's climate, held in Toronto in 1988, the prime ministers of Norway and Canada agreed to a 20 percent reduction in carbon emissions by the year 2005; if greenhouse warming is to be slowed, more policymakers — and those representing the major polluters — must agree to restrictions that are at least this farsighted.

OZONE DEPLETION

Ozone (O_3) represents a molecular form of oxygen. When it is near the ground, ozone contributes to air pollution, especially photochemical smog. But when it is in the upper atmosphere, it behaves more benevolently, absorbing dangerous ultraviolet radiation and preventing it from reaching the ground. (Excessive ultraviolet radiation can cause sunburn, skin cancer, and blindness.) Atmospheric scientists have noted that the ozone layer, especially above the Antarctic, has been thinning dangerously, with a hole about as large as the area covered by the United States. A major culprit is the class of chemicals known as chlorofluorocarbons, which have been widely used in industry, as aerosol propellants and refrigerants, and in the manufacture of polystyrene foam.

As with the greenhouse effect, the precise extent of ozone depletion is difficult to assess, and even its effects are diffuse. Unlike wars, epidemics, or famines, atmospheric deterioration generally does not photograph well or lend itself to dramatic thirty-second "sound bites." But for all its subtlety, it is no less real. Once again, we face a kind of tragedy of the commons, in that individuals and individual industries have little motivation to behave responsibly toward the atmosphere unless others are persuaded or coerced into behaving similarly. The same applies to countries: Unless all states can be persuaded to act together, there is little motivation for any one to act separately. Thus, there is likely to be an immediate economic cost, for example, in taxing carbon emissions or forbidding the use of CFCs.

This makes it especially heartening that, in the case of ozone depletion at least, some cooperation has been achieved. In 1987, twenty-four nations agreed to the Montreal Protocol, pledging themselves to a 50 percent cut in CFC production by 1999. The heavily industrialized countries agreed to undertake the bulk of this transition, a major triumph for the United Nations Environment Programme. Although it affects only one of the many environmental problems that require attention — and in the opinion of many experts, even in this case, it is too little and possibly even too late — the Montreal Protocol represents an important political and psychological victory for planetary, environmental consciousness.

TROPICAL RAIN FORESTS

The world's tropical rain forests are the greatest repositories of biological diversity — sheer numbers of species — on Earth. They are also among the most endangered. Although they cover only about 7 percent of the Earth's surface, they are home to a staggering 50 to 80 percent of all plant and animal species. Of the estimated 5–30 million species on Earth, only about 1.7 million have even been identified. It is difficult to assess the value of such species, that is, their value to *Homo sapiens*. Moreover, seen as entities in themselves, with their own intrinsic worth, each is irreplaceable and priceless. In addition, obscure species often prove of direct human benefit: The bark of the seemingly worthless cinchona tree yields the antimalarial drug quinine, chemicals derived from certain oysters are used to treat Parkinson's disease, and so on. Furthermore, forests tend to counter the greenhouse effect by "fixing" carbon in the biomass of trees. Destroying forests not only renders them unable to absorb excess carbon dioxide, but also releases additional quantitites through burning and decomposition.

Tropical rain forests are immensely complex biological entities; once disrupted, they take a very long time to recover, perhaps hundreds of years or more. Long before this recovery took place, many (perhaps most) tropical rain forest species would be extinct. Once this happens, they can never be brought back. Many people are misled by the luxuriance of tropical rain forests, thinking that their soils must be exceptionally productive. In fact, most of the nutrients in tropical soils are held in the vegetation itself; once this is cleared and burned, the soils typically can support agriculture only for a few years. After this, they revert to a hard, cement-like material called "laterite," transformed essentially into barren wasteland.*

Economic Pressures on Rain Forests

Nonetheless, land hunger and government/investor eagerness for "development" has resulted in the destruction of vast amounts of tropical rain forests, particularly in South America, Africa, and Indonesia. Regions that are especially threatened include the island of Madagascar (home to many "endemic" species — those that are found only in a given region) where more than 90 percent of the original vegetation is gone, the eastern slope of the Andes, the monsoon forests of the low Himalayas, the Atlantic coastal forests of Brazil, and Malaysia. Less than one twentieth of the world's tropical forests are under any protection whatsoever, and those that are, often are "protected" on paper only: They are still subject to extensive poaching, lumbering, grazing, and so on, largely because of human poverty, overpopulation, and greed.

Economic factors typically loom large in this ongoing tragedy. Tropical rain forests grow in Third World countries, which are often desperately poor, and hence eager to attempt anything that promises economic improvement, even if the "gains" are only short-lived. Moreover, these countries tend to suffer from painfully high national debt, so that funds are desperately needed to make the interest payments. Central American countries, for example, have been clearing their remaining rain forest to raise beef so as to earn money from U.S. fast-food restau-

rants, and South Asian states export teak and mahogany, destroying their own countryside in the process, for similar reasons.

In the meantime, the world's unique and irreplaceable rain forests are being demolished. Every year, 11 million hectares of tropical forests are cleared — about the area of Virginia. In 1987 alone, 8 million hectares of Brazilian rain forest were burned to clear land for cattle ranching. And about 100 of the world's species become extinct every day. Senator Albert Gore asked, "If, as in a science fiction movie, we had a giant invader from space clomping across the rain forests of the world with football field–size feet — going boom, boom, boom every second — would we react?"[3] His point is that this is happening right now.

Responses to the Problem

As worldwide awareness of the plight of the rain forests has increased, so has international pressure on those states that are currently devastating theirs. But this too raises difficulties. For one thing, many large corporations are profiting from rain forest destruction, which reduces the incentive for governments to preserve them. For another, having largely wiped out the indigenous inhabitants of North America, and greatly abused their own environment (also making themselves rich in the process), North Americans are on shaky ground lecturing Brazilians to refrain from destroying their "frontier." And after years of selfish, destructive ecological imperialism in Africa, Europe has little moral basis for urging the Zaire government to spare the Congo watershed. Imagine the response if the British government had sought to prevent the United States from slaughtering its own indigenous bison herds during the nineteenth century. The environmental and social challenge in the Third World is to emulate the prosperity of the industrial states without repeating their mistakes. Conservation efforts must also contend with a fierce nationalism, often evoked when the wealthy North lectures the impoverished South about what the latter should do with its own lands. Few issues, short of war itself, better illuminate absurdity of state sovereignty in

---

*The great temples of Angor Wat, in Kampuchea, are build essentially of laterite.

Burnt section of tropical rainforest, Ivory Coast, Africa.
(Greenpeace/C. Plowden)

an interdependent world. But Brazil, for example, has its ancient battle cry, *A Amazonia e nossa* ("The Amazon is ours").

It will not be easy to persuade Third World inhabitants and governments — or the rest of us, for that matter — that the Amazon, the upper Congo watershed, the New Guinea lowlands, and indeed, all of the planet, belongs to all of us. But there is also some cause for hope. Worldwide awareness of the plight of the rain forests has increased greatly. Funds have been established to help preserve these irreplaceable regions. The field of "restoration ecology" has also gathered momentum, investigating ways to restore previously devastated lands. Local governments have begun to realize that their own economic, social, cultural, and even political health requires that they preserve a healthy environment.

And some organizations have begun experimenting with "debt for nature swaps," in which the external debt of certain Third World countries is purchased at a substantial discount (say, 50¢ on the dollar), and then used, in turn, to guarantee nature reserves. In this way, countries like Ecuador and Bolivia have been able to retire some of their debt while also preserving some of their natural environment . . . to everyone's benefit. The field of "ecotourism" has also been blossoming, giving countries that are wildlife-rich but cash-poor a financial incentive to preserve their living resources; the African state of Ruanda, for example, has been able to reap substantial income by providing opportunities for wealthy, nature-loving tourists to observe free-living gorillas. (The alternative is to clear the forests and destroy the gorillas, for short-lived subsistence farming, which is also less remunerative.) More than 10 percent of Costa Rica's land is now protected, much of it in national parks; if the environmental movement continues to show the political vitality it has demonstrated in recent years, other countries can be expected to follow suit.

RENEWABLE RESOURCES

One of the most fundamental principles of environmental stewardship is that we must respect the natural cycles on which all life depends. There is simply no viable alternative to some form of global balance: between carbon emissions and carbon fixation, between soil erosion and soil formation, between tree cutting and burning and tree planting and growth, between births and deaths. In the long run, we simply cannot take more away from the land than we — or nature — put back. Moreover, we must plan for the long run. It is ethically unacceptable, and ultimately impractical as well, to purchase short-term gratification and growth while robbing the future. (Similarly, we cannot displace material from one part of a natural cycle into another without courting trouble; for example, as previously noted, the greenhouse effect results from the unbalanced shift of carbon from fossil fuels to the atmosphere.)

Soil

Forests and soils provide especially poignant and worrisome cases of renewable resources that are being dangerously disrupted. Over geological time, for example, soils were formed more rapidly than they eroded, thereby bequeathing to all of us a life-sustaining layer of topsoil averaging about 6–10 inches deep. But deforestation, erosion, overgrazing, and so on have dangerously degraded this natural legacy. It may be difficult to believe, but in ancient times, North Africa was the granary of Rome. Today, it is desert, and that desert is advancing south across Africa at a frightening pace.

In some cases, deserts are caused by simple drought, a natural absence of water. In others, the process of "desertification" is largely responsible. Desertification is a major threat to soil. It is not a natural process, but rather the consequence of human mistreatment, whereby the rich organic substance is washed or blown away, leaving relatively coarse, rocky materials, which cannot sustain plant life and also are unable to retain moisture, thereby contributing to erosion and further degradation. The resulting sand dunes or gullies are nonproductive and very difficult to reclaim, even for wildlife habitat.

According to a 1984 assessment by the United Nations Environmental Programme, 4.5 billion hectares — 35 percent of the Earth's land surface — are threatened by desertification. Of this vast region, three-quarters has already been at least somewhat degraded. In the United States today, farmers lose 6 tons of topsoil for every one ton of produce grown. Atmospheric sensing stations in Hawaii can detect when spring plowing begins in China because of the increase in particulate matter as precious soil becomes airborne. Worldwide, approximately 25 billion tons of topsoil are lost to erosion every year; this is nearly equivalent to what now covers the wheatlands of Australia.

As Third World economies decline and population pressure rises, marginal land is brought under cultivation, leading to further erosion by wind and water, desertification, and additional loss of long-term productivity. Until the midtwentieth century, worldwide crop production increased at least in part because additional lands were brought under cultivation. Then, further increases in agricultural yields were achieved during the 1950s and 1960s through the "green revolution" of improved genetic varieties, fertilizers, and pesticides. But the limits of such advances are rapidly being reached. Per capita productivity in Africa, for example, has actually begun *declining*, and no major new regions can be brought under cultivation, at least not for long. Furthermore, overuse of existing croplands can exact a heavy price. In addition to erosion and desertification, for example, millions of acres are being destroyed by "salinization": When underground soil drainage is insufficient, irrigation water — loaded with fertilizer and other salts — puddles up and evaporates, leaving an implacable manmade saline desert, which already covers vast areas of previously productive land, and is expanding rapidly. Deforestation also contributes to this problem because tree roots normally suck up excess ground water that is then transpired by the leaves; this allows subsurface salts to remain underground. With the trees destroyed, excess ground water carries these poisonous salts to the surface, which is then unable to support plant life.

The World Bank has introduced a new concept, "food insecurity," which refers to those people who lack enough food for normal health and physical activity. African states are especially food insecure, notably Ethiopia, Zaire, Uganda, Chad, Somalia, and Mozambique. The drought of 1988 revealed that such insecurity may be potentially more widespread than many realize, and moreover, developed states may not be immune. Thus, the U.S. grain harvest that year fell below consumption rates for the first time in recent history. It was only because of record amounts of grain in storage at the beginning of the 1987 crop year that the ensuing poor harvests of 1988 and 1989 did not result in widespread famine among other countries, who rely upon U.S. exports.

The destruction of productive soil is very difficult, but not impossible, to reverse. Overgrazed and overcultivated land must be allowed to lie fallow, sometimes for many years. Land that is especially vulnerable must be taken out of active production. The United States has led the way in this regard; the Food Surplus Act of 1985 is intended to shift 45 million acres of highly erodable land into meadows or forests. (This represents fully one-eighth of U.S. cropland, but it does not actually constitute a sacrifice, since such land is not highly productive, and moreover, it cannot produce worthwhile yields for very long, before being seriously degraded.)

Forests

The basic principle of sustainability applies to forest growth and regeneration as well. In short, if we destroy more than is created, we are cutting into the productive substance of the planet. And such imbalance cannot continue for long. If we cut and burn more than grows in that same period of time, then forests (or other resources) are diminished, weakened, and ultimately, destroyed. In Third World countries, forest cover is declining at a dangerous rate, due to logging, land clearing, and firewood gathering. Between 1973 and 1981—a mere eight years—India lost 16 percent of its forest cover; as a result, fuelwood prices in India's forty-one largest cities increased by nearly one half, exacting a painful toll on that nation's poor. It doesn't take a higher degree in mathematics or forestry to see that such trends cannot continue very long, and that such depredations must inevitably have devastating effects on wildlife, soil formation and maintenance, water quality, atmospheric equilibrium, and—not least—human well-being. In central Europe and North America, acid rain generated by industrial air pollution, especially coal-fired power-generating plants, has already damaged up to 25 percent of the forests, and rendered thousands of lakes uninhabitable by fish and other aquatic life. Forest destruction, in turn, leads to soil erosion, further degradation of water quality, and increased runoff. For example, years of forest destruction in the Himalayan foothills above Bangladesh contributed to devastating floods in 1988, which took an enormous toll in lives and property.

The Bangladesh tragedy exemplifies several important environmental themes:

1. Political boundaries are virtually irrelevant to the world's ecology. Forest-cutting in north-eastern India, Nepal, and Bhutan resulted in widespread destruction in Bangladesh, which is downstream.

2. Environmental issues are not only the legitimate worry of the affluent. Poor people—and often poor countries—typically are located where the environment has been most severely abused, and are liable to suffer most seriously from environmental disasters.

3. Environmental abuse can generate short-term profits, but invariably at the cost of long-term declines. Natural systems underpin all natural economies; as the former deteriorate, so will the latter. As a result, sensible policies must reflect environmental wisdom no less than economic, social, and political realities.

4. Natural processes must be respected. Human beings can intervene in those processes—we can unbalance them, and sometimes even restore them—but we cannot transcend them.

It is possible, fortunately, to turn the tide on forest loss. Tree-planting on a massive scale will help overcome greenhouse warming, reverse erosion, provide fuel and wildlife habitats, and improve water and air quality. South Korea has begun to do just this, China is on the verge, and India at least has developed a forward-looking plan to reclaim its forests. Celebrating its one hundredth year of statehood, North Dakota pledged in 1989 to plant 10 million trees. Trees do grow back, and reforestation is generally feasible, so long as the money is available and people understand the need to do it.

Food Production

One of the most important renewable resources is the production of food itself. Nontechnologic farmers obtain small yields, and are often thought to be inefficient compared with modern, high-tech agriculture. But in fact, much of the productivity of agro-industry is achieved by using vast amounts of energy. On average, every one calorie expended by nontechnologic farmers (as human and animal labor) yields five to fifty calories of food energy. By contrast, U.S. farming expends five to ten calories of energy (mostly as petroleum, some as fertilizer and pesticide) to produce just one calorie of food. We grow a lot of food, but we do so by expending even more energy, which not only contributes to greenhouse warming, but also depletes our most important nonrenewable resource, fossil fuels.

THE PROBLEM OF ENERGY

Energy, defined as the capacity to do work, represents a fundamental human need. As civilization has grown, human and animal energy has been supplemented by mechanical and chemical energy, the former provided by wind and water, the latter by combustion of wood and fossil fuels, notably coal, oil, and natural gas. More recently, nuclear energy has been tapped as well.

Nuclear Energy

Nuclear energy was originally hailed as being "too cheap to meter," but it now presents major problems: soaring costs because of safety problems, risks of accidental radioactive releases, the possible diversion of nuclear power to produce nuclear weapons, and the nearly intractable problem of safely storing the highly radioactive by-products. In addition, public confidence in nuclear power was severely shaken by several major accidents, including one at Three Mile Island in Pennsylvania in 1979, and the much more serious explosion and fire at the Chernobyl nuclear power plant in the Soviet Union in 1986. The Chernobyl disaster resulted in perhaps 50 deaths, 100 immediate injuries, 135,000 people evacuated from their homes, and more than $3 billion in direct financial costs. Even more critically, not only was European agriculture greatly disrupted, but experts estimate that anywhere from hundreds to possibly tens of thousands of cancer deaths will result in future years. Nuclear power still retains substantial popular and governmental support in one country: France. Elsewhere, worldwide enthusiasm for nuclear power has dropped dramatically. In fact, the proportion of the world's energy to be provided by nuclear power apparently

will be lower in the year 2000 than it was in 1987. No new nuclear power plants have been ordered in the United States since 1974, and without substantial government subsidies, the nuclear power industry clearly would fail the test of the marketplace. (On the other hand, some argue that with growing concern over acid rain and the greenhouse effect, nuclear power may get a new lease on life, since, for all its liabilities, nuclear power does not produce carbon dioxide or oxides of nitrogen or sulfur.)

Fossil Fuels

Nonnuclear energy sources can roughly be divided into two categories: renewable and nonrenewable. Of these, the nonrenewable energy sources currently supply the largest proportion. They are also the most polluting, and of course — by definition — once they are used up, they cannot be replenished. Fossil fuels essentially have powered the Industrial Revolution, and the use of fossil fuels has parelleled industrialization and modernization. Thus in 1900, worldwide fossil fuel use totaled the equivalent of one billion tons of coal; by 1950, that figure had increased to 3 billion tons; and by 1986, 12 billion. At the same time, total carbon emissions from fossil fuels increased as well, peaking at more than 5 billion metric tons per year in 1980 (deforestation adds about another 1–3 billion tons annually). Since 1980, the Gross World Product has continued to increase, whereas carbon emissions have more or less stabilized; greater efficiency of fuel use appears to be responsible. This, in turn, is largely a result of dramatic increases in the prices of fuel — especially oil — during the 1970s. It further suggests that one way for governments to encourage conservation is to make energy more expensive. We can expect governments to resist this solution, however, because of internal pressures from the petroleum industry, as well as a reluctance to hamper their own economy and put it at a short-term disadvantage relative to other countries. It will also be argued (correctly) that the poor would suffer most from increased fuel costs.

Following the twin Mideast oil crises of 1974 and 1979 (the first in response to Arab anger over

U.S. support of Israel during the Yom Kippur War, and the second as a result of the Iran hostage situation), oil costs rose dramatically, and interest in oil conservation increased proportionately. However, with the temporary "oil glut" of the 1980s—itself largely a consequence of political disarray within OPEC—prices dropped from $36 per barrel in 1982 to less than $12 per barrel in 1988. American consumers have responded by once again turning toward larger, less fuel-efficient vehicles, and greater profligacy overall.

But sometime in the twenty-first century, alternatives to petroleum must be found. By the mid-1980s, almost one half of all the oil discovered on Earth had already been consumed, including four-fifths of North America's known reserves. As with many natural resources, the distribution of oil bears little relationship to world population. The Indian subcontinent, with nearly one billion people in 1990 and another billion expected before population growth finally stabilizes in the next century, has less than 1 percent of the world's petroleum. China, with more than a billion people, has only about 3 percent. By contrast, the Middle East, with only 4 percent of the world's population, sits on 56 percent of global oil reserves. Advanced industrial societies—in particular, Western Europe and Japan—rely heavily on oil, but have very little of their own.

Each world region can be categorized as to its "carrying capacity," the number of people who can be supported by the natural resources of that region. Many states are overextended ecologically, living beyond their means. In some cases (Bangladesh, Indonesia, Haiti), this overextension generates severe, chronic poverty; in others (Japan, Western Europe, the United States), it has given rise to imperialism—military and/or economic—whereby the resources of other states are appropriated. In the latter cases, fossil fuels in particular have served as a kind of "subsidy," allowing these countries to expand economically beyond their natural carrying capacities.

Coal is the most abundant fossil fuel worldwide, with the largest deposits in China, the U.S.S.R., and the United States. Unfortunately, coal is also environmentally destructive, since, on combustion, it releases not only large amounts of carbon dioxide (contributing to greenhouse warming) but also nitrogen and sulfur oxides, which make up a major component of acid rain.

Oil Spills

Oil has been especially troubling, not only because of the industrial world's addiction to it and the pollution caused by burning it, but also because of its penchant to spill and cause additional environmental damage. In March 1989, the United States experienced the worst oil spill in its history, when a supertanker, the *Exxon Valdez*, ran aground on a reef in Prince William Sound, Alaska. It dumped 240,000 barrels of oil (about 11 million gallons) onto one of the world's most scenic and environmentally sensitive regions, and it could not have happened at an ecologically more sensitive time: Migrating birds, by the tens of thousands, were about to start touching down in the area, and the tiny fry at numerous fish hatcheries were especially vulnerable. Many thousands of birds died, along with hundreds of sea otters and seals, as well as uncounted hundreds of thousands—perhaps millions—of fish. It has been estimated that the local ecosystem, as well as the economy (based largely on fishing), will take decades to recover, and that in part, it may never do so. In fact, oil spills are quite common, with an average of 2.9 million barrels being dumped annually onto the world's oceans. It is particularly ironic that loss of a scarce and precious commodity such as oil would also become a major source of pollution, and that in the spilling of vast quantities of oil, the environment is itself substantially degraded.

The *Exxon Valdez* disaster occurred at a time when the U.S. Congress was considering opening up additional Alaskan lands for oil exploration and drilling, notably the Arctic National Wildlife Refuge, along the North Slope, whose tundra ecosystem is even more vulnerable to oil spills and other disturbances. Supporters of such "development" point to what they see as the inevitable need to extract, process, and combust the planet's petroleum resources. We are simply too dependent on petroleum, they assert, to be paralyzed by environmental concerns.

Conservation, Increased Efficiency, and Renewable Sources

Energy use is an area in which change is particularly necessary if we are to create a prosperous, healthy world. But if nuclear power is too dangerous, coal too polluting, and oil too limited and geopolitically troublesome, what options remain? In the long term, there seems little choice but to pursue increased development of renewable energy sources: hydroelectric, wind, solar (photovoltaic), and possibly tidal as well. In the short term, however, most of the world's energy balance must be met by increased conservation and enhanced efficiency. Such solutions are not intrinsically exciting; they lack the romantic allure of dramatically discovering some new, high-tech source of energy. But in the real world of diminishing resources and increasing pollution as well as economic disparity, no better hope for a balanced and enduring future seems to exist.

National investments in conservation and increased efficiency currently represent only a tiny fraction of energy investment overall, yet they provide a far better return than efforts to increase the supply of energy. The so-called soft path — a combination of renewable energy sources, increased efficiency, and conservation — must be the route to the future. Even now, solar collectors provide a large proportion of domestic hot water in Israel, wind power generates substantial electricity in California, and geothermal energy is important in Iceland and the Philippines. Worldwide, wind power alone generates about 2,000 megawatts of electricity, which displaces more than 500,000 tons of carbon emissions annually. It can be expected that rural electrification of Third World villages will add substantially to atmospheric carbon dioxide; on the other hand, an international commitment to employ photovoltaics for this purpose would constitute a major savings, and one that is well within the reach of modern technology.

Since 1973, world energy efficiency has increased by about 25 percent, displacing $250 billion in coal, oil, gas, and nuclear expenditures annually; the advantages, clearly, are not just financial, but environmental as well. Conservation leaders, such as Amory Lovins of the Rocky Mountain Institute in Aspen, Colorado, note that enormous additional savings could be effected if Americans simply stopped living in leaky houses, and stopped driving gas-guzzling automobiles. Some specific options include the following:

- Newly designed "superwindows," which insulate two to four times better than triple-glazed windows, would save more oil and gas annually than the total annual Alaskan production.

- Weatherizing uninsulated and badly insulated oil- and gas-heated homes would save 1.65 billion barrels. This would cost about $27 billion, in contrast to the $45 billion currently budgeted for projecting military forces into the Persian Gulf, an operation whose purpose is to protect the major source of foreign oil supplies.

- Toughened efficiency standards for home appliances alone (which to some degree are already on the books) will displace more than 300 million tons of carbon emissions per year.

- Every one mile per gallon (mpg) improvement in gas consumption among U.S. automobiles would save the amount of oil that is annually produced in all of Alaska. The average U.S. car currently releases its weight in carbon into the atmosphere every year. Cars and trucks consume so much petroleum that every one mpg increase in mileage will reduce carbon dioxide emissions by about 40 billion pounds annually, equivalent in output to six large coal-fired power plants. And yet, in 1986, the Reagan administration announced a three-year rollback in requirements for average fuel efficiency, reducing the new-car minimum from 27.5 to 26 mpg. The average U.S. car gets 18.3 mpg, whereas the average new car gets about

30 mpg. Volvo has announced a new model that averages 71 mpg, while a Renault prototype exceeds 100 mpg. Furthermore, a sea-change in public attitude, away from private vehicles and toward mass transmit, could lead to massive energy and environmental savings, equivalent to discovering several Middle Easts full of oil, but resulting in one tenth the pollution.

- Switching from high-sulfur eastern coal to low-sulfur western supplies would reduce the deadly burden of sulfuric acid in rainfall. In addition, various promising technologies now exist that can greatly reduce sulfur dioxide emissions from coal-burning power plants, which constitute the largest single cause of acid rain. Currently, two-thirds of the energy from such plants goes up the chimney as waste heat; it is possible to enhance the efficiency of such operations by so-called fluidized bed combustion, from 33 percent to 70 percent and greater. Switching to natural gas would also be very helpful, since natural gas emits only half the carbon of coal (greenhouse warming), less nitrogen (smog), and no sulfur (acid rain).

- A carbon emission tax could accurately reflect the global costs of polluting technologies, while also raising large amounts of revenues that could be directed toward reconstructing the environment, and also sponsoring energy-efficient technologies. Such a tax would also make renewable energy sources more competitive with their polluting, nonrenewable counterparts.

For some global problems—for example, the nuclear arms race—difficulties revolve especially around what governments do, and have done. In others, such as the environmental crisis, the problem is ongoing, *unless* governments do something to intervene. Yet, doing something always seems more costly than doing nothing, and doing just a little bit (to satisfy public demand) always seems cheaper than actually doing a lot. But when it comes to environmental protection, inaction will, in the long run, be far more costly than action. This is because the worldwide ecological situation, if left to itself, will not remain at the same level; rather, it is bound to deteriorate.

ACTIVISM

Within the United States

Environmental activism takes many forms. Within the United States, it is largely expressed through the following means: legislative, legal, and direct action. Legislative environmentalism involves the passing of laws designed to protect environmental values, to preserve wild and open space, to restrict pollution (typically by establishing air or water standards to which states and local municipalities are required to comply), to prohibit the sale of materials derived from endangered species, and so on. A landmark piece of legislation, the National Environmental Policy Act of 1970, requires that, before expending federal funds on any major project, an environmental impact statement must first be prepared and evaluated; this statement is expected to employ scientific studies to evaluate the extent of the impact, to determine whether it can be diminished, and to provide objective information as to whether the project should be permitted to go forward.

Often, legislative remedies are incomplete, in part because governments may hesitate to enforce regulations that they see as harmful to business interests. In such cases, citizens may have access to legal procedures, obtaining court injunctions to prevent illegal actions, and in some cases, forcing governments to enforce their own laws. The field of environmental law has grown rapidly, and groups such as the Environmental Defense Fund bring polluters and land despoilers to court. There has also been some progress in identifying environmental values (the right to clean air, water, an environment containing wildlife) as having legal standing similar to personal property rights or the right to privacy.

Finally, there is the question of direct action, analogous in many ways to nonviolent resistance against war. Groups such as Greenpeace have

Greenpeace activists plugging a polluting outflow pipe in Ashtabula, Ohio. (Greenpeace/Rob Visser)

sel *Rainbow Warrior*, which had been protesting French nuclear weapons testing in the South Pacific.

Not surprisingly, there has been some tension between large, relatively wealthy and well-connected environmental organizations that often are headquartered in Washington, D.C. — such as the Sierra Club, Wilderness Society, National Wildlife Federation, Audubon Society — which lobby members of Congress and seek to exert influence at the national level, and local, grass-roots activists, who are often on the "front lines" in disputes over leaky toxic dump sites, nuclear power plants, and so on. Nonetheless, the environmental movement in the United States has been gaining strength, although there seems little prospect for an influential U.S. Green party modeled on the European experience.

In Other Countries

Grass-roots environmentalism has, if anything, been developing more strongly in other countries. One of the most remarkable is the Chipko, or "Hug-the-Tree," movement of India. Beginning in the 1970s, Chipko developed in remote villages in the southern foothills of the Himalayas. It arose spontaneously, based on a cultural heritage that held a deep respect for the region's lofty mountains, magnificent forests, and clear streams. A series of disastrous floods undeniably resulted from extensive deforestation; local activists responded by literally hugging the great trees, and, in time-honoured Gandhian fashion (see Chapter 23), lying down in front of logging operations. The Chipko strategy has since been used to save other natural areas in India, and it has also spread to other countries, where environmental concern is often most strongly developed among the poor, who rely most deeply on the land. (The poor are typically in a difficult bind, forced by the necessities of day-to-day subsistence into environmentally destructive practices, and yet also painfully aware of their dependence on natural eco-systems.)

Another epic struggle has pitted indigenous Amazonian tribes, rubber-tappers (who earn their

blockaded whaling ships and sewage outfalls, and by a variety of dramatic and often courageous acts, including boycotts and sit-ins, called public attention to other environmental abuses, such as the clubbing of baby seals or improper disposal of nuclear waste. Such actions often entail civil disobedience, and can be controversial. The radical environmental organization Earth First! sometimes resorts to ecological sabotage ("ecotage"), by vandalizing land-clearing equipment, or "spiking" trees (hammering large nails into them, thereby making it dangerous to cut them into lumber). Governments have occasionally responded with violence and outright terrorism, as when French intelligence agents blew up the Greenpeace ves-

Biography

Lester R. Brown

Lester R. Brown has been called, by the *Telegraph* of Calcutta, "the guru of the global environmental movement." His original training was in agriculture and he spent six months studying in India and ten years growing tomatoes. He also served as an international agricultural analyst for the U.S. Department of Agriculture. In 1974 he founded the Worldwatch Institute, a private, nonprofit, Washington-based research institute devoted to the analysis of global environmental, demographic, and economic issues.

He launched an annual series of the *State of the World* reports in 1984, designed to raise consciousness, impart environmental information, and suggest solutions to the world's environmental problems. He also launched *World Watch*, a bimonthly magazine that reports on the Worldwatch Institute's research and policy recommendations.

Lester Brown has appeared on many television and radio talk shows, including *The Today Show, Meet the Press, Nightline,* and National Public Radio, emphasizing the need for public attention and government action with respect to the worldwide environment. His books include *Man, Land, and Food, World Without Borders, By Bread Alone,* and *Building a Sustainable Society.*

---

living extracting latex sap from free-growing rubber trees), anthropologists, and environmentalists against Brazilian land development interests. In this case, ecological exploitation has been intimately connected with violence, in the form of genocidal extermination of whole villages and indigenous tribes, by private "armies" hired by landowners, and abetted by the Brazilian military. In 1989, the conflict betweeen environmental exploiters and defenders received worldwide attention with the murder of noted ecologist and rubber-tapper organizer Chico Mendez.

Small-scale, grass-roots organizing continues to occur worldwide on behalf of the environment and its people. Tens of thousands of community development groups operate in India alone, and their focus, increasingly, is on ecologically sensitive, sustainable development. Ecological issues have become a major focus for the more than 100,000 "Christian base communities" that have sprung up in Brazil, while in Africa and Asia in particular, women have been especially prominent in struggling for local reforestation, soil preservation, and so forth. Although it cannot honestly be said that the tide has turned—every year, in fact, the planet seems on balance to be losing rather than gaining— at least the battle has been joined.

A SUSTAINABLE FUTURE

A sustainable society is one that is fundamentally in equilibrium with its environment, that meets its needs without diminishing the prospects of future generations. The alternative—nonsustainable exploitation—can produce short-term benefits but long-term disaster. Ecosystems, and presumably, entire planets, can be destroyed by thoughtlessness and a failure to take the long view. Consider one small example, a cautionary tale that can be extended to other resources. The Peruvian anchovy fishery expanded rapidly from 4 million tons (1960) to 8 million tons (1965) and then to 13 million tons

(1970). In contrast with the rosy predictions of economists and fishing industry officials, ecologists had long been warning that the anchovy fishery could not sustain catches above 9 million tons; then, in the early 1970s, yields plummeted to less than 2 million tons annually. And there they have remained. As with the industrial benefits of exploiting fossil fuels, or the agricultural benefits of denuding the world's tropical rain forests, the Peruvian fishery was cannibalizing its own underlying resource base, at a rate that could not be sustained. As a consequence, it appears to have been seriously, and perhaps permanently, injured.

There is little question that human societies must ultimately meet the fundamental criterion of sustainability. It has been suggested that some of the world's great civilizations — Sumerian, Mayan, Roman — may have declined in part because they were destabilized internally, by depletion of their underlying resource base. Today, very few knowledgeable people question the ultimate desirability, even the necessity, of a sustainable world economy. There is considerable debate, however, over the best route to sustainability, and even about when the limits to growth must be faced. Some people retain faith that technology will somehow save us, as it often appeared to have done in the past.* Others maintain that the Earth is blessed with abundant resources — natural as well as human — sufficient to see us through any crisis that will arise, at least for the foreseeable future. And yet others trust in God, or capitalism, or communism.

Faith in Technology

One argument holds that as resources are used up the resulting shortages will serve as incentive to (1) find new reserves, (2) reduce the rate of consumption, for example, by increasing efficiency,

and (3) substitute abundant resources for those in short supply, for example, making telephone lines out of fiber-optic tubes instead of copper. Necessity (or more precisely, higher prices) will be the mother of invention as a resource-poor world finds new solutions to old problems. In the recent past, fossil fuels largely replaced wood and animal power in providing energy for heavy industry, and aluminum has to some degree supplemented iron as a construction material. Who is to say that humanity will not continue to be equally inventive? New resources, new forms of energy, new ways of replenishing the earth may be just over the horizon.

The difficulty with such thinking is that innovations cannot be counted on,† whereas the depletion of known resources is absolutely certain. Moreover, even when they do prove successful, "solutions" often carry a new array of problems along with them: Fossil fuels pollute the atmosphere, high-technology mining operations are often energy-intensive themselves, and so on. A starry-eyed confidence that technology or inventiveness will always save us — like Flash Gordon or the Lone Ranger riding heroically to the last-minute rescue — may well have tragic consequences.

Thresholds

Many experts fear, in addition, that we cannot continue on our present course much longer without causing irreversible damage. There may be key thresholds in the planetary environment that, once crossed, may permanently impair the Earth's ability to meet our needs in the future. If the atmospheric load of greenhouse gases becomes too high, the ozone layer too sparse, soils too eroded, air and water pollution too severe (or some combination of these and other factors), if forest clearing and

---

*It should be noted that many of these supposed "solutions" were short-term only, resulting in situations that were no better, or even worse, than before the technological "savior" appeared.

†There was immense excitement in the late 1980s about the possibility that "cold fusion" could provide cheap, abundant, clean energy; that hope now appears illusory, and we must conclude that there probably is no free lunch in our environmental future.

Ground-clearing in what had been a lush African rainforest. Modern technology, such as the highly efficient, specially designed bulldozer pictured here, often proves to be part of the problem rather than the solution. (Greenpeace/C. Plowden)

desertification go too far, then at some point, the planet may simply become incapable of nurturing life, regardless of our attempts to remedy things. Thus, it seems likely that the current generation has the enormous responsibility of determining the future habitability of our planet — and not just for ourselves but for myriad other species as well. In this regard, time is not on our side. Soil, once eroded away, can take centuries to be replenished; certain forms of contamination (plastics, nuclear waste, long-lived pesticides) will "live" longer than human history has thus far endured; the atmosphere, once warmed, may be impossible to cool; and species, once extinct, can never be re-created.

As we have seen, however, there are solutions, some of them short-term stopgaps, others more promising for the long haul. Certain countries — notably the wealthy ones — have even stabilized their population (see Chapter 22), which, by definition, is a major step toward sustainability. Others — such as China — are working hard to do so. Energy efficiency can be increased dramatically,

and alternative, renewable sources can be expanded. Reforestation, soil conservation, wildlife preservation, and strict antipollution controls are all eminently feasible. In most cases, the sticking point is political will. In this respect, several major issues can be identified.

Human Perception

Many dramatic human achievements require that a perceptual threshold be crossed. Before this happens, relatively few people have any deep dissatisfactions with the status quo; the result is business as usual. Then, charismatic leaders, catastrophic events, or successful education campaigns may combine to force a dramatic perceptual shift, after which the world appears transformed . . . and after this, sometimes, the world itself can actually be changed. These events often have a distinct ethical/religious component, but appeals to simple self-preservation may also be effective — consider the increasing worldwide revulsion toward nuclear weapons. Perhaps, with the various combined threats to the worldwide environment, and the intense publicity they have generated in recent years, ecological wholeness is about to receive the attention and action that it warrants.

Interconnections

A world at peace is one in which environmental, human rights, and economic issues all cohere to foster maximum growth and well-being. Ecological harmony cannot realistically be separated from questions of human rights or economic justice.* The right to a safe environment, clear air, and pure water is no less a human right than the right to freedom of expression or dissent, equal employment opportunity, or participation in the political process. Environmental degradation is also intimately connected to poverty; as we have seen, wealthy states are often able to export their most odious environmental abuses, and impoverished states are often forced by their poverty to accept the situation. In addition, within any given state, wealthy people are able to purchase environmental amenities, while the poor find themselves living in polluted, degraded surroundings. The plowing of steep, erosion-prone slopes — which permanently destroys soil — as well as large-scale intrusions onto wildlife habitats (which contributes to extinction) is in large part a response to land hunger in rural Third World countries, where a small minority of wealthy people own the great majority of the arable land, thereby pushing people to environmentally abusive behavior.

Ecological wholeness cannot be achieved piecemeal. The rain forests will continue to be abused so long as there are too many people and not enough land; indeed, overpopulation has an impact on every environmental issue (see Chapter 22). Poverty leads to land degradation, as hungry,

desperate people clear and cultivate regions that should be left untouched. The burning of fossil fuels produces air pollution as well as greenhouse gases; greenhouse warming will greatly increase food insecurity by reducing agricultural productivity; accordingly, solutions to these and other problems must be intimately tied to providing adequate, safe energy.

Environmental problems are integrated in another sense as well. Many of the most severe ecological threats are worldwide in scope, including the greenhouse effect, air and water pollution that affects many states, and the threat to the planet's ozone layer. Others, although occurring within national boundaries, affect the world economy and/or the worldwide quality of life, such as the loss of species diversity, soil destruction, and unsustainable demands on the world's renewable resources as well as the heedless depletion of nonrenewables. Deforestation in Nepal causes flooding in Bangladesh; water overuse by the United States deprives Mexico of water from the Colorado River; pollution of the Rhine by Swiss and West German chemical industries makes its water toxic for the Dutch who live downstream; whaling by the Japanese destroys these magnificent animals for everyone; and so on.

Finally, the various environmental and social issues are themselves interlocking. Thus, population stabilization, as we shall see, will likely occur only when poverty is reduced; Third World countries will be able to devote themselves to the preservation of their unique wild resources only if and when their debt burden is relieved; energy use will be sustainable only if it does not burden the air and water with additional pollutants; and so forth. Undeniably, world cooperation on the environment is every bit as necessary as on economic matters, or on issues of military security and disarmament.

Tensions Between Economics and the Environment

In the long run, there is only compatibility between economics and ecology, because what destroys the environment also destroys economies. But economic planners typically look only to the immediate future, and in the short run, jobs, profits, and

---

*This point could equally well be made in Chapters 20, 21, or 22, but since the concept of interconnections is so fundamental to ecological thinking, it seems most appropriate to emphasize it in this chapter.

development often conflict with environmental preservation. Air and water pollution controls cost money, and installing them may make an industry less profitable, leading to plant closings and loss of jobs. A sound environment may demand that wetlands be preserved (to absorb variations in the water table, as breeding grounds for fish and other aquatic organisms, and so on), but such preservation may come at the cost of restrictions on development (fewer new shopping centers, housing sites, industrial parks, and so on). Environmentalists warn that we cannot continue plundering the planet and still have a decent home left for ourselves; when stated this way, nearly everyone agrees. But for many economists and growth advocates, "plundering the planet" is another phrase for "standard of living," and everyone also agrees that living standards should be high. Something, it seems, has to give.

Ultimately, economic development and environmental protection are not antagonistic; they are intimately connected. Living standards cannot remain high if they are built on a crumbling environmental infrastructure. Vast numbers of people rely directly on the natural surpluses produced by a healthy environment: harvesting fish from wild populations in oceans, rivers, and lakes, obtaining game from the land and fuel from the forests. A Mauritanian cattle-herder does not need advanced training in ecology to know that "the land is tired," nor does a Filipino fisherman require a degree in marine biology to recognize that fish don't thrive where the ocean is polluted. Guatemalan peasants know all too well the consequences of plowing land that is too steep, and it is not only wealthy, amateur bird-watchers who mourn the loss of brilliant animals such as the quetzal, which has a prime place in the cultural identity of Central American Indians.

But it is not only the Third World "primitives" who are immersed in the environment; we all depend on stable hydrological cycles for water, on atmospheric processes for air, on a stable world climate, on the productivity of the world's organic soils. Environmental degradation, in the long run, translates directly not only into a less interesting and less beautiful planet— one deprived of wildlife, for example, or scenic values—but also into thirst, hunger, poverty, sickness, and misery. The World Bank has recently reorganized its priorities, recognizing that many of its past projects have been environmental disasters: dams that fill up with silt, land-clearing that quickly reverts to virtual desert, "forestry" that makes timber companies wealthy while depriving indigenous people (and various plant and animal species as well) of their ways of life. As a result, ecological issues are now supposed to be fully considered in evaluating proposals for development assistance.

Nonetheless, in many cases, battle lines continue to be drawn between those who see themselves as defending the environment and those who champion jobs and economic development. In the Pacific Northwest of the United States, for example, a major controversy has erupted between conservationists and the timber industry. A rare bird species, the spotted owl, nests only in relatively large, undisturbed tracts of old-growth forest. These forests are unique in the world, and only a small remnant of their previous grandeur still persists. But the timber in these forests is also coveted by loggers. Whether a long-term accommodation can be reached in this and other acute conflicts between economics and ecology remains in doubt. It should be emphasized, however, that in the long run, a successful timber industry requires a continuing supply of trees, just as the spotted owl does. Accordingly, it seems not only possible that a "win–win" solution can be achieved, but also necessary, because neither the economy nor the environment can be victorious if the other is defeated.

Political Ideologies

Critics of environmental policies in the West sometimes assume that capitalism is largely to blame; after all, a system that exalts profits above everything seems likely to disregard environmental values. And without doubt, the industrialism of capitalist states is intimately connected to their many environmental abuses. But socialist states are no more sensitive to environmental issues, and in

Spotted owl. This rare species is found only in the ancient forests of northwest North America and is the focus of intense controversy about jobs versus environment. (Robert Ashbaugh)

many cases, less so. In the U.S.S.R. and other communist states, the single-minded pursuit of production goals takes precedence over profits, and the environment — no less than in capitalist states — is seriously abused. Within the Soviet Union, for example, the once-majestic Aral Sea has dropped forty feet because of destructive, short-sighted dam and irrigation projects. The Neva River, just outside Leningrad's Hermitage Museum, is befouled with oil. Swimming is regularly curtailed at Black Sea resorts, due to typhoid and dysentery contamination. Environmental restrictions on development of Siberia are almost nonexistent, and ignored when present. Forest destruction in East Germany, Czechoslovakia, and Poland is among the most severe on Earth, and many regions of Poland in

particular have become drastically polluted by chemical and other toxic wastes.* The difference between traditional economics and sustainable economics (whether market-oriented or centrally planned) is that the former is concerned with how to produce what for whom, whereas the latter expands the definition of "for whom" to include future generations and the living Earth as well.

Because of the "discipline of the market," the economies of capitalist states are generally more efficient than those that are centrally planned; for example, the market-oriented states of Japan, Sweden, France, West Germany, the United States, and Great Britain average about 5 kilograms sulfur dioxide emitted per $1,000 GNP, whereas the communist states of Czechoslovakia, East Germany, Hungary, Romania, and the U.S.S.R. average about 30 kgs. In other words, the communist states were six times more inefficient, and inefficiency, in this case, translates into resource wastage as well as increased environmental pollution. Socialist states also use more energy per unit of GNP, and they are, if anything, even more polluted than capitalist states. (It is thus especially sobering to imagine the condition of the world's atmosphere, as well as its oil reserves, if China — which currently relies heavily on bicycles for transportation — was to achieve the per capita automobile ownership now enjoyed, say, by the United States.)

In the Marxist perspective, human problems are seen as deriving from the structure of social relationships, not the relationships of people to their environment. The ideology of growth is therefore deeply established (as it is in capitalism), along with the determination to build a Marxist utopia based on the abolition of material scarcity. Abandoning such a goal would be virtually to abandon the goal of Marxism itself. Accordingly, production and material expansion has long been the narrowly focused goal of socialist economic planners, with

---

*In fact, widespread dissatisfaction over environmental pollution was an important factor driving the anticommunist upheavals in Eastern Europe.

only token concern for the environment. And widespread state ownership has made the tragedy of the commons even more widespread than in market-oriented societies; private greed, insensitivity, and indifference have largely been replaced by public greed, insensitivity, and indifference.

Environmental activists in the United States often bemoan the American love affair with free enterprise and private land ownership. They point out how much ecological destruction has resulted from insistence that pursuit of profit justifies just about anything (pollution, resource depletion, and so on), and they emphasize how ruination of the natural environment has been brought about by the insistence that the "owners" have the right to destroy their own property (strip-mine it, sell it to developers of condominiums or shopping centers, and so forth). Their answer: more public ownership and public regulation of the environment. At the same time, ironically, environmental activists in the Soviet Union — of which there are growing numbers — increasingly bemoan the Soviet insistence on communism and public land ownership. They point out how much ecological destruction has resulted from pursuit of bureaucratically defined production goals and the fact that, since the land has no "owners," people don't feel committed to protecting it. Their answer: more private ownership and less public regulation of the environment. One might say that the grass is indeed greener on the other side of the ideological fence, with the added proviso that, when considering environmental issues, green is indeed the appropriate color for envy. It is sometimes said that the difference between capitalism and communism is that in the former, people exploit people, whereas in the latter, it is the other way around! In both cases, it is the environment — and ultimately, everyone — that loses.

There is, however, no theoretical reason why centrally planned economies could not exhibit greater environmental sensitivity than they now show. Given their structure, such "command economies" would in fact be better situated to include such considerations, by governmental fiat, in their economic planning. What is needed is the political/ideological resolve to do so. (It should be noted that under Mikhail Gorbachev, the Soviet Union has finally begun to include environmental preservation in its economic and social planning.) Similarly, there is no reason why market-oriented states could not exhibit greater sensitivity to the environment, although once again, this would require a modification of traditional ideology: Industry and the public would probably have to tolerate increased government insistence on strict environmental standards.

Making Peace

A world of increasingly scarce and endangered resources might be one in which people are motivated to cooperate, for everyone's benefit. But it might also be one in which conflict and violence are exaggerated, as wealthy states seek to maintain access to raw materials and to hold onto their advantages, while poor states attempt to translate their existing resources into power, or simply to retain them in the face of growing demands. It would be especially tragic if a world made tense by ecological scarcity drifted into a war that, in addition to its human toll, destroyed yet more of the nonhuman environment.

To get a feeling for the profoundly antiecological nature of modern war — even when it is nonnuclear — consider these consequences of the Vietnam War: 18 million gallons of Agent Orange and other chemical defoliants, dropped from airplanes, poisoned hundreds of thousands of acres in southeast Asia, and dramatically increased the number of miscarriages and birth deformities among the populace. Approximately 40 percent of Vietnam's land was rendered unfit for forestry or agriculture by the extensive use of defoliants, napalm, and high-explosive bombs.

But we are not doomed to repeat the mistakes of the past. The future can be reclaimed. Doing so, however, requires not only forbearance with respect to war, but an active commitment to peace. This, in turn, must involve not only measures directed at preventing war, but also those needed to build peace, including public as well as private commitment to invest heavily in environmental protection and restoration. But such investments require time, effort, and money. The following goals are minimal, but also achievable: reforesting the Earth and stopping current deforestation; slowing and eventually stabilizing population growth; increasing energy efficiency and developing renewable energy sources; protecting topsoil from erosion, desertification, and salinization; preserving representative, adequate-sized samples of the planet's pristine ecosystems and its wildlife; putting an end to poaching and to the trade in products from endangered species; and protecting the water, and land from harmful, persistent pollution. However, such accomplishments will not come cheaply. Some estimates suggest that they would require annual expenditures, over the next few decades, in the range of $200 billion per year. (The General Accounting Office estimates that it will cost about $150 billion just to clean up the mess already existing at U.S. nuclear production facilities.) And with so many pressing demands on government budgets, it is not clear where such funds would come from.

At the same time, who can argue that the goal — a habitable, sustainable planet — isn't worth such a cost? Moreover, even a price tag of $200 billion annually is only about one fifth of the world's annual military expenditures, which currently approach $1 *trillion* per year. Given the financial constraints alone (not to mention the spiritual or philosophical ones), it may well be that we cannot make peace with the planet until we make peace with one another. If national security is eventually redefined in broader terms than mere military security, such a transformation may well be possible. After all, the Netherlands currently spends about 6 percent of its GNP defending itself against the ocean — a far greater expenditure for its national security than it spends on NATO. And China has made impressive strides to demilitarize its economy, using the resources that have been released to invest in its own future. In 1977, China spent 13 percent of its GNP on the military, one of the highest percentages of the world. Ten years later, the military's share of China's economy had dropped by about one half, to approximately 6 percent, while investments in family planning, food production, and reforestation have paid off handsomely. China's

forests had been so devastated that by 1960, just 8 percent of that country remained tree-covered; by 1986, the figure had risen to 13 percent, with a realistic goal of 20 percent by the year 2000. At the same time, population growth has been dramatically reduced, and between 1977 and 1987, per capita food production rose by 50 percent.

On the other hand, we do not need to wait for the dawning of universal love and solidarity to make a major contribution toward correcting the sad state of the world's environment. Certain key states, by acting decisively, could greatly mitigate our current environmental difficulties. For example, the United States, China, and the Soviet Union produce fully 50 percent of the world's CO_2 emissions; Brazil, Indonesia, and Zaire hold 48 percent of all remaining virgin tropical rain forest; China and India together account for 35 percent of the world's annual population increase; and the northern tier of industrial states are responsible for virtually all of the world's acid rain production.

The result is a two-pronged lesson. First, as we have seen, making peace with the Earth may well require that we make peace with one another. But second, just as some people claim that "peace begins with me," impressive strides toward environmental peace can begin with the actions of individual countries, industries, groups, and people as well, not only to showcase what can be done, but also to get results. Otherwise, before the physical and biological limitations of the Earth take a more direct toll, a period of Hobbesian strife might ensue; chaos and war — with all its profoundly anti-ecological effects — may add to the devastation. Our shared environmental plight may inspire human beings to unite as inhabitants of a shared and threatened planet, or, more narrowly and destructively, as competitive members of separate and embattled nation-states.

Environmental Ethics

This chapter — like the rest of the book — has been motivated by a need to identify real-world problems and suggest real-world solutions. Thus, it is driven more by considerations of practicality than

Eucalyptus trees planted to stabilize sand dunes — a result of desertification — in Senegal. (United Nations/ Jeffrey Foxx)

by ethics. However, just as there is an underlying ethic to Peace Studies itself (the rightness of peace and the wrongness of violence), we can also identify deep-seated ethical components to environmental sensitivity. In the Indian cultural heritage, for example, human activity is guided by three values of life: *Artha* (essentially, resources), *Kama* (the needs and desires of human beings), and *Dharma* (right conduct, or what people *ought* to do as opposed to what they *want* to do.) Dharma also entails the proper utilization of resources, restricting their use to the satisfaction of one's primary needs, and not appropriating the resources of others. To do otherwise is to steal from others and from the world. In this worldview, Dharma consists of mediating skillfully and thoughtfully between desires and resources; there is therefore a close link between justice, ecological harmony, and social harmony. Activities that are wasteful or destructive of natural resources must therefore be rejected, on ethical grounds as well as for practical reasons.

As historian Lynn White pointed out in an influential essay,[4] the primary thrust of Judeo-Christian tradition has been, if anything, antinature. Al-

though an undertone of creation-centered spirituality can be found within both Judaism and Christianity, both religions emphasize a separation between human beings, on the one hand, and the biological world of beasts and fields, on the other. Human beings are thought to have been created in the image of God, as against the gross and nonspiritual material world. We have been told to "go forth and multiply," and to "subdue the earth." Having emphasized such a distinction between people and the natural world, Judeo-Christian teaching established a context for destruction and exploitation, providing the intellectual and emotional underpinning to what has since become our ecological crisis. White concludes his essay by describing an alternative tradition in Western theology: the gentle, nature-centered, and compassionate acceptance of Saint Francis of Assissi. He proposed Francis as the patron saint of ecologists.

Other thinkers have also proposed the establishment of ethics on a less homocentric and more tolerant and diversity-oriented basis. There may be deep benefits to adopting such a perspective, a more humble and accommodating view of the world and our place in it. If human beings saw themselves as part of the life-process rather than its most celebrated rulers, the result could be a more thoughtful, tolerant, and gentler way of living, not only with our planet, but also with one another.

It seems likely that the great environmental struggles, on which the future viability of the world's ecology will depend, will be played out during the decade of the 1990s. After that, it may well be too late. If people are to rise to this challenge, they must see themselves as part of planetary processes, not set apart. They must follow the rate of soil erosion as closely as the rate of inflation, and expend at least as much concern about keeping up with air and water quality standards as about keeping up with the Soviet Union in nuclear weapons. They must begin to reconsider basic questions about common benefit versus individual rights. They may be able to afford two automobiles, for example, or a large family, but, they must ask themselves, can the planet?

Environmental ethics, as proposed by Henry David Thoreau and later John Muir, and more recently by Aldo Leopold and others, seeks to respect the living (and nonliving) world as having value in itself, not simply because of its possible utility or threat to human beings. This perspective emphasizes that peace may ultimately require a much broader view of the human community, in which people are not only responsible for their own actions, the actions of other people, and their effects on other people, but also their effects on all other life-forms. We have long had a code of interpersonal ethics, the Ten Commandments. In the eighteenth and nineteenth centuries, we developed codes of societal ethics: capitalism, democracy, liberalism, conservatism, socialism. To complete this triumvirate, perhaps what is needed from the twentieth century is a code of environmental ethics.

A FINAL NOTE ON ECOLOGICAL WHOLENESS

Perhaps the fundamental lesson to be derived from a search for ecological wholeness is that of underlying unity. All things, quite literally, are linked to all others, such that any striving for peace must take account of this connectedness: living things to the soil and to the atmosphere as well as to all other living things, people to their natural environment as well as to their man- and woman-made social systems and to each other, the past to the future of this planet, and risks to opportunities for every one and every thing.

"What is man without the beasts?" asked a native American, Chief Seattle, in 1854.

> If all the beasts are gone, man would die from a great loneliness of spirit. For whatever happens to the beasts, soon happens to man. All things are connected. You must teach your children that the ground beneath their feet is the ashes of our grandfathers. So that they still respect the land, tell your children that the earth is rich with the lives of our kin. Teach your children what we have taught our children — that the earth is our mother. Whatever befalls the earth befalls the sons of the earth.[5]

Study Questions

1. How do environmental/ecological concerns qualify as matters of national security?

2. Explain how the following serve as examples of the Tragedy of the Commons in action: the slaughter of whales, the deforestation of India.

3. Consider recycling: Is it reasonable to propose that societal problems are susceptible to individual solutions?

4. A solution to the greenhouse effect must ultimately deal with basic questions about the organization of production and consumption in modern society. Elaborate.

5. Describe some connections between the problems of rain forest destruction, wildlife conservation, desertification, deforestation, and the greenhouse effect.

6. To what extent will conservation aid in ameliorating the energy crisis? In solving it?

7. It has been said that ecological awareness is a luxury to be indulged in by the middle and upper classes. Agree or disagree.

8. Discuss the concept of sustainability, applied specifically to a natural resource problem.

9. Demonstrate the connections between ecological wholeness and social processes, considering a current issue of environmental controversy.

10. Environmental issues transcend the East–West split, but are more central to the North–South division. Explain.

Suggestions for Further Reading

Harold H. Sprout. 1971. *Toward a Politics of the Planet Earth*. Van Nostrand Reinhold: New York.

William Ophuls. 1977. *Ecology and the Politics of Scarcity*. Freeman: San Francisco.

Andre Gorz. 1980. *Ecology as Politics*. South End Press: Boston.

Oran R. Young. 1989. *International Cooperation: Building Regimes for Natural Resources and the Environment*. Cornell University Press: Ithaca, N.Y.

Lester R. Brown et al. (The Worldwatch Institute) published annually. *The State of the World*. Norton: New York.

Source Notes

1. John F. Kennedy. Speech at The American University, June, 1963.

2. Garrett Hardin. 1961. "The Tragedy of the Commons." *Science* 162: 1243–1248.

3. *Time*, Jan. 2, 1989, p. 66.

4. Lynn White. 1967. "The Historical Roots of Our Ecologic Crisis." *Science* 155: 1203–1207.

5. Chief Seattle. 1984. *Chief Seattle's Speeches*. Friends of the Earth: Seattle, WA.

22

Economic Well-Being

If a free society cannot help the many who are poor, it cannot help the few who are rich.
John F. Kennedy

Peace implies a state of tranquility, calm, and satisfaction. It is very difficult to be tranquil or calm, or satisfied, however, when denied such basic needs as food, clothing, shelter, education, and medical care. Many people are even hard-pressed to establish ethical guidelines — let alone abide by them — when fundamental necessities are not available. Bertolt Brecht puts it well in his play *The Threepenny Opera:*

> First feed the face, and then tell right from wrong.
> Even noblemen may act like sinners,
> Unless they've had their customary dinners.[1]

Even when their bellies are at least minimally full, people rarely feel peaceful when they perceive that their economic condition is far inferior to that of others. Not surprisingly, therefore, there is little peace in a world characterized by painful differences between the rich and poor, between the haves and the have-nots. Poverty, as we have seen, may not lead directly to war, but it certainly is not conducive to peace. Revolutions in particular have been stimulated and maintained by grinding economic privation. And one of the most important, though rarely acknowledged, reasons why the rich states maintain large military forces may be that they are concerned with preventing any fundamental reorganization in the worldwide distribution of power and wealth. Saint Francis, commenting on the "plight" of the wealthy, noted that "he who has property also needs weapons and warriors to defend it."[2] Or, as we learn in the song "I Got Plenty of Nothin'," from the musical *Porgy and Bess*,

> Folks with plenty of plenty, got a lock on da' door;
> don't want nobody to get what's in
> while they're out gettin' some more.[3]

But most of all, inequality in resources and opportunities represents a direct burden on the poor themselves (this includes poor people as well as poor countries). When poverty is persistent, degrading, miserable, life-shortening, life-threatening, and life-denying, it is an affront to human dignity. The search for peace, accordingly, must include a search for human economic and social betterment.

Most of the world's people are in fact so preoccupied with their own immediate problems (of which poverty looms especially large) that wider preoccupations such as nuclear weapons, and even peace and war, seem almost irrelevant. The political imagination of most human beings typically is constrained by such immediacies: in Latin America, debt, democratization, and poverty; in Africa, famines, displaced persons, debt, and ethnic and religious violence; and so on. The concrete day-to-day struggles of normal people to lead tolerable lives occupies most of the energies of the overwhelming majority.

Efforts to eliminate poverty, or — not necessarily the same thing — to maximize wealth, have stimulated some of the major socioeconomic schemes of modern times, notably capitalism and communism. Accordingly, we shall not attempt, in this limited chapter, to reinvent the wheel by drafting a blueprint for the preferred world economy. We shall instead try to sketch out some of the primary issues, identify some of the major controversies, and point toward possible courses of action.

Like war, poverty is not an abstraction, although we often speak of it in general terms. Just as

there are specific wars, there are specific, flesh-and-blood people, and specific regions of particularly bleak poverty, even in so-called wealthy countries. As with war, there are also questions of definition and identification: What is poverty? Is it getting better or worse? How do regions and countries differ? Yet, just as theory helps us identify and understand the causes and prevention of war generally, it can do the same for poverty . . . even though, as in efforts to understand war, theory yields many different explanations, some of them conflicting in their interpretations and recommendations.

THE PROBLEM OF POVERTY

In its simplest terms, poverty exists when people do not have access to the "good life." Of course, one person's good life is another's luxury. For a middle-class American, the good life may require a house, two cars, a color TV, at least one vacation (paid) annually, and the ability to send one's children to the college of their choice. For a resident of Manila's Tondo slum, it may entail regular meals, access to a sewer system, one day off per month, and the ability to keep one's children from dying of diarrhea. The "poverty level" in the United States would be considered a luxury level in much of the Third World.* Indeed, the most dramatic examples of poverty on a global scale concern the Third World countries, or states of the South. Variously labeled "underdeveloped," "developing," "have-nots," "less-developed countries" (or LDCs), these states clearly are significantly poorer than their Northern, industrial neighbors. In addition, Third World states generally (although not universally) have been subject to colonization and exploitation by the wealthier states, at least in the past.

---

*By the same token, consider the following figures for the technologically advanced countries: 80 percent of suicides, 74 percent of heart attacks, 75 percent of television "zombies," 56 percent of impotence and frigidity, 98 percent of illicit drug consumption[4] — out of only 10 percent of the world's population.

Physical and Psychological Effects

One of the most important, if least recognized, aspects of poverty is its psychological effects, the bitter pill of perceived injustice and inequality that must be swallowed by those who observe the affluence of others while still mired in their own poverty. Even if one's own purchasing power is adequate for survival, it can be painful to witness a dramatically higher level of consumption on the part of others — and with increased communication and transportation, even the most isolated people, living traditional and impoverished lives, are exposed to examples of affluence. The results are deep mental suffering: envy, shame, and either despair or anger. (And, as we shall see, along with "development" in the Third World, there seems to be an inevitable widening of the gap between rich and poor.)

Beyond the phenomenon of envy is the painful physical fact of deep, absolute poverty. Hunger is the most obvious manifestation, with disease being inevitably associated as well. Other sufferings are also associated with poverty. Poor housing and inadequate sanitation, for example, contribute to disease, as does inadequate nutrition. Health care is minimal or nonexistent. Educational opportunities are very limited, both because areas of extreme poverty frequently have few and typically inadequate schools, and because the very poor often need their children to work, so they are denied whatever limited educational opportunities may be available. The result is a deepening of the cycle of poverty, making it even more difficult for such people, or their descendants, to escape. Not surprisingly, lifespans are significantly shorter among the very poor.

National and Global Inequalities: Some Numbers

Poverty may be measured in absolute terms (sheer deprivation, of food, health, life expectancy, and so on), or in comparative measures (inequality in the distribution of wealth, such that a small proportion of the population monopolizes more than its share of wealth, leaving the majority with very little per capita). In addition, trends in poverty are also important. Thus, the per capita income in Argentina,

Venezuela, and Peru was lower in 1989 than in 1970. In Mexico, workers currently earn 40 percent less, in real wages, than they did in 1980.

National Inequality.   But the relative inequality in wealth is perhaps even more appalling. In Brazil, 40 percent of the population takes home scarcely 7 percent of that country's GNP; half of the country obtains more than 90 percent of the GNP. Distribution in the United States is only somewhat more equitable: The top 20 percent of the U.S. population receives more than 40 percent of the annual GNP, while the lowest 40 percent gets less than 20 percent of the nation's wealth. Interestingly, communist states are not substantially more egalitarian; in Bulgaria, for example, the top 20 percent earns 33 percent, and the bottom 40 percent earns 27 percent. (Communist states are actually somewhat more equitable than such statistics might imply, however, since health care and education are free, housing and food is government-subsidized and thus quite inexpensive, and some degree of employment is more or less guaranteed.)

Global Inequality.   Global inequality in wealth is even greater than national inequality. Thus, in the world as a whole, the top one fifth — the industrialized countries — rakes in nearly three-quarters of the world's economic product, while the remaining four-fifths get what is left. At the bottom end, the poorest one fifth of the world's people garner less than 2 percent of the world's GNP. The average income in the industrialized countries averages more than fifteen times that of the poorer countries. Forty-three percent of the world's population receives less than 4 percent of its income, so that the poorer countries wind up with a scant one thirty-eighth the income of the industrialized countries. Moreover, the absolute gap between global rich and poor is widening.

This difference between industrial and Third World states corresponds roughly to the distinction between a poor South and an affluent North. The United States, Japan, the Western European states, and the oil-rich Middle Eastern states have per capita GNPs in excess of $8,000; by contrast, sub-Saharan Africa (excluding South Africa), China, the Indian subcontinent, and much of east Asia (excluding Taiwan, South Korea, Hong Kong, and Singapore), have per capita GNPs of $1,000 and less. Latin America averages about $2,000, and the Soviet bloc generally stands at about $5,000, midway between Latin America and the affluent North.

Quality of Life and Frequency of Death. Life expectancy parallels this global division of wealth, with a strong positive correlation between life expectancy and per capita GNP. In addition to deaths attributable to structural violence, inhabitants of the impoverished South also suffer far more than their share of mortality due to overt violence. Thus, if mortality due to violence was distributed evenly with respect to numbers, the North, with 30 percent of the world's population, could be expected to experience 30 percent of all violent deaths. In reality, however, the North has endured only about 9 percent of total deaths from international wars (leaving the other 91 percent of all war deaths to be suffered by Southern peoples). Similarly, less than one tenth of 1 percent of all worldwide deaths attributable to civil violence took place in the North (or 99.9 percent in the South), and approximately 4 percent of all deaths due to structural violence occurred in the North, which means that 96 percent of such deaths fell upon people of the South.[5] An estimated 40,000 babies, for example, die of malnutrition every *day* in the Third World.

The three poorest regions of the world (Africa, south Asia and east Asia) earn less than 20 percent of the world's economic product, but along with that comes 83 percent of all infant deaths, 83 percent of those without adequate water, 88 percent of adult illiterates, and 96 percent of the malnourished. Health care budgets in the Third World (including Latin America) average a mere $10.50 per capita, one quarter of their military budgets, and one fiftieth the expenditures on health care in the developed countries. In 1985, Third World countries spent an average of $150 on the education of each school-age child; by contrast, the industrialized countries spent an average of $2,250. (It should be emphasized that the deplorable situation of

Third World conditions does not mean that some people in the industrialized countries do not also experience poverty; as of 1989, for example, one fifth of all children in the United States were born into poverty.)

The Third World is a world of widespread and appalling contrasts; gleaming high-tech development alongside chronic and unremitting poverty. In many cases, the degree of deprivation is hidden by governmental manipulation of statistics. In Chile, for example, instead of assessing malnutrition by considering a child's weight in relation to his or her age, it is estimated by weight in relation to height; thus, a child whose growth is stunted is declared adequately nourished! Examples abound of governmental callousness toward the poor, in large part because the poor tend to have a very small say in governmental decision making, which generally takes place on behalf of the wealthy and powerful. During the Reagan administration, for example, an effort was made to cut school lunch programs for the poor by declaring ketchup a vegetable.

By most measures, the plight of the world's most impoverished people is desperately bad, and getting worse. Per capita Gross Domestic Product has declined by about 4 percent per year in sub-Saharan Africa (excluding the Republic of South Africa). The World Bank estimates that per capita income in this region will be less in 1995 than it was in 1973 — and this in the face of worldwide inflation in the prices of certain basic materials, such as petroleum. As a result, Africans will find themselves forced to spend more money for various essentials — notably, fuel — at the same time that they actually have less money in their pockets. The minimum wage in Kenya has already declined by 42 percent from 1975 to 1984. The most realistic measures take account of the purchasing power of wages: Someone earning the minimum wage in Chile could purchase 313 kilograms of bread each month during 1971; in 1989, this had fallen to 85 kilograms.

Identifying the Impoverished

Although poverty is a worldwide phenomenon, it is not homogeneously distributed. There are poor people living in rich countries (parts of Appalachia, for example, within the United States) and wealthy people in the poorest countries (multimillionaire plantation owners in Bangladesh or the Philippines). Poverty, however, is generally easy to identify, wherever it is found: high levels of unemployment, poor nutrition, inadequate health care and education, little or no savings, high levels of indebtedness, low levels of investment, and often, ecologically depleted environments. As the Brandt Commission* put it,

> Few people in the North have any detailed conception of the extent of poverty in the Third World or of the forms that it takes. Many hundreds of millions of people in the poorer countries are preoccupied solely with survival and elementary needs. For them work is frequently not available or, when it is, pay is very low and conditions often barely tolerable. Homes are constructed of impermanent materials and have neither piped water nor sanitation. Electricity is a luxury. Health services are thinly spread and in rural areas only rarely within walking distance. Primary schools, where they exist, may be free and not too far away, but children are needed for work and cannot easily be spared for schooling. Permanent insecurity is the condition of the poor. There are no public systems of social security in the event of unemployment, sickness or death of a wage-earner in the family. Flood, drought or disease affecting people or livestock can destroy livelihoods without hope of compensation. In the North, ordinary men and women face genuine economic problems — uncertainty, inflation, the fear if not the reality of unemployment. But they rarely face anything resembling the total deprivation found in the South. Ordinary people in the South would not find it credible that the societies of the North regard themselves as anything other than wealthy.[6]

It should also be emphasized that, although urban slums suffer from devastating impoverishment, and typically receive the bulk of public attention, in fact the *favelas* of São Paulo, the *barrios* of Mexico City, the slums of Cairo or Kinshasa are a relatively recent and minor phenomenon; despite their terrible squalor, the urban poor are generally better off than their rural cousins. This is part of the reason why the population in Third World cities is doubling every ten to fifteen years, as impoverished, landless peasants flock to the cities, creating situations that become ever more desperate and unmanageable. Even now, however, more than 70 percent of the world's poor still live in rural villages, in India, Africa, Indonesia, and so on. Among the rural poor, illiteracy and the great epidemic diseases — malaria, cholera, tuberculosis — are at an all-time low, but the good things in life (and some of the necessities, such as an adequate diet) are no more available than they were before. Historically, rural interests have been overrepresented in Western democratic republics, notably England and the United States. By contrast, rural people — especially the very poor — are characteristically underrepresented in Third World government decision making.

Measuring Poverty and Relative Advantage

As we have seen, per capita GNP (or alternatively, Gross Domestic Product, if the value of imports and exports is omitted), is a useful index of wealth, by which different countries or regions can be compared. Alternatively, we can measure Gross National Product as a percentage of Total World Product; to be meaningful, this figure must then be adjusted for population in each country or region. When this is done, we obtain the "coefficient of advantage" — the percentage of total world product obtained by a given country or region divided by the percentage of total world population encompassed by that country or region. For example, North America contains about 6.2 percent of the world's population; it obtains, however, 31.5 percent of the world's GNP, for a coefficient of advantage of 31.5/6.2 = 5.08. By contrast, Africa has 8.7 percent of the world's population, but only 2.0 percent of the world's GNP, for a coefficient of (dis)advantage of 2.0/8.7 = 0.23. A coefficient of advantage of 1.0 would indicate an equitable per capita division of the world's resources. (It should

---

*An independent commission, chaired by former West German chancellor Willy Brandt, that reported on the problems and prospects facing the world's less-developed countries.

be noted, however, that even in this case, divisions of wealth *within* countries or regions could still be extreme.)

The Lorenz Curve and the Gini Coefficient.   Two other measures are important in assessing worldwide distribution of wealth: the Lorenz curve and the Gini coefficient. A Lorenz curve is drawn by graphing the share of world product against the share of world population. As depicted in Figure 22.1, if wealth was evenly distributed according to population, this "curve" would be a straight line. However, it clearly isn't; rather, the Lorenz curve is bowed inward, because certain regions (North America, Oceania, Western Europe) obtain a larger share of the world's wealth than would be indicated by their population, while others (Latin America, Africa, Asia) obtain less. A useful procedure, then, is to determine the amount of area below the diagonal in this curve. This is known as the Gini coefficient, or G, and is commonly used as a measure of inequality in distribution. Gini coefficients can be computed for the world, as in Figure 22.1, or for individual countries, plotting ethnic groups, cities, and the like on the ordinate (vertical axis).

Patterns of Inequality.   Our focus is primarily on worldwide patterns. In this regard, it is interesting to note that three world regions are characterized by different patterns of inequality. Europe shows a comparatively low level of income inequality (G averaging around 20), but a high level of inequality in ownership of land; Great Britain has the lowest G figure for Western European income (5.0), but the highest (72.3) for land. By contrast, the countries of Southeast Asia tend to have relatively equitable distribution of land ownership, but substantial variations in income (from $G = 14.9$ in Japan to $G = 43.0$ in Thailand). And in Central and South America, inequalities are marked in both income and land ownership. For Peru, $G = 39.8$ for income and a whopping 93.3 for land.

These patterns reflect historical trends as well as current socioeconomic conditions. The concentration of land ownership in Western Europe is a

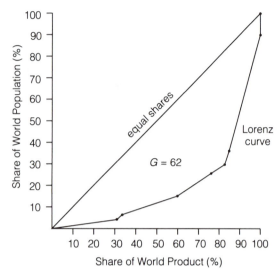

FIGURE 22.1   Lorenz Curve

holdover from the preindustrial, feudal era, when a landed aristocracy held sway. Income has become more equalized as a result of industrialization and the success of labor unions. In Southeast Asia, agriculture is relatively intensive, with large numbers of small private holdings, but also fabulously wealthy princes, merchants, manufacturers, and miserably impoverished landless peasants. In much of Latin America and Africa, land ownership and wealth coincide, largely through ranching, plantations, or mines, leaving the vast majority with neither land nor income.

Although the United States is, by many measures, the wealthiest country in the world, it does not always rank high in socioeconomic conditions for its people: fifth in worldwide literacy rate, seventh in public school expenditures per capita, eighth in life expectancy, eighth in public health expenditures per capita, sixteenth in percentage of women enrolled in universities, eighteenth in infant mortality rate, and twentieth in teachers per school-age population. There are 30,000 homeless people on the streets of New York City, the world's richest city, and an estimated 23 million Americans are functionally illiterate. One child in five is born into poverty.[7]

The situation among Third World countries, on the other hand, is much worse. In the Philippines, more than one half of that country's 60 million people don't have adequate food, clothing, or shelter. Per capita income is not even $600, or less than $2 per day. Much of the problem, as in most agrarian societies, revolves around unequal distribution of land. The World Bank reports, for example, that wealthy people in the Philippines have so much land that there simply is very little left for the poor. And as we have seen, rural poverty is even more serious than its urban counterpart. "The immense majority of arable land," wrote Guatemala's Roman Catholic bishops in 1988,

> is in the hands of a numerically insignificant minority, while most *campesinos* [poor peasants] have nowhere to grow their crops. Far from approaching a solution, this situation is becoming more difficult and painful every day. . . . The Guatemalan *campesino* is in a desperate situation. The immense majority receives none of the services the state is obliged to provide to all Guatemalans, not education, not sanitary programs or social security of any kind, not housing that meets minimum conditions of hygiene and dignity. . . . All who live in our nation must awaken to the gravity of this problem.[8]

In Guatemala, as in many other Latin American countries, the current experiment with democracy is a fragile one. Although the government is ostensibly civilian, in fact the military operates autonomously, essentially beyond the control of government officials. Moreover, failures of this and other governments to deliver on their promises of social and economic reform have led to increased rumblings of discontent, which could easily lead to violent insurrection, a return to military dictatorship . . . or both.

CAUSES OF POVERTY

"The rich are different from you and I," F. Scott Fitzgerald is said to have commented to Ernest Hemingway, whereupon Hemingway supposedly responded, "Yes, they have more money."

It is one thing to conclude that poverty is caused by failure to own land. But in a sense, this is equivalent to saying that poverty is caused by an absence of money. What, then, is the underlying cause? There have been many explanations, some of which may even be correct. In certain cases, the natural resources of a country are so poor that wealth is virtually impossible to create. The African state of Chad, for example, is so arid as to be agriculturally unproductive, and it also lacks significant mineral deposits. By contrast, wealthy countries such as the United States tend to be naturally well endowed. But this argument is not altogether satisfying. Japan, for example, has relatively few natural resources, yet it has become an economic giant; this is also the case with Hong Kong, South Korea, Singapore, and Taiwan, as well as certain wealthy but resource-poor European states such as Belgium and the Netherlands. In a sense, some states can be considered especially resource-rich (Venezuela, Saudi Arabia, Kuwait), while others are capital-rich (Singapore, South Korea, Hong Kong, Taiwan, Japan). Some — notably the United States — are rich in both resources and capital, whereas others — Chad, Bangladesh — appear to be poor in both. Clearly, however, resources alone do not explain everything.

Self-Perpetuation

To some degree, poverty compounds itself. For example, by a process known as "urban-pull and rural-push," landless peasants tend to be drawn toward Third World cities, and pushed away from rural areas where their future looks especially bleak. The crush of unskilled people in these cities overwhelms social supports, including the availability of jobs, housing, sanitation, water supplies, food, medical treatment, and education. Meanwhile, back on the farm, poor peasants lack irrigation, fertilizers, pest control, credit, crop advice, and good seed, so they harvest less than their wealthier counterparts. One hectare in China yields an average of $2,300; in Taiwan, that figure is nearly doubled, to $4,000; and in South Korea, it is $5,400. By contrast, a hectare in the Philippines yields only $500. In this way, the poor find themselves mired in a no-win situation. As we shall see,

Vietnamese woman gathering rice plants by hand. Poor countries, lacking effective technology, are likely to remain poor, while wealthy countries are able to enhance their wealth. (Oxfam America/John Hammock)

rapid population growth also contributes mightily to the disparity in per capita income between the rich and poor. And of course, this vicious cycle of poverty operates on a personal level as well: People deprived of an education, for example, are unable to compete effectively for higher-paying jobs, and their children, in turn, are likely to be relatively uneducated, thereby perpetuating the cycle.

Government Policies

Government policies can also contribute substantially to poverty. Many analysts have attempted to explain the "economic miracle" of Japan; a general conclusion is that social organization—in Japan's case, most notably a powerful work ethic—has helped boost economic productivity. Alternatively, where poverty is widespread and has existed for thousands of years with little sign of improvement, a kind of fatalistic lethargy often sets in. Government policies can have substantial impact in such cases, either encouraging grass-roots self-help or deepening the plight of a country's majority. The country of Zaire, for example, is "rich," as measured by natural resources, yet 80 percent of Zaireans are desperately poor, and real wages are only about one tenth what they were when Zaire gained independence in 1960. At least some of the responsibility must be borne by Zairean dictator Mobuto,

who has stolen more than $5 billion directly from the national treasury. National wealth was similarly plundered by Marcos in the Philippines, Somoza in Nicaragua, Batista in Cuba, and Duvalier in Haiti. Fiscal mismanagement and irresponsibility—often bolstered by a rigid adherence to discredited ideology—has also resulted in economic degradation. An example is Romania, a country that is abundantly endowed with natural resources (notably oil), but that was reduced to painful poverty by destructive, Stalinist-style policies.

Governments frequently take power with promises to represent the oppressed and underprivileged. Once in office, however, rulers often find it advantageous to cater to the powerful (that is, in most cases, the wealthy). Carlos Menem, for example, was elected president of Argentina in 1989 by espousing a "Peronist" economic policy, which historically has allied itself with organized labor and Argentina's impoverished peasantry. Once in office, however, and pressured by rampant inflation as well as a massive international debt, Menem promptly began cutting back on Argentina's welfare state. A similar transition occurred with Corazon Aquino's government in the Philippines, which has backpedaled on promised land reform. There are many reasons for such policy shifts, including keeping the military happy (thereby allowing the government to remain in power) and satisfying the demands of foreign bankers (particularly the World Bank and the International Monetary Fund, both of which typically insist on domestic fiscal "austerity" in return for debt relief), as well as the occasional lure of personal payoffs. It should also be reiterated that, short of revolution or the overt threat of revolution, the very poor generally have a disproportionately small voice in government decision making.

Political Ideology

Social and political factors also can contribute significantly to income disparities. According to Marxists, capitalism itself is largely to blame: Capitalist societies are stratified by economic class, with the bosses exploiting the workers, thereby keeping them poor. According to capitalist theory, wealth is more likely to be generated by an unfettered free market; poverty is due to lack of effort, will, or ability, to bad luck, or, to the repressive influence of government interference. According to the economist Adam Smith, private enterprise, if left to its own devices, will act as though guided by an "unseen hand," to produce the maximum economic good for the maximum number of people. Implicit in capitalist theory is the idea that some people will inevitably do less well than others. This difference is presumably due at least in part to unavoidable differences between them; it is not the job of society to establish equality in such cases. Moreover, if government intervenes to redistribute wealth, this will not only diminish the efficiency with which new wealth is produced, but also constitute a major blow to individual liberty.

Even most capitalist societies, however, do not subscribe to laissez-faire theories, in which governments are expected to take a purely hands-off attitude. Various "safety net programs" have been established in the United States, for example, Head Start, Aid to Families with Dependent Children, and so on. And most other Western democracies are substantially more involved at the governmental level, seeking to maintain and improve the economic lot of their poorest citizens. In the past, conservative ideologies attributed poverty to natural inferiority; more recently, the scapegoating process tends to be more subtle, pointing to social circumstances, and thereby relieving society of responsibility in such cases.

This is a particularly pernicious attitude, one that essentially blames the victim by attributing poverty to various characteristics of the poor: inadequate education, ill health, old age, low motivation, high crime rates. It is one thing to identify a "culture of poverty" that makes it difficult for the poor to better themselves. It is quite another to maintain that the poor are poor because they do not deserve anything better, or because they choose it.

Racism

Poverty is widespread even within the wealthiest countries, and in certain cases, substantial racist attitudes are involved. Consider the case of blacks in the United States. By 1987, in a time of general economic "recovery," identified black unemployment was still 13 percent (in 1965, it had been 8.1 percent), and one of every three blacks was below the poverty line. (It has been estimated that, in fact, about 50 percent of black men may actually be unemployed or substantially underemployed.) Such circumstances seemingly are a result of persistent racism and its social effects: In 1989, more black men were in jail, for instance, than in college. Among black college graduates, unemployment is four times higher than among their white counterparts. The median incomes of black men employed full-time fell 10 percent from 1979 to 1987, and by 1989, more than one half of all new full-time jobs for blacks paid less than $11,610 — poverty wages for a family of four. In 1987 and 1988, U.S. blacks actually experienced a *decline* in their average lifespan; of all the world's Western industrialized countries, this is the only known example of such a negative demographic trend among a major subset of the population.

War and Military Preparations

Finally, there is a complex causative relationship between poverty and war. Preparing for war occasionally yields economic benefits: Many advances in the aircraft industry, radar, computers, and so on were stimulated by military research and development. On balance, however, domestic progress, if it was the goal, clearly would be produced far more effectively by targeting financial resources explicitly at domestic needs. Moreover, considering the immense destructiveness of war itself, there can be no question that, on balance, war is impoverishing (in fact, it is only made possible by the industries of peace). War is essentially a parasite, feeding off the economic and social strength of societies; and like most parasites, it weakens its host.

As we noted previously, military industries provide employment, but they actually create fewer jobs than if comparable sums were expended in the civilian sector. Similarly, military expenditures are by their nature inflationary, and they do not contribute to equitable distributions of wealth, since they are strongly biased toward high-tech materials and highly trained white-collar employees. And perhaps

A Korean family salvaging bricks with which to rebuild their wrecked house. Economic progress is often stymied by the destructiveness of war. (United Nations)

most important, military spending uses funds that could otherwise be used for environmental protection, social programs, the alleviation of poverty, or the rebuilding of the national infrastructure.

THIRD WORLD "DEVELOPMENT"

The stark contrast between rich and poor is nowhere more painfully real than in the Third World. Franz Fanon, a black psychiatrist and political radical, described the contrast in his angry and influential book, *The Wretched of the Earth*.

> The settler's town is a strongly-built town, all made of stone and steel. It is a brightly-lit town; the streets are covered with asphalt, and the garbage-cabs swallow all the leavings, unseen, unknown and hardly thought about. The settler's feet are never visible, except perhaps in the sea; but there you're never close enough to see them. His feet are protected by strong shoes although the streets of his town are clean and even, with no holes or stones. The settler's town is a well-fed town, an easy-going town, its belly is always full of good things. The settler's town is a town of white people, of foreigners.
>
> The town belonging to the colonized people, or at least the native town, the Negro village, the medina, the reservation, is a place of ill fame peopled by men of evil repute. They are born there, it matters little where or how; they die there, it matters not where nor how. It is a world without spaciousness: men live there on top of each other, and their huts are built one on top of the other. The native town is a hungry town, starved of bread, of meat, of shoes, of coal, of light. The native town is a crouching village, a town on its knees, a town wallowing in the mire. It is a town of niggers and dirty Arabs. The look that the native turns on the settler's town is a look of lust, of envy.[9]

And, we might add, sometimes it is a look of exhaustion, of despair, and of rage.

Development Theory

During the 1950s and 1960s, "development" was seen as the key to the Third World's economic future. As President John Kennedy put it, "a rising tide lifts all boats." The idea was to improve the economic situation in the world generally, and in the Third World most especially, as a result of which, some economic benefits would be enjoyed by everyone, including the poorest countries and the poorest segments of society. In the jargon of the 1980s, a dynamic world economy would convey benefits that would "trickle down" to everyone.

Growth and Modernization.

During its heyday, development theory (also sometimes referred to as "modernization" or "growth" theory) contrasted with "containment" theory, which sought to prevent the U.S.S.R. from expanding its control, and rather simplistically equated revolutionary nationalism with international communism. The idea of development theory, quite simply, was that economic progress would spread from the industrialized states to the Third World — variously known as the UDCs (underdeveloped countries), LDCs (less-developed countries), or DCs (developing countries). Theorists argued that foreign aid, as well as enhanced trade and credit provided by the North, would help speed the process. Instead of dividing up the global pie differently, the wealthy states would simply help to bake a larger pie.

Development theory gave rise to numerous government programs, including the Alliance for Progress (within the Western Hemisphere) and the Peace Corps. Development theory is closely allied to classical free enterprise economic theory, which espouses the basic theme of "grow now, redistribute later." Developing countries, according to this view, should strive to attract more, not less, foreign capital, and to emphasize efficiency and growth as their goals. There have been some dramatic success stories in development, notably the so-called east Asian Gang of Four: Hong Kong, Singapore, South Korea, and Taiwan, as well as the most dramatic of all, Japan. Moreover, those economies that have been least integrated into the world free market system, such as Albania and Burma, have been among the least dynamic.

Disappointments.

Development theory still persists in various forms. But the great majority of poor countries have not had positive experiences with growth and development in recent decades, which has led to growing dissatisfaction and increasingly militant demands on the part of the world's poor.

One of the major disappointments of Third World "development" has been a phenomenon sometimes referred to as "marginalization," whereby increased wealth in the middle and upper classes is actually accompanied by deeper poverty for the very poor. There will always be relative poverty — some people at the poor end of the income spectrum — just as there will always be those who are comparatively wealthy. The tragedy of marginalization is that it involves an increase in the absolute amount of poverty. In short, the benefits of economic growth in the Third World have not reached the lowest levels, and the poorest of the poor are pushed more and more to the margins of subsistence.

This pattern of uneven development was first described by economist Simon Kuznets in 1955.[10] The so-called Kuznets curve suggests that per capita GNP and inequality in income distribution often take the form of an inverted U: As per capita income increases, so does unequal distribution. This inequality supposedly reaches a maximum — that is, greatest disparity between rich and poor — when total overall wealth is intermediate; as wealth continues to grow, it eventually becomes more equitably distributed, as in modern industrial states. Certain industrial states, however, such as France, have retained unusually high levels of income inequality, whereas many Third World countries — Zambia, Ivory Coast, Kenya, Peru, Brazil, Mexico, Malaysia, the Philippines — have not managed to reach the "descending," or increasingly equitable, conditions on the far side of the Kuznets curve. This condition, whereby development causes increased disparity in income, is associated with low per capita school enrollment and high birth rates. Regardless of its causes and correlates, however, the distressing fact remains that, in many if not most cases, development has been a cruel joke, as the already low-income poor have faced the prospect and reality of *declining* incomes.

The Search for Alternatives.   Responding to this, some countries have begun to move away from a simple progrowth and development model, to one emphasizing social services and self-reliance. Sri Lanka, for example, has succeeded in eliminating abject poverty by devoting half of its national budget to free rice, education, and health services, and subsidized food and transportation. As a result, life expectancy has risen dramatically, approaching that of other, more "developed" countries. (Tragically, ethnic conflict — between Tamils and Sinhalese — has interfered with, and to some degree overshadowed, the remarkable social accomplishments of Sri Lanka.)

For most Third World governments, development poses a difficult dilemma. On the one hand, a system emphasizing free markets, open trade, and foreign investment offers the prospect of efficient, rapid growth and potentially massive production. On the other hand, such a system also tends to enhance the schism between rich and poor.

The New International Economic Order

UNCTAD, the United Nations Conference on Trade and Development, first convened in 1964, whereupon the "Group of 77," comprising the seventy-seven poorest countries, joined to form a pressure group, whose goal was to achieve a "profound reorganization of economic relations between the rich and poor countries." More specifically, the poor countries sought to obtain improved terms of trade, credit, the transfer of resources and technology for development, and enhanced control over their own natural resources — human and cultural as well as natural. Since then, the Group of 77 has expanded to more than 100 countries. Among other things, it has demanded that 1 percent of the rich countries' GNP be transferred to the poor states, not as charity or extortion, but as their just due; according to their argument, the wealth of the rich states has been at least partly stolen from the poorer ones, and the poor countries want that wealth to be redistributed. Not surprisingly, the wealthy states have not embraced this idea.

Yet by the early 1970s, global economic issues had entered the agenda of world politics; this amalgam of demands and requests was known as the New International Economic Order, or NIEO. By the 1970s, the poorer countries, despite their poverty, felt a degree of empowerment in part because of a growing confidence in their ability to manage their own natural resource base, combined with the success of decolonization throughout the world, which fostered a strong spirit of national self-reliance. It was thought that pressure from the Third World could force a reorganization of the global economy in ways more favorable to them. And if nothing else, the NIEO movement did at least succeed in widening the scope of global concern about poverty, expanding it from its earlier focus on income disparities *within* states to include the issue of disparities *between* states.

Unfortunately, by the late 1980s the realignment goals of the NIEO were virtually dead. Weakening economies and fragmented political structures have virtually destroyed any leverage on the part of the South. At the same time, another perspective — quite different from development theory — has been gaining credibility. According to this influential critique, often known as *dependencia* theory, "development" has actually been harmful to Third World people.

Dependencia Theory

This perspective on Third World poverty was originally applied to the economic situation in Latin America, a region that has long been economically and politically subservient to the United States. Under the influence of radical economic theorists such as André Gunder Frank, the term *dependencia*, based on the Spanish word for "dependency," has also been applied to other Third World regions, wherever indigenous peoples and resources are believed to be exploited by the wealthier, industrialized states of the North.

The basic idea of dependencia is that poverty in what Johan Galtung called the "periphery" (the Third World) occurs in large part because of affluence in the "center" (the industrialized North; see Chapter 11). The poor countries are not so much underdeveloped as overexploited, and Third World poverty results not from neglect by the wealthy North, but from altogether too much attention. Countries such as Zaire, Indonesia, Brazil, India, and Malaysia are rich; only their people are poor. According to this view, not only did the North exploit the South overtly during the days of colonialism, but such exploitation has continued, covertly, even after outright imperial control was terminated. Even now, the wealthy, powerful North takes advantage of the South, by manipulating markets, credit, and trade balances. In the past, repressive control was exerted directly, by armed forces of occupation; now, such control is indirect, through surrogate local rulers (the so-called *comprador* class), who are clients of the wealthy states, and who profit personally by impoverishing their own people while being essentially in league with the Northern powers. As a result, the great majority of Third World people are victimized by their own governments as well as by the industrialized states. Unlike the relationship between, say, the United States and West Germany, in which benefits flow in both directions, exchanges between either of these wealthy Northern powers and Mauritania, for example, are likely to be exploitative and distinctly one-sided.

According to one radical critic, three Hollywood-style images have strongly influenced the way the Western public views imperialism:

- *The Walt Disney Idyllic.* The White colonizers arrive in what is a fertile but empty land. Seeing nobody around, they stake out a claim. After fighting off some predatory animals and enduring a few hardships, they manage to build nice homes and settle down on their farms.

- *The South Seas Romance.* The White colonizers arrive to be greeted by smiling natives who offer gifts and throw their country open to the wise and beneficial rule of the newcomers. The White leader falls in love with the friendly chief's beautiful daughter and a happy time is had by all.

- *The Thin-Red-Line Heroic Epic.* White colonizers arrive peacefully intended, only to be attacked by shrieking, bloodlusting savages inexplicably bent on committing fiendish acts. In self-defense, the brave, outnumbered White colonizers fight back

and eventually exterminate the horrid savages and establish civilized order.[11]

To these, we can add a fourth image:

- *The Benevolent Uncle.* After a period of tutelage, the colonies are granted full and complete independence, after which the grateful natives continue to receive care and assistance from the generous Great White Fathers, who help the colonials modernize, grow, and assume their rightful place in the sun.

The truth, not surprisingly, is more complicated and less complimentary to the colonizers: The process of imperialism typically involves military subjugation, divide-and-conquer, and at last, self-government. But even then, the former colonies often remain dependent on their original colonizer, or on the wealthier states in general. Thus begins the process of "dependent development," which is characterized by the following:

1. The Third World's natural resources are plundered by the advanced capitalist nations, and its industrial development is suppressed or retarded, in some cases for centuries.

2. The Third World's economic infrastructure is distorted, organized around a few extractive industries and export agriculture. Growing capital investments from richer nations bring a limited industrial development whose goal is to use the available cheap labor to produce commodities for affluent Western consumer markets.

3. The needs of Third World people for housing, food, medical care, and education become superfluous to this process of capital extraction.

4. The homegrown capitalist classes of the Third World use their money for high-living consumption and external investment. The more politically influential among them engage in a wide-scale plunder of public monies and resources. Like the foreign investors, they contribute nothing while taking a good deal out of their own nation's economy.[12]

According to this view, Third World economies have been interpenetrated by the North, and forcibly geared to fulfill its needs: tin from Bolivia, mahogany from Malaysia, and so on. The South essentially provides raw materials and some simple manufactured goods, while the North concentrates on complex and often high-tech industrial products (such as automobiles and computers) and services (such as banking, insurance, and communication). Those with faith in development maintain that the underdevelopment of the South is largely a temporary stage en route to industrialization and modernization, of the sort that eventually took place in the North. By contrast, dependency theorists argue that Third World poverty is the result of the North having its way with the South, keeping the latter at an essentially precapitalist (feudal) level. Presumably, conditions in the South therefore will not improve unless dependency on the North is terminated.

Dependency theorists point out that the Third World situation has been deteriorating vis-à-vis the industrialized world. For example, in the 1930s, Third World countries essentially fed themselves, producing a surplus of 12 million metric tons of grain; in 1980, they had to import 88 million tons. Commodities and raw materials (exported by the Third World) have regularly been devalued on the world trading markets, whereas manufactured goods (exported by the industrial states) have enjoyed increasingly favorable terms of trade. Each of more than two dozen developing countries rely on just one commodity for more than one half of their export earnings, and another thirteen rely on just two. This situation, encouraged by the industrial states, enhances the economic and political dependency of those states whose wealth is largely in the form of raw materials. Along with concentrating on a small number of exports, dependent countries find themselves dealing with a very limited number of trading partners, so that they are doubly dependent: on a limited range of products and also on a limited range of partners. Their economies are typically distorted, with very uneven development. Rather than growing needed and highly nourishing crops like soy or corn, for example, Third World countries find themselves compelled to raise income-generating crops such as tobacco, coffee, and sugar, which satisfy needs in the industrialized North while also providing some immediate cash for the South, but at the same time diminish their own economic self-sufficiency.

Certain states, such as China, have rejected dependency and emphasized autonomy and self-reliance. Others, like Sri Lanka, have self-consciously chosen to invest relatively heavily in social and human services, against the urgings and pressures of the international financial community.

The Debt Problem

In addition to poverty itself, most Third World countries have another problem, one that saps revenues, limits domestic spending options, and sits like an ogre, waylaying countries that seek to progress along the path of economic betterment. That problem is debt. Mexico, for example, pays out about $9 billion annually on a foreign debt of $104 billion. With such a drain on its finances, Mexico has virtually no hope of achieving prosperity, as it is literally unable to invest in its own economy. Economic growth had averaged 6 percent annually from 1940 to 1980, but during the 1980s the Mexican GNP actually declined, in some years by as much as 4 percent. Real incomes (measured by purchasing power, and thus discounted for inflation) were down 40 percent by 1989 as compared with 1980 levels, while the inflation rate was 60 percent.

In 1980, the rich nations of the world transferred $35 billion to the poor nations, $25 billion as overseas investments and $10 billion as aid. In 1982, before the debt crisis erupted, Third World states were still taking in $18 billion more than they paid out. But by 1989, the annual net transfer was $30 billion, *flowing in the other direction*, from the poor nations to the rich, as payment on national indebtedness. As of 1989, total indebtedness was about $1.32 *trillion*,* which represents a staggering

---

*In an equally astonishing turnaround, the United States has become the world's largest debtor nation. The strength of the U.S. economy, however, is such that there are no serious doubts about U.S. ability to pay its obligations; moreover, servicing the foreign debt has not noticeably crippled domestic investments.

blow to the potential well-being of the poor countries, occurring just when funds are desperately needed to finance domestic improvements. And so, desperately poor inhabitants of Africa, South Asia, and Latin America witness the spectacle of their governments using scarce national revenues to build twenty-story luxury hotels and condominiums, seeking to attract foreign tourists and their money.

The debt crisis was precipitated in large part by a widespread recession among the wealthy states. The stage was set during the 1970s, when costs skyrocketed for petroleum, weapons, and food—all of which were purchased by Third World countries, in part using funds that Northern banks eagerly made available. By the 1980s, interest rates rose dramatically while commodity prices plummeted, whereupon Third World states found themselves increasingly hard-pressed to meet the interest payments on their loans. Ever since, the poor countries have been falling ever further behind in their capacity to pay. Their plight has been like that of the coal workers in the song "Sixteen Tons": "You load sixteen tons and what do you get? Another day older and deeper in debt."

Under certain circumstances, the International Monetary Fund permits rescheduling of this crushing debt burden, but only if the debtor country agrees to "austerity programs," which typically require drastic cutbacks in government subsidies of food, transportation, health care, and education, as well as antiinflation policies that substantially increase unemployment and underemployment. A related strategy has been to provide new loans to enable debtors to pay the interest on old loans . . . a "solution" that is unlikely to inspire much long-term confidence.

The human cost of international debt has been staggering. A UNICEF report in 1988 estimated that during 1987, 500,000 children died because of economic decline or stagnation in the world's poorest states, which generated government cutbacks in basic health services, primary education, and food and fuel subsidies. This all occurred when family incomes for a billion people were *declining*, especially in Africa, South America, and south Asia.

Transportation for the rich and the poor in modern-day Sudan. (Oxfam America/Sukop)

Perhaps not surprisingly, therefore, some of the most impoverished and indebted states have threatened to default on their loans.

Development Models

There are several models of suggested Third World development, which we shall briefly summarize:

1. *Classic capitalism.* Emphasizes growth, efficiency, free markets, integration into the world economy through foreign investment, the production of money-generating exports, and a minimal role of the government except in military affairs. "Grow now, redistribute later" could serve as a motto.

2. *Classic socialism.* Involves radical redistribution of wealth, often by revolutionary takeover, egalitarian social relations, and a highly centralized and planned economy.

3. *Liberal capitalism.* Modifies classic capitalism by admitting a role for the government in achieving some small degree of redistribution, providing basic social services, and so on.

4. *Liberal Marxism.* Emphasizes meeting basic needs of the population, even at the cost of growth.

5. *Communitarian and self-reliant.* Involves participatory social relations and grass-roots development with decentralization.

The United States government strongly favors classic capitalism as a model for Third World development; the Soviet Union, classic socialism. Modifications of these ideologies — liberal capitalism and liberal socialism — have increasingly been replacing their more doctrinaire antecedents, as Western-oriented Third World dictatorships such as those in the Philippines, South Korea, and Brazil give way to governments with more sensitivity to the downtrodden. At the same time, even the giant socialist states such as China and the U.S.S.R. itself have begun incorporating free enterprise and diminishing the role of the state in centralizing economic policy. As of now, communitarian models of development exist largely in theory, and as occasional, small-scale experimental efforts.

ETHICS AND WEALTH INEQUITIES

Amid all these conflicting ideologies and models, a fundamental question remains: Why should the wealthy states agree to any kind of New International Economic Order, or indeed, to any policies designed to reduce the inequities in world wealth? Do the wealthy countries have any obligation toward the poor ones? Some claim that no such obligation exists. An extension of laissez-faire capitalism and the ideology of "rugged individualism" is that poverty is the unavoidable consequence of differences (among countries no less than among individuals), and that such inequality should not only be tolerated but even celebrated, since it indicates that merit is being rewarded. By this argument, redistributing wealth in fact is immoral, since such redistribution necessarily involves taking away resources that rightfully belong to someone.

On the other hand, there are many reasons for opposing inequalities in global wealth. One is moral obligation, a virtually universal sense that gross inequity is of itself unfair, even if it is not the result of unjust practices. Certainly, there is something ethically repugnant about the spectacle of dire, unremitting, life-threatening poverty coexisting with extreme luxury. For some, it is an imperative based

essentially on charity: When suffering exists, people have a moral duty to attempt to alleviate it.

The ethicist John Rawls has developed a theory of rights that emphasizes liberty and equity. According to this influential view, "Social and economic inequalities are to be arranged so that they are . . . to the greatest benefit of the least advantaged."[13] Rawls proposes that we evaluate any social institution from "behind the veil of ignorance" — that is, considering every system as though we have no foreknowledge as to our own specific place within that system: Not knowing whether we would be privileged or not, how would we feel about being part of a given social form? (Our view of the Hindu caste system would probably be affected if we had a high probability of being an "untouchable," for example.)

Moreover, it is not unreasonable to suggest that the poverty of the many is somehow connected to the extreme wealth of the privileged few. Wealth amidst poverty is often the result of extortion, theft, unmerited good luck, and so on. But aside from issues of fairness and merit, there are the questions of "distributive justice." Should society intervene to assure equitable distribution of wealth? Or should certain minimum levels of economic welfare be established? If so, then how? And what should they include — housing, education, medical care, assured employment? If so, how can we make room for individual initiative, and assure that people will contribute their "fair share"?

A classic Marxist maxim is "from each according to his ability, to each according to his need." But in practice, it has proven difficult to assess and reward need, and even more difficult to induce people to contribute according to their ability, unless they perceive that a direct personal benefit will flow from their labors; hence, the low productivity of many socialist economies. Beyond this, is it necessarily true that everyone should be treated equally? With respect to legal entitlements or political rights, most people would agree that the answer is yes, but in other respects, it is clearly no. Criminals, for instance, are treated differently than law-abiding citizens. What about reward for special effort or skill? Is inequality of compensation in itself unjust? And what about unequal wages between farmer and factory worker, police officer and physician, villager and city-dweller, Eskimo and Polynesian? Is inequality any more acceptable between different countries than within a single country?

A simple, practical argument in favor of social policies that diminish poverty is that change of one sort or another is going to take place in any event, so it may as well be peaceful and orderly. People who are well fed and basically satisfied with their situation in life should be less likely to turn to violence, whether personal or at the level of states. Hence, the wealthy have a selfish interest in the welfare of the underprivileged. And for practitioners of realpolitik, if the demand for distributive justice seems likely to result in change, then the opportunity arises to orchestrate that change in a way most consistent with national policy goals. Foreign aid is one of the more obvious and presumably benevolent techniques in this respect.

Although to some extent foreign aid may appear to be well intentioned, in fact, most of it appears to be selfishly motivated. Japanese and U.S. foreign assistance, for example, is strongly biased toward "helping" other countries purchase Japanese and U.S. goods. More than three-quarters of all U.S. foreign aid is bilateral, typically following channels of geopolitical interest rather than social or economic need; the top four recipients of U.S. aid are, in order, Israel, Egypt, Turkey, and South Korea. And much foreign aid, even when it goes to needy countries, is siphoned off to the wealthy within those countries, much of it via corrupt government officials. Critics (and some cynics) have suggested, therefore, that foreign aid — since it is raised by taxes, like any other government expenditure — essentially involves a process whereby the poor people in wealthy countries help enrich the wealthy people in poor countries.

On the other hand, well-designed foreign aid seems unavoidable as a moral imperative as well as a realpolitik necessity. The trick, for those concerned about improving the lot of the world's needy, is to make it effective, that is, to have it benefit those who need it most. In this respect, there is an observation that is no less cogent for having become a cliché: Give someone a fish and you feed him for a day; teach someone to fish, and you feed him for a lifetime.*

HUNGER

Perhaps the most painful index of poverty is inadequate nutrition. And unfortunately, it will take more than a few fishing lessons to resolve the problem of world hunger. Approximately 15–20 percent of the human population currently suffers from being undernourished, primarily lacking sufficient protein and/or calories. About 70 percent of the world's hunger is found in nine countries: India, Bangladesh, Pakistan, Indonesia, the Philippines, Zaire, Kampuchea, Brazil, and Ethiopia.

The Extent of the Problem

The average inhabitant of south Asia consumes fewer than 2,000 calories per day, as compared to more than 3,000 for the average American. The average Asian consumes about 400 pounds of grain per year, almost all of it directly as grain. The average American, by contrast, consumes an extraordinary 2,000 pounds of grain per year, but of this, only about 150 pounds are eaten directly as grain (the most energy-efficient way); about 100 pounds are consumed as alcohol, and most of the remainder much less efficiently, as meat. (When calories are transferred from grain to livestock and the meat then eaten by human beings, between 75 and 90 percent of the calories are lost.) Approximately one billion people in the Third World are chronically undernourished, even while food imports have increased, emphasizing Third World dependence on such imports as well as vulnerability to droughts, hurricanes, floods, earthquakes, and the like.

---

*Assuming that the waters remain unpolluted and not overfished, and also that local warfare doesn't make it impossible to go fishing safely.

Five million children died from hunger-related illnesses in sub-Saharan Africa alone during 1984. UNICEF estimates that 25–30 percent of all Third World children die before the age of four, because of malnutrition and related diseases. In Bangladesh, 150,000 children go blind every year because of malnutrition, particularly insufficient vitamin A. In Africa alone, more than 100 million people have been characterized by the World Bank as "food insecure." One third of the Ethiopian population (about 15 million people) is undernourished, along with nearly 14 million Nigerians. Among many African countries, more than 40 percent of the population suffer from chronic food insecurity; these states include Uganda, Mozambique, Chad, Somalia, Ethiopia, Zambia, and Zaire.

The simple ability to raise food is certainly relevant, and in this respect, it is especially troubling that per capita food production in many Third World states, notably in Africa, actually went *down* during the 1980s. Poor countries produce less food, at least in part because, being poor, they cannot afford modern agricultural technology. Rice yields in India and Nigeria, for example, are only one third that of Japan, and Brazil's corn yields are only one third that of the United States. Approximately one tenth of the world's land surface is now under cultivation, but little increase in farmland can be anticipated: Most of the remaining land is desert, mountainous, arctic, or otherwise uncultivable. Nonetheless, despite serious problems of desertification, erosion, and pollution, worldwide agriculture raises 2.5 times the grain needed for human consumption. Inequities in such consumption, however, are dramatic.

A Matter of Distribution

To a large extent, the problem of world hunger is not really so much a production problem as it is a *distribution* problem. In Mexico, for example, where as many as 80 percent of the country's rural children are undernourished, livestock consumes more grain than the entire rural population . . . and the meat is then exported to the United States.

Throughout much of Africa, land that once grew sorghum and corn, for local consumption, is now owned by multinational agribusiness conglomerates, and produces cotton and coffee, for export. Local people are thereby denied native grains while also being unable to pay for imported wheat and rice, which tend to be relatively expensive because of transportation and distribution costs. People may have desperate needs, but in economic terms, this doesn't constitute "demand" unless they can pay for what they want. Moreover, the rich have greater influence on the politics of decision making. As a result, when poor countries are capable of production, there is a tendency to make luxury goods, for export, rather than necessities, for domestic consumption.

Fewer than 3 percent of landowners — many of them absentee and/or large agribusiness firms — own nearly 75 percent of the world's cultivatable land. In some areas, this inequity is even greater. One percent of the population of northeast Brazil, for example, owns fully 45 percent of the land, much of it used to grow sugar, which generates money for the owners, but virtually no food for the vast majority of the population. For their part, national governments tend to encourage such activity, since it generates cash that is desperately needed to make foreign debt payments. Meanwhile, peasant farmers, desperate to raise their own food, find themselves forced to cultivate erodible hillsides and infertile terrain, which in turn is quickly overcultivated and depleted, leading to ecological ruin and yet more poverty and famine.

In 1974, Frances Moore Lappé wrote *Diet for a Small Planet*, in which she argued the need for people to eat lower on the food chain (less meat, more grain, and so on). In 1986, in her book *World Hunger*, she saw the problem differently: World grain production alone, she estimated, is enough to provide 3,600 calories per capita per day — enough to make everyone overweight. The World Bank has agreed, estimating that world grain production alone could provide 3,000 calories and 65 grams of protein per person per day, more than the highest estimates of minimum nutritional requirements. If only 2 percent of the world's grain output were redirected toward those who need it, hunger would essentially be eliminated from the world. But, Lappé points out, the greed of agribusiness shippers and brokers, plus control of land by a small elite, leaves hundreds of millions of people hungry every day. The politics of scarcity, which dominate the lives of Third World people, have scarcely been examined in the overfed First World.

POPULATION

As we have seen, positive peace involves a web of interconnected relationships. This is especially true of the population problem. Population — the sheer press of human numbers — makes itself felt in every aspect of the human condition, but the environmental and economic impact of human population is particularly acute. On the one hand, the negative impact that human beings exert on their environment is clearly a function of technology. (Compare the damage done to a tropical rain forest, for example, by 10,000 indigenous hunters, gatherers, and horticulturists — who have lived in relative balance with the forest for thousands of years — with the damage wrought by 10,000 people armed with bulldozers, dynamite, asphalt, and guns, who threaten to destroy whole ecosystems in a matter of years.) And yet, the sheer number of people also contributes substantially to environmental problems. Even among Third World countries using minimal technology, expanding population threatens to destroy major wildlife forms because of habitat destruction (for example, the fencing and plowing of land otherwise needed for jaguar habitats in Belize) and hunting (for example, poaching of elephants and rhinos in Tanzania). Too many people results in too much consumption, which in turn pollutes the air and water, creates unmanageable quantities of solid waste, and threatens to exceed the productive capacity of any given region — and ultimately, the entire planet — to provide nourishment, decent living conditions, and an acceptable environment. Many of our problems doubtless can be ameliorated greatly by social, po-

litical, and technological innovations; even with the best of policies, however, there must ultimately be a stabilization of the human population, or else no solutions will ever hold for the long haul.

This is especially true of attempts at economic self-betterment. All too often, countries seem poised to make real gains in their living standards, only to have the progress nullified by an exploding population. No country can "pull itself up by its bootstraps" if the weight of its human population is so great as to tear those straps.

Some Numerical Trends

The human species is several million years old. World population, however, did not reach the 1 billion mark until about the year A.D. 1600. This increase was due largely to the Agricultural Revolution, begun around 8,000 B.C., with the domestication of plants and animals. This, in turn, resulted in better diets, more reliable food supplies, and the opportunity for division of labor. After the long journey to that first billion, it took only 300 years to add the next billion. This happened around 1900, stimulated in large part by the Industrial Revolution (which made energy available via mechanization and the use of fossil fuels), as well as advances in public hygiene, vaccination procedures, and the control of major epidemics like typhoid, typhus, and cholera. The third billion arrived in just one sixth that time, by 1950, and the fourth by 1975. As of 1986, the total was 5 billion, and still climbing. In short, not only has the world population been growing, the rate of that increase has itself increased, because, as the English economist Malthus pointed out, human population increases geometrically (or exponentially).

As recently as the 1940s, world population was rising, but at a modest pace of about 1 percent per year. Then, the worldwide rate of population increase more than doubled, exceeding 2 percent, and in certain countries, 3 percent and even more. The result has been little short of cataclysmic. In some cases — notably, the developed economies of the West — population trends are cause for hope rather than alarm, as they have bucked the world-wide trend. About 30 percent of the world's people live in developed countries, but the percentage of world population increase attributable to these countries is less than 10 percent. It is anticipated, for example, that the U.S. population will actually decline slightly by early in the next century, after the momentum of the "baby boomers" carries the population from 248 million in 1989 to about 300 million. Similarly, West Germany is expected to decline by 10 percent, from 60 million to 54 million, by the year 2025. Switzerland's population is similarly likely to drop, by 8 percent, and Sweden's, by 6 percent.

Third World Population Growth.   And yet, total world population will increase wildly, doubling in another forty years. In 1989 alone, world population increased by 85 million, the equivalent of adding a new Mexico. More than 90 percent of this growth occurred in the Third World: As the old adage says, the rich get richer and the poor get children. Of the world's new people, 16.5 million were African, 9.6 million were Latin American and 51.7 million were Asian. The cause of this increase, quite simply, is an excess of births over deaths, and the effect, as we shall see, is a deepening of the planetary ecological crisis, plus a deepening of the poverty within which such population growth takes place. To maintain a constant population size, women must bear, on average, 2 children in their lifetime. The U.S. average is currently 1.8, Canada 1.7, Denmark 1.4, and West Germany 1.3; in rapidly expanding populations such as Mexico, however, the average woman bears 4.0 children. In Nigeria and Kenya, the numbers reach a whopping 6.6 and 8.0, respectively.

This tidal wave of population growth means that in Third World countries alone, approximately 665 million people have been added since 1950, more than currently live in all of Oceania, Japan, the Soviet Union, Europe, and North America. Take the situation in just one country, Nigeria, the most populous in Africa. Since 1950, Nigeria has grown from 43 million to 105 million persons, and by 2025, that number is expected to swell to over 300 million! Some people contend that concern about overpopulation—especially on the part of Caucasians—is actually a concealed form of racism. This accusation is at least plausible, since rapid population increases are occurring largely in non-Caucasian nations, in Africa, Latin America, and parts of Asia. But it should be emphasized that the costs of overpopulation are born overwhelmingly by the people who are themselves overcrowded. Countries in which resources are already stretched to the limit are required, by virtue of their expanding human populations, to increase demands on water, soil, wildlife habitats, and education, health, and other human service budgets that are already dangerously depleted. Struggling, debt-ridden governments have, in many cases, already reached or surpassed their abilities to provide even basic services to their people. In 1969, for example, Mexico City had a population of 9 million people; in 1989, there were 20 million people in this huge, almost ungovernable city.

Widening the Gap.   Consider Nigeria again for a moment. Already struggling to provide decent conditions for more than 100 million persons, Nigeria will have to provide for the additional schooling, transportation, communication, health, and other needs of a population exceeding that of North America in the early 1990s. An economy that is already painfully overstretched must somehow find nearly 200 million new, productive jobs. When a population grows at a rate of 3.3 percent or higher annually (which is true for Kenya, Zimbabwe, Iraq, Jordan, Thailand, Honduras, Nicaragua, and the Dominican Republic), it must *double* its industrial and agricultural production every twenty-nine years, a feat that is virtually impossible. And for economic improvement to be made, such increases must be even more rapid. This population plight of the poorer countries brings to mind the Red Queen's observation to Alice in *Adventures Through the Looking Glass:* You have to run if you merely want to stay in the same place; to get anywhere, you must go faster yet.

For another example, take the Philippines, whose population has been growing at 2.5–3.0 percent per year, one third higher than that of Asia as a whole. In terms of the Philippine economy, this means 700,000 new job-seekers every year, added to 6,000,000 already unemployed. In 1989, 55 percent of all Filipinos were poor; this is actually a substantial improvement from the situation under Ferdinand Marcos in 1984, when 70 percent of Filipinos were impoverished. Because of the country's rapid population growth, however, the absolute numbers of poor actually *increased* by two-thirds during the five-year period from 1984 to 1989. Under such conditions, concern about overpopulation must be seen as humanitarian, not racist.

The worldwide economic disparity between rich and poor can only be accentuated by current population trends. In 1970, for example, the world income was $881 per person, actually an average of $2,701 per capita in the richer countries, and $208 per capita in the poorer ones. Even if the latter attempt economic self-improvement, rapid population growth makes a mockery of such efforts. Imagine, for example, that income increased 5 percent per year in rich and poor countries alike, but at the same time, population increased by 0.5 percent per year among the rich countries and 2.5 percent among the poor (these are current rates). The 5 percent increase in income thus becomes 4.5 percent for the wealthy countries, and 2.5 percent for the poor ones. The result is a widening gap in per capita income between rich and poor. Starting at $2,701 per capita income in 1970, an increase of 4.5 percent per year produces a threefold increase in twenty-five years, to more than $8,000 in 1995; during that same time, under our assumptions, the per capita increase in income in the poorer countries, from $208 to $386, will not even have doubled. The grandchildren of the present rich-country generation, in 2020, will be enjoying a per capita income of more than $24,000, while their poor-country "peers" will be earning only $715 . . . less than the world average in 1970.

The point is that high population growth in the poorer countries will not only prevent a closing of the economic gap between rich and poor, it will actually *widen* that gap. The rates of income growth in rich and poor countries are roughly comparable;

accordingly, it is the different rate of *population* growth that keeps the latter from catching up. This problem is particularly acute in the Indian subcontinent, Africa, and Latin America.

The Demographic Transition

Many European states, including the Soviet Union, and the United States as well, have virtually attained zero population growth, whereas in Latin America the population growth rate is about 2.7 percent, in Africa 2.6 percent, and in Asia 2.0 percent. But there is some reason to hope that these high rates of population increase will decline in the future, as women experience an improvement in their social and economic status, and as (assuming they do) Third World countries experience general social and economic improvements. This expectation is based on one of the most important trends in human population, known as the "demographic transition": Birth rates consistently decline as a result of industrialization, urbanization, and a general improvement in economic conditions.

In nonindustrial, rural societies experiencing the first stage of this demographic process, birth rates and death rates both tend to be high, and the population therefore remains relatively stable. Then, with public health measures, increased immunizations, widespread food distribution, and so on, death rates decline while birth rates remain high, and population therefore increases dramatically. But in the final stage of the demographic transition, social and economic conditions improve, and this, along with lowered infant mortality, produces a desire for smaller families, as parents realize they do not need large numbers of children to serve as field hands, to compensate for high mortality, or to provide social security in their old age. Moreover, parents recognize that to provide their children with such benefits as a higher education, they must have fewer of them. As a result, in the final stage of the demographic transition, populations eventually level off.

Many countries have successfully made this transition, including much of Europe, Oceania, and, increasingly, the United States and the Soviet

Union. Fertility has also gone down impressively among those "Fourth World" Asian countries that have experienced substantially improved economic conditions: South Korea averages 1.8 children per family, Singapore 1.7, and Japan 2.1. The correlation between financial success and reduced family size is imperfect, however. In some cases, religious and social traditions that favor large families have proved to be especially stubborn. For example, Saudi Arabia and the United Arab Emirates, two of the world's richest countries as measured by per capita GNP, average 7.1 and 5.9 children per family, respectively. China has brought its fertility rate down to 2.4 children per family, in part by social coercion, but also by making family planning and health care available, as well as by widespread public education regarding the societal benefits of family planning. (Even so, there have been some problems. In particular, Chinese society — like many others — has traditionally valued male offspring over female. Because one-child families are socially sanctioned, parents apparently have sometimes killed their infant daughters, thereby enabling themselves to "try again" for a son.)

The Demographic/Economic/Environmental Trap

On the other hand, there is a real danger that some states may never make it to the third and stabilizing stage of the demographic transition; rather, they could get stuck in the second stage, caught in what might be termed a "demographic/economic/environmental (D-E-E) trap." In such cases, rapid population growth results in increased demands on natural and socioeconomic systems, which are then overtaxed and begin to collapse. People may respond with higher birth rates, which in turn produce yet more ecological and socioeconomic pressure, and which ultimately impoverish the land and the people, leading to catastrophic mortality, from starvation and epidemics, and possibly direct violence as well.

Population levels, ecological factors, and economic conditions are all intimately related. Thus, every environment can be said to have a "carrying capacity" — the number of people who can be supported by the soil, forestlands, grasslands, croplands, water, and other resources of that region. If demand exceeds carrying capacity, the effect is like mining capital rather than living off one's interest: It cannot be sustained for long. For example, in many areas of the world, wood is used for fuel. More people means more demand for wood, which leads to cutting, perhaps in excess of the amount that grows annually. As forests dwindle, wood becomes scarce and expensive, adding to the misery of the poor, while the deforestation itself seriously diminishes wildlife values, contributes to the greenhouse effect, and generates erosion and downstream flooding. (Devastating floods in Bangladesh during 1988, which killed tens of thousands of people and left hundreds of thousands homeless, were due to the destruction of forests in the foothills of the Himalayas, above that country.)

The forestlands of India in 1982 could support an annual harvest of 39 million tons of wood, whereas fuelwood demand was for 133 million tons. The gap — 94 million tons — was met by overcutting (which compromised future forest production), or by burning cow dung, which robbed the soil of needed fertility. If India's forests continue to shrink while its population expands, this gap will become even larger, with possibly irrevocable long-term effects. A similarly tragic pattern can take place with regard to supplies of fresh water (if demand exceeds the recharge rate of underground aquifers, lakes and reservoirs, or the flow rate of rivers.) The productivity of grasslands or croplands can be similarly abused, with very serious consequences. A study of nine countries in southern Africa, for example, found that cattle exceeded the carrying capacity of local grasslands by 50 to 100 percent. Clearly, these problems cannot be solved simply by cutting down more trees, digging deeper wells (which temporarily provide more water but eventually lower the water table and exhaust aquifers), adding more fertilizer, and the like. And even though the acute problem of world hunger is, to some extent, one of distribution rather than production, even a distribution problem is exacerbated

Temporary settlements constructed by "eco-refugees" in Ethiopia. (United Nations/Peter Magubane)

by the presence of too many mouths, to whom food must somehow be distributed. And underlying this, of course, is the problem of sustainability.

Another significant consequence of the demographic/economic/environmental trap is the production of large numbers of so-called eco-refugees, people who are forced to leave their ancestral homes because of environmental degradation. Land-hungry farmers are increasingly driven onto wildlife preserves and marginal land that is highly erodible and easily destroyed. The result is desertification, a process that is immensely destructive of the natural ecosystems upon which human socioeconomic health ultimately depends. The increasing numbers of eco-refugees congregate in cities and refugee centers, where they become heavily dependent on government assistance, and are highly susceptible to disease and — as has occurred in drought-stricken sub-Saharan Africa — massive starvation, when and if relief efforts run into political, economic, or logistical difficulties.

Uncontrolled population growth in subsistence economies threatens not only a country's environment, but also its social and economic capacities. Universal public education becomes virtually impossible when school systems are drowned beneath a tidal wave of youngsters. When population is constant (as in West Germany or Switzerland), a 2 percent increase in economic growth results in increased prosperity; when the population increases by 3 or 4 percent, that same 2 percent economic growth results in painfully declining living standards. As the 1990s begin, "The world is dividing largely into countries where population growth is slow or nonexistent and where living conditions are improving, and those where population growth is rapid and living conditions are deteriorating or in imminent danger of doing so."[14]

It is difficult to make a cogent case that more people are needed, in any part of the world. Those regions that we generally consider to be "unpopulated" usually possess few people because the land and its climate can only support small populations. Deserts, high mountain slopes, or low-lying marsh- or swampland that is regularly inundated by floods cannot — and should not — be heavily populated. The planet Earth does not appear to contain any Shangri-las: regions that are currently unpopulated,

Dead cow in a drought-stricken area in Senegal. (United Nations / John Isaac)

but that could provide idyllic, well-balanced lives for substantial numbers of people. Moreover, as we have seen, Third World countries are already dangerously overextended in their ability to care for their current population.

On the other hand, overpopulation can easily be exaggerated as a cause of human misery. Some of the most horribly impoverished regions of the Earth—such as the Sudan or Chad in Africa, or northeastern Brazil—are among the most sparsely populated. (Ecologists would note that such regions, because of their environmental limitations, should not be heavily populated in the first place; given the extreme susceptibility of tropical soils to destruction, and the extreme dryness of much of northern Africa, for example, it seems likely that the natural "carrying capacity" of such regions for human population is necessarily low.) The extreme poverty of India, Pakistan, and Indonesia is often blamed on high birthrates and population density, yet these countries have fewer people per square mile than England, Wales, Japan, Holland, Belgium, West Germany, and Italy, among others.

During the 1950s, Cuba—with a population of 5 million—suffered devastating poverty and widespread starvation; today, with more than twice the population, the Cuban people are well nourished. Clearly, then, although population can be a problem, and can add to existing problems, it is not the entire problem.

A world of zero population growth might also have some disadvantages. For example, there would be fewer interactions between adults and children. In rapidly growing Kenya, 53 percent of the population is under age 15; in Sweden, with a stable population, only 18 percent of the population is under 15. This means, of course, that the demands upon Sweden's educational system are much less than those placed on Kenya's. On the other hand, societies with a younger age structure have fewer current problems meeting the special needs of an elderly population: 17 percent of Sweden's population is over age 65, as opposed to only 2 percent of Kenya's. In the United States, there is concern that an increasingly aged population will place heightened demands on the social security system, with proportionately fewer tax-paying citizens paying for the retirement needs of proportionately more elderly retirees. On balance, however, the transition to a more stable age structure would make relatively few demands on society as a whole. Rather, it requires a shift in priorities: fewer pediatricians and more gerontologists, fewer elementary schools and more senior centers.

Efforts at Birth Control

Successful birth control programs require an accurate understanding of the causes and effects of population growth. There are four basic theories correlating population growth with socioeconomic situations:

1. Reproduction leads to poverty. People have too many children, forcing them to try to feed too many mouths, and to divide their land and their resources among too many individuals.

2. Poverty leads to reproduction. People have children because they are needed to work to help support their families; moreover, children don't cost very much if you don't buy VCRs and computers for them, or send them to college. In addition, under conditions of poverty, a relatively small number of children survive, which generates pressure for having large numbers of children.

3. Suppression of women leads to reproduction. Women would have fewer children if they had greater control over their lives, especially an increase in status and access to inexpensive, reliable family planning techniques.

4. (Actually a variant of theory 3) Male pig-headedness leads to increased numbers of children. Population growth is due to the influence of men, who equate large families with sexual virility and other "macho" characteristics.

To some extent, all of these theories seem to be true; they are not mutually exclusive. Large families, for example, are often a result of poverty and the low status of women, and they also generally lead to a vicious cycle of yet more poverty and sexism.

At present, about two-thirds of all birth control users live in the industrialized world. In some cases, Third World hesitation regarding birth control can be attributed to cultural factors, such as the "macho" societies of Latin America, which equate manhood with the production of children; to opposition from Catholic authorities in such states as Mexico, the Philippines, and Kenya; and to Moslem traditions in Egypt, Iran, Pakistan, and India. However, there is reason to believe that birth control technology, if widely available, would voluntarily be used. UN surveys, for example, have found that one half of all married women do not want any more children than they now have. And yet, contraceptive research and development funding, worldwide, was just $57 million in 1983, and population-assistance funding from the United States to the UN Fund for Population Activities and the International Planned Parenthood Federation declined from 1985 to 1987, to about $230 million. The Reagan administration was generally antagonistic to family planning, both domestically and globally. The World Bank estimated that it would cost $8 billion (about ten days worth of U.S. military spending) to make birth control easily available worldwide by the year 2000.

Breast-feeding is a moderately effective means of birth control, or at least, of birth spacing: Lactation tends to inhibit ovulation. (This is one reason why campaigns to convince Third World mothers to substitute artificial infant formula for breast-feeding are especially pernicious.) Sterilization is also becoming increasingly popular: About 98 million women and 35 million men are sterilized annually. Approximately 28 million abortions are performed annually in the Third World and about 26 million in industrialized countries; of these, roughly one half are illegal, and thus, likely to be performed by unskilled people and under unsafe conditions. Abortion is a highly charged issue for many people; even its supporters concede that it is a relatively violent means of family planning and thus, less desirable than contraception. Nonetheless, when other means of birth control have failed, access to safe abortions would seem preferable to enforced childbearing.

Iranian women attending a literacy class. Improvements in the educational, economic, and social status of women generally lead to a reduction in the birth rate. (United Nations)

Reproductive Rights for Women.   Perhaps the most effective way to reduce population growth is to improve the status of women. For example, when the government of Bangladesh initiated a program of financial loans designed to help rural women develop their own small businesses, contraceptive use among the recipients increased from an average of 35 percent to 75 percent. The relatively low social and economic status of women worldwide undoubtedly contributes to high birth rates, in several ways. Thus, married women — typically subordinate to their husbands — are often denied social permission to say no to their husband's demands for more children. In much of Africa, for example, social pressures are especially strong, since at marriage, the husband essentially purchases his wife's labor as well as her future children; each additional child solidifies the mother's place within the household.

When women are denied access to education and other forms of advancement, childbearing also becomes the only accepted rite of passage to adulthood. As one authority concludes:

> Improving the status of women, or, more specifically, reducing their economic dependence on men, is a crucial aspect of development. Until female education is widespread — until women gain at least partial control over the resources that shape their economic lives — high fertility, poverty, and environmental degradation will persist in many regions.[15]

It is also noteworthy that birth control and family planning are related to matters to public health. For example, complications arising from pregnancy and childbirth are the leading killers of Third World women in their twenties and thirties. More than 3,000 maternal deaths occur per 100,000 live births in regions of Ethiopia and Bangladesh, as compared with 10 in the United States and only 2 in Norway. This all adds up to a cogent argument in favor of reproductive rights for women. The case would be very strong simply as a matter of human rights alone.* With the addition of economic and ecological arguments, it becomes overwhelming.

Government Policies.   China began its "one-family, one-child" program in 1979. The goal was no more than 1.2 billion Chinese by the year 2000. Violators are punished by fines and dismissal from government jobs, while better housing and stipends are available to one-child households. The results have been mixed. There is some reason to believe, as noted previously, that female infanticide increased, as parents sought to make their one child a boy. Moreover, only 19 percent of Chinese families have just one child. Chinese population policy has been concentrated among urban, ethnic Chinese, whereas minorities and rural people have been to some extent exempted. Population growth in China, however, has decreased, from nearly 3 percent to 1.4 percent, largely because of a tendency to marry and bear children at a later age, and because of the active efforts of the Chinese government. (One very effective way of slowing population growth is for women to delay reproduction until later in life — for example, age 32 instead of 17 — one reason for the reduced population growth in Ireland, for example.)

Government efforts are clearly needed, especially if the D-E-E trap is to be avoided. For perhaps the first time in history, Third World governments must seek to lower birth rates during a time of deteriorating living conditions . . . so that they do not get worse yet. This goes against the traditional tendency of people to increase family size when mortality is high (the first demographic stage). Societal efforts can include, as we have seen,

increasing the status of women, improving social and economic conditions generally, improving education, enhancing access to contraception (a wide range of methods is currently available, including birth control pills, condoms, IUDs, surgically implanted hormone releasers that operate for up to five years), and positive inducements for small families (subsidies, housing, education, and medical benefits) and, possibly, various negative incentives for large ones. The latter, not surprisingly, can be especially controversial. India, for example, followed a rather aggressive population policy in the early 1970s, which led to charges of coerced abortions and sterilization programs. The result was a widespread backlash, which created resistance to subsequent efforts at family planning. The lesson to be learned is that, although population policies are necessary, they must be based on volition rather than compulsion; that is, governments and agencies should educate, provide incentives and technology, and minister to existing demand, without being heavy-handed.

Unmet Need.   There is, in fact, a very large unmet need with respect to limitation of family size. For example, women of reproductive age were surveyed in four Third World countries: India, Egypt, Peru, and Ghana. The percentage indicating that they did not want any more children was, respectively, 50, 56, 70, and 90. The percentage using contraception was, in turn, 28, 30, 25, and 10. Subtracting the latter from the former, we get the proportion of women who wish to limit their family size, but are not employing any form of birth control: 22 percent in India, 26 percent in Egypt, 45 percent in Peru, and a staggering 80 percent in Ghana. The unmet need for contraception is clearly enormous, and whereas it can be seen as a personal, family, national, and global tragedy, it also provides population planners with an immense opportunity — a chance to reduce the catastrophic increase in human population while at the same time satisfying the desires of the people involved.

There has been some progress. In the last twenty years, average fertility in the Third World

---

*It should be noted that of all birth control and fertility reduction techniques, abortion is by far the most controversial. Opponents of abortion argue forcefully that the "right to life" is also a human right. Many fewer people support the rights of the "unconceived." Accordingly, there is far more support worldwide for contraception than for abortion.

has dropped from six children per woman to four; use of contraceptives by potentially reproductive, married women has increased from 9 percent to 43 percent, and as a result, the rate of world population increase has slowed from 2.1 percent per year to 1.7 percent. But do not be deceived; we are talking here about a reduction in the *rate of increase*, not a decline in world population itself. In addition, population growth is not evenly spread; typically, states that are already pressing hard on their economic and ecologic resource base — and that, accordingly, are most threatened by increasing numbers of people — are likely to be experiencing the most rapid population growth.

An enlightened population policy commends itself on financial grounds as well. Mexico, for example, discovered that for every peso spent on family planning, there is a savings of nine pesos that would otherwise have been spent on maternal and infant health care, not even counting education. Although birth control programs are no substitute for investment in education, health care, or economic and environmental betterment, it is clear that fertility reduction is essential if any of these social programs are ultimately to be meaningful and to have any chance of succeeding.

The Developed Countries

As we have seen, poor countries tend to reduce their rate of population growth as they become more wealthy, and wealthy countries (like the United States and the nations of Western Europe) have relatively low rates of population increase. However, this is no reason to be complacent or self-righteous, because the wealthy countries use far more resources per capita than do the poor ones, and they also produce proportionately more pollution. The United States is about twice as prodigal as the other developed states — with about 6 percent of the world's population, it consumes more than 30 percent of the world's resources, five times its "rightful" share. Or look at it this way: The average U.S. citizen is about twenty times as hurtful to the world's supply of resources as is the average Third Worlder.

Additionally, the United States consumes one quarter of the world's energy each year (eleven times the world average, per capita), and it uses this energy inefficiently: For the energy expended, the United States produces only one half the economic output of Japan or West Germany. The United States, which contains 6 percent of the world's population, belches out 15 percent of the world's sulfur dioxide emissions and 25 percent of its carbon and nitrogen oxides. It produces 3.5 pounds of trash per person per day, and owns 135 million cars, fully one third of the world's total — with all that implies in terms of the consumption of nonrenewable metals (in constructing automobiles) and of petroleum (in driving them), as well as the generation of pollution, including greenhouse gases.

Clearly, population growth in Third World countries is a serious social, environmental, and economic problem for the residents of these countries. However, when considering the planetary costs of overpopulation, population growth in developed states such as the United States is far more serious. Americans, in short, have no justification for blaming others for the effects of their fertility on the world's environmental plight; we are not only part of the problem, but the largest part of it.

FUTURE DIRECTIONS

An overcrowded, overarmed world, increasingly divided between haves and have-nots, is not an acceptable prospect, either in terms of basic morality or in its more practical consequences: misery, disruption, and perhaps, greater probability of violence. Writing in 1974, the economist Robert Heilbroner predicted possible "wars of redistribution," driven by the rage of the impoverished, subsisting in a world of obscene luxury.[16] But poor people are unlikely to march aggressively into the rich countries, especially so long as the latter are guarded by abundant lethal weaponry. Unlike a ghetto riot, in which poverty and frustration erupt into the looting of a local department store, poverty is more apt to continue generating its own kind of structural violence, eroding the quality of human life. It may also continue to generate political instability, especially in the poor countries themselves. Heilbroner envisions

> the descent of large portions of the under-developed world into a condition of steadily worsening social disorder, marked by shorter life expectancies, further stunting of physical and mental capacities, political apathy intermingled with riots and pillaging when crops fail . . . ruled by dictatorial governments serving the interests of a small economic and military upper class and presiding over the rotting countryside with mixed resignation, indifference, and despair. This condition could continue for a considerable period, effectively removing these areas from the concern of the rest of the world, and consigning the billions of their inhabitants to a human state comparable to that which we now glimpse in the worst regions of India or Pakistan.[17]

As with other questions discussed in Peace Studies, it is easier to outline the problem of poverty than to suggest solutions. It is also a major accomplishment just to appreciate the problem, since — like human rights and environmental degradation — it is vast and multidimensional. Without first acknowledging its magnitude and complexity, no effective solutions can be possible. As to the prospects for a future socioeconomic system, changes clearly must take place. The plight of the poor is not just temporary, but at the same time, it need not necessarily be eternal. One of the greatest impediments to effective action in this respect is the inclination of powerful governments — representing people who are essentially satisfied with the status quo — to ignore the problem, minimize it, and, if pressed, pay only lip service to its urgency. There is a near-universal tendency, especially among the relatively wealthy and self-satisfied, to opt for the easiest and most short-sighted, temporary palliatives, such as targeted foreign aid or improved terms of trade in specific cases. Among the more general, long-range suggestions raised, the following may have particular merit:

- Recognizing that whereas growth is to some degree desirable, growth in itself does not necessarily lead to a greater sharing of prosperity, either between states or within them.

- Establishing an internationally accepted floor below which poverty shall not be permitted, analogous to the "safety net" currently in place in most Western democracies.

- Making birth control universally available, either free or at minimal cost.

- Developing and implementing a worldwide literacy program, plus upgrading of educational facilities and opportunities, especially in the Third World.

- Enhancing the role and effectiveness of local, grass-roots activities that promote economic growth along with environmental protection.

- Providing massive debt relief for Third World states, coupled with reorientation of their economies to satisfy domestic needs.

- Making serious efforts toward accomplishing self-reliant "ecodevelopment," which is neither stagnation nor ecological exploitation, but rather a differentiated and autonomous development, respecting the cultural heterogeneity of the Third World, as well as the need to work with nature rather than against it.

- Recognizing that resource-guzzling technologies will likely be hurtful for many if not most Third World countries as well as for the developed world; in addition, realizing that high-technology procedures put relatively few people to work, whereas unemployment is a major contributor to poverty. It should be emphasized, however, that, even though technology has often been misused, the real barriers to human betterment are not technological but social, political, and economic. "Alternative technology," based on the notion that "small is beautiful," can be helpful, but alternative social and political forms are likely to be a prerequisite for a sustainable development process.

- Redirecting a large proportion of planetary resources, currently eaten up by military spending, to upgrading the living conditions of the world's people. For a painful example of

United States B-2 (stealth) bomber. These airplanes will cost over $800 million apiece. (U.S. Department of Defense)

misplaced priorities, consider that in a time of diminishing East–West tensions combined with horrifying poverty and dreadful environmental abuse, the United States remains nonetheless committed to purchasing 75 B-2 Stealth bombers, at $813 million apiece, for a total price tag of $61 billion.

All of this will entail a willingness of inhabitants of the Northern industrial countries in particular to accept a degree of belt-tightening of their own, that is, a less wasteful and ostentatious lifestyle. Just as ecologists have long argued that "there is no such thing as a free lunch," the world's wealthy must realize that a reduction of planetary inequity will have to involve some sacrifices on their part. Instead of maximizing accumulation, typically by a few, a successful assault on world poverty may require a different orientation, toward maximizing and expanding collective welfare. It will be an especially difficult task to accomplish this reorientation—which will involve some collectivization of goals and methods—while also preserving and in some cases even enhancing the free enterprise systems that have shown themselves capable of such impressive production. Long-term changes are morally, economically, and environmentally necessary; the question is whether the world's wealthy will acknowledge this, and respond in time.

In this regard, the current thaw in the U.S.-Soviet Cold War is especially promising, not only because it diminishes the likelihood of a Third

World War, but also because it could help release resources now consumed by the military on both sides, and desperately needed for constructive purposes. The experience of Costa Rica may be instructive. This small Central American state has no army, and just a small national police force. Whereas Guatemala and Honduras, by contrast, spend 15 percent of their GNP on their military, Costa Rica spends only about 3 percent of its GNP on its police. These savings permit Costa Rica to devote 11 percent of its GNP to health and education, more than twice the proportional expenditure of Honduras, and three times that of Guatemala. As a result, polio and diphtheria have been eradicated in Costa Rica, and whooping cough, tetanus, and measles are nearly gone. Infant mortality has plummeted, as has birthrate, which declined 35 percent from 1960 to 1983. During the 1980s, the U.S. government regularly pressured Costa Rica to reverse its priorities, and invest in national armed forces, ostensibly as defense against communism (but, in fact, as part of the Reagan administration's desire to put military pressure on Nicaragua). It seems likely, however, that the demilitarized, prosocial policy of Costa Rica is a surer ultimate path to stability and security. Costa Rica may yet represent the wave of the future.

A FINAL NOTE ON ECONOMIC WELL-BEING

As we have seen, many of the world's people are poor. Some are so poor that their lives are shortened or made miserable; others are prevented from experiencing their full potential. Only a small proportion enjoy substantial material advantages. Indirect violence is thus widespread and, despite advances in science and technology, in many areas it is increasing. Overpopulation exacerbates this problem as well as the disparity between the haves and the have-nots (who, not surprisingly, are also "want-mores"). Solutions, however, do exist, including various redistribution strategies, development programs, and family planning. The problem of poverty—like that of human rights, the environment, and war itself—is ancient, but not necessarily intractable. Enough resources exist on the planet Earth to provide a decent material life for everyone, especially if human numbers are eventually controlled. The greatest obstacle to economic well-being appears to be the social and political inclinations of human beings themselves, but whether this leads to optimism or pessimism is best left to the reader.

Study Questions

1. Compare and contrast differences in wealth within a country with differences among different countries.

2. Describe various ways of measuring poverty.

3. Define the Lorenz curve and the Gini coefficient.

4. How does poverty lead to a vicious cycle of inequity and further poverty?

5. What is meant by "uneven development," or "increased marginalization despite development"?

6. Discuss at least four different explanations for why there is so much poverty and inequity in wealth in the Third World.

7. What is meant by the NIEO?

8. Briefly define *dependencia* theory, and apply it to a specific Third World situation.

9. Describe various ethical approaches to poverty. Why should relatively affluent people in the United States be concerned with starvation in, say, Ethiopia?

10. How does the demographic transition offer hope to the problem of Third World overpopulation? What can be done to facilitate it?

Suggestions for Further Reading

Michael P. Todaro. 1981. *Economic Development in the Third World*. Longman: New York.

Ruth Leger Sivard. (Published annually). *World Military and Social Expenditures*. World Priorities: Washington, DC.

Gerald Meier. 1984. *Emerging from Poverty: The Economics That Really Matters*. Oxford University Press: New York.

Chadwick Alger and Michael Stohl (eds.). 1989. *A Just Peace Through Transformation*. Westview Press: Boulder, CO.

Edward Weisband (ed.). 1989. *Poverty Admidst Plenty*. Westview Press: Boulder, CO.

Source Notes

1. Bertolt Brecht. 1956. *Threepenny Novel*. Grove Press: New York.

2. St. Francis of Assisi. 1959. *Writings*. Mowbray: London.

3. George Gershwin. 1935. *Porgy and Bess*.

4. Roy Preiswerk. 1981. "Could We Study International Relations As If People Mattered?" In *Peace and World Order Studies*. Institute for World Order: New York.

5. G. Kohler. 1978. "Global Apartheid." *Alternatives: A Journal of World Policy*. 4.

6. The Independent Commission on International Development Issues (the Brandt Commission). 1980. *North–South: A Programme for Survival*. MIT Press: Cambridge, MA.

7. All data from Ruth Leger Sivard. 1988–1989. *World Military and Social Expenditures*. World Priorities: Washington, DC.

8. *The New York Times*, May 10, 1988.

9. Franz Fanon. 1963. *The Wretched of the Earth*. Grove Press: New York.

10. Presidential address to the American Economic Association, 1955.

11. Michael Parenti. 1989. *The Sword and the Dollar*. St. Martin's: New York.

12. Parenti. *Sword*.

13. John Rawls. 1973. *A Theory of Justice*. Harvard University Press: Cambridge, MA.

14. Lester Brown. 1987. "Analyzing the Demographic Trap." In L. Brown et al. (eds.), *State of the World, 1987*. Norton: New York.

15. Jodi Jacobson. 1988. "Planning the Global Family." In Brown et al. *State*.

16. Robert Heilbroner. 1974. *An Inquiry into the Human Prospect*. Norton: New York.

17. Ibid.

23

Nonviolence

Nonviolence is intimately associated with certain ethical and religious traditions, especially Buddhism and Christian pacifism (see Chapter 19). However, it has achieved such stature, as a goal and as a practical strategy in the struggle for peace — both positive peace and the avoidance of war — that it deserves a separate treatment. Because Mohandas Gandhi is unarguably the major teacher of nonviolence in modern times, we begin this chapter with a brief consideration of his life.

MOHANDAS K. GANDHI

Mohandas Gandhi is revered by Indians as the founder of their nation, and also by millions of others as the leading exponent of nonviolence and as a virtual modern-day saint. He pioneered the use of nonviolent resistance as both a spiritual/philosophical approach to life and an intensely practical technique of achieving political and social change. Gandhi was widely known among Indians as "Mahatma" (Great Soul), for his courage, simplicity, and penetrating insight, and for the extraordinary impact of his teachings and his life.

Central to Gandhi's worldview was the search for truth, and indeed, he titled his autobiography *My Experiments with Truth*. Gandhi considered that truth (*ahimsa*, in Sanskrit) was achievable only through love and tolerance for other people; moreover, it required continual testing, experimentation, occasional errors, and constant, unstinting effort. His teachings emphasized courage, directness, friendly civility, absolute honesty, nonviolence to all living creatures, and adherence to the truth. Perhaps the most important Gandhian concept is *satyagraha*, literally translated as "soul-force" or "soul-truth." *Satyagraha* requires a clear-headed adherence to goals of love and mutual respect, and it demands a willingness to suffer, if need be, to achieve these goals.

Early Years

Gandhi was born in India, in 1869; his parents were merchant-caste Hindus. He remained a devout Hindu throughout his life, although his thinking incorporated elements from numerous other religious and ethical traditions. He was strongly influenced by pacifist Christianity, as well as by the writings of Thoreau and Tolstoy on the rights and duties of individuals to practice civil disobedience when governmental authorities are insensitive to higher morality. He married very young (he and his wife were both 13), and studied law in London. After a brief time in India, the young barrister went to South Africa, where he was outraged by that country's system of racial discrimination (there was, and still is, a large Asian — especially Indian — population in South Africa). He remained there for twenty-one years, leading numerous campaigns for Indian rights, editing a newspaper, and developing his philosophy of nonviolent action as well as specific techniques for implementing it. He was physically abused and arrested many times by British authorities, but also served courageously on the British side when he agreed with their positions; for example, he organized an Indian Ambulance Corps during the Boer War (1899–1902) and the Zulu Rebellion (1906), for which he was decorated by the government.

Gandhi as a young attorney in South Africa. (*Gandhi the Man*, by E. Easwaran, courtesy of Nilgiri Press, Petaluma, Ca.)

Return to India

After achieving some notable reforms, Gandhi returned to India in 1915, and within a few years became the leader of the Indian nationalist movement, seeking independence from colonial Britain. When the British government made it illegal to organize political opposition, Gandhi led a successful *satyagraha* campaign against these laws. In 1919, British troops fired into a crowd of unarmed Indian men, women, and children, who had been demonstrating peacefully; nearly 400 were killed in what became known as the Amritsar Massacre. This slaughter served to highlight the difference between the steadfast nonviolence of Gandhi's followers and the relative brutality of the colonial government; it also moved Gandhi to refine and further develop his techniques of *satyagraha*. In particular, he took the great Hindu war epic, the *Bhagavad-Gita*, to be an allegory not about war, but about the human soul, and the need for all people to devote themselves, unselfishly, to the attainment of their goals. He urged that for real success, it is necessary to "reduce yourself to zero," that is, to remove the self-will and striving for personal aggrandizement that so often leads to arrogance or even tyranny.

Gandhi frequently employed fasts to emphasize the importance of personal suffering and to protest the violence that periodically broke out, as less disciplined Indian nationalists rioted against British rule, notably during the Bombay riots in 1921 and the Chauri-Chaura riots in 1922. Following these painful experiences, Gandhi temporarily called off his struggle for Indian independence. During the 1920s, Gandhi continued to fight for the rights of the lowest Hindu caste, the Untouchables — whom he renamed the *Harijan* (children of God) — and for miners, factory workers, and poor peasants. He urged Indians to develop cottage industries, such as spinning and weaving, so as to deprive Great Britain of its major economic advantage in occupying India: markets for English textile products. Hand weaving contributed to the potential of Indian national self-sufficiency, while also emphasizing the dignity of labor.

When Britain introduced the Salt Acts, requiring that all salt must be purchased from the government, Gandhi led a massive march, 320 kilometers to the sea, where he and his followers made salt from seawater, in defiance of the law. In all, Gandhi spent about seven years in various jails for his numerous acts of nonviolent resistance, making it respectable — indeed, honorable — for protesters to be imprisoned for their beliefs. He was a small, slight man with indomitable moral certitude and remarkable physical stamina. He was an ascetic and intensely frugal, and he also possessed a biting sense of humor; once, when he visited the British king in London, the half-naked Gandhi was asked whether he felt a bit underdressed for the occasion, to which he replied, "His Majesty wore enough for the two of us." Another time, when asked what he thought of Western civilization, he replied, "I think it would be a good idea."

Gandhi was deeply grieved by the intense periodic violence between Hindus and Moslems, and

Gandhi working at a spinning wheel. (Library of Congress)

he opposed the partition of British colonial India into an independent Moslem Pakistan and Hindu India. He was assassinated (by a high-ranking Hindu who opposed his insistence on religious tolerance) in 1948, the year after India won its independence from Britain. However, Gandhi accomplished what many thought impossible: He led his country of 400 million people to freedom, against one of the mightiest empires on Earth, without firing a shot. He also showed that a highly spiritual concept — nonviolence — can be an intensely practical tool in the quest for peace, even in the twentieth-century world of realpolitik, power, and violence.

NONVIOLENCE IN THEORY

Unfortunately, Gandhian *satyagraha* has often been translated into English as "passive resistance." This is akin to translating *light* as "nondarkness," or defining *good* as "absence of evil." It omits the positive, creative component of its subject. *Satyagraha* is passive only insofar as it espouses self-restraint rather than the active injuring of others. In all other respects, it is active and assertive, requiring great energy and courage.

Nonviolent Love and Suffering

A key to understanding Gandhi's efforts at nonviolence is embodied in the word for nonviolent love, *ahimsa*, the bedrock of *satyagraha*. As Gandhi expressed it, "Ahimsa and Truth are so intertwined that it is practically impossible to disentangle and separate them. . . . Nevertheless, ahimsa is the means; truth is the end."[1] *Ahimsa* is often defined as "nonviolence." As with the term *passive resistance*, however, such usage does violence to the underlying concept, which instead is far more active: in the case of *ahimsa*, active love. It is closer to Albert Schweitzer's principle of "reverence for life," a concept that is not only negative — determination not to destroy living things — but also positive — a commitment in favor of life, especially the life of other human beings. *Ahimsa* requires deep respect for the opponent's humanity, an insistence upon meeting the other with sympathy and kindness . . . but also with absolute, unwavering firmness. It is not meek, or mild, or retiring. It implies nothing less than the willingness of each individual to take unto her- or himself the responsibility for reforming the planet, and, necessarily, to suffer in the process. Gandhi emphasized that

> ahimsa in its dynamic condition means conscious suffering. It does not mean meek submission to the will of the evil-doer, but it means pitting of one's whole soul against the will of the tyrant. Working under this law of our being, it is possible for a single individual to defy the whole might of an unjust empire to save his honor, his religion, his soul, and lay the foundation for that empire's fall or its regeneration.[2]

And again,

> Suffering is the law of human beings; war is the law of the jungle. But suffering is infinitely more powerful than the law of the jungle for converting the opponent and opening his ears, which are otherwise shut, to the voice of reason. Nobody has probably drawn up more petitions or espoused more forlorn causes than I, and I have come to this fundamental conclusion that if you want something really important to be done you must not merely satisfy the rea-

son, you must move the heart also. The appeal of reason is more to the head, but the penetration of the heart comes from suffering. It opens up the inner understanding in man. Suffering, not the sword, is the badge of the human race.[3]

The basis for this suffering (termed *tapasya* by Gandhi) is several-fold. For one thing, unless one is prepared to suffer, the depth of one's commitment can be questioned. Moreover, since any serious conflict must lead to suffering, the nonviolent resister's devotion to justice will almost certainly precipitate suffering. *Tapasya* therefore indicates willingness to undergo this suffering oneself, and not to shift its burden onto anyone else — including the opponent — as a consequence of one's commitment to the truth of nonviolence.

Gandhi's emphasis on suffering is especially difficult for many people to understand or accept. It tends — probably more than any other aspect of his thought and practice — to make Gandhian nonviolence relatively inaccessible to many Westerners. And yet, *tapasya* should not be altogether foreign, especially to Christian tradition, given the central importance attributed to Christ's redeeming agony on the cross. In addition, it is not stretching Gandhi's concept too greatly to substitute "courage" for "willingness to suffer." This has the added benefit of helping dispel the frequent misunderstanding that practitioners of nonviolence are cowards, seeking an easy way out of conflict.

Nonviolence as an Active Force

Gandhi strongly emphasized that *satyagraha* must be distinguished from passive acquiescence or the desire to avoid pain or death at any price. The middle class in particular has often been scorned as having an excessive fear of conflict and a corresponding desire to be comfortable at all costs. There is nothing middle class about Gandhian nonviolence. "The inability of the bourgeois to dream great dreams and ambition noble deeds," according to one observer,

> is revealed in their timidity in the face of violence and conflict, by their willingness to make unholy

compromises or concede a point of principle in the face of violent threats. This cowardice also shows itself in what may be called the mercenary impulse, the impulse to hire others to fight one's own battles. This impulse has such concrete manifestations as hiring additional police to suppress domestic unrest or in spending money for a so-called all volunteer army, rather than personally accepting the obligations of citizenship. While many people see such practices as sensible and less conflictual approaches to social problems, they represent what Gandhi called the nonviolence of the weak. Such nonviolence he took to be counterfeit, a cloak for passivity and cowardice, a form of apathy and indifference.[4]

Gandhian nonviolence at its best is the nonviolence of the strong, the courageous, the outraged . . . not merely passive acquiescence by the weak, the cowardly, or the comfortable. "My creed of nonviolence is an extremely active force," wrote Gandhi. "It has no room for cowardice or even weakness. There is hope for a violent man to be some day nonviolent, but there is none for a coward."[5]

Gandhian nonviolence suggests answers to some fundamental questions. For example, what is the more important measure of worth, the individual or the society? It can be a prescription for anarchy to make individuals the supreme measure of moral action; alternatively, when the "the group," "society," or the state is rendered supreme, the door is opened to despotism. Nonviolent civil disobedience seeks to recognize both aspects of humanity: the right of individual choice, and also the obligation of each individual to experience the consequences of that choice, as judged and determined by the society of which he or she is a part.

But the nonviolent answer is not an easy one. Beatings, imprisonment, even death, are all seen as part of the nonviolent struggle. Individuals are called upon to function, and to suffer, for the good of all. The *satyagrahi* (practitioner of *satyagraha*) must be prepared to accept such suffering. Because of the clarity it evokes in the *satyagrahi*, as well as the confusion, self-doubt, and empathy it evokes in the opponent, nonviolence unleashes a remarkable kind of power, a "force" with which most people are unaccustomed.

Satyagraha, the means whereby *ahimsa* is expressed and nonviolent victory attained, also requires respect for the opponent and perseverance in weaning the opponent from error, rather than trying to injure or annihilate him or her. A nonviolent campaign must be conducted without hate, aimed at policies, not persons. It must be based on absolute truthfulness. It must take the opponent seriously, and seek to engage him/her in dialogue and self-examination. It must respect the opponents and permit them to change direction without loss of face.

Traditionally, when conflicts are resolved by violence, they simply involve the triumph of one protagonist over the other. Such a "resolution" may occur via threat, persuasion, or naked force, but in any event, the presumption is that one side wins and the other loses — what mathematicians call a "zero sum game" (as in most competitive sports, where for every winner there is a loser, so that the sum total of wins and losses equals zero). Even when overtly seeking a compromise — hence, a "win–win" or "positive sum game" solution — each side typically attempts to profit at the other's expense, and to compromise only when it has no alternative. By contrast, *satyagraha* aims to resolve the source of the conflict, rather than to defeat or annihilate the opponent. In *satyagraha*, the goal is to persuade the adversary that all parties have more to gain by acting in harmony and love than by persevering in discord and violence. Rather than viewing the adversary as an enemy to be overcome, the *satyagrahi* considers him or her a participant in a shared search for a just (that is, "truthful") solution to the problem at hand.

Ends Versus Means

Gandhi was unalterably opposed to any doctrine in which the end justifies the means. He maintained that there was "the same inviolable connection between the means and the end as there is between the seed and the tree."[6] Of course, a seed can be distinguished from a tree, but nonetheless, the two are inseparably linked; French philosopher Jacques

Maritain wrote that the means of achieving a goal is "in a sense the end in the process of becoming."[7] When the means are pure, the end will be desirable; if the route to political protest is sullied with violence or hatred, the end also will be spoiled. Philosopher Hannah Arendt seconded this, adding that "the practice of violence, like all action, changes the world, but the most probable change is to a more violent world."[8]

For nonviolent activists schooled in the Gandhian mold, violence is reactionary: the more violence, the less revolution. By using violent methods, revolutions and antiwar movements can build up reservoirs of resentment and hatred, as well as possibly laying the foundations for additional injustice and yet more violence. This stands not only as a warning against violence, but also as a caution against letting frustration drive peaceful protest into violent and often self-destructive avenues. In the late 1960s, for example, Thomas Merton, one of the towering figures of nonviolence in the United States, warned that the peace movement "may be escalating beyond peaceful protest. In which case it would also be escalating into self-contradiction."[9]

By contrast, political activists of the far left and right are generally prone to make moral compromises, convinced that their vision of the world-as-it-should-be justifies almost any means of attaining it. Lenin, for instance, announced that "to achieve our ends, we will unite even with the Devil."[10] For Lenin, any tendency to moralize about the evil of using violent means to achieve revolutionary ends was "the petty hypocrisy of sentimentalists drawn from the dominant but doomed class."[11] In his poem "To Posterity," Bertolt Brecht, playwright and Marxist, warned about how violence has corrupted and perverted the noblest intentions:

> Even anger against injustice
> Makes the voice grow harsh. Alas, we
> Who wished to lay the foundations of kindness
> Could not ourselves be kind.[12]

Similarly, ideologues of the far right have not hesitated to make common cause with oppressive dictatorships—Somoza in Nicaragua, Marcos in the Philippines, Pinochet in Chile, Duvalier in Haiti, the shah in Iran, Suharto in Indonesia—in the interest of a presumed greater good, the defeat or containment of international communism. "Extremism in the cause of liberty is no vice," proclaimed a prominent campaign slogan used by presidential candidate Barry Goldwater (one of the patron saints of modern-day conservatism) in 1964. In the 1980s, the Reagan administration enlisted the aid of drug-dealing Panamanian military strongman Manuel Noriega in its efforts to overthrow the Sandinistas of Nicaragua, and also secretly sold arms to the Iranian government, while publicly promoting an antidrug campaign as well as urging U.S. allies to boycott the Khomeini regime as one that supports terrorism.

Neither the far left nor the far right have shared Gandhi's acute sensitivity to the relationship between means and ends. And whereas everyone would agree that it is desirable to avoid aggression and international intimidation, a Gandhian would also question the legitimacy of employing (that is, deploying) nuclear weapons, or any instruments of violence, as means toward those ends.

NONVIOLENCE IN PRACTICE

Cicero, in *The Letters to His Friends*, asks, "What can be done against force, without force?" Students of nonviolence would answer, "Plenty." In fact, they would question whether anything effective, lasting, or worthwhile can be done against force, *with* force. The Reverend Martin Luther King, Jr., nonviolent leader of the civil rights movement in the United States, and a visionary who, like Gandhi, was also intensely practical and result-oriented, wrote that "returning violence for violence multiplies violence, adding deeper darkness to a night already devoid of stars. Darkness cannot drive out darkness; only light can do that. Hate cannot drive out hate; only love can do that."[13] As Gandhi put it,

> Noncooperation with evil is as much a duty as is cooperation with good. But in the past, noncooperation has been deliberately expressed in violence to

the evil-doer. I am endeavoring to show to my countrymen that violent noncooperation only multiplies evil, and that as evil can only be sustained by violence, withdrawal of support of evil requires complete abstention from violence.[14]

This did not mean, however, that the *satyagrahi* was forbidden anger, even hatred; rather, these feelings were carefully directed toward the various *systems* of evil, rather than toward individuals. Gandhi wrote:

> I can and do hate evil wherever it exists. I hate the system of government that the British people have set up in India. I hate the ruthless exploitation of India even as I hate from the bottom of my heart the hideous system of untouchability for which millions of Hindus have made themselves responsible. But I do not hate the domineering Englishman as I refuse to hate the domineering Hindus. I seek to reform them in all the loving ways that are open to me. My noncooperation has its roots not in hatred, but in love.[15]

For Gandhi and his followers, it was impossible to elevate oneself by debasing others. Similarly, it debases others if they are permitted to dominate oneself.

Nonviolent Action and Government Reaction

In practice, Gandhi's *satyagraha* and King's nonviolent action took many forms: marches, boycotts, picketing, leafleting, strikes, civil disobedience, the nonviolent occupation of various government facilities, vigils and fasts, mass imprisonments, refusals to pay taxes, and a willingness at all times to be abused by the authorities and yet to respond nonviolently, with politeness, courage, and determination. This, as Gandhi was fond of pointing out, demanded far more strength than is required to pull a trigger, far more courage than is needed to fight, or to fight back.

But the practitioner of nonviolence does not cease struggling; indeed, the nonviolent struggle is, if anything, more intense than its violent counterpart. Gandhian techniques do not offer an alternative to fighting; rather, they provide other, nonviolent ways of doing so. During the famous "salt *satyagraha*" of 1930, for example, Gandhi arrived at the Dharasana Salt Works with 2,500 marchers. According to a Western eyewitness, the men arrived at a police stockade in complete silence, then approached and were in turn battered on the head with steel-shod clubs, while no one so much as even raised an arm in self-protection:

> From where I stood I heard the sickening whack of the clubs on unprotected skulls. The waiting crowd of marchers groaned and sucked in their breath in sympathetic pain at every blow.... The survivors, without breaking ranks, silently and doggedly marched on until struck down.[16]

This event, like the Amritsar Massacre, not only underscored the courage and humaneness of the Indian *satyagrahis*, it also contrasted dramatically with the ugly violence of the government, thereby helping to sway world opinion as well as the British electorate — which became increasingly sympathetic to Gandhi's cause.

Violent governmental overreaction historically has had the effect of transforming victims into martyrs, who become symbols of their regime's callous wrong-headedness. For example, in 1819, a nonviolent crowd in Manchester, England, was attacked by soldiers while listening to speeches calling for the repeal of the Corn Laws. This so-called Peterloo Massacre became a rallying cry for radicals who eventually succeeded in their demands. The slaughter of participants in the Paris Commune of 1871 led to greater solidarity among the French working class. Violence and brutality directed toward U.S. civil rights workers in the 1960s led to widespread revulsion and moral indignation against the system of racial segregation in the South. The Kent State killings in 1970 galvanized sentiment opposed to the Vietnam War, just as the "police riot" at the Democratic Party Convention in Chicago, in 1968, led to widespread condemnation of the political system. More recently, the 1988 Israeli policy of beating Palestinian protesters who sought an end to Israeli occupation of the West Bank has led to solidification of Palestinian sentiment and an outpouring of criticism against the Israeli govern-ment, including protests from many in the U.S. Jewish community.*

Enduring and Transforming Violence

For nonviolent campaigns to be successful, the campaigners must have immense determination, self-respect, and also (Gandhi would add) respect for the opponent. A popular phrase among radical activists in the United States during the 1960s was "power to the people." Followers of nonviolence believe that the people are most powerful when they have sufficient moral courage to be immune, not only to the threat of violence directed toward them, but also to the inclination to employ violence themselves. The latter comes from having sufficient clarity of purpose (Gandhi would call it "selfless-ness"). As Gandhi saw it, this does not involve a purging of anger, but rather a transforming of it: "I have learnt through bitter experience the one su-preme lesson to conserve my anger and as heat con-served is transmuted into energy, even so our anger controlled can be transmuted into a power which can move the world."[17]

When a victim responds to violence with yet more violence, he or she is responding in predict-able, perhaps even instinctive ways. Although vio-lent responses may seem justified, such actions tend to validate the original attacker, and even, in a way, to vindicate the original violence as far as the at-tacker is concerned: Since the victim is so violent, then presumably he or she deserved it. Moreover, there is a widespread expectation of countervailing power analogous in the social sphere to Newton's

First Law, which states that for every action there is an equal and opposite reaction. In most aspects of life, from the personal to the international, the ex-ercise of power usually produces a countervailing response: Abused children often become abusing adults, laissez-faire capitalism gave rise to commu-nism, European liberal democracy and socialism helped spawn fascism, U.S. nuclear weapons have helped generate Soviet nuclear weapons, Reagan administration militarism in the early 1980s gave impetus to the nuclear freeze and other movements for nonintervention in Central America and else-where.

If A hits B, and then B hits back, this nearly always encourages A to strike yet again. Gandhi was not fond of the Biblical injunction "an eye for an eye, a tooth for a tooth," pointing out that if we all behaved that way, soon the whole world would be blind and toothless! Instead, if B responds with nonviolence, this not only breaks the chain of anger and hatred (analogous to the Hindu chain of birth and rebirth), it also puts A in a unexpected posi-tion. "I seek entirely to blunt the edge of the tyrant's sword," wrote Gandhi, "not by putting up against it a sharper-edged weapon, but by disappointing his expectation that I would be offering physical resistance."[18] Accustomed to counterviolence — and even, perhaps, hoping for it — the violent per-son who encounters a nonviolent opponent who is courageous and respectful, even loving, becomes a "victim" of a kind of moral jujitsu, in which the attacker's own energy is redirected, knocking him or her off balance. "It would at first dazzle him and at last compel recognition from him," wrote Gan-dhi, "which recognition would not humiliate him but would uplift him."[19] And in fact, Gandhi's most bitter opponents were almost inevitably won over.

Consider this account of a meeting between the young Gandhi and the legendary General Jan Smuts of South Africa. Gandhi spoke first:

> "I have come to tell you that I am going to fight against your government."
>
>   Smuts must have thought he was hearing things. "You mean you have come here to tell me that?" he laughs. "Is there anything more you want to say?"

---

*It is interesting that in this case, a Palestinian, Mu-barak Awad, was expelled from the Israeli-occupied West Bank for advocating Gandhian nonviolence, in-cluding refusal to cooperate with Israeli authorities as well as nonpayment of taxes. Some observers suggest that the Israeli authorities considered Awad's nonviolent tactics a greater threat than the prospects of Palestinian violence, because violence can readily be countered with yet more violence, whereas nonviolence leaves the authorities in a much more difficult quandary.

Gandhi with a group of supporters. (Library of Congress)

understand force," and therefore, they cannot be moved by anything other than force or the threat of force. The truth, however, may be precisely the opposite: Those who understand and expect force can generally deal with it effectively. *Satyagraha* — soul-force rather than physical force — may be more likely to disconcert and move those who understand violence, but have had little experience with Gandhi's Truth.

Part of the goal of *satyagraha* is to make the oppressor reflect on his or her unity with the resister, and to change internally. One sympathetic student used the analogy of an iceberg: In warm water, an iceberg melts below the water line, invisibly, until suddenly, as the weight shifts, it may flip over.[21] In this way, the consciousness of the oppressor may be changed suddenly and dramatically. "If my soldiers began to think," wrote Frederick the Great, "not one would remain in the ranks."[22] Nonviolence, adroitly and persistently practiced, has the power of causing soldiers — and government leaders — to think.

MARTIN LUTHER KING, JR. AND THE U.S. CIVIL RIGHTS MOVEMENT

Second to Gandhi, the most influential modern exponent and practitioner of nonviolence was the Reverend Martin Luther King, Jr., who consciously adapted *satyagraha* for use in the American South during the 1950s and 1960s. King studied Gandhi's philosophy and methods, traveled to India, and emerged as the chief spokesperson, architect, and spiritual leader of the nonviolent civil rights campaign in the United States. Like Gandhi, King spent much time behind bars for his nonviolent defiance of unjust laws supporting racial discrimination. His "Letter from a Birmingham Jail" is one of the classic statements of the philosophy of nonviolence and the evils of racial intolerance. In it, King also expressed a sense of outrage and urgency:

> We know from painful experience that freedom is never voluntarily given by the oppressor; it must be demanded by the oppressed. . . . I guess it is easy for those who have never felt the stinging darts of segregation to say "wait." But when you have seen

"Yes," says Gandhi. "I am going to win."

Smuts is astonished. "Well," he says at last, "and how are you going to do that?"

Gandhi smiles. "With your help."[20]

Years later, Smuts recounted this meeting, noting — with humor — that Gandhi was correct.

Nonviolence as a Proactive Force

Nonviolence is often described as nonviolent *resistance*, implying that it is a reaction, a response to some initial force. In fact, however, nonviolence as practiced by Gandhi and his followers (including notably the Reverend Martin Luther King, Jr., in the United States) was *pro*active much more than *re*active. These very successful practitioners of politically active nonviolence became masters at initiating their struggles, keeping their opponents off balance. Their tactics were unpredictable, spontaneous, radical, experimental . . . and not surprisingly, government authorities found them baffling and exasperating in the extreme. It is said — of some people and some nations — that "they only vicious mobs lynch your mothers and fathers at will and drown your sisters and brothers at whim; when you see hate-filled policemen curse, kick, brutalize and even kill your black brothers and sisters with impunity; when you see the vast majority of your twenty million Negro brothers smothering in an airtight cage of poverty in the midst of an affluent society . . . then you will understand why we find it difficult to wait.[23]

During the 1950s and 1960s, transportation, restaurants, sports events, restrooms, libraries, schools, and churches were often racially segregated in the South, with superior facilities reserved for "whites only." Voting rights were often denied or severely restricted by poll taxes, literacy tests, and outright intimidation. Lynching of blacks was relatively common, and racial violence was widespread, led especially by the Ku Klux Klan, a semisecret band of white supremacists.

Perhaps the seminal event in King's leadership of the civil rights movement was the Montgomery (Alabama) bus boycott, which started in December 1955, when Ms. Rosa Parks refused to take a seat in the back of a public bus. After thousands of blacks walked miles to work rather than ride on segregated buses, public facilities eventually were integrated. Later, Freedom Riders, seeking to desegregate interstate bus transportation (in accord with a 1960 Supreme Court decision), endured frequent beatings and mob violence, while the state police often failed to provide protection, and typically arrested the Riders instead. Sit-ins began at segregated lunch counters in February 1960, in Greensboro, North Carolina, at the soda fountain of a five-and-ten cent store. With King's encouragement, these nonviolent sit-ins, boycotts, and marches quickly spread to more than 100 cities, and succeeded in integrating restaurants throughout the South.

These were the years when Governor George Wallace stood in the doorway of the University of Alabama to deny admission to black students, whose right to attend had been upheld by the U.S. Supreme Court. President John Kennedy dispatched federal troops to the University of Mississippi when that school was finally forced to accept

James Meredith as its first black student; 2 people were killed and 375 injured in the ensuing riot. Lester Maddox was elected governor of Georgia largely because he had distributed axe-handles to the customers of his restaurant, urging that they be used against would-be integrators. Three civil rights workers — James Chaney, Michael Schwerner, and Andrew Goodman — were kidnapped and brutally slain in Mississippi; no jury could be found to convict the accused murderers. Mrs. Violet Liuzzo, also a civil rights worker, was gunned down on an Alabama road. Medgar Evers, Mississippi state leader of the NAACP (National Association for the Advancement of Colored People) was shot in the back and killed outside his home. Electric cattle prods, police dogs, and high-pressure water hoses were used against peaceful demonstrators in Birmingham, Alabama. Nonviolent civil rights marchers were herded to jail in Jackson, Mississippi, with the police harassing the marchers and offering them no protection against abusive crowds. Four young black girls were killed by a bomb blast while at Sunday School in a Birmingham Baptist Church. Through all this, King maintained a steadfast devotion to nonviolence, based on his perception of Christian principles. "Let no man pull you so low," he was fond of saying, "as to make you hate him."

It is no small task, though, to separate hatred of offenses — or of offending institutions — from hatred of the offenders: to hate murder but love the murderer, to hate oppression but not the oppressor, to hate torture but not the torturer. In this, King once again showed himself to be a disciple of Gandhi, showing uncompromising respect, even love, for his opponents, while being equally uncompromising in pursuit of the Truth as he saw it. And Martin Luther King, Jr., was himself assassinated, just as Gandhi had been.

But like Gandhi, King also mobilized a nonviolent army of followers, awakened the conscience of millions, and achieved monumental reforms. He founded the Southern Christian Leadership Conference, which emphasized nonviolence and grassroots, community action, and in 1963, he organized the "March on Washington for Jobs and Freedom," also known as the "Poor People's March," which brought about 500,000 people to the U.S. capital. This effort represented a new dimension of King's nonviolent campaign: extending it from integration and civil rights to a broader concern with social justice for all people. His campaign in favor of the Voting Rights Act also helped lead to its passage in 1965. The year before, Martin Luther King, Jr., had been awarded the Nobel Peace Prize.

One assessment of King's work, by a white theologian, is that in addition to the impact of his example as a remarkable human being,

> he restored and renewed in his own nation, and perhaps in other parts of the world, the awareness that all social relationships are essentially ethical in character, and we ignore the ethical quality of them at our own peril. For gross inequities in a society cannot long sustain the social fabric and are an imminent peril to us all. He also demonstrated that the freedoms of a people are only to be preserved, appreciated and enjoyed in and through action. His insistence upon militant nonviolence, especially as that stressed the refusal to cooperate in one's own abasement or enslavement, is a clear reminder that the ethical shape of a society is altogether dependent upon the ethical character and behavior of the individuals in that society. It is a function of their willingness to assume personal responsibility for the shape of society and cannot be left to some system. Systems, structures and institutions are essential to human existence, but they need not be determinative of our existence. They can and at times should be changed, and that is possible without the use of violence.[24]

Shortly before his death, King also started speaking out in opposition to the Vietnam War and the nuclear arms race. "If we assume that humankind has a right to survive," he once wrote,

> then we must find an alternative to war and destruction. In a day when sputniks dash through outer space and guided ballistic missiles are carving highways of death through the stratosphere, nobody can win a war. The choice today is no longer between violence or nonviolence. It is between nonviolence or nonexistence.[25]

Martin Luther King, Jr., about to address the crowd during the "Poor People's March" in Washington, DC, 1963. (Library of Congress)

NONVIOLENT SUCCESSES

Nonviolence has relatively few dramatic successes that can be celebrated. By contrast, there have been far more examples of successful violence, if we measure "success" by the achievement of immediate goals: conquest of territory or people, acquisition of booty, imposition of a particular social system, forcible defeat of would-be aggressors, and so on. But it can also be argued that violence, by its nature, mitigates against lasting success and sows the seeds for further violence. When "peace" is imposed by violence or the threat of violence, it is not really peace, but rather a temporary disequilibrium maintained by the constant input of energy and fear. It is violence that is temporarily suppressed, held in abeyance, not eliminated. The situation in South Africa is a good example: A kind of "peace" is maintained, but only through massive structural violence, and direct violence as well. Such situations, and other, similar ones in which societal relations are founded on violence, are likely to be unstable, as well as destructive of human values. Indeed, the turmoil of human history — some of which has been chronicled in this text, and the horrors of which have motivated its writing — can itself be seen as a monument to the *failure*, not the success, of violence.

In any event, there have been cases of successful nonviolent action, beyond the best-known examples of Indian independence and the U.S. civil rights movement. Gandhi himself pointed out that, in fact, nonviolence is far more pervasive in ordinary human life than most of us realize, and far more frequently (and successfully) employed than violence:

> The fact that there are so many men still alive in the world shows that it is based not on the force of arms but on the force of truth or love. Therefore, the greatest and most unimpeachable evidence of the success of this force is to be found in the fact that, in spite of the wars of the world, it still lives on. Thousands, indeed tens of thousands, depend for their existence on a very active working of this force. Little quarrels of millions of families in their daily lives disappear before the exercise of this force. Hundreds of nations live in peace. History does not and cannot take note of this fact. History is really a record of every interruption of the working of the force of love or of the soul. Two brothers quarrel; one of them repents and re-awakens the love that was lying dormant in him; the two again begin to live in peace; nobody takes note of this. But if the two brothers, through the intervention of solicitors or some other reason, take up arms or go to law — which is another form of the exhibition of brute force — their doing would be immediately noticed in the press, they would be the talk of their neighbors and would probably go down in history. And what is true of families and communities is true of nations . . . . History, then, is a record of an interruption of the course of nature.[26]

The Third World

As to major political events in the realm of states, probably the most notable example of the recent triumph of nonviolence was the toppling of Philippine dictator Ferdinand Marcos by the "people power" of Corazon Aquino's supporters, in February 1986. This virtually bloodless coup occurred after Marcos loyalists attempted to rig an election in the dictator's favor. The ensuing protest revolved around persistent nonviolence by Filipino civilians, who at one point interposed themselves between armed forces loyal to Marcos and a small band of military dissidents who had declared their support for Aquino and her followers. Newspapers worldwide printed remarkable photographs showing Catholic nuns inserting flowers in the barrels of automatic rifles carried by Philippine army soldiers. Marcos relinquished power, and went into exile in the United States, when it became evident that his own military would not fire on the unarmed Filipino populace.

Within a few months, a similar popular expression of discontent drove Jean-Claude Duvalier, son of long-time Haitian dictator "Papa Doc" Duvalier, from power. The departure of Duvalier has not restored democracy to impoverished Haiti, which has the highest illiteracy rate and lowest per capita income in the Western Hemisphere, as well as a long tradition of autocratic governments. Nonetheless, in the case of Haiti and the Philippines, spontaneous nonviolent movements succeeded in deposing military dictatorships that appeared deeply entrenched, and that had received substantial assistance (military as well as economic) from the United States; in both cases, traditional violent revolution probably would have led to an enormous number of casualties.

In 1987, popular discontent with the military dictatorship of South Korea's Chun Doo Hwan led to a series of largely nonviolent demonstrations, which in turn caused Chun to relinquish power and permit the first democratic elections ever held in that country. As it happened, Chun's hand-picked successor, Roh Tae Woo, won that election, largely because the opposition ran two candidates, thereby dividing the vote. Nonetheless, South Korea finally seems set on the road to democracy, and nonviolence is largely responsible. It is also noteworthy that in the cases of Haiti, the Philippines, and South Korea, violent excesses on the part of these dictatorships contributed heavily to the popular discontent that ultimately toppled their governments.

Eastern Europe

Under reformist leader Alexander Dubček, the Czechoslovak government in 1968 began granting a range of political and economic freedoms, seeking to establish "socialism with a human face." The U.S.S.R. apparently felt threatened by these developments, and organized an invasion of Czechoslovakia later that summer, crushing the brief and ill-fated "Prague spring." Most Americans think of that Soviet-led invasion as an overwhelming victory for the forces of communist repression. In fact, however, the people of Czechoslovakia mounted a remarkable program of nonviolent resistance at the time. Although essentially no military resistance was offered to the invading force of nearly 500,000 troops, the Czech people prevented the installation of a collaborationist government for eight months, using general strikes, work slowdowns, clandestine radio broadcasts, and noncooperation on the part of government employees. A compromise (the so-called Moscow Protocols) was even reached, which allowed most of the reform leaders to remain in authority; only when riots occurred at Aeroflot offices in Prague — that is, when nonviolent discipline broke down — did Soviet occupying forces remove the reformers, and subdue the country.

Twenty-one years later, in the autumn of 1989, massive peaceful demonstrations finally drove the Communist party from its preeminent place in Czechoslovakia. It may be significant that this occurred within days after Czech security forces brutally suppressed one of the initial prodemocracy demonstrations; outrage at this "police violence" appears to have fueled Czech determination to replace the discredited government. In contrast to the Czech experience, the overthrow of Romanian dictator Nicolai Ceausescu involved violence. Significantly, however, it was public outrage at the brutal military response to a nonviolent, citizens' protest in the city of Timisoara that ignited the country-wide revolt.

The Polish trade union movement "Solidarity" has also followed a strenuously nonviolent path, one that has ultimately been successful, serving in many ways as a model for the electrifying events in Eastern Europe during 1989. After being banned in a Soviet-inspired government crackdown in 1981 — which included the imposition of martial law — continued nonviolent agitation, including boycotts and strikes, led to official government recognition of Solidarity and its affiliates. By 1989, Solidarity leaders, some of whom had been in prison shortly before, were elected to positions in a noncommunist Polish government that is becoming increasingly democratic.

During the autumn of 1989, prodemocracy demonstrations shook the states of Eastern Europe, and the results have been extraordinary. A noncommunist government was established in Poland, and the Hungarian Communist party reformed itself and agreed to popular elections, which it was certain to lose. The totalitarian leadership in East Germany and Czechoslovakia has also agreed to eliminate the guaranteed "privileged place" of the Communist party in these two states, and to permit political freedoms. Moreover, the Berlin Wall — longtime symbol of the Cold War and the East–West division of Europe — has essentially been dismantled. In the words of Polish Solidarity leader Lech Walesa, these formidable events, some of the most remarkable in modern times, were accomplished without "so much as breaking a single window-pane."

China

Also in 1989, the world witnessed the spectacle of China — the world's most populous country, and one that has, since 1949, been in the grip of a rigidly authoritarian communist government — convulsed by demands for reform and democratization. For several weeks, nonviolent protesters, led by college students but including a wide cross section of the population, occupied Tiananmen Square in the heart of Beijing, with popular demonstrations involving more than one million people. Supporters in other major cities — Shanghai, Nanking, Hunan, Hong Kong — also made themselves heard, and even after martial law was declared and the protesters ordered to disperse, "people power" nonviolently persuaded Chinese troops to refrain from moving against the students.

Then, the government cracked down, with a brutal military assault; the precise number of casualties are not known, but probably thousands were killed. The ultimate outcome of the democratic reform movement remains in doubt, in China and throughout the communist world. It seems very likely, however, that the process itself will continue. And the bitterness sown by the Chinese government's violent repression — which in many ways resembles the British army's Amritsar Massacre in colonial India — will almost certainly have consequences for the future of China and other governments that practice brutality against nonviolent protesters.

There is, as Gandhi noted, a special outrage associated with such one-sided uses of lethal force. The "Tiananmen Massacre," occurring on a Sunday in June, was not the first "Bloody Sunday" in world history. In 1905, a mass of nonviolent Russian peasants in St. Petersburg (now Leningrad), led by Father Gapon, attempted to submit a petition to Czar Nicholas, whose troops responded by slaughtering hundreds of unarmed people. This led to a general strike, which ushered in some limited democratic reforms on the part of the government, but which also signaled the beginning of the end for czarist tyranny. When the Russian Revolution finally took place, thirteen years later in 1918, it represented, in some ways, the culmination of mounting anger and revulsion that had been sown by the Russian government's history of wanton violence toward its own people.

A similar case can be made for the "Kent State Massacre" in the United States, although the numbers involved were far smaller, and the public response was far short of revolution. In this incident, Ohio National Guardsmen shot four students who were part of a crowd peacefully demonstrating in

opposition to the U.S. bombing of Cambodia in 1970. It generated widespread outrage in the United States, and marked a turning point in citizen respect for the federal government and its prosecution of the Vietnam War.

The point is that nonviolence, especially when contrasted with a brutal government response, has an extraordinary power to influence the human mind. Hence, it may well have a profound role to play in practical politics, even — and perhaps especially — against violent, heavily armed, repressive regimes. In China, just as in Russia eighty-four years before, the populace, as well as many military leaders themselves, were shocked and infuriated by the heavy-handed use of violence against peaceful demonstrators: "The People's Army," exhorted one communique from the Chinese military itself, "absolutely must not attack the people!" When it does so, such a regime likely will quickly lose its legitimacy, its popular support, and ultimately, its power.

Interstate Examples

These recent examples of nonviolent successes and near-successes all occurred in conflicts taking place within a given state, rather than between states; examples of successful nonviolence operating between states are more difficult to come by. To some extent, the Palestine *intifada*, or uprising, in which Arabs inhabiting the West Bank and Gaza have sought to free themselves from Israeli occupation, may be an example of nonviolence, or at least, reduced violence, in action. Although it has not (yet) been successful, the *intifada* has generated extreme discomfort and soul-searching among the Israeli citizenry and within the government. In addition, it illustrates the highly critical public reaction that tends to result when a government responds violently to nonviolent protest.

Although Palestinian extremists have made substantial use of terrorism and other violence in their struggle with Israel, the *intifada* has been mostly peaceful, with violence largely restricted to rock-throwing. The Israeli response, by contrast, has been significantly more violent, although it has stopped short of mass murder. During its first year (December 1987–December 1988), 350 Palestinian

Arabs were killed and tens of thousands wounded; by contrast, 2 Israeli soldiers and 6 civilians were killed and 1,100 wounded. Israeli defense minister Yitzak Rabin initially announced that "The first priority is to use force, might, beatings," to end the uprising. This, in turn, generated worldwide condemnation, and the whole episode greatly discomforted Israeli public opinion, since most Israelis — like most Britons during the 1920s and 1930s, when Gandhi was leading his campaign for Indian independence — think of themselves as highly civilized and moral.

There are some historical examples of the successful international use of nonviolence. (As we have already seen, there are numerous governmental techniques of conflict resolution short of violence: diplomacy and negotiation, international law, and so on. We are concerned here with nonviolence as a direct, popular, grass-roots campaign.) During the midnineteenth century, for example, Austria was seeking to dominate its partner in union, Hungary. The Hungarians were militarily weaker than the Austrians, and they recognized that physical resistance would be useless and probably counterproductive. Instead, Hungarians responded by boycotting Austrian goods, refusing to recognize or cooperate with Austrian authorities, and establishing independent Hungarian industrial, agricultural, and educational systems. Noncompliance proved a powerful tool. For example, Hungarians refused to pay taxes to Austrian collectors. When the resisters' property was seized, no Hungarian auctioneers would sell it, so Austrian auctioneers were imported. But then, no Hungarian would buy the property, so Austrian purchasers had to be imported as well. Not surprisingly, Austrian authorities ended up with a net financial loss. Austria also sought to enforce compulsory military service and the billeting of Austrian soldiers in local homes, but Hungarian noncompliance was such that in 1867, the Austrian emperor consented to a constitution giving Hungary full rights within the Austro-Hungarian union.

Many people associate successful independence movements with war and armed rebellion, such as the American Revolution, the liberation of the Netherlands from Spanish control, or the independence of Algeria from France or Kenya from Britain. In fact, however, independence has been achieved, in many cases, by nonviolent means: Canada in the nineteenth century, numerous colonies in the decades following World War II, and so on. In 1905, to take an example little known to Americans, Norway was granted its independence from Sweden, with no violence whatever. Shortly before, Norwegian nationalists had declared their country to be a free and independent state, almost precipitating a war; but in a subsequent plebiscite, all but 184 Norwegians voted for independence, and the Swedish government relented.

Several decades later, during the Second World War, Norway again became a notable site of nonviolent resistance. Germany invaded Norway in April 1940, and quickly put down Norwegian military resistance; overcoming the people, however, was much more difficult. A pro-Nazi Norwegian, Vidkun Quisling, was set up as dictator (since then, a "Quisling" has entered the lexicon as a collaborator who helps form a puppet government). Norwegian society spontaneously and persistently undermined the Quisling government, with shows of solidarity on the part of students, the clergy, and especially, public school teachers, who refused to participate in mandated pro-Nazi indoctrination programs for their students. The Nazis responded by imprisoning and killing many civilians, but the refusals continued, and the country gradually became increasingly ungovernable. As President Franklin Roosevelt put it, Norway became "at once conquered and unconquerable."

During the autumn of 1943, when Denmark was occupied by German armed forces, large numbers of Danes prevented Nazi authorities from seizing more than 90 percent of the 8,000 Danish Jews and deporting them to concentration camps. Using improvised methods of communication and transportation, the outnumbered and vastly outgunned Danish citizens succeeded in smuggling most of these would-be victims to safety in Sweden. Another successful resistance tactic was for large numbers of Danes to defy the German authorities by wearing the Star of David, which supposedly was used to identify a Jew. Virtually the entire country — government officials, religious leaders, trade unionists, professionals — opposed the Nazi efforts at liquidating the Jewish population, and they were largely successful.

Abundant evidence suggests that military force has its political and social limits, even when (as in the modern world) such force is technologically almost unlimited. It is questionable whether a mailed fist — whether Israeli, South African, Polish, or Chinese — can long oppress a resistant population. Most public opinion, at least in the West, holds that it cannot. Nonetheless, it is questionable whether governments will move in the near future to deemphasize significantly the use of violence or the threat of violence in their internal and international affairs.

CIVILIAN-BASED DEFENSE

Advocates of nonviolence are not limited to religious zealots and high-minded moralists. Increasingly, people are questioning fundamental assumptions about peace, defense, and security, as the limitations and dangers of traditional military "solutions" become increasingly clear. A classic case, epitomizing what for many is the paradox of reliance of military means of defense, was the Vietnamese village of Ben Tre, which, according to a U.S. major, had to be destroyed "in order for us to save it." The notion of being defended with nuclear weapons leaves many people similarly incredulous.

If nonviolence is to have any practical effect on international affairs, however, it must be seen, not as the divine idiosyncrasy of uniquely empowered saints and martyrs, but rather as a hard-headed approach that can be employed by the great majority of people, who are no more than human. Among the practical suggestions for applying nonviolence to national defense, the most organized and — possibly — realistic involve so-called civilian-based defense, or CBD. (This must be distinguished from "civil defense," the much less realistic government plans for protecting citizenry in the event of a nuclear war.) CBD embraces a variety of nonviolent techniques that are intended to make it very difficult, if not impossible, for a conquering state to govern another and to gain any benefit from its "victory."

The major theorist of civilian defense, Gene Sharp,[27] has identified more than 146 specific techniques of nonviolent action, ranging from general strikes, boycotts, and nonpayment of taxes to removal of street signs and sabotage of electrical services. Civilian defenders would not violently resist the occupation of their country, and they would undoubtedly expose themselves to substantial hardship, suffering, and even death. But military defenders must also anticipate great amounts of hardship, suffering, and death, even in a "successful" war. Advocates of civilian-based defense emphasize that to be successful, substantial training would be required, as well as a populace willing to commit itself to the success of the enterprise. There is, however, nothing new in this: Military training also requires time, effort, and sacrifice, as well as a committed populace. Moreover, most efforts at nonviolent resistance — Hungary in the midnineteenth century, Norway in the early 1940s, Czechoslovakia in 1968 — were spontaneous, unprepared, and largely leaderless. Serious civilian defense, well rehearsed and planned in advance, has never been tried. Given its impressive track record as a form of resistance when it was essentially extemporized on the spot, the future of civilian defense might well be bright indeed if it was ever carried out by a well-trained and -prepared populace. And the prospects of facing a determined and highly disciplined populace, one committed to denying the invader virtually all fruits of conquest, just might serve to deter invasion no less effectively than the amassing of military forces . . . and at substantially reduced cost and risk.

Even beyond its deterrent value, CBD — based on an organized determination never to surrender, even if overrun by an adversary — could well hold out even greater prospects for "victory" than more traditional military tactics and strategies. This is because, as weapons become ever more destructive, doctrines of national security based on traditional military techniques offers less and less prospect of defense, or even of narrowly defined battlefield success.

Looking specifically at Europe, Sharp has argued persuasively that NATO has not enhanced Western security; rather, "The capacity to defend in order to deter has been replaced by the capability to destroy massively without the ability to defend."[28] By contrast, a civilian-based defense would aim to

> deny the attackers their objectives and to make society politically indigestible and ungovernable by the attackers. . . . Potential attackers are deterred when they see that their objectives will be denied them, political consolidation prevented, and that as a consequence of these struggles unacceptable costs will be imposed on them politically, economically, and internationally.[29]

Rather than focusing on moral considerations, Sharp emphasizes the prospects of civilian defense based on "hard-headed" strategic and cost-effectiveness grounds. He also points out that if nuclear deterrence fails, the results will be catastrophic. By contrast, if deterrence based on civilian defense fails, the result will be the first opportunity to attempt to implement a truly nonviolent defense.

In short, according to Sharp, civilian defense differs from reliance on military means primarily in that it offers hope for the future:

> Increased confidence in civilian defense and liberation by nonviolent action could produce a chain reaction in the progressive abolition of both war and tyranny. If this happened, the whole course of history would be altered. Some of the gravest fears and insecurities of the modern world would be lifted. Civilian defense could make it possible to face the future realistically, without fear or panic, but with courage, confidence, and hope.[30]

PROSPECTS FOR NONVIOLENCE

Despite the appeal of nonviolence, it seems unlikely that states will soon give over their defense to such strategies — whether Gandhian *satyagraha* or civilian defense. In the long run, however, it can be argued that nonviolence, in whatever form, offers hope, whereas violence does not. Nonviolence, in fact, is not limited to tactics of defending a given people; rather, it is directed toward overthrowing an entire system of relationships that is fundamentally based on violence, oppression, and the unfair dominance of some by others. Thus, nonviolence is directly relevant not only to the prevention of war, but also to the establishment of social justice, environmental protection, and the defense of human rights. It does not aim at achieving simply a more effective national defense, but rather a defense of all humanity and of the planet against destructiveness and violence, by seeking to change the terms within which individuals and groups interact.

It can be argued, for example, that the destructive patterns whereby people and states interact violently with one another are also reflected in the destructive style that characterizes the interaction of people with their environment. The destruction of rain forests, the clear-cutting of temperate zone woodlands, the gouging of the Earth in the course of strip-mining, the pollution of water and air, the extinction of plant and animal species, even, according to some people, the eating of meat and the use of internal combustion engines — all these may be considered forms of violence, and all result, in a sense, from a lack of *ahimsa*, in Gandhian terms.

These are problems for the United States no less than other parts of the world. As black power leader H. Rap Brown has emphasized, violence is as American as cherry pie. Sometimes this is presented as reassuring; that is, violence in the United States is nothing new and therefore nothing to get alarmed about. More appropriately, however, it is a warning: Violence is widely considered inimical to decent values. Accordingly, it has become commonplace to decry the prevalence of violence in American life, applied not only to international affairs, but also to interpersonal patterns, including homicide and abuse of children and spouses, as well as the wider, deeper patterns of structural violence, including homelessness, drug abuse, environmental destruction, unemployment, poverty, unequal career options, inadequate medical care, and low-quality education.

Among some persons deeply committed to nonviolence, the legitimate outrage against violence is sometimes carried to excess; some would claim, for example, that education is violence, child-rearing is violence, marriage is violence. If so, then perhaps even eating, sleeping, and breathing are violent (consider the destructive action of our molars, not to mention digestive acids). At this point, clearly, a serious distinction has been trivialized, and that is regrettable. But this is a minority and extreme view, and should not be allowed to diminish the importance of identifying and opposing violence.

The leading advocates of nonviolence in the twentieth century, Gandhi and King, each derived the core of their philosophy and the wellsprings of their activism from deeply felt religious faith: Gandhi was a devout Hindu, King an ordained Southern Baptist minister. Others, by contrast, have emphasized the practical aspects of nonviolence as a tactic for achieving results in the social sphere. For example, Gene Sharp bases his commitment to nonviolence largely on the utilitarian need for alternatives to violence in meeting social injustice, as well as domestic tyranny and international aggression. As Sharp sees it,

> Both moral injunctions against violence and exhortations in favor of love and nonviolence have made little or no contribution to ending war and major political violence. . . . Only the adoption of a substitute type of sanction and struggle as a functional alternative to violence in acute conflicts — where important issues are, or are believed to be at stake — can possibly lead to a major reduction of political violence in a manner compatible with freedom, justice and human dignity.[31]

In the United States, advocates of nonviolence have been accused of being unpatriotic, not only because they recommend a less bellicose attitude toward the Soviet Union (among others), but also because their efforts are in some ways subversive of accepted American values. In a memorandum solicited by the Kerner Commission (convened by President Johnson to investigate the causes of violence in American life, following the domestic riots of the mid-1960s), Thomas Merton warned that the sources of violence can be found "not in esoteric groups but in the very culture itself, its mass media, its extreme individualism and competitiveness, its inflated myths of virility and toughness, and its overwhelming preoccupation [with various means of destruction]."[32] In another essay, Merton warned that

the struggle against war is directed not only against the bellicosity of the Communist powers, but against our own violence, fanaticism and greed. Of course, this kind of thinking will not be popular in the tensions of the cold war. No one is encouraged to be too clear-sighted, because conscience can make cowards, by diluting the strong conviction that our side is fully right and the other side is fully wrong.[33]

So, nonviolence is likely to be resisted because it will be seen as weakening our position in the world. There will be other problems. Government leaders find it much easier to preside over the rape and pillage of national resources, reaping short-term advantage (including election and reelection), rather than facing the daunting task of working toward a self-sustaining natural ecology that might remain viable into the indefinite future. A domestic society purged of structural violence would also require a serious rearrangement of current attitudes toward wealth, property, and privilege. And imagine a state whose military forces are dismantled, which is prepared to defend itself only nonviolently. Wouldn't it be vulnerable to coercion and attack, leading to loss of freedom and very high casualties? In this respect, Costa Rica is once again worth considering. This small Central American country abolished its army in 1948 after the military supported an unpopular dictator who was subsequently overthrown. Yet, it has persisted as a model democracy that has never been invaded, despite the fact that Costa Rica's neighbors are dictatorships and Central America is hardly a peaceful region. (On the other hand, as Central America became increasingly a focus of Cold War concerns in the 1980s, Costa Rica has been subject to growing U.S. pressures for militarization.)

Pacifism is largely tolerated in the United States and many other countries, so long as it is performed by small and uninfluential groups. But as Merton points out, "There is also an implication that any minority stand against war on grounds of conscience is ipso facto a kind of deviant and morally eccentric position, to be tolerated only because there are always a few religious half-wits around in any case, and one has to humor them in order to preserve

Greenpeace boats nonviolently blockading a U.S. warship to protest the presence of nuclear weapons on board. (Greenpeace/Randy Thomas)

the nation's reputation for respecting individual liberty."[34]

Would it ever be practical to rest a state's defense on nonviolent, civilian-based tactics and strategies? Some claim that Gandhi only succeeded in India and King in the United States because both Britain and the United States had a long tradition of humane, civilized treatment of others. In fact, the opposite can also be argued: British response to Third World insurrection was characterized by extraordinary brutality, and the U.S. government did not exactly treat its own native Americans with forbearance, at Wounded Knee and other massacres. It is certainly questionable whether even a Gandhi could have prevailed against a Stalin or a Hitler. Civilian-based defense, for that matter, would be helpless against bombardment attacks, especially using nuclear weapons . . . but of course, military defense is equally helpless. Opponents of nonviolence as a national strategy often point to the slaughter that might take place if a nonviolent country were to be invaded by a violent opponent. Supporters can point out, however, that in this case the

casualties might very well be lower than if such an invasion was met with countervailing military force.

The question remains: Beyond nonviolence as a theoretical ideal, or as a profound personal witness, or even as it may someday inform domestic policy and contribute to positive peace, what about the realistic prospects of nonviolence in the realm of military affairs? Will the avoidance of war ever rest on a studied refusal to engage in violence?

Admittedly, it is neither psychologically nor politically appealing to contemplate a strategy that "allows" an aggressor to take over one's country. But neither is it pleasant to contemplate military defense. It may be that military force is something with which we are considerably more familiar, not that it is necessarily more effective . . . especially if the billions of dollars now expended on the military were to be redirected toward nonviolent means. It may also be that governments would be vigorously opposed to instituting widespread nonviolent training, not only because it would compete with traditional military efforts, but also because such training would empower the population to resist that government, thereby posing a threat — even to democracies, which, like most governments, are more comfortable responding to violent provocations and armed resistance than to unarmed, nonviolent protest.

A national policy of nonviolent defense would also require that a state largely renounce its interventionist goals in other countries, or at least, it would have to forgo the prospect of direct military intervention in support of economic and political "neo-imperialism" (see Chapter 22). A populace trained and organized for civilian defense might or might not be able to deter an aggressor, but it assuredly could not invade or intimidate a distant country. For some people, this is an added advantage of civilian defense; for others, a liability.

In the military sphere, there is little chance that CBD will soon be adopted as the defense strategy of any major state. However, it need not be initiated in an all-or-nothing manner. There is no reason why CBD training could not be gradually integrated into existing military doctrine, after which it will be available to assume a more significant role as part of a transition from offensively oriented forces to those concerned — at first primarily, and then exclusively — with defense. Highly respected military and political planners in several European states have been studying the prospects for such a transition; it represents a revolution in security policy, one that is currently bubbling just below the level of official policy, but that might well emerge in the 1990s, especially if — as seems increasingly likely — the Cold War is finally ending.

Paradoxically, there is some danger that, in deemphasizing the role of traditional military forces, and placing the primary burden of defense on the shoulders of the civilian population, CBD would contribute to a kind of militarizing of national cultures, as civilians find themselves forced to confront the nitty-gritty of national security. The greatest problem, however, is probably a deeply ingrained distrust of nonviolence as a workable strategy, combined with a widespread fascination with violence and a tendency to rely upon it as a last resort, when — in a revealing phrase — "push comes to shove."

NONVIOLENCE AT HOME

Governments have had abundant experience with violence, both its perpetration and suppression. They are relatively unfamiliar, by contrast, with nonviolence. How would governments respond if faced with massive nonviolent protest? Most tax collection systems, for example, rely almost entirely on voluntary compliance. What if people, nonviolently, stopped complying? Most systems of conscription rely, fundamentally, on the willingness of the population to "be drafted." What if governments held a war and nobody came?

In the Christian worldview of Martin Luther King, Jr., social sin as well as personal sin exists; thus, sinfulness can be a condition of human life and an aspect of social institutions, no less than a consequence of individual acts. The eradication of social sin — originally defined specifically as racism and segregation, but later, as King's interests expanded, encompassing other evils as well — demands a personal commitment. This commitment, in turn, is only rarely realized alone. In most cases, it is an enterprise to be attempted in the company of others, thereby establishing a loving and dedicated community, typically one that is centered around the Christian concept of *agape*, or divine, redeeming love.* (It must be emphasized, however, that such love is not the sloppy, sentimentalized kind. Although it aims ultimately at forgiveness and reconciliation rather than revenge or vindication, it stubbornly insists on identifying wrong, and correcting it.)

Despite his emphasis on socially responsible action, for Gandhi in particular the nonviolent calling was also a deeply personal one. It required — and for today's Gandhians, it still requires — that individuals make a painful and important choice, one that gives them the chance of affirming their

---

*In some cases, such communities literally establish meeting or even living places, as in the nationwide networks of "Agape houses." In others, these communities are more symbolic and metaphoric, linking those engaged in a common, nonviolent struggle.

humanity. Gandhian nonviolence, however, promises to be much more than an inspiration for mass protest; it also offers a possibility for transformation in one's personal life. Thus, in Gandhi's view,

> It did not matter if the adversaries were the Indian Congress and the British raj, a group of peasants and their landlord, or a husband and wife; satyagraha may be used, he said, "by individuals as well as by communities. It may be used as well in political as in domestic affairs. Its universal applicability is a demonstration of its permanence and invincibility."[35]

According to its practitioners, *satyagraha* can apply as readily to interactions within a family as to efforts at reforming an oppressive governmental policy. Gandhi himself relates how his initial encounters with nonviolence were due to his wife Kasturbai: Early in their marriage, Gandhi was dictatorial and domineering, but his wife persevered, and ultimately reformed him through love, a willingness to suffer without retaliating, and an implacable will.

Satyagraha, in a sense, is no more a technique than love, or courage, or honesty is a technique. Rather, it is an internal condition, a pervasive personal attitude, a fundamentally private affair that is complete unto itself, and that serves to complete the *satyagrahi* as well. As we have seen, Gandhi also insisted that part of the discipline of *satyagraha* is the renunciation of self; this predominantly Eastern ideal implies a transcending of self-interest, rising above the "opposing currents of love and hatred, attachment and repulsion," as advised in Gandhi's beloved *Bagavad-Gita*. The first struggle, then, for a would-be practitioner of Gandhian nonviolence — and perhaps the most difficult one of all — is a kind of "self-*satyagraha*," in which selfish individualism, ego, and other troublesome attachments are overcome.

It should be clear from this brief overview that nonviolence offers more than a way of establishing nonmilitary defense, or resisting improper authority, or even achieving socially desirable goals. It represents an entire way of being, and one of the most hopeful, yet difficult, opportunities for redefining self and society and achieving a lasting, positive peace. It has been attempted by many people other than Gandhi and King, with varied results. During the 1970s, the Chicano labor leader Cesar Chavez successfully employed Gandhian nonviolent tactics, including extensive fasting, in support of improved working conditions for migrant fruit-pickers. In the 1980s, Mitch Snyder, of the Center for Creative Nonviolence, has employed various imaginative techniques to publicize the plight of the nation's homeless people. The Greenham Commons women's peace camp — established to oppose the introduction of cruise missiles into England during the early 1980s — has relied heavily on the principles of *satyagraha*, as have the efforts of the proenvironment, antinuclear Green party, and the environmental group Greenpeace. Bishop Desmond Tutu and Chief Albert Luthuli have waged courageous nonviolent campaigns against apartheid in South Africa. East German dissidents, wishing to liberalize the East German state without themselves emigrating to the West, successfully opposed the long-time neo-Stalinist government of Erich Honecker by nonviolent means, such as mass demonstrations and displays of lighted candles in home windows as a sign of solidarity with prodemocracy elements. Nationwide, nonviolent general strikes were particularly effective in demonstrating to the Czechoslovak Communist party that it had been rejected by the great majority of the Czech people.

According to the most influential proponents of nonviolence — Gandhi, King, and before them, Tolstoy, Thoreau, Christ — the key to success in such endeavors rests not with the opponent but with each individual, in the depth and honesty of his or her commitment. In his writings on nonviolence, Leo Tolstoy emphasized the responsibility of individuals, not only in their personal relationships, but also in their refusal to participate in violence organized by the state. He had contempt for such traditional liberal responses to war as the convening of meetings, the passing of resolutions, even attempts to establish and invoke international law. Rather, Tolstoy believed that the abolition of war — even more crucial, in his view, than the establishment of social justice — fundamentally required a decision by individuals to say No, and to say it un-equivocally. He argued that governments them-selves reveal what kind of antiwar actions are most threatening to the state-sponsored system of war:

> Liberals entangled in their much talking, socialists, and other so-called advanced people may think that their speeches in Parliament and at meetings, their unions, strikes, and pamphlets are of great impor-tance; while the refusals of military service by pri-vate individuals are unimportant occurrences not worthy of attention. The governments, however, know very well what is important to them and what is not. And the governments readily allow all sorts of liberal and radical speeches in Reichstags, as well as workmen's associations and socialist demonstra-tions, and they even pretend themselves to sympa-thize with those things, knowing that they are of great use to them in diverting people's attention from the great and only means of emancipation. But governments never openly tolerate refusals of mili-tary service, or refusals of war taxes, which are the same thing, because they know that such refusals expose the fraud of governments and strike at the root of their power.[36]

As we have seen, William James emphasized that the war against war was not going to be a picnic. This will almost certainly be true, whether or not the campaign is waged nonviolently, and whether or not it is limited to a struggle against war or ex-panded to include such positive goals as social jus-tice and environmental integrity. In the meantime, it might be worth pondering the following words, seen on a bumper sticker: "The Meek Are Getting Ready."*

A FINAL NOTE ON NONVIOLENCE

Serious nonviolence, not as an ideal but as an im-mediate policy — personal as well as national — seems foreign to most Westerners, including most professed Christians. "Christianity has not been tried and found wanting," noted the English writer G. K. Chesterton, "it has been found difficult and left untried."[37] What, we may ask, is the future of nonviolence? That is for you, the readers of this book, to determine. Or, alternatively, we might ask: Does the world have a future *without* nonviolence? In his masterpiece, *Leaves of Grass*, the nineteenth-century American poet Walt Whitman gives us his simple answer:

> Were you looking to be held together by lawyers?
> Or by an agreement on a paper? Or by arms?
> Nay, nor the world, nor any living thing, will so cohere.
> Only those who love each other shall become indi-visible.[37]

Study Questions

1. What aspects of Gandhi's philosophy are most dif-ficult for Westerners to understand?

2. What aspects of Gandhi's philosophy are most accessible to Western traditions of thinking and acting?

3. What is wrong with the phrase *passive resistance?*

4. Explain what is meant by Gandhi's insistence that *satyagraha* must be done by the strong, not the weak.

5. Discuss the impact of nonviolent resistance on oth-ers who are accustomed to violence, both in their behavior and in the response of their opponents.

6. Discuss similarities and differences between the U.S. civil rights movement and the struggle for In-dian independence from Britain.

7. What common patterns can be recognized in other nonviolent successes around the world? In failures?

8. What is meant by civilian defense? Assess its pros-pects for success.

9. Suggest nonreligious bases for nonviolence, as a so-cial practice and as a way of life.

10. What would be some requirements for nonprovoc-ative defense to be successful? What do you think Gandhi would think about it?

---

*It should be clear by now that nonviolence actually has nothing to do with being meek . . . but this phrase seemed too delicious to omit!

Suggestions for Further Reading

Richard B. Gregg. 1959. *The Power of Nonviolence*. Schocken Books: New York.

Joan V. Bondurant. 1965. *Conquest of Violence: The Gandhian Philosophy of Conflict*. University of California Press: Berkeley.

Gene Sharp. 1973. *The Politics of Non-Violent Action*. Porter Sargent: Boston.

James Hanigan. 1984. *Martin Luther King, Jr. and the Foundations of Nonviolence*. University Press of America: New York.

Robert L. Holmes (ed.). 1990. *Nonviolence in Theory and Practice*. Wadsworth: Belmont, CA.

Source Notes

1. Quoted in E. Easwaran. 1978. *Gandhi the Man*. Nilgiri Press: Petaluma, CA.

2. Ibid.

3. Quoted in N. K. Bose (ed.). 1957. *Selections from Gandhi*. Navajivan: Ahmedabad, India.

4. James P. Hanigan. 1984. *Martin Luther King, Jr. and the Foundations of Nonviolence*. University Press of America: New York.

5. M. K. Gandhi. 1940. *An Autobiography: The Story of My Experiments with Truth*. Navajivan: Ahmedabad, India.

6. Quoted in P. Regamey. 1966. *Nonviolence and the Christian Conscience*. Darton, Longmann, and Todd: London.

7. Ibid.

8. Hannah Arendt. 1969. *On Violence*. Harcourt, Brace & World: New York.

9. Thomas Merton. 1980. *The Non-Violent Alternative*. Farrar, Straus & Giroux: New York.

10. Quoted in Jean Bethke Elshtain. 1987. *Women and War*. Basic Books: New York.

11. Ibid.

12. Bertolt Brecht. 1976. *Poems*. Methuen: London.

13. Quoted in Alan Geyer. 1982. *The Idea of Disarmament*. The Brethren Press: Elgin, IL.

14. M. K. Gandhi. 1968. *Selected Works*. S. Narayan (ed.). Navajivan: Ahmedabad, India.

15. Gandhi. *Autobiography*.

16. Quoted in Erik Erikson. 1969. *Gandhi's Truth*. Norton: New York.

17. Quoted in Joan Bondurant. 1971. *Conflict: Violence and Nonviolence*. Aldine Atherton: Chicago.

18. Bose. *Selections*.

19. Ibid.

20. Easwaran. *Gandhi*.

21. Richard Gregg. 1960. *The Power of Nonviolence*. James Clarke: London.

22. Quoted in Gregg, ibid.

23. Martin Luther King, Jr. 1964. *Why We Can't Wait*. New American Library: New York.

24. James Hanigan. 1984. *Martin Luther King, Jr. and the Foundations of Nonviolence*. University Press of America: New York.

25. Martin Luther King, Jr. "My Pilgrimage to Nonviolence." Reprinted in *The Catholic Worker*, Jan./Feb. 1983.

26. M. K. Gandhi. 1951. *Non-Violent Resistance*. Schocken Books: New York.

27. Gene Sharp. 1978. *The Politics of Nonviolent Action*. Porter Sargent: Boston.

28. Gene Sharp. 1985. *Making Europe Unconquerable: The Potential of Civilian-Based Deterrence and Defense*. Ballinger: Cambridge, MA.

29. Ibid.

30. Gene Sharp. 1970. "National Defense Without Armaments." *War/Peace Report* 10:3–10.

31. Sharp. *The Politics of Nonviolent Action*.

32. Quoted in Merton. *The Non-Violent Alternative*.

33. Ibid.

34. Ibid.

35. Timothy Flinders. "How Satyagraha Works." In E. Easwaran, *Gandhi the Man*. Nilgiri Press: Petaluma, CA.

36. Leo Tolstoy. 1987. "Letter on the Peace Conference." In *Writings on Civil Disobedience and Nonviolence*. New Society Publishers: Philadelphia.

37. Quoted in D. Attwater. 1947. *Modern Christian Revolutionaries*. Devin-Adair: New York.

38. Walt Whitman. 1968. *Leaves of Grass*. Norton: New York.

24

Personal Transformation

There are moments when things go well and one feels encouraged. There are difficult moments and one feels overwhelmed. But it's senseless to speak of optimism or pessimism. The only important thing is to know that if one works well in a potato field, the potatoes will grow. If one works well among men, they will grow—that's reality. The rest is smoke. It's important to know that words don't move mountains. Work, exacting work, moves mountains.

Danillo Dolci

This will be a brief chapter, not because there isn't much to say, but because personal transformation is fundamentally, well, personal. Concern with peace works in different ways for each of us. Some of you, treating Peace Studies as a course like any other, will simply obtain a grade and file it—along with whatever you may have learned along the way—away in your academic repertoire to be variously forgotten or half-remembered. For others, exposure to Peace Studies may expand your consciousness in some significant way, influencing your subsequent behavior and perceptions. This book will have been successful in proportion to the number of readers in the latter category.

INTERNAL AND EXTERNAL TRANSFORMATIONS

When exposed to issues that are particularly relevant, or arguments that are especially cogent, or simply when emotions and other subconscious factors "click" in a mysterious and little-known way, people may suddenly see the world in a different way. People who have experienced a religious conversion often speak of having been "born again," after which everything seems new and different.

"Peace begins with me?" Marine recruits during basic training. (U.S. Department of Defense)

Peace Studies does not necessarily aim for a comparable conversion experience, although it sometimes happens. Personal transformation can assume many forms, from the intense and mystical to a practical determination to vote differently, give money to or get directly involved in a particular cause, read another book, take another course, or develop a lifelong vocation.

Many people currently are working in various ways to help establish a world at peace. Richard Falk calls them "citizen/pilgrims," and they typically focus on specific goals, such as economic conversion, the abolition of nuclear weapons, an end to military interventionism, the elimination of poverty or malnutrition, the eradication of political oppression or environmental destruction, the defense of human rights, or the restoration of a relationship between people and their planet and/or one another. The route of such citizen/pilgrims, like that of the earlier pilgrims hundreds of years ago, is likely to be long and difficult, but not impossible.

It has widely been claimed that peace must start within each individual, then spread outward: "Peace begins with me." This implies not only examining one's own life and making changes that seem consistent with one's beliefs, but also identifying those personal patterns that may rein-

force societywide systems of oppression. Such self-examination may, in turn, lead to some painful conclusions and decisions: recognizing how one's own life has involved oppression of others, questioning what balance is desirable (and feasible) between relative personal privilege and selfless devotion to a cause. For some people, fighting oppression requires breaking out of their own oppression. "A liberal," goes the saying, "fights for other people's liberation; a radical fights for his or her own." In this context, breaking out of oppressive personal relationships may well be a prerequisite for helping alleviate the oppression of others.

To some degree, the world will be a better and less violent place if each individual makes peace in his or her own life. Important as it is, however, the personal transformation involved in making one's own inner peace is only part of the necessary equation; peace must be made not only internally, but also externally, out "there" in the real and sometimes nasty world. No amount of "centeredness," "organic living," "alternative lifestyles," or personal peace will solve the problem of apartheid, of surrogate war in the Third World, of poverty, of the denial of human rights, or of environmental abuse, to say nothing of the danger of nuclear war. You can think pure thoughts, eat only organic foods, and never think ill of another, but this won't prevent destruction of the rain forests, or provide a decent education for a little girl in Mozambique, or prevent your dying in a nuclear war. Peace may begin with each of us, but war, at least, is likely to begin elsewhere (such as the Pentagon or the Kremlin), and peace must end with changes in the world at large. It may be satisfying — and even necessary — to "liberate" oneself, but it is not sufficient.

In the course of becoming involved in the struggle for peace, an awkward collision may be unavoidable, between a personal, ethical commitment to nonviolence and some of the harsh realities of a world in which the achievement of "freedom," "equality," and "liberation" may require conflict — at the very least — if any meaningful change is to occur.

STUMBLING BLOCKS TO PERSONAL TRANSFORMATION

All of these are personal decisions, deeply personal ones that everyone will confront in his or her unique way. For some people, the decision to become involved in solving the world's problems derives from ethical/religious conviction. For others, a sense of outraged humanism opens their eyes to the injustices and dangers afflicting this planet. Sometimes, a commitment to peace derives from a kind of transformative experience, perhaps a sudden crash of insight, what has been called a moment of "epiphany," when things suddenly are seen with a unique and breathtaking clarity. At other times, it comes slowly and gradually, with the progressive realization that something long suspected is indeed true — as facts, ideas, and personal experiences fit into a coherent whole. Sometimes, the appeal is primarily logical, at other times emotional and deeply personal.

For others, of course, it doesn't come at all. The thrust of this final chapter is that personal transformation is a prerequisite for the achievement of peace. (Not that everyone must be transformed. For most successful social movements, it is only necessary that a critical number — perhaps fewer than 10 percent of the population — become sin-

cerely committed to the outcome; for a major restructuring of society, perhaps 40 to 50 percent will be needed.) In any event, the greatest barrier to peace may well be less the intractability of world problems than the fact that those problems are psychologically, and thus politically, invisible. Moreover, those who do perceive them tend to respond either with a feeling of hopelessness or with self-defeating violence.

Violence generally evokes its own response, comparably violent. As for hopelessness, there are several avenues. One is to point out the various genuine possibilities for action, as we have tried to do in this book. Another is to adopt the existential view that hopelessness is itself fundamental to the human condition, which in turn necessitates that we struggle — without hope — because that is what it *means* to be human. And yet another is to embrace despair (especially in regard to long-term nuclear and environmental anxiety) as an indication of our fundamental love for the planet and its living creatures. After all, if we did not care, we would not grieve. And, paradoxically, out of that recognition can come renewed strength.

Hopelessness can result from two different sources. On the one hand, there is the literal lack of hope, a denial that solutions even exist, or could ever be implemented. On the other, there is a frustration that derives from being a small, isolated individual in a very large and complicated world. The issue in this case is not so much an absence of hope as a lack of power, or rather, a perception of one's powerlessness. One purpose of Peace Studies thus is to provide some empowerment, on both levels.

There are those who refuse to see the world's plight out of concern that the problem of peace is so vast that, if they opened themselves to its immensity, they would be sucked in, as into an irresistible black hole. To these people we point out that, insofar as they see the problem this way, they have already been engulfed, whether they recognize it or not. Admitting their concerns and anxieties, and allowing themselves to act on them, will be refreshing in the extreme, even exhilarating. And of course, they do not really have to devote themselves 100 percent, body, mind, and soul. They can support peace, with their votes, some volunteer time, occasional financial contributions, and the like, without necessarily disrupting their entire lives. Of course, they can also make a deeper commitment; there is no objective right or wrong in such cases.

Those who fail to see the planetary plight, on the other hand, tend to be reacting to one of three circumstances: (1) a sense that the world's ills are inevitable, part of the natural landscape, like many people once imagined slavery to be; (2) a refusal to admit that which is discomfiting — in other words, practicing denial — because of an understandable inclination to spare themselves emotional pain; and (3) a lack of awareness of the problems. In a society that in some ways does not really want to confront the world's difficulties (and especially, its own complicity in creating them), it is relatively easy to avoid thinking very much about nuclear weapons, environmental deterioration, and Third World poverty, not to mention genocide against what are (for us) obscure populations in, say, Brazil or the Philippines.

But what is "easy" may not be what is right. And since the world is small and getting smaller, as the problems begin to mount, no one will long be insulated from their effects. We are rapidly approaching the point where only an ostrich, head determinedly buried in the sand, will be able to avoid the fundamental issues of avoiding war and establishing peace.

The Brazilian social activist Paulo Freire has coined the term "conscientization," referring to the achievement of first personal and then group awareness. He is primarily concerned with the establishment of social justice, and he calls, accordingly, for "humanization," which is "thwarted by injustice, exploitation, oppression, and the violence of the oppressors; it is affirmed by the yearning of the oppressed for freedom and justice, and by their struggle to recover their lost humanity."[1]

As Freire notes, one of the most important aspects of personal transformation is the role of empowerment. In some cases, to be sure, individuals commit themselves to a cause despite a certainty that they will ultimately fail; the most notable example is that of the French existentialists, such as Albert Camus, who emphasized that death makes life absurd, and that, as a result, it is fundamental to the human condition that we each define ourselves by our struggle against so uncaring a universe . . . even though, like Sisyphus, we are necessarily doomed to failure. But for most of us, commitment and action are not forthcoming without a sense of hope. The image of ultimate failure is not usually considered a reassuring one, likely to recruit a large number of enthusiastic followers. "In order for the oppressed to wage the struggle for their liberation," writes Freire,

> they must perceive the reality of oppression not as a closed world from which there is no exit, but as a limiting situation which they can transform. This perception is a necessary but not a sufficient condition for liberation; it must become the motivating force for liberating action.[2]

MOTIVATING FACTORS IN PERSONAL TRANSFORMATION

Although oppression is most blatant in the *favelas* of São Paulo, the grinding rural poverty of Chad and Ethiopia, or in the treatment of political prisoners in Cuba, Israel, and South Africa, it should be clear even to relatively fortunate college students in the United States that they, too, are both contributors to and victims of what Richard Falk calls "invisible oppression," from environmental abuse to economic maldistribution to the state-sponsored terrorism of the nuclear arms race. This is a large part of my personal motivation in writing this text: to contribute to the awakening and empowering of Peace Studies students. But even knowledge and information, taken alone, are not enough. Also needed is a sense of personal responsibility and, in most cases, of the prospects for success.

Dr. Helen Caldicott used to recruit antinuclear activists by urging each individual in her audience to "take the world upon your shoulders, like Atlas." It may be a heavy load, but it is somewhat lighter when shared. And furthermore, if each of us doesn't do it, who will? Law professor Roger Fisher made one of the most effective pleas for personal involvement, speaking at an antinuclear symposium.

He began by recounting a friend's reaction to the title of his presentation, which was "Preventing Nuclear War." His friend's response was, "Boy, have *you* got a problem!" Here are Professor Fisher's own words:

> That reaction a few minutes ago to the title of these remarks reminded me of an incident when during World War II, I was a B-17 weather reconnaisance officer. One fine day we were in Newfoundland test-flying a new engine that replaced one we had lost. Our pilot's rank was only that of flight officer because he had been court martialed so frequently for his wild activities; but he was highly skillful.
>
> He got us up to about 14,000 feet and then, to give the new engine a rigorous test, he stopped the other three and feathered their propellers into the wind. It is rather impressive to see what a B-17 can do on one engine. But then, just for a lark, the pilot feathered the fourth propeller and turned off that fourth engine. With all four propellers stationary, we glided, somewhat like a stone, toward the rocks and forests of Newfoundland.
>
> After a minute or so the pilot pushed the button to unfeather. Only then did he remember: In order to unfeather the propeller you had to have electric power, and in order to have electric power you had to have at least one engine going. As we were buckling on our parachutes, the co-pilot burst out laughing. Turning to the pilot he said "Boy have *you* got a problem!"[3]

Fisher then went on to discuss some of the difficulties of, as well as the prospects for, preventing nuclear war. At the end of his talk, he returned to the hapless B-17, with himself inside, without power and about to crash:

> Well, we didn't crash; we weren't all killed. On that plane we had a buck sergeant who remembered that back behind the bomb bay we had a putt-putt generator for use in case we had to land at some emergency air field that did not have any electric power to start the engines. The sergeant found it. He fiddled with the carburetor; wrapped a rope around the flywheel a few times; pulled it and pulled it; got the generator going and before we were down to 3,000 feet we had electricity. The pilot restarted the engines, and we were all safe. Now saving that plane was not the sergeant's job in the sense that he created the risk. The danger we were in was not his

fault or his responsibility. But it was his job in the sense that he had an opportunity to do something about it.[4]

It can be argued that each of us has a duty to contribute to world peace, if only because — like the crew in Roger Fisher's stricken B-17 — we are all in this world together, and it is definitely at risk. There aren't even any parachutes. At least as important, however, is the fact that each of us can make a contribution.

Social psychologists have determined, in fact, that of the various factors that seem likely to motivate people to change their behavior, the most powerful is the simple message "You can do it" — that is, evidence that individual behavior will be effective in generating some desirable effect. For example, in an experiment, subjects were given three different kinds of information about cigarette smoking, automobile injuries, and sexually transmitted disease.[5] The purpose was to determine which information was most effective in changing the behavior of the subjects: (1) details about the noxious consequences of the events (interviews with lung cancer patients, gruesome photos of automobile and sexually transmitted disease victims), (2) statistical data about the probability of experiencing or contracting these outcomes if behavior remained unchanged, or (3) information specifying what preventive measures could be taken and emphasizing their likely effectiveness. The results showed clearly that the third factor, the "efficacy of coping responses," was the most influential in inducing people to change their behavior. Moreover, the first consideration — appeals to fear by emphasizing the noxiousness of the threat — actually served to *reduce* the likelihood that subjects would engage in adaptive behavior, apparently because such appeals evoked powerful psychological resistances in the subjects.

The implications for Peace Studies may be important. If people are to change, to break through their crust of denial and selfish indifference, it may be most effective to appeal to their sense of efficacy rather than to their rational evaluation of danger, or to their raw fear. The latter, in fact, may even be counterproductive. Thus, we turn next to the question of efficacy. But first, an additional motivating factor deserves mention: fun. The ironic truth is that it can be great fun trying to bring peace to the world. For Roger Fisher, it is

> an exciting venture. It is a glorious world outside. There are people to be loved and pleasures to share. We should not let details of past wars and threat of the future take away the fun and joy we can have working together on a challenging task. I see no reason to be gloomy about trying to save the world. There is more exhilaration, more challenge, more zest in tilting at windmills than in any routine job. Be involved, not just intellectually but emotionally. Here is a chance to work together with affection, with caring, with feeling. Feel some of your emotions. Don't be uptight. You don't have to be simply a doctor, a lawyer, or a merchant. We are human beings. Be human.
>
> People have struggled all of their lives to clear ten acres of ground or simply to maintain themselves and their family. Look at the opportunity we have. Few people in history have been given such a chance — a chance to apply our convictions, our values, our highest moral goals with such competence as our skills may give us. A chance to work with others — to have the satisfaction that comes from playing a role, however small, in a constructive enterprise. It's not compulsory. So much the better. But what challenge could be greater? We have an opportunity to improve the chance of human survival.[6]

THE EFFICACY OF PERSONAL ACTION

No one can accurately assess the prospects of establishing peace in the world. Certainly, the problems can be identified, and some of the proposed solutions can be discussed. This we have attempted to do. Many of them may be feasible, especially if initiated in combination rather than alone: a switch to nonprovocative defense, substantially reduced nuclear arsenals, redistribution of global expenditures from the military to social needs, protection of the environment and human rights, strengthening of various world peacekeeping systems in the context of establishing global rather than national security, a widespread shift toward nonviolence, and so on.

As to the efficacy of personal action, it cannot be stated too strongly that individuals *can* make

a difference, and not only larger-than-life figures such as Mother Teresa or Martin Luther King, Jr. In a democracy, individuals count, each one of us. Moreover, powerlessness is a self-fulfilling prophecy, but then, so is empowerment. When people are convinced that they are helpless, and that their behavior is insignificant, then they will behave helplessly and without significance. But the opposite is also true. "It is within our power," wrote Thomas Paine more than two hundred years ago, "to begin the world anew." To some degree, that is exactly what happened when a state was formed based on the principle of democracy and self-government. And the prospect of major, transformative change — not only within individuals, but in their society as well — is no less true in our time than it was in his. (Interestingly, Edmund Burke, writing at about the same time as Paine, but espousing a very different view of what the world should be like, noted that "the only thing necessary for the triumph of evil is for good men* to do nothing.")

In addition, there is some reason for optimism. Nuclear weapons are becoming increasingly delegitimized in the minds of leaders and citizens alike, and war itself may be headed in a similar direction; next can come the elimination of major violent conflict — and throughout, the increasing realization of positive peace. For this process to continue (to some degree it has already begun), three things are needed: (1) belief in the possibility of peace, (2) belief in one's personal power and efficacy, and (3) motivation to proceed. We shall emphasize the first of these.

A primary stumbling block to the establishment of peace is not so much the difficulty of achieving it, but rather the inability or refusal of many people to imagine peace as a realistic prospect. The widespread disbelief that peace is possible is a major hindrance to its ever being achieved: Before anything can be done, it must first be imagined, and the importance of effective imagery cannot be overestimated. In a commencement address at Johns Hopkins University in 1985, James

---

*Make that, "good *people*."

Rouse said this about the importance of visualizing one's goal:

> It is a way of thinking that raises up images of what might be — should be — and thereby helps people to see potential that otherwise might not be understood and evokes action that might not otherwise occur. These images generate energy and forestall early compromise with lesser results. Such images are often dismissed as visionary and impractical. And the state of mind that often evokes that response is one of the burdens of our society. It is a state of mind that inhibits movement towards goals that may be widely accepted as valid and important by discounting them in advance as unachievable.[7]

Athletic coaches, business leaders, and others have come to recognize the value of visualization: imagining one's body perfectly coordinated during a gymnastics exercise, envisioning oneself achieving a new sales record, and so on. Subtly, unconsciously, the mind can be essentially "reprogrammed," resulting in the accomplishment of things previously thought out of reach. Personal transformation does occur, but only after people believe in the possibility of themselves changing, and have a positive image of the kind of change they desire. Similarly, for the world to be transformed toward peace, people must believe in the *possibility* of peace, or their efforts are liable to be half-hearted, if they make any at all. And they must begin imagining a world at peace. Such an image need not be finished in all its fine points and details, but it must be realistic and feasible. It must not project so far into the future that it seems irrelevant to the present, and it must not make excessive demands on human capacities as we know them. At the same time, it must be idealistic enough to be inspirational, to be worth striving for.

THE FUTURE

Many people believe that the world today stands at the brink of a major transformation. "The core concept," write two proponents of this viewpoint,

> is of an "age," as in "the modern age" or the "Middle Ages." World civilization, according to this idea, is about to shift from the modern, industrial age into another age — just as Western civilization shifted from the Middle Ages to the modern age. This coming age is often simply referred to as the "next age" or the "new age."
>
> One should not underestimate the sweep and power of an idea that assumes that *all* aspects of social life and institutions may change profoundly. The analogy of the shift from the Middle Ages to the modern age is illuminating; almost every dimension and aspect of society was affected. The general organization of society, the structure of economies, the relationships between local and large political units, the meaning and purpose of politics, the role of religion, and many other key aspects of life and society were altered enormously between medieval times and the late seventeenth century. Implicit in the anticipation of a new age is the belief that such profound changes in human society could occur again.[8]

There is nothing necessarily fixed and immutable about the world as it exists today. A world system based on states could give way to one based on local, semiautonomous communities, just as reliance on nuclear weapons is being replaced by widespread revulsion toward them. Nonviolence could swell and violence shrink in human affairs. Alternatively, many aspects of a world at peace, discussed in the preceding chapters, could be instituted with only minimal alteration in the basic face of human society as it now exists. As progress is made and new systems are institutionalized, change would then be evolutionary rather then revolutionary. It may also be lasting.

A FINAL NOTE ON PERSONAL TRANSFORMATION

The achievement of peace is only secondarily a problem of "hardware," to be solved by the manipulation of structures whether physical or social. Primarily, it is a problem in human "software," in the ways we think, and often stubbornly refuse to do so. And herein lies the hope, because there is enormous potential within the human species, not only to remove the "bugs" from our own program, but also to recreate our lives as we rebuild our world. A generation ago, Lewis Mumford wrote that

Antinuclear protestor being arrested after sitting on the tracks outside the Trident submarine base at Bangor, Washington. Some people, as in this case, are willing to make a personal, solitary "witness" in favor of peace; others prefer being part of a group and engaging in activities that range from civil disobedience to lobbying or stuffing envelopes. (Bill Wahl)

every transformation of man . . . has rested on a new metaphysical and ideological base; or rather, upon a new picture of the cosmos and the nature of man. . . . We stand on the brink of a new age. . . . In carrying man's self-transformation to this further stage, world culture may bring about a fresh release of spiritual energy that will unveil new potentialities, no more visible in the human self today than radium was in the physical world a century ago, though always present.[9]

Let us emphasize: This is not simply a soft-headed appeal to quasimysticism and "feel-good" pop psychology; it is the stuff of which conceptual (and sometimes, flesh-and-blood) revolutions are made. Social organizer Saul Alinsky coined a valuable phrase for would-be activists: "Think globally, act locally." There are many avenues for personal involvement, numerous organizations to join, a large number of which are active on the local as well as the national or global level. Most people find it

difficult to persevere alone; this is why such groups are so important. They also tend to have a larger voice than a solitary individual. The Appendix contains a selective list; some are lobbying organizations, most put out publications of one sort or another. Feel free to contact them. After all, when was the last time you stood up for something you believed in? And do you *really* have anything better to do?

Source Notes

1. Paulo Freire. 1970. *Pedagogy of the Oppressed.* Continuum: New York.

2. Ibid.

3. Roger Fisher. 1981. "Preventing Nuclear War." In Ruth Adams and Susan Cullen (eds.), *The Final Epidemic.* Educational Foundation for Nuclear Science: Chicago.

4. Ibid.

5. Ronald W. Rogers and C. Ronald Mewborn. 1976. "Fear Appeals and Attitude Change: Effects of a Threat's Noxiousness, Probability of Occurrence, and the Efficacy of Coping Responses." *Journal of Personality and Social Psychology* 34: 54–67.

6. Fisher. "Preventing Nuclear War."

7. Quoted in H. B. Hollins, A. L. Powers, and M. Sommer. 1989. *The Conquest of War*. Westview Press: Boulder, CO.

8. Richard Smoke with Willis Harman. 1987. *Paths to Peace*. Westview Press: Boulder, CO.

9. Lewis Mumford. 1956. *The Transformations of Man*. Harper: New York.

Appendix

Peace-Related Organizations

American Committee on Africa
198 Broadway
New York, NY 10038

American Committee on East–West Accord
109 11th St. SE
Washington, DC 20003

American Friends Service Committee
1501 Cherry St.
Philadelphia, PA 19105

Amnesty International
304 W. 58th St.
New York, NY 10019

Arms Control Association
11 Dupont Circle NW
Washington, DC 20036

Center for Defense Information
600 Maryland Ave. SW
Washington, DC 20024

Committee for National Security
2000 P Street NW, Suite 515
Washington, DC 20036

Consortium on Peace, Research, Education and
    Development (COPRED)
Center for Conflict Resolution
George Mason University
4400 University Dr.
Fairfax, VA 22030

Council on Economic Priorities, Conversion
    Information Center
30 Irving Place
New York, NY 10003

Educators for Social Responsibility
23 Garden St.
Cambridge, MA 02138

Fellowship of Reconciliation
P.O. Box 271
Nyack, NY 10960

Friends of the Earth
1045 Sansome
San Francisco, CA 94111

Greenpeace USA
2007 R St. NW
Washington, DC 20009

Institute for Defense and Disarmament Studies
20001 Beacon St.
Brookline, MA 02146

Institute for Food and Development Policy
1885 Mission St.
San Francisco, CA 94103

Institute for Policy Studies
1901 Q St. NW
Washington, DC 20009

International Center for Research on Women
1717 Massachusetts Ave. NW
Washington, DC 20036

International League for Human Rights
236 E. 46th St.
New York, NY 10017

International Peace Academy
777 United Nations Plaza
New York, NY 10017

International Peace Research Association
Mershon Center
199 West 10th Ave.
Columbus, OH 43201

Mobilization for Survival
853 Broadway, Room 2109
New York, NY 10003

National Resources Defense Council
1725 I St. NW
Washington, DC 20006

Oxfam-America
115 Broadway
Boston, MA 02216

Peace Research Institute
25 Dundas
Ontario L9H 4E5 Canada

Peace Studies Association
c/o The Kansas Institute for Peace and Conflict
    Resolution
Bethel College
North Newton, KS 67117

The Population Council
1 Dag Hammarskjold Plaza
New York, NY 10017

SANE/Freeze
711 G St. SE
Washington, DC 20003

Women's International League for Peace and
    Freedom
1213 Race St.
Philadelphia, PA 19107

World Federalists Association
418 Seven St. SE
Washington, DC 20003

World Policy Institute
777 United Nations Plaza
New York, NY 10017

Worldwatch Institute
1776 Massachusetts Ave. NW
Washington, DC 20036

Index